W9-CON-570

FAMILY THERAPY

FAMILY THERAPY

A Bibliography, 1937-1986

COMPILED BY

Bernard Lubin,
Alice W. Lubin, Marion G. Whiteford,
and Rodney V. Whitlock

FOREWORD BY

Luciano L'Abate

Bibliographies and Indexes in Psychology, Number 4

Greenwood Press
New York • Westport, Connecticut • London

Library of Congress Cataloging-in-Publication Data

Lubin, Bernard, 1923-
  Family therapy : a bibliography, 1937-1986 / compiled by Bernard Lubin,
Alice W. Lubin, Marion G. Whiteford, and Rodney V. Whitlock ; foreword by Luciano L'Abate.
    p.   cm. — (Bibliographies and indexes in psychology, ISSN
0742-681X ; no. 4)
  Bibliography: p.
  Includes indexes.
  ISBN 0-313-26172-5 (lib. bdg. : alk. paper)
  1. Family psychotherapy—Bibliography.   I. Title.   II. Series.
Z6665.7.F35L83   1988
[RC488.5]
016.61689'156—dc 19   88-18682

British Library Cataloguing in Publication Data is available.

Library of Congress Catalog Card Number: 88-18682
ISBN: 0-313-26172-5
ISSN: 0742-681X

First published in 1988

Greenwood Press, Inc.
88 Post Road West, Westport, Connecticut 06881

Printed in the United States of America

The paper used in this book complies with the
Permanent Paper Standard issued by the National
Information Standards Organization (Z39.48-1984).

10 9 8 7 6 5 4 3 2 1

Contents

Foreword

Luciano L'Abate

An individual's accomplishments provide an important perspective on his identity -- so too with an intellectual movement, a professional-technical area, and a field of study. What we have here is a record of 50 years of accomplishment in the field of family therapy. From modest beginnings, publication has grown rapidly. This bibliography compiles 6,167 books, chapters in books, book reviews, articles, and monographs. The care and thoroughness with which this comprehensive listing has been assembled assures its accuracy and usefulness.

It would be easy to overlook the very large amount of work involved in searching, verifying, checking and rechecking, etc. that went into the production of this comprehensive bibliography. The fields of family, couples and marital therapy will be grateful to Bernard Lubin and his associates for this labor of love. It not only documents the past accomplishments in a thorough way, it also will encourage additional scholarship and research.

Preface

Although publication in the area of family therapy is only at the half century mark (the earliest publication located with family therapy in the title was in 1937), the quickening pace of publication and the indications of general vitality in this field would seem to warrant a compilation of the literature at this time. We undertook this task with the hope that the outcome would facilitate scholarship, research, theory development and clinical reporting even further.

Because of their relationship to the family therapy domain, this bibliography also compiles the literature for the fields of marital therapy and couples therapy. We have not attempted to distinguish between therapy, psychotherapy, and counseling in making decisions about inclusion.

This bibliography contains 6,167 cross-referenced entries and represents a thorough search of Psychological Abstracts, Sociological Abstracts, Cumulated Index Medicus, Cumulative Index to Nursing and Allied Health Literature, International Nursing Index, Dissertation Abstracts, Current Contents, Books in Print, and reference lists from relevant books in the areas of "family therapy", "marital therapy", and "couples therapy". A subject index and an author index are provided.

We would like to express our gratitude and appreciation to Patricia Falk for her assistance with the typing of the entries, to Kenneth West, II, for his assistance with the compilation activity, and to Kimberly Seaton for assisting with the printing and with the proofreading. Our thanks also go to Dr. Arthur M. Bodin and Sage Publishing Co. for making suggestions and sharing materials. Our special gratitude and appreciation go to Carol Rust whose skills, knowledge, and generous time commitment to the word processing aspect of this project were invaluable.

It is clear that research and publication in family therapy is both robust and increasing. As mentioned earlier, our hope is that this bibliography will facilitate this important development still further, and, by making the literature a bit more accessible, will assist in improving both the quality and quantity of writing in this field even further.

Bibliography

1. Abarbanel, A.R., and Back, G. (1959), Group psychotherapy for the infertile couple. International Journal of Fertility, 4, 151.

2. Abbott, D.W. (1976), The effects of open forum family counseling on perceived family environments and on behavior change of the child while controlling for the relationship styles of the parents. Dissertation Abstracts International, 36, 8335A.

3. Abbott, J.M., and Ladd, G.M. (1970), Any reason why this mentally retarded couple should not be joined together. Mental Retardation, 8, 45-48.

4. Abel, T.M. (1978), Introducing family therapy in Iran. Transatlantic Mental Health Research Newsletter, 20(4), 1.

5. Abel, T.M. (1983), Comparisons between group and family therapy. In L.R. Wolberg and M.L. Aronson (Eds.), Group and family therapy 1982. New York: Brunner/Mazel.

6. Abel, T.M., Bruzzese, D.A., and Wilson, J. (1974), Short-term family therapy for short-term hospitalized patients: A vehicle for training as well as treatment. In: L.R. Wolberg and M.C. Aronson (Eds.), Group therapy 1974: An overview. New York, NY: Stratton Intercontinental Medical Book Corp.

7. Abell, R.G. (1983), A dedication to Berne, Eric. In L.R. Wolberg and M.L. Aronson (Eds.), Group and family therapy 1982. New York: Brunner/Mazel.

8. Abels, B.S., and Brandsma, J.M. (1977), Therapy for couples. San Francisco: Jossey-Bass.

9. Abelsohn, D. (1983), Dealing with the abdication dynamic in the post-divorce family: A context for adolescent crisis. Family Process, 22, 359-383.

10. Able, S.E., and Jacques, M.M. (1973), A systems theory approach to the identification of judgmental errors in family treatment of decisions. International Journal of Social Psychiatry, 19, 110-113.

11.   Ablon, J. (1974), Al-Anon family groups. American Journal of
      Psychotherapy, 28, 30-45.

12.   Abramowitz, C.V. (1977), Blaming the mother: An experimental
      investigation of sex-role bias in countertransference. Psychology of
      Women, 2, 24-34.

13.   Abramowitz, S.I. (1976), Sex role related counter transference in
      psychotherapy. Archives of General Psychiatry, 33(1), 71-73.

14.   Abramowitz, S.I., Roback, H.B., Schwartz, J.M., Yasjna, A., Abramonitz,
      C.V., and Gomes, B. (1976), Sex bias in psychotherapy: A failure to
      confirm. American Journal of Psychiatry, 133(6), 706-709.

15.   Abramowitz, S.I., and Abramowitz, C.V. (1976), Sex role
      psychodynamics in psychotherapy. American Journal of Psychotherapy,
      30(4), 583-592.

16.   Abramowitz, S.I., and Sewell, H.H. (1980), Marital adjustment and sex
      therapy outcome. Journal of Sex Research, 16(4), 325-337.

17.   Abramson, H.A., and Peshkin, M.M. (1960), Psychosomatic group
      therapy with parents of children with intractable asthma: Adaptive
      mechanisms. Annals of Allergy, 18, 87-91.

18.   Abramson, H.A., and Peshkin, M.M. (1978), Psychosomatic group
      therapy with parents of children with intractable asthma. VIII. The
      Kohl family. Journal of Asthma Research, 16(1), 21-40.

19.   Abramson, H.A., and Peshkin, M.M. (1980), Psychosomatic group
      therapy with parents of children with intractable asthma. XIII: The
      Goldey Family. Part III. Journal of Asthma Research 17, 123-47.

20.   Abramson, H.A., and Peshkin, M.M. (1979), Psychosomatic group
      therapy with parents of children with intractable asthma: VIII. The
      Kohl family: II. Journal of Asthma Research, 16(2), 63-81.

21.   Abramson, H.A., and Peshkin, M.M. (1979), Psychosomatic group
      therapy with parents of children with intractable asthma. IX. The
      Peters family: I. Journal of Asthma Research, 16(3), 103-117.

22.   Abramson, H.A., and Peshkin, M.M. (1979), Psychosomatic group
      therapy with parents of children with intractable asthma: X. The
      Peters family: II. Journal of Asthma Research, 16(4), 149-164.

23.   Abramson, M. (1975), Group treatment of families of burn-injured
      patients. Social Casework, 56, 235-241.

24.   Abrioux, M.L., and Zingle, H.W. (1979), An exploration of the marital
      and life satisfactions of middle-aged husbands and wives. Canadian
      Counselor, 13(2), 85-92.

25.   Abroms, G.M. (1981), Family therapy in a biomedical context. Journal
      of Marriage & Family Therapy, 7(3), 385-390.

26.   Abroms, G.M., Fellner, C.H., and Whitaker, C.A. (1971), The family
      enters the hospital. American Journal of Psychiatry, 127, 1363-1370.

27.   Ack, M., Beale, E., and Ware, L. (1975), Parent guidance:
      Psychotherapy of the young child via the parent. Bulletin of the
      Menninger Clinic, 35(5), 436-447.

28.   Ackerman, N.A. (1984), A theory of family systems. New York:
      Gardner Press.

29.   Ackerman, N.W (1962), Family psychotherapy and psychoanalysis: The
      implications of a difference. Family Process, 1, 30-43.

30.   Ackerman, N.W. (1962), Adolescent problems: A symptom of family
      disorder. Family Process, 1(2), 202-213.

31.   Ackerman, N.W. (1964), The family approach to marital disorders.
      American Journal of Orthopsychiatry, 34, 223-224.

32.   Ackerman, N.W. (1964), Family therapy in schizophrenia: Theory and
      practice. International Psychiatric Clinics, 1, 929-943.

33.   Ackerman, N.W. (1960), Family focused therapy of schizophrenia. In
      S.C. Sher, and H.R. Davis (Eds.), The outpatient treatment of
      schizophrenia. New York: Grune and Stratton.

34.   Ackerman, N.W. (1961), Emergence of family psychotherapy on the
      present scene. In: M.I. Stein (Ed.), Contemporary psychotherapies. New
      York: Free Press.

35.   Ackerman, N.W. (1958), Toward an integrative therapy of the family.
      American Journal of Psychiatry, 114, 727-733.

36.   Ackerman, N.W. (1959), Theory of family dynamics. Psychoanalytic
      Review, 46, 33-50.

37.   Ackerman, N.W. (1966), Family psychotherapy: Theory and practice.
      American Journal of Psychotherapy, 20, 405-414.

38.   Ackerman, N.W. (1966), Family psychotherapy today: Some areas of
      controversy. Comprehensive Psychiatry, 7, 375-388.

39.   Ackerman, N.W. (1954), Interpersonal disturbances in the family.
      Psychiatry, 17, 359-368.

40.   Ackerman, N.W. (1968), Treating the troubled family. New York, NY:
      Basic Books.

41.   Ackerman, N.W. (1968), The emergence of family psychotherapy: A
      personal account. In J.A. Peterson (Ed.), Marriage and family
      counseling: Perspectives and prospect. New York: Association Press.

42.   Ackerman, N.W. (1971), The growing edge of family therapy. Family
      Process, 10, 143-156.

43.   Ackerman, N.W. (1970), Family psychotherapy today. Family Process,
      9, 123-236.

44.   Ackerman, N.W. (1970), Family interviewing: The study process.
      International Psychiatry Clinics, 7, 3-19.

45.   Ackerman, N.W. (1970), The art of family therapy. Psychiatry Clinics, 7, 21-26.

46.   Ackerman, N.W. (1970), Disturbances in the family. Psychiatry, 17, 359-368.

47.   Ackerman, N.W. (1978), The functions of a family therapist: A personal viewpoint. Dynamische Psychiatrie, 1(2), 99-109.

48.   Ackerman, N.W. (Ed.) (1970), Family therapy in transition. Boston, MA: Little, Brown.

49.   Ackerman, N.W., Beatman, F.L., and Sherman, S.N. (Eds.) (1961), Exploring the base for family therapy. New York: Family Service Association of America.

50.   Ackerman, N.W., and Behrens, M.L. (1956), The family group and family therapy: The practical application of family diagnosis. Issue and Studies, 1, 52-54.

51.   Ackerman, N.W., and Behrens, M.L. (1968), The family approach and levels of intervention. American Journal of Psychotherapy, 22(1), 5-14.

52.   Ackerman, N.W., and Behrens, M.L. (1967), The uses of family psychotherapy. American Journal of Orthopsychiatry, 37, 391-392.

53.   Acosta, F.X. (1982), Group psychotherapy with Spanish-speaking patients. In R.M. Becerra, M. Karno and J.I. Escobar (Eds.), Mental health and Hispanic Americans: Clinical perspectives. New York: Grune and Stratton.

54.   Acworth, A., and Bruggen, P. (1985), Family therapy when one member is on the death bed. Journal of Family Therapy, 7, 379-386.

55.   Adam, D., and Gingras, M. (1982), Short and long-term effects of a marital enrichment program upon couple functioning. Journal of Sex and Marital Therapy, 8, 97-118.

56.   Adamoyurka, E.A. (1981), A primary prevention program for reconstituted or blended families. Dissertation Abstracts International, 42, 1593-B.

57.   Adams, G.R. (1980), Runaway youth projects: Comments on care programs for runaways and throwaways. Journal of Adolescence, 3, 321-34.

58.   Adams, K. (1947), Counseling against family breakdown. Marriage and Family Living, 8-10.

59.   Adams, P.L. (1982), Family as consensus. Psychiatric Annals, 12, 875-886.

60.   Adams, R., and Hill, G. (1983), The labours of Hercules: Some good reasons why social workers should not try to be different, and practice family therapy. Journal of Family Therapy, 5, 71-80.

61.   Adams, W.J. (1968), Clients, counselors, and fees: Ingredients of a myth? Family Coordinator, 17, 288-292.

62.   Adams, W.J. (1979), Counsellor's assessment of love development in mate selection and marriage. Canadian Counselor, 1(2), 93-97.

63.   Adamson, W.C. (1972), Helping parents of children with learning disabilities. Journal of Learning Disabilities, 5, 326-330.

64.   Addario, D., and Rodgers, A. (1974), Some techniques for the initial interview in couples therapy. Hospital and Community Psychiatry, 25, 799-800.

65.   Addis, M., Schulman-Miller, J., and Lightman, M. (1984), The cult clinic helps families in crisis. Social Casework, 65, 515-522.

66.   Addis, M., and Lightman, M. (1983), The cult clinic of the Jewish Family Service. Los Angeles. Help for families in need. Praxis in Kinderpsychologie und Kinderpsychiatrie, 32, 145-64.

67.   Adelson, G., and Peress, E. (1979), Single-couple and group sex therapy. Social Casework, 60, 471-478.

68.   Adelson, J.P., and Talmade, W.C. (1976), Tips for clients: How to screw up your marriage counseling. Family Therapy, 3(2), 93-95.

69.   Adler, R., Bongar, B., and Katz, E.R. (1982), Psychogenic abdominal pain and parental pressure in childhood athletics. Psychosomatics, 23, 1185-1186.

70.   Adler, T.S., Katz, M., and Yehezkiel, A. (1975), An interdisciplinary programme for family planning among North African families in the developmental towns of the Neger. Israel Annals of Psychiatry, 13, 105-116.

71.   Adsett, C.A., and Bruhn, J.G. (1968), Short-term group psychotherapy for post-myocardial infarction patients and their wives. Canadian Medical Association Journal, 99, 577-584.

72.   Afoa, I.A. (1980), Divorce counseling with Samoan couples. Dissertation Abstracts International, 41, 1235-A.

73.   Aguinik, P.L. (1970), The spouse of the phobic patient. British Journal of Psychiatry, 117, 59-67.

74.   Ahlvik, H., Arrajarri, T., Penttimen, A., and Talvinko, S. (1979), Cases descriptive of the stages of family counseling. Psychiatria Fennica, 75, 25-32.

75.   Ahrons, C.R., and Perlmutter, M.S. (1982), Therapy with remarriage families: III. The relationship between former spouses: A fundamental subsystem in the remarriage family. Family Therapy Collections, 2, 31-46.

76.   Akhtar, S. (1978), Obessional neurosis, marriage, sex and fertility: Some transcultural comparisons. International Journal of Social Psychiatry, 24, 164-166.

77.   Alanen, Y.O. (1963), Round table conference on family studies and family therapy of schizophrenic patients. Acta Psychiatrica Scandanavia, 39, Suppl. 169, 420-425.

78. Alanen, Y.O. (1973), On family therapy of young schizophrenics. Acta Psychiatrica Scandanavia, Supplement, 243.

79. Alanen, Y.O., and Kinnunen, P. (1974), Marriage and the development of schizophrenia: A study of 30 married couples after one spouse had fallen ill with schizophrenia during the marriage, the Consensus Rorschach reflecting the dynamics. Psychiatrica Fennica, 70 121-143.

80. Albert, H.D., Olds, C.D., Davis, D.M., and Hoffman, J.S. (1980), Sexual therapy for patients without partners. American Journal of Psychotherapy, 34(2), 228.

81. Alberti, G. (1965), Ways of its appearance in group psychotherapy of the families of chronic schizophrenics. Ospedische Psychiatria, 33, 597-610.

82. Alberti, R.E., and Emmons, M.L. (1976), Assertion training in marital counseling. Journal of Marriage and Family, 2(1), 49-54.

83. Albretsen, C.S. (1964), Family life and psychiatric treatment. Examples of practical psychiatric work with "family oriented" therapy. Nordische Psychiatrische Tidschrift, 18, 538-541.

84. Albretsen, C.S. (1964), Training of psychiatric personnel with focus in interactional problems: A group approach by means of a projected fantasy-family. Acta Psychiatrica Scandanavia, 40 (Suppl. 180), 249-256.

85. Albretsen, C.S. (1968), Treatment of post-partum psychosis with hospitalization of the baby, the patient and her husband. Sykepleien, 55, 82-84.

86. Albretsen, C.S. (1968), Hospitalization of post partum psychotic patients, together with babies and husbands. Acta Psychiatrica Scandanavia Supplement, 203, 179.

87. Albretsen, C.S. (1966), Married couples in group psychotherapy. Nordische Psychiatrica Tidschrift, 20, 113-125.

88. Albretsen, C.S. (1971), A closed multi-family group. Journal of Oslo City Hospital, 21, 56-60.

89. Albretsen, C.S. (1976), Family therapy models and some therapeutic and prophylactic considerations. Acta Psychiatrica Scandanavia, 265, 33-34.

90. Albretsen, C.S. (1981), Couples and multi-family groups: Therapeutic and administrative viewpoints. Journal of Oslo City Hospital, 3(2), 27-29.

91. Albretson, C.S. (1968), A multifamily group. Nordische Psychiatrische Tidschrift, 22, 319-323.

92. Alcorn, L.P. (1978), Interpersonal behavior traits and perceived marital adjustment of married couples in marital counseling and not in marital counseling. Dissertation Abstracts International, 39, 3360A.

93. Aldous, N.R. (1973), Mechanisms of stale mate in conjoint marital therapy. Canadian Journal of Psychiatry, 18, 191-199.

94. Aldridge, D. (1984), Family interaction and suicidal behavior: A brief review. Journal of Family Therapy, 6(4), 309-322.

95. Aldridge, R.G. (1984), An ecological approach to family therapy. Corrective and Social Psychiatry and Journal of Behavior Technology, Methods and Therapy, 30(3), 74-75.

96. Aleksandrowicz, D.R. (1978), Interminable mourning as a family process. Israeli Annals of Psychiatry, 16, 161-169.

97. Alexander, I.E. (1963), Family therapy. Marriage and Family Living, 25, 146-154.

98. Alexander, I.E. (1983), Review of S. Waorondskinner's Development in family therapy: Theories and applications since 1948. Contemporary Psychology, 28, 120.

99. Alexander, J., and Parsons, B.V. (1982), Functional family therapy. Monterey, CA: Brooks-Cole.

100. Alexander, J.F., Barton, C., Schiaro, R., and Parsons, B.V. (1976), Systems-behavioral intervention with families of delinquents: Therapist characteristics, family behavior, and outcome. Journal of Consulting and Clinical Psychology, 44, 656-664.

101. Alexander, J.F., Waldron, H., Warburton, J., and Mas, C.H. (1985), The misuse of functional family therapy: A non-sexist rejoinder. Journal of Marital and Family Therapy, 11(2), 139-144.

102. Alexander, J.F., and Parsons, B.V. (1973), Short-term behavioral intervention with delinquent families: Impact on family process and recidivism. Journal of Abnormal Psychology, 81, 219-225.

103. Alexy, W.E. (1982), Dimensions of psychological counseling that facilitate the grieving process of bereaved parents. Journal of Counseling Psychology, 29, 498.

104. Alfred, G.H. (1976), How to strengthen your marriage and family. Provo, UT: Brigham Young University Press.

105. Alger, I. (1981), Marital crises. Current Psychiatric Therapies, 21, 83-93.

106. Alger, I. (1967), Joint psychotherapy of marital problems. Current Psychiatric Therapies, 7, 112-117.

107. Alger, I. (1973), Audio-visual techniques in family therapy. In: D.A. Bloch (Ed.), Techniques of family psychotherapy: A primer. New York: Grune and Stratton.

108. Alger, I. (1985), Instructional videotapes for use in family therapy. Hospital and Community Psychiatry, 36(1), 13-19.

109. Alger, I. (1983), Family therapy, psychoanalysis, and change. Journal of the American Academy of Psychoanalysis, 11, 575-592.

110. Alger, I. (1983), Continuing education and training. American Journal of Family Therapy, 11, 59.

111.   Alger, I., and Hogan, P. (1967), The use of videotape recording in
       conjoint marital therapy. American Journal of Psychiatry, 123, 1425-
       1430.

112.   Alger, I., and Hogan, P. (1969), Enduring effects of videotape playback
       experience on family and marital relationships. American Journal of
       Orthopsychiatry, 39, 86-94.

113.   Alkire, A.A., and Brunse, A.J. (1974), Impact and possible casualty from
       videotape feedback in marital therapy. Journal of Consulting and
       Clinical Psychology, 42, 203-210.

114.   Alkire, A.A., and Brunse, A.J. (1974). Impact and possible casualty
       from videotape feedback in marital therapy. Journal of Clinical
       Psychology, 30, 351-354.

115.   Allen, D.T. (1966), Psychodrama in the crib and in the family. Group
       Psychotherapy, 19, 22-28.

116.   Allen, J.D. (1976), Peer group supervision in family therapy. Child
       Welfare, 55, 183-189.

117.   Allen, J.E., and Cole, L.P. (1975), Clergy skills in family planning
       education and counseling. Journal of Religion and Health, 14(3), 198-
       205.

118.   Allen, T.W. (1975), "For our next act....": An unsystematic prescript to
       marriage and family counseling: A counseling psychologist's view.
       Counseling Psychologist, 5, 3-15.

119.   Allred, G.H., and Kersey, F.L. (1977), The AIAC, a design for
       systematically analyzing marriage and family counseling: A progress
       report. Journal of Marriage and Family Therapy, 3, 17-25.

120.   Almeida, J.I., and Pereira, A.C. (1972), Family meeting in therapeutic
       community. Neurobiology, 35, 215-218.

121.   Alonao, B.J., and Lazar, A.L. (1981), Nurse's role in counseling parents
       of defective newborns. Journal of Special Educators, 17, 326-334.

122.   Alonso, A., and Rutan, J.S. (1981), Couples therapy and the new sexual
       politics. Family Therapy, 3, 149-157.

123.   Altenberg, H.E. (1968), Changing priorities in child psychiatry. Voices,
       4, 36-39.

124.   Altmannherz, U. (1985), Review of Psychoanalytical method and family
       therapy. Praxis der Kinder psychologie und Kinderpsychiatrie, 34(1), 23.

125.   Alvarez, N. (1977), Structural character of the therapeutic intervention
       and various psychodynamic aspects in family therapy. Acta Psiquiatrica
       Y Psicologia De America Latina, 23, 131-138.

126.   Amatea, E.S., Munson, P.A., Anderson, L.M., and Rudner, R.A. (1980),
       Short-term training program for case workers in family counseling.
       Social Casework, 61, 205-214.

127.   Amatea, E.S., and Finnette, F. (1981), Family systems counseling: A
        positive alternative to traditional counseling. Elementary School
        Guidance and Counseling, 15, 223–236.

128.   Ambrosino, S. (1979), Integrating counseling, family life education, and
        family advocacy. Social Casework, 60(10), 579.

129.   Amendolara, F.R. (1974), Group therapy for mothers of drug addicts.
        British Journal of Addiction, 69(2), 181–182.

130.   American Husband, (The). (1978), Statistical Bulletin of Metropolitan
        Life Insurance Company, 59, 12–13.

131.   American Wife, (The). (1978), Statistical Bulletin of Metropolitan Life
        Insurance Company, 59, 14–15.

132.   Ammann, A. (1982), Sexuality in adolescence—psychological and family
        therapeutic aspects (author's transl.). Therapeutische Umschau Revue
        Therapeutic, 39, 434–7.

133.   Ammon, G. (1972), Group and aggression: A psychoanalytic research on
        aggression dynamics of a family group. Group Psychotherapy, 20, 181–
        190.

134.   Ammon, G. (1978), Psychoanalytic work with parents within group
        dynamics. Dynamische Psychiatry, 1(1), 64–67.

135.   Amster, F. (1944), Collective psychotherapy of mothers of emotionally
        disturbed children. American Journal of Orthopsychiatry, 14, 44–52.

136.   Anderson, C. (1982), The community connection: The impact of social
        networks on family and individual functioning. In F. Walsh (Ed.), Normal
        family processes. New York: Guilford Press.

137.   Anderson, C., and Mayes, P. (1982), Treating family sexual abuse: The
        humanistic approach. Journal of Child Care, 1, 31–46.

138.   Anderson, C., and Stewart, S. (1983), Mastering Resistance: A practical
        guide to family therapy. New York: Guilford Press.

139.   Anderson, C.M. (1977), Family intervention with severely disturbed
        inpatients. Archives of General Psychiatry, 34, 697–702.

140.   Anderson, C.M., Hogarty, G.E., and Reiss, D.J. (1980), Family
        treatment of adult schizophrenic patients: A psycho-educational
        approach. Schizophrenia Bulletin, 6, 490–505.

141.   Anderson, C.M., and Malloy, E.S. (1976), Family photographs: In
        treatment and training. Family Process, 15, 259–264.

142.   Anderson, C.N., and Janosko, R.E. (1978), Family therapy in paranoia.
        Current Psychiatric Therapies 18, 107–116.

143.   Anderson, C.W. (1981), The handicapped child's effect on parent-child
        relations: A useful model for school psychologists. School Psychology
        Review, 10, 82–90.

144.   Anderson, D.A. (1974), The family growth group: Guidelines for an emerging means of strengthening families. Family Coordinator, 2 (1), 7.

145.   Anderson, D.B. (1976), An operational framework for working with rural families in crisis. Journal of Marriage and Family Therapy, 2, 145-154.

146.   Anderson, D.B. (1969), Nursing therapy with families. Perspectives in Psychiatric Care, 7, 21-27.

147.   Anderson, E.D. (1971), The impact of suggestions: Their effect on children. Journal of the American Institute of Hypnosis, 12, 61-63.

148.   Anderson, E.K. (1972), A review of communication theory within the family framework. Family Therapy, 1, 15-34.

149.   Anderson, L.M., and Shafer, G. (1979), The character-disordered family: A community treatment model for family sexual abuse. American Journal of Orthopsychiatry, 49, 436-445.

150.   Anderson, P.W. (1979), The effects of simulated families therapy on selected students in an introductory marriage and family counseling course. Dissertation Abstracts International, 40, 3190A.

151.   Anderson, R.A. (1977), The left-out child: An observation of a role function in certain families. Family Therapy., 4, 11-15.

152.   Anderson, S.A., Atilano, R.B., Bergen, L.P., Russell, C.S., and Jurich, A.P. (1985), Dropping out of marriage and family therapy: Intervention strategies and spouse perceptions. American Journal of Family Therapy, 13(1), 39.

153.   Anderson, S.A., and Russell, C.S. (1982), Utilizing process and content in designing paradoxical interventions. American Journal of Family Therapy, 10, 48-60.

154.   Anderson, S.C., and Henderson, D.C. (1983), Family therapy in the treatment of alcoholism. Social Work in Health Care, 9, 79-94.

155.   Anderson, S.K. (1977), Early identification and primary prevention of potential parent-child interaction problems. Dissertation Abstracts International, 38, 2352B.

156.   Andolfi, M. (1978), A structural approach to a family with an encopretic child. Journal of Marriage and Family Therapy, 4, 25-29.

157.   Andolfi, M. (1978), Report on the second international conference on family therapy in the community. International Journal of Family Counseling, 6, 102.

158.   Andolfi, M. (1979), Redefinition of family therapy. American Journal of Family Therapy, 7, 5-15.

159.   Andolfi, M. (1979), Family therapy: An interactional approach. New York, NY: Plenum.

160.   Andolfi, M. (1980), Prescribing the families' own dysfunctional rules as a therapeutic strategy. Journal of Marital and Family Therapy, 8, 29-36.

161. Andolfi, M., and Angelo, C. (1981), The therapist as director of the family drama. Journal of Marital and Family Therapy, 7, 255-264.

162. Andolfi, M., and Angelo, C. (1983), Behind the family mask: Therapeutic changes in rigid family systems. New York: Brunner-Mazel.

163. Andolfi, M., and Menghi, P. (1977), The prescription in family therapy: Therapeutic paradox II. Archivis Psicologia, Neurologia Psichiatria, 38, 57-76.

164. Andolfi, M., and Menghi, P. (1976), Prescriptions in family therapy I. Archivis Psicologia, Neurologia Psichiatria, 37, 434-456.

165. Andolfi, M., and Zwerling, I. (Eds.) (1980), Dimensions of family therapy. New York: Guilford Press.

166. Andreozzi, L.L. (1985), The effects of short-term structural-analytic oriented family therapy on families with a presenting child problem. Dissertation Abstracts International, 45, 3325-B.

167. Andrews, E. (1972), Experiential role-play in the training of family therapists. American Journal of Orthopsychiatry, 42, 313-314.

168. Andrews, E.E. (1970), The group marathon method with married couples. Summary of workshops. Newsletter of the American Orthopsychiatric Association, 14, 16.

169. Andrews, R.J., and Apelt, W.C. (1972), The role of the special school in the integration of mentally retarded children into the community. Australian Journal of Mental Retardation, 2, 54-58.

170. Andrey, B., Burille, P., Martinez, J.P., and Rey, Y. (1978), (Treatment of a case of school maladjustment by brief family therapy.) Enfance, 2-3, 143-164.

171. Andron, L., and Strum, M.L. (1973), Is "I do" in the repertoire of the retarded? A study of the functioning of married retarded couples. Mental Retardation, 11, 31-34.

172. Andron, L., and Strum, M.L. (1973), Is "I do" in the repertoire of the retarded? A study of the functioning of married retarded couples. Journal of South Carolina Medical Association, 69, 390-395.

173. Angel, P., and Sternschuss, A.S. (1983), The family of the addict: Critical review of the literature. Psychiatrie De L'Enfant, 26, 237-255.

174. Angleo, C. (1981), The use of the metaphoric object in family therapy. American Journal of Family Therapy, 9, 69-78.

175. Annett, M. (1979), Family handedness in three generations predicted by the right shift theory. Annuals of Human Genetics, 42, 479-491.

176. Anonymous. (1979), Counseling services for parents of sudden infant death syndrome cases. Australian Family Physician, 8(2), 203-204.

177. Anonymous. (1980), Family psychiatry versus family therapy. Psychiatric Annals, 10(2), 42.

178.   Anonymous. (1981), Social work, sociology and the context of family therapy. Journal of Family Therapy, 3(3), 263.

179.   Anonymous. (1982), Therapy: Families of schizophrenics help them stay well. Psychology Today, 16(11), 77.

180.   Anonymous. (1948), Psychodrama of a pre-marital couple. Sociatry, 2, 103-120.

181.   Anonymous. (1980), Marriage guidance counseling in general practice. Drug and Therapeutics Bulletin, 18(8), 32.

182.   Antebi, E. (1981), The paradoxical nature of family art therapy. Pratt Institute Creative Arts Therapy Review, 2, 37-45.

183.   Antelyes, J. (1973), The veterinarian in marriage and practice. I. Human relations: Home and office. Veterinary Medicine - Small Animal Clinic, 68, 961.

184.   Antelyes, J. (1973), The veterinarian in marriage and practice. II. Personal fulfillment: Home and office. Veterinary Medicine - Small Animal Clinic, 68, 1171.

185.   Anthony, E.J. (1972), An introduction to family group therapy. In: H.I. Kaplan and B.J. Sadock (Eds.), Group treatment of mental illness. New York: E.P. Dutton.

186.   Antley, M.A., Antley, R.M., and Hartlage, L.C. (1973), Effects of genetic counseling on parental self concepts: Down's syndrome. Journal of Psychology, 83, 335-338.

187.   Anton, R.F., Hogan, I., Jalali, B., Riordan, C.E., and Kleber, H.D. (1981), Multiple family therapy and naltrexone in the treatment of opiate dependence. Drug and Alcohol Dependence, 8, 157-168.

188.   Antonic, Z. (1977), Adolescent crisis and the family. Psihijatrija Danas, 9, 349-353.

189.   Antonucci, T., Gillett, N., and Hoyer, F.W. (1979), Values and self-esteem in three generations of men and women. Journal of Gerontology, 34, 415-422.

190.   Apfelbaum, B. (1977), A contribution to the development of the behavioral analytic sex therapy model. Journal of Sex and Marital Therapy, 3(2), 128-138.

191.   Aponte, H. (1980), Family therapy and the community. In: M.S. Gibbs, J.R. Lachenmeyer, and J. Sigal (Eds.), Community psychology: Theoretical and empirical approaches. New York: Gardner Press.

192.   Aponte, H., and Hoffman, L. (1973), The open door: A structural approach to a family with an anorectic child. Family Process, 12, 1-44.

193.   Aponte, H.J. (1974), Organizing treatment around the family's problems and their structural bases. Psychiatric Quarterly, 48, 209-222.

194.   Aponte, H.J. (1979), Diagnosis in family therapy. In: C.B. Germain (Ed.), Social work practice. New York, NY: Columbia University Press.

195. Apostoles, F.E., Anderson, C.J., and Hoye, C.L. (1974), The use of closed-circuit television in marital therapy. Journal of Psychiatric Nursing and Mental Health Services, 12, 10-16.

196. Appel, M.J. (1964), Changes in attitudes of parents of retarded children effected through group counseling. American Journal of Mental Deficiency, 68, 807-812.

197. Appelle, M. (1977), The effect of group marital therapy on self-disclosure, social distance and self-spouse perception. Dissertation Abstracts International, 37(12), 6312-B.

198. Appenzeller, S.N. (1984), Review of R.J. Green and J.L. Framo's Family therapy - major contributions. Psychiatric Forum, 12(1), 76.

199. Appolone, C. (1978), Preventive social work intervention with families of children with epilepsy. Social Work Health Care, 4, 139-148.

200. Apprey, M. (1983), The myth of the matriarch who holds all the cards: II. Journal of Psychoanalytic Anthropology, 6, 163-178.

201. Apter, M.J., and Smith, K.C. (1979), Psychological reversals: Some new perspectives on the family and family communication. Family Therapy, 2, 89-100.

202. Aradi, N.S., and Piercy, F.P. (1985), Ethical and legal guidelines related to adherence to treatment protocols in family therapy outcome research. American Journal of Family Therapy, 13, 60-65.

203. Aradine, C.R. (1978), The family and you. Collaborating to foster family attachment. Part 3. MCN: American Journal of Maternal-Child Nursing, 3, 92-98.

204. Aradine, C.R. and Hansen, M.F. (1970), Interdisciplinary teamwork in family health care. Nursing Clinical of North America, 5, 211.

205. Arajarvi, T., Huttunen, M.O., and Talvinko, S. (1977), Family counseling in the prevention of children's psychiatric disorders: A preliminary report. Psychiatrica Fennica, 73, 89-95.

206. Arrajarri, T., Nupponen, O., Sipila, M. L., and Talvinko, S. (1981), Family counseling in the prevention of psychiatric disorders in children. Acta Paedopsychiatrica, 47, 81-9.

207. Araoz, D.L. (1977), Marital problems and the exceptional child. International Journal of Family Counseling, 5, 64-69.

208. Araoz, D.L. (1972), Marital therapy with former priests. Psychotherapy: Theory, Research and Practice, 9(4), 337-339.

209. Araoz, D.L. (1977), Biorhythm in couple counseling. International Journal of Family Counseling, 5, 34-39.

210. Araoz, D.L. (1985), Review of M. Ritterman, Using hypnosis in family therapy. Contemporary Psychology, 30(1), 42-43.

211. Araoz, D.L., and Negleyparker, E. (1985), Family hypnotherapy. American Journal of Family Therapy, 13, 11-15.

212.   Araoz, D.T. (1975), The Edwards Personal Preference Schedule in couple therapy. International Journal of Family Counseling, 3, 46-51.

213.   Araoz,D.T. (1978), Clinical hypnosis in couple therapy. Journal of the American Society of Psychiatrists in Dental & Medical Schools, 25, 58-67.

214.   Arbogast, R.C., Scratton, J.M., and Krick, J.P. (1978), The family as patient: Preliminary experience with a recorded assessment schema. Journal of Family Practice, 7, 1151-1157.

215.   Ard, B.N., Jr. (1969), Basic books for the marriage counselor. In: B.N. Ard, Jr., and C.C. Ard (Eds.), Handbook of marriage counseling. Palo Alto, CA: Science and Behavior Books.

216.   Ard, B.N., Jr. (1969), Communication theory in marriage counseling: A critique. In: B.N. Ard, Jr., and C.C. Ard (Eds.), Handbook of marriage counseling. Palo Alto, CA: Science and Behavior Books.

217.   Ard, B.N., Jr. (1967), The a-b-c of marriage counseling. Rational Living, 2, 10-12.

218.   Ard, B.N., Jr., and Ard, C.C. (1969), Laws regarding marriage counseling. In: B.N. Ard, Jr., and C.C. Ard (Eds.), Handbook of marriage counseling. Palo Alto, CA: Science and Behavior Books.

219.   Ard, B.N., Jr., and Ard, C.C. (Eds.) (1969), Handbook of marriage counseling. Palo Alto, CA: Science and Behavior Books.

220.   Ard, C.C. (1969), Information-gathering techniques in marriage counseling. In: B.N. Ard, Jr., and C.C. Ard (Eds.), Handbook of marriage counseling. Palo Alto, CA: Science and Behavior Books.

221.   Areisin, L. (1965), Practical experience with marital and sex counseling. Deutsche Gesundheitswesen, 20, 1692-1696.

222.   Arentzen, W.P. (1978), Impact of alcohol misuse on family life. Alcoholism, 2, 349-351.

223.   Argles, P. (1983), Identifying separation threats in family therapy. Journal of Marital and Family Therapy, 9, 209-211.

224.   Ariel, S., Carel, C.A., and Tyano, S. (1985), Uses of children's make-believe play in family therapy: Theory and clinical examples. Journal of Marital and Family Therapy, 11(1), 47-60.

225.   Ariel, S., Carol, C.H., and Tyano, S. (1984), Why family therapy should be both homostatic and coherent: A Kuhnian reply to Dell. Journal of Marital and Family Therapy, 10, 357-360.

226.   Ariel, S., Carol, C.H., and Tyano, S. (1984), A formal explication of the concept of family homostasis. Journal of Marital and Family Therapy, 10, 337-350.

227.   Armer, L.G. (1980), Sex-role attitudes, perceived sex-role behaviors and marital adjustment of clients from a family counseling agency. Dissertation Abstracts International, 40, 3879-A.

228.   Armstrong, H., Morris, R.M., Amerongen, M., and Kernaghan, P. (1983), Group therapy for parents of delinquent children. International Journal of Group Psychotherapy, 33, 85-98.

229.   Armstrong, M.C. (1981), Toward a marital contract: A model for marital counseling. Social Casework, 62(9), 520.

230.   Armstrong, R.G. (1975), Subgroups in married couples group sessions. Group Psychotherapy and Psychoanalysis, 28, 60-65.

231.   Armstrong, R.G., and Schur, D. (1972), Warm-up techniques in a married couples group. Group Psychotherapy, 25, 93-101.

232.   Arnkoff, D.B. (1985), Review of A. Freeman, (Ed.), Cognitive therapy with couples and groups. Contemporary Psychology, 30(1), 44.

233.   Arnold, A. (1962), The implications of two-person and three-person relationships for family psychotherapy. Journal of Health and Human Behavior, 3, 94-97.

234.   Arnold, E.L. (Ed.) (1978), Helping parents help their children. New York: Brunner/Mazel.

235.   Arnold, L.E., and Estreicher, D.G. (1985), Parent-child group therapy: Building self-esteem in a cognitive-behavioral group. Lexington, MA: Lexington Books.

236.   Arnon, A., and Levav, I. (1978), The family at a glance — a computerized family care flow-chart. Journal of Family Practice, 7, 1235-1238.

237.   Asen, K., Stein, R., Stevens, A., McHugh, B., Greenwood, J., and Cooklin, A. (1982), A day unit for families. Journal of Family Therapy, 4, 345-258.

238.   Assev, A. (1980), Family therapy in Norway. Journal of Marital and Family Therapy, 6(1), 85-87.

239.   Astigueta, F.D. (1983), T-groups for medical students: Some clinical notes. In L.R. Wolberg and M.L. Aronson (Eds.), Group and family therapy 1982. New York: Brunner/Mazel.

240.   Aston, P.J., and Dobson, G. (1972), Family interaction and social adjustment in a sample of normal school children. Journal of Child Psychology and Psychiatry, 13, 77-90.

241.   Athanasion, R., and Sarkin, R. (1974), Premarital sexual behavior and postmarital adjustment. Archives of Sexual Behavior, 3, 207-225.

242.   Attneave, C.L. (1969), Therapy in tribal settings and urban network intervention. Family Process, 8, 192-210.

243.   Aubert, C., Torrado, and DeSilva, M. (1981), Family treatment of a young prepsychotic child. Acta Paedopsychiatrica, 47, 197-205.

244.   Aubertin, C. (1968), Un projet-pilote de traitement pour alcooliques: La dimension familiale. (A pilot project for treatment of alcoholics: The familiar dimension.) Toxicomanies, 1, 217-219.

245.   Aubry, J., and Bargues, R. (1964), Les nourrices d'un placement familial curatif des carences affectives graves de la primiere enfance. (Foster mothers in charge of disturbed children.) L'Evolution Psychiatrique, 29(3), 411-436.

246.   Auckenthaler, A. (1982), Marital therapy and conceptions of relationships: Conservative contents of a "progressive" method of therapy. Partnerberatung, 19, 57-68.

247.   Auerswald, E.H. (1985), Thinking about thinking in family therapy. Family Process, 24(1), 1-12.

248.   Augenbraun, B., and Tasem, M. (1966), Differential techniques in family interviewing with both parents and preschool child. Journal of the American Academy of Child Psychiatry, 5, 721-730.

249.   Aumage, M. (1978), (The father in conjoint family therapy where one family member is a psychiatric patient.) Etudes, 9, 109-114.

250.   Authier, J. (1979), The family life cycle seminars: An innovative health care psychology program. Professional Psychology, 10, 451-457.

251.   Authier, J., and Land, T. (1978), Family: The unique component of family medicine. Journal of Family Practice, 7, 1066-1068.

252.   Authier, K. (1983), Incest and sexual violence. Family Therapy Collections, 10, 101-128.

253.   Avery, A.W., Ridley, C.A., Leslie, L.A., and Milholland, T. (1980), Relationship enhancement with premarital dyads: A six-month follow-up. American Journal of Family Therapy, 8(3), 23-30.

254.   Avery, N.C. (1982), Family secrets. Psychoanalytic Review, 69, 471-486.

255.   Avesar, A. (1974). Towards a more humanistic approach to family therapy. Dissertation Abstracts International, 34, (10-B).

256.   Avis, J.M. (1985), The politics of functional family therapy: A feminist critique. Journal of Marital and Family Therapy, 11(2), 127-138.

257.   Ayers, G.W. (1976), A time-limited approach to marital therapy. Psychiatric Forum, 5, 24-30.

258.   Azrin, N.H., Naster, B.H., and Jones, R. (1973), Reciprocity counseling: A rapid learning-based procedure for marital counseling. Behaviour Research and Therapy, 11, 365-382.

259.   Azrin, N.H., Nunn, R.G., and Frantz, S.E. (1980), Comparison of reciprocity and discussion-type counseling for marital problems. American Journal of Family Therapy, 8, 21-28.

260.   Babchuk, N. (1978-79), Aging and primary relations. International Journal of Aging and Human Development, 9, 137-151.

261.   Baber, W.S., and Lindsay, J.S.B. (1965), Family psychiatry. New Zealand Medical Journal, 64, 17-22.

262. Babineau, R. (1975), University mental health professionals and the avoidance of family. Journal of American College Health Association, 24, 75-79.

263. Bach, O. (1972), Effect of family therapy in psychiatric treatment. Ceskoslovenska Psychiatrie, 58, 193-198.

264. Bach, O., Feldes, D., Kriegel, A., and Smolivsky, B. (1972), Group therapy with married couples. Psychiatrie, Neurologie Un Medizinische Psychologie, 24(2), 90-97.

265. Bach, O., Feldes, D., and Gruss, U. (1972), The importance of family therapy in psychiatric treatment. Ceskoslovensa Psychiatrica, 68, 193-198.

266. Bach, R., and Moylan, J.J. (1975), Parents administer behavior therapy for inappropriate urination and encopresis: A case study. Journal of Behavior Therapy and Experimental Psychiatry, 6(3), 239-241.

267. Backman, A., and Feldes, D. (1981), Chronic asthma in children: A medico-psycho-social approach. Psychiatria Fennica, 77, 85-95.

268. Badenoch, A., Fisher, J., Hafner, J., and Swift, H. (1984), Predicting the outcome of spouse-aided therapy for persisting psychiatric disorders. American Journal of Family Therapy, 12(1), 59-72.

269. Bader, E. (1982), Redecisions in family therapy: A study of a change in an intensive family therapy workshop. Transactional Analysis Journal, 12(1), 27.

270. Bader, E. (1976), Redecisions in family therapy: A study of change in an intensive family therapy workshop. Dissertation Abstracts International, 37, 2491-2492B.

271. Bader, E., Microys, G., Sinclair, C., Willett, E., and Conway, B. (1980), Do marriage preparation programs really work? A Canadian experiment. Journal of Marriage and Family Therapy, 6(2), 171-179.

272. Badoud, F. (1982), Review of A. Ruffiot's Psychoanalytic family therapy. Psychologie, 41, 336.

273. Baer, P.E. (1983), Conflict management in the family: The impact of paternal hypertension. In J.P. Vincent (Ed.), Advances in Family Intervention, Assessment and Theory, Vol. 3. Greenwich: JAI Press.

274. Baethge, G. (1981), Child therapy or family therapy? Considerations as to their indication. Praxis Der Kinderpsychologie Und Kinderpsychiatrie, 30, 159-165.

275. Bagarozzi, D.A. (1982), The family therapist's role in treating families in rural communities: A general systems approach. Journal of Marital and Family Therapy, 8, 51-58.

276. Bagarozzi, D.A. (1980), Family therapy and the black middle class: A neglected area of study. Journal of Marriage and Family Therapy, 6(2), 159-166.

277.   Bagarozzi, D.A. (1980), Holistic family therapy and clinical supervision: Systems, behavioral and psychoanlaytic perspectives. Family Therapy, 7, 153-165.

278.   Bagarozzi, D.A. (1984), Family measurement techniques. American Journal of Family Therapy, 12(4), 59-62.

279.   Bagarozzi, D.A. (1983), Contingency contracting for structural and process changes in family systems. In L.R. Wolberg and M.L. Aronson (Eds.), Group and family therapy 1982. New York: Brunner/Mazel.

280.   Bagarozzi, D.A. (1983), Review of G. Thorman's Helping troubled families: A social work perspective. American Journal of Family Therapy, 11, 82-83.

281.   Bagarozzi, D.A., Jurich, A., and Giordano, J. (Eds.). (1982), Marital and family therapy: New perspectives in theory, research and practice. New York: Human Sciences Press.

282.   Bagarozzi, D.A., and Anderson, S. (1982), The evolution of family mythological systems: Considerations for meaning, clinical assessment, and treatment. Journal of Psychoanalytic Anthropology, 5, 71-90.

283.   Bagarozzi, D.A., and Atilano, R.B. (1982), SIDCARB: A clinical tool for rapid assessment of social exchange inequities and relationship barriers. Journal of Sex and Marital Therapy, 8, 325.

284.   Bagarozzi, D.A., and Bagarozzi, J.I. (1980), Financial counseling: A self control model for the family. Family Relations, 29, 396-403.

285.   Bagarozzi, D.A., and Giddings, C.W. (1983), Conjugal violence: A critical review of current research and clinical practices. American Journal of Family Therapy, 11, 3-15.

286.   Bagarozzi, D.A., and Ginnings, C.W. (1984), Behavioral marital therapy: Empirical status, current practices, trends and future directions. Clinical Social Work Journal, 11(3), 263-279.

287.   Bagarozzi, D.A., and Rauen, P. (1981), Pre-marital counseling: Appraisal and status. American Journal of Family Therapy, 9(3), 13-27.

288.   Bagarozzi, D.A., and Wodarski, J.S. (1978), Behavioral treatment of marital discord. Clinical Social Work Journal, 6, 135-154.

289.   Baideme, S.M., Hill, H.A., and Serritella, D. (1978), Conjoint family therapy following divorce: An alternative strategy. International Journal of Family Counseling, 1, 55-59.

290.   Baideme, S.M., Kern, R.M., and Taffel-Cohen, S. (1979), The use of Adlerian family therapy in a case of school phobia. Journal of Individual Psychology, 35(1), 58-69.

291.   Baird, E., and Redfering, D.L. (1975), Behavior modification in marriage counseling. Journal of Family Counseling, 3, 59-64.

292.   Baird, J.P. (1973), Changes in patterns of interpersonal behavior among family members following brief family therapy. Dissertation Abstracts International, 34, 404-B.

293. Baisden, M.J., and Baisden, J.R. (1979), Profile of women who seek counseling for sexual dysfunction. American Journal of Family Therapy, 7(1), 68-77.

294. Baither, R.C. (1978), Family therapy with adolescent drug abusers: A review. Journal of Drug Education, 8, 337-343.

295. Baker, A.A. (1952), The misfit family: A psychodramatic technique used in a therapeutic community. British Journal of Medical Psychology, 25, 235-243.

296. Baker, F.P. (1983), Framo's method of integration of family of origin with couples therapy: A follow-up study of an intergenerational approach. Dissertation Abstracts International, 44, 295-B.

297. Baker, O.V., Druckman, J.M., and Flagle, J.E. (1981), The identification and development of three intervention models for youth and families experiencing separation and divorce. Conciliation Courts Review, 19, 41-46.

298. Baldus, D. (1984), Deep psychological conflict analysis of problems among couples (Review of P. Seidman). Analytische Psychologie, 15, 71.

299. Baldwin, B.A. (1978), Moving from drugs to sex: New directions for youth-oriented peer counseling. Journal of the American College of Health Association, 27(2), 75-78.

300. Baldwin, C. (1985), Development of a question classification scale for family therapy. Dissertation Abstracts International, 45, 2762-A.

301. Balester, L., and Renzi Gaustalla, B. (1967), Intervento psicoterapico nei rapporti interpersonali di un gruppo familiare. (Psychotherapeutic intervention in the interpersonal relationships of a family group.) Rivista Di Psychiatrica, 2, 582-588.

302. Balint, E. (1966), Marital conflicts and their treatment. Comprehensive Psychiatry, 7(5), 407.

303. Balis, S., and Zirpoli, E. (1982), Four plus four: A short-term family group for relatives of alcoholics. Social Work With Groups, 5, 49-55.

304. Ball, J.D., and Ball, O. (1979), Strengthening families through marriage enrichment. In: N. Stinnett, B., Chesser, and J. Defrain (Eds.), Building family strengths. Lincoln, NE: University of Nebraska Press.

305. Ball, J.D., and Henning, L.H. (1981), Rational suggestions for premarital counseling. Journal of Marriage and Family Therapy, 7(1), 69-73.

306. Balmer, J.V., Becvar, R.J., and Hinckley, M. (1977), Patterns of redundancy in marriage and family systems. Family Therapy, 4, 113-119.

307. Balrop, J.L. (1975), Marital therapy: An existential approach. Family Therapy, 2(3), 269.

308. Balswick, J.K (1979), The importance of developmental task achievement to early marital adjustment. Family Therapy, 6(3), 145.

309.   Bambrick, A.F. (1980), Defining the terms of go-between process. International Journal of Family Therapy, 2, 99–105.

310.   Bancroft, J. (1975), The behavioral approach to marital problems. British Journal of Medical Psychology, 48, 147–152.

311.   Bander, K., Fein, E., and Bishop, G. (1982), Child sex abuse treatment: Some barriers to program operation. Child Abuse and Neglect, 6, 185–191.

312.   Bandler, R., Grinder, J., and Satir, V. (1976). Changing with families: A book about further education for being human. Palo Alto, CA: Human Science and Behavior Books.

313.   Bang, R. (1961), Understanding and helping in the care of single cases/casework: With special reference to prerequisites in marriage counseling work. Praxis der Kinderpsychologie und Kinder Psychiatrie, 10, 228–237.

314.   Bank, S., and Kahn, M.D. (1976), Sisterhood-brotherhood is powerful: Sibling subsystems and family therapy. Annual Progress in Child Psychiatry, 7, 493–518.

315.   Bank, S., and Kahn, M.D. (1975), Sisterhood-brotherhood is powerful: Sibling subsystems and family therapy. Family Process, 14(3), 311–337.

316.   Banmen, J. (1982), The incidence, treatment, and counseling of incest. International Journal for the Advancement of Counseling, 5(3), 201.

317.   Banning, A. (1979), The attraction of opposites: An object-relations understanding of family intervention over three generations. Australian and New Zealand Journal of Psychiatry, 13(3), 241–247.

318.   Baptiste, D.A. (1985), Review of C. Obudho (Ed.). Black marriage and family therapy. Family Relations, 34(1), 138–139.

319.   Baptiste, D.A., Jr. (1984), Marital and family therapy with racially/culturally intermarried stepfamilies: Issues and guidelines. Family Relations, 33(3), 373–380.

320.   Barash, D.A. (1979), Dynamics of the pathological family system. Perspectives in Psychiatric Care, 17, 17–25.

321.   Barcai, A. (1981), Normative family development. Journal of Marital and Family Therapy, 7, 353–359.

322.   Barcai, A. (1971), Family therapy in the treatment of anorexia nervosa. American Journal of Psychiatry, 128, 286–290.

323.   Barcai, A. (1967), An adventure in multiple family therapy. Family Process, 6, 185–192.

324.   Barcai, A., and Rabkin, L.Y. (1972), Excommunication as a family therapy technique. Archives of General Psychiatry, 27, 804–808.

325.   Barcai, A., and Rabkin, R.Y. (1975), Family therapy for the 'incorrigible' adolescent. Current Psychiatric Therapies, 15, 65–70.

326.   Bard, M. (1970), Training police as specialists in family crisis
       intervention. Washington, D.C.: National Institute of Law Enforcement
       and Criminal Justice, U.S. Department of Justice, Law Enforcement
       Assistance Administration.

327.   Bard, M. (1969), Family intervention police teams as a community
       mental health resource. Journal of Criminal Law, 60, 247-250.

328.   Bardill, D.R. (1976), The simulated family as an aid to learning family
       group treatment. Child Welfare, 55, 703-709.

329.   Bardis, P.D. (1959), A familism scale. Marriage and Family Living, 21,
       340-341.

330.   Barette, J., and Marsden, C.D. (1979), Attitudes of families to some
       aspects of Huntington's chorea. Psychological Medicine, 9, 327-336.

331.   Barker, P. (1981), Basic family therapy. Baltimore, MD: University
       Park.

332.   Barker, P. (1978), "The impossible child": Some approaches to
       treatment. Canadian Psychiatric Association Journal, 23, 1-21.

333.   Barker, W. (1979), Realities and problems of intervention in a study of
       zoo parent-child dyads. Bulletin of the British Psychological Society, 32,
       148.

334.   Barlow, D.H., Mavissakalian, M., and Hay, L.R. (1981), Couples
       treatment of agoraphobia: Changes in marital satisfaction. Behaviour
       Research and Therapy, 19, 245-55.

335.   Barlow, D.H., O'Brien, G.T., and Last, C.G. (1984), Couples treatment
       of agoraphobia. Behavior Therapy, 15, 41-58.

336.   Barlow, D.H., and Seidner, A.L. (1983), Treatment of adolescent
       agoraphobics: Effects on parent-adolescent relations. Behaviour
       Research and Therapy, 21, 519-526.

337.   Barmettler, D., and Fields, G.L. (1975-76), Using the group method to
       study and treat parents of asthmatic children. Social Work and Health
       Care, 1(2), 167-176.

338.   Barnard, C.P., and Corrales, R.G. (1981), The theory and technique of
       family therapy. Springfield, IL: Charles C. Thomas.

339.   Barnes, G.G. (1980), Family therapy in social work settings: A survey
       by questionnaire 1976 to 1978. Journal of Family Therapy, 2, 357-378.

340.   Barnes, G.G. (1982), Initial work with the family. In A. Bentovim, G.G.
       Barnes, and A. Cooklin (Eds.), Family therapy. I. Complementary
       frameworks of theory and practice. London: Academic Press.

341.   Barnes, G.G. (1982), Pattern and intervention: Research findings and
       the development of family therapy theory. In A. Bentovim, G.G. Barnes,
       and A. Cooklin (Eds.), Family therapy. I. Complementary frameworks
       of theory and practice. London: Academic Press.

342.   Barnes, G.G. (1983), A difference that makes a difference: Brief intervention in family pattern. 1. Journal of Family Therapy, 5, 37-52.

343.   Barnes, G.G., Bentovim, A., Bynghall, J., and Cooklin, A. (1982), Dialogues in a family in treatment. In. A. Bentovim, G.G. Barnes, and A. Cooklin (Eds.), Family therapy. I. Complementary frameworks of theory and practice. London: Academic Press.

344.   Barnes, G.G., Chabon, R.S., and Hertzberg, L.J. (1974), Team treatment for abusive families. Social Casework, 55(10), 600.

345.   Barnett, L.R., and Nietzel, M.T. (1979), Relationship of instrumental and affectional behaviors and self-esteem to marital satisfaction in distressed and nondistressed couples. Journal of Consulting and Clinical Psychology, 47(5), 946-957.

346.   Barnhill, L.R. (1979), Healthy family systems. Family Coordinator, 28, 94-100.

347.   Barnhill, L.R. (1980), Basic interventions for violence in families. Hospital and Community Psychiatry, 31, 547-551.

348.   Barnhill, L.R., and Longo, D. (1978), Fixation and regression in the family life cycle. Family Process, 17, 469-478.

349.   Barnwell, J.E. (1960), Group treatment of older adolescent boys in a family agency. Social Casework, 41, 247-253.

350.   Barocas, H.A. (1972), Psychodrama techniques in training police in family crisis intervention. Group Psychotherapy and Psychoanalysis, 25, 30-31.

351.   Baron, R. (1978), Probation officers, family crisis counseling and juvenile diversion: I and II. Dissertation Abstracts International, 38, 3462-B.

352.   Barr, J.P. (1984), Review of L.R. Barnhill's Clinical approaches to family violence: The family therapy collections. Contemporary Psychology, 29(7), 593.

353.   Barrabee, P. (1957), The family as a unit of treatment in mental health therapy. Marriage and Family Living, 19, 182-186.

354.   Barrett, B.N. (1976), Enterprising principles of counseling the low-income black family. Journal of Nonwhite Concilliation and Personnel Guidance, 5, 14-22.

355.   Barrett, D.L., and Fine, H.J. (1980), A child has been beaten: The therapy of battered children as adults. Psychotherapy: Theory, Research and Practice, 17(3), 285-294.

356.   Barrett, M.J. (1983), Review of C. Madanes' Strategic family therapy. American Journal of Family Therapy, 11, 78-79.

357.   Barron, E., and Richardson, J.A. (1978), Counseling women for tubal sterilization. Health and Social Work, 3(1), 49-58.

358. Barrows, S.E. (1981), Family therapy in Europe: An interview with Maurizio Andolfi. American Journal of Family Therapy, 9(4), 70-75.

359. Barrows, S.E. (1982), Interview with Palazzoli, Mara Selvini and Prata, Giuliana. American Journal of Family Therapy, 10, 60-69.

360. Barrows, S.E. (1982), Nathan W. Ackerman as a therapist and individual: A interview with Donald Bloch and Kitty La Perriere. American Journal of Family Therapy, 10, 63-70.

361. Barrozzi, R.L., Park, D., and Watson, E.L. (1982), A family agency integrates advocacy, counseling, and FLE. Social Casework, 63(4), 227.

362. Barry, A. (1979), Research project on successful single-parent families. American Journal of Family Therapy, 7, 65-73.

363. Barry, M.P. (1972), Feedback concepts in family therapy. Perspectives in Psychiatric Care, 10, 183-189.

364. Barthe, H.J. (1984), Review of S. Minuchin and H.C. Fishman's Practice of Structural family therapy, strategies and techniques. Praxis der Kinderpsychologie und Kinderpsychiatrie, 33(4), 161.

365. Bartlett, D. (1975), The use of multiple family therapy groups with adolescent drug addicts. In: M. Sugar (Ed.), The adolescent in group and family therapy. New York, NY: Brunner/Mazel.

366. Bartoletti, M.D. (1969), Conjoint family therapy with clinic team in a shopping plaza. International Journal of Social Psychiatry, 15, 251-257.

367. Bartoletti, M.D., Bourke, P., and MacDonald, E.M. (1982), Therapy with remarriage families: VI. The supportive separation system: a joint legal and marital counseling alternative. Family Therapy Collections, 2, 79-91.

368. Barton, C. (1983), Communication, cognitions, and contingencies in delinquent and control families. Dissertation Abstracts International, 44, 1584-B.

369. Barton, C., Alexander, J.F., Waldron, H., Turner, C.W., and Warburton, J. (1985), Generalizing treatment effects of functional family therapy: Three replications. American Journal of Family Therapy, 13, 16-26.

370. Barton, C., and Alexander, J.F. (1977), Therapists' skill as determinants of effective systems-behavioral family therapy. International Journal of Family Counseling, 5, 11-19.

371. Barton, W.E., and Davidson, E.M. (1961), Psychotherapy and family care. Current Psychiatric Therapies, 1, 204-249.

372. Bartone, J.C. (1985), Family therapy: Medical subject analysis with research bibliography. Washington, D.C.: ABBE Pubs Assn.

373. Bartusis, M.A. (1981), Infidelity, separation, and divorce. Current Psychiatric Therapies, 21, 95-101.

374. Bartusis, M.A. (1982), The integration of marital therapy into private practice. Psychiatric Annals, 12(7), 677.

375.   Barzillai, R. (1973), Factors in the psycho-pathology of the child. Acta Biochimica et Biophysica Academiae Scientiarum Hungaricae, 21, 7-9.

376.   Basamania, B.W. (1961), The family as the unit of study and treatment: IV. The emotional life of the family: Inferences for social casework. Workshop, 1959. American Journal of Orthopsychiatry, 31, 74-86.

377.   Basecgz, G. (1968), Conjoint family psychotherapy. Acta Psychiatrica Belgica, 68, 383-391.

378.   Basecqz, G. (1974), Familial interrelational approach in psychiatry: A "philosophy" rather than a technique. Acta Psychiatrica Belgica, 74(4), 389-404.

379.   Bashford, M.B. (1977), An assessment of direct and observational communication training as marital quasi-therapy. Dissertation Abstracts International, 38, 2353B.

380.   Basquin, M., Dubuisson, P., Lajevnes, B., and Testemal, G. (1969-1970), Reflections on the therapeutic couple in psychodrama. Bulletin of Psychologie, 23(13-16), 775-778.

381.   Bassoff, E.S. (1982), Identifying, preventing, and treating disturbances between parents and their infants. Personnel and Guidance Journal, 60, 228-232.

382.   Bastoe, O. (1973), Marriage guidance. A family therapeutic offer of treatment. Zeitschrift fur Psychosomatische Medizin und Psychoanalyse, 19, 272-278.

383.   Bastoe, O. (1974), Marriage guidance. A family therapeutic offer of treatment. Tidsskrift for den Norske Laegeforening, 94, 581-584.

384.   Bastoni, J.B. (1980), Psychotherapy with wives of sexual deviants. American Journal of Psychotherapy, 34(1), 20-25.

385.   Bate Boerop, J.L. (1975), General systems theory and family therapy in practice. Family Therapy, 2, 69-77.

386.   Bates, J.E., Skilbeck, W.M., and Smith, K.V. (1975), Intervention with families of gender-disturbed boys. American Journal of Orthopsychiatry, 45, 150-157.

387.   Battegay, R. (1983), Review of U. Rauchfleish's According to best judgment and conscience: The ethical responsibility of psychology and psychotherapy - new contributions to educational and family counseling, Vol. 6. Gruppenpsychotherapie und Gruppendynamik, 18, 257.

388.   Battin, D., Ankin, A., and Wiener, A. (1975), Telephone intervention in the therapy of bereaved families. Journal of Thanatology, 3(1), 43-48.

389.   Baublitz, J.I. (1978), Transitional treatment of hostile married couples. Social Work, 23, 321-323.

390.   Baucom, D.H. (1982), A comparison of behavioral contracting and problem-solving/communications training in behavioral marital therapy. Behavior Therapy, 13, 162-174.

391. Baucom, D.H. (1983), Assessing change in the clinical practice of marital therapy. American Journal of Family Therapy, 11, 67-70.

392. Baucom, D.H. (1983), Conceptual and psychometric issues in evaluating the effectiveness of behavioral marital therapy. In J.P. Vincent (Ed.), Advances in family intervention, assessment and theory, Vol. 3. Greenwich: JAI Press.

393. Bauelas, J.B. (1984), Analogue research and the family therapist: Rejoinder. Family Process, 23(3), 346.

394. Bauer, R. (1979), Gestalt approach to family therapy. American Journal of Family Therapy, 7, 41-45.

395. Bauers, W. (1983), Family therapy in connection with clinical psychotherapy for children and teenagers. Praxis Der Kinderpsychologie und Kinderpsychiatrie, 32, 224-233.

396. Baum, M.C. (1978), The short-term, long-term, and differential effects of group versus bibliotherapy relationship enhancement programs for couples. Dissertation Abstracts International, 38, 6132-6133B.

397. Baum, V. (1981), Counseling families of deaf children. Journal of Rehabilitation of the Deaf, 15(1), 16.

398. Baumann, M., and Von Orelli, R. (1961), Functional relationship between child, parents, and therapist in child psychotherapy. Praxis Der Kinderpsychologie Und Kinderpsychiatrie, 10, 1.

399. Bayard, R.T. (1975), Nonverbal communication between spouses. Dissertation Abstracts International, 36, 1959B.

400. Beach, S.R., and Arias, I. (1983), Assessment of perceptual discrepancy: Utility of Primary Communication Inventory. Family Process, 22, 309-316.

401. Beach, S.R.H., Jouriles, E.N., and O'Leary, K.D. (1985), Extramarital sex: Impact on depression and commitment in couples seeking marital therapy. Journal of Sex and Marital Therapy, 11, 99-108.

402. Beal, D., and Dukro, P. (1977), Family counseling as an alternative to legal action for the juvenile status offender. Journal of Marital and Family Therapy, 3, 77-81.

403. Beal, E.M. (1980), Teaching family therapy: Theory, technique and supervision. Psychiatric Annals, 10, 31-44.

404. Beal, E.W. (1979), Children of divorce: A family systems perspective. Journal of Social Issues, 35(4), 140.

405. Beal, E.W. (1976), Current trends in the training of family therapists. American Journal of Psychiatry, 133, 137-141.

406. Beal, E.W. (1978), Use of the extended family in the treatment of multiple personality. American Journal of Psychiatry, 135, 539-542.

407. Beatman, F.L. (1964), The training and preparation of workers for family-group treatment. Social Casework, 45, 202-208.

408. Beatman, F.L., and Ackerman, N.W. (1966), Current issues in family treatment. Social Casework, 47, 75-81.

409. Beauchamp, S.P. (1979), Educating patient and family for CV surgery. Association of Operating Room Nurses Journal, 29, 860-862.

410. Beaver, W.A. (1978), Conjoint and pseudo-disjunctive treatment in communication skills for relationship improvement with marital couples. Dissertation Abstracts International, 39, 3361A.

411. Beavers, W.R. (1982), Indications and contraindications for couples therapy. Psychiatric Clinics of North America, 5, 469-478.

412. Beavers, W.R. (1981), A systems model of family for family therapists. Journal of Marriage and Family Therapy, 7(3), 299-307.

413. Beavers, W.R. (1983), Learning a systems orientation from parents. Family Therapy Collections, 6, 54-65.

414. Beavers, W.R. (1985), Psychotherapy and growth: A family systems perspective. New York: Brunner/Mazel.

415. Beavers, W.R. (1983), Healthy, midrange, and severely dysfunctional families. In F. Walsh (Ed.), Normal family processes. New York: Guilford Press.

416. Beavers, W.R. (1982), Review of D.B. Wile's Couples therapy: A non-traditional approach. International Journal of Group Psychotherapy, 32, 556.

417. Beavers, W.R. (1983), Review of J.L. Framo's Explorations in marital and family therapy. Family Process, 22, 121-122.

418. Beavers, W.R., and Voeller, M.N. (1983), Family models: Comparing and contrasting the Olson circumplex model with the Beavers systems model. Family Process, 22, 85-98.

419. Bechosian, R.C. (1978), Family therapy: Full length case studies. International Journal of Family Counseling, 6, 89.

420. Beck, D.F. (1975), Research findings on the outcomes of marita# counseling. Social Casework, 56, 153-181.

421. Beck, H.L. (1959), Counseling parents of retarded children. Children, 6, 225-230.

422. Beck, H.W. (1977), Dream analysis in family therapy. Clinical Social Work Journal, 5, 53-57.

423. Beck, M. (1977), Family therapy as reciprocal emotional induction. Family Therapy, 4, 151-161.

424. Beck, M. (1976), Some reflections on the life and death struggle in the treatment of schizophrenically involved families. Family Therapy, 3, 141-149.

425. Beck, M. (1975), Therapeutic management of aggression in family therapy. Family Therapy, 2, 137-140.

426.   Beck, M.J (1977), The therapist's response to the family's aggression. Journal of Marital and Family Therapy, 3, 67-69.

427.   Beck, M.J. (1977), Treatment of the character-disordered family member. Family Therapy, 4, 43-48.

428.   Beck, M.J. (1975), Respiratory resistance in family therapy. Journal of Family Counseling, 3(1), 77-78.

429.   Beck, M.J. (1979), Pathological narcissism and the psychology of the married victim. Family Therapy, 6(3), 155.

430.   Beck, M.J., Levinson, F., and Bloom, M. (1975), Modern psychoanalytic treatment of narcissistic families. Family Therapy, 2, 63-68.

431.   Beck, R.L. (1982), Family psychiatry and the medical student: The marital and family assessment seminar. Journal of Psychiatric Education, 6, 94-100.

432.   Beck, R.L. (1982), Process and content in the family-of-origin group. International Journal of Group Psychotherapy, 32, 233-44.

433.   Beck, R.L. (1983), The couple's assessment outline: A teaching tool for psychiatric training. Clinical Supervision, 1, 5-15.

434.   Beck-Dvorzak, M. (1967), Parents' personality and psychotherapy of the neurotic child. Neuropihijatrija, 15, 75-81.

435.   Becker, B.J. (1978), Holistic, analytic approaches to marital therapy. American Journal of Psychoanalysis, 38, 129-142.

436.   Becker, J. (1963), "Good premorbid" schizophrenic wives and their husbands. Family Process, 2, 34-51.

437.   Becker, J.V., Skinner, L.J., and Abel, G.G. (1982), Treatment of a 4-year-old victim of incest. American Journal of Family Therapy, 10, 41-46.

438.   Becker, M. (1948), The effects of activity group therapy on sibling rivalry. Journal of Social Casework, 29, 217-221.

439.   Becker, M.C. (1945), The effects of group therapy on sibling rivalry. Smith College Studies in Social Work, 16, 131-132.

440.   Becker, S. (1981), Counseling the families of deaf children: A mental health worker speaks out. Journal of Rehabilitation of the Deaf, 15(1), 10.

441.   Beckman, D., and Junker, H. (1973), Structures of married couples in the Glessen test (Author's translation). Zeitschrift fur Psychotherapie Medizin und Psychologie, 23, 140-150.

442.   Beckman, K., Marsella, A.J., and Finney, R. (1979), Depression in the wives of nuclear submarine personnel. American Journal of Psychiatry, 136, 524-526.

443.   Beckman-Brindley, S., and Tavormin, J.B. (1978), Power relationships in families: A social-exchange perspective. Family Process, 17, 423-436.

444.   Becvar, D.S. (1982), The family is not a group—or is it? Journal for Specialists in Group Work, 7, 88-95.

445.   Becvar, R.J., and Becvar, D.S. (1982), Systems theory and family therapy: A primer. Lanham, MD: University Press of America

446.   Bedford, S. (1969), The "new morality" and marriage counseling. In: B.N. Ard, Jr., and C.C. Ard (Eds.), Handbook of marriage counseling. Palo Alto, CA: Science and Behavior Books.

447.   Bedrosian, R.C. (1982), Clinical approaches to family violence: VIII. Using cognitive and systems intervention in the treatment of marital violence. Family Therapy Collections, 1, 117-138.

448.   Bedrosian, R.C. (1979), Review of M. Berger, Beyond the double-bind. American Journal of Family Therapy, 7, 87.

449.   Bedrosian, R.C. (1979), Review of P. Papp, Family therapy: Full-length case studies. International Journal of Counseling, 6, 89.

450.   Beecher, W., and Beecher, M. (1957), Re-structuring mistaken family relationships. Journal of Individual Psychology, 13, 176-181.

451.   Beels, C.C. (1978), Social networks, the family, and the schizophrenic patient: Introduction to the issue. Schizophrenic Bulletin, 4, 512-521.

452.   Beels, C.C. (1975), Family and social management of schizophrenia. Schizophrenia Bulletin, 13, 97-118.

453.   Beels, C.C., and Ferber, A. (1969), Family therapy: A view. Family Process, 8, 280-318.

454.   Beels, C.C., and McFarlane, W.R. (1982), Family treatments of schizophrenia: Background and state of the art. Hospital and Community Psychiatry, 33, 541-550.

455.   Beese, F. (1972), Neurosis structure and family dynamics: Theoretical bases. Praxis Der Kinderpsychologie und Kinderpsychiatrie, 21, 114-120.

456.   Beeson, G.W. (1982), Pastoral response to marital alienation. Pastoral Psychology, 30, 185-192.

457.   Behr, H. (1979), Cohesiveness in families and therapy groups Group Analysis, 12, 9-12.

458.   Behr, H. (1979), Review of S. Wolrond-Skinner's Family and marital psychotherapy. Group Analysis, 12, 275.

459.   Behr, H.L. (1977), Introducing medical students to family therapy using simulated family interviews. Journal of Medical Education, 11, 32-38.

460.   Beigel, H. (1953), Prevarication in marriage counseling. Marriage and Family Living, 15, 332-337.

461.   Beigner, R.M. (1974), The development and evaluation of a training videotape for the resolution of marital conflict. Dissertation Abstracts International, 34(7), 3485B.

462.   Beit-Hallahme, B., and Colon, F. (1974), Involving family members in student counseling. Psychotherapy: Theory, Research and Practice, 11(3), 265-269.

463.   Beitchman, J.H. (1981), A sick father and his son: A clinical case and some therapeutic considerations. Bulletin of the Menninger Clinic, 45(1), 29-42.

464.   Beland, H. (1980), Review of S. Minuchin, Families and family therapy. Gruppenpsychotherapie und Gruppendynamik, 16, 171-174.

465.   Belfie, M.J. (1976), An exploratory study of the effects of family relationships of a parent-teen communication workshop. Dissertation Abstracts International, 37, 905-906A.

466.   Belgum, J.A. (1948), Group therapy in a court setting with parents of delinquent children. Unpublished Masters Thesis, New York School of Social Work.

467.   Bell, D.F. (1970), Family participation in hospital care for children. Children, 17, 154.

468.   Bell, J.E. (1975), Recent advances in family group therapy. In: M. Rosenbaum and M.M. Berger (Eds.), Group psychotherapy and group function. (2nd Ed.). New York, NY: Basic Books.

469.   Bell, J.E. (1977), Family in medical and psychiatric treatment: Selected clinical approaches. Journal of Operational Psychiatry, 8, 57-65.

470.   Bell, J.E. (1978), Family context therapy: A model for family change. Journal of Marital and Family Therapy, 4, 111-126.

471.   Bell, J.E. (1961), Family group therapy: A method for the psychological treatment of older children, adolescents, and their parents. Public Health Monograph, 64, 1-52.

472.   Bell, J.E. (1964), The family group therapist: An agent of change. International Journal of Group Psychotherapy, 14, 72-83.

473.   Bell, J.E. (1962), Recent advances in family group therapy. Journal of Child Psychology and Psychiatry and Applied Disciplines, 3, 1-15.

474.   Bell, J.E. (1963), A theoretical position for family group therapy. Family Process, 2, 1-14.

475.   Bell, J.E. (1967), Contrasting approaches in marital counseling. Family Process, 6, 16-26.

476.   Bell, N.W. (1962), Extended family relations of disturbed and well families. Family Process, 1(2), 175-193.

477.   Bell, S. (1978), The effects of sociodrama on the behaviors and attitudes of elementary school boys. Group Psychotherapy, Psychodrama, and Sociometry, 31, 117-135.

478.   Bellman, M. (1971), Is family therapy an alternative to the established methods of treatment in child psychiatry? Lakartidningen, 68, 1234-1242.

479.   Bellucci, M.T. (1975), Treatment of latency-age adopted children and parents. Social Casework, 56, 297-301.

480.   Bellville, T.P., Raths, O.N., and Bellville, C.J. (1969), Conjoint marriage therapy with a husband-and-wife team. American Journal of Orthopsychiatry, 39, 473-483.

481.   Belmont, L.P., and Jasnow, A. (1961), The utilization of cotherapists and of group therapy techniques in a family-oriented approach to a disturbed child. International Journal of Group Psychotherapy, 11, 319-328.

482.   Belove, L. (1980), First encounters of the close kind (FECK): The use of the story of the first interaction as an early recollection of a marriage. Journal of Individual Psychology, 36(2), 191-208.

483.   Belson, R. (1975), The importance of the second interview in marriage counseling. Counseling Psychology, 5, 27-31.

484.   Belson, R. (1980), International politics and family systems: Some observations on tactics. International Journal of Family Therapy, 2(4), 212-229.

485.   Beltrami, E., Dupras, A., and Tremblay, R. (1977), Effect of sexual fantasy frequencies on outcome of short-term treatment program of sexual inadequacy in heterosexual couples. In: R. Gemme and C.C. Wheeler (Eds.), Progress in sexology: Perspectives in sexuality. New York, NY: Plenum Pres.

486.   Belzer, H. (1983), The effectiveness of a psychosocial intervention with cancer patients and their families in facilitating their adapation to living with cancer. Dissertation Abstracts International, 43, 2700-B.

487.   Ben-Ami, V.I. (1976), The effects of pretreatment training on certain intake interview behaviors of family members. Dissertation Abstracts International, 37, 3060-3061B.

488.   Benjamin, L.S. (1977), Structural analysis of a family in therapy. Journal of Consulting and Clinical Psychology, 45, 391-406.

489.   Bennett, H.G., Collins, S., Fisher, G.D., Hughes, S.E., and Reinhart, J.B. (1982), SCAN: A method of community collaboration. Child Abuse and Neglect, 6, 81-85.

490.   Bennett, I.B. (1973), Use of ego psychology concepts in family service intake. Social Casework, 54, 290-293.

491.   Benningfield, A.B. (1978), Multiple family therapy systems. Journal of Marital and Family Therapy, 4, 25-34.

492.   Benningfield, A.B. (1980), Multiple family therapy systems. Advances in Family Psychiatry, 2, 411-424.

493.   Bennington, K.F. (1972), Counseling the family of the deafened adult. Journal of Applied Rehabilitation Counseling, 3, 178-187.

494.   Bennum, I. (1984), Review of E. Kaufman and P. Kaufman's Family
       therapy of drug and alcohol abuse. British Journal of Addiction, 79(3),
       349.

495.   Bennun, I. (1985), Prediction and responsiveness in behavioral marital
       therapy. Behavioural Psychotherapy, 13, 186-201.

496.   Benoit, J.C. (1977), Schizophrenia, communication, and psychiatric
       institution: Therapeutic advantage of the familial interview in the
       presence of the psychotic. Etudes Psychotherapie, 8, 111-116.

497.   Benoit, J.C. (1984), Family interventions in psychiatry. Family therapy
       or planned group conferences. Soins Psychiatrie, 29, 3-8.

498.   Benoit, J.C., Daigremont, A., Guitton, C., Porot, D., and Rabean, B.
       (1978), Collective interviews of couples in sectorized psychiatry.
       Annals of Medical Psychology, 136, 901-909.

499.   Benoit, J.C., Daigremont, A., Kossmann, L., Pruss, P., and Roume, D.
       (1980), Multi-family encounter group in a residence for chronic
       patients. Annals of Medical Psychology, 138, 1253-60.

500.   Benoit, J.C., Daigremont, A., Rabeau, B., and Angst, M. (1977), The
       family interview in the presence of a psychotic: Positive results with
       chronically hospitalized schizophrenics. Annals of Medical Psychology,
       135, 802-811.

501.   Benson, L., Berger, M. and Mease, W. (1975), Family communication
       systems. Small Group Behavior, 6, 91-105.

502.   Benton, D.W. (1979), Family therapy: Problems encountered in
       defocusing the identified patient. Journal of Psychiatric Nursing, 17(5),
       28-32.

503.   Bentovim, A. (1971), Behandlung psychisch geosturter kinder durch
       familientherapie. (Treatment of mentally disturbed children with family
       therapy.) Praxis der Kinderpsychologie und Kinderpsychiatrie, 20, 74-78.

504.   Bentovim, A. (1970), Psychoanlayses unde psychotherapie bei kindern
       und jugendlichen. (Psychoanalysis and psychotherapy with children and
       adolescents.) Praxis der Kinderpsychologie und Kinderpsychiatrie, 19,
       68-74.

505.   Bentovim, A. (1976), Disobedience and violent behavior in children:
       Family pathology and family treatment--I. British Medical Journal;
       Clinical Research Edition, 1, 947-949.

506.   Bentovim, A. (1976), Disobedience and violent behavior in children.
       Family pathology and family treatment--II. British Medical Journal;
       Clinical Research Edition, 1, 1004-1006.

507.   Bentovim, A. (1982), A family therapy approach in making decisions in
       child care cases. In A. Bentovim, G.G. Barnes, and A. Cooklin (Eds.),
       Family therapy. 2. Complementary frameworks of theory and
       practice. London: Academic Press.

508.   Bentovim, A. (Ed.) (1982), Family therapy: Complementary frameworks
       of theory and practice, Vol. 1. New York: Grune and Stratton.

509. Bentovim, A. (Ed.). (1982), Family therapy: Complementary frameworks of theory and practice, Vol. 2. New York: Grune and Stratton.

510. Bentovim, A., Bynghall, J., Barnes, G.G., Cooklin, A., and Skynner, R. (1982), Different view of a healthy family. In A. Bentovim, G.G. Barnes, and A. Cooklin (Eds.), Family therapy. I. Complementary frameworks of theory and practice. London: Academic Press.

511. Bentovim, A., and Gilmour, L. (1981), A family therapy interactional approach to decision making in child care, access, and custody cases. Journal of Family Therapy, 3(2), 65-78.

512. Bentovim, A., and Kinston, W. (1978), Brief focal family therapy when the child is the referred patient: I. Clinical. Journal of Child Psychology and Psychiatry, 19, 1-12.

513. Benz, M.G. (1940), Family counseling service in a university community. Teacher's College Contributions to Education, No. 800.

514. Berc, K.M. (1974), Letter: Wives of homosexual men. American Journal of Psychiatry, 131, 832-833.

515. Berensen, D. (1976), A family approach to alcoholism. Psychiatric Quarterly, 13, 33-38.

516. Berenson, G. (1976), Attachment theory, object relations theory and family therapy. Family Therapy, 3, 483-495.

517. Berenson, G. (1977), The family therapist. Family Therapy, 4, 17-30.

518. Berenson, G. (1970). Critical incidents in the context of family therapy. Critical incident No.1. International Psychiatry Clinics, 7, 261-272.

519. Berenson, G. (1970), Critical incidents in the context of family therapy. Critical incident No. 4. International Psychiatry Clinics, 7, 299-308.

520. Berenson, G., and White, H. (Eds.) (1980), Annual review of family therapy. Vol. 1. New York, NY: Human Sciences Press.

521. Berenstein, I. (1963), Psicoterapia asistencial de la familia: Un sociograma familiar. (Social psychotherapy of the family: A family sociogram.) Acta Psiquiatrica Y Psicologia de America Latina, 9(1), 39-46.

522. Berenstein, J. (1968), The family group: Psychotherapeutic process and setting. Acta Psiquiatrica Y Psicologia de Americana Latina, 14(3), 238-251.

523. Berent, N. (1972), Knowledge of family planning and marital counseling among student nurses. Harefuah, 82, 131-135.

524. Berezowsky, J. (1979), Intimacy, individuation, and marriage. Canadian Counselor, 13(2), 98-101.

525.   Berg, B. (1978), Learning family therapy through simulation. Psychotherapy, Theory Research and Practice, 15, 56-60.

526.   Berg, B., and Rosenblum, N. (1977), Fathers in family therapy: A survey of family therapists. Journal of Marital and Family Therapy, 3, 85-91.

527.   Berg, C.D. (1978), Helping children accept death and dying through group counseling. Personnel and Guidance Journal, 57(3), 169-172.

528.   Berg, T. (1980), The "couple's Rorschach" and the "post-Rorschach": Two methods in marital diagnostion. Tidsskrift For Norsk Psykologforening, 17, 333-345.

529.   Bergantino, L. (1983), I asked Carl Whitaker to teach me family therapy and this is what happened. American Journal of Family Therapy, 11, 59-66.

530.   Berge, A. (1965), (Psychotherapy of the family group.) Revue Neuropsychiatrie Infantile et D'Hygeine Mentale de L'Enfance, 13, 651-657.

531.   Bergen-Wallach, C.H. (1980), Family therapy: An evaluation from the families' perspective. Dissertations Abstracts International, 41, 1902B. (University Microfilms No. 8024943).

532.   Berger, D.M. (1983), Review of F.M. Sander's Individual and family therapy: Toward integration. Canadian Journal of Psychiatry, 28, 148.

533.   Berger, H. (1973), Patterns of change in body position during family therapy. Dissertation Abstracts International, 34, 2920-2921B.

534.   Berger, M. (1984), Practicing family therapy in diverse settings: New approaches to the connections among families, therapists and treatment settings. San Francisco, CA: Jossey-Bass.

535.   Berger, M.E. (1975), A note on luring a resistant spouse into marital therapy. Journal of Marriage and Family Counseling, 1(4), 387-388.

536.   Berger, M.M. (1978), Use of videotape in the integrated treatment of individuals, couples, families, and groups in private practice. In M.M. Berger (Ed.), Videotape techniques in psychiatric training and treatment. New York, NY: Brunner/Mazel.

537.   Berger, M.M. (1979), Couple therapy by a married couple. Journal of the American Academy of Psychoanalysis, 7, 219-240.

538.   Berger, M.M. (1972), The use of videotape in the integrated treatment of individuals, couples, families, and groups in private practice. In: H.I. Kaplan and B.J. Sadock (Eds.), New models for group therapy. New York, NY: E.P. Dutton.

539.   Berger, M.M. (1973), Multifamily psychosocial group treatment with addicts and their families. Group Process, 5, 31-45.

540.   Berger, M.M. (1973), Multifamily psychosocial group treatment with addicts and their families. In: M. Rosenbaum (Ed.), Drug abuse and drug addiction. London: Gordon and Breach.

541.   Berger, M.M. (1975), Multifamily psychosocial group treatment with addicts and their families. In: M. Rosenbaum and M.M. Berger (Eds.), Group psychotherapy and group function. (2nd Edition). New York, NY: Basic Books.

542.   Berger, M.M. (1979), Men's new family roles: Some duplications for therapists. Family Coordinator, 28, 638.

543.   Bergman, A.S. (1980), Marital stress and medical training: An experience with a support group for medical house staff wives. Pediatrics, 65, 944-947.

544.   Bergman, J.S. (1983), Prescribing family criticism as a paradoxical intervention. Family Process, 22, 517-522.

545.   Bergner, R.M. (1979), The use of systems-oriented illustrative stories in marital psychotherapy. Family Therapy, 6(2), 109-118.

546.   Bergner, R.M. (1973), The development and evaluation of a training videotape for the resolution of marital conflict. Dissertation Abstracts International, 34, 3485B.

547.   Bergquist, B. (1984), The remarried family: An annotated bibliography, 1979-1982. Family Process, 23(1), 107-120.

548.   Berk, R.A. (1981), On the compatibility of applied and basic sociological research: An effort in marriage counseling. American Sociologist, 16(4), 204.

549.   Berkey, B.R. (Ed.) (1976), Save your marriage. Chicago, IL: Nelson-Hall.

550.   Berkman, A.S., and Fleet-Berkman, C. (1984), The supervision of cotherapist teams in family therapy. Psychotherapy: Theory, Research and Practice, 21(2), 197-205.

551.   Berkovitz, I.H., and Sugar, M. (1975), Indications and contraindications for adolescent group psychotherapy. In: M. Sugar (Ed.), The adolescent in group and family therapy. New York, NY: Brunner/Mazel.

552.   Berkowitz, D.A. (1977), On the reclaiming of denied affects in family therapy. Family Process, 16, 495-501.

553.   Berkowitz, L. (1972), Factors affecting the rehabilitation of youths after discharge from a mental hospital: A post hoc analysis of participants' perceived values of components in a family-centered resocialization program and subject characteristics as related to outcome. Dissertation Abstracts International, 33, 2339B.

554.   Berkowitz, R. (1984), Therapeutic intervention with schizophrenic patients and their families: A description of a clinical research project. Journal of Family Therapy, 6(3), 211-234.

555.   Berley, R.A., and Jacobsen, N.S. (1984), Causal attributions in intimate relationships: Toward a model of cognitive behavioral marital therapy. In P.C. Kendall (Ed.), Advances in Cognitive-Behavioral Research and Therapy, Vol. 3. Orlando, FL: Academic Press.

556. Berlin, I.N. (1974), Minimal brain dysfunction: Management of family distress. Journal of the American Medical Association, 229, 1454-1456.

557. Berlin, I.N. (1981), Familial treatment of severe adolescent problems. Current Psychiatric Therapies, 21, 61-9.

558. Berlin, I.N. (1979), A developmental approach to work with disorganized families. Journal of American Academy of Child Psychiatry, 18, 354-365.

559. Berlin, I.N., McCullough, G., Liska, E.S., and Szurek, S.A. (1957), Intractable episodic vomiting in a three-year-old child. Psychiatric Quarterly, 31, 228-249.

560. Berlin, J.B. (1979), Marriage contracts and couple therapy. Family Coordinator, 28, 142.

561. Berman, E., and Dixon Murphy, T.F. (1979), Training in marital and family therapy at free-standing institutes. Journal of Marital and Family Therapy, 5, 29-42.

562. Berman, E.L. (1978), The effectiveness of parent counseling as an intervention to promote change in the academically "at risk" student. Dissertation Abstracts International, 38, 5345A.

563. Berman, E.M. (1982), The individual interview as a treatment technique in conjoint therapy. American Journal of Family Therapy, 10, 27-37.

564. Berman, E.M. (1983), Review of L. L'Abate's Values, ethics, legalities and the family therapist. Journal of Marital and Family Therapy, 9, 217.

565. Berman, E.M., Miller, W. R., Vines, N., and Lief, H.I. (1977), The age 30 crisis and the 7-year-itch. Journal of Sex and Marital Therapy, 3, 197-204.

566. Berman, E.M., and Lief, H.I. (1975), Marital therapy from a psychiatric perspective: An overview. American Journal of Psychiatry, 132, 583-592.

567. Berman, G. (1967), Communication of affect in family therapy. Archives of General Psychiatry, 17, 154-158.

568. Berman, G. (1982), Family therapy training: Learning an attitude. Canadian Journal of Psychiatry, 27, 561.

569. Berman, G. (1978), Review of M. Bowen's Family therapy in clinical practice. Canadian Journal of Psychiatry, 23, 588.

570. Berman, K.K. (1966), Multiple family therapy: Its possibilities in preventing readmission. Mental Hygiene, 50, 367-370.

571. Berman, K.K., (1969), Use of test findings in marital group therapy. Journal of Medicine and Society, 66, 612-615.

572. Berman, L., and Ruane, C. (1981), The "tag-alongs": A profile of depressive and phobic delinquents. Family and Child Mental Health Journal, 7, 90-99.

573.   Bermann, E. (1980), Review of I. Goldenberg and H. Goldenberg's Family therapy: An overview. Contemporary Psychology, 25, 696.

574.   Bermudez, P. (1979), Vector therapy: An aspect of family psychiatry. Revista Colombiana de Psiquiatria, 8, 49-56.

575.   Bernal, G. (1982), Punctuation of interactions and marital distress: A qualitative analysis. Family Therapy, 4, 289-298.

576.   Bernal, G., and Alvarez, A.I. (1983), Culture and class in the study of families. Family Therapy Collections, 8, 33-50.

577.   Bernal, G., and Baker, J. (1980), Multi-level couple therapy: Applying a metacommunicational framework of couple interactions. Family Process, 19, 367-76.

578.   Bernal, G., and Flores-Ortiz, Y. (1982), Latino families in therapy: Engagement and evaluation. Journal of Marital and Family Therapy, 8, 357-365.

579.   Bernal, M.E. (1980), Outcome evaluation, parent training and client-centered parent counseling for children with conduct problems. Journal of Applied Behavior Analogs, 13(4), 677-691.

580.   Bernard, H.S. (1979), When a child's distress is a family affair. Nursing Clinics of North America, 5, 677.

581.   Bernard, H.S. (1977), The women's movement: A new challenge for the psychotherapist. Family Therapy, 4, 1-10.

582.   Bernard, H.S., and Schwartz, A.J. (1977), A family workshop for college students. Journal of the American College Health Association, 26, 331-333.

583.   Bernard, J. (1959), Counseling techniques for arriving at optimum compromises: Game and decision theory. Marriage and Family Living, 21, 264-274.

584.   Bernard, J.M., and Nesbitt, S. (1981), Divorce: An unreliable predictor of children's emotional predispositions. Journal of Divorce, 5, 31-42.

585.   Bernardez, T. (1980), Separating the sexes in group therapy: An experiment with men's and women's groups. International Journal of Group Psychotherapy, 29(2), 493-502.

586.   Bernardo, M.L. (1981), Pre-marital counseling and the couple with disabilities: A review and recommendation. Rehabilitation Literature, 42, 7-8, 213.

587.   Bernheim, K.F. (1982), Supportive family counseling. Schizophrenia Bulletin, 8, 634-640.

588.   Bernstein, B.E. (1982), Values, ethics, legalities, and the family therapist: VI. Ignorance of the law is no excuse. Family Therapy Collections, 1, 87-102.

589.   Bernstein, B.E. (1977), Lawyer and counselor as an interdisciplinary team: Points for a woman to ponder in considering the basic finances of divorce. Family Coordinator, 26(4), 421-428.

590.   Bernstein, B.E. (1976), Lawyer and counselor as an interdisciplinary team: The timely referral. Journal of Marriage & Family Therapy, 2, 347-354.

591.   Bernstein, B.E. (1979), Lawyer and therapist as an interdisciplinary team: Trial preparation. Journal of Marriage and Family Therapy, 5, 93-100.

592.   Bernstein, B.E. (1974), Lawyer and counselor as an interdisciplinary team: One lawyer's suggestions. Family Coordinator, 23, 41-44.

593.   Bernstein, R.M., Brown, E.M., and Ferrier, M.J. (1984), A model for collaborative team processing in brief systemic family therapy. Journal of Marital and Family Therapy, 10(2), 151-156.

594.   Berry, S.L., and Roath, M. (1982), Family treatment of a borderline personality. Clinical Social Work Journal, 10, 3-14.

595.   Besalel, V.A., and Azrin, N.H. (1981), The reduction of parent-youth problems by reciprocity counseling. Behavior Research and Therapy, 19(4), 297.

596.   Betof, N.G. (1978), The effects of a forty week family therapy training program on the organization and trainees. Dissertation Abstracts International 39, 768A.

597.   Bettschart, W. (1977), Some reflexions on therapeutic measures with parents at a child's day hospital. Acta Paedopsychiatrica, 43, 23-31.

598.   Bettschart, W. (1982), Ten years' activity in the day clinic with psychotic children and their families. Praxis der Kinderpsychologie und Kinderpsychiatrie, 31, 87-92.

599.   Bettschart, W., Hoffet, J. F., and Galland, S. (1980), Parents' relations with the Day Hospital. Revue Medicale Suisse Romande, 100, 601-6.

600.   Beukenkamp, C., Jr. (1959), Anxiety activated by the idea of marriage as observed in group psychotherapy. Mental Hygiene, 43, 532-538.

601.   Beutler, L.E. (1971), Attitude similarity in marital therapy. Journal of Consulting and Clinical Psychology, 37, 298-301.

602.   Bey, D.R., and Lange, J. (1974), Waiting wives: Women under stress. American Journal of Psychiatry, 131, 283-286.

603.   Bhatti, R.S., Janakiramaiah, N., and Channabasavanna, S.M. (1980), Family psychiatric ward treatment in India. Family Process, 19, 193-200.

604.   Bhatti, R.S., Janakiramaiah, N., and Channabasavanna, S.M. (1982), Group interaction as a method of family therapy. International Journal of Group Psychotherapy, 32, 103-114.

605.   Bichler, G.R. (1983), Behavioral-systems marital therapy. In. J.P. Vincent (Ed.), Advances in family intervention, assessment and theory, Vol. 3. Greenwich: JAI Press.

606.   Bicksler, P. (1950), Four marriage counseling cases illustrating the helpful relationship. Family and Childrens Society, Miemo. 1.

607.   Biddle, J.R. (1978), Working with families within inpatient settings. Journal of Marriage and Family Therapy, 4, 43-51.

608.   Biderman, R. (1983), The effects of the Minnesota Couples Communication Program on communication, adaptability, and cohesion: A quasi-experimental investigation. Dissertation Abstracts International, 43, 2600-A.

609.   Biele, H., and Farber, H. (1969), (Child guidance in pediatric psychiatry: Group discussions with the parents of behaviorally disturbed children as a special form of therapy.) Psychiatrie, Neurologie, und Medizinsche Psychologie, 21, 99-106.

610.   Bielicka, I. (1965), Theoretical principles of "family psychotherapy" of children with developmental defects. Ceskoslovenska Pediatrie, 20, 906-908.

611.   Bierber, I., and Bieber, T.B. (1978), Post-partum reactions in men and women. Journal of the American Academy of Psychoanalysis, 6, 511-519.

612.   Bierenbaum, H., and Bergey, S.F. (1980), Family therapy training in a pediatric setting. Journal of Pediatric Psychology, 5(3), 263-276.

613.   Bierer, J. (1976), The total separation treatment (T.S.T.): A method for the treatment of marital difficulties and disharmonies in patients suffering from the E.I.M.P. syndrome. International Journal of Social Psychiatry, 22, 206-213.

614.   Bierer, J. (1976), Love-making - an act of murder: The "golem" syndrome. International Journal of Social Psychiatry, 22, 197-199.

615.   Bierman, G. (1963), The role of the father in educational counseling. Praxis der Kinderpsychologie und Kinderpsychiatrie, 12, 298-308.

616.   Bierman, G. (1967), Mother's role in educational counseling and psychotherapy. Praxis der Kinderpsychologie und Kinderpsychiatrie, 16, 249-254.

617.   Bigney, R.E. (1978), Intrapsychic and interpersonal personality and temperament changes in marital dyads resulting from a marriage enrichment program based on rational-emotive therapy. Dissertation Abstracts International, 39, 4723A.

618.   Bilelo, F. (1979), Making marriages grow. Transactional Analysis Journal, 9, 74-76.

619.   Billings, A. (1979), Conflict resolution in distressed and nondistressed married couples. Journal of Consulting and Clinical Psychology, 47, 368-376.

620.   Billings, A.G., Kessler, M., Gomberg, C.A., and Weiner, S. (1979), Marital conflict resolution of alcoholic and non-alcoholic couples during drinking and nondrinking sessions. Journal of Study of Alcoholism, 40, 183-195.

621.   Bilson, A., and Ross, S. (1981), The use of structured experiences in family therapy. Journal of Family Therapy, 3(1), 39-50.

622.   Bingley, L., Leonard, J., Hensman, S., Lask, B., and Wolff, O. (1980), Comprehensive management of children on a paediatric ward: A family approach. Archives of Disease in Childhood, 55, 555-61.

623.   Birchard, C. (1967), Family therapy training project. Canadian Mental Health, 16, 31-32.

624.   Birchler, G.R. (1975), Live supervision and instant feedback in marriage and family therapy. Journal of Marriage and Family Therapy, 1, 331-342.

625.   Birchler, G.R., Clopton, P.L., and Adams, N.L. (1984), Marital conflict resolution: Factors influencing concordance between partners and trained copers. American Journal of Family Therapy, 12(2), 15-28.

626.   Birchler, G.R., and Spinks, S.H. (1982), Behavioral-systems marital therapy: Dealing with resistance. Family Process, 21(2), 169-185.

627.   Birchler, G.R., and Spinks, S.H. (1980), Behavioral-systems marital and family therapy: Integration and clinical application. American Journal of Family Therapy, 8, 6-28.

628.   Bird, H.R., and Canino, G. (1982), The Puerto Rican family: Cultural factors and family intervention strategies. Journal of the American Academy of Psychoanalysis, 10, 257-268.

629.   Bird, H.W., and Schuham, A.I. (1978), Meeting families' treatment needs through a family psychotherapy center. Hospital and Community Psychiatry, 29, 175-178.

630.   Birleson, P., and Sills, J. (1981), The use of a double-blind drug trial in family therapy to demedicalize a problem. Journal of Family Therapy, 3(1), 31-38.

631.   Birmingham, V.H., and Smith, A. D. (1977), Implementing a parent involvement program in a state hospital and school for children....Gaebler Children's Unit Hospital, School of Metropolitan State Hospital, Waltham, Massachusetts. Children Today, 6, 20-23.

632.   Biron, A. (1975), "Couple disease" and therapeutic approach. Semain Des Hopitaux Therapeutique, 51, 491-495.

633.   Birtchnell, J. (1975), The special place of psychotherapy in the treatment of attempted suicide, and the special type of psychotherapy required: Observations derived from the experience of treating by psychotherapy and research series of young married suicide attempters. Psychotherapy and Psychosomatics, 25, 315-318.

634.   Birtchnell, J. (1979), Review of L. Headley's Adults and their parents in family therapy: New directions in treatment. British Journal of Psychiatry, 134, 645.

635.   Birtchnell, J. (1984), Review of A. Lange and O. Vanderhart's Directive family therapy. British Journal of Psychiatry, 145, 311-315.

636.   Bishop, B.R., and Stumphauzer, J.S. (1973), Behavior therapy of thumbsucking in children: A punishment, time out, and generalization effect: What's a mother to do? Psychological Reports, 33(3), 939-944.

637.   Bishop, D., Byles, J., and Horn, D. (1984), Family training methods: Minimal contact with an agency. Journal of Family Therapy, 6(4), 323-334.

638.   Bishop, S.M., and Lynn, A.G. (1983), Multi-level vulnerability of adolescent marriages: An ecosystem model for clinical assessment and intervention. Journal of Marital and Family Therapy, 9, 271-282.

639.   Bistline, J.L. (1983), The impact of live supervision on the family therapist's level of immediacy, anxiety, responsiveness, and genuineness. Dissertation Abstracts International, 43, 2327-B.

640.   Bittner, G. (1976), Non-escapism: Remarks on a new concept of family therapy based on psychoanalysis. Zeitschrift Fur Pedagogik, 22, 775-780.

641.   Bjorklund, R.C. (1980), Exploring marriage: A relational workshop. Dissertation Abstracts International, 41, 1085-A.

642.   Bjorksten, O.J. (1985), New clinical concepts in marital therapy. Washington, D.C.: American Psychiatric Association.

643.   Bjorksten, O.J.W. (1984), Current marital trends and outcome of marriage counseling in Japan: 1982. Journal of Sex and Marital Therapy, 10(2), 123-136.

644.   Blaaderen-Stok, C.L. (1970), An approach to family therapy along analytic lines. International Journal of Group Psychotherapy, 20, 241-244.

645.   Black, D. (1985), Review of A. Treacher and J. Carpenter (Eds.), Using family therapy. Journal of Family Therapy, 7(1), 72.

646.   Black, D. (1982), Custody and access: A literary lesson. Journal of Family Therapy, 4, 247-256.

647.   Black, D. (1982), Family therapy in child guidance clinics. In A. Bentovim, G.G. Barnes, and A. Cooklin (Eds.), Family therapy. 2. Complementary frameworks of theory and practice. London: Academic Press.

648.   Black, D. (1982), Handicap and family therapy. In A. Bentovim, G.G. Barnes, and A. Cooklin (Eds.), Family therapy. 2. Complementary frameworks of theory and practice. London: Aacademic Press.

649.   Black, J.M. (1978), Families with handicapped children: Who helps whom and how. Child Care, 4(4), 239-245.

650.   Black, K.M. (1970), Teaching family process and intervention. Nursing Outlook, 18, 54-58.

651.   Black, L., Herscher, L., and Steinschneider, A. (1978), Impact of the
        apnea monitor on family life. Pediatrics, 62, 681-685.

652.   Black, R.B. (1980), Parents' evaluations of genetic counseling. Patient
        Counseling and Health Education, 2(3), 142.

653.   Blanck, T., Cederbald, M., and Dorner, E. (1973), Varieties of family
        therapy at a child guidance clinic in Stockholm. Acta Psychiatrica
        Scandinavica, 243, 18.

654.   Blankstein, J.H. (1968), Family therapy: A theoretical exploration.
        Maanbladvoor de Geestelyke Volksgezondheid, 23(5), 177-192.

655.   Blankstein, J.H. (1968), Family therapy: Report of a course in family
        therapy. Tijdschrift voor Maatschappelijk Werk, 22(5), 100-104.

656.   Blankstein, J.H. (1970), Family therapy or the problem of antithesis of
        intrapsychic and intrapersonal dynamics. Fortschritte der
        Psychoanalyses, 4, 174-188.

657.   Blanton, S. (1965), The contributions of the religio-psychiatric approach
        to family life. Pastoral Counseling, 3(1), 3-6.

658.   Blau, H.J. (1977), Group talks with parents of leukemic children.
        Kinderaerztl Praxis, 45(6), 278-280.

659.   Blau, J.S. (1978), Changes in assertiveness and marital satisfaction after
        participation in an assertive training group. Dissertation Abstracts
        International, 39, 971B.

660.   Blechman, E.A. (1979), Marital therapy and child management
        training. American Journal of Family Therapy, 7, 79-80.

661.   Blechman, E.A. (1974), The family contract game. Family Coordinator,
        23, 269-281.

662.   Blechman, E.A. (1980), Family problem-solving training. American
        Journal of Family Therapy, 8(3), 3-21.

663.   Blechman, E.A., Budd, K.S., Szykula, S., Embry, L.H., Oleary, K.D.,
        Christopher, E.R., Wahler, R., Kogan, K., and Riner, L.S. (1981),
        Engagement in behavioral family therapy: A multi-site investigation.
        Behavior Therapy, 12, 461-472.

664.   Blechman, E.A., Olson, D.H., and Schornagel, C.Y. (1976), Family
        contract game: Technique and case study. Journal of Consulting and
        Clinical Psychology, 44, 449-455.

665.   Blechman, E.A., Taylor, C.J., and Schrader, S.M. (1981), Family problem
        solving versus home notes as early intervention with high-risk children.
        Journal of Consulting and Clinical Psychology, 49, 919-926.

666.   Blechman, E.A., and Rabin, C. (1982), Concepts and methods of explicit
        marital negotiation training with the marriage contract game.
        American Journal of Family Therapy, 10, 47-56.

667.   Bleck, E.E., and Headley, L. (1961), Treatment and parent counseling
        for the preschool child with cerebral palsy. Pediatrics, 27, 1026-1032.

668.   Bleckmann, K.H. (1971), The destiny of so-called "risk children" in the
       light of parental counseling. Praxis der Kinderpsychologie und
       Kinderpsychiatrie, 20(4), 125-132.

669.   Bleichmar, H.B. (1970), (The family system: Theory of the technique of
       psychotherapy.) Acta Psichiatrica Y Psicologica de America Latina, 16,
       148-154.

670.   Blinder, M. (1982), Marital dissolution and child custody: A primer for
       family therapists and divorce attorneys. Family Therapy, 9, 1-20.

671.   Blinder, M.G., Coleman, A.D., Curry, A.E., and Kessler, D.R. (1965),
       "MCFT": Simultaneous treatment of several families. American Journal
       of Psychiatry, 19, 559-569.

672.   Blinder, M.G., and Kirschenbaum, M. (1968), Married couple group
       therapy. In: J.H. Masserman (Ed.), Current psychiatric therapies. New
       York, NY: Grune and Stratton.

673.   Blinder, M.G., and Kirschenbaum, M. (1967), The technique of married
       couple group therapy. Archives of General Psychiatry, 17, 44-52.

674.   Bloch, D., and Simon, R. (Eds.) (1982), The strength of family therapy:
       Selected papers of Nathan W. Ackerman. New York: Brunner/Mazel.

675.   Bloch, D.A. (1980), Family therapy. In: C.K. Holling and J.M. Lewis
       (Eds.), Family: Evaluation and treatment. New York, NY:
       Brunner/Mazel.

676.   Bloch, D.A. (1974), Nathan W. Ackerman: The first family paper. In:
       L.R. Wolberg and M.L. Aronson (Eds.), Group therapy 1974: An
       overview. New York, NY: Stratton Intercontinental Medical Book Corp.

677.   Bloch, D.A. (1976), Family therapy, group therapy. International
       Journal of Group Psychotherapy, 26, 289-299.

678.   Bloch, D.A. (1973), Audio-visual techniques in family therapy. In D.A.
       Bloch (Ed.), Techniques of family psychotherapy: A primer. New York:
       Grune and Stratton.

679.   Bloch, D.A. (1979), AAMFT; AFTA. Family Process, 18, 99-101.

680.   Bloch, D.A. (Ed.) (1973), Techniques of family psychotherapy: A
       primer. New York, NY: Grune and Stratton.

681.   Bloch, D.A. and Weiss, H. M. (1981), Training facilities in marital and
       family therapy. Family Process, 20, 133-146.

682.   Bloch, D.A., Brown, S.L., Lief, I., and Lewis, J.M. (1980), Controversial
       issues in family therapy: Panel discussion. In: C.K. Hofling, and J.M.
       Lewis (Eds.), Family: Evaluation and treatment. New York, NY:
       Brunner/Mazel.

683.   Bloch, D.A., and Laperriere, K. (1973), Techniques of family therapy: A
       conceptual frame. Seminars in Psychiatry, 5(2), 121-140.

684.   Blood, R.O. (1976), Research needs of a family life educator and
       marriage counselor. Journal of Marriage and Family Living, 38, 7-12.

685.   Bloom, B.L. (1985), A factor analysis of self-report measures of family functioning. Family Process, 24, 225-240.

686.   Bloom, L.G. (1980), A Delphi study to determine methods to aid the terminally ill patient and their families. Dissertation Abstracts International, 40, 4480-A.

687.   Bloomfield, S., Nielsen, S., and Kaplan, L. (1984), Retarded adults, their families, and larger systems: A new role for the family therapist. Family Therapy Collections, 11, 138-149.

688.   Bloomfield, S.I. (1982), Foster care: An interactional perspective. Dissertation Abstracts International, 43, 1044-A.

689.   Blotcky, A.D., Tittles, B.L., Friedman, S., and DeCarlo, T.J. (1980), An exploration of change in parent child relationships during the course of a family oriented treatment program. Family Therapy, 7(2), 139-145.

690.   Blotcky, M.J. (1978), Family mailer: Parent guide to homosexuality. International Journal of Family Counseling, 6, 91.

691.   Blotcky, M.J., Grace, K.D., and Looney, J.G. (1984), Treatment of adolescents in family therapy after divorce. Journal of the American Academy of Child Psychiatry, 23, 222-225.

692.   Blotcky, M.J., Looney, J.C., and Grace, K.D. (1982), Treatment of the adopted adolescent: Involvement of the biologic mother. Journal of the American Academy of Child Psychiatry, 21, 281-5.

693.   Blumberg, M.L. (1980), Review of J.A. Kroth's Child sexual abuse: Analysis of a family therapy approach. American Journal of Psychotherapy, 34, 278.

694.   Blumberg, M.L. (1979), Collateral therapy for the abused child and the problem parent. American Journal of Psychotherapy, 3(3), 339-353.

695.   Blumberry, W.M. (1983), Review of L. Bergantino's Psychotherapy, insight and style: The existential moment. Journal of Sex and Marital Therapy, 9, 90.

696.   Blumberry, W.M. (1983), Review of R. Fisch, J.H. Weakland, and L. Segal's The tactics of change: Doing therapy briefly. Journal of Sex and Marital Therapy, 9, 89.

697.   Blumberry, W.M. (1983), Review of J.L. Framo's Explorations in marital and family therapy: Selected papers of Framo, James, L. Journal of Sex and Marital Therapy, 9, 88.

698.   Blumenstein, H. (1985), Review of A. Bross's Family therapy: Principles of strategic practice. Social Work, 30, 83.

699.   Blumenstein, H. (1983), Review of L.R. Wolberg and M.L. Aronson's Group and family therapy. Social Work, 28, 224.

700.   Blumenstein, H. (1983), Review of G.H. Zuk's Family therapy: A triadic-based approach. Social Work, 28, 224.

701. Boals, G.F., Peterson, D.R., Farmer, L., Mann, D.F., and Robinson, D.L. (1982), The reliability, validity, and utility of three data modes in assessing marital relationships. Journal of Personality Assessment, 46, 85-95.

702. Boas, B.A. (1978), Review of S. Minuchin's Families and family therapy. Australian Psychologist, 13, 405.

703. Boas, C.V.E. (1962), Intensive group psychotherapy with married couples. International Journal of Group Psychotherapy, 12, 142-153.

704. Boas, C.V.E. (1953), The necessity of group therapy in marriage guidance clinics. International Journal of Sexology, 7, 79-80.

705. Boatman, B., Borkan, E.L., and Schetky, D.H. (1981), Treatment of child victims of incest. American Journal of Family Therapy, 9, 43-51.

706. Bodin, A.M. (1969), Family therapy training literature: A brief guide. Family Process, 8, 272-279.

707. Bodin, A.M. (1969), Videotape applications in training family therapists. Journal of Nervous and Mental Disease, 148, 251-261.

708. Boe, J. (1979), Saving the children. Nursing Forum, 18(1), 60-68.

709. Boeckhorst, F.W. (1983), The cyclical course of a family therapy session. Tijdschrift Voor Psychotherapie, 9, 201-207.

710. Boekelheide, P.D. (1980), All in the family. Journal of the American College Health Association, 28, 69-73.

711. Boer, A.K., and Lantz, J.E. (1974), Adolescent group therapy membership selection. Clinical Social Work Journal, 2, 172-181.

712. Boettcher, R.E. (1977), Interspousal empathy, marital satisfaction, and marriage counseling. Journal of Social Service Research, 1(1), 105-113.

713. Bogdan, J.L. (1982), Paradoxical communication as interpersonal influence. Family Process, 21, 443-52.

714. Bogdan, J.L. (1984), A family is a family is a family - rejoinder. Family Process, 23(3), 395-400.

715. Bogdan, J.L. (1984), Family organization as an ecology of ideas: An alternative to the reification of family systems. Family Process, 23(3), 375-388.

716. Bogliolo, C., and Bacherini, A.M. (1977), Terapia familiare e psichiatria di territorio. Firenze: Unicini Pierucci.

717. Bograd, M. (1984), Family systems approaches to wife battering: A feminist critique. American Journal of Orthopsychiatry, 54, 558-568.

718. Boh, K. (1979), Intervention strategies and health outcome measures: Family and community support policies. Social Science Medicine, 13A, 563.

719.   Bohman, M. (1974), The family and illness. Lakartidningen, 71, 2542-2544.

720.   Bohman, M. (1974), The family and illness. Tidsskrift for den Norske Laegeforening, 94, 581-584.

721.   Boideme, S.M. (1978), Conjoint family therapy following divorce: Alternative strategy. International Journal of Family Counseling, 6, 55-59.

722.   Bolman, W.M. (1968), Preventive psychotherapy for the family: Theory, approaches, and programs. American Journal of Psychiatry, 125, 458-472.

723.   Bonier, R.J., and Koplovsky, A. (1971), The borderline adolescent in crises intervention. Proceedings of the Annual Convention of the American Psychological Association, 6, 437-438.

724.   Bonnefil, M.C. (1979), Therapist, save my child: A family crisis case. Clinical Social Work Journal, 7, 6-14.

725.   Bonnefil, M.C., and Jacobson, G.F. (1979), Family crisis intervention. Clinical Social Work Journal, 7, 200-213.

726.   Bono, M. (1985), Review of B.B. Wolman and G. Strickler (Eds.). Handbook of family and marital therapy. Canadian Journal of Psychiatry, 30(2), 160.

727.   Boodish, H.M. (1953), An experiment in group counseling on marriage and family. Marriage and Family Living, 15, 121-125.

728.   Bopp, M.J., and Weeks, G.R. (1984), Dialectical metatheory in family therapy. Family Process, 23, 49-61.

729.   Borecky, V. (1977), Family scenotest. Psychologia a Patopsychologia Dietata, 12, 55-66.

730.   Borens, R. (1974), Experiences with the family of schizophrenic patients. Schweizer Archiv Fur Neurologie, und Psychiatre, 115, 323-336.

731.   Boris, S.K. (1971), The development of a rating scale to measure the effectiveness of the initial phase of marriage counseling. Dissertation Abstracts International, 32(1), 540-A.

732.   Borlick, M.M. (1971), Implications of family therapy for community health nursing. Virginia Nurse Quarterly, 39, 7-12.

733.   Bornstein, P.H., Ballweg, B.S., Weissler, C.E., Fox, S.G., Kirby, K.L., Andre, J.C., Sturm, C.A., Wilson, G.L., and McLellary, R.W. (1983), Treatment acceptability of alternative marital therapies: A comparative analysis. Journal of Marital and Family Therapy, 9, 205-208.

734.   Bornstein, P.H., Fisher, D.C., and Balleweg, B.J. (1982), Problem-solving in couples: A guide for clinical research and applied practice. Scandinavian Journal of Behaviour Therapy, 11, 1-13.

735.   Bornstein, P.H., Hickey, J.S., Schulein, M.J., Fox, S.G., and Scolatti, M.J. (1983), Behavioural-communications treatment of marital interaction: Negative behaviors. British Journal of Psychology, 84, 41-48.

736.   Bornstein, P.H., and Knapp, M. (1981), Behavioral communications treatment of marital discord: Positive behaviors. Behavioral Counseling Quarterly, 10, 189-201.

737.   Borrero, G., Krynski, J., and Short, K. (1975), Parent-child communication workshop: A developmental approach. Psychiatric Communication, 16, 41-63.

738.   Bos, P. (1974), Family Rorschach: A method for detection of family dynamics. Ceskoslovenska Psychiatrica, 70, 167-173.

739.   Bos, P. (1973), The application of projective methods in studying family communication. Psychiatrie, Neurologie, und Medizinische Psychologie, 25, 736-740.

740.   Bos, P. (1968), Family psychotherapy and its significance for child psychiatry. Ceskoslovenska Psychiatrica, 64, 263-269.

741.   Bosch, J. (1984), Systematic family therapy of psychosomatic disease in juveniles. Schweizerische fur Rundschau Medicale Praxis, 34, 225-228.

742.   Bosch, J., and Bachmann, U. (1983), Marital therapy by the family physician. I: The concept of marital collusion. Praxis, 22, 251-55.

743.   Boss, P.G. (1979), The corporate executive wife's coping patterns in response to routine husband-father absence. Family Process, 18, 79-86.

744.   Boswell, J. (1981), The dual-career family: A model for Egalitarian family politics. Elementary School Guidance and Counseling, 15, 262-268.

745.   Boszormenyi-Nagy, I. (1974), Ethical and practical implications of intergenerational family therapy. Psychotherapy and Psychosomatics, 24, 261-268.

746.   Boszormenyi-Nagy, I. (1978), Review of H. Stierlin's Psychoanalysis and family therapy: Selected papers. American Journal of Psychiatry, 135, 1011.

747.   Boszormenyi-Nagy, I. (1962), Symposium: Family treatment of schizophrenia. The concept of schizophrenia from the perspective of family treatment. Family Process, 1(1), 103-113.

748.   Boszormenyi-Nagy, I. (1966), From family relationships to a psychology of relationships: Fictions of the individual and fictions of the family. Comprehensive Psychiatry, 7, 408-423.

749.   Boszormenyi-Nagy, I. (1970), Critical incidents in the context of family therapy. International Psychiatry Clinics, 7, 251-260.

750.   Boszormenyi-Nagy, I., and Framo, J.L. (1963), Psychotherapy with the family in schizophrenia. Journal of the Medical Association of Georgia, 52, 366-367.

751.   Boszormenyi-Nagy I., and Spark, G.M. (1973), Invisible loyalties:
Reciprocity in intergenerational family therapy. New York, NY: Harper
and Row.

752.   Bottom, W.D. (1979), Family violence: The sickness of a system.
Alabama Journal of Medical Science, 16, 124-130.

753.   Boudet, R. (1956), Family counseling. Paris: Paris Association of
French Family Counsels.

754.   Boudreault, M., and Maziade, M. (1980), Training in family therapy in
Quebec. Neuropsychiatrie de L'Enfance de L'Adolescence, 28, 259-264.

755.   Boudry, C.L., and Pfaehler, P. (1976), Double-focus treatment of a
psychotic young girl and her parents. Revue Neuropsychiatrie Infantile
et D'Hygeine Mentale de L'Enfance, 24, 25-33.

756.   Boulier, B., and Rosenweig, M.R. (1978), Age, biological factors, and
socioeconomic determinants of fertility: A new measure of cumulative
fertility for use in the empirical analysis of family size. Demography,
15, 487-497.

757.   Bour, P. (1960), Psychotherapie croisee d'un couple nevrotique.
(Overlapping therapy with a neurotic couple.) Evolution Psychiatrique,
25, 255-269.

758.   Bowen, M. (1972), Family therapy and family group therapy. In: H.I.
Kaplan, and B.J. Sadock (Eds.), Group treatment of mental illnes. New
York, NY: Dutton.

759.   Bowen, M. (1974), Alcoholism as viewed through family systems theory
and family psychotherapy. Annals of the New York Academy of
Sciences, 233, 115-122.

760.   Bowen, M. (1978), Family therapy in clinical practice. New York:
Aronson.

761.   Bowen, M. (1961), The family as the unit of study and treatment: I.
Family psychotherapy. Workshop, 1959. American Journal of
Orthopsychiatry, 31, 40-60.

762.   Bowen, M. (1966), The use of family theory in clinical practice.
Comprehensive Psychiatry, 7, 345-374.

763.   Bowen, M. (1974), Alcoholism as viewed through family systems theory
and family psychotherapy. American Journal of Psychiatry, 28, 397-408.

764.   Bowers, J.E., and McNally, K. (1979), Obesity in children: An ecological
approach. Journal of Continuing Education in Nursing, 10, 40-49.

765.   Bowers, J.E., and McNally, K. (1983), Family-focused care in the
psychiatric inpatient setting. Images: Journal of Nursing Scholarship,
14, 26-31.

766.   Bowman, T. (1976), Developing strengths in families. Family
Coordinator, 25, 169-174.

767. Box, S. (1978), An analytic approach to work with families. Journal of Adolescence, 1, 119-134.

768. Box, S. (1981), Change in families: Some concluding thoughts. In S. Box, B. Copley, J. Magagna, and E. Moustaki (Eds.), Psychotherapy with families: An analytic approach. London: Routledge and Kegan Paul Ltd.

769. Box, S. (1981), Space for thinking in families: Introduction. In S. Box, B. Copley, J. Magagna, and E. Moustaki (Eds.), Psychotherapy with families: An analytic approach. London: Routledge and Kegan Paul Ltd.

770. Box, S. (1981), Working with the dynamics of the session. In S. Box, B. Copley, J. Magagna, and E. Moustaki (Eds.), Psychotherapy with families: An analytic approach. London: Routledge and Kegan Paul Ltd.

771. Box, S., Copley, B., Magagna, J., and Moustaki, E.(Eds.) (1981), Psychotherapy with families: An analytic approach. Boston, MA: Routledge and Kegan.

772. Boyd, E., Clark, J., Kempler, H., Johannet, P., Leonard, B., and McPherson, P.(1974), Teaching interpersonal communication to troubled families. Family Process, 13, 317-336.

773. Boyd, J.H. (1979), The interaction of family therapy and psychodynamic individual therapy in an inpatient setting. Psychiatry, 42, 99-111.

774. Boyd, J.L., McGill, C.W., and Falloon, R.H. (1981), Family participation in the community rehabilitation of schizophrenics. Hospital and Community Psychiatry, 32(9), 629-632.

775. Boyd, L.A., and Roach, A.J. (1977), Interpersonal communication skills differentiating more satisfying from less satisfying marital relationships. Journal of Counseling Psychology, 24, 540-542.

776. Boyd, N.J. (1977), Clinicians' perceptions of black families in therapy. Dissertation Abstracts International, 38, 346B.

777. Boyd, R.E. (1974), Working with parents and community resources. In: H.A. Moses (Ed.), Student personnel work in general education: A humanistic approach. Springfield, IL: Charles C. Thomas.

778. Boyd, W.H., and Bolen, D.W. (1970), The compulsive gambler and spouse in group psychotherapy. International Journal of Group Psychotherapy, 20, 77-90.

779. Boyer, C.L. (1960), Group therapy with married couples. Marriage and Family Living, 22, 21-24.

780. Boyer, J.P., and Paris, M.C. (1983), Family stories. Neuropsychiatrie de L'enfance et de L'adolescence, 31, 31-38.

781. Boyer, P.A. (1984), A guide for the family therapist: The family as an international kaleidoscope. New York: Aronson.

782.   Bracefield, H. (1979), Family therapy. New Zealand Nursing Journal, 72(4), 23-25.

783.   Brackmann, S. (1978), (Supervision within a family treatment oriented team.) Praxis der Kinderpsychologie und Kinderpsychiatrie, 27, 10-14.

784.   Bradley, M., and DeCook, J.W. (1977), Conjoint marital therapy: Counseling for couples in difficulties. Part 1. Nursing Times, 73, 318-319.

785.   Bradley, M., and DeCook, J.W. (1977), Conjoint marital therapy. II. Nursing Times, 73, 351-353.

786.   Bradley, R.W. (1982), Using birth order and sibling dynamics in career counseling. Personnel and Guidance Journal, 61(1), 25.

787.   Bradley, S.E. (1978), Anglo-American views of health and the family. (Editorial). Annals of Internal Medicine, 89, 569.

788.   Bradnan, W.A., Talmage, J.B., and Vansickle, G.R. (1972), Familial communicational patterns of a patient with gilles-de-la-tourette syndrome. Journal of Nervous and Mental Disease, 154, 60-68.

789.   Brady, C.A., and Ambler, J. (1982), Therapy with remarriage families: X. Use of group educational techniques with remarried couples. Family Therapy Collections, 2, 145-157.

790.   Brady, J.P. (1977), An empirical study of behavioral marital therapy in groups. Behavior Therapy, 8, 512-513.

791.   Braiman, S.G. (1977), The establishment of a therapeutic alliance with parents of psychiatrically hospitalized children. Social Work and Health Care, 3, 19-27.

792.   Brainerd, G.L. (1978), The effect on marital satisfaction of a communication training program for married couples, administered by paraprofessional personnel. Dissertation Abstracts International, 38, 3382B.

793.   Brajsa, P. (1981), Relation psychodynamics of married life and family. Socijalna Psihijatrija, 9, 21-28.

794.   Brajsa, P. (1981), Relation psychodynamics of premarital and marital counseling. Socijalna Psihjatrija, 9, 225-244.

795.   Brajsa, P. (1974), What is family psychotherapy? Anali Zavoda za Mentalno Zdravise, 6, 55-59.

796.   Brajsa, P. (1975), Mental hygiene and family planning. Socijalna Psihijatrija, 3, 157-167.

797.   Brajsa, P. (1981), Therapy of parents and family therapy from the aspect of related psychodynamics. Psihijatrija Danas, 13, 47-59.

798.   Bramer, T.E. (1984), Before family therapy: Responding to potential life threatening, drug related crisis. Psychiatry, 30(1), 14-20.

799.   Branch, H. (1982), Review of J.S. Horewitz's Family therapy and transactional analysis. International Journal of Social Psychiatry, 28, 119.

800.   Brandon, J.M. (1983), An application of strategic and systematic family therapy analysis perspectives to organizational development. Dissertation Abstracts International, 44, 1268-B.

801.   Brandreth, A. (1967), Assessment of marriage counseling in a small family agency. Social Work, 12, 34-39.

802.   Brandzel, E. (1965), Working through the Oedipal struggle in family-unit sessions. Social Casework, 46, 414-422.

803.   Branson, H.K. (1970), The terminal patient and his family. Bedside Nurse, 3, 21.

804.   Brashear, D.B. (1973), Abortion counseling. Family Coordinator, 22(4), 429-435.

805.   Brassard, J.P. (1969), Family counseling: Comparative study of French and British experiences. Pour la Vie, 113, 133-177.

806.   Brassington, R. (1982), The changing family constellation in single-parent families. Individual Psychology: Journal of Adlerian Theory, Research, and Practice, 38, 369-379.

807.   Braswell, M., and Meeks, R. (1982), The police officer as a marriage and family therapist: A discussion of some issues. Family Therapy, 4, 189-200.

808.   Bratter, T.E. (1974), Helping affluent families help their acting-out, alienated, drug abusing adolescent. Journal of Family Counseling, 2, 22-31.

809.   Braun, B.G. (1984), Hypnosis and family therapy. American Journal of Clinical Hypnosis, 26(3), 182-186.

810.   Braun, S.J., and Reiser, N.R. (1970), Teacher-parent work in the home: An aspect of child guidance clinical services. Journal of the Academy of Child Psychiatry, 9, 495-514.

811.   Braverman, S. (1974), Living-in as part of the treatment of a family. Family Therapy, 1, 179-192.

812.   Braverman, S. (1982), Family of origin as a training resource for family therapists. Canadian Journal of Psychiatry, 27, 629-633.

813.   Braverman, S. (1980), Family therapist: Technician or clinician. Canadian Journal of Psychiatry, 25, 666-670.

814.   Braverman, S. (1981), Family of origin: The view from the parents' side..marital conflict after a relatively stable long-term marriage. Family Process, 20, 431-437.

815.   Braverman, S., Hoffman, L., and Szkrumel, N. (1984), Concommitant use of strategic and individual therapy in treating a family. American Journal of Family Therapy, 12, 29-38.

816.   Bray, G.P. (1980), Team strategies for family involvement in
       rehabilitation. Journal of Rehabilitation, 46, 20-23.

817.   Bray, G.P. (1978), Rehabilitation of spinal cord injured: A family
       approach. Journal of Applied Rehabilitation Counseling, 9, 70-78.

818.   Breece, J.N. (1978), Loss of spousal consortium. Legal Aspects of
       Medical Practice, 6, 47-51.

819.   Breit, M., Im-Won, G., and Wilner, R. (1983), Strategic approaches with
       resistant families. American Journal of Family Therapy, 11, 51-58.

820.   Bremgman, Z. (1981), Family-behavior therapy of an oppositional
       child. Israeli Journal of Psychology & Counseling in Education, 14, 30-
       38.

821.   Brendtro, L.K., and Ness, A.R. (1982), Perspectives on peer group
       treatment: The use and abuse of guided group interaction/positive peer
       culture. Children and Youth Services Review, 4, 307-324.

822.   Brenes, A., and Cooklin, A. I. (1983), Videotape feedback effects on
       interpersonal perception accuracy in families undergoing therapy.
       Journal of Psychiatric Treatment and Evaluation, 25, 345-352.

823.   Brenes-Chacon, A. (1979), (The marital communication laboratory: A
       preventive service for marital problems.) Anuario Psychologie, 21, 107-
       132.

824.   Brenk, E., Dominicus, R.D., Hauer, I., and Jochinke, C. (1978), (Training
       in mutual communication of married couples addicted to alcohol.)
       Psychiatrische Praxis, 5, 159-166.

825.   Breon, S., and Mises, R. (1980), Psychotherapy of a child accompanied
       by his mother during a course of treatment in an institution.
       Neuropsychiatrie, 28(9), 383-387.

826.   Breslow, D.B., and Hron, B.G. (1977), Time-extended family
       interviewing. Family Process, 16, 97-103.

827.   Bresnick, E.R. (1981), A holistic approach to the treatment of the crisis
       of infertility. Journal of Marital and Family Therapy, 7, 181-188.

828.   Bretz, J.M. (1975), Family therapy in treatment of a depressed
       patient. Psychiatric Quarterly, 12(6), 38-42.

829.   Breunlin, D.C., Cornwell, M., and Cade, B. (1983), International trade in
       family therapy: Parallels between societal and therapeutic values.
       Family Therapy Collections, 11, 91-107.

830.   Breunlin, D.C., Schwartz, R.C., and Cade, B. (1983), Therapy in stages:
       A life cycle view. Family Therapy Collections, 11, 1-11.

831.   Breunlin, D.C., Schwartz, R.C., and Krause, M.S. (1983), Evaluating
       family therapy training: The development of an instrument. Journal of
       Marital and Family Therapy, 9, 37-47.

832.   Breunlin, D.C., and Cade, B. (1981), Intervening in family systems with
       observer messages. Journal of Marital and Family Therapy, 3, 453-460.

833.   Breunlin, D.C., and Southgate, P. (1978), An interactional approach to dysfunctional silencing in family therapy. Family Process, 17, 207-216.

834.   Breunlin, C., and Breunlin, D.C. (1979), Family therapy approach to adolescent disturbances: Review of the literature. Journal of Adolescence, 2, 153-170.

835.   Briard, F.K. (1976), Counseling parents of children with learning disabilities. Social Casework, 57(9), 581-585.

836.   Bridgman, R. (1959), Counseling matrimonial clients in family court. National Probation and Parole Association Journal, 5, 187-199.

837.   Briggs, D. (1971), The trainee and the borderline client: Countertransference pitfalls marital group therapy. Clinical Social Work Journal, 7, 133-146.

838.   Briggs, J.P., and Briggs, M.A. (1979), Treating the marital crisis with the two-marriage equation. Journal of Sex and Marital Therapy, 5, 28-40.

839.   Briggs, J.W. (1968), A comparison of client-centered vs. directive group counseling with high school students. Alberta Journal of Education, 14(3), 193-201.

840.   Brightman, R.P., Baker, B.L., Clark, D.B., and Ambrose, S.A. (1982), Effectiveness of alternative parent training formats. Journal of Behavior Therapy and Experimental Psychiatry, 13, 113-118.

841.   Brink, N.F. (1982), Metaphor creation for use within family therapy. American Journal of Clinical Hypnosis, 24, 258-265.

842.   Brink, T.L. (1976), Geriatric counseling: A practical guide. Family Therapy, 3, 163-168.

843.   Brinkley-Birk, A., and Birk, L. (1975), Sex therapy for vaginismus, primary impotence, and ejaculatory incompetence in an unconsummated marriage. Psychiatric Quarterly, 12, 38-42.

844.   Briscoe, C.W., and Smith, J.B. (1973), Depression and marital turmoil. Archives of General Psychiatry, 29, 811-817.

845.   Briscoe, C.W., and Smith, J.B. (1974), Psychiatric illness—marital units and divorce. Journal of Nervous and Mental Disease, 158, 440-445.

846.   Britton, R. (1981), Re-enactment as an unwitting professional response to family dynamics. In S. Box, B. Copley, M. Mgagna, and E. Moustaki (Eds.), Psychotherapy with families: An analytic approach. London: Routledge and Kegan Paul Ltd.

847.   Broadbent, D.E. (1980), Effects of specific analysis and communication training on marital problem solving and positive interactions. Dissertation Abstracts International, 41, 682-B.

848.   Broadhead, G.D., and Rarick, G.L. (1978), Family characteristics and gross motor traits in handicapped children. Research Quarterly, 49(4), 421-429.

849.   Broadhurst, D.D. (1978), What schools are doing about child abuse and neglect. Children Today, 7, 22-24.

850.   Brock, G.W., and Sanderson, B. (1984), Social exchange in the initial family therapy interview. Journal of Marital and Family Therapy, 10(3), 317-320.

851.   Broderick, C.B. (1983), The therapeutic triangle: A sourcebook on marital therapy. Beverly Hills, CA: Sage.

852.   Brodey, W.M. (1968), Changing the family. New York, NY: Clarkson N. Potter.

853.   Brodey, W.M. (1961), The family as the unit of study and treatment: III. Image, object and narcissistic relationships. Workshop, 1959. American Journal of Orthopsychiatry, 31, 69-73.

854.   Brodkin, A.M. (1977), Redemption through "retribulization": A sociology of knowledge analysis of the family therapy movement. Dissertation Abstracts International, 38, 3084A.

855.   Brodkin, A.M. (1980), Family therapy: The making of a mental health movement. American Journal of Orthopsychiatry, 50, 4-17.

856.   Brodoff, A.S. (1983), Assessing marital stress by life stages. Patient Care, 17, 140, 145, 148-149.

857.   Brodoff, A.S. (1983), Using the history in marriage counseling. Patient Care, 17, 95-97, 100-101, 104-108.

858.   Brodoff, A.S. (1983), Ensuring optimal premarital counseling. Patient Care, 17, 147-150, 155-156, 158.

859.   Brodoff, A.S. (1983), Marriage counseling: Deciding when separation is best. Patient Care, 17, 210-211, 214-215, 218-220.

860.   Brodoff, A.S. (1983), Marriage counseling: Helping couples with sexual problems. Patient Care, 17, 87-89, 93, 96-97.

861.   Brodoff, A.S. (1983), Marriage counseling: Intervening in patient-child problems. Patient Care, 17, 141-143, 145.

862.   Brodoff, A.S. (1983), Marriage counseling: Treating marital problems effectively. Patient Care, 17, 193-196, 198, 201-205.

863.   Brodoff, A.S. (1982), Detecting hidden marital difficulties...family doctor as chief counselor. Patient Care, 16, 39-41, 44-45.

864.   Brodoff, A.S. (1982), Taking a stand on marriage counseling: How each of these doctors does or avoids doing marriage counseling. Patient Care, 16, 20-22, 24, 31-32.

865.   Brodsky, R. (1953), Family-centered psychotherapy and counseling. Jewish Social Services Quarterly, 29, 387-396.

866.   Brody, E.B. (1956), Modification of family interaction patterns by group interview technique. International Journal of Group Psychotherapy, 6, 38-47.

867.   Brody, S. (1961), Simultaneous psychotherapy of married couples. Current Psychiatric Therapies, 1, 139-144.

868.   Brody, S. (1961), Simultaneous psychotherapy of married couples: Preliminary observations. Psychoanalytic Review, 48(4), 94-107.

869.   Brody, V.A. (1978), A developmental play: A relationship-focused program for children. Child Welfare, 57(9), 591-599.

870.   Brody, W.M., and Hayden, M. (1957), Intrateam reactions: Their relation to the conflicts of the family in treatment. American Journal of Orthopsychiatry, 27, 349-355.

871.   Broeck, E. (1974), The extended family center. "A home away from home" for abused children and their parents. Child Today, 3, 2-6.

872.   Bromberg, H. (1977), Counseling heart patients and their families...Airport Marina Counseling Service and Clinic, Los Angeles, California. Health and Social Work, 2, 158-172.

873.   Bromberg, P. (1980), Reaching high risk infants via their high risk fathers. Infant Mental Health Journal, 1(3), 161-167.

874.   Bronson, M. (1983), An integration of individual and family therapy. In N.B. Ebeling and D.A. Hill (Eds.), Child abuse and neglect: A guide with case studies for treating the child and family. Littleton: John Wright PSG, Inc.

875.   Brook, J.S., Lukoff, I.F., and Whiteman, M. (1978), Family socialization and adolescent personality and their association with adolescent use of marijuana. Journal of Genetic Psychology, 133, 261-271.

876.   Brookman, R.R. (1984), Review of S.W. Henggeler's Delinquency and adolescent psychopathology: A family ecological systems approach. Journal of Adolescent Health Care, 5(3), 218.

877.   Brooks, B. (1982), Families in treatment for incest. Dissertation Abstracts International, 42, 3408.

878.   Brooks, C.E. (1975), A justification and a program of development for religiously based family life/counseling centers. Dissertation Abstracts International, 35, 4975-4976B.

879.   Bross, A. (1983), Family therapy. New York: Guilford Press.

880.   Bross, R.B. (1954), The family unit in group psychotherapy. International Journal of Group Psychotherapy, 4, 393-408.

881.   Brosseau, M., LeTourmeux, M.C., and Morin, Y. (1970), An experience in family therapy in an adult psychiatric department of a general hospital. Laval Medical, 41, 484-489. (French)

882.   Brousseau, K. (1937), Psychological service at the Los Angeles Institute of Family Relations. Journal of Counseling Psychology, 3, 49.

883.   Browe, M.J. (1974), Conjoint marital therapy: Advise or interpretation? Journal of Psychology, 86, 35-47.

884. Brown, A. (1978), A case study in family systems consultation for community health nurses working with Sudden Infant Death Syndrome (SIDS) families. Family Therapy, 5, 233-244.

885. Brown, B.M. (1958), Ministerial marriage counseling in a lower class setting. Coordinator, 7, 10-15

886. Brown, E.M. (1981), Divorce and the extended family: A consideration of services. Journal of Divorce, 5, 159-171.

887. Brown, E.M., Pitkin, E., and Bates, C. (1973), Multiple family therapy with hospitalized drug addicts and their families. American Journal of Orthopsychiatry, 43, 256(a).

888. Brown, J.R. (1980), Back to the beanstalk: Enchantment and reality for couples. La Jolla, CA: Psychology and Consulting Associates Press.

889. Brown, P., and Manela, R. (1977), Client satisfaction with marital and divorce counseling. Family Coordinator, 26, 294-303.

890. Brown, R. (1979), A dialogic existential perspective from the teachings of Martin Buber in the context of family therapy. Dissertation Abstracts International, 40(9), 4472B.

891. Brown, R.A. (1973), Feedback in family interviewing. Social Work, 18, 52-59.

892. Brown, R.E. (1980), The effects of a seven week structured group experience on the marital adjustment of parents of preschool learning imparied children. Dissertation Abstracts International, 40, 5784A. (University Microfilms No. 8009976.)

893. Brown, S.L. (1964), Clinical impressions of the impact of family group interviewing on child and adolescent psychiatric practice. Journal of the American Academy of Child Psychiatry, 3, 688-696.

894. Brown, S.L. (1966), Family therapy viewed in terms of resistance to change: Psychiatric research reports. American Psychiatric Association, 20, 132-139.

895. Brown, S.L., Augenbraum, B., and Reid, H.L. (1967), Breakdown in family developmental process and the psychiatric preschool center as a therapeutic agent. American Journal of Orthopsychiatry, 37, 312-313.

896. Brown, S.R. (1980), Reconciliation in pastoral marriage counseling: A theological study linking the concept of reconciliation in light of Emil Brunner with actual case studies of pastoral marriage counseling. Dissertation Abstracts International, 41, 1098-A.

897. Brownell, K.D., Heckerman, C.L., Westlake, R.J., Hayes, S.C., and Monti, P.M. (1978), Effect of couples training and partner co-operativeness in behavioral treatment of obesity. Behavior Research and Therapy, 16, 322-323.

898. Brownell, K.D., and Stunkard, A. J. (1981), Couples training, pharmacotherapy, and behavior therapy in the treatment of obesity. Archives of General Psychiatry, 37, 1224-9.

899. Brownlee, A. (1978), The family and health care: Explorations in cross-cultural settings. Social Work Health Care, 4, 179-188.

900. Broxton, E.H. (1980), Marital enrichment: Some research and observations on effectiveness. Dissertation Abstracts International, 41, 1715-B.

901. Bruce, T. (1982), Family work in a secure unit. In A. Bentovim, G.G. Barnes, and A. Cooklin (Eds.), Family therapy. 2. Complementary frameworks of theory and practice. London: Academic Press.

902. Brueton, M. (1975), The crippled tree and the fair blossom: Critical early intervention in family life. Child Psychiatry Quarterly, 8, 9-12.

903. Bruggen, P. (1979), Review of S. Waldronskinner's Family and marital psychotherapy: Critical approach. British Journal of Psychiatry, 135, 377.

904. Bruggen, P. (1982), Action speaks louder: A handbook of non-verbal group techniques. Journal of Family Therapy, 4, 323.

905. Bruggen, P. (1984), Review of D. Bloch and R. Simon's The strength of family therapy: Selected papers of Nathan W. Ackerman. British Journal of Medical Psychology, 57, 197-198.

906. Bruggen, P., and Davies, G. (1977), Family therapy in adolescent psychiatry. British Journal of Psychiatry, 131, 433-447.

907. Brunelle, P. (1954), Exploring skills of family life at school: Sociodrama with a fourth-grade group. Group Psychotherapy, Psychodrama, and Sociometry, 6, 227-255.

908. Bruninga, C.L. (1967), Group marriage counselling in a state hospital. Hospital and Community Psychiatry, 18, 379-380.

909. Brunner, E.J. (1982), Interaction analysis in the field of family therapy. Praxis Der Kinderpsychologie Und Kinderpsychiatrie, 31, 300-307.

910. Bruno, V., Truppi, M.C., and Zugaro, M. (1982), Preliminaries on alcoholism and family therapy. Minerva Medica, 73, 1473-80.

911. Brunschwig, H. (1982), Family Therapy. Soins Psychiatrie, 27, 47-9.

912. Brunworth, B.J. (1983), The efficacy of a marriage enrichment weekend only vs. a marriage enrichment plus follow-up support. Dissertation Abstracts International, 43, 2802-A.

913. Bubolz, M.M., and Whiren, A.P. (1984), The family of the handicapped: An ecological model for policy and practice. Family Relations: Journal of Applied Family and Child Studies, 33, 5-12.

914. Bucher, B. (1979), Classroom treatment of psychotic children. Behavior Modification, 3, 63-72.

915. Buchholz, M.B. (1981), Psychoanalysis—family therapy—system theory: Critical remarks upon the theory concerning a change of paradigm. Praxis Der Kinderpsychologie Und Kinderpsychiatrie, 30, 48-55.

916. Buchholz, M.B. (1983), Psychoanalytic aspects of communication:
      Reflections on a frequently used family therapeutic concept. Psyche,
      37(7), 624-641.

917. Buchmueller, A.D., Porter, F., and Gildea, M.C. (1954), A group therapy
      project of behavior problem children in public schools. Nervous Child,
      10, 415-424.

918. Buchmueller, A.D., and Gildea, M.C. (1955), Group therapy for parents
      of behavior problem children in public schools. International Journal of
      Social Psychiatry, 1, 51-56.

919. Buchmueller, A.D., and Gildea, M.C. (1949), A group therapy project
      with parents of behavior problem children in public schools. American
      Journal of Psychiatry, 106, 46-52.

920. Buchness, S.G., and Ryerson, M.S. (1981), Family functioning as a
      prognostic tool for drug abusers Family and Child Mental Health
      Journal, 7, 83-89.

921. Buck, M. (1970), Dysphasia: The patient, his family, and the nurse.
      Cardiovascular Nursing, 6, 51.

922. Buckland, C.M. (1972), Toward a theory of parent education: Family
      learning centers in the post industrial society. Family Coordinator, 21,
      151-162.

923. Buckland, C.M. (1977), An educational model of family consultation.
      Journal of Marital and Family Therapy, 3, 49-56.

924. Buckles, N.J., Parker, A.T., and Austin, T. (1974), Married couples
      workshop: Problems and process. Journal of the American College
      Health Association, 22, 431-434.

925. Buckley, T.J. (1977), Commonalities and differences in theories and
      techniques of family therapy. In: T.J. Buckley, J.J. McCarthy, E.
      Norman, and M.A. Quaranta (Eds.), New directions in family therapy.
      Oceanside: Dabor Science Publications.

926. Buda, B. (1978), Familien-und partnerbeziehungen in theorie und
      praxis. (Family and partner-relationships in theory and practice of
      dynamic psychiatry.) Dynamische Psychiatrie, 52/53, 484-495.

927. Buddeberg, B. (1982), Combination of individual and family therapy in a
      psychotic child: Case report of a four-year treatment. Acta
      Paedopsychiatrica, 18, 111-122.

928. Buddeberg, C., and Buddeberg, B. (1982), Family conflicts as collusion:
      A psychodynamic perspective for family therapy. Praxis der
      Kinderpsychologie und Kinderpsychiatrie, 31, 143-50.

929. Buddeburg, B. (1979), Family therapy of anorexia nervosa. Praxis der
      Kinderpsychologie und Kinderpsychiatrie, 28, 37-42.

930. Budman, S.H., and Clifford, M. (1979), Short-term group therapy for
      couples in a health maintenance organization. Professional Psychologist,
      10, 419-429.

931.   Buehler, C., and Wells, B. (1981), Counseling the romantic. Family Relations, 30, 452-458.

932.   Bugental, D.E. and Love, L.R. (1972), Videotaped family interaction: Differences reflecting presence and type of child disturbance. Journal of Abnormal Psychology, 79, 285-290.

933.   Buhrmann, M.V., and Gqomfa, J.N. (1982), The Xhosa healers of Southern Africa: 3. A family therapy session with a dream as a central content. Journal of Analytische Psychologie, 13, 41-57.

934.   Buie, D.J., Jr. (1977) Discussion of the paper by E.R. Shapiro, R.L. Shapiro, J. Zinner, and D.A. Berkowitz on the borderline ego and the working alliance: Indications for family and individual treatment in adolescence. International Journal of Psycho-analysis, 58, 89-93.

935.   Bulbulyan, A.A. (1969), The psychiatric nurse as a family therapist. Perspectives in Psychiatric Care, 7, 58-69.

936.   Bullock, D., and Kobayashi, K. (1978), The use of live consultation in family therapy. Family Therapy, 5, 245-250.

937.   Bullock, D., and Thompson, B. (1979), Guidelines for family interviewing and brief therapy by the family physician. Journal of Family Practice, 9, 837-81.

938.   Bullock, S.C., and Mudd, E.H. (1959), The interrelatedness of alcoholism and marital conflict: II. The interaction of alcoholic husbands and their nonalcoholic wives during counseling. Symposium, 1958. American Journal of Orthopsychiatry, 29, 519-527.

939.   Bulluck, L. (1977), The relationship between expectations and perceptions of the marital counseling process and unplanned terminations among blue-collar, as compared to white-collar couples. Dissertation Abstracts International, 39, 5731A.

940.   Burak, R.L. (1980), Conjoint family drawing: A family interaction assessment tool. Dissertation Abstracts International, 40, 3383-B.

941.   Burch, C. (1982), Review of A. French's Distracted children and their families. Journal of Family Therapy, 4, 326.

942.   Burch, C. (1982), Review of R. Lansdown's More than sympathy The everyday needs of sick and handicapped children and their families. Journal of Family Therapy, 4, 327.

943.   Burgess, R.L. (1978), Family interaction in abusive, neglectful, and normal families. Child Development, 49, 1163-1173.

944.   Burke, C.W. (1979), Marriage matters. (letter). British Medical Journal, 1, 1424.

945.   Burks, H.L. (1965), The use of family therapy and brief hospitalization. Diseases of the Nervous System, 26, 804-806.

946.   Burlingame, V.S. (1982), The family therapy tapestry: A multidisciplinary history of the family therapy movement in the United

States from 1900 to 1957. Dissertation Abstracts International, 43, 1953-B.

947. Burnett, M. (1976), Review of G.H. Zuk's Process and practice in family therapy. Contemporary Psychology, 21, 29.

948. Burns, C.W. (1972), Effectiveness of the basic encounter group in marriage counseling. Dissertation Abstracts International, 33, 1281B.

949. Burns, D.R. (1968), The "absent member" in family therapy of schizophrenia: A review. Pennsylvania Psychiatric Quarterly, 8, 5-9.

950. Burquest, B. (1979), Severe female delinquency: When to involve the family in treatment. Adolescent Psychiatry, 7, 516-523.

951. Burton, G. (1962), Group counseling with alcoholic husbands and their nonalcoholic wives. Marriage and Family Living, 24, 56-61.

952. Burton, G., Kaplan, H.M., and Hudd, E.H. (1968), Marriage counseling with alcoholics and their spouses. I. A critique of the methodology of a follow-up study. British Journal of Addictions, 63, 151-159.

953. Burton, G., and Kaplan, H.M. (1968), Group counseling in conflicted marriages where alcoholism is present: Clients' evaluation of effectiveness. Journal of Marriage, 30, 74-79.

954. Burton, G., and Kaplan, H.M. (1968), Marriage counseling with alcoholics and their spouses. II. The correlation of excessive drinking behavior with family pathology and social deterioration. British Journal of Addictions, 63, 161-170.

955. Burton, G.E., and Young, D.R. (1962), Family crisis in group therapy. Family Process, 1, 214-223.

956. Busch, H., Kormandy, E., and Feuerlein, H. (1973), Partners of female alcoholics. British Journal of Addictions, 68, 179-184.

957. Buschman, P. (1976), Child with leukemia: Group support for parents. American Journal of Nursing, 76, 1121.

958. Bussod, N., and Jacobson, N.S. (1983), Cognitive behavioral marital therapy. Counseling Psychologist, 12, 57-63.

959. Butehorn, L. (1978), A plan for identifying priorities in treating multiproblem families. Child Welfare, 57, 365-372.

960. Butler, J., Bow, I., and Gibbons, J. (1979), Task-centered casework with marital problems. British Journal of Social Work, 8, 393-410.

961. Butts, W.M. (1962), Psychodrama with students and their wives. Group Psychotherapy, Psychodrama, and Sociometry, 15, 55-57.

962. Buvat, J. (1976), Approach to the couple in the treatment of sexual dysfunctions. Lille Medical, 21, 363-368.

963. Byles, J.A., Bishop, D.S., and Horn, D. (1983), Evaluation of a family therapy training program. Journal of Marital and Family Therapy, 9, 299-304.

964.   Byng-Hall, J. (1983), On the use of family myths as defense in family therapy. Etudes Psychotherapiques, 14, 87-98.

965.   Byng-Hall, J. (1980), Symptom bearer as marital distance regulator: Clinical implications. Family Process, 19, 355-365.

966.   Byng-Hall, J. (1982), Dysfunction of feeling: Experiential life of the family. In A. Bentovim, G.G., Barnes, and A. Cooklin (Eds.), Family therapy. I. Complementary frameworks of theory and practice. London: Academic Press.

967.   Byng-Hall, J. (1982), Family legends: Their significance for the family therapist. In A. Bentovim, G.G. Barnes, and A. Cooklin (Eds.), Family therapy. I. Complementary frameworks of theory and practice. London: Academic Press.

968.   Byng-Hall, J. (1982), Grandparents, other relatives, friends and pets. In A. Bentovim, G.G. Barnes, and A. Cooklin (Eds.), Family therapy. 2. Complementary frameworks of theory and practice. London: Academic Press.

969.   Byng-Hall, J. (1983), Review of J. Alexander and B.V. Parson's Functional family therapy. Family Process, 22, 246-248.

970.   Byng-Hall, J., and Bruggen, P. (1974), Family admission decisions as a therapeutic tool. Family Process, 13(4), 443-459.

971.   Byng-Hall, J., and Campbell, D. (1981), Resolving conflicts in family distance regulation: An integrative approach. Journal of Marital and Family Therapy, 7, 321-330.

972.   Bynum, E.B. (1980), The use of dreams in family therapy. Psychotherapy: Theory, Research and Practice, 17, 227-231.

973.   Byrne, D., Cherry, F., Lamberth, J., and Mitchell, H.E. (1973), Husband-wife similarity in response to erotic stimuli. Journal of Personality, 41, 385-394.

974.   Cable, L. (1977), The effectiveness of a leader-created agenda parent counseling model in changing parental attitudes of parents of trainable mentally retarded adolescents. Dissertation Abstracts International, 38, 1989-1990A.

975.   Cabrespine, J.L., and Delafraye, J.P. (1982), Family therapy. Soins Psychiatrie, 27, 27-30.

976.   Cade, B.W. (1980), Resolving therapeutic deadlocks using a contrived team conflict. International Journal of Family Therapy, 2(4), 253-262.

977.   Cade, B.W. (1980), Strategic therapy. Journal of Family Therapy, 2(2), 89.

978.   Cade, B.W. (1979), Family therapy: An interactional approach to problems. Health Visit, 52, 33-34.

979.   Cadogan, D.A. (1973), Marital group therapy in the treatment of alcoholism. Quarterly Journal of Studies on Alcohol, 34, 1187-1194.

980.   Cahill, T.J. (1976), The effectiveness of familial involvement on the psychodynamics of adolescent drug user therapy. Dissertation Abstracts International, 36, 4128-4129B.

981.   Cahn, R., Weill, D., and Dion, Y. (1974), Understanding the parents of psychotic children by means of the countertransference process. Psychiatrie de L'Enfant, 17, 413-478.

982.   Cahners, S.S. (1978), Group meetings for families of burned children. Health and Social Work, 3, 165-172.

983.   Cahners, S.S., and Bernstein, N.R. (1979), Rehabilitating families with burned children. Scandavian Journal of Plastic Reconstructive Surgery, 13, 173-175.

984.   Caille, P. (1982), The evaluation phase of systemic family therapy. Journal of Marital and Family Therapy, 8, 29-39.

985.   Caille, P. (1978), Family therapy. Psychotherapy of the psychotic patient and his family? The treatment process in the framework of theory. Psychotherapy and Psychosomatics, 29(1-4), 217-220.

986.   Caille, P. (1981), How therapeutic intervention does create the prerequisites of change in human relations. Journal of Marital and Family Therapy, 7(3), 281-290.

987.   Caille, P., Abrahamsen, P., Buhl, C., and Sorbye, B. (1979), Levels of communication and the systems approach in the psychotic family. Evolution Psychiatrique, 44, 439-455.

988.   Caille, P., Abrahamsen, P., Girolami, C., and Sorbye, B. (1977), A systems theory approach to a case of anorexia nervosa. Family Process, 16, 455-465.

989.   Caille, P., and Sorbye, B. (1977), Family psychiatry. Tidschrift For Den Norske Laedeforening, 97, 1621-1624.

990.   Calhoun, S.H. (1970), Power relations in the setting of family pathology: Alignments and oppositions. Dissertation Abstracts International, 31, 4330B.

991.   Callaghan, K.A. (1970), Practical management of the battered baby syndrome. Medical Journal of Australia, 1, 1282-1284.

992.   Cameron, M. (1976), Family care nursing at Sturt CAE. Australian Nurses Journal, 5, 59-60.

993.   Camp, H. (1973), Structural family therapy: An outsider's perspective. Family Process, 12, 269-278.

994.   Campbell, D. (1982), Adolescence in families. In A. Bentovim, G.G. Branes, and A. Cooklin (Eds.), Family therapy. 2. Complementary frameworks of theory and practice. London: Academic Press.

995.   Campbell, D., and DeCarteret, J. (1984), Guidelines for clinicians considering family therapy research. Journal of Family Therapy, 6(2), 131-148.

996.   Campbell, D., and Draper, R. (Eds.) (1985), Applications of systemic family therapy: The Milan approach. New York: Grune and Stratton.

997.   Campbell, D.M. (1980), Review of N.S. Jacobson and G. Margolin, Marital therapy: Strategies based on social learning and behavior exchange principles. British Journal of Psychiatry, 136, 604.

998.   Campbell, D.M. (1983), Review of C. Madanes' Strategic family therapy. Journal of Family Therapy, 5, 99.

999.   Campbell, P.G. (1983), Streit family workshops: Creating change in a family environment. Journal of Drug Education, 13, 223-227.

1000.   Campbell, R.V., O'Brien, S., Bickett, A.D., and Lutzker, J.R. (1983), In-home parent training, treatment of migraine headaches, and marital counseling as an ecobehavioral approach to prevent child abuse. Journal of Behavior Therapy and Experimental Psychiatry, 14, 147-154.

1001.   Campbell, T.W., Van Gee, S.J., Brock, G., and Greenfield, G. (1980), Use of a multiple family group for crisis intervention. General Hospital Psychiatry, 2, 95-9.

1002.   Campion, J. (1982), Young Asian children with learning and behavior problems: A family therapy approach. Journal of Family Therapy, 4(2), 153.

1003.   Campion, J. (1984), Psychological services for children: Using family therapy in the setting of a school psychological service. Journal of Family Therapy, 6(1), 47-62.

1004.   Campion, J., and Fry, E. (1985), The contribution of Kleinian psychotherapy to the treatment of a disturbed five-year old girl and her family. Journal of Family Therapy, 7, 341-356.

1005.   Campos, R.L. (1980), Family therapy and the Chicano drug abuser. In: B.G. Ellis (Ed.), Drug abuse from the family perspective. Rockville: National Institute of Drug Abuse.

1006.   Canavan, D.I. (1983), Impaired physicians program: Aftercare. Journal of the Medical Society of New Jersey, 80, 849.

1007.   Cancrini, L. (1974), Family psychotherapy with a case of a depresesd woman: Reflections on Sigmund Freud's concept of "mourning and melancholia." Rivista Psychiatrica, 9, 185-202.

1008.   Candib, L., and Glenn, M. (1983), Family medicine and family therapy: Comparative development, methods, and roles. Journal of Family Practice, 12, 773-779.

1009.   Candy, M.M. (1979), Birth of a comprehensive family-centered maternity program. Journal of Obstetrical and Gynecological Nurses, 8, 80-84.

1010.   Canevaro, A. (1981), Family therapy with psychotic patients: An institutional approach. Journal of Marital and Family Therapy, 7, 375-383.

1011.   Canevars, A.A. (1977), Toward a clinical structural theory of family therapy. Acta Psiquirtrica Y Psychologica de America Latina, 23, 139-142.

1012.   Canino, G., and Canino, I.A. (1982), Culturally, syntonic family therapy for migrant Puerto Ricans. Hospital and Community Psychiatry, 33, 299-303.

1013.   Canino, I.A., and Canino, G. (1980), Impact of stress on the Puerto Rican family: Treatment considerations. American Journal of Orthopsychiatry, 50, 535-41.

1014.   Cantoni, L. (1975), Family life education: A treatment modality. Child Welfare, 54, 658-665.

1015.   Cantor, D.W. (1982), Divorce: Separation or separation-individuation?. American Journal of Psychoanalysis, 42, 307-313.

1016.   Cantor, D.W., and Drake, E.A. (1983), Divorced parents and their children: A guide for mental health professionals. New York: Springer Publishing.

1017.   Cantor, P. (1975), The effects of youthful suicide on the family. Psychiatric Opinion, 12(6), 6-11.

1018.   Cantwell, D.P. (1979), Families of autistic and dysphasic children. I. Family life and interaction patterns. Archives of General Psychiatry, 36, 682-687.

1019.   Caplan, H. (1968), Some aspects of parent guidance in child psychiatry. Canadian Journal of Psychiatry, 13, 311-315.

1020.   Caplan, R.T. (1973), Attitude change of couples involved in a sexual therapy program. Dissertation Abstracts International, 34, 3053A.

1021.   Car, M.A. (1977), A family in conflict: An analysis of discourse spanning six months of family therapy. Dissertation Abstracts International, 38, 2089A.

1022.   Carder, J.H. (1972), New dimension to family agency from family life education. Social Casework, 53, 355-360.

1023.   Cardillo, J.P. (1971), The effects of teaching communication roles on interpersonal perception and self-concept in disturbed marriages. Dissertation Abstracts International, 32, 2392-2393B.

1024.   Carek, D.J. (1964), Treatment of a family involved in fratricide. Archives of General Psychiatry, 11, 533-542.

1025.   Carel, A. (1982), "Parents-infant" psychotherapy. Research on the autistic process. Neuropsychiatrie de L'Enfance et de L'Adolescence, 30, 209-15.

1026.   Carel, C.A., and Tyano, S. (1983), Family evaluation and family therapy when a child or adolescent is the identified patient. In L.R. Wolberg and M.L. Aronson (Eds.), Group and family therapy 1982. New York: Brunner/Mazel.

1027.   Carey, A. (1977), Helping the child and the family cope with death. International Journal of Family Counseling, 5, 58-63.

1028.   Carkhuff, R.R., and Berenson, B.G. (1972), The utilization of black functional professionals to reconstitute troubled families. Journal of Clinical Psychology, 28, 92-93.

1029.   Carl, D. (1981), Review of J.K. Zeig's Ericksonian approaches to hypnosis and therapy. Journal of Marital and Family Therapy, 9, 216.

1030.   Carl, D., and Jurkovic, G.J. (1983), Agency triangles: Problems in agency-family relationships. Family Process, 22, 441-451.

1031.   Carlson, J., Portes, P., and Fullmer, D. (1977), Developing family competencies: An Adlerian model. International Journal of Family Counseling, 5, 32-40.

1032.   Carlyne, M.J. (1980), A paediatric home therapy programme for developmental progress in severely handicapped infants. Child Care, Health and Development, 6(6), 339-350.

1033.   Carnes, P.J. (1980), Educating interactionally impaired adults: An analysis of curriculum impact on family environment. Dissertation Abstracts International, 41, 1967-A.

1034.   Carnes, P.J., and Laube, H. (1975), Becoming us: An experiment in family learning and teaching. Small Group Behavior, 6, 106-120.

1035.   Caroli, F. (1978), The treatment of psychotic children in a day-clinic. Acta Paedopsychiatrica, 43, 145-148.

1036.   Caron, C.L., and Caron, M. (1970), Child psychiatry and child centers. Revue de Neuropsychiatrie Infantile et de Mentale de L'Enfance, 18, 913-925.

1037.   Carone, P.A., (Ed.) (1985), Mental health problems of workers and their families. New York: Human Science Press.

1038.   Carozza, P.M., and Heirsteiner, C.L. (1982), Young female incest victims in treatment: Stages of growth seen with a group art therapy model. Clinical Social Work Journal, 10, 165-175.

1039.   Carpenter, J. (1984), Making training relevant: A critical view of family therapy training in the U.K. Journal of Family Therapy, 6, 235-246.

1040.   Carpenter, J., Treacher, A., Jenkins, H., and Oreilly, P. (1983), Oh no - not the Smiths again: An exploration of how to identify and overcome stuckness in family therapy. 2. Stuckness in the therapeutic and supervisory systems. Journal of Family Therapy, 5, 81-96.

1041.   Carroll, E.J. (1960), Treatment of the family as a unit. Pennsylvania Medical Journal, 63, 57-62.

1042.   Carroll, E.J., Cambor, C.G., Leopold, J.V., Miller, M.D., and Reis, W.J. (1963), Psychotherapy of marital couples. Family Process, 2, 25-33.

1043.   Carter, D.C. (1970), The diagnosis and treatment of husband paranoidism. West Virginia Medical Journal, 66, 345-348.

1044.   Carter, D.K. (1977), Counseling divorced women. Personnel and Guidance Journal, 55(9), 537-541.

1045.   Carter, J.A. (1981), Couples' perceptions of relationship variables, marital adjustment and change before and after treatment. Dissertation Abstracts International, 41, 3172-B.

1046.   Carter, R.D., and Thomas, E.J. (1973), Modification of problematic marital communication using corrective feedback and instruction. Behavior Therapy, 4(1), 100.

1047.   Carter, W.W. (1968), Group counseling for adolescent foster children. Children, 15, 22-27.

1048.   Caruso, G.J. (1963), Family oriented psychotherapy: A review. Journal of the Louisiana Medical Society, 115, 312-316.

1049.   Case history method in the study of family process (1970), Group For The Advancement Of Psychiatry: GAP Reports, 6, 237-380.

1050.   Cassidy, M.J. (1973), Communication training for marital pairs. Dissertation Abstracts International, 34, 3054A.

1051.   Castro-Guevara, N.P. (1967), La entrevista con el nino y sus padres en una clinica de la conducta. (Interview with child and parents in a behavior clinic.) Revista de Clinica de la Conducta, 1, 17-25.

1052.   Catanzaro, R.J. (1973), Combined treatment of alcoholics, drug abusers, and related problems in a "family residential center." Drug Forum, 2, 203-212.

1053.   Catanzaro, R.J., Pisani, V.D., Fox, R., and Kennedy, E.R. (1973), Familization therapy: An alternative to traditional mental health care. Diseases of the Nervous System, 34, 212-218.

1054.   Catham, M.A. (1978), The effect of family involvement on patient's manifestations of postcardiotomy psychosis. Heart Lung, 7, 995-999.

1055.   Caust, B.L., Libow, J.A., and Raskin, P.A. (1981), Challenges and promises of training women as family systems therapists. Family Process, 20, 439-47.

1056.   Cavan, R.S. (1973), Speculations on innovations to conventional marriage in old age. Gerentologia Clinica, 15, 124-132.

1057.   Cavanagh, J. (1957), Fundamental marriage counseling: A Catholic viewpoint. Milwaukee, WI: Bruce.

1058.   Cazzullo, C.L. (1978), Psychotherapy of the family as a measure for preventing relapses and improving the prognosis in schizophrenic patients. Acta Psychiatrica Belgica, 78, 256-268.

1059.   Cecobert, S. (1973), The concept of the therapeutic couple (apropos of the experience of a therapeutic couple in a group of couples). Revue Francaise de Psychanalyse, 36, 83-110.

1060.   Cermak, I. (1973), Family crisis and psychosomatic illness.
        Psychotherapy and Psychosomatics, 22, 250-254.

1061.   Cermak, I. (1972), Family therapy. Praxis der Psychotherapie, 17, 104-
        112.

1062.   Cermak, L. (1971), Family crisis and psychosomatic illness. Progress in
        Neurology and Psychiatry, 26, 459-472.

1063.   Cermak, T.L., and Brown, S. (1982), Interactional group therapy with
        the adult children of alcoholics. International Journal of Group
        Psychotherapy, 32(3), 375.

1064.   Chabot, D.R. (1976), Family therapy with court-committed,
        institutionalized, acting-out male adolescents. Clinical Psychologist, 29,
        8-9.

1065.   Chafetz, L., and Galliard, J. (1978), The impact of a therapeutic nurse-
        family relationship on post graduate public health nursing students.
        Geneva School of Nursing. International Journal of Nursing Studies,
        15(1), 37-49.

1066.   Chalpin, G. (1966), The fathers-group: An effective therapy medium for
        involving fathers in a child psychiatric clinic treatment program.
        Journal of the American Academy of Child Psychiatry, 5, 125-133.

1067.   Chamberlain, C., and Awad, G. (1975), Psychiatric service to the
        juvenile court: A model. Canadian Journal of Psychiatry, 20, 599-605.

1068.   Chamow, L. (1975), A functional approach to family assessment.
        Family Therapy, 2, 259-268.

1069.   Chance, E. (1959), Families in treatment: From the viewpoint of the
        patient, the clinician, and the researcher. New York: Basic Books.

1070.   Chandler, E. (1968), Treatment of a psychotic family in a family
        psychiatry setting. Psychotherapy and Psychosomatics, 16, 339-347.

1071.   Chapman, G.E. (1974), Treating parents of disturbed adolescents. Mt.
        Siani Journal of Medicine New York, 41, 520-523.

1072.   Chapman, G.E. (1974), Treating parents and disturbed adolescents.
        Nursing Times, 70, 154-155.

1073.   Chappelear, E.M., and Fried, J.E. (1967), Helping adopting couples come
        to grips with their new parental roles. Children, 14, 223-226.

1074.   Charny, I.W. (1962), Family interviews in redefining a "sick" child's role
        in the family problem. Psychological Reports, 10, 577-578.

1075.   Charny, I.W. (1966), Integrated individual and family psychotherapy.
        Family Process, 5, 179-198.

1076.   Charny, I.W. (1972), Parental intervention with one another on behalf of
        their child: A breaking-through tool for preventing emotional
        disturbance. Journal of Contemporary Psychotherapy, 5, 19-29.

1077.   Charny, I.W. (1981), Structuralism, paradoxical intervention and existentialism: The current philosophy and politics of family therapy. Fokus po Familien, 9(1), 14-30.

1078.   Charny, I.W. (1980), Why are so many (if not really all) people and families disturbed? Journal of Marital and Family Therapy, 6(1), 37-47.

1079.   Charny, I.W. (1983), Structuralism, paradoxical intervention, and existentialism - the current philosophy and politics of family therapy. In L.R. Wolberg, and M.L. Aronson (Eds.), Group and family therapy 1982. New York: Brunner/Mazel.

1080.   Chase, A.M., Crowley, C.D., and Weintraub, M.K. (1979), Treating the throwaway child: A model for adolescent service. Social Casework, 60, 538-546.

1081.   Chassin, L., Perelman, M., and Weinberger, G. (1974), Reducing parental resistance to examining family relationships: The therapeutic use of a child management task. Psychotherapy: Theory, Research and Practice, 11, 387-390.

1082.   Chastulik, F. (1981), A comparison of the effects of a structured experimental learning group and a structured marital enrichment group on the reduction of disparity in interpersonal perceptions between married couples. Dissertation Abstracts International, 42, 1582-B.

1083.   Chatagnon, P.A. (1977), Prevention and control of child and juvenile delinquency and criminality. The home of the child and its parents. Annales Medico-Psychologiques, 1, 211-226.

1084.   Chazan, R. (1974), A group family therapy approach to schizophrenia. Israeli Annals of Psychiatry, 12, 177-193.

1085.   Cheek, F.E., Franks, C.M., Laucius, J., and Burtle, V. (1971), Behavior modification training for wives of alcoholics. Quarterly Journal for Studies on Alcohol, 32, 456-461.

1086.   Chelune, G.J., Sultan, F.E., Vosk, B.N., Ogden, J.K., and Waring, E.M. (1984), Self-disclosure patterns in clinical and non-clinical couples. Journal of Clinical Psychology, 40, 213-215.

1087.   Chelune, G.J., Sultan, F.E., Vosk, B.N., Ogden, J.K., and Waring, E.M. (1984), Self-disclosure and its relationship to marital intimacy. Journal of Clinical Psychology, 40, 216-219.

1088.   Chernus, L.A. (1982), Marital treatment following early infant death. Clinical Social Work Journal, 10, 28-38.

1089.   Chescheir, M.W. (1975), Boundaries in the person and in the family: Theory and practice in family therapy. Dissertation Abstracts International, 35, 5520-5521A.

1090.   Chesney, A.P., Blakeney, P.E., Chan, F.A., and Cole, C.M. (1981), The impact of sex theapy on sexual behaviors and marital communciaton. Journal of Sex and Marital Therapy, 7, 70-9.

1091.   Chesney, A.P., Blakeney, P.E., Cole, C.M., and Chan, F.A. (1981), A
comparison of couples who have sought sex therapy with couples who
have not. Journal of Sex and Marital Therapy, 7, 131-40.

1092.   Chessick, R.D. (1977), Intensive psychotherapy for the psychiatrist's
family. American Journal of Psychotherapy, 31, 516-524.

1093.   Chester, R. (1973), Health and marital breakdown: Some implications
for doctors. Journal of Psychosomatic Medicine, 17, 317-321.

1094.   Chethik, M. (1976), Work with parents: Treatment of the parent-child
relationship. Journal of the American Academy of Child Psychiatry, 15,
453-463.

1095.   Chichilinsky, S. (1962), Familial occupational therapy: The adaptive
home. Semana Medica, 121, 748-758.

1096.   Childs-Jackson, G.J. (1983), Extended family networking: A therapeutic
approach for inner-city minority families. Dissertation Abstracts
International, 44, 1954-B.

1097.   Chiles, J., Stauss, F.S., and Benjamin, L.S. (1980), Marital conflict and
sexual dysfunction in alcoholic and non-alcoholic couples. British
Journal of Psychiatry, 141, 266-273.

1098.   Choi, M.W. (1978), Birth crisis: Parental and professional responses to
the birth of a child with a defect. Comprehensive Pediatric Nursing, 2,
1-10.

1099.   Chope, H.D., and Blackford, L (1963), The chronic problem family: San
Mateo County's experience. American Journal of Orthopsychiatry, 33(3),
462-469.

1100.   Christensen, A. (1976), Cost effectiveness in behavioral family
therapy. Dissertation Abstracts International, 37, 3066B.

1101.   Christensen, A., Johnson, S.M., Phillips, S., and Glasgow, R.E. (1980),
Cost effectiveness in behavioral family therapy. Behavior Therapy, 11,

1102.   Christensen, B., and DeBlassie, R.R. (1980), Counseling with parents of
handicapped adolescents. Adolescence, 15(58), 397-408.

1103.   Christensen, B.L. (1977), A family systems treatment program for
families of delinquent adolescent boys: And the effects of the
treatment program on the family environment and individual personality
traits of delinquent adolescent boys in a residential institution.
Dissertation Abstracts International, 37, 6092A.

1104.   Christensen, D.N. (1983), Postmastectomy couple counseling: An
outcome study of a structured treatment protocol. Journal of Sex and
Marital Therapy, 9, 266-275.

1105.   Christiansen, N.H. (1985), A preliminary contribution to an
understanding of the use of playfulness in family therapy. Dissertation
Abstracts International, 46, 1517-A.

1106.   Christie-Seely, J. (1981), Teaching the family system concept in family
medicine. Journal of Family Practice, 13(1), 391-401.

1107. Christman, C. (1967), Family group therapy: Implications for music therapy. Journal of Music Therapy, 4, 100–105.

1108. Church, A.S. (1979), An evaluation of parent effectiveness training (PET) in families of school-age children. Dissertation Abstracts International, 40, 906B.

1109. Churchill, S.R. (1965), Social group work: A diagnostic tool in child guidance. American Journal of Orthopsychiatry, 35(3), 581–588.

1110. Churven, P. (1984), Review of A. Lange and O. Van der Hart's Directive family therapy. Australian and New Zealand Journal of Psychiatry, 18(4), 403–404.

1111. Churven, P. (1984), Review of F.W. Kaslow's The international book of family therapy. Australian and New Zealand Journal of Psychiatry, 18(1), 104.

1112. Churven, P.G. (1979), Family intervention for beginners: A rationale for a brief problem-oriented approach in child and family psychiatry. Australian and New Zealand Journal of Psychiatry, 13(3), 235–239.

1113. Churven, P.G. (1980), Families: Parental attitudes to family assessment in a child psychiatry setting. Advances in Family Psychiatry, 2, 209–220.

1114. Churven, P.G. (1978), Families: Parental attitudes to family assessment in a child psychiatry setting. Journal of Child Psychology and Psychiatry and Allied Disciplines 19, 33–41.

1115. Churven, P.G., and Cintio, B. (1983), An application of strategic family therapy to a residential child and family psychiatry service: Redbank House. Australian and New Zealand Journal of Psychiatry, 17, 191–195.

1116. Churven, P.G., and McKinnon, T. (1982), Family therapy training: An evaluation of a workshop. Family Process, 21, 345–52.

1117. Ciani, N. (1974), Family psychiatry and the pragmatics of communication. Rivista Psychiatrica, 9, 1–40.

1118. Ciani, N. (1972), Family psychotherapy: Clinical and theoretical aspects. Rivista Psychiatrica, 7, 72–96.

1119. Cierpka, M. (1982), The juvenile diabetic and his family. Zeitschrift Fur Psychosomatische Medizin Und Psychoanalyse, 28, 363–384.

1120. Cirincione, D., Hart, J., Karle, W., and Switzer, A. (1980), The functional approach to using dreams in marital and family therapy. Journal of Marital and Family Therapy, 6, 147–152.

1121. Citrin, R.S. (1981), Reciprocity counseling in the extended family: A field study. Dissertation Abstracts International, 41, 3005-A.

1122. Clancy, H. (1970), A group family holiday: An innovation in the therapeutic management of the autistic child. Slow Learning Children, 17, 149–162.

1123. Clark, A. (1981), Therapy—that's a different story. Journal of Family Therapy, 3, 211–225.

1124.   Clark, A. (1982), Review of P. Watzlawick's The language of change. Journal of Family Therapy, 4, 324-325.

1125.   Clark, C.C. (1977), Psychotherapy with the resistant child. Perspectives in Psychiatric Care, 15(3), 122-125.

1126.   Clark, J., and Kempler, H.L. (1973), Therapeutic family camping: A rationale. Family Coordinator, 22, 437-442.

1127.   Clark, M.E. (1984), Review of J.C. Wynne's Family therapy in pastoral ministry. Personnel and Guidance Journal, 62(7), 436.

1128.   Clark, S. (1981), An experimental study of two approaches to the treatment of marital dysfunctioning. Dissertation Abstracts International, 41, 4838-A.

1129.   Clark, T., Zalis, T., and Sacco, F. (1982), Outreach family therapy. New York: Aronson.

1130.   Clarke, C. (1969), The family as an integral part of management: The physician's role in guidance. Texas Medical Journal, 65, 60-63.

1131.   Clarke, J.I. (1981), Self-esteem: A family affair leader guide. Minneapolis, MN: Winston Press.

1132.   Clarke, M. (1974), Treating frigidity means treating the couple. Medical Journal of Australia, 2(11), 405-409.

1133.   Clarkin, J.F. (1984), Review of G.R. Patterson's Coercive family process. Family Process, 23(1), 122.

1134.   Clarkin, J.F., Frances, A., and Moodie, J. (1979), Selection criteria for family therapy. Family Process, 18, 391-405.

1135.   Clarkin, J.F., and Glick, I.D. (1982), Recent developments in family therapy: A review. Hospital and Community Psychiatry, 33, 550-6.

1136.   Clarkin, J.F., and Glick, I.D. (1982), Supervision of family therapy. In M. Blumenfield (Ed.), Applied supervision in psychotherapy. New York: Grune and Stratton.

1137.   Clavan, S. (1974), Review of C.S. Sager and H.S. Kaplan (Eds.), Progress in group and family therapy. Journal of Marriage and the Family, 36, 209.

1138.   Cleghorn, J.M., and Levin, S. (1973), Training family therapists by setting learning objectives. American Journal of Orthopsychiatry, 43, 439-446.

1139.   Clemens, A.H. (1953), The cana movement in the United States: Summary of a survey made under the auspices of the marriage counseling center of the Catholic University of America. Washington, DC: Catholic University of America.

1140.   Clemensschroner, B.L. (1968), Family guardian and family therapy. Tijdschrift voor Maatshappelijk Werk, 22(17), 383-389.

1141.   Clement, J.A. (1977), Family therapy: The transferability of theory to practice. Journal of Psychiatric Nursing, 15, 33-37.

1142.   Clement, P.W. (1971), Please mother, I'd rather you did it yourself: Training parents to treat their own children. Journal of School Health, 41, 65-69.

1143.   Clement, U. (1980), Sexual unresponsiveness and orgastic dysfunction: An empirical comparison. Journal of Sex and Marital Therapy, 6(4), 274-281.

1144.   Clement, U., and Pfaeffkune, F. (1980), Changes in personality scores among couples subsequent to sex therapy. Archives of Sexual Behavior, 9(3), 235-244.

1145.   Clement, U., and Schmidt, G. (1983), The outcome of couple therapy for sexual dysfunctions using three different formats. Journal of Sex and Marital Therapy, 9, 67-78.

1146.   Clementel, C., and Crockatt, P. (1979), Problems in a creative marriage following the birth of the first child: An account of a conjoint marital therapy. British Journal of Medical Psychology, 52, 163-168.

1147.   Clements, I.W., and Buchanan, D.E. (1982), Family therapy: A nursing perspective. New York: John Wiley and Sons.

1148.   Clercksachsse, R.D. (1978), (Several problems of family counseling and family therapy in context with institutional goals.) Praxis der Kinderpsychologie und Kinderpsychiatrie, 27, 309.

1149.   Cleveland, M. (1979), Family adaptation to the traumatic spinal cord injury of a son or daughter. Social Work and Health Care, 4, 459-471.

1150.   Cleveland, M. (1976), Sex in marriage: At 40 and beyond. Family Coordinator, 25, 233-240.

1151.   Cleveland, M. (1981), Families and adolescent drug abuse: Structural analysis of children's roles. Family Process, 20, 295-304.

1152.   Cleveland, M., and Irvin, K. (1982), Custody resolution counseling: An alternative intervention. Journal of Marital and Family Therapy, 8, 105-111.

1153.   Cline, V.B., Mejia, J., Coles, J., Klein, N., and Cline, R.A. (1984), The relationship between therapist behaviors and outcome for middle and lower-class couples in marital therapy. Journal of Clinical Psychology, 40(3), 691-704.

1154.   Cloninger, C.R., Rice, J., and Reich, T. (1979), Multifactorial inheritance with cultural transmission and associative mating. III. Family structure and the analysis of separation experiments. American Journal of Human Genetics, 31, 366-388.

1155.   Clower, C.G., and Brody, L. (1964), Conjoint family therapy in outpatient practice. American Journal of Psychotherapy, 18, 670-677.

1156.   Clyman, R.I. (1979), What pediatricians say to mothers of sick newborns: An indirect evaluation of the counseling process. Pediatrics, 63(5), 719-723.

1157.   Cobb, D.E. (1978), Determinants of effectiveness in parental counseling. Journal of Community Psychology, 6(3), 229-240.

1158.   Cobb, J. (1980), Review of F.M. Sander's Individual and family therapy: Toward an integration. British Journal of Psychiatry, 137, 488.

1159.   Cobb, J., McDonald, R., Marks, I., and Stern, R. (1980), Marital versus exposure therapy: Psychological treatments of co-existing marital and phobic-obsessive problems. Behavioural Analysis and Modification, 4(1), 3.

1160.   Cobb, J.P. (1982), The interaction between neurotic problems and marriage: Implications for the therapist. Partnerberatung, 19, 105-111.

1161.   Coben, E.L. (1981), The clinical role of the marital and family therapist as perceived by primary care and non-primary care physicians. Dissertation Abstracts International, 42, 1600-B.

1162.   Coche, J. (1978), (Thoughts on a nosology in family therapy.) Gruppenpsychotherapie und Gruppendynamik, 13, 342-353.

1163.   Coche, J., Frohman, B., Yantis, S., and Thomas, R. (1978), (Short-term multiple family group therapy - Some guidelines.) Grupenpsychotherapie und Gruppendynamik, 13, 217-227.

1164.   Cochrane, N. (1973), Some reflections on the unsuccessful treatment of a group of married couples. British Journal of Psychiatry, 123, 395-401.

1165.   Coe, W.C. (1972), A behavioral approach to disrupted family interactions. Psychotherapy: Theory, Research and Practice, 9, 80-85.

1166.   Coe, W.C., and Black, D.R. (1976), An exploratory study evaluating a behavioral approach to disrupted family interactions. Corrective and Social Psychiatry, 22, 46-49.

1167.   Coggins, D.R. (1978), Review of A.C.R. Skynner's, Systems of family and marital psychotherapy. American Journal of Psychiatry, 125, 630.

1168.   Cohen, C.J., and Corwin, J. (1978), A further application of balance theory to multiple family therapy. International Journal of Group Psychotherapy, 28, 195-209.

1169.   Cohen, I.M. (1966), Family structure, dynamics and therapy. Washington, D.C.: American Psychiatric Association.

1170.   Cohen, J.S. (1977), Marital counseling in general practice. Proceedings of the Royal Society of Medicine, 20, 495-496.

1171.   Cohen, M., Goldenberg, I., and Goldenberg, H. (1977), Treating families of bone marrow recipients and donors. Journal of Marital and Family Therapy, 3, 45-51.

1172.   Cohen, M.M., and Wellisch, D.K. (1978), Living in limbo: Psychosocial intervention in families with a cancer patient. American Journal of Psychotherapy, 32, 561-571.

1173.   Cohen, P.M. (1983), A group approach for working with families of the elderly. Gerontologist, 23, 248-50.

1174.   Cohen-Matthijsen, T. (1970), The battered child syndrome. Nederlands Tijdschrift Voor Geneeskunde, 114, 142-149.

1175.   Cohler, B.J., and Geyer, S. (1982), Psychological autonomy and interdependence within the family. In F. Walsh (Eds.), Normal family processes. New York: Guilford Press.

1176.   Cohn, A.H. (1979), An evaluation of three demonstration child abuse and neglect treatment programs. Journal of American Academy of Child Psychiatry, 18, 283-291.

1177.   Cohn, C.K., and Talmadge, J.M. (1976), Extended family presents. Family Therapy, 3, 235-244.

1178.   Colas, Y. (1984), Family and mental disorders in the aged. Planned perspective at admission. Soins Psychiatrie, 29, 15-20.

1179.   Colas, Y. (1983), Observation techniques in systematic family therapy. Perspectives Psychiatriques, 21, 256-262.

1180.   Cole, C.L. (1983), Review of L. Hof, and W.R. Miller's Marriage enrichment: Philosophy, process and program. American Journal of Family Therapy, 11, 80-81.

1181.   Cole, C.M. (1978), The role of brief family therapy in medical rehabilitation. Journal of Rehabilitation, 44, 29.

1182.   Cole, C.M. (1983), Sexual disorders and the family therapist. Family Therapy Collections, 6, 49-61.

1183.   Cole, C.M., Blakeney, P.E., Chan, F.A., Chesney, A.P., and Creson, P.L. (1979), The myth of symptomatic versus asymptomatic partners in the conjoint treatment of sexual dysfunction. Journal of Sex and Marital Therapy, 5(2), 79-89.

1184.   Colebrook, E.P. (1981), Anorexia Nervosa: Delineation of six phases with implications for diagnosis and structural family therapy. Dissertation Abstracts International, 42, 1957-A.

1185.   Coleman, E. (1982), Bisexual and gay men in heterosexual marriage: Conflicts and resolutions in therapy. Journal of Homosexuality, 7(2-3), 93.

1186.   Coleman, J.C. (1953), Group therapy with parents of mentally deficient children. American Journal of Mental Deficiency, 57, 700-704.

1187.   Coleman, K.H. (1980), Conjugal violence: What 33 men report. Journal of Marital and Family Therapy, 6(2), 207-213.

1188.   Coleman, R.E., and Miller, A.G. (1975), The relationship between depression and marital maladjustment in a clinic population: A multitrait-multimethod study. Journal of Consulting and Clinical Psychology, 43(5), 647-651.

1189.   Coleman, S.B. (1978), An index for measuring agency involvement in family therapy. Family Process, 17, 479-483.

1190.   Coleman, S.B. (1978), Sib group therapy: A prevention program for siblings from drug addicted families. International Journal of the Addictions, 13, 115-127.

1191.   Coleman, S.B. (Ed.) (1985), Failures in family therapy. New York: Guilford Press.

1192.   Coleman, S.B., and Davis, D.I. (1978), Family therapy and drug abuse: A national survey. Family Process, 17, 21-29.

1193.   Coleman, S.B., and Kaplan, J.D. (1978), A profile of family therapists in the drug abuse field. American Journal of Drug Abuse, 5, 171-178.

1194.   Colliander, C. (1962), Family counseling as a profession. Nordisk Medcin, 68, 1205-1209.

1195.   Collins, L.E., and Zimmerman, N. (1983), Homosexual and bisexual issues. Family Therapy Collections, 8, 82-100.

1196.   Collins, M.C. (Ed.) (1978), Child abuse: A study of child abusers in self-help group therapy. Littleton, MA: P&G Publishing Co.

1197.   Collison, C.R., and Futrell, J. (1982), Family therapy for the single-parent family system. Journal of Psychosocial Nursing and Mental Health Services, 20, 16-20.

1198.   Colman, A.D. (1976), The effect of group and family emphasis on the role of the psychiatric resident of an acute treatment ward. International Journal of Group Psychotherapy, 15, 516-525.

1199.   Colman, W. (1975), Occupational therapy and child abuse. American Journal of Occupational Therapy, 29(7), 412-417.

1200.   Colon, F. (1978), Family ties and child placement. Family Process, 17, 289-312.

1201.   Combrinck, G.L., Gursky, E.J., and Brendler, J. (1982), Hospitalization of single-parent families of disturbed children. Family Process, 21, 141-52.

1202.   Combrinck, G.L., and Higley, L.W. (1984), Working with families of school-aged handicapped children. Family Therapy Collections, 11, 18-29.

1203.   Combrinck-Graham, L. (1974), Structural family therapy in psychosomatic illness: Treatment of anorexia nervosa and asthma. Clinical Pediatrics, 13(10), 827-833.

1204.   Commaille, J. (1983), Divorce and the child's status: The evolution in France. Journal of Comparative Family Studies, 14, 97-116.

1205.   Committee on the family. (1970), The field of family therapy, Report No. 78. New York: Group for the Advancement of Psychiatry.

1206.   Compernolle, T. (1981), J.L. Moreno: An unrecognized pioneer of
        family therapy. Family Process, 20, 331-335.

1207.   Compernolle, T. (1980), Basic premises for training curriculum in
        structural family therapy. In: W. Demoor and H.R. Wijngaarden (Eds.),
        Psychotherapy: Research and training. Amsterdam: Elsevier.

1208.   Compher, J.V. (1983), Home services to families to prevent child
        placement. Social Work, 28, 360-364.

1209.   Condini, A., Pavan, L., and Esposito, E. (1972), Results of psychotherapy
        with the families of adolescents with suicidal tendency. Rivista
        Psychiatrica, 7, 459-468.

1210.   Confal, J.D., and Brock, G.W. (1979), Parent-child relationship
        enhancement: Skills training approach. In: N. Stinnett, B. Chessler and
        J. Defrain (Eds.), Building family strengths. Lincoln, NE: University of
        Nebraska Press.

1211.   Confer, H.P. (1980), The effects of a marital enrichment program upon
        spousal perception of the dyadic relationship. Dissertation Abstracts
        International, 41, 2507-A.

1212.   Conger, J.P. (1979), Family therapy and the concept of sprezzatura.
        Family Therapy, 6(1), 1-3.

1213.   Connolly, C. (1978), Counseling parents of school age children with
        special needs. Journal of School Health, 48(2), 115-118.

1214.   Conrad, D. (1977), A starving family. Bulletin of the Menninger Clinic,
        41, 487-495.

1215.   Conrad, G.J., and Elkins, H.K. (1959), The first eighteen months of
        group counseling in a family service agency. Social Casework, 40, 123-
        129.

1216.   Constantine, J.A., Piercy, F.P., and Sprenkle, D.H. (1984), Live
        supervision-of-supervision in family therapy. Journal of Marital and
        Family Therapy, 10, 95-97.

1217.   Constantine, L.L. (1984), Dysfunction and failure in open family
        systems: II. Clinical issues. Journal of Marital and Family Therapy, 10,
        1-17.

1218.   Constantine, L.L. (1978), Family sculpture and relationship mapping
        techniques. Journal of Marital and Family Therapy, 4, 13-23.

1219.   Constantine, L.L. (1976), Designed experience: A multiple, goal-
        directed training program in family therapy. Family Process, 15, 373-
        387.

1220.   Contreras, R., and Scheingold, L. (1984), Couples groups in family
        medicine training. Journal of Family Practice, 11, 293-296.

1221.   Conture, E.G. (1982), Youngsters who stutter: Diagnosis, parent
        counseling and referral. Journal of Developmental and Behavior
        Pediatrics, 3(3), 163.

1222. Conway, D.F. (1971), The effects of conjoint family play sessions: A potential preventive mental health procedure for early identified children. Dissertation Abstracts International, 32, 3631B.

1223. Cookerly, J.F. (1974), Comparative results of the six major forms of marriage counseling. Dissertation Abstracts International, 35, 184A.

1224. Cookerly, J.R. (1974), The reduction of psychopathology as measured by the MMPI clinical scales in three forms of marriage counseling. Journal of Marriage and the Family, 36, 332-335.

1225. Cookerly, J.R. (1980), Does marital therapy do any lasting good? Journal of Marital and Family Therapy, 6, 393-397.

1226. Cookerly, J.R. (1973), The outcome of the 6 major forms of marriage counseling compared: A pilot study. Journal of Marriage and the Family, 35, 608-612.

1227. Cooklin, A. (1978), Family therapy in British context-Cultural reflections in practice. Family Process, 17, 99-106.

1228. Cooklin, A. (1982), Change in here-and-now systems vs. systems over time. In A. Bentovim, G.G. Barnes, and A. Cooklin (Eds.), Family therapy. I. Complementary frameworks of theory and practice. London: Academic Press.

1229. Cooklin, A. (1984), Review of F. Kaslow's The international book of family therapy. British Journal of Psychiatry, 144, 445.

1230. Cooklin, A. (1983), Review of J. Willi's Couples in collusion. Family Process, 22, 250.

1231. Cooklin, A., Miller, A.C., and McHugh, B. (1983), An institution for change: Developing a family day unit. Family Process, 22, 453-468.

1232. Cooklin, A.I. (1979), Family therapy in adolescence. Irish Medical Journal, 72, 377-382.

1233. Coombs, L.C. (1979), Underlying family-size preferences and reproductive behavior. Study of Family Planning, 10, 25-36.

1234. Coombs, L.C. (1978), How many children do couples really want? Family Planning Perspective, 10, 303-308.

1235. Cooney, K.M. (1978), Nursing care of emotionally abused and deprived children. Issues in Comprehensive Pediatric Nursing, 3, 54-62.

1236. Cooper, A., Rampage, C., and Soucy, G. (1981), Family therapy training in clinical psychology programs. Family Process, 20, 155-66.

1237. Cooper, B. (1980), Review of P. Papp's Family therapy: Full length case studies. Journal of Marital and Family Therapy, 6, 242.

1238. Cooper, E.B. (1978), Facilitating parental participation in preparing the therapy component of the stutterer's individualized education program. Journal of Fluency Disorders, 3(3), 221-231.

1239. Coopersmith, E. (1978), Intergenerational relatedness and attitudes toward aging: A case study in family therapy. Dissertation Abstracts International, 38, 5244A.

1240. Coopersmith, E. (1980), The family floor plan: A tool for training, assessment and intervention in family therapy. Journal of Marital and Family Therapy, 6, 141–146.

1241. Copley, B. (1983), Introducing families to family work. In S. Box, B. Copley, J. Magagna, and E. Moustaki (Eds.), Psychotherapy with families: An analytic approach. London: Routledge and Kegan Paul Ltd.

1242. Copley, B. (1983), Work with a family as a single therapist with special reference to transference manifestations. Journal of Child Psychotherapy, 9, 103–118.

1243. Coppersmith, E.I. (1983), Diagnosis and assessment in family therapy: IV. The family and public service systems: An assessment method. Family Therapy Collections, 6, 83–99.

1244. Coppersmith, E.I. (1980), Expanding uses of the telephone in family therapy. Family Process, 19(4), 411–417.

1245. Coppersmith, E.I. (1982), From "hyperactive" to "normal but naughty": A multisystem partnership in de-labeling. International Journal of Family Psychiatry, 3, 131–144.

1246. Coppersmith, E.I. (1983), The place of family therapy in the homeostasis of larger system. In. L.R. Wolberg and M.L. Aronson (Eds.), Group and family therapy 1982. New York: Brunner/Mazel.

1247. Coppersmith, E.I. (1984), Review of C.M. Anderson and S. Stewart's Mastering Resistance: A practical guide to family therapy. Family Process, 23(1), 127.

1248. Coppersmith, E.I. (1984), A special "family" with handicapped members: One family therapist's learnings for the l'arche community. Family Therapy Collections, 11, 150–159.

1249. Corder, B.F., Page, P.V., and Corder, R.F. (1974), Parental history, family communication and interaction patterns in adolescent suicide. Family Therapy, 1, 285–290.

1250. Cornen, V.E., Johnson, K.M., and Lannamann, J.W. (1982), Paradoxes, double binds, and reflective loops: An alternative theoretical perspective. Family Process, 21, 91–112.

1251. Corney, R.H. (1978), Group work with single parents—the consumer's viewpoint: Participants' impressions. Health and Social Services Journal, 88, 30–32.

1252. Cornman, S.K. (1948), An experiment in family role-changing. Sociatry, 2, 242–243.

1253. Cornwell, M., and Pearson, R. (1980), Cotherapy teams and one-way screen in family therapy practice and training. Family Process, 20(2), 199–209.

1254.　Corpaci, A., and Stefanile, C. (1981), Psycho-social needs and family advisory services in Toscana. Bollettino Di Psicologia Applicata, 51, 51-77.

1255.　Cortney, B. (1969), A community's use of family counseling as a mental health service. Mental Hygiene, 53, 90-99.

1256.　Costa, L.A. (1981), The effects of a marriage encounter program on marital communication, dyadic adjustment, and the quality of the interpersonal relationship. Dissertation Abstracts International, 42, 1850-A.

1257.　Costanzo, J.P. (1983), The use of family therapy with special needs children and their families. Dissertation Abstracts International, 44, 1026A.

1258.　Costell, R.M., and Reiss, D. (1982), The family meets the hospital. Clinical presentation of a laboratory-based family typology. Archives of General Psychiatry, 39, 433-8.

1259.　Costello, C.G. (1969), Communication patterns in family systems. Nursing Clinics of North America, 5, 77.

1260.　Costello, R.M. (1977), "Chicana liberation" and the Mexican-American marriage. Psychiatric Annals, 7(12), 64-73.

1261.　Cotton-Huston, A.L., and Wheeler, K. A. (1983), Preorgasmic group treatment: Assertiveness, marital adjustment and sexual function in women. Journal of Sex and Marital Therapy, 9, 296-302.

1262.　Coughlan, W.G. (1948), Marriage counseling in Australia and New Zealand. International Journal of Sexology, 2, 118-123.

1263.　Coughlin, F., and Wimberger, H.C. (1968), Group family therapy. Family Process, 7, 37-50.

1264.　Coulshed, V. (1981), Engaging in family therapy: Problems for the inexperienced, uninvited therapist. Journal of Family Therapy, 3(1), 51-58.

1265.　Coulshed, V.A. (1983), The family as the unit of treatment: A case record. British Journal of Social Work, 13, 39-55.

1266.　Counts, R.M. (1974), Further thoughts on family therapy: Reply to Zaphiropoulas, Spiegel, and Harrell. Contemporary Psychoanalysis, 10(4), 492-501.

1267.　Counts, R.M. (1973), Family therapy as a parameter of individual psychotherapy. Contemporary Psychoanalysis, 9, 502-514.

1268.　Counts, R.M. (1967), Family crisis and the impulsive adolescent. Archives of General Psychiatry, 17, 64-71.

1269.　Courtois, C.A., and Watts, D.L. (1982), Counseling adult women who experienced incest in childhood or adolescence. Personnel and Guidance Journal, 60(5), 275.

1270. Cowie, V. (1967), Parental counseling and spinal bifida. Developmental Medicine and Child Neurology, 9, 110-112.

1271. Cowley, A.S. (1978), Family integration and mental health. Saratoga, CA: R & E Pubs.

1272. Cox, E.S. (1983), Family structure and external openness: A two-dimensional model. Dissertation Abstracts International, 43, 3428-A.

1273. Coyne, J.C. (1984), Strategic therapy with depressed married persons: Initial agenda, themes, and interventions. Journal of Marital and Family Therapy, 10, 53-62.

1274. Coyne, J.C. (1984), Paradoxical techniques in strategic family therapy: A behavioral analysis. Journal of Behavior Therapy and Experimental Psychiatry, 15(3), 221-228.

1275. Coyne, J.C., Denner, B., and Ransom, D.C. (1982), Undressing the fashionable mind. Family Process, 21, 391-396.

1276. Crafoord, C. (1980), Put the booze on the table: Some thoughts about family therapy and alcoholism. Journal of Family Therapy, 2, 71-85.

1277. Crafoord, C. (1973), Family therapy orientated community mental health program in Lulea, Sweden. Acta Psychiatrica Scandinavica, 243, 26.

1278. Craig, T.J., and Vannatta, P.A. (1979), Influence of demographic characteristics on two measures of depressive symptoms: The relation of prevalence and persistence of symptoms with sex, age, education and marital status. Archives of General Psychiatry, 36, 149-154.

1279. Crandall, J.W. (1976), Pathological nurturance: The root of marital discord. Journal of Family Counseling, 4(2), 62-68.

1280. Crandall, J.W. (1981), A study in pathological nurturance: The marriage of Gustav Mahler. Clinical Social Work Journal, 9, 91-100.

1281. Crandall, J.W. (1973), Diagnostic uses of early spouse memories in marriage counseling. Journal of Family Counseling, 1, 17-27.

1282. Crane, D.R. (1985), Single-case experimental designs in family therapy research: Limitations and considerations. Family Process, 24(1), 69-78.

1283. Crane, D.R., Newfield, N., and Armstrong, D. (1984), Predicting divorce at marital therapy intake: Wives distress and the marital status inventory. Journal of Marital and Family Therapy, 10(3), 305-312.

1284. Crane, D.R., and Mead, D.E. (1980), The marital status inventory: Some preliminary data on an instrument to measure marital dissolution potential. American Journal of Family Therapy, 8, 31-35.

1285. Crase, D.R., and Crase, D. (1975), Death and the young child: Some practical suggestions for support and counseling. Clinical Pediatrics, 14(8), 747-450.

1286. Crawford, R.J. (1983), Spouses of alcoholics (letter). New Zealand Medical Journal, 93, 545.

1287.   Crisler, D.A. (1978), New family constellations: Dimensions and effects of systematic culture shock. Dissertation Abstracts International, 38, 3870-3871B.

1288.   Crist, J.R. (1955), An experiment in marriage counseling training. Journal of Counseling Psychology, 2, 35-37.

1289.   Crist, J.R. (1958), Marriage counseling involving a passive husband and an aggressive wife. Marriage and Family Living, 20, 121-126.

1290.   Critchley, D.L. (1982), Interventions with disorganized parents of disturbed children. Issues Mental Health Nursing, 4, 199-215.

1291.   Critchley, D.L. (1981), The child as patient: Assessing the effects of family stress and disruption on the mental health of the child. Perspectives in Psychiatric Care, 19, 144-155.

1292.   Critchley, D.L., and Berlin, I.N. (1979), Day treatment of young psychotic children and their parents: Interdisciplinary issues and problems. Child Psychiatric Quarterly, 9, 221-237.

1293.   Croake, J.W. (1984), Review of O.C. Christiansen and T.G. Schramski's Alderian family counseling. American Journal of Family Therapy, 12(2), 83.

1294.   Croake, J.W., and Hinckle, D.E. (1983), Adlerian family counseling education. Individual Psychology: Journal of Adlerian Theory, Research and Practice, 39, 247-258.

1295.   Croake, J.W., and Kelly, F.D. (1985), Adlerian family therapy with schizophrenic and depressed patients. Individual Psychology, 41, 302-312.

1296.   Croake, J.W., and Lyon, R.S. (1978), Research design in marital adjustment studies. International Journal of Family Counseling, 6(2), 32-35.

1297.   Crohn, H. (1982), Therapy with remarriage families: XI. A basis for understanding and treating the remarried family. Family Therapy Collections, 2, 159-186.

1298.   Crolla-Baggen, M. (1982), Psychotherapy with older married couples. Tijdschrift Voor Psychotherapie, 8, 217-221.

1299.   Cromwell, R.E. (1979), Review of L.S. Dodson and D. Kurpius' Family counseling: A systems approach. Family Coordinator, 28, 288.

1300.   Cromwell, R.E., Olson, D.K.A., and Fournier, D.G. (1976), Tools and techniques for diagnosis and evaluation in marital and family therapy. Family Process, 15, 1-49.

1301.   Cromwell, R.E., and Kenney, B.P. (1979), Diagnosing marital and family systems: A training model. Family Coordinator, 29, 101-108.

1302.   Cromwell, R.E., and Peterson, G.W. (1983), Multisystem-Multimethod family assessment in clinical contexts. Family Process, 22, 147-63.

1303. Cromwell, R.E., and Thomas, L.V. (1976), Developing resources for
       family potential: A family action model. Family Coordinator, 25, 13-26.

1304. Cronin-Stubbs, D. (1978), Family crisis intervention: A study. Journal
       of Psychiatric Nursing, 16, 36-44.

1305. Crosby, H.W. (1983), The consensus Rorschach and personal constructs:
       Couples' transactions and change. Dissertation Abstracts International,
       43, 3354-B.

1306. Cross, D.G. (1985), Family therapy and the notion of accountability:
       With reference to trends in individual psychotherapy. International
       Journal of Family Therapy, 7(1), 25-37.

1307. Croteau, J.G. (1971), Thoughts on three years of family therapy
       practice with middle-class French Canadians. Interpretation, 5(4), 105-
       118.

1308. Crotty, C.J. (1967), An exploratory study of the expressions of self-
       inadequacy of male marriage counseling clients. Dissertation Abstracts
       International, 27(9-A), 3139-3140.

1309. Croufer-North, E., Bobon-Schrod, H., and Fraipont, J. (1978), A propos
       d'un groupe therapeutique de couples. Psychotherapie and
       Psychosomatics, 29, 125-219.

1310. Crowe, M. (1982), The treatment of marital and sexual problems: A
       behavioural approach. In A. Bentovim, G.G. Barnes, and A. Cooklin
       (Eds.), Family therapy. I. Complementary frameworks of theory and
       practice. London: Academic Press.

1311. Crowe, M.J. (1978), Conjoint marital therapy: A controlled outcome
       study. Psychological Medicine, 8, 623-636.

1312. Crowe, M.J. (1973), Conjoint marital therapy: Advice or
       interpretation? Journal of Psychosomatic Medicine, 17, 309-315.

1313. Crowe, M.J. (1974), Conjoint marital therapy: Advice or
       interpretation? Journal of Psychology, 86, 35-47.

1314. Crowe, M.S. (1984), Review of R.T. Segraves' Marital therapy: A
       combined psychodynamic behavioral approach. Behaviour Research and
       Therapy, 22(5), 594.

1315. Crowle, M.E. (1982), The family money management counseling
       service: A community project of the College of Home Economics.
       Canadian Home Economics Journal, 32(2), 67.

1316. Crozzoli, L.A., Menarini, M.G., and Onnis, L. (1976), (The symmetric
       relationship: An analysis of the problem in a couple's interaction).
       Rivista Psichiatrica, 11(4), 291-318.

1317. Cruzat, M.F. (1974), Various practical considerations on the treatment
       of childhood epilepsy. Revista Chilena de Pediatria, 45, 536-540.

1318. Cuber, J. (1948), Marriage counseling practice. New York: Appleton-
       Century-Crofts.

1319.   Cuber, J.F. (1945), Functions of the marriage counselor. Marriage and Family Living, 7, 3-5.

1320.   Cummings, S.T., and Stock, D. (1962), Brief group therapy of mothers of retarded children outside the specialty clinic setting. American Journal of Mental Deficiency, 66, 739-748.

1321.   Cunningham, A., and Saayman, G.S. (1984), Effective functioning in dual career families: An investigation. Journal of Family Therapy, 6(4), 365-380.

1322.   Cunningham, J.M., and Matthews, K.L. (1982), Impact of multiple-family therapy approach on a parallel latency-age/parent group. International Journal of Group Psychotherapy, 32, 91-102.

1323.   Curry, A.E. (1965), Therapeutic management of multiple family groups. International Journal of Group Psychotherapy, 15, 90-96.

1324.   Curry, A.E. (1966), The family therapy situation as system. Family Process, 5, 131-141.

1325.   Curtis, J. (1981), Current resources in family therapy. Jonesboro, TN: Pilgrimage, Inc.

1326.   Curtis, J., and Greene, J. (1979), Premarital, marital and family therapy: An annotated bibliography. Jonesboro, TN: Pilgrimage Inc.

1327.   Curtis, J.H. (1979), Marriage and family counselor: Improved image and accessibility. In: N. Stinnett, B. Chesser, and J. DeFrain (Eds.), Building family strengths. Lincoln, NE: University of Nebrasks Press.

1328.   Curtis, J.H. (1977), A response to L.V. Harvey's "A comment on an argument for the use of paraprofessional counselors in premarital and marital counseling." Famiy Coordinator, 26(1), 71-74.

1329.   Curtis, J.H. (1980), Review of I.D. Glick and D.R. Kessler's Marital and family therapy. Fammily Relations, 29, 258.

1330.   Curtis, J.H. (1980), Review of P. Papp's Family therapy: Full length case studies. Family Relations, 29, 259.

1331.   Curtis, J.H., and Miller, M.E. (1976), An argument for the use of paraprofessional counselors in premarital and marital counseling. Family Coordinator, 25(1), 47-50.

1332.   Curtis, R. (1977), Psychotherapy with children of divorce. Canada's Mental Health, 25(2), 33.

1333.   Cutler, D.L., and Madore, E. (1980), Community-family network therapy in a rural setting. Community Mental Health Journal, 16, 144-55.

1334.   Cutrow, R.J. (1977), A child's self-concept and its correlation to maternal perceptions, attitudes, and behavioral evaluations. Dissertation Abstracts International, 37, 4670B.

1335.   Cutting, A.R. (1979), Family oriented mental health consultation to a naval research group. Social Casework, 60, 236-242.

1336.   D'Afflitti, J.G., and Swanson, D. (1975), Group sessions for the wives of home-hemodialysis patients. American Journal of Nursing, 75(4), 633-635.

1337.   D'Afflitti, J.G., and Weitz, G.W. (1974), Rehabilitating the stroke patient through patient-family groups. International Journal of Group Psychotherapy, 24, 323-332.

1338.   Dagoni-Weinberg, E. (1969), From total isolation to social communication: Treatment of a case of early infantile autism. Alta Paedopsychiatrica, 36, 153-165.

1339.   Dahlgren, L. (1979), Female alcoholics. IV. Marital situation and husbands. Acta Psychiatry in Scandanavia, 59, 59-69.

1340.   Dailey, D.M. (1974), Family therapy with the homosexual: A search. Homosexual Counseling Journal, 1, 7-15.

1341.   Daines, B., and Holdsworth, V. (1980), Marital therapy: Breaking up over a baby. Nursing Mirror, 151, 26.

1342.   Daines, B., and Holdsworth, V. (1980), Marital therapy: Do you know the one about my mother-in-law?. Nursing Mirror, 151(8), 34.

1343.   Daines, B., and Holdsworth, V. (1980), Marital therapy: Holding hands. Part 7. Nursing Mirror, 151, 42.

1344.   Daines, B., and Holdsworth, V. (1980), Marital therapy: Losing interest. Nursing Mirror, 151(5), 24.

1345.   Daines, B., and Holdsworth, V. (1980), Marital therapy: Uncomfortable feelings...the couple suddenly stops coming to therapy. Part 4. Nursing Mirror, 151, 32.

1346.   Daines, B., and Holdsworth, V. (1980), Marital therapy: When two is not company. Part 6. Nursing Mirror, 151, 29.

1347.   Daines, B., and Holdsworth, V. (1980), Marital therapy: 'You could have a laugh'...a case of dyspareunia. Nursing Mirror, 151(4), 20.

1348.   Daitzman, R.J. (1977), Methods of self-confrontation in family therapy. Journal of Marital and Family Therapy, 3, 3-9.

1349.   Dakan, E.A. (1951), Changes in concept of self and of partner for married couples in nondirective group therapy. Unpublished doctoral dissertation, Columbia University.

1350.   Dale, P. (1981), Family therapy and incomplete families. Journal of Family Therapy, 3(1), 3-20.

1351.   Dalton, D.R. (1982), Efficacy of the home setting for conducting Adlerian family counseling. Dissertation Abstracts International, 42, 3438-B.

1352.   Dalton, J., and Epstein, H. (1963), Counseling parents of mildly retarded children. Social Casework, 44, 523-530.

1353.   Dalton, P. (1983), Family treatment of an obsessive-compulsive child:
         A case report. Family Process, 22, 99-108.

1354.   Dammann, C.A. (1984). Review of M. Andolif, C. Angelo, P. Menghi
         and A.M. Nicolocorigliano's Behind the family mask: Therapeutic change
         in rigid families. Family Process, 23(1), 121.

1355.   Damnjanovic, M. (1980), Family cooperation in the rehabilitation of
         mental patients. Psihijatrija Danas, 12, 413-417.

1356.   Danesh, H.B. (1980), The angry group for couples: A model for short-
         term group psychotherapy. Psychiatric Journal of the University of
         Ottawa, 5, 118-124.

1357.   Daniels, N. (1967), Participation of relatives in a group-centered
         program. International Journal of Group Psychotherapy, 17, 336-341.

1358.   Danziger, S. (1982), Major treatment issues and techniques in family
         therapy with the borderline adolescent. Journal of Psychosocial Nursing
         and Mental Health Services, 20, 27-34.

1359.   Danziger, S.K. (1979), Treatment of women in childbirth: Implications
         for family beginnings. American Journal of Public Health, 9, 895-901.

1360.   Dar, H., Winter, S.T., and Tal, Y. (1974), Families of children with cleft
         lips and palates: Concerns and counseling. Developmental Medicine and
         Child Neurology, 16, 513-517.

1361.   Dare, C. (1985), The family therapy of anorexia nervosa. Journal of
         Psychiatric Research, 19, 435-444.

1362.   Dare, C. (1975), A classification of interventions in child and conjoint
         family therapy. Psychotherapy and Psychosomatics, 25, 116-125.

1363.   Dare, C. (1982), What do they learn at school: Family systems and the
         school-going child. In A. Bentovim, G.G. Barnes, and A. Cooklin (Eds.),
         Family therapy. 2. Complementary frameworks of theory and
         practice. London: Academic Press.

1364.   Dare, C. (1982), The empty nest: Families with older adolescents and
         models of family therapy. In A. Bentovim, G.G. Barnes, and A. Cooklin
         (Eds.), Family therapy. 2. Complementary frameworks of theory and
         practice. London: Academic Press.

1365.   Dasilva, G. (1963), The role of the father with chronic schizophrenic
         patients: A study in group therapy. Canadian Psychiatric Association
         Journal, 8, 190-203.

1366.   Dato, R. (1979), Review of J.F. Perez's Family counseling, therapy and
         practice. Journal of Marital and Family Therapy, 5, 115.

1367.   Davanzo, H. (1962), The family group in dynamic psychiatric diagnosis.
         International Journal of Group Psychotherapy, 12, 496-502.

1368.   Davenport, Y.B., Adland, M.L., Gold, P.W., and Goodwin, F.K. (1979),
         Manic-depressive illness psychodynamic features of multigenerational
         families. American Journal of Orthopsychiatry, 49, 24-35.

1369. Davenport, Y.B., Ebert, M.H., Adland, M.L., and Goodwin, F.K. (1977), Couples group therapy as an adjunct to lithium maintenance of the maniac patient. American Journal of Orthopsychiatry, 47, 495-502.

1370. David, A.C. (1970), Using audiotape as an adjunct to family therapy: Three case reports. Psychotherapy: Theory, Research and Practice, 7, 28-32.

1371. David, J. (1979), Theology of Bowen, Murray or the marital triangle. Psychology and Theology, 7, 259-262.

1372. David, J.R. (1981), The effects of a structured family enrichment program upon selected dimensions of a psychosocial functioning of intact families. Dissertation Abstracts International, 42, 2501-B.

1373. David, J.R., and Orton, J.W. (1980), Marriage and family therapy: A separate discipline. Military Medicine, 145, 431-434.

1374. David, M.J. (1983), Family intervention models. Archives of Physical Medicine and Rehabilitation, 64, 389.

1375. Davidoff, I.F. (1982), Review of G.L. Schulman's Family therapy: Teaching, learning, doing. Family Process, 21, 498.

1376. Davids, M. (1955), Integration of activity group therapy for a 10 year old boy with casework services to the family. International Journal of Group Psychotherapy, 5, 31-44.

1377. Davidson, D.M. (1979), The family and cardiac rehabilitation. Journal of Family Practice, 8, 253-261.

1378. Davidson, S., and Yftach, R. (1976), The therapy of the unconsummated marriage. Psychotherapy: Theory, Research, and Practice, 13(4), 418-419.

1379. Davies, I.J., Ellenson, G., and Young, R. (1966), Therapy with a group of families in a psychiatric day center. American Journal of Orthopsychiatry, 36, 134-146.

1380. Davis, A.J., Jr. (1983), Short-term family counseling. Nebraska Medical Journal, 58, 299-302.

1381. Davis, D. (1979), Review of T.J. Paolino and B.S. McCrady's Alcoholic marriage: Alternative perspectives. American Journal of Family Therapy, 7, 86.

1382. Davis, D.I. (1978), Family therapy for the drug user: Conceptual and practical considerations. Drug Forum, 6, 197-205.

1383. Davis, D.I. (1980), Alcoholics Anonymous and family therapy. Journal of Marital and Family Therapy, 6, 65-73.

1384. Davis, D.I. (1980), Why family therapy for drug abuse: From the clinical perspective. In: B.G. Ellis (Ed.), Drug abuse from the family perspective. Rockville, MD: National Institute of Drug Abuse.

1385. Davis, D.R. (1968), Interventions into family affairs. British Journal of Medical Psychology, 41, 73-79.

1386.   Davis, D.R. (1978), Family processes in schizophrenia. British Journal of Hospital Medicine, 20, 524-531.

1387.   Davis, E.L. (1983), Uncensored versus measured communication treatments in therapy for marital adjustment. Dissertation Abstracts International, 44, 988A.

1388.   Davis, G.M. (1979), The differential effect of married couple communication training in groups with the spouse present and spouse not present. Dissertation Abstracts International, 49, 4023-B.

1389.   Davis, I.P. (1975), Advice giving in parent counseling. Social Casework, 56(6), 343-347.

1390.   Davis, P.H., and Osherson, A. (1978), Some effects of cultural stereotyping on fathering. Journal of Contemporary Psychotherapy, 10, 32-38.

1391.   Davis, P.H., and Osherson, A. (1977), The concurrent treatment of a multiple-personality woman and her son. American Journal of Psychotherapy, 31, 504-515.

1392.   Davis, R.C. (1977), Professional self-concept and behavior of marriage/family counselors as a function of professional identity. Dissertation Abstracts International, 38, 6528A.

1393.   Davis, R.E. (1969), Issues in professional training for family therapy. Newsletter of the American Orthopedic Association, 13, 41-42.

1394.   Davis, S., and Marcus, L.M. (1980), Involving parents in the treatment of severely communication disordered children. Journal of Pediatric Psychology, 5(2), 189-198.

1395.   Davis, S.L., and David, D.I. (1983), Neuro-linguistic programming and family therapy. Journal of Marital and Family Therapy, 9, 283-291.

1396.   Davis, S.L., and Davis, D. (1982), NLP and marital and family therapy. Family Therapy Networks, 6(3), 19-21.

1397.   Davis, T.S. (1979), In-home support for recovering alcoholic mothers and their families: The family rehabilitation coordinator. Journal of Studies on Alcohol, 40, 313-317.

1398.   Dawley, A. (1939), Trends in therapy: Interrelated movement of parent and child in therapy with children. American Journal of Orthopsychiatry, 9, 748-755.

1399.   Dawling, E., and Hones, H.V. (1978), Small children seen and heard in family therapy. Journal of Children in Psychotherapy, 4, 87-96.

1400.   Dayringer, R. (1978), Family therapy techniques for the family physician. Journal of Family Practice, 6, 303-307.

1401.   De-Nour, A.K., Fisher, G., Mass, M., and Czackes, J.W. (1974), Diagnosis and therapy of families of patients on chronic hemodialysis. Mental Health and Society, 1, 251-256.

1402. DeBella, G.A.W. (1979), Family psychotherapy with the homosexual family: Community psychiatry approach to homosexuality. Community Mental Health, 15, 41-46.

1403. DeElejalde, F. (1971), Inadequate mothering: Patterns and treatment. Bulletin of the Menninger Clinic, 35, 182-198.

1404. DeFries, J.C., Johnson, R.C., Kuse, A.R., McClearn, G.E., Polovina, J., Vandenberg, S.G., and Wilson, J.R. (1979), Familial resemblance for specific cognitive abilities. Behavioral Genetics, 9, 23-43.

1405. DeJesus, A. (1981), (Instruments, goals and satisfaction in prematrimonial counseling of clients.) Reviste LatinoAmericana de Psicologia, 13(1), 131-138.

1406. DeLio, A.R. (1982), An investigation of the effectiveness of intervention strategies on juvenile anti-social behaviors. Dissertation Abstracts International, 43, 1466A.

1407. DeNayer, A., and Muller, C. (1978), (The sociopsychological notions of status: The role and norm and the systematic mechanisms in the psychotic family.) Annals Medico-Psychologiques, 136(5), 689-709.

1408. DePreneuf, C., and Collomb, H. (1971), (Social change and family psychotherapy in Senegal: Some practical problems.) Revue Neuropsychiatrie Infantile et D'Hygeine Mentale de L'Enfance, 19, 581-588.

1409. DeShazer, S. (1974), On getting unstuck: Some chance-initiating tactics for getting the family moving. Family Therapy, 1, 19-26.

1410. DeShazer, S. (1975), The confusion technique. Family Therapy, 2, 23-30.

1411. DeShazer, S. (1977), The optimist-pessimist technique. Family Therapy, 4, 93-100.

1412. DeShazer, S. (1982), Patterns of brief family therapy. New York: Guilford Press.

1413. DeShazer, S. (1982), Some conceptual distinctions are more useful than others. Family Process, 21, 71-84.

1414. DeShazer, S. (1979), Brief therapy with families. American Journal of Family Therapy, 7, 83-94.

1415. DeShazer, S. (1980), Brief family therapy: A metaphorical task. Journal of Marital and Family Therapy, 6(4), 471-476.

1416. DeShazer, S. (1978), Brief therapy with couples. International Journal of Family Counseling, 6, 17-30.

1417. DeShazer, S. (1983), Diagnosis and assessment in family therapy: VI. Diagnosing = Researching + Doing Therapy. Family Therapy Collections, 6, 123-132.

1418. DeShazer, S. (1984), The death of resistance. Family Process, 23, 11-21.

1419.   DeShazer, S. (1983), Some bonuses of using a team approach to family therapy. In L.R. Wolberg and M.L. Aronson (Eds.), Group and family therapy 1982. New York: Brunner/Mazel.

1420.   DeShazer, S. (1982), Review of G.R. Weeks and L. L'Abate's Paradoxical psychotherapy: Theory and practice with individuals, couples, and families. Family Proces, 21, 488-489.

1421.   DeShazer, S., and Molnar, A. (1984), Four useful interventions in brief family therapy. Journal of Marital and Family Therapy, 10(3), 297-304.

1422.   DeShazer, S.D. (1975), Brief therapy: 25 company. Family Process, 14(1), 79-93.

1423.   DeStefano, R. (1984), Review of H.I. McCurrin and C.R. Figley's Stress and the family, Vol. 2, Coping with catastrophe. Family Process, 23(3), 458.

1424.   DeStefano, T.J. (1982), Family therapy compared to individual play therapy in the treatment of young children for behavioral and emotional problems. Dissertation Abstracts International, 42, 4187-B.

1425.   DeSuide, I.B., Garsd, S., Mor Riog, M., and de Bergallo, A.T. (1977), Family therapy in an institutional setting. Acta Psiquiatrica & Psychologia de America Latina, 23, 143-150.

1426.   DeVore, W. (1983), Ethnic reality: The life model and work with black families. Social Casework, 64, 525-531.

1427.   DeWitt, D.J. (1982), A combined premarital and early marital counseling program based on Adler's individual psychology. Dissertation Abstracts International, 43, 868B.

1428.   DeWitt, K.N. (1978), The effectiveness of family therapy: A review of outcome research. Archives of General Psychiatry, 35, 549-561.

1429.   DeYoung, A.J. (1979), Marriage encounter: A critical examination. Journal of Marital and Family Therapy, 5(2), 27.

1430.   DeYoung, C.D. (1968), Nursing's contribution in family crisis treatment. Nursing Outlook, 16, 60-62.

1431.   Death, E. (1982), Power and influence in the environment of family therapy. Journal of Family Therapy, 4, 229-246.

1432.   Debbane, E.G. (1972), Family psychiatry: A perspective. Perspectives in Psychiatric Care, 37, 15-27.

1433.   Debow, S.L. (1975), Identical twins concordant for anorexia nervosa: A preliminary case report. Canadian Journal of Psychiatry, 20, 215-217.

1434.   Dechenne, T.K. (1973), Experiential facilitation in conjoint marriage counseling. Psychotherapy: Theory, Research and Practice, 10, 212-214.

1435.   Dechesaro, C. (1970), Treatment of outpatients, adolescents, and their parents in separate-simultaneous group psychotherapy. Psychiatric Communication, 13(1), 29-33.

1436. Defazio, V.J., and Klenbort, T. (1975), A note on the dynamics of psychotherapy during marital dissolution. Psychotherapy: Theory, Research and Practice, 12(1), 101-104.

1437. Deitcher, S., and Rolsky, J.N. (1974), A new model of family evaluation and brief treatment: The "family-assessment evening" and multiple-family concurrent short-term therapy. American Journal of Orthopsychiatry, 44, 217-218.

1438. Del Castillo, G., and Grainich, A. (1971), The inpatient treatment of a child drug abuser in a mixed age group. Psychiatric Quarterly, 45(4), 593-602.

1439. Del Sordo, K. (1982), Group family counseling: An aid to long-term care. Journal of Long-term Care Administration, 10, 37-42.

1440. DelCampo, R.L. (1985), Review of C. Anderson and S. Stewart's Mastering resistance: A practical guide to family therapy. Family Process, 34(1), 148.

1441. Delgado, M. (1978), A Hispanic foster parents program. Child Welfare, 57, 427-431.

1442. Delgado, M. (1984), Review of M. Goldrick, J.K. Pearce and J. Giordano's Ethnicity and family therapy. Social Casework, 65, 56-57.

1443. Dell, D.F. (1980), Review of F. Farrelly and J. Brandsma's Provocative therapy. Journal of Marital and Family Therapy, 6, 93.

1444. Dell, P.F. (1977), Family therapy process in a family therapy seminar. Journal of Marital and Family Therapy, 3, 43-48.

1445. Dell, P.F. (1982), In search of truth: On the way to clinical epistemology. Family Process, 21, 407-14.

1446. Dell, P.F. (1982), Beyond homeostasis: Toward a concept of coherence. Family Process, 21, 21-41.

1447. Dell, P.F. (1980), The Hopi family therapist and the Aristotelian parents. Journal of Marital and Family Therapy, 6(2), 123-130.

1448. Dell, P.F. (1984), Why family therapy should go beyond homeostasis: A Kuhnian reply to C. Ariel and S. Tyano. Journal of Marital and Family Therapy, 10, 351-356.

1449. Delson, N., and Clark, M. (1981), Group therapy with sexually molested children. Child Welfare, 60(3), 175-182.

1450. Delvaux, B.L. (1978), Husband-wife attitudes toward child rearing (abstract). American Journal of Nursing, 78, 1907.

1451. Delvey, J. (1982), Parenting errors and their correction in group psychotherapy. American Journal of Psychotherapy, 36(4), 523.

1452. Delvey, J. (1984), Review of B.B. Wolman and G. Stricker's Handbook of family and marital therapy. American Journal of Psychotherapy, 38(2), 307.

1453.   Dematatis, C.G. (1982), A comparison of the traditional filial therapy program to an integrated filial-IPR program. Dissertation Abstracts International, 42, 4187B.

1454.   Demopoulos, R.I., and Kammerman, S. (1979), The association of parity and marital status with the development of ovarian carcinoma: Clinical implications. Obstetrics and Gynecology, 54, 150-155.

1455.   Dempsey, R.J. (1980), Marital adjustment, improved communication, and greater self-disclosure as the effects of a weekend marriage encounter. Dissertation Abstracts International, 40, 4258A.

1456.   DenBleyker, S. (1970), Family nursing. Frontier Nursing Service Quarterly Bulletin, 46, 31.

1457.   Denicola, J., and Sadler, J. (1980), Training abusive parents in child management and self control skills. Behavior Therapy, 11(2), 263-270.

1458.   Denny, J.M. (1980), Review of H.Y. Kwiatkowska's Family therapy and evaluation through art. Journal of Nervous and Mental Disease, 168, 190.

1459.   Dentch, G.E., O'Farrell, T.J., and Cutter, H.S.G. (1980), Readability of marital assessment measures used by behavioral marriage therapists. Journal of Consulting and Clinical Psychology, 48, 790-792.

1460.   Depotovic, A. (1974), Alcoholism, drug-addictions and the family. Anali Zavoda za Mentalno Zdravije, 6, 191-202.

1461.   Derdeyn, A.P., and Waters, D.B. (1981), Unshared loss and marital conflict. Journal of Marital and Family Therapy, 7, 481-487.

1462.   Dettinger, G.B. (1979), Defending the military family. (letter). American Journal of Psychiatry, 136, 855-856.

1463.   Dettmann, D.F., and Colangelo, N. (1980), A functional model for counseling parents of gifted students. The Gifted Child Quarterly, 24(4), 158-162.

1464.   Deutsch, D. (1967), Family therapy and family life style. Journal of Individual Psychology, 23, 217-223.

1465.   Deutsch, D. (1967), Group therapy with married couples: The birth pangs of a new family life style in marriage. Individual Psychology Bulletin, 4(2), 56-62.

1466.   Deutsch, R.A. (1978), Sex-linked role behavior, philosophical orientation, and coping styles in three marital groups. Dissertation Abstracts International, 39(12), 6192B.

1467.   Deykin, E.Y. (1972), Life functioning in families of delinquent boys: An assessment model. Social Service Review, 46, 90-102.

1468.   DiBella, G.A. (1979), Family psychotherapy with the homosexual family: A community psychiatric approach to homosexuality. Community Mental Health Journal, 15, 41-46.

1469. DiCocco, B.E., and Lott, E.F. (1982), Family/school strategies in dealing with the troubled child. International Journal of Family Therapy, 4, 98-106.

1470. DiGiacomo, P. (1983), An elementary pragmatic approach in systems-therapy. International Journal of Family Psychiatry, 4, 331-340.

1471. DiGiuseppe, R., and Wilner, R.S. (1980), An eclectic view of family therapy: When is family therapy the treatment of choice? When is it not? Journal of Clinical and Child Psychology, 9, 70-72.

1472. DiLeonardi, J.W. (1981), Correlating treatment outcomes of parents and young children. Child Welfare, 60, 245-253.

1473. Diament, C. (1978), Evaluation of behavioral group counseling for parents of learning disabled children. Journal of Abnormal Child Psychology, 6(3), 385-400.

1474. Diamond, J.D. (1951), Group counseling in the family agency. Social Casework, 32, 207-214.

1475. Diatkine, G. (1979), Families without qualities: Language and thinking troubles in families with multiple problems. Psychiatrie De L'Enfant, 22, 237-273.

1476. Dickes, R., and Strauss, D. (1980), Adverse reaction of the apparently healthy partner in response to improvement in the overtly dysfunctional partner. Journal of Sex and Marital Therapy, 6, 109-15.

1477. Dickie, J.R., and Gerber, S.C. (1980), Training in social competence: The effect on mothers, fathers, and infants. Child Development, 51(4), 1248-1251.

1478. Dicks, R.L. (1950), Creative listening as a method in marital counseling. Marriage and Family Living, 12, 91-94.

1479. Dicks, R.L. (1945), Methods for effective counseling. Marriage and Family Living, 7, 85.

1480. Dickson, M. (1974), Involvement of the spouse in the treatment of the alcoholic. Nursing Mirror and Midwives Journal, 139, 77-79.

1481. Dieckhofer, K. (1980), Psychiatric family care. The Geel community as an example for future development. Muenchener Medizinische Wochenschrift, 1819-21.

1482. Dielman, C., Stevens, K., and Frederick, G. (1984), The strategic use of symptoms as metaphors in family therapy: Some case illustrations. Journal of Strategic and Systemic Therapies, 3, 29-34.

1483. Diepold, B. (1979), Group therapy with children. Gruppenpsychotherapie und Gruppendynamics, 14, 84.

1484. Dietz, C.R., and Costello, M.E. (1956), Reciprocal interaction in the parent-child relationship during psychotherapy. American Journal of Orthopsychiatry, 26, 376-393.

1485. Digiulio, J.F., and Janosik, G.J. (1982), Successful partners: Credit counseling and family services. Social Casework, 63, 482-488.

1486. Diihrssen, A. (1968), Preventive measures in the family. Psychotherapy and Psychosomatics, 16, 319-332.

1487. Dillard, C.K. (1981), Marriage enrichment: A critical assessment of the couples communication program model. Dissertation Abstracts International, 42, 2882A.

1488. Dimitriou, E.C. (1983), A behavioral approach to marital therapy: A Greek experiment. Psychotherapy and Psychosomatics, 36, 144-153.

1489. Dimmock, B., and Dungworth, D. (1983), Creating maneuverability for family systems therapists in social services departments. Journal of Family Therapy, 5, 53-70.

1490. Dinaberg, P., Glick, I.D., and Felgenbaum, E. (1977), Marital therapy of women alcoholics. Journal of Studies on Alcohol, 38, 1247-1258.

1491. Dinges, N.G., Yazzie, M.L., and Tollefson, G.D. (1974), Developmental intervention for Navajo family mental health. Personnel and Guidance Journal, 52, 390-395.

1492. Dinicola, V.F. (1984), Road map to schizo-land: Mara Selvini Palazzoli and the Milan model of systemic family therapy. Journal of Strategic and Systemic Therapies, 3, 50-62.

1493. Dinkmeyer, D., and Dinkmeyer, D., Jr. (1981), Adlerian family therapy. American Journal of Family Therapy, 9, 45-52.

1494. Dinkmeyer, D., and Dinkmeyer, J. (1982), Adlerian marriage therapy. Individual Psychology: Journal of Adlerian Theory, Research, and Practice, 38, 115-122.

1495. Dinkmeyer, D., and Dinkmeyer, J. (1983), Adlerian family therapy. Individual Psychology: Journal of Adlerian Theory, Research and Practice, 20, 116-124.

1496. Dinkmeyer, P., Sr. (1984), The marital therapy techniques of Richard Stuart. Individual Psychology, 40(2), 196-200.

1497. Dinnen, A., and Bell, D.S. (1975), Psychotherapy in a large open family group. Australian and New Zealand Journal of Psychiatry, 9, 93-98.

1498. Dinning, W.D. (1978), Factor structure of behavioral content measures in seven therapeutic modalities in disturbed adolescents. Dissertation Abstracts International, 38, 5010B.

1499. Dixen, J., and Jenkins, J.O. (1981), Incestuous child sexual abuse: A review of treatment strategies. Clinical Psychology Review, 34, 211-222.

1500. Dlabacova, E., Capponi, V., and Gbelcova, E. (1977), (Uses of group psychotherapy in marital consultation service.) Ceskoslovenska Psychiatrica, 73, 85-89.

1501.   Dlabacova, E., and Planava, I. (1979), Work with groups in marital and premarital advisory centers. Ceskoslovenska Psychiatrie, 75, 21-25.

1502.   Doane, J.A. (1978), Family interaction and communication deviance in disturbed and normal families: Review of research. Family Process, 17, 357-376.

1503.   Doane, J.A. (1978), Family interaction and communication deviance in disturbed and normal families. Questions of strategy: Rejoiner to Jacobs and Grounds. Family Process, 17, 389-394.

1504.   Dobson, J.E. (1984), An Afrocentric educational manual: Toward a non-deficit perspective in services to families and children. Knoxville, TN: University of Tennessee School of Social Work.

1505.   Dodge, J.S. (1981), Family health counseling: An education program for counselors. New Zealand Medical Journal, 94(694), 310-312.

1506.   Dodinral, P.A. (1973), Distribution of matrimonial migrations in Belgium. Gerontologist, 13, 409-411.

1507.   Dodson, L.S. (1983), Intertwining Jungian depth psychology and family therapy through use of action techniques. Journal of Group Psychotherapy, Psychodrama and Sociometry, 35, 155-164.

1508.   Doering, R.L. (1961), Physiology: The neglected discipline in family life education. Marriage and Family Living, 23, 267-269.

1509.   Doerr, B.C., and Jones, J.W. (1979), Effect of family preparation on the state anxiety level of the CCU patient. Nursing Research, 28, 315-316.

1510.   Doherty, W.J. (1982), Review of F.I. Nye's Family relationships: Rewards and costs. American Journal of Family Therapy, 10, 82.

1511.   Doherty, W.J., McCabe, P., and Ryder, R.G. (1978), Marriage encounter: Critical appraisal. Journal of Marital and Family Therapy, 4, 99-114.

1512.   Doherty, W.J., and Baird, M.A. (1983), Family therapy and family medicine. New York: Guilford Press.

1513.   Doherty, W.J., and Colangelo, N. (1984), The family FIRO Model: A modest proposal for organizing family treatment. Journal of Marital and Family Therapy, 10, 19-29.

1514.   Doherty, W.J., and Ryder, R.G. (1980), Parent Effectiveness Training (P.E.T.): Criticisms and caveats. Journal of Marital and Family Therapy, 6(4), 409-419.

1515.   Doherty, W.J., and Walker, B.J. (1982), Marriage encounter casualties: A preliminary investigation. American Journal of Family Therapy, 10, 15-25.

1516.   Dohner, O., and Angermeyer, M.C. (1981), Social group work with relatives of mental patients (parents of schizophrenic adolescents) (author's transl.). Psychotherapie, Psychosomatik, Medizinische Und Psychologie, 31, 70-3.

1517.   Dolber, A., Greenberg, W.D., and Linder, R. (1977), From symptom to problem in living: Family approach to the treatment of the hospitalized psychiatric patient. Psychotherapy: Theory, Research and Practice, 14, 52-56.

1518.   Dolberg, G. (1966), On the establishing of medical-psychological marriage and sex counseling as a part of marriage and family counseling. Deutsches Gesundheitswesen, 21, 1768-1775.

1519.   Dolger, H. (1970), The young diabetic and family stress. Medical Insight, 2, 32.

1520.   Doll, E.A. (1953), Counseling parents of severely mentally retarded children. Journal of Clinical Psychology, 9, 114-117.

1521.   Dollinger, S.J. (1983), A case report of dissociative neurosis (depersonalization disorder) in an adolescent treated with family therapy and behavior modification. Journal of Consulting and Clinical Psychology, 51, 479-484.

1522.   Dominian, J. (1979), Introduction of marital pathology: Management, basic counseling. British Medical Journal, 2, 915-916.

1523.   Dominian, J. (1979), Introduction to marital pathology: Management, sexual counseling. British Medical Journal, 2, 1053-1054.

1524.   Dominian, J. (1979), Introduction to marital pathology. Management: Psychodynamics. British Medical Journal, 2, 987-989.

1525.   Donner, A. (1978), The number of families required for detecting the familial aggregation of a continuous attribute. American Journal of Epidemiology, 108, 425-428.

1526.   Donner, A. (1979), The use of correlation and regression in the analysis of family resemblance. American Journal of Epidemiology, 110, 335-342.

1527.   Donner, J., and Gamson, A. (1968), Experience with multifamily, time limited, outpatient groups at a community psychiatric clinic. Psychiatry, 31, 126-137.

1528.   Donofrio, A.F. (1976), Parent education vs. child psychotherapy. Psychology in the Schools, 13, 176-180.

1529.   Donofrio, D.S. (1969), The effect of therapist variables on parents and their children as a function of work with parent counseling groups. Dissertation Abstracts International, 3, 2904B.

1530.   Donofrio, J.C. (1979), A comparison of family verbal interaction patterns in families with an asthmatic, diabetic, and non-disabled child. Dissertation Abstracts International, 40, 4477B.

1531.   Donovan, L.P. (1976), Family environment: Significance for continuance in a day treatment program. Journal of Clinical Psychology, 29, 10-12.

1532.   Dooley, B.K. (1976), Family communication during the process of multi-family group counseling and its effect on the school performance of the adolescent family members. <u>Dissertation Abstracts International</u>, <u>37</u>, 1400-1401A.

1533. Dor, J., Homburg, R., and Rabau, E. (1977), An evaluation of etiologic factors and therapy in 665 infertile couples. <u>Fertility and Sterility</u>, <u>28</u>(7), 718-722.

1534. Dorfman, E. (1968), Content-free study of marital resemblances in group therapy. <u>Journal of Abnormal Psychology</u>, <u>73</u>, 78-80.

1535. Dorgan, B.J., and Dorgan, R.E. (1972), A theoretical rationale for total family therapy with stutterers. <u>British Journal of Social Psychiatry</u>, <u>6</u>, 214-222.

1536. Dorgan, J.P. (1977), A study of the effectiveness of a programmed strategy of behavioral intervention for parents of children with learning and behavior disorders. <u>Dissertation Abstracts International</u>, <u>38</u>, 1887A.

1537. Dorr, D. (1981), Conjoint psychological testing in marriage therapy: New wine in old skins. <u>Professional Psychology</u>, <u>12</u>, 549-555.

1538. Douglas, J. (1981), Behavioral family therapy and the influence of a systems framework. <u>Journal of Family Therapy</u>, <u>3</u>(4), 327.

1539. Douglas, M.D. (1979), Contextual determinants of the reciprocity of control strategy behaviors for marital dyads. <u>Dissertation Abstracts International</u>, <u>41</u>(2), 685B.

1540. Douglas, R.R. (1968), Dinnertime dynamics. <u>Family Coordinator</u>, <u>17</u>, 181-184.

1541. Dovinval, P.A. (1973), Distribution of matrimonial migrations in Belgium. <u>Human Heredity</u>, <u>23</u>, 59-68.

1542. Dowling, E. (1985), The struggle for control in family therapy: A means to an end or an end in itself. <u>Journal of Family Therapy</u>, <u>7</u>, 297-300.

1543. Dowling, E., Cade, B., Breulin, D.C., Frude, N., and Seligman, P. (1982), A retrospective survey of students views on a family therapy training program. <u>Journal of Family Therapy</u>, <u>4</u>(1), 61.

1544. Dowling, E., and Seligman, P. (1980), Description and evaluation of a family therapy training model. <u>Journal of Family Therapy</u>, <u>2</u>, 123-130.

1545. Dowling, E.M., and Jones, H.V. (1978), Small children seen and heard in family therapy. <u>Journal of Children in Psychotherapy</u>, <u>4</u>(4), 87-96.

1546. Downes, C. (1982), How endings are experienced in time limited family placement of difficult adolescents. <u>Journal of Adolescence</u>, <u>5</u>, 379-94.

1547. Downing, C.J. (1974), Worry workshop for parents. <u>Elementary School Guidance and Counseling</u>, <u>9</u>, 124-131.

1548. Downing, C.J. (1983), A positive way to help families. <u>Elementary School Guidance and Counseling</u>, <u>17</u>, 208-213.

1549.   Dowsling, J.L. (1980), Sex therapy for recovering alcoholics: An essential part of family therapy. International Journal of the Addictions, 15(8), 179-1190.

1550.   Doyle, A.M. (1974), Role processing applied to marital counseling. Personnel and Guidance Journal, 52(10), 681-685.

1551.   Doyle, A.M., and Dorlac, C. (1978), Treating chronic crisis bearers and their families. Journal of Marital and Family Therapy, 4, 37-42.

1552.   Dozink-Litynska, A. (1973), The family. Pielegniarka i Polozna, 10, 15.

1553.   Drake, B. (1975), Psychoanalytically oriented psychodrama with multiple family groups. American Journal of Orthopsychiatry, 45, 260-261.

1554.   Dreikurs, R. (1972), Family counseling: A demonstration. Journal of Individual Psychology, 28, 207-222.

1555.   Dreikurs, R. (1951), Family group therapy in the Chicago community child-guidance center. Mental Hygeine, 35, 291-301.

1556.   Dreikurs, R. (1949), Counseling for family adjustment. Individual Psychology Bulletin, 7, 119-137.

1557.   Dreikurs, R., Corsini, R., Lowe, R., and Sonstegard, M. (Eds.) (1959), Adlerian family counseling: A manual for counseling center. Eugene, OR: University Press.

1558.   Dreman, S.B. (1977), Secrecy, silk gloves and sanctions: A family approach to treating an encopretic child. Family Therapy, 4, 171-177.

1559.   Dreman, S.B., and Cohen, E.C. (1982), Children of victims of terrorist activities: A family approach to dealing with tragedy. American Journal of Family Therapy, 10, 39-47.

1560.   Dreyfus, E.A. (1979), Counseling the divorced father. Journal of Marital and Family Therapy, 5, 79-86.

1561.   Drob, S., Stewart, S., and Bernard, H. (1982), Psychotherapy with borderline patients. Group, 6, 14-22.

1562.   Drotar, D. (1977), Family oriented intervention with the dying adolescent. Journal of Pediatric Psychology, 2, 68-71.

1563.   Druckman, J.M. (1979), Family-oriented policy and treatment program for female juvenile status offenders. Journal of Marriage and Family, 41, 627-636.

1564.   Druckman, J.M., and Rhodes, C.A. (1977), Family impact analysis: Application to child custody determination. Family Coordinator, 26, 451-458.

1565.   Dube, S., and Mohan, D. (1977), Towards a distinction between psychopathology and sociopathology in short-term conjoint marital therapy. Indian Journal of Behavior, 1(2), 30-34.

1566. Duckert, K. (1973), Family in a purely polyclinic family institution. Acta Psychiatrica Scandinavica, 243, 20–22.

1567. Duddle, C.M. (1975), The treatment of marital psycho-sexual problems. British Journal of Psychiatry, 127, 169–170.

1568. Duehn, W.D., and Mayadas, N.S. (1975), Behavioral rehearsals in group counseling with parents. American Journal of Orthopsychiatry, 45(2), 261–262.

1569. Duff, R.S. (1981), Counseling with families and deciding care of severly defective children: A way of coping with medical Vietnam. Pediatrics, 67(3), 315–320.

1570. Duffy, M. (1984), Review of M. Little's Family breakup: Understanding marital problems and the mediating of child custody decisions. Contemporary Psychology, 29(3), 231.

1571. Dugan, C.M. (1979), Evaluation of a family style group home treatment program. Dissertation Abstracts International, 41(2), 670B.

1572. Duhl, B.S. (1983), Review of D.S. Freeman's Techniques of family therapy. Family Process, 22, 128.

1573. Duhl, F.J. (1981), The use of the chronological chart in general systems family therapy. Journal of Marital and Family Therapy, 7(3), 361–373.

1574. Duhl, F.J., and Duhl, B.S. (1979), Structured spontaneity: Thoughtful art of integrative family therapy at BFI. Journal of Marital and Family Therapy, 5, 59–76.

1575. Duhrssen, A. (1980), Review of W. Toman's Family therapy: Basis, empirical data and practice. Psychosomatik Medizinische Und Psychoanalyzes, 26, 394.

1576. Duhsler, K. (1976), Family therapy by means of symbol interpretation. Praxis Der Kinderpsychologie Und Kinderpsychiatrie, 25, 96–99.

1577. Dukic, T. (1978), Problems of the therapist in the home treatment of family groups. Pishijatrija Danas, 10, 113–115.

1578. Dulfano, C. (1978), Family therapy of alcoholism. In: S. Zimberg, J. Wallace, and S.B. Blume (Eds.), Practical approaches to alcoholism psychotherapy. New York, NY: Plenum Press.

1579. Dulicai, D. (1977), Nonverbal assessment of family systems: A preliminary study. Art in Psychotherapy, 4, 55–62.

1580. Dunivin, D.L. (1982), Review of A.E. Carter and M. McGoldrick's The family life cycle: A framework for family therapy. Journal of Contemporary Psychotherapy, 13, 103.

1581. Dunlop, J., Skorney, B., and Hamilton, J. (1982), Group treatment for elderly alcoholics and their families. Social Work With Groups, 5, 87–92.

1582. Dunn, G., and Rosen, B. (1982), When family must change too...each member of the family is an influencing factor in mental illness. Nursing Mirror, 155, 28–29.

1583.   Dunn, M.E., and Dickes, R. (1977), Erotic issues in cotherapy. Journal of Sex and Marital Therapy, 3, 205-211.

1584.   Dunne, D.E. (1976), Psychological factors relating to infertility of couples and the implications for counseling and psychotherapy. Dissertation Abstracts International, 35, 7288A.

1585.   Durell, V.G. (1969), Adolescents in multiple family group therapy in a school setting. International Journal of Group Psychotherapy, 19, 44-52.

1586.   Durkin, J.E. (1983), Epistemology, psychotherapy, and psychopathology: Conference at Houston. American Journal of Family Therapy, 11, 74-77.

1587.   Durrant, M. (1984), Review of A.S. Gurman and D.P. Kniskern's Handbook of family therapy. Australian Psychologist, 19(1), 107.

1588.   Durrett, D.D., and Kelly, P.A. (1974), Can you really talk with your child? A parental training program in communication skills toward the improvement of parent-child interaction. Group Psychotherapy, Psychodrama, and Sociometry, 27(1-4), 98-109.

1589.   Duryee, M.A. (1980), Development of a family therapist: Training in an interethnic deinstitutionalization-of-status-offenders agency. Dissertation Abstracts International, 41, 1971B. (University Microfilms No. 8024940.)

1590.   Dwyer, J.H., Menk, M.C., and Van Houten, C. (1965), The caseworker's role in family therapy with severely disturbed children. Family Process, 4, 21-31.

1591.   Dwyer, J.H., Menk, M.C., and Van Houten, C. (1964), The caseworker's role in family therapy on a residential treatment service for disturbed children. American Journal of Orthopsychiatry, 24, 246-247.

1592.   Dydyk, B., French, G., Gertsman, C., and Morrison, N. (1982), Admission of whole families. Canadian Journal of Psychiatry, 27, 640-643.

1593.   Dyer, D. (1959), A comparative study relating to marital happiness to university course helpful in marital adjustment. Marriage and Family Living, 21, 230-232.

1594.   Dyer, R. (1979), Pre-psychotherapy characteristics of prematurely, unilaterally discontinuing families at a community mental health center. Dissertation Abstracts International, 39, 6115B.

1595.   Dym, B.M. (1984), Review of W.S. Doherty and M.A. Baird's Family therapy and family medicine. General Hospital Psychiatry, 6(3), 236.

1596.   Dysinger, R.H. (1961), The family as the unit of study and treatment: II. A family perspective on the diagnosis of individual members. Workshop, 1959. American Journal of Orthopsychiatry, 31, 61-68.

1597.   Dysinger, R.H., and Bowen, M. (1959), Problems for medical practice presented by families with a schizophrenic member. American Journal of Psychiatry, 116, 514-517.

1598.   Eager, M. (1977), Longdistance nurturing of the family bond. Part 3.
        Journal of Maternal Child Nursing, 2, 293-294.

1599.   Earle, R.H. (1970), Family group therapy: A relevant model for the
        pastoral counselor. Dissertation Abstracts International, 31(5), 2980B.

1600.   Easson, W.M. (1970), The dying child: The management of the child or
        adolescent who is dying. Springfield, IL: Charles C. Thomas.

1601.   Eastman, J.N., and Mesibov, G.B. (1981), Family interventions in a
        private pediatric practice. Journal of Marital and Family Therapy, 7,
        461-466.

1602.   Eastman, J.N., and Saur, W.G. (1979), Group model for building
        strengths in families with handicapped children. In: N. Stinnett, B.
        Chesser, and J. DeFrain (Eds.), Building family strengths. Lincoln, NE:
        University of Nebraska Press.

1603.   Eastman, W.F., and Reifler, C.B. (1969), Marriage counseling in the
        student health service. Journal of the American College Health
        Association, 17, 289-295.

1604.   Eaton, M., and Livingstone, D. (1962), Marriage counseling by the family
        doctor. New Zealand Medical Journal, 61, 357-363.

1605.   Eberhart, A. (1979), Therapeutic storytelling with preschoolers. Journal
        of American Academy of Child Psychiatry, 18, 119-127.

1606.   Ebert, B. (1978), Homeostasis. Family Therapy, 5, 171-175.

1607.   Ebigbo, P.O., Onyeama, W.P., Ihezue, U.H., and Ahanotu, A.C. (1981),
        Family therapy with polygamous families. Zeitschrift Fur
        Psychosomatische Medizin Und Psychoanalyse, 27, 180-191.

1608.   Ebigbo, P.O., Onyeama, W.P., Nkemena, A., and Ahanotu, A.C. (1982),
        Family therapy with monogamous Nigerian families. International
        Journal of Family Psychiatry, 3, 215-229.

1609.   Ecke, S.A. (1980), The role of the significant other in alcoholism.
        Dissertation Abstracts International, 41, 1499B.

1610.   Eckerle, R.A. (1976), "Interact", a family oriented community based
        juvenile delinquency intervention program. Dissertation Abstracts
        International, 37, 1226A.

1611.   Eddy, J., and Lawson, D. (1983), Religious concepts and short-term
        therapy for troubled parents. Counseling and Values, 27, 186-189.

1612.   Edelson, R.I., and Seidman, E. (1975), Use of videotaped feedback in
        altering interpersonal perceptions of married couples: A therapy
        analogue. Journal of Consulting and Clinical Psychology, 43(2), 244-250.

1613.   Edelston, H. (1973), A reply to the new relations in sex and marriage: A
        saner view. Community Health, 5, 131-136.

1614.   Eden, D.M. (1985), A study of counselor trainees on the variables of self
        concept, gender, styles of counseling and choice of family therapy as a
        speciality. Dissertation Abstracts International, 46, 1192-A.

1615.   Edsler, R.M. (1974), Effects of assertive training on marital interaction. Archives of General Psychiatry, 30, 643-649.

1616.   Edwards, D.G. (1973), The family: A therapeutic model for the treatment of drug addiction. Clinical Social Work Journal, 4, 3-12.

1617.   Egger, G.J. (1978), Early adolescent antecedents of narcotic abuse. International Journal of Addiction, 13, 773-781.

1618.   Egolf, D.B. (1972), The use of parent-child interaction patterns in therapy for young stutterers. Journal of Speech and Hearing Disorders, 37(2), 222-232.

1619.   Ehrentraut, G. (1976), The effects of premarital counseling of juvenile marriages on marital communication and relationship patterns. Dissertation Abstracts International, 36, 3571B.

1620.   Ehrenwald, J. (1974), Family dynamics and the transgenerational treatment effect. In: L.R. Wolberg and M.C. Aronson (Eds.) Group therapy 1974: An overview. New York, NY: Stratton Intercontinental Medical Book Corp.

1621.   Family therapy and training in child psychiatry. Journal of the American Academy of Child Psychiatry, 12, 461-472.

1622.   Eichel, E. (1978), Assessment with a family focus. Journal of Psychiatric Nursing, 16, 11-14.

1623.   Eidelson, R.J., and Epstein, N. (1982), Cognition and relationship maladjustment development of a measure of dysfunctional relationship beliefs. Journal of Consulting and Clinical Psychology, 50, 715-20.

1624.   Eiduson, B.T., and Livermore, J.B. (1953), Complications in therapy with adopted children. American Journal of Orthopsychiatry, 23, 795-802.

1625.   Eila, A.D. (1960), Teamwork in premarital counseling. Pastoral Psychology, 10, 33-38.

1626.   Einstein, G., and Moss, M.S. (1967), Some thoughts on sibling relationships. Social Casework, 48, 549-555.

1627.   Eisdorfer, C., and Cohen, D. (1981), Management of the patient and family coping with dementing illness. Journal of Family Practice, 10, 831-837.

1628.   Eisenberg, M.G., and Rustad, L.C. (1976), Sex education and counseling program on a spinal cord injury service. Archives of Physical Medicine and Rehabilitation, 57(3), 135-140.

1629.   Eisler, R.M. (1973), Behavior techniques in family oriented crisis intervention. Archives of General Psychiatry, 28, 111-116.

1630.   Eisler, R.M. (1972), Crisis intervention in the family of a firesetter. Psychotherapy: Theory, Research and Practice, 9(1), 76-79.

1631.   Eisler, R.M. (1976), Behavioral techniques in family crisis. Current Psychiatric Therapies, 16, 255-262.

1632.   Eisler, R.M., Miller, P.M., and Hersen, R. (1974), Effects of assertive training on marital interaction. Archives of General Psychiatry, 30, 643-649.

1633.   Eist, H.I., and Mandel, A.U. (1968), Family treatment of ongoing incest behavior. Family Process, 7, 216-232.

1634.   Ekberg, M., and Strom, R.J. (1977), Family therapy in anorexia nervosa: An alternative treatment. Lakartidningen, 74, 647-650.

1635.   Eklof, C. (1974), The family as a disease entity. Sairaanhoitaja, 50, 41-42.

1636.   Elbaum, P.L. (1981), The dynamics, implications, and treatment of extramarital sexual relationships for the family therapist. Journal of Marital and Family Therapy, 7, 489-495.

1637.   Elder, M.E., and Weinberger, P.E. (1971), A family centered project in a state mental hospital. Mental Hygiene, 55, 337-343.

1638.   Eldred, C.A., and Washington, M.N. (1975), Female heroin addicts in a city treatment program: The forgotten minority. Psychiatry, 38(1), 75.

1639.   Eldridge, W.D. (1983), Therapist's use of information and dynamics from extramarital relationships to stimulate growth in married couples. Family Therapy, 10, 1-11.

1640.   Elgon, A. (1982), The birth of a baby and the pre-school years. In A. Bentovim, G.G. Barnes and A. Cooklin (Eds.), Family therapy. 2. Complementary frameworks of theory and practice. London: Academic Press.

1641.   Elias, M.J., Chinsky, J.M., Larcen, S.W., and Allen, G.J. (1982). A multilevel behavioral-perspective school program: Process, problems, and potential. In A.M. Jeger, and R.S. Slotnick (Eds.), Community mental health and behavioral-ecology: A handbook of theory, research, and practice. New York: Plenum Publishing Corporation.

1642.   Elkaim, M. (1982), Anorexia nervosa: Individual and family therapy approaches. A systems approach to several cases of anorexia nervosa. Feuillets Psychiatriques de Liege, 15, 252-265.

1643.   Elkaim, M. (1981), Non-equilibrium, chance and change in family therapy. Journal of Marital and Family Therapy, 7(3), 291-297.

1644.   Elkaim, M., Prigogine, I., Guattari, F., Stengers, I., and Denenbourg, J.L. (1982), Openness: A round-table discussion. Family Process, 21, 57-70.

1645.   Elkin, M. (1977), Postdivorce counseling in a conciliation court. Journal of Divorce, 1, 55-65.

1646.   Elkin, M. (1977), Premarital counseling for minors: The Los Angeles experience. Family Coordinator, 26, 429-443.

1647.   Elkin, M. (1975), Licensing marriage and family counselors: A model act. Journal of Marital and Family Therapy, 1, 237-249.

1648. Elkins, J.R. (1977), A counseling model for lawyering in divorce cases. Notre Dame Lawyer, 53(2), 229-265.

1649. Elliot, H. (1974), Marriage counseling with deaf clients. Journal of Rehabilitation of the Deaf, 8(2), 29-36.

1650. Elliott, J. (1979), The G.P. obstetrician as husband and father. Australian Family Physician, 8, 523-525.

1651. Ellis, A. (1975), The treatment of sexual disturbance. Journal of Marital and Family Therapy, 1, 111-121.

1652. Ellis, A. (1960), Marriage counseling with demasculinizing wives and demasculinized husbands. Journal of Marriage and Family Living, 22, 13-21.

1653. Ellis, A. (1961), A rational approach to premarital counseling. Psychological Reports, 8, 333-338.

1654. Ellis, A. (1956), A critical evaluation of marriage counseling. Journal of Marriage and Family Living, 18, 65-71.

1655. Ellis, A. (1953), Marriage counseling with couples indicating sexual incompatibility. Marriage and Family Living, 15, 53-58.

1656. Ellis, A. (1978), Family therapy: A phenomenological and active directive approach. Journal of Marriage and Family Therapy, 4, 43-50.

1657. Ellis, T. (1982), The marriage enrichment weekend: A qualitative study of a particular weekend experience. Dissertation Abstracts International, 43, 1955B.

1658. Elmore, J.R. (1969), A comparison of attitudes toward pre-marital consultation obtained from a representative sample of protestant clergymen and church-related engaged couples. Dissertation Abstracts International, 30, 37-22-A.

1659. Elton, A. (1982), Maintaining family motivation during treatment. In A. Bentovim, G.G. Barnes, and A. Cooklin (Eds.), Family therapy. I. Complementary frameworks of theory and practice. London: Academic Press.

1660. Elwell, M.E. (1979), Sexually assaulted children and their families. Social Casework, 60, 227-235.

1661. Elwood, R.W., and Jacobson, N.S. (1982), Spouses' agreement in reporting their behavioral interactions: A clinical replication. Journal of Consulting and Clinical Psychology, 50, 783-784.

1662. Ely, A.L. (1971), Efficacy of training in conjugal therapy. Dissertation Abstracts International, 31(8), 4988B.

1663. Embree, T.J. (1981), A descriptive analysis of supervision in marital and family therapy. Dissertation Abstracts International, 42, 2315A.

1664. Emde, R.N., Boyd, C., and Mayo, G.A. (1968), Family treatment of folie de deux. Psychiatric Quarterly, 42, 689-711.

1665.   Emde-Boas, C. (1962), Intensive group psychotherapy with married
        couples. International Journal of Group Psychotherapy, 12, 142-153.

1666.   Emer, J. (1979), Counseling in relation to changing and different family
        structures in Turkey. International Journal for the Advancement of
        Counseling, 2(3), 165.

1667.   Emshoff, J.G. (1980), The diversion of juvenile delinquents: A
        comparison of intervention with the family and intervention with all life
        systems. Dissertation Abstracts International, 41, 1159B.

1668.   Engebretson, J.C. (1982), Stepmothers and first-time parents: Their
        needs and problems. Pediatric Nursing, 8, 387-390.

1669.   Engel, L.B. (1973), Perceived effects of fair fight training: A system of
        marital therapy. Dissertation Abstracts International, 33(11), 5510B.

1670.   Engeln, R., Knutson, J., Laughy, L., and Garlington, W. (1968), Behavior
        modification techniques applied to a family unit: A case study. Journal
        of Child Psychology, Psychiatry and Related Disciplines, 9, 245-252.

1671.   Entine, A.D. (1977), Counseling for midlife and beyond. Vocational
        Guidance Quarterly, 25(4), 332-336.

1672.   Epperson, M.M. (1977), Families in sudden crisis: Process and
        intervention in a critical care center....Maryland Institute for
        Emergency Medicine. Social Work in Health Care, 2, 265-273.

1673.   Epstein, G.M. (1977), Evaluating the bereavement process as it is
        affected by variation in the time of intervention. Dissertation Abstracts
        International, 38, 2362B.

1674.   Epstein, L.H., Wing, R.R., Koeske, R., Andrasik, F., and Ossip, D.J.
        (1981), Child and parent weight loss in family-based behavior
        modification programs. Journal of Consulting and Clinical Psychology,
        49, 674-685.

1675.   Epstein, N. (1976), Techniques of brief therapy with children and
        parents. Social Casework, 57, 317-323.

1676.   Epstein, N. (1982), Cognitive therapy with couples. American Journal
        of Family Therapy, 10, 5-16.

1677.   Epstein, N., Jayne-Lazarus, C., and DeGiovanni, I.S. (1979), Cotrainers
        as models of relationships: Effects of the outcome of couples therapy.
        Journal of Marital and Family Therapy, 5, 53-60.

1678.   Epstein, N., and Eidelson, R.J. (1981), Unrealistic beliefs of clinical
        couples: Their relationship to expectations, goals, and satisfaction.
        American Journal of Family Therapy, 9, 13-22.

1679.   Epstein, N., and Jackson, E. (1978), An outcome study of short-term
        communication training with married couples. Journal of Consulting and
        Clinical Psychology, 46, 207-212.

1680.   Epstein, N., and Shainline, A. (1974), Paraprofessional parent-aides and
        disadvantaged families. Social Casework, 55, 230-236.

1681.   Epstein, N., and Slavson, S.R. (1962), Further observations on group
psychotherapy with adolescent delinquent boys in residential
treatment. I. "Breakthrough" in group treatment of hardened delinquent
adolescents. International Journal of Group Psychotherapy, 12, 199-210.

1682.   Epstein, N.B. (1966), Some issues in family therapy. Laval Medical, 37,
146- 50.

1683.   Epstein, N.B. (1985), Discussion of Cross. International Journal of
Family Therapy, 7(1), 38-39.

1684.   Epstein, N.B. (1984), Review of C.M. Anderson and S. Stewart's
Mastering resistance: A practical guide to family therapy.
Contemporary Psychology, 29(10), 809.

1685.   Epstein, N.B. (1970), Family therapy today: An overview. Laval
Medical, 41, 835-844.

1686.   Epstein, N.B., Baldwin, L.M., and Bishop, D.S. (1983), The McMaster
family assessment device. Journal of Marital and Family Therapy, 9,
171-180.

1687.   Epstein, N.B., Bishop, D.S., and Baldwin, L.M. (1982), McMaster model
of family functioning: A view of the normal family. In F. Walsh (Ed.).
Normal family processes. New York: Guilford Press.

1688.   Epstein, N.B., and Bishop, D.S. (1981), Problem centered systems
therapy of the family. Journal of Marital and Family Therapy, 7, 23-31.

1689.   Epstein, N.B., and Bishop, D.S. (1973), Position paper - Family therapy:
State of the art - 1973. Canadian Journal of Psychiatry, 18, 175-184.

1690.   Epstein, N.B., and Levin, S. (1973), Training for family therapy within a
faculty of medicine. Canadian Journal of Psychiatry, 18, 203-208.

1691.   Epstein, N.B., and Sanmbarbara, J. (1975). Conflict behavior in clinical
couples: Interpersonal perceptions and stable outcomes. Family
Process, 14, 51-66.

1692.   Erickson, G. (1973), Teaching family therapy. Education for Social
Work, 9, 9-15.

1693.   Erlich, I. (1978), Polish women students: Attitudes toward career and
marriage. Journal of the American College Health Association, 26, 334-
337.

1694.   Eshelman, M.A. (1981), A comparison of the temporal orientations,
interventions, and leadership styles of expert family therapists
representing differing theoretical perspectives. Dissertation Abstracts
International, 42, 2026B.

1695.   Esser, P.H. (1971), Evaluation of family therapy with alcoholics. British
Journal of Addiction, 66(4), 251-256.

1696.   Esser, P.H. (1968), Conjoint family therapy for alcoholics. British
Journal of Addiction, 63, 177-182.

1697.   Esser, P.H. (1970), Conjoint family therapy with alcoholics—a new approach. British Journal of Addiction, 64, 272-286.

1698.   Essig, J.D. (1972), Prediction accuracy as a method of evaluating the Adlerian approach to improving family adjustment. Dissertation Abstracts International, 32, 4945A.

1699.   Esterson, A. (1965), Results of family oriented therapy with hospitalized schizophrenics. British Medical Journal, 5476, 1462-1465.

1700.   Esterson, H., Feldman, C., Krigsman, N., and Warshaw, S. (1973), Time limited group counseling with parents of preadolescent underachievers: A pilot program. Proceedings of the 81st Annual Convention of the American Psychological Association, 8, 701-702.

1701.   Estes, N.J. (1974), Counseling the wife of an alcoholic spouse. American Journal of Nursing, 74, 1251-1255.

1702.   Estreicher, D.G. (1983), The development of family therapy techniques for families with developmentally disabled children. Dissertation Abstracts International, 43, 3384B.

1703.   Euster, S.D., Ward, V.P., and Varner, J.G. (1982), Adapting counseling techniques. Child Welfare, 61(6), 375.

1704.   Evans, D.M. (1980), Some aspects of parent counseling in schools for the deaf. The Teacher of the Deaf, 4(3), 81.

1705.   Evans, H.A., Chagoya, L., and Rakoff, V. (1971), Decision-making as the choice of family therapy in an adolescent in-patient setting. Family Process, 10, 97-110.

1706.   Evans, R.C. (1978), Keith - Case study of structural family therapy: Comments. Family Process, 17, 353.

1707.   Evans, R.C. (1976), Marital therapy when one spouse has a primary affective disorder (letter). American Journal of Psychiatry, 133, 1346.

1708.   Evans, S. (1968), More about the baby pool. Journal of Emotional Education, 8, 21-24.

1709.   Evenson, M.L. (1981), An Adlerian activity approach to family enrichment. Dissertation Abstracts International, 41, 4287A.

1710.   Everaerd, W., and Dekker, J. (1981), A comparison of sex therapy and communication therapy: Couples complaining of orgasmic dysfunction. Journal of Sex and Marital Therapy, 7, 278-89.

1711.   Everett, C.A. (1977), An analysis of clinical supervisors as agents of professional socialization: A study of the American Association of Marriage and Family Counselors. Dissertation Abstracts International, 38, 3085A.

1712.   Everett, C.A. (1979), Masters degree in marriage and family therapy. Journal of Marital and Family Therapy, 5, 7-14.

1713.   Everett, C.A. (1976), Family assessment and intervention for early adolescent problems. Journal of Marital and Family Therapy, 2, 155-165.

1714.   Everett, C.A. (1985), Review of A. Lange and O. Van der Hart's
         Directive family therapy. Family Relations, 34(1), 144.

1715.   Everett, C.A. (1985), Review of B.B. Wolman and G. Stricker's
         Handbook of family and marital therapy. Contemporary Psychology, 30,
         724.

1716.   Everett, C.A. (1980), An analysis of AAMFT supervisors: Their identity,
         roles and resources. Journal of Marriage and Family Therapy, 6(2), 215.

1717.   Everett, H.C. (1967), The "adversary" system in married couples' group
         therapy. Sandoz Psychiatric Spectator, 4, 5-6.

1718.   Everett, H.C. (1969), The "adversary" system in married couples' group
         therapy. In: J.H. Masserman (Ed.), Current psychiatric therapies. New
         York, NY: Grune and Stratton.

1719.   Everett, H.C. (1968), The "adversary" system in married couples' group
         therapy. Inernational Journal of Group Psychotherapy, 18, 70-74.

1720.   Everson, S. (1977), Sibling counseling. American Journal of Nursing, 77,
         644-646.

1721.   Eveson, M., and Eveson, S. (1974), Role repertoire in marriage. Group
         Psychotherapy, 27, 119-122.

1722.   Ewart, C.K. (1978), Behavior contracts in couple therapy: An
         experimental evaluation of quid pro quo and good faith models.
         Dissertation Abstracts International, 39, 4575B.

1723.   Ewell, L.W., Nance, W.E., Corey, L.A., Boughman, J.A., and Winter,
         P.M. (1978), Blood pressure studies on monozygotic twins and their
         families. Progress in Clinical and Biological Research, 24, 29-38.

1724.   Ewing, C.P. (1976), Family crisis intervention and traditional child
         guidance: A comparison of outcomes and factors related to success in
         treatment. Dissertation Abstracts International, 36, 4686B.

1725.   Exum, H.A. (1983), Key issues in family counseling with gifted and
         talented black students. Roeper Review, 5, 28-31.

1726.   Eyberg, S.M., and Robinson, E.A. (1982), Parent-child interaction
         training: Effects on family functioning. Journal of Clinical Child
         Psychology, 11, 130-137.

1727.   Eysenck, H.J. (1980), Review of N.S. Jacobson and G. Margolin's Marital
         therapy: Strategies based on social learning and behavior exchange
         principles. Behavior Research and Therapy, 18, 513.

1728.   Ezzo, F.R. (1980), A comparative outcome study of family therapy and
         positive parenting with court-referred adolescents. Dissertation
         Abstracts International, 40, 6198A.

1729.   Ezzo, F.R. (1980), Family psychiatry vs. family therapy. Psychiatric
         Annals, 10, 42.

1730.   Fagin, C.M. (1968), Family therapy in Czechoslovakia. Canada's Mental
         Health, 16, 23-24.

1731.   Fagin, C.M. (1970), Family-centered nursing in community psychiatry: Treatment in the home. Philadelphia, PA: Davis.

1732.   Falbo, T. (Ed.) (1984), The single-child family. New York: Guilford Press.

1733.   Falek, A. (1973), Issues and ethics in genetic counseling with Huntington's disease families. Psychiatric Forum, 4, 51-60.

1734.   Falicov, C.J. (1984), Review of M. Karpel and E. Strauss' Family evaluation. Family Process, 23(3), 461-463.

1735.   Falicov, C.J., Constantine, J.A., and Breunlin, D.C. (1981), Teaching family therapy: A program based on training objectives. Journal of Marital and Family Therapy, 7, 497-505.

1736.   Falicov, C.J., and Karrer, B.M. (1984), Therapeutic strategies for Mexican American families. International Journal of Family Therapy, 6(1), 16-30.

1737.   Falloon, I.R., Boyd, J.L., McGill, C.W., Razani, J., Moss, H.B., and Gilderman, M. (1982), Family management in the prevention of exacerbations of schizophrenia: A controlled study. New England Journal of Medicine, 306, 1437-1440.

1738.   Falloon, I.R., Boyd, J.L., and McGill, C.W. (1984), Family care of scihozphrenia: A problem-solving approach to the treatment of mental illness. New York: Guilford Press.

1739.   Falloon, I.R., Boyd, J.L., and Mcgill, C.W. (1982), Behavioral family therapy for schizophrenia. In J.L. Curran, and P.M. Monti (Eds.), Social skills training: A practical handbook for assessment and treatment. New York: Guilford Press.

1740.   Falloon, I.R., Liberman, R.P., Lillie, F.J., and Vaughn, C.E. (1981), Family therapy of schizophrenics with high risk of relapse. Family Process, 20(2), 211-221.

1741.   Family symposium. (1976), American Journal of Psychology, 133, 669-687.

1742.   Family conflict — the starting point. (1980), Community Outlook, 6, 260-261.

1743.   Family groups in joint meetings learn to correct communication distortions. Roche Report: Frontiers in Clinical Psychiatry, (1974), 6, 5-6.

1744.   Family therapy helps addict. (1979), Journal of American Medical Association, 241, 546-551.

1745.   Family: Group therapies: Digests of papers. American Orthopsychiatric Association. (1975), American Journal of Orthopsychiatry, 45, 260-270.

1746.   Fanelli, J.P. (1978), Family decision making: Ecosystem approach. International Journal of Family Counseling, 6, 92-93.

1747.   Fanshell, D., and Moss, F. (1971), Playback: A marriage in jeopardy examined. New York: Columbia University Press.

1748.   Farley, F.H., and Davis, S.A. (1978), Arousal, personality, and assortative mating in marriage: Generalizability and cross-cultural factors. Journal of Sex and Marital Therapy, 4, 50-53.

1749.   Farley, J.E. (1979), Family separation - individuation tolerance: A developmental conceptualization of the nuclear family. Journal of Marital and Family Therapy, 5, 61-67.

1750.   Farrer-Meschan, R. (1971), Importance of marriage counseling to infertility investigation. Obstetrics and Gynecology, 38, 316-325.

1751.   Farris, D.W., and Avery, A.W. (1980), Training marital couples in problem-solving skills: An evaluation of a weekend training format. Family Therapy, 7, 83-96.

1752.   Fasting, C. (1973), Active psychotherapy in family crisis: II. Technical aspects clinical samples. Acta Psychiatrica Scandinavica, 243, 42.

1753.   Fatis, M., and Konewko, P.J. (1983), Written contracts as adjuncts in family therapy. Social Work, 28, 161-165.

1754.   Fattal, T., and Fattal, E. (1977), Cash flow forecasting: A marriage counseling tool. International Journal of Family Counseling, 5(1), 48-54.

1755.   Faulk, R.E. (1982), The effects of a two-weekend marital enrichment program on self-disclosure and marital adjustment. Dissertation Abstracts International, 42, 3398B.

1756.   Faulkner, J., and Kich, G.K. (1983), Assessment and engagement stages in therapy with the interracial family. Family Therapy Collections, 11, 78-90.

1757.   Federico, J. (1979), The marital termination period of the divorce adjustment process. Journal of Divorce, 3(2), 93-106.

1758.   Feinleib, M., Ware, J.H., Garrison, R.J., Borhani, N., Christian, J.C., and Rosenman, R. (1978), An analysis of variance for major coronary heart disease risk factors in twins and their brothers. Progress in Clinical and Biological Research, 24, 13-19.

1759.   Feinstein, H.M. (1981), Family therapy for the historian? — The case of William James. Family Process, 20, 97-107.

1760.   Feld, B. (1982), Countertransference in family therapy. Group, 6, 3-13.

1761.   Feldes, D., and Bach, O. (1970), (Basics on family group therapy in comparison with the hypotheses of sociological and psychologic research direction in schizophrenia and psychoses similar to schizophrenia.) Psychiatrie, Neurologie, und Medizinische Psychologie, 22, 321-328. (German).

1762.   Feldman, G.C. (1981), Three's company: Family therapy with only-child families. Journal of Marital and Family Therapy, 7(1), 43-46.

1763.   Feldman, H.S. (1980), Family therapy: Its role in the prevention of criminality. Journal of Forensic Science, 25, 15-19.

1764.   Feldman, H.S. (1971), Treating emotional illness arising in marital discord: An evaluation of psychotherapy and psychotropic medication. Psychosomatics, 12, 123-126.

1765.   Feldman, L.B. (1979), Marital conflict and marital intimacy-Integrative psychodynamic-behavioral-systematic model. Family Process, 18, 69-78.

1766.   Feldman, L.B. (1976), Depression and marital interaction. Family Process, 15, 389-395.

1767.   Feldman, L.B. (1982), Dysfunctional marital conflict: An integrative interpersonal-intrapsychic model. Journal of Marital and Family Therapy, 8, 417-428.

1768.   Feldman, L.B. (1980), Styles and strategies of family therapy. Psychiatric Annals, 10, 253-260.

1769.   Feldman, L.B. (1976), Processes of change in family therapy. Journal of Family Counseling, 4, 14-22.

1770.   Feldman, L.B. (1976), Strategies and techniques of family therapy. American Journal of Psychotherapy, 30, 14-28.

1771.   Feldman, L.B. (1976), Goals of family therapy. Journal of Marital and Family Therapy, 2, 103-113.

1772.   Feldman, L.B. (1982), Sex roles and family dynamics. In F. Walsh (Ed.), Normal family processes. New York: Guilford Press.

1773.   Feldman, L.B., and Pinsof, W.M. (1982), Problem maintenance in family systems: An integrative model. Journal of Marital and Family Therapy, 8, 285-294.

1774.   Feldman, M.J. (1967), Privacy and conjoint family therapy. Family Process, 6, 1-9.

1775.   Feldman, R.B., and Feldman, S. (1982), Resident training systems and family systems training: Limits of compatability. Canadian Journal of Psychiatry, 27, 559-560.

1776.   Felice, M. (1980), Follow-up counseling of adolescent rape victims. Medical Aspects of Human Sexuality, 14(3), 67-68.

1777.   Fellner, C. (1976), Use of teaching stories in conjoint family therapy. Family Process, 15, 427-431.

1778.   Fenell, D.L. (1980), The effects of choice awareness marriage enrichment program on participants' marital satisfaction, self-concepts, accuracy of perception of spouses, and choosing behaviors. Dissertation Abstracts International, 40, 4894-A.

1779.   Fenell, D.L. (1982), Review of J.R. Bemporad's Child development in normality and psychopathology. American Journal of Family Therapy, 10, 89.

1780.   Fengler, J. (1975), Feedback technique in marriage and family therapy. Praxis der Psychotherapie, 20, 34-48.

1781.   Fenton, N. (1959), The prisoner's family: A study of family counseling in an adult correctional facility. Palo Alto, CA: Pacific Books.

1782.   Fenyes, C. (1976), The family pride factor in family therapy. Family Therapy, 3, 129-132.

1783.   Fenyes, C. (1976), Kiss the frog: A therapeutic intervention for refraining family rules. Family Therapy, 3, 123-128.

1784.   Ferber, A., Mendelsohn, M., and Napier, A. (1972), The book of family therapy. New York: Science House.

1785.   Ferber, A., and Mendelsohn, M. (1969), Training for family therapy. Family Process, 8, 25-32.

1786.   Ferber, A.S.   (1970), Changing family behavior programs. International Psychiatry Clinics, 7, 27-55.

1787.   Feres-Carneiro, T. (1980), (Marital psychotherapy: The conjugal relationship and its repercussions in the behavior of the children). Arquivos Brasileiros De Psicologia, 32, 51-61.

1788.   Ferguson, B.B. (1979). A parents' group. Journal of Psychiatric Nursing, 17, 24-27.

1789.   Ferguson, L. (1979), The family cycle: Orientation for interdisciplinary training. Professional Psychology, 10, 863-867.

1790.   Ferrara, M. (1982), The case of little Hans: A prototype of family therapy? Revista de Psicologica Normale et Patologica, 74, 163-176.

1791.   Ferraro, K.J. (1983), Review of J. Monahan's Predicting violent behavior: An assessment of clinical techniques. American Journal of Family Therapy, 11, 75.

1792.   Ferraro, K.J. (1983), Review of M.D. Pagelow's Woman-battering: Victims and their experiences. American Journal of Family Therapy, 11, 75.

1793.   Ferraro, K.J. (1983), Review of R.B. Stuart's Violent behavior: Social learning approaches to prediction, management and treatment. American Journal of Family Therapy, 11, 75.

1794.   Ferraro, K.J. (1983), Review of M.E. Wolfgang, and F. Ferracuti's The subculture of violence: Towards an integrated theory in criminology. American Journal of Family Therapy, 11, 75.

1795.   Ferreira, A.J. (1967), Family therapy in alcoholism. Psychotherapy and Psychosomatics, 15, 20.

1796.   Ferreira, A.J. (1967), Family therapy and the concept of mental health. Voices, 3, 18-21.

1797.   Ferreira, A.J. (1967), Family therapy: A new era in psychiatry. Western Medicine, 8, 83-87.

1798. Ferreira, A.J. (1967), Psychosis and family myth. American Journal of Psychotherapy, 21, 186–197.

1799. Ferreira, A.J., and Winter, W.D. (1966), Stability of interactional variables in family decision-making. Archives of General Psychiatry, 14, 352–355.

1800. Ferson, J. (1971), The "monster complex" in children who have seizures. Proceedings of the Annual Convention of the American Psychological Association, 6, 625–626.

1801. Fertel, N.S., and Feuer, E.G. (1981), Treating marital and sexual problems in the Orthodox Jewish community. Journal of Psychology and Judaism, 6, 85–94.

1802. Fibush, E.Q. (1957), The evaluation of marital interaction in the treatment of one partner. Social Casework, 38, 303–307.

1803. Ficher, I.V. (1984), Review of G. Arentewicz and G. Schmiat's The treatment of sexual disorders. Family Process, 23(1), 125.

1804. Ficher, I.V., and Linsenberg, M. (1976), Problems confronting the female therapist doing couple therapy. Journal of Marriage and Family Counseling, 2(4), 331–339.

1805. Fichten, C., and Wright, J. (1983), Videotape and verbal feedback in behavioral couple therapy: A review. Journal of Clinical Psychology, 39, 216–221.

1806. Fichten, C.S., Libman, E., and Brender, W. (1983), Methodological issues in the study of sex therapy: Effective components in the treatment of secondary orgasmic dysfunction. Journal of Sex and Marital Therapy, 9, 191–202.

1807. Field of family therapy (1970), GAP Report, 7, 525–644.

1808. Field, W.E. (1982), Review of I.W. Clements and D.M. Buchanan's Family therapy: A nursing perspective. American Journal of Nursing, 82, 1633.

1809. Fielding, B.B. (1966), The utilization of dreams in the treatment of couples. Psychotherapy and Psychosomatics, 14, 81–89.

1810. Fields, S. (1974), All in the family therapy: I. Treating the family system. Innovations, 1, 3–7.

1811. Fields, S. (1974), All in the family therapy: II. Changing units of treatment. Innovations, 1, 9–10.

1812. Fields, S. (1974), All in the family therapy: III. Day care: Another kind of problem. Innovations, 1, 11.

1813. Fieldsteel, N.D. (1974), Family therapy-individual therapy: A false dichotomy. In: L.R. Wolberg and M.L. Aronson, Group therapy 1974: An overview. New York: Stratton Intercontinental Medical Book Corp.

1814. Fieldsteel, N.D. (1980), Therapist or leader: Group and family therapy experiences. Group, 4, 40–42.

1815.   Fife, B.L., and Gant, B.L. (1980), The resolution of school phobia through family therapy. Journal of Psychiatric Nursing, 18, 13-16.

1816.   Figley, C.R., Sprenkle, D.H., and Denton, W. (1976), Training marriage and family counselors in an industrial setting. Journal of Marriage and Family Counseling, 2, 167-177.

1817.   Figley, C.R., and Sprenkle, D.H. (1978), Delayed stress response syndrome: Family therapy implications. Journal of Marriage and Family Counseling, 4, 53-60.

1818.   Figueiredo, E., Germond, A., and Louca, A.L. (1977) (A contribution to the pathogenesis and treatment of post-partum schizophrenia episodes: A collective and familial therapy in a day unit.) Annales Medico-Psychologiques, 2, 461-470.

1819.   Filpot, G., and Rucquoy, G. (1973), Comparative study using Rorschach test of couples in conflict and the personality structure of their members compared with those in general psychiatric consultation. Acta Psychiatrica Belgica, 73, 762-784.

1820.   Filsinger, E.E. (1983), Choices among marital observation coding systems. Family Process, 22, 317-335.

1821.   Filsinger, E.E. (Ed.) (1983), Marriage and family assessment: A sourcebook for family therapy. Beverly Hills, CA: Sage.

1822.   Filsinger, E.E., McAvoy, P., and Lewis, R.A. (1982), An empirical typology of dyadic formation. Family Process, 21, 321-336.

1823.   Fincham, F., and O'Leary, K.D. (1983), Causal inferences for spouse behavior in maritally distressed and nondistressed couples. Journal of Social and Clinical Psychology, 23, 42-57.

1824.   Fine, M.J., and Holt, P. (1983), Corporal punishment in the family: A systems perspective. Psychology in the Schools, 20, 85-92.

1825.   Fine, P. (1982), Play and family therapy as core skills for child psychiatry: Some implications of Piaget's theory for integrations in training and practice. Child Psychiatry and Human Development, 13, 79-96.

1826.   Fine, P. (1973), Family networks and child psychiatry in a community health project. Journal of the American Academy of Child Psychiatry, 12, 675-689.

1827.   Fine, S. (1973), Family therapy and a behavioral approach to childhood obsessive-compulsive neurosis. Archives of General Psychiatry, 28, 695-697.

1828.   Fine, S. (1974), Troubled families: Parameters for diagnosis and strategies for change. Comprehensive Psychiatry, 15, 73-77.

1829.   Fine, S. (1980), Children in divorce, custody, and access situations: The contribution of the mental health professional. Journal of Child Psychology Psychiatry and Allied Disciplines, 21, 353-361.

1830.   Finger, S. (1965), Concurrent group therapy with adolescent unmarried mothers and their parents. Confinia Psychiatrica, 8, 21-26.

1831.   Fink, H.K. (1958), Adaptations of the family constellation in group psychotherapy. Acta Psychotherapie, Psychsomatik y Orthopsychiatrie, 6, 43-56.

1832.   Fink, P. (1981), The relatives group: Treatment for parents of adult chronic schizophrenics. International Journal of Group Psychotherapy, 31, 453-68.

1833.   Finkelhor, D. (1978), Psychological, cultural, and family factors in incest and family sexual abuse. Journal of Marriage and Family Counseling, 4(4), 41-49.

1834.   Finkelstein, N.E. (1980), Family-centered group care. Child Welfare, 59, 33-41.

1835.   Finol, G.J. (1973), The influence of three methods of interpersonal process recall upon parental verbal interaction with a mentally retarded child using short-term family psychotherapy. Dissertation Abstracts International, 34, 1274B.

1836.   Finzan, A. (1979), Family therapy: Encounters with a therapeutic fashion. Psychiatrische Praxis, 6, 100-106.

1837.   Firestone, E., and Moschetta, P. (1975), Behavioral contracting in family therapy. Journal of Family Counseling, 3, 27-31.

1838.   Fisch, M. (1976), Homeostasis: A key concept in working with alcoholic families. Family Therapy, 3, 133-139.

1839.   Fischer, B.L. (1978), Therapists: Perception of healthy functioning. International Journal of Family Counseling, 6, 9-18.

1840.   Fischer, J. (1966), Group treatment of families with schizophrenic sons. Social Casework, 47, 438-445.

1841.   Fischer, J., Anderson, J.M., Arveson, E., and Brown, S. (1978), Adlerian family counseling: An evaluation. International Journal of Family Counseling, 6(2), 42-44.

1842.   Fish, L.S., Fish, R.C., and Sprenkle, P.H. (1984), Treating inhibited sexual desire: A marital therapy approach. American Journal of Family Therapy, 12(3), 3-12.

1843.   Fishburn, S.D. (1982), An appeal to the APA for a division of family therapy. American Psychologist, 37, 973-4.

1844.   Fisher, B.L., Giblin, P.R., and Hoopes, M.H. (1982), Healthy family functioning: What therapists say and what families want. Journal of Marital and Family Therapy, 8, 273-284.

1845.   Fisher, E.O. (1973), A guide to divorce counseling. Family Coordinator, 22(1), 55-61.

1846.   Fisher, E.P. (1975), Divorce counseling and values. Journal of Religion and Health, 14(4), 265-270.

1847.   Fisher, H.S. (1977), Adolescent group psychotherapy: Collaborative opportunity for patients, parents, and therapist. International Journal of Group Psychotherapy, 27(2), 233-240.

1848.   Fisher, J. (1978), Essence of being stuck: It takes one to think you know one or work on the therapist's own family. International Journal of Family Counseling, 6, 36-41.

1849.   Fisher, J.V., Barnett, B.L., and Collins, J. (1976), The post-suicide family and the family physician. Journal of Family Practice, 3, 263-267.

1850.   Fisher, L. (1976), Dimensions of family assessment: A critical review. Journal of Marriage and Family Counseling, 2(4), 367-382.

1851.   Fisher, L. (1977), On the classification of families: A progress report. Archives of General Psychiatry, 34, 424-433.

1852.   Fisher, L. (1981), Types of paradoxial intervention and indications/contraindications for use in clinical practice. Family Process, 20, 25-35.

1853.   Fisher, L. (1982), Transactional theories but individual assessment: A frequent discrepancy in family research. Family Process, 21, 313-320.

1854.   Fisher, L. (1978), On the impossibility of overriding the influence of the family. American Journal of Diseases of Children, 132, 1075-1076.

1855.   Fisher, L., and Warren, R.C. (1972), The concept of role assignment in family therapy. International Journal of Group Psychotherapy, 22, 60-76.

1856.   Fisher, R.E. (1974), The effect of two group counseling methods on perceptual congruence in married pairs. Dissertation Abstracts International, 35(2-A), 885.

1857.   Fisher, S., and Mendell, D. (1958), The spread of the psychotherapeutic effects from the patient to his family group. Psychiatry, 21, 133-140.

1858.   Fisher, S.G. (1980), The use of time limits in brief psychotherapy: A comparison of six-session, twelve-session, and unlimited treatment with families. Family Process, 19, 377-392.

1859.   Fisher, S.G. (1984), Time-limited brief therapy with families: A one-year follow-up study. Family Process, 23, 101-106.

1860.   Fishman, H.C. (1983), Diagnosis and assessment in family therapy: III. Reflections on assessment in structural family therapy. Family Therapy Collections, 11, 63-81.

1861.   Fitchett, G. (1979), Family therapy and communion. Pastoral Psychology, 27, 202-210.

1862.   Fitzgerald, R.G. (1972), Mania as a message: Treatment with family therapy and lithium carbonate. American Journal of Psychotherapy, 26, 547-554.

1863.   Fitzgerald, R.V. (1969), Conjoint marital psychotherapy: An outcome and follow-up study. Family Process, 8, 260-271.

1864. Fivaz, E., Fivaz, R., and Kaufmann, L. (1981), Dysfunctional transactions and therapeutic functions: An evolutive model. Journal of Marital and Family Therapy, 7, 309-320.

1865. Fix, A.G. (1974), Neighborhood knowledge and marriage distance: The Semai case. Annals of Human Genetics, 37, 327-332.

1866. Flach, F.F. (1979), Marriage: New therapeutic dimensions. Psychiatric Annals, 9(6), 296-301.

1867. Flaherry, J.A. (1979), Self-disclosure in therapy: Marriage of the therapist. American Journal of Psychotherapy, 33(3), 442-452.

1868. Flanzer, J.P. (1978), Family focused management: Treatment of choice for deviant and dependent families. International Journal of Family Counseling, 6, 25-31.

1869. Fleck, S. (1976), A general systems approach to severe family pathology. American Journal of Psychiatry, 133, 669-673.

1870. Fleck, S. (1979), The family in the treatment of schizophrenics. Journal of the National Association of Private Psychiatric Hospitals, 10(4), 22.

1871. Fleck, S. (1980), Family and marital therapy combined with individual psychotherapy. In: T.B. Karasu and I. Bellak (Eds.), Specialized techniques in individual psychotherapy. New York: Brunner/Mazel, 441-461.

1872. Fleck, S. (1965), Some general and specific indications for family therapy. Confinia Psychiatrica, 8, 27-36.

1873. Fleck, S. (1966), An approach to family pathology. Comprehensive Psychiatry, 7, 307-320.

1874. Fleck, S. (1968), Symposium on family research and family therapy. Psychotherapy and Psychosomatics, 16(6), 293-296.

1875. Fleck, S. (1985), Review of M.R. Lansky's Family therapy and major psychopathology. International Journal of Family Therapy, 6, 205-208.

1876. Fleck, S. (1983), Review of M.R. Lansky's Family therapy and major psychopathology. American Journal of Psychiatry, 140, 362.

1877. Fleischer, G. (1975), Producing effective change in impoverished, disorganized families. Is family therapy enough? Family Therapy, 2, 277-289.

1878. Fleischman, M.J. (1979), Using parenting salaries to control attrition and cooperation in therapy. Behavior Therapy, 10, 111-116.

1879. Fleischman, M.J., & Hoyne, A. M. (1979), Working with families: A social learning approach. Contemporary Education, 50, 66-71.

1880. Fleming, M.J. (1977), An evaluation of a structured program designed to teach communication skills and concepts to couples: A field study. Dissertation Abstracts International, 37, 7633-7634A.

1881.   Flinn, S.K., and Brown, L.O. (1977), Opening moves in crisis intervention with families of chronic psychotics. In: T.J. Buckley, J.J. McCarthy, E. Norman, and M.A. Quaranta (Eds.), New directions in family therapy. Oceanside: Dabor Science Publications.

1882.   Flint, A.A., Jr., and MacLennan, B.W. (1962), Some dynamic factors in marital group psychotherapy. International Journal of Group Psychotherapy, 12, 355-361.

1883.   Flomenhaft, K. (1984), Review of L.R. Wolberg and M.L. Aronson's Group and family therapy: 1982. Contemporary Psychology, 29(5), 424.

1884.   Flomenhaft, K., and Carter, R.E. (1977), Family therapy training: Program and outcome. Family Process, 16, 211-218.

1885.   Flomenhaft, K., and Carter, R.E. (1974), Family therapy training: A statewide program for mental health centers. Hospital and Community Psychiatry, 25, 789-791.

1886.   Flomenhaft, K., and Christ, A.E. (Eds.) (1980), The challenge for family therapy: A dialogue for child psychiatric educators. New York: Plenum.

1887.   Flores, J.L. (1979), Becoming a marriage, family and child counselor: Notes from a Chicano. Journal of Marital and Family Therapy, 5, 17-22.

1888.   Flowers, J.V. (1978), A simulation game to systematically improve relationship communication. Journal of Marriage and Family Counseling, 4(4), 51-57.

1889.   Floyd, F.J., and Markman, H.J. (1984), An economical observational measure of couple's communication skill. Journal of Consulting and Clinical Psychology, 52(1), 97-103.

1890.   Floyd, G.J. (1973), Managing member silence in family therapy. Journal of Psychiatric Nursing, 11, 20-24.

1891.   Floyd, H.H. (1982), Values assessment-comparison (VAC): A family therapy technique. Family Therapy, 9, 279-288.

1892.   Floyd, W.A. (1974), The use of MMPI in marital counseling and research. Journal of Family Counseling, 2(1), 16-21.

1893.   Floyd, W.A. (1976), A new look at research in marital and family therapy. Journal of Family Counseling, 4, 19-23.

1894.   Fogarty, J.F. (1975), The family emotional self system. Family Therapy, 2, 75-97.

1895.   Fogelman, E. (1979), Therapeutic groups for children of holocaust survivors. International Journal of Group Psychotherapy, 29, 211-236.

1896.   Fogle, D.M. (1980), Art and poetry therapy combined with talking therapy with a family of four in an out-patient clinic. Arts in Psychotherapy, 7, 27-34.

1897.   Foley, V.D. (1980), Current leadership styles in family therapy. Group, 4, 19-28.

1898.   Foley, V.D. (1980), Review of C.P. Barnard and R.G. Corrales's The theory and technique of family therapy. International Journal of Family Therapy, 2, 205

1899.   Foley, V.D. (1979), Review of A.C.R. Skynner's Systems of family and marital psychotherapy. International Journal of Group Psychotherapy, 29, 122-123.

1900.   Foley, V.D. (1975), Family therapy with black disadvantaged families: Some observations on roles, communication, and technique. Journal of Marriage and Family Counseling, 1, 29-38.

1901.   Foley, V.D. (1974), Family therapy with black, disadvantaged families. American Journal of Orthopsychiatry, 44, 220-226.

1902.   Foley, V.D. (1974), An introduction to family therapy. New York: Grune and Stratton.

1903.   Foley, V.D. (1971), Conceptual roots of conjoint family therapy: A comparative analysis of major therapists. Dissertation Abstracts International, 32(4), 2219A.

1904.   Foley, V.D. (1978), Review of A.C.R. Skynner's Systems of family and marital psychotherapy. International Journal of Family Counseling, 6, 95.

1905.   Foley, V.D. (1976), Alcoholism: A family system approach. Journal of Family Counseling, 4, 12-18.

1906.   Foley, V.D. (1978), Review of H. Grunebaum and J. Christ's Contemporary marriage: Structure, dynamics, and therapy. Contemporary Psychology, 23(8), 573.

1907.   Foley, V.D. (1983), Multiple family therapy with urban blacks. In L.R. Wolberg and M.L. Aronson (Eds.), Group and family therapy: 1982. New York: Brunner/Mazel.

1908.   Foley, V.D., and Dyer, W.W. (1974), "Timing" in family therapy : The "when", "how", and "why" of intervention. Family Coordinator, 23, 373-382.

1909.   Folkins, C., Pepitone, A., Rockwell, F., Vando, R.F., Vando, A., Spensley, J., and Rockwell, D. (1982), A leaderless couples group postmortem. International Journal of Group Psychotherapy, 32, 367-373.

1910.   Follingstad, D.R., and Haynes, S.N. (1981), Naturalistic observation in assessment of behavioral marital therapy. Psychological Reports, 44, 471-479.

1911.   Fong, J.Y. (1978), Symposium on directions in psychiatric nursing. Multiple family group therapy with a tri-therapist team. Nursing Clinics of North America, 13, 685-699.

1912.   Fontaine, P.J. (1975), Training group at the University Center for Child Guidance at Wolvwe (Brussels). Acta Psychiatrica Belgica, 75, 899-904.

1913.   Fontane, A.S. (1979), Using family of origin material in short-term marriage counseling. Social Casework, 60(9), 529.

1914.   Ford, B.G., and West, L.W. (1979), Human relations training for families: A comparative strategy. Canadian Counselor, 13, 102-107.

1915.   Ford, F.R. (1983), Rules: The invisible family. Family Process, 22, 135-145.

1916.   Ford, F.R., and Herrick, J. (1974), Family rules: Family life styles. American Journal of Orthopsychology, 44, 61-69.

1917.   Ford, J.D., Bashford, M.B., and DeWitt, K.N. (1984), Three approaches to marital enrichment: Toward optimal matching of participants and interventions. Journal of Sex and Marital Therapy, 10, 41-48.

1918.   Forehand, R., Griest, D.L., Wells, K., and McMahon, R.J. (1982), Side effects of parent counseling on marital satisfaction. Journal of Counseling Psychology, 29(1), 104.

1919.   Forehand, R.L., and McMahon, R.J. (1981), Helping the non-compliant child: A clinician's guide to parent training. New York: Guilford Press.

1920.   Foreman, S., and Seligman, L. (1983), Adolescent abuse. School Counselor, 30, 17-25.

1921.   Forrest, T. (1978), A synthesis of individual theory and therapy with family concepts. Psychoanalytic Review, 65, 507-521.

1922.   Forrest, T. (1969), Treatment of the father in family therapy. Family Process, 8, 106-118.

1923.   Fosson, A.R., Elam, C.L., and Broaddus, D.A. (1982), Family therapy in family practice: A solution to psychosocial problems? Journal of Family Practice, 16, 461-465.

1924.   Fost, N. (1981), Counseling families who have a child with a severe congenital anomaly. Pediatrics, 67(3), 321-324.

1925.   Foster, A.L. (1978), Changes in marital sexual relationships following treatment for sexual dysfunctioning. Journal of Sex and Marital Therapy, 4, 186-197.

1926.   Foster, R.G. (1937), Servicing the family through counseling agencies. American Sociological Review, 2, 764-770.

1927.   Foster, R.M. (1973), A basic strategy for family therapy with children. American Journal of Psychotherapy, 27, 437-445.

1928.   Foster, S.I. (1980), Review of J.B. Reid (Ed.), A social learning approach to family intervention. Volume II: Observation in home settings. Behavioral Assessment, 2, 303-305.

1929.   Foster, S.L., Prinz, R.J., and O'Leary, K.D. (1983), Impact of problem-solving communication training and generalization procedures on family conflict. Child and Family Behavior Therapy, 7, 1-23.

1930.   Foster, S.L., and Hoier, T.S. (1982), Behavioral and sytems family therapies: A comparison of theoretical assumptions. American Journal of Family Therapy, 10, 13-23.

1931.   Foster, S.W. (1984), Review of L.R. Wolberg and M.L. Aronson, (Eds.).
         Group and family therapy 1983. Journal of Marital and Family Therapy,
         10(4), 440-441.

1932.   Foster, S.W., and Gurman, A.S. (1983), On talking systems and treating
         people. In L.R. Wolberg and M.L. Aronson (Eds.), Group and family
         therapy: 1982. New York: Brunner/Mazel.

1933.   Fowler, P.C. (1982), Factor structure of the Family Environment
         Scale: Effects of social desirability. Journal of Clinical Psychology, 38,
         285-92.

1934.   Fox, A.J., Bulosu, L., and Kinlen, L. (1979), Mortality and age-
         differences in marriage. Journal of Biosocial Science, 11, 117-131.

1935.   Fox, G.L. (1979), The families influence on adolescent sexual behavior.
         Child Today, 8, 21-25, 36.

1936.   Fox, R., and Whelley, J. (1982), Preventing placement: Goal attainment
         in short-term family treatment. Child Welfare, 61, 231-238.

1937.   Fox, R.E. (1976), Family therapy. In: I.B. Weiner (Ed.), Clinical
         methods in psychology. New York, NY: John Wiley & Sons.

1938.   Fox, R.E. (1969), Issues in professional training for family therapy.
         Newsletter of the American Orthopedic Association, 13, 41.

1939.   Fox, R.E. (1968), The effect of psychotherapy on the spouse. Family
         Process, 7, 7-16.

1940.   Frager, S. (1978), Multiple family therapy: A literature review. Family
         Therapy, 5, 105-120.

1941.   Fraiberg, S., and Bennett, J. (1978), Intervention and failure to thrive:
         A psychiatric outpatient treatment program. Birth and the Family
         Journal, 5, 227-230.

1942.   Framer, E.M., and Sanders, S.H. (1980), The effects of family
         contingency contracting on disturbed sleeping behaviors in a male
         adolescent. Journal of Behavior Therapy and Experimental Psychiatry,
         11(3), 235-237.

1943.   Framo, J. (1979), A personal viewpoint on training in marital and family
         therapy. Professional Psychology, 10, 868-875.

1944.   Framo, J.L. (1982), Explorations in marital and family therapy:
         Selected papers of James L. Framo. New York: Guilford Press.

1945.   Framo, J.L. (1962), Symposium: Family treatment of schizophrenia:
         The theory of the technique of family treatment of schizophrenia.
         Family Process, 1(1), 119-131.

1946.   Framo, J.L. (1973), Marriage therapy in a couples group. Seminar in
         Psychiatry, 5(2), 207-217.

1947.   Framo, J.L. (1979), Family theory and therapy. American Psychologist,
         34, 988-992.

1948.   Framo, J.L. (1976), Family of origin as a therapeutic resource for adults in marital and family therapy: You can and should go home again. Family Process, 15, 193-210.

1949.   Framo, J.L. (1972), Family interventions: A dialogue between family researchers and family therapists. New York, NY: Springer Publishing.

1950.   Framo, J.L. (1975), Personal reflections of a family therapist. Journal of Marriage and Family Counseling, 1, 15-28.

1951.   Framrose, R. (1982), Adolescent enmeshment: A case for brief strategic therapy. Journal of Adolescence, 5, 149-57.

1952.   Framrose, R. (1982), Review of M.R. Lansky's Family therapy and major psychopathology. Journal of Adolescence, 5, 302.

1953.   Frances, A. (1980), Review of F.M. Sander, Individual and family therapy. Hospital and Community Psychiatry, 31, 710.

1954.   Frances, A., Clarkin, J.F., and Perry, S. (1984), DSM-III and family therapy. American Journal of Psychiatry, 141, 406-409.

1955.   Francis, J.L. (1977), Toward the managment of heterosexual jealousy. Journal of Marriage and Family Counseling, 3, 61-69.

1956.   Frank, C. (1984), Contextual family therapy. American Journal of Family Therapy, 12(1), 3-6.

1957.   Frank, C., and Boszormenyi-Nagy, I. (1984), Major constructs of contextual therapy: An interview with Ivan Boszormenyi-Nagy. American Journal of Family Therapy, 12(1), 7-14.

1958.   Frank, E., Anderson, C., and Kupfer, D.J. (1976), Profiles of couples seeking sex therapy and marital therapy. American Journal of Psychiatry, 133(1), 559-562.

1959.   Frank, E., Anderson, C., and Rubinstein, D. (1979), Marital role strain and sexual satisfaction. Journal of Consulting and Clinical Psychology, 47(6), 1096-1103.

1960.   Frank, E., Anderson, C., and Rubinstein, D. (1980), Marital role ideals and perception of marital role behavior in distressed and non-distressed couples. Journal of Marital and Family Therapy, 6, 55-63.

1961.   Frank, E., and Kupfer, D.J. (1976), In every marriage there are two marriages. Journal of Sex and Marital Therapy, 2, 137-143.

1962.   Frank, I., and Frank, R.K. (1980), Review of T.J. Paolino and B.S. McCrady's Marriage and marital therapy. Psychosomatics, 21, 435.

1963.   Frank, J.A. (1951), Counseling in infertility, frigidity, and homosexuality. In A.H. Clemens (Ed.), Marriage education and counseling. Washington, D.C.: Catholic University of America Press.

1964.   Frank, O.S. (1979), Review of M.K. Hinchliffe, O. Hooper, and M.K. Roberts's Melancholy marriage: Depression in marriage and psychosocial approaches to therapy. British Journal of Psychiatry, 135, 377.

1965.   Frank, O.S. (1979), Review of T.J. Paolino and B.S. McCrady's Marriage and marital therapy: Psychoanalytic, behavioral and systems theory perspectives. British Journal of Psychiatry, 135, 377.

1966.   Frankfurt, M. (1982), Review of J.C. Hansen and D. Rosenthal's Strategies and techniques in family therapy. Family Process, 21, 495-497.

1967.   Franklin, P. (1969), Family therapy of psychotics. American Journal of Psychoanalysis, 29, 727-736.

1968.   Fraser, J.S. (1982), Structural and strategic family therapy: A basis for marriage, or grounds for divorce? Journal of Marital and Family Therapy, 8, 13-22.

1969.   Frederickson, C.G. (1977), Life stress and marital conflict: A pilot study. Journal of Marriage and Family Counseling, 3, 41-47.

1970.   Frederickson, J. (1983), Exorcism as a process of family projective identification and indigenous psychotherapy. Family Therapy, 10, 165-172.

1971.   Freed, A.O. (1982), Building theory for family practice. Social Casework, 63, 472-481.

1972.   Freedman, B.J., and Rice, D.G. (1977), Marital therapy in prison: One partner "couple therapy." Psychiatry, 40, 175-183.

1973.   Freedman, D.S., and Thornton, A. (1979), The long term impact of pregnancy at marriage on the families economic circumstances. Family Planning Perspectives, 11, 6-13, 18-21.

1974.   Freedman, J., and Jacobsen, N.S. (1978), Review of R.F. Stahman and W.J. Hiebert's Klemer's counseling in marital and sexual problems: A clinicians handbook. Journal of Marriage and Family Counseling, 4, 120-121.

1975.   Freedman, J.S. (1979), Review of S. Minuchin, B. Rosman, and L. Baker's Psychosomatic families: Anorexia nervosa in context. American Journal of Family Therapy, 7, 83-84.

1976.   Freeman, D.R. (1965), Counseling engaged couples in small groups. Social Work, 10, 36-42.

1977.   Freeman, D.S. (1979), Person-to-person communication in the family. Canadian Mental Health, 27, 2-4.

1978.   Freeman, D.S. (1979), Person to person communication in the family. Family Therapy, 5, 277-287.

1979.   Freeman, D.S. (1981), Techniques of family therapy. New York: Aronson.

1980.   Freeman, D.S. (1976), The family as a system: Fact or fantasy? Comprehensive Psychiatry, 17, 735-747.

1981.   Freeman, D.S. (1976), Phases of family treatment. Family Coordinator, 25, 265-271.

1982.   Freeman, D.S. (1976), A systems approach to family therapy. Family Therapy, 3, 61-73.

1983.   Freeman, D.S. (1977), The family systems practice model: Underlying assumptions. Family Therapy, 4, 57-65.

1984.   Freeman, D.S. (1977), The use of time in family therapy. Family Therapy, 4, 195-206.

1985.   Freeman, D.S., and Trute, B. (1983), Ecological perspectives in family and community mental health practice. Canadian Journal of Community Mental Health, 10, 3-6.

1986.   Freeman, S.J., Lwavens, E.J., and McCulloch, D.J. (1969), Factors associated with success or failure in marital counseling. Family Coordinator, 18(2), 125-128.

1987.   Freeman, V.J. (1964), Differentiation of unity family therapy approaches prominent in the United States. International Journal of Social Psychiatry, Special Edition, 2, 35-46.

1988.   Freeman, V.J., Klein, A.F., Riehman, L.M., Lukoff, I.F., and Heisey, V.E. (1963), "Family group counseling" as differentiated from other "family therapies." International Journal of Group Psychotherapy, 13, 167-175.

1989.   French, A.P. (1977), Disturbed children and their families: Innovations in evaluation and treatment. New York, NY: Human Sciences Press.

1990.   French, A.P. (1979), Disturbed children and their families. Revised edition. New York, NY: Human Sciences Press.

1991.   Freund, J.C., and Cardwell, G. (1977), A multi-faceted response to an adolescent's school failure. Journal of Marriage and Family Counseling, 3, 49-57.

1992.   Frey, J. (1984), A family systems approach to illness-maintaining behaviors in chronically ill adolescents. Family Process, 23(2), 237-250.

1993.   Freyberger, H. (1978), Review of H. Stierlin, J. Ruckerembden, N. Wetzel, and M. Wirsching's Family therapy. Psychotherapy and Psychosomatics, 30, 243.

1994.   Frick, V., and Roemer, H. (1973), Proceedings: Marital conflicts and their psychosomatic effects. Archive fur Gynaekologie, 214, 31-33.

1995.   Friedell, R. (1980), Review of N.S. Jacobson and G. Margolin's Marital therapy. Journal of Sex and Marital Therapy, 6, 146.

1996.   Friedemann, A. (1967), (Diagnostic and therapeutic approach to the problem marriage.) Praxis der Psychotherapie, 12, 265-275.

1997.   Friedlander, M.L., and Highlen, P.S. (1984), Spatial view of the interpersonal structure of family interviews: Similarities and differences across counselors. Journal of Counseling Psychology, 31, 478-488.

1998.   Friedman, A.S. (1975), Interaction of drug therapy with marital therapy in depressive patients. Archives of General Psychiatry, 32, 619-637.

1999.   Friedman, A.S. (1963), The incomplete family in family therapy. Family Process, 2, 288-301.

2000.   Friedman, A.S. (1962), Symposium: Family treatment of schizophrenia: Family therapy as conducted in the home. Family Process, 1(1), 132-140.

2001.   Friedman, A.S. (1965), Psychotherapy for the whole family. New York, NY: Springer Publishing.

2002.   Friedman, A.S., and Friedman, C.J. (1971), Therapy with families of sexually acting-out girls. New York, NY: Springer Publishing.

2003.   Friedman, D. (1979), Blaming: An impasse in marital conflict-strategies for intervention. Journal of Psychiatric Nursing, 17, 8-13.

2004.   Friedman, D.B., and Hanson, H. (1968), Family therapy in pediatrics. Clinical Pediatrics, 7, 665-669.

2005.   Friedman, D.H., and Friedman, S. (1982), Day care as a setting for intervention in family systems. Social Casework, 63, 291-295.

2006.   Friedman, H.J. (1984), Review of M. Andolphi, C. Angelo, P. Menghi and A.M. Nicolocorigliano's Behind the family mask: Therapeutic change in rigid family systems. American Journal of Psychiatry, 141(6), 818.

2007.   Friedman, P.H. (1981), Integrative family therapy. Family Therapy, 8, 171-178.

2008.   Friedman, P.H. (1979), Review of J. Bell's Family therapy. Family Process, 18, 218-220.

2009.   Friedman, P.H. (1979), Review of L. Headley's Adults and their parents in family therapy: New directions in treatment. Contemporary Psychology, 24, 783.

2010.   Friedman, P.H. (1980), An integrative approach to the creation and alleviation of disease within the family. Family Therapy, 7(3), 179-195.

2011.   Friedman, P.H. (1974), Outline (alphabet) of 26 techniques of family and marital therapy: A through Z. Psychotherapy: Theory, Research and Practice, 11, 259-264.

2012.   Friedman, P.H. (1982), The multiple roles of the integrative marital psychotherapist. Family Therapy, 9, 109-118.

2013.   Friedman, R. (1971), Structured family-oriented therapy for school behavior and learning disorders. Child Welfare, 49, 187-195.

2014.   Friedman, R. (1978), Using the family school in the treatment of learning disabilities. Journal of Learning Disabilities, 11, 378-382.

2015.   Friedman, R. (1977), Techniques for rapid engagement in family therapy. Child Welfare, 56, 509-517.

2016.   Friedman, R. (1979), Review of E.B. Visher and J.S. Visher's Stepfamilies: A guide to working with stepparents and stepchildren. Child Welfare, 58, 555.

2017.   Friedman, R., Dreisen, K., Harris, L., Schoen, P., and Shulman, P. (1978), Parent power: Holding technique in the treatment of omnipotent children. International Journal of Family Counseling, 6(1), 66-73.

2018.   Friedman, W.H., Jelly, E., and Jelly, P. (1978), Group therapy in family medicine: II. Establishing the group. Journal of Family Practice, 6, 1243-1247.

2019.   Friedman, W.H., Jelly, E., and Jelly, P. (1978), Group therapy in family medicine: III. Starting the group. Journal of Family Practice, 7(2), 317-320.

2020.   Friedman, W.H., Jelly, E., and Jelly, P. (1978), Group therapy in family medicine. IV: A case report. Journal of Family Practice, 7(3), 501-503.

2021.   Friedman, W.H., Jelly, E., and Jelly, P. (1979), Group therapy for psychosomatic patients at a family practice center. Psychosomatics, 20, 671-677.

2022.   Friedrich, W.N., and Copeland, D.R. (1983), Brief family-focused intervention on the pediatric cancer unit. Journal of Marital and Family Therapy, 9, 293-298.

2023.   Friedrich, W.N., and Loftsgard, S.O. (1978), Comparison of two alcoholism scales with alcoholics and their wives. Journal of Clinical Psychology, 34, 784-786.

2024.   Friedrich, W.N., and Pollack, S.L. (1982), Extreme interpersonal sensitivity in family members. American Journal of Family Therapy, 10, 27-34.

2025.   Friesen, J. (1976), Family counseling: A new frontier for school counselors. Canadian Counselor, 10, 180-184.

2026.   Friesen, J.D. (1983), An ecological systems approach to family counseling. Canadian Counselor, 17, 98-104.

2027.   Friesen, V.I. (1983), The family in the etiology and treatment of drug abuse: Toward a balanced perspective. Advances in Alcohol and Substance Abuse, 3, 77-89.

2028.   Friesen, V.I. (1981), Family therapy and the historical movement. Family Therapy, 8, 211-221.

2029.   Friesen, V.I. (1979), On shame and the family. Family Therapy, 6(1), 39-58.

2030.   Friesen, V.I., and Casella, N.T. (1982), The rescuing therapist: A duplication of the pathogenic family system. American Journal of Family Therapy, 10, 57-62.

2031.   Froelich, J.E. (1978), Family crises intervention. Juvenile and Family Court Journal, 29, 3-12.

2032. Frohlich, H.H. (1982), Characteristics of therapist-patient relations in marital, sex and family counseling. Zeitschrift fur Arztliche Fortbildung (Jena), 76, 747-50.

2033. Frohlich, H.H. (1982), Factors in partner conflict. Zeitschrift fur Arztliche Fortbildung (Jena), 76, 168-72.

2034. Froiland, D.J., and Hozman, T.L. (1977), Counseling for constructive divorce. Personnel and Guidance Journal, 55(9), 525-529.

2035. Frommer, E.A. (1969), A day hospital for mentally disturbed children. Tidskrift voor Liekenverples, 22, 635-636.

2036. Frommer, E.A., and O'Shea, G. (1973), The importance of childhood experience in relation to problems of marriage and family-building. British Journal of Psychiatry, 123, 157-160.

2037. Frosh, S. (1982), Review of P. Baker's Basic family therapy. The British Journal of Psychology, 73, 562.

2038. Frosh, S. (1984), Review of G.R. Weeks and L.L. L'Abate's Paradoxical psychotherapy: Theory and practice with individuals, couples and families. British Journal of Psychology, 75, 136.

2039. Froyd, H.E. (1973), Counseling families of severely visually handicapped children. New Outlook, 67, 251-257.

2040. Frude, N. (1980), Methodological problems in the evaluation of family therapy. Journal of Family Therapy, 2, 29-44.

2041. Frude, N., and Dowling, E. (1980), A follow-up analysis of family therapy clients. Journal of Family Therapy, 2, 149-162.

2042. Frzier, F.L. (1975), Parent education: A comparison of the impact of the Adlerian and the behavioral approaches. Dissertation Abstracts International, 35, 4155-4156-A.

2043. Fuhr, R.A., Moos, R.H., and Dishotsky, N. (1981), The use of family assessment and feedback in ongoing family therapy. American Journal of Family Therapy, 9(1), 24-36.

2044. Fujda, E. (1970), Report about marital therapy. Protialkoholicky Obzor, 5(6), 149-151.

2045. Fulcomer, D.M., Edelman, S.K., and Lewis, E.C. 1961), Interdisciplinary marriage counseling in a university counseling service. Journal of Marriage and Family Living, 23, 273-275.

2046. Fuller, G.M., and Pew, W.L. (1978), Family and marriage education "recording". Individual Psychology, 15, 46-52.

2047. Fullmer, D.W. (1972), Family group consultation. Elementary School Guidance and Counseling, 7, 130-136.

2048. Fulmer, R.H. (1977), Families with schizophrenic sons: A description of family characteristics and a strategy for family therapy. Family Therapy, 4, 101-111.

2049.   Fulmer, R.H. (1983), A structural approach to unresolved mourning in single parent family systems. Journal of Marital and Family Therapy, 9, 259-269.

2050.   Fulmer, R.H., Cohen, S., and Monaco, G. (1985), Using psychological assessments in structural family therapy. Journal of Learning Disabilities, 18(3), 145.

2051.   Fulton, W.C. (1974), Counseling as an insured benefit: Perspectives from the insurance industry. Family Coordinator, 23(3), 291-294.

2052.   Funk, J.B. (1983), Special problems in divorce management. Journal of Developmental and Behavioral Pediatrics, 4, 108-112.

2053.   Furman, B. (1983), A review of the history of family therapy. Psykologia, 42, 93-99.

2054.   Furman, B., Lounavaara, and Rintala, H. (1983), Systems theory and family therapy. Duodecim, 103, 1719-1725.

2055.   Furnam, E.P. (1978), The death of a newborn: Care of the parents. Birth and Family Journal, 5, 214-218.

2056.   Furniss, T. (1983), Mutual influence and interlocking professional-family process in the treatment of child sexual abuse and incest. Child Abuse and Neglect, 7, 207-223.

2057.   Furniss, T., Bentovim, A., and Kinston, W. (1983), Clinical process recording in focal family therapy. Journal of Marital and Family Therapy, 9, 147-170.

2058.   Furrer, W. (1970), Analytical group therapy of couples. Ehe, 4, 162-168.

2059.   Furstenberg, F.F., Jr., and Crawford, A.G. (1978), Family support: Helping teenage mothers to cope. Family Planning Perspectives, 10, 322-333.

2060.   Fuzeki, B. (1973), Family psychotherapy. Orvosi Hetilap, 114, 2416-2418.

2061.   Gabriel, A., and Halpert, A. (1952), The effect of group therapy for mothers on their children. International Journal of Group Psychotherapy, 2, 159-171.

2062.   Gacic, B., Ivanovic, M., and Sedmak, T. (1981), Compensation and decompensation crisis in the family system in developing and treated alcoholism. Psihijatrija Danas, 13, 229-237.

2063.   Gagnier, T.T. (1977), Individual psychopathology and the family system: An exploratory study. Dissertation Abstracts International, 38, 895-896B.

2064.   Gagnon, J.H., Rosen, R.C., and Lieblum, S.R. (1982), Cognitive and social aspects of sexual dysfunction: Sexual scripts in sex therapy. Journal of Sex and Marital Therapy, 8(1), 44.

2065.   Gaines, T. (1978), Factors influencing failure to show for a family evaluation. International Journal of Family Counseling, 6, 57-61.

2066. Gaines, T. (1978), A technique for reducing parental obsessions in family therapy. Family Therapy, 5, 91-94.

2067. Gaines, T., and Stedman, J.M. (1976), Influence of separate interviews on clinicians' evaluative perceptions in family therapy. Journal of Consulting and Clinical Psychology, 47, 1138-1139.

2068. Gaines, T., and Stedman, J.M. (1981), Factors associated with dropping out of child and family treatment. American Journal of Family Therapy, 9, 45-51.

2069. Gaines, T., and Stedman, J.M. (1979), The influence of therapist experience upon evaluative perceptions of family members. American Journal of Family Therapy, 7, 44-48.

2070. Gajdos, K.C. (1984), A study of the development of family therapy as a treatment modality. Dissertation Abstracts International, 44, 2359-A.

2071. Gale, A. (1974), Group therapy for married couples. Australian New Zealand Journal of Psychiatry, 8, 187-192.

2072. Galinson, M.L. (1976), A study of the California statues regulating or related to the practice of marriage and family counseling. Dissertation Abstracts International, 37, 2477-B.

2073. Gallagher, C. (1975), The marriage encounter. Garden City, NY: Doubleday and Co., Inc.

2074. Gallant, D.M., Bishop, M.P., Stoy, B., Faulkner, M.A., and Paternoski, L. (1970), Group psychotherapy with married couples: A successful technique in New Orleans Alcoholism Clinic patients. Journal of the Louisiana Medical Society, 122, 41-44.

2075. Gallego, I., Katz de Salmun, F., Paniza, G., and Veiga, C. (1979), Psychotherapy of a plurifamiliar group of inpatients in a therapeutic community. Acta Psiquiatrica Y Psicologica de America Latina, 25, 212-218.

2076. Gallo, F.T. (1977), Counseling the breast cancer patient and her family. Family Therapy, 4, 247-253.

2077. Galper, M.F. (1981), The cult phenomenon: Behavioral science perspectives applied to therapy. Marriage and Family Review, 4(3/4), 141-149.

2078. Gambrill, E.D. (1978), Marital communication and decision making analysis assessment and change. International Journal of Family Counseling, 6, 90-91.

2079. Gammer, C. (1983), Phased family therapy. Psykisk Halsa, 24, 91-121.

2080. Ganahl, G.F. (1982), Effects of client, treatment, and therapist variables on the outcome of structured marital enrichment. Dissertation Abstracts International, 43, 4576-B.

2081. Gangsel, L.B. (1971), Manual for the group premarital education and counseling of protestant young adults. Dissertation Abstracts International, 31(11), 6342-A.

2082.   Gansheroff, N., Boszormenyi-Nagy, I., and Matrullo, J. (1980), Clinical and legal issues in the family therapy record. Advances in Family Psychiatry, 2, 221-226.

2083.   Gansheroff, W., Boszormenyi-Nagy, I., and Matrullo, J. (1977), Clinical and legal issues in the family therapy record. Hospital and Community Psychiatry, 28, 911-913.

2084.   Gant, B.L. (1979), Behavioral approach to building more positive marriage and family relationships. In: N. Stinnet, B. Chesser, and J. Defrain (Eds.), Building family strengths. Lincoln, NE: University of Nebraska Press.

2085.   Gant, B.L., Barnard, J.D., Kuehn, F.E., Jones, H.H., and Christopher, E.R. (1981), A behaviorally based approach for improving intrafamilial communication patterns. Journal of Clinical Child Psychology, 10(2), 102-106.

2086.   Gantman, C.A. (1980), A closer look at families that work well. International Journal of Family Therapy, 2, 106-119.

2087.   Garb, R., and Kutz, I. (1980), Families in transition: The role of the father. Group Analysis, 13, 124-127.

2088.   Garcia, V.L. (1975), Case study: Family art evaluation in a Brazilian guidance clinic. American Journal of Art Therapy, 14, 132-139.

2089.   Garfield, R. (1979), Integrative training model for family therapists: Hahnemann master of family therapy program. Journal of Marital and Family Therapy, 5, 15-22.

2090.   Garfield, R. (1979), Review of H. Kwiatkowska's Family therapy and evaluation through art. Art in Psychotherapy, 6, 199.

2091.   Garfield, R., and Schwoeri, L. (1981), A family consultation model: Breaking a therapeutic impasse. International Journal of Family Psychiatry, 2, 251-267.

2092.   Garfinkel, H.N. (1981), Family systems personality profile: An assessment instrument based on the Bowen theory. Dissertation Abstracts International, 41, 2757-B.

2093.   Garland, D.R. (1979), The effects of active listening skills training upon interaction behavior, perceptual accuracy, and marital adjustment of couples participating in a marriage enrichment program. Dissertation Abstracts International, 40(7), 3481-B.

2094.   Garrett, L.D. (1979), Group behavioral therapy versus family behavioral therapy in treatment of obese adolescent females. Dissertation Abstracts International, 40, 1364-1365-B.

2095.   Garrigan, J.J., and Bambrick, A. (1977), Family therapy for disturbed children: Some experimental results in special education. Journal of Marriage and Family Counseling, 3, 83-93.

2096.   Garrigan, J.J., and Bambrick, A.F. (1977), Introducing novice therapists to go-between techniques of family therapy. Family Process, 16, 237-246.

2097.   Garrigan, J.J., and Bambrick, A.F. (1975), Short term family therapy
        with emotionally disturbed children. Journal of Marriage and Family
        Counseling, 1, 379-385.

2098.   Garrigan, J.J., and Bambrick, A.F. (1979), New findings in research on
        go-between process. International Journal of Family Therapy, 1, 76-85.

2099.   Garrison, C., and Weber, J. (1981), Famiy crisis intervention using
        multiple impact therapy. Social Casework, 62(10), 585.

2100.   Garrison, J.E. (1979), Review of J.F. Perez's Family counseling.
        Contemporary Psychology, 24, 848.

2101.   Garrison, T. (1979), Alcoholism can be a family problem. Life Health,
        94, 13-15.

2102.   Gartner, D. (1979), Group sessions for adolescents and for parents
        awaiting therapy in a child guidance clinic. Hospital and Community
        Psychiatry, 30, 161-162.

2103.   Gartner, R.B., Bass, A., and Wolbert, S. (1979), The use of the one-way
        mirror in restructuring family boundaries. Family Therapy, 6(1), 27-37.

2104.   Gartner, R.B., Fulmer, R.H., Weinshel, M., and Goldklank, S. (1978), The
        family life cycle: Developmental crises and their structural impact on
        families in a community mental health center. Family Process, 17, 47-
        58.

2105.   Garvey, M., and Tuason, V.B. (1979), Physician marriages. Journal of
        Clinical Psychiatry, 40, 129-131.

2106.   Garwood, D.S., and Augenbraun, B. (1968), Coordinated
        psychotherapeutic approach to a familial dysautonomic preschool boy
        and his parents. Psychoanalytic Review, 55, 62-78.

2107.   Garza, M.K. (1978), The status of marriage and family counseling in
        graduate counselor education programs. Dissertation Abstracts
        International, 39, 3372-A.

2108.   Gaspard, N.J. (1970), The family of the patient with long-term illness.
        Nursing Clinics of North America, 5, 77.

2109.   Gatti, F., and Coleman, C. (1976), Community network therapy: An
        approach to aiding families with troubled children. American Journal of
        Orthopsychiatry, 46, 608-617.

2110.   Gattringer, B. (1977), The problem child in the neurological practice:
        New findings in family research. Wiener Medizinische Wochenschrift,
        127, 376-379.

2111.   Gattringer, B. (1977), Retrospective study of one year of family therapy
        in a neurological practice. Nervenarzt, 48, 326-330.

2112.   Gauron, E.F., and Breeden, S.A. (1975), A married couple in separate
        therapy groups. Journal of Family Counseling, 3, 24-28.

2113.   Gavilo, H.M. (1983), Family therapy and behavior therapy approach to treating a child with elective mutism. Dissertation Abstracts International, 43, 3014-B.

2114.   Gear, M.C., and Liendo, E.C. (1976), Psychoanalysis, semiology and family communication. Evolution Psychiatrique, 41, 239-272.

2115.   Geddes, M., and Medway, J. (1977), The symbolic drawing of the family life space. Family Process, 16, 219-228.

2116.   Gee, A.S. (1967), The values of marriage counselors. Dissertation Abstracts International, 27, 3269-B.

2117.   Gehring, T.M. (1983), Diagnostic significance of the system-oriented initial family interview in ambulatory child psychiatry. Praxis der Kinderpsychologie und Kinderpsychiatrie, 32, 218-224.

2118.   Gehrke, S., and Kirschenbaum, M. (1967), Survival patterns in family conjoint therapy. Family Process, 6, 67-80.

2119.   Gehrke, S., and Moxom, J. (1962), Diagnostic classifications and treatment techniques in marriage counseling. Family Process, 1(2), 253-264.

2120.   Geismar, L.L., and Ayres, B. (1959), A method for evaluating the social functioning of families under treatment. Social Work, 4, 101-108.

2121.   Geiss, S.K., and O'Leary, K.D. (1981), Therapist ratings of frequency and severity of marital problems: Implications for research. Journal of Marital and Family Therapy, 7, 515-520.

2122.   Geist, R.A. (1979), Onset of chronic illness in children and adolescents: Psychotherapeutic and consultative intervention. American Journal of Orthopsychiatry, 49, 4-23.

2123.   Gelcer, E. (1983), Mourning in a family affair. Family Process, 22, 501-516.

2124.   Gelinas, D.J. (1978), Conceptual frameworks in psychology: A modified Kuhnian analysis of the emergence of double bind family therapy. Dissertation Abstracts International, 39, 1477-B.

2125.   Gelinas, P.M. (1979), A family life education program. Canadian Mental Health, 27, 12.

2126.   Gellert, S.D., and Wilson, G. (1978), Family therapy. Transactional Analysis Journal, 8, 38-43.

2127.   Gendreau, P. (1984), Stanton, Todd and Associates: The family therapy of drug abuse and addiction (Review). Canadian Journal of Criminology, 26(1), 112-113.

2128.   Genovese, R.J. (1975), Marrige encounter. Small Group Behavior, 6, 45-56.

2129.   Genthner, R.W., and Veltkamp, L.J. (1977), A scale for assessing family dysfunction-function. International Journal of Family Counseling, 5(1), 79-85.

2130.   Gentili, P., and De Petris, R. (1981), The sphere of the "between" in systematic family therapy. Psichiatria Generale E Dell'eta Evolutiva, 73, 293–305.

2131.   Genton, M. (1983), Marriage counseling: For which motives? Krankenpflege (Bern), 4, 54–56.

2132.   Gentry, C.E. (1980), Review of J.A. Kroth's Child sexual abuse: Analysis of a family therapy approach. Social Work, 25, 416.

2133.   Gentry, C.E., and Eaddy, V.B. (1980), Treatment of children in spouse abusive families. Victimology, 5, 240–250.

2134.   Gerace, L. (1981), Phenomenon of early engagement in family therapy. Journal of Psychiatric Nursing, 19, 29–32.

2135.   Gerard, D. (1982), Sexual functioning after mastectomy: Life vs. lab. Journal of Sex and Marital Therapy, 8, 305–315.

2136.   Gerber, D. (1984), Aggression, possible family therapy in child abuse. Don't seek the culprits in the parents. Krankenpflegel, 5, 32–33.

2137.   Gerber, G.L. (1977), Review of P.A. Martin's A marital therapy manual. Group, 1, 205–207.

2138.   Gerhardt, U. (1981), Family therapy in theory and practice. Praxis der Kinderpsychologie und Kinderpsychiatrie, 30, 274–285.

2139.   Gerlicher, K. (1983), Tooth, mouth, and jaw problems from the viewpoint of psychoanalytically-oriented family therapy. Fortschrift der Kieferorthopadie, 67, 224–231.

2140.   Gerrish, M.J. (1970), The family therapist is a nurse. Journal of Nursing, 17, 63–67.

2141.   Gershenson, J., and Cohen, M.S. (1978), Through the looking glass: The experiences of two family therapy trainees with live supervision. Family Process, 17, 225–230.

2142.   Gerson, M.T., and Barsky, M. (1979), New family therapist: Glossary of terms. American Journal of Family Therapy, 7, 15–30.

2143.   Gerstenberg, W. (1979), Psychodrama in ambulatory psychotherapy with parents and children. Praxis der Kinderpsychologie und Kinderpsychiatrie, 28, 293–302.

2144.   Gerver, J., Peterson, R., and Arrill, M. (1965), Family therapy: A selected annotated bibliography. Washington, D.C.: Government Printing Office, National Clearinghouse for Mental Health Information.

2145.   Giannini, M.J., and Goodman, L. (1963), Counseling families during the crisis reaction to Mongolism. American Journal of Mental Deficiency, 67, 740–747.

2146.   Gibbs, H.W., and Achterberg-Lawlis, J. (1979), The spouse as facilitator for esophageal speech: A research perspective. Journal of Surgical Oncology, 11, 89–94.

2147.   Giblin, P., Sprenkle, P.H., and Sheehan, R. (1985), Enrichment outcome research: A meta-analysis of premarital, marital and family interventions. Journal of Marital and Family Therapy, 11, 257-272.

2148.   Gilbert, G.C. (1974), Counseling black adolescent parents. Social Work, 19(1), 88-95.

2149.   Gilbert, R., Christensen, A., and Margolin, G. (1984), Patterns of alliances in nondistressed and multiproblem families. Family Process, 23(1), 75-88.

2150.   Gilder, R., Buschman, P.R., Sitarz, A.L., and Wolff, J.A. (1978), Group therapy with parents of children with leukemia. American Journal of Psychotherapy, 32(2), 276-288.

2151.   Gill, H., and Temperley, J. (1974), Time-limited marital treatment in a foursome. British Journal of Medical Psychology, 47, 153-162.

2152.   Gill, H.S., and Singh, N. (1972), Treatment of the marital dyad in a foursome: An illustrative case study. Postgraduate Medical Journal, 48, 555-562.

2153.   Gillette, T.L. (1959), Toward a student-centered marriage course: A progress report. Marriage and Family Living, 21, 155-159.

2154.   Gilmore, A. (1973), Attitudes of the elderly to marriage. Gerontologia Clinica, 15, 124-132.

2155.   Ginck, G.H., Reiner, B.S., and Smith, B.O. (1965), Group counseling with unmarried mothers. Journal of Marriage and the Family, 27, 224-229.

2156.   Gingras, M., Adam, D., and Chagnon, G.J. (1983), Marital enrichment: The contribution of sixteen process variables to the effectiveness of a program. Journal of Sex and Marital Therapy, 9, 121-136.

2157.   Gingras-Baker, S. (1976), Sex role stereotyping and marriage counseling. Journal of Marriage and Family Counseling, 2(4), 355-366.

2158.   Ginsberg, C. (1967), Versuch einer gross familie: Die "family by choice als mittel zur rehabilitierung des menschlichen. (The trial of an extended family: The "family by choice" as a means of rehabilitating the human element.) Psychotherapy and Psychosomatics, 15, 24-25.

2159.   Ginsberg, C.K. (1968), Experiment with a "greater family." The "family by choice" as means for the rehabilitation of human values. Psychotherapy and Psychosomatics, 16, 119-127.

2160.   Gladding, S.T. (1984), Training effective family therapists: Data and hope. Journal of Counseling and Development, 63, 103-104.

2161.   Glaser, D., Furniss, T., and Bingley, L. (1984), Focal family therapy: The assessment stage. Journal of Family Therapy, 6, 265-274.

2162.   Glass, J.R. (1974), Family therapy: An overview. Intellect, 102, 106-108.

2163.   Glasser, L.N., and Glasser, P.H. (1977), Hedonism and the family: Conflict in values? Journal of Marriage and Family Counseling, 3, 11-18.

2164.   Glasser, P.H. (1963), Changes in family equilibrium during
        psychotherapy. Family Process, 2, 245-264.

2165.   Gleason, J., and Prescott, M.R. (1977), Group techniques for pre-marital
        preparation. Family Coordinator, 26, 277-280.

2166.   Glendening, S.E., and Wilson, A.J., III (1972), Experiments in group pre-
        marital counseling. Social Casework, 53, 551-562.

2167.   Glick, I., and Haley, J. (1981), Family therapy and research: An
        annotated bibliography. Second edition. New York: Grune and Stratton.

2168.   Glick, I.D., and Borus, J.F. (1984), Marital and family therapy for
        troubled physicians and their families: A bridge over troubled waters.
        Journal of the American Medical Association, 25, 1855-1888.

2169.   Glick, I.D., and Haley, J. (1971), Family therapy and research: An
        annotated bibliography of articles and books. New York: Grune and
        Stratton.

2170.   Glick, I.D., and Kessler, D., (Eds.) (1980), Marital and family therapy:
        An introductory text. ed. 2. New York: Grune and Stratton.

2171.   Glick, I.D., and Kessler, D.R. (1974), Marital and family therapy. New
        York: Grune and Stratton.

2172.   Glick, I.D., and Patten, J.T. (1983) Review of R.J. Green and J.L.
        Framo's Family therapy: Major contributions. Journal of the American
        Academy of Child Psychiatry, 22, 212.

2173.   Glick, I.D., and Spencer, J.H. (1985), Inpatient family therapy: On the
        boundary between past and present. Family Process, 24, 349-351.

2174.   Gliedman, L.H., Rosenthal, D., Frank, J.D., and Nash, H.T. (1956),
        Group therapy of alcoholics with concurrent group meetings of their
        wives. Quarterly Journal of Studies on Alcohol, 17, 655-670.

2175.   Glisson, D.H. (1976), A review of behavioral marital counseling: Has
        practice turned out theory? Psychological Record, 26(1), 95-104.

2176.   Gogan, J.L., Koocher, G.P., Fine, W.E., Foster, D.J., and O'Malley, J.E.
        (1979), Pediatric cancer survival and marriage: Issues affecting adult
        adjustment. American Journal of Orthopsychiatry, 49, 423-430.

2177.   Golann, S. (1984), Review of L. L'Abate's Family psychology. American
        Journal of Family Therapy, 12(4), 71.

2178.   Gold, J.H., and Gold, E. (1981), The belittled wife: Social, legal, and
        psychotherapeutic considerations. Canadian Journal of Psychiatry, 26,
        402-405.

2179.   Goldberg, C. (1975), Courtship contracts in marital therapy. Journal of
        Family Counseling, 3, 40-45.

2180.   Goldberg, D.C. (Ed.) (1985), Contemporary marriage: Special issues in
        couples therapy. Homewood, IL: Dorsey Press.

2181.   Goldberg, H.K. (1979), Hearing impairment: A family crisis. Social Work in Health Care, 5, 33-40.

2182.   Goldberg, K. (1979), Review of Psychoanalysis and family therapy. Canadian Mental Health, 27, 26.

2183.   Goldberg, M. (1982), The dynamics of marital interaction and marital conflict. Psychiatric Clinics of North America, 5, 449-467.

2184.   Goldberg, M. (1967), Counseling sexually incompatible marriage partners. Postgraduate Medicine, 42, 62-68.

2185.   Goldberg, M. (1974), The uses of dreams in conjoint marital therapy. Journal of Sex and Marital Therapy, 1, 75-81.

2186.   Golden, D.A., and Davis, J.G. (1974), Counseling parents after the birth of an infant with Down's syndrome. Children Today, 3(2), 7-11.

2187.   Golden, J.S, Price S., Heinrich, A.G., and Lobitz, W.C. (1978), Group vs. couple treatment of sexual dysfunctions. Archives of Sexual Behavior, 7, 593-602.

2188.   Golden, J.S. (1982), Review of M. Cook and R. McHenry's Sexual attraction. Journal of Sex and Marital Therapy, 8, 253.

2189.   Golden, J.S. (1982), Review of A.K. Offit's Night thoughts: Reflections of a sex therapist. Journal of Sex and Marital Therapy, 8, 254.

2190.   Golden, K.M. (1977), Psychiatry: The physician as family therapist. Postgraduate Medical Journal, 62, 209-223.

2191.   Golden, N., Chirlin, P., and Shone, B. (1970), Tuesday children: Therapy in groups for children with learning disabilities and their mothers. Social Casework, 51, 599-605.

2192.   Goldenberg, I., Stier, S., and Preston, T.A. (1975), The use of multiple family marathon as a teaching device. Journal of Marriage and Family Counseling, 1, 343-349.

2193.   Goldenberg, I., and Goldenberg, H. (1975), A family approach to psychological services. American Journal of Psychoanalysis, 35, 317-328.

2194.   Goldenberg, I., and Goldenberg, H. (1979), Family therapy: An overview. Monterrey, CA: Brooks/Cole.

2195.   Goldenburg, I., and Goldenburg, H. (1984), Treating the dual career couple. American Journal of Family Therapy, 12(2), 29-37.

2196.   Golder, V. (1985), Feminism and family therapy. Family Process, 24(1), 31-48.

2197.   Goldfried, M.R. (1979), Review of T.J. Paolino and B.S. McCrady's Marriage and marital therapy: Psychoanalytic, behavioral, and systems theory perspectives. American Journal of Family Therapy, 7, 96-98.

2198.   Goldklank, S. (1983), My family made me do it: The influence of family of origin process on family therapists' occupational choice. Dissertation Abstracts International, 43, 2336-B.

2199.   Goldman, H.H. (1980), The post-hospital mental patient and family therapy: Prospects and populations. Journal of Marital and Family Therapy, 6(4), 447-452.

2200.   Goldman, J., and Coane, J. (1977), Family therapy after the divorce: Developing a strategy. Family Process, 16, 357-362.

2201.   Goldsmith, J. (1983), Review of E. Visher and J. Visher's How to win as a stepfamily. Journal of Marital and Family Therapy, 9, 218.

2202.   Goldsmith, J.M., and Lang, J. (1981), Direct treatment of children in the family and children's agency: Toward an integrated practice. Family and Child Mental Health Journal, 7, 138.

2203.   Goldsmith, M.J. (1979), The Rhode Island connection: A family day care training program. Child Today, 8, 2-5, 37.

2204.   Goldstein, H. (Ed.). (1969), Readings in family therapy. New York: Irvington.

2205.   Goldstein, H.K., Cohen, A., Thames, M., and Galloway, J.P. (1974), The influence of group therapy with relatives on rehabilitation clients and their families. Small Group Behavior, 5, 374-384.

2206.   Goldstein, M.J. (1980), Family therapy during the aftercare treatment of acute schizophrenia. In: J.S. Strauss, M. Bowers, J.W. Downey, S. Fleck, S. Jackson, and I. Levine (Eds.), Psychotherapy of schizophrenia, pp. 77-89. New York: Plenum.

2207.   Goldstein, M.J., Rodnick, E.H., Evans, J.R., May, P.R., and Steinberg, M.R. (1978), Drug and family therapy in the aftercare of acute schizophrenics. Archives of General Psychiatry, 35, 1169-1177.

2208.   Goldstein, M.Z. (1977), Fathering: A neglected activity. American Journal of Psychoanalysis, 37, 325-336.

2209.   Goll, K. (1979), Role structure and subculture in families of elective mutists. Family Process, 18, 55-68.

2210.   Gomberg, M.R. (1946), The Gold case: A marital problem. In: J. Taft (Ed.), Counseling and protective service as family case work. Philadelphia, PA: School of Social Work.

2211.   Gomberg, R.M., and Levinson, F.T. (1951), Diagnosis and process in family counseling. New York: Family Service Association.

2212.   Gomersall, J.D. (1972), Family therapy. Drugs and Society, 1, 12-14.

2213.   Goodall, J. (1979), Malnutrition and the family: Deprivation in Kwashiorkor. Proceedings of the Nutrician Society, 38, 17-27.

2214.   Goodman, B., and Goodman, N. (1976), Effects of parent orientation meetings on parent-child communication about sexuality and family life. Family Coordinator, 24, 284-291.

2215.   Goodman, E.S. (1973), Marriage counseling as science: Some research considerations. Family Coordinator, 22(1), 111-116.

2216.   Goodrich, W. (1972), Changes in child psychiatry training required by developmental-adaptive theory. Journal of Nervous and Mental Disease, 154, 213-220.

2217.   Goodrich, W. (1975), Review of S. Minuchin's Families and family therapy. Contemporary Psychologist, 20, 395-396.

2218.   Goodstein, R.K. (1977), Psychotherapy with phobic patients: The marriage relationship as the source of symptoms and focus of treatment. American Journal of Psychotherapy, 31(2), 285-293.

2219.   Goodwin, H.M. (1974), The functional approach in the private practice of marriage counseling. Journal of the Otto Rank Association, 9(1), 26-29.

2220.   Goodwin, H.M. (1966), Indication for marriage counseling: Methods and goals. Comprehensive Psychiatry, 7, 454-462.

2221.   Goodwin, R.H. (1972), The family life educator as change agent: A participant in problems and solutions. Family Coordinator, 21, 303-312.

2222.   Goolishian, H.A. (1979), Review of M. Bowen's Family therapy in clinical practice. Journal of Marital and Family Therapy, 5, 120.

2223.   Goolishian, H.A. (1962), Family treatment approaches: II. A brief psychotherapy program for disturbed adolescents. American Journal of Orthopsychiatry, 32, 142-148.

2224.   Goolishian, H.A. (1983), Review of L. Hoffman's Foundations of family therapy: A conceptual framework for systems change. Contemporary Psychology, 28, 17.

2225.   Goolishian, H.A., Anderson, H.K., and Epstein, N.B. (1980), Engagement techniques in family therapy. International Journal of Family Therapy, 2, 95-98.

2226.   Gootnick, A.T. (1976), The use of the minicontract in family therapy. Family Therapy, 3, 169-173.

2227.   Gordon, R.H., and Kilpatrick, C.A. (1977), Program of group counseling for men who accompany women seeking legal abortions. Community Mental Health Journal, 13(4), 291-295.

2228.   Gordon, R.M. (1983), Systems-object relations view of marital therapy: Revenge and re-raising. In L.R. Wolberg and M.L. Aronson (Eds.), Group and family therapy: 1982. New York: Brunner/Mazel.

2229.   Gordon, S., and Waldo, M. (1984), The effects of assertiveness training on couples relationships. American Journal of Family Therapy, 12(1), 73-78.

2230.   Gordon, S.B. (1979), Responsive parenting: An approach to training parents of problem children. American Journal of Community Psychology, 7, 45-56.

2231.   Gordon, S.B. (1975), Multiple assessment of behavior modification with families. Journal of Consulting and Clinical Psychology, 43, 917-919.

2232.   Gorecki, J. (1965), Marriage counseling in the light of divorce studies. Kultura I Spoleczenstwo, 9(1), 119-126.

2233.   Goren, S. (1979), A systems approach to emotional disorders of children. Nursing Clinics of North America, 14, 457-465.

2234.   Gorton, T.A., Doerfler, D.L., Hulka, B.S., and Tyroler, H.A. (1979), Intrafamilial patterns of illness reports and physician visits in a community sample. Journal of Health and Social Behavior, 20, 37-44.

2235.   Goss, B.E. (1978), An investigation of the effects of expressed need for marital counseling and of gender on marital satisfaction. Dissertation Abstracts International, 39, 2496-B.

2236.   Gottlieb, A., and Pattison, E.M. (1966), Married couples group psychotherapy. Archives of General Psychiatry, 14, 143-152.

2237.   Gottlieb, S.B. (1960), Group psychotherapy for married couples. Unpublished doctoral dissertation, Columbia University.

2238.   Gottlieb, S.B. (1960), Response of married couples included in a group of single patients. International Journal of Group Psychotherapy, 10, 143-159.

2239.   Gottman, J.M. (1980), Consistency of nonverbal affect and affect reciprocity in marital interaction. Journal of Consulting and Clinical Psychology, 48, 711-717.

2240.   Gottschalk, L.A., Brown, S.B., Bruney, E.H., Shumate, L.W., and Uliana, R.L. (1973), An evaluation of a parents' group in a child-centered clinic. Psychiatry, 36, 157-171.

2241.   Gould, E., and Degroot, D. (1981), Inter- and intrafamily interaction in multi-family group therapy. American Journal of Family Therapy, 9, 65-73.

2242.   Gould, E., and Glick, I.D. (1977), The effects of family presence and brief family intervention on global outcome for hospitalized schizophrenic patients. Family Process, 16, 503-510.

2243.   Graber, A.L., Christman, B., and Boehm, F.H. (1978), Planning for sex, marriage, contraception, and pregnancy. Diabetes Care, 1, 202-203.

2244.   Grady, M. (1975), An assessment of the behavioral scientist's role with the dying patient and the family. Military Medicine, 140(11), 789-792.

2245.   Graeven, D.B., and Schaef, R.D. (1978), Family life and levels of involvement in adolescent heroin epidemic. International Journal of Addiction, 13, 747-771.

2246.   Graff, R.W., and Hornf, A.M. (1973), Counseling needs of married students. Journal of College Student Personnel, 14(5), 438-442.

2247.   Graham, F.W., Kadis, A.L., Berger, M.M., and McCormick, C.G. (1960), Discussion – group treatment of married couples: A symposium. International Journal of Group Psychotherapy, 10, 160-173.

2248.   Graham, P. (1974), Child psychiatry and psychotherapy. Journal of
         Child Psychology and Psychiatry and Allied Disciplines, 15, 59-66.

2249.   Grainick, A. (1969), Family therapy in a private hospital setting.
         Current Psychiatric Therapy, 9, 179-181.

2250.   Gralnick, A. (1962), Family psychotherapy: General and specific
         considerations. American Journal of Orthopsychiatry, 32, 515-526.

2251.   Gralnick, A. (1962), The family in psychotherapy. Psychiatric
         Quarterly, Supplement, 36, 269-277.

2252.   Gralnick, A. (1963), Conjoint family therapy: Its role in rehabilitation
         of the inpatient and family. Journal of Nervous and Mental Disease, 136,
         500-506.

2253.   Gralnick, A., and D'Elia, F. (1973), "Administration" as therapy of the
         inpatient's family. Journal of the National Association of Private
         Psychiatric Hospitals, 5, 22-27.

2254.   Granat, J.P. (1978), Marital disintegration among parents of mentally
         retarded adults and adolescents: Implications for psychological
         counseling. Dissertation Abstracts International, 39, 3469-A.

2255.   Grand, H. (1983), Unique transference elements in co-therapy groups.
         In L.R. Wolberg and M.L. Aronson (Eds.), Group and family therapy:
         1982. New York: Brunner/Mazel.

2256.   Grando, R. (1975), An approach to family crisis intervention. Family
         Therapy, 2(3), 201.

2257.   Granger, J.A. (1974), Including the younger child in conjoint family
         evaluation and therapy. Psychiatric Forum, 4, 21-26.

2258.   Granite, U., and Goldman, S.B. (1975), Rehabilitation therapy for burn
         patients and spouses. Social Casework, 56(10), 593-598.

2259.   Granvold, D.K., and Tarrant, R. (1983), Structured marital separation as
         a marital treatment method. Journal of Marital and Family Therapy, 9,
         189-198.

2260.   Grauer, H., Betts, D., and Birnborn, F. (1973), Welfare emotions and
         family therapy in geriatrics. Journal of the American Geriatric Society,
         21(1), 21-24.

2261.   Graves, M.H. (Ed.) (1970), Help for troubled parents. New York:
         Vantage.

2262.   Gray, C.B. (1976), Comparison of basic couples' encounters and
         marriage encounters. Small Group Behavior, 7, 197-220.

2263.   Gray, E., and Morgan, D.K. (1979), Desired family size and sex of
         children in Botucatu, Brazil. Journal of Heredity, 70, 67-69.

2264.   Gray, J.D. (1980), Counseling women who want both a profession and a
         family. Personnel and Guidance Journal, 59(1), 43-48.

2265.   Green, R. (1948), Trends in orthopsychiatric therapy: Treatment of
         parent-child relationships. American Journal of Orthopsychiatry, 18,
         442-446.

2266.   Green, R., Ferguson, L.R., Framo, J.L., Shapiro, R.J., and LaPerriere,
         K. (1979), A symposium on family therapy training for psychologists.
         Professional Psychology, 10, 859-862.

2267.   Green, R., and Fuller, M. (1973), Group therapy with feminine boys and
         their parents. International Journal of Group Psychotherapy, 23(1), 54-
         68.

2268.   Green, R.J., and Framo, J.L., Eds. (1980), Family therapy: The major
         approaches. New York: International Universities Press.

2269.   Green, R.J., and Saeger, K.E. (1982), Learning to "think systems": Five
         writing assignments. Journal of Marital and Family Therapy, 8, 285-294.

2270.   Green, R.R. 1978), Counseling techniques for working with the family of
         the hearing impaired child. Hearing Rehabilitation Quarterly, 3, 17-20.

2271.   Greenbaum, H. (1983), On the nature of marriage and marriage
         therapy. Journal of the American Academy of Psychoanalysis, 11, 283-
         297.

2272.   Greenbaum, H. (1973), Marriage, family, and parenthood. American
         Journal of Psychiatry, 130, 1262-1265.

2273.   Greenberg, G.S. (1980), Review of T. J. Paolino and B.S. McCrady's
         Marriage and marital therapy: Psychoanalytic, behavioral and systems
         theory perspectives. Family Process, 19, 203.

2274.   Greenberg, G.S. (1978), Review of P. Papp's Family therapy: Full-
         length case studies. Family Process, 7, 231.

2275.   Greenberg, G.S. (1977), The family interactional perspective: A study
         and examination of the work of Don D. Jackson. Family Process, 16,
         385-412.

2276.   Greenberg, G.S. (1974), Conjoint family theory: An entree to a new
         behavior therapy. Dissertation Abstracts International, 35, 3878-3879-
         A.

2277.   Greenberg, G.S. (1983), Diagnosis and assessment in family therapy:
         VII. The beginning family therapist and dilemmas in diagnosis. Family
         Therapy Collections, 11, 133-142.

2278.   Greenberg, I.M., Glick, I., Match, S., Riback, S.S., and Oaks, G. (1964),
         Family therapy: Indications and rationale. Archives of General
         Psychiatry, 10, 7-23.

2279.   Greenberg, M.T., and Calderon, R. (1984), Early intervention:
         Outcomes and issues. Topics in Early Childhood Special Education, 11,
         1-9.

2280.   Greenberg, S. (1983), The family in later life: A descriptive study.
         Dissertation Abstracts International, 44, 1387A.

2281.   Greendorfer, S.L., and Lewko, J.H. (1978), Role of family members in sport socialization of children. Research Quarterly, 49, 146–152.

2282.   Greene, B.L., Broadhurst, B.P., and Lustig, N. (1964), Psychotherapy of marital disharmony: The combined approach. American Journal of Orthopsychiatry, 34, 320–321.

2283.   Greene, B.L., Lee, R.R., and Lustig, N. (1973), Transient structured distance as a maneuver in marital therapy. Family Coordinator, 22(1), 15–22.

2284.   Greene, B.L., Lee, R.R., and Lustig, N. (1975), Treatment of marital disharmony where one spouse has a primary affective disorder (manic depressive illness): I. General overview - 100 couples. Journal of Marriage and Family Counseling, 1, 39–50.

2285.   Greene, B.L., Lustig, N., and Lee, R.R. (1976), Marital therapy when one spouse has a primary affective disorder. American Journal of Psychiatry, 133(7), 827–830.

2286.   Greene, L.R. (1983), The patient-staff community meeting as therapeutic agent for borderline personality disorders. In L.R. Wolberg and M.L. Aronson (Eds.), Group and family therapy: 1982. New York: Brunner/Mazel.

2287.   Greenley, J.R. (1972), The psychiatric patient's family and length of hospitalization. Journal of Health and Social Behavior, 13, 25–37.

2288.   Greer, S.E., and D'Zurilla, T.J. (1975), Behavioral approaches to marital discord and conflict. Journal of Marriage and Family Counseling, 1, 299–315.

2289.   Gregg, G.S. (1968), Comprehensive professional help for the retarded child and his family. Hospital and Community Psychiatry, 19, 122–124.

2290.   Griedman, A.A. (1965), Psychotherapy for the whole family. New York: Springer Publishing.

2291.   Griest, D.L., and Wells, K.C. (1983), Behavioral family therapy with conduct disorders in children. Behavior Therapy, 14, 37–53.

2292.   Grob, M.C., Eisen, S.V., and Berman, J.S. (1978), Three years of follow-up monitoring: Perspectives of formerly hospitalized patients and their families. Comprehensive Psychiatry, 19, 491–499.

2293.   Groce, P.C. (1973), Bargaining: A system of marital counseling for the family practitioner. Journal of Maine Medical Association, 64, 224–225.

2294.   Groce, P.C. (1974), Bargaining: A system of marital counseling for the practitioner. Journal of the Kentucky Medical Association, 72, 77–81.

2295.   Grolnick, L. (1983), Ibsen's Truth, family secrets, and family therapy. Family Process, 22, 275–288.

2296.   Gross, G. (1979), The family angel: The scapegoat's counterpart. Family Therapy, 6, 133–136.

2297.   Gross, G. (1975), Foster home placements: Conjoint family therapy for the foster family's role dilemma. Family Therapy, 2, 57-61.

2298.   Grosser, G.H., and Paul, N.L. (1964), Ethical issues in family group therapy. American Journal of Orthopsychiatry, 34, 875-884.

2299.   Grotjahn, M. (1965), Clinical illustrations from psychoanalytic family therapy. In: B. Green (Ed.), The psychotherapies of marital disharmony. New York, NY: The Free Press.

2300.   Grotjahn, M. (1963), Clinical observations about the dynamics of the family neurosis. Psychological Reports, 13(3), 830.

2301.   Grotjahn, M. (1959), Analytic family therapy: A survey of trends in research and literature. In: J.H. Masserman (Ed.), Science and psychoanalysis. New York, NY: Grune and Stratton.

2302.   Grotjahn, M. (1968), The aim and technique of psychiatric family consultations. In: W. Mendel and P. Solomon (Eds.), The psychiatric consultation. New York, NY: Solomon, Grune and Stratton.

2303.   Grotjahn, M. (Ed.) (1960), Psychoanalysis and the family neurosis. New York, NY: W.W. Norton and Co.

2304.   Gruher, M. (1979), Family counseling and the status offender. Juvenile and Family Court Journal, 30(1), 23-29.

2305.   Grunebaum, H. (1979), Review of L. Headley's Adults and their parents in family therapy: New directions in treatment. American Journal of Psychiatry, 135, 874.

2306.   Grunebaum, H. (1979), Middle age and marriage: Affiliative men and assertive women. American Journal of Family Therapy, 7, 46-50.

2307.   Grunebaum, H. (1979), Selection of couples for group therapy. American Journal of Family Therapy, 7, 6-8.

2308.   Grunebaum, H. (1984), Schizophrenia and the family. 2. Adverse effects on family therapy comments. Family Process, 23(3), 421-424.

2309.   Grunebaum, H., Christ, J., and Nieberg, N. (1969), Diagnosis and treatment planning for couples. International Journal of Group Psychotherapy, 19, 185-201.

2310.   Grunebaum, H., and Christ, J. (1968), Interpretation and the task of the therapist with couples and families. International Journal of Group Psychotherapy, 18, 495-503.

2311.   Grunspun, H. (1959), A criaga digofrenica: Sua psicopldagogia. (The mentally retarded child: His psychopedagogy.) Revista Psicologica Normal y Patologica, 5, 311-376.

2312.   Grunwald, H. (1957), Group counseling in a family and children's agency. International Journal of Group Psychotherapy, 7, 318-326.

2313.   Gubi, M., and Dobo, M. (1976), Group therapy with the parents of children treated in the department for neurotics. Magyar Pszichologiai Syemle, 33, 24-31.

2314. Guerin, P.J.   (1984), Review of G. Shipman's Handbook for family analysis. Family Process, 23(1), 123-124.

2315. Guerin, P.J. (Ed.) (1976), Family therapy: Theory and practice. New York: Halsted Press.

2316. Guerin, P.J., and Fogarty, T.F. (1972), The family therapist's own family. International Journal of Psychiatry, 10, 6-22.

2317. Guerney, B. (1985), Family therapy research: What are the most important variables? International Journal of Family Therapy, 7(1), 40-49.

2318. Guerney, B., Coufal, J., and Vogelsong, E. (1983), Relationship enhancement versus a traditional approach to therapeutic/preventative/enrichment parent-adolescent programs. International Journal of Eclectic Psychotherapy, 4, 31-43.

2319. Guerney, B., Jr., Coufal, J., and Vogelsong, E. (1981), Relationship enhancement versus a traditional approach to therapeutic/preventive/enrichment parent-adolescent programs. Journal of Consulting and Clinical Pyschology, 41, 927-939.

2320. Guerney, B., Jr., and Guerney, L.F. (1964), Choices in initiating family therapy. Psychotherapy: Theory, Research and Practice, 1, 119-123.

2321. Guerney, B.G. (1984), Review of D.R. Mace's Close companions: The marriage enrichment handbook. American Journal of Family Therapy, 12(1), 80-81.

2322. Guldner, C.A. (1978), Family therapy for the trainee in family therapy. Journal of Marriage and Family Counseling, 4, 127-132.

2323. Guldner, C.A. (1983), Comments on the theme issue: Family therapy. Journal of Group Psychotherapy, Psychodrama and Sociometry, 35, 134.

2324. Guldner, C.A. (1983), An essential bibliography in family therapy. Journal of Group Psychotherapy, Psychodrama and Sociometry, 35, 178.

2325. Guldner, C.A., and Tummon, P.P. (1983), A brief history of the family therapy movement. Journal of Group Psychotherapy, Psychodrama and Sociometry, 35, 134.

2326. Gullerud, E.N., and Harlan, V.L. (1962), Four way joint interviewing in marital counseling. Social Casework, 43, 532-537.

2327. Gullotta, T.P., and Donohue, K.C. (1981), The corporate family: Theory and treatment. Journal of Marital and Family Therapy, 7, 151-157.

2328. Gumina, J.M. (1980), Sentence-completion as an aid to sex therapy. Journal of Marital and Family Therapy, 19, 201-206.

2329. Gumper, L.L. (1979), Adaptation of the induced affect procedure for conjoint treatment of marital discord: An initial study of process effects with high and low functioning married couples. Dissertation Abstracts International, 40(9), 4483-B.

2330.   Gumper, L.L., and Sprenkle, D.H. (1981), Privileged communication in therapy: Special problems for the family and couples therapists. Family Process, 20, 11-23.

2331.   Gunberg, E.W. (1983), Review of C.P. Barnard and R.G. Corrales' The theory and technique of family therapy. Family Relations, 32, 301.

2332.   Gunderson, S.S. (1980), Advocacy in family therapy. Journal of Psychiatric Nursing, 18, 24-28.

2333.   Gunn, A.D. (1970), The breaking marriage. Nursing Times, 66, 1484-1485.

2334.   Guntern, G. (1981), System therapy: Epistemology, paradigm and pragmatics. Journal of Marital and Family Therapy, 7, 265.

2335.   Guntern, G. (1980), System therapy: The child with psychosomatic disease and its family. Paediatrica et Paedologiques, 15, 1-10.

2336.   Gunther, E. (1972), (Andrological aspects in marriage and sex counseling services.) Deutsche Gesundheitswesen, 27, 2250-2253.

2337.   Gurman, A.A. (1982), Changing collusive patterns in marital therapy. American Journal of Family Therapy, 10, 71-72.

2338.   Gurman, A.S., and Knudson, R.M. (1978), Behavioral marriage therapy. I. A psychodynamic-systems analysis and critique. Family Process, 17, 121-138.

2339.   Gurman, A.S. (1978), Contemporary marital-therapies: Critique and comparative analysis of psychoanalytic, behavioral and systems-theory-approaches. In: T.J. Paolini and B.S. McCardy (Eds.), Marriage and marital therapy: Psychoanalytic, behavioral and systems theory perspectives. New York: Brunner/Mazel.

2340.   Gurman, A.S. (1979), Dimensions of marital therapy: A comparative analysis. Journal of Marital and Family Therapy, 5, 5-16.

2341.   Gurman, A.S. (1982), Using paradox in psychodynamic marital therapy. American Journal of Family Therapy, 10, 72-74.

2342.   Gurman, A.S. (1980), Behavioral marriage therapy in the 1980's: The challenge of integration. American Journal of Family Therapy, 8(2), 86-96.

2343.   Gurman, A.S. (1973), Marital therapy: A content-coded bibliography, 1928-1972. Catalog of Selected Documents in Psychology, 3, 55-56.

2344.   Gurman, A.S. (1973), Marital therapy: Emerging trends in research and practice. Family Process, 12, 45-54.

2345.   Gurman, A.S. (1973), The effects and effectiveness of marital therapy: A review of outcome research. Family Process, 12, 145-170.

2346.   Gurman, A.S. (1971), Group marital therapy: Clinical and empirical implications for outcome research. International Journal of Group Psychotherapy, 2, 174-189.

2347.   Gurman, A.S. (1975), Couples' facilitative communication skill as a dimension of marital therapy outcome. Journal of Marital and Family Therapy, 1, 163-174.

2348.   Gurman, A.S. (1975), Evaluating the outcomes of couples groups. In: A. Gurman and D. Rice (Eds.), Couples in conflict. New York, NY: Jason Aronson.

2349.   Gurman, A.S. (1979), Family therapy research in community clinics. American Journal of Family Therapy, 7, 9-10.

2350.   Gurman, A.S. (1979), Psychotherapy and growth: Family systems perspectives. Family Process, 18, 107-108.

2351.   Gurman, A.S. (1983), Family therapy research and the "new epistemology." Journal of Marital and Family Therapy, 11, 227-234.

2352.   Gurman, A.S. (1981), Sources of influence in the family therapy field: Publication trends in three major journals. Journal of Marital and Family Therapy, 7(1), 81-87.

2353.   Gurman, A.S. (1983), The virtues and dangers of a life-cycle perspective in family therapy. American Journal of Family Therapy, 11, 67-74.

2354.   Gurman, A.S. (1984), Transference and resistance in marital therapy. American Journal of Family Therapy, 12(2), 70-73.

2355.   Gurman, A.S. (1984), Analogue research and the family therapist. Family Process, 23(3), 341-345.

2356.   Gurman, A.S. (Ed.) (1981), Questions and answers in the practice of family therapy, Vol. 1. New York: Brunner/Mazel.

2357.   Gurman, A.S., Knudson, R.M., and Kniskern, D.P. (1978), Behavioral marriage therapy: IV. Take two aspirin and call us in the morning. Family Process, 17, 165-180.

2358.   Gurman, A.S., and Kniskern, D.P. (1978), Research on marital and family therapy: Progress, perspective and prospect. In: S.L. Garfield and A.E. Bergin (Eds.), Handbook of psychotherapy and behavior change: An empirical analysis. New York: John Wiley and Sons.

2359.   Gurman, A.S., and Kniskern, D.P. (1978), Behavioral marriage therapy. II. Empirical perspectives. Family Process, 17, 139-148.

2360.   Gurman, A.S., and Kniskern, D.P. (1978), Deterioration in marital and family therapy: Empirical, clinical, and conceptual issues. Family Process, 17, 3-20.

2361.   Gurman, A.S., and Kniskern, D.P. (1977), Enriching research on marital enrichment programs. Journal of Marital and Family Therapy, 3, 3-11.

2362.   Gurman, A.S., and Kniskern, D.P. (1981), Handbook of family therapy. New York: Brunner/Mazel.

2363.   Gurman, A.S., and Kniskern, D.P. (1978), Technolatry, methodolatry, and the results of family therapy. Family Process, 17, 275-281.

2364.   Gustavsdottir, K. (1973), Experiences from the family therapy program at Kleppsspitlainn, Reykjavik. Acta Psychiatrica Scandinavica, Supplement, 243, 45-46.

2365.   Gutheil, T.G., and Avery, N.C. (1977), Multiple overt incest as family defense against loss. Family Process, 16, 105-116.

2366.   Gutierrez-Murillo, E. (1973), Prematrimonial elementary sex education of women. Gaceta Medica de Mexico, 106, 352-354.

2367.   Guttmacher, J.A. (1976), Review of M. Sugar's The adolescent in group and family therapy. International Journal of Group Psychotherapy, 26, 117-119.

2368.   Guttman, H.A. (1973), A contraindication for family therapy: The prepsychotic or postpsychotic young adult and his parents. Archives of General Psychiatry, 29, 352-355.

2369.   Guttman, H.A. (1972), A time unit method of coding intrafamilial interaction from the audiotape. Psychotherapy: Theory, Research and Practice, 9(3), 267-268.

2370.   Guttman, H.A. (1977), The new androgyny: Therapy of "liberated" couples. Canadian Journal of Psychiatry, 22, 225-229.

2371.   Guttman, H.A. (1982), Transference and countertransference in conjoint couple therapy: Therapeutic and theoretical implications. Canadian Journal of Psychiatry, 27, 92-97.

2372.   Guttman, H.A. (1975), The child's participation in conjoint family therapy. Journal of the American Academy of Child Psychiatry, 14, 490-499.

2373.   Guttman, H.A., Spector, R.M., Sigal, J.J., Epstein, N.B., and Rakoff, V. (1972), Coding of affective expression in family therapy. American Journal of Psychotherapy, 26, 185-194.

2374.   Guttman, H.A., Spector, R.M., Sigal, J.J., Rakoff, V., and Epstein, N.B. (1971), Reliablity of coding affective communication in family therapy sessions: Problems of measurement and interpretation. Journal of Consulting and Clinical Psychology, 37, 397-402.

2375.   Guttman, H.A., and Sigal, J.J. (1978), Teaching family psychodynamics in a family practice center: One experience. International Journal of Psychiatric Medicine, 8, 383-392.

2376.   Gwyn, F.S., and Kilpatrick, A.C. (1981), Family therapy with low-income blacks: A tool or turn-off? Social Casework, 62, 259-266.

2377.   Haagen, E.K. (1976), A group therapy experience with unwed mothers: Repairing the mother-child bond. Transnational Mental Health Research Newsletter, 18(1), 11-15.

2378.   Haas, L.J., and Alexander, J.F. (1980), Review of T.J. Paolino and B.S. McCardy's Marriage and marital therapy: Psychoanalytic, behavioral and systems theory perspectives. Contemporary Psychology, 25, 256-257.

2379. Haber, J. (1981), Family therapy with single, young adults. Perspectives in Psychiatric Care, 19, 174-9.

2380. Hackett, T.J. (1976), Psychological assistance for the dying patient and his family. Annual Review of Medicine, 27, 371-378.

2381. Hackney, G.R., and Ribordy, S.C. (1980), An empirical investigation of emotional reactions to divorce. Journal of Clinical Psychology, 36, 105-110.

2382. Hackney, H. (1983), Review of E.O. Fisher's Impact of divorce on the extended family. American Journal of Family Therapy, 11, 84.

2383. Hader, M. (1965), The importance of grandparents in family life. Family Process, 4(2), 228-238.

2384. Hadley, T.R., Jacob, T., Milliones, J., Caplan, J., and Spitz, D. (1974), The relationship between family developmental crisis and the appearance of symptoms in a family member. Family Process, 13, 207-214.

2385. Hafner, R.J. (1981), Spouse-aided therapy in psychiatry: An introduction. Australian and New Zealand Journal of Psychiatry, 15, 329-337.

2386. Hafner, R.J. (1982), Marital interaction in persisting obsessive-compulsive disorders. Australian and New Zealand Journal of Psychiatry, 16, 171-178.

2387. Hafner, R.J., Badenoch, A., Fisher, J., and Swift, H. (1983), Spouse-aided versus individual therapy in persisting psychiatric disorders: A systematic comparison. Family Process, 22, 385-399.

2388. Hafner, R.J., Gilchrist, P., Bowling, J., and Kalucy, R.S. (1981), The treatment of obsessional neurosis in a family setting. Australian and New Zealand Journal of Psychiatry, 15(2), 145-151.

2389. Hafner, R.J., Hatton, P., and Larkin, F. (1981), Spouse-aided therapy and psychiatric nursing: A preliminary report. Australian Journal of Family Therapy, 2(3), 143-153.

2390. Hagglund, T.B., and Pylkkanen, K. (1974), Psychotherapy of drug using adolescents as inpatients and outpatients in a hospital special care unit. Psychiatrica Fennica, 14, 249-256.

2391. Hahlweg, K., Kraemer, M., Schindler, L., and Revenstorf, D. (1980), Behavioral marital therapy: An empirical analysis. Zeitschrift Fur Klinische Psychologie Forschung Und Praxis, 28, 159-169.

2392. Hahlweg, K., Revenstorf, D., Schindler, L., and Brengelmann, J.C. (1982), Current issues in marital therapy. Analysis Y Modificacion de Conducta, 6, 3-27.

2393. Hahlweg, K., Revenstorf, D., and Schindler, L. (1982), Treatment of marital distress: Comparing formats and modalities. Advances in Behaviour Research and Therapy, 4, 57-74.

2394.   Hahlweg, K., Revenstorf, D., and Schindler, L. (1983), The Munich
        marital therapy study: Practical implications. Partnerberatung, 20, 13-
        25.

2395.   Hahlweg, K., Revenstorf, D., and Schindler, L. (1984), Effects of
        behavioral marital therapy on couples' communication and problem-
        solving skills. Journal of Consulting and Clinical Psychology, 52(4), 553-
        566.

2396.   Haldane, D., and McCluskey, U. (1981), Working with couples:
        Psychiatrists, clinical psychologists and social workers compared.
        Journal of Family Therapy, 3(4), 363.

2397.   Haldane, D., and McCluskey, U. (1982), Existentialism and family
        therapy: A neglected perspective. Journal of Family Therapy, 4(2), 117.

2398.   Haldane, J.D. (1984), Review of A.S. Gurman's Questions and answers in
        the practice of family therapy, Vol. 2. Journal of Family Therapy, 6(4),
        405.

2399.   Hale, B.J. (1978), Gestalt techniques in marriage counseling. Social
        Casework, 59, 382-432.

2400.   Haley, J. (1980), How to be a marriage therapist without knowing
        practically anything. Journal of Marital and Family Therapy, 6, 385-391.

2401.   Haley, J. (1962), Whither family therapy? Family Process, 1, 69-100.

2402.   Haley, J. (1967), Speech sequences of normal and abnormal families
        with two children present. Family Process, 6, 81-97.

2403.   Haley, J. (1963), Marriage therapy. Archives of General Psychiatry, 8,
        213-234.

2404.   Haley, J. (1982), The contribution to therapy of Milton H. Erickson,
        M.D. Family Therapy Networker, 6(1), 3-4, 6, 36-38.

2405.   Haley, J. (1981), On the right to choose one's own grandchildren.
        Family Process, 21, 367-8.

2406.   Haley, J. (1975), Why a mental health clinic should avoid family
        therapy. Journal of Marriage and Family Counseling, 1(2), 3-13.

2407.   Haley, J. (1971), Family therapy. International Journal of Psychiatry, 9,
        233-242.

2408.   Haley, J. (1973), Strategic therapy when a child is presented as the
        problem. Journal of the American Academy of Child Psychology, 12,
        675-689.

2409.   Haley, J. (1984), Marriage or family therapy. American Journal of
        Family Therapy, 12(2), 1-14.

2410.   Haley, J. (Ed.) (1971), Changing families: A family therapy reader.
        New York: Grune and Stratton.

2411.   Haley, J., and Hoffman, L. (1968), Techniques of family therapy. New
        York: Basic Books.

2412.   Haley, W.E. (1983), A family behavioral approach to the treatment of the cognitively impaired elderly. Gerontologist, 23, 18-20.

2413.   Hall, C.M. (1979), The Bowen family theory and its uses. New York: Sason Aronson.

2414.   Hall, R.C., and Simmons, W.C. (1974), The POW wife: A psychiatric appraisal. Archives of General Psychiatry, 29, 690-694.

2415.   Halleck, S.L. (1976), Family therapy and social change. Social Casework, 57, 483-493.

2416.   Haller, L.L. (1974), Family systems theory in psychiatric intervention. American Journal of Nursing, 74, 462-463.

2417.   Hallowitz, D. (1975), Counseling and treatment of the poor black family. Social Casework, 56(8), 451-459.

2418.   Hallowitz, D. (1970), The problem-solving component in family therapy. Social Casework, 51, 67-75.

2419.   Hallowitz, D. (1966), Individual treatment of the child in the context of family therapy. Social Casework, 47, 82-86.

2420.   Hallowitz, E., and Stephens, B. (1959), Group therapy with fathers. Social Casework, 40, 183-192.

2421.   Hallund, K., and Andersen, H. (1981), Experience in family therapy at the clinic for child psychiatry. Ugeskrift For Laeger, 143, 893-896.

2422.   Halperin, D.A., and Hoyt, M.L. (1973), Psychiatrists and group psychotherapy: The reluctant marrige. Groups, 5, 53-56.

2423.   Halperin, S.M., and Smith, T.A. (1983), Differences in stepchildren's perceptions of their stepfathers and natural fathers: Implications for family therapy. Journal of Divorce, 7, 19-30.

2424.   Halpern, H.A., Canale, J.R., Grant, B., and Bellemy, C. (1979), A systems crisis approach to family treatment. Journal of Marital and Family Therapy, 5, 87-94.

2425.   Halsen, A.W. (1973), Active psychotherapy in family crisis: II. Theoretical aspects and follow-up study. Acta Psychiatrica Scandinavica, 243, 42.

2426.   Halton, A., and Magagna, J. (1981), Making a space for parents. In S. Box, B. Copley, J. Magagna, and E. Moustaki (Eds.), Psychotherapy with families: An analytic approach. London: Routledge and Kegan Paul Ltd.

2427.   Halvorson, P.A. (1980), A family service agency follow-up study of outcome of therapy. Dissertation Abstracts International, 40, 5732-A. (University Microfilms No. 8009776.)

2428.   Hamann, E.E. (1983), Comparison of marital adjustment of couples who bring a child for therapy and couples who bring themselves for therapy. Dissertation Abstracts International, 44, 1593-A.

2429.   Hamberg, S.R. (1983), Reading aloud as an initial assignment in marital therapy. Journal of Marital and Family Therapy, 9, 81-88.

2430.   Hamburg, S.R. (1985), Leaving the consulting room to provoke enactment in marital therapy. Journal of Marital and Family Therapy, 11(2), 187-192.

2431.   Hammer, L.I. (1967), Family therapy with multiple therapists. Current Psychiatric Therapies, 7, 103-111.

2432.   Hammond, D.C. (1983), Ethics in marital and sex therapy. American Psychologist, 38, 502-503.

2433.   Hammond, D.C. (1974), Dimensions of helpfulness in saturation marathon couples group-therapy with prison inmates and their partners. Dissertation Abstracts International, 74, 3510-B.

2434.   Hammond, J.M. (1981), Divorce group counseling for secondary school students. Ann Arbor, MI: Cranbrook Publishing Co.

2435.   Hammond, J.M. (1981), Loss of the family unit: Counseling groups to help kids. Personnel and Guidance Journal, 59(6), 392-394.

2436.   Hampel, C. (1972), A contribution to the problem of family therapy. Praxis der Kinderpsychologie und Kinderpsychiatrie, 21, 241-246.

2437.   Hampshire, P.A. (1981), Family therapy with lower socioeconomic juvenile offenders: Engagement and outcome. Dissertation Abstracts International, 41, 2761-B.

2438.   Hanben, R.J.B. (1977), History of marriage counseling with implications for present practice. Dissertation Abstracts International, 38(4), 2360-A.

2439.   Hancock, E. (1980), The dimensions of meaning and belonging in the process of divorce. American Journal of Orthopsychiatry, 50, 18-27.

2440.   Hancock, E. (1976), Crisis intervention in a new born nursery intensive care unit. Social Work and Health Care, 1, 421-432.

2441.   Handlarz, M.C., Deschmer, M.C., Waingort, D., Cervone, N., and Farias, M.A. (1976), Study and treatment of the drug addict and his family. Acta Psiquiatrica y Psicologica de America Latina, 72, 289-294.

2442.   Handlon, J.H. (1962), Symposium: Family treatment of schizophrenia. Discussion. Family Process, 1(1), 146-152.

2443.   Handlon, J.H., and Parloff, M.B. (1962), The treatment of patient and family as a group: Is it group psychotherapy? International Journal of Group Psychotherapy, 12, 132-141.

2444.   Hanley, D.F. (1974), Changes in parent attitudes related to a parent effectiveness training and a family enrichment program. Dissertation Abstracts International, 34, 7044-A.

2445.   Hanley, F.W. (1967), Some comments on family and individual therapy. Canadian Journal of Psychiatry, 12, 70-72.

2446.   Hannemann, E. (1979), Short-term family therapy with juvenile status offenders and their families. Dissertation Abstracts International, 40, 1894-B.

2447.   Hannum, J.W. (1980), Some cotherapy techniques with families. Family Process, 19, 161-168.

2448.   Hansen, C.C. (1968), An extended home visit with conjoint family therapy. Family Process, 7, 67-87.

2449.   Hansen, D.A. (1979), Sex-role stereotyping, marital adjustment, and marital communication. Dissertation Abstracts International, 40(5), 1894-B.

2450.   Hansen, J., and L'Abate, L. (1982), Approaches to family therapy. New York: MacMillan.

2451.   Hansen, J.C., and Himes, B.S. (1979), Application of a cyclical diagnostic model with families. Family Therapy, 6(2), 101-107.

2452.   Hansen, J.C., and Rosenthal, D. (1981), Strategies and techniques in family therapy. Springfield, IL: C.C. Thomas.

2453.   Hansen, L.S. (1979), Counseling issues related to changing roles of women and men in work and family. International Journal for the Advancement of Counseling, 2(1), 66-77.

2454.   Harari, C. (1969), Family emotional patterns in relation to children's problems. Dissertation Abstracts International, 30, 2419-B.

2455.   Harbin, H. (1975), Some advantages and disadvantages of conducting individual and conjoint family therapy by the same therapist. Diseases of the Nervous System, 36, 20-23.

2456.   Harbin, H.T. (1979), A family-oriented psychiatric inpatient unit. Family Process, 18, 281-291.

2457.   Harbin, H.T. (1980), Episodic dyscontrol and family dynamics. Advances in Family Psychiatry, 137, 163-170.

2458.   Harbin, H.T. (1980), Family therapy training for psychiatric residents. American Journal of Psychiatry, 137, 1595-1598.

2459.   Harbin, H.T. (1981), Family therapy with personality disorders. In J.L. Lion (Ed.), Personality disorders: Diagnosis and management (reviewed for DMS III), 2nd Edition. Baltimore, MD: Williams and Wilkins.

2460.   Hardcastle, D.R. (1973), The effects of a family counseling program on parents family satisfaction, perceived integration and congruence and on specific behavior patterns in the family. Dissertation Abstracts International, 3(5), 2766-A.

2461.   Hardcastle, D.R. (1972), Measuring effectiveness in group marital counseling. Family Coordinator, 21, 213-218.

2462.   Hardin, J.M. (1977), The effect of group counseling on sex role expectations of unmarried couples. Dissertation Abstracts International, 37(9), 4648-B.

2463.   Hardin, S.B., and Skerrett, K. (1981), Counseling working mothers. Journal of Nurse-Midwifery, 26(4), 19.

2464.   Hardy, K.V. (1980), Attitudes toward marriage counseling: A study of middle and lower class blacks. Dissertation Abstracts International, 41, 1232-A.

2465.   Hardy, R.E., and Gull, J.G. (Eds.) (1974), Therapeutic needs of the family: Problems, descriptions and therapeutic approaches. Springfield, IL: Charles C. Thomas.

2466.   Hardy-Fanta, C., and MacMahon-Herrera, E. (1981), Adapting family therapy to the Hispanic family. Social Casework, 62, 138-148.

2467.   Hare, R.T., and Umbarger, C. (1973), A structural approach to therapy with schizophrenic families. Proceedings of the 81st Annual Convention of the American Psychological Association, 8, 1059-1060.

2468.   Hare-Mustin, R.T. (1979), Family therapy and sex role stereotypes. Counseling Psychology, 8, 31-32.

2469.   Hare-Mustin, R.T. (1979), Sexism in family therapy. American Journal of Family Therapy, 7, 81-83.

2470.   Hare-Mustin, R.T. (1979), Family therapy following the death of a child. Journal of Marital and Family Therapy, 5, 51-60.

2471.   Hare-Mustin, R.T. (1976), Paradoxical tasks in family therapy: Who can resist? Psychotherapy: Theory, Research and Practice, 13, 128-130.

2472.   Hare-Mustin, R.T. (1980), Family therapy may be dangerous for your health. Professional Psychology, 11(6), 935-938.

2473.   Hare-Mustin, R.T. (1982), China's marriage law: A model for family responsibilities and relationships. Family Process, 2, 477-382.

2474.   Hare-Mustin, R.T., and Lamb, S. (1984), Family counselors attitudes toward women and motherhood - a new cohort. Journal of Marital and Family Therapy, 10, 419-422.

2475.   Hareven, T.K. (1982), American families in transition - historical perspectives on change. In F. Walsh (Ed.), Normal family processes. New York: Guildford Press.

2476.   Harley, A.B., Jr. (1963), Group psychotherapy for parents of disturbed children. Mental Hospital, 14, 14-19.

2477.   Harman, R.L. (1978), Gestalt marriage and family therapy. Gestalt Journal, 1(2), 92-103.

2478.   Harms, E. (1965), Propaedeutic for a family psychiatry. Psychotherapy and Psychosomatics, 13, 387-396.

2479.   Harms, E. (1964), A socio-genetic concept of family therapy. Acta Psychotherapie, (Basel), 12, 53-60.

2480.   Harper, G. (1983), Varieties of parenting failure in anorexia nervosa: Protection and parentectomy, revisited. Journal of the American Academy of Child Psychiatry, 22, 134-39.

2481.   Harper, M.S. (1964), Changes in concepts in mental health, illness and perception as a result of family therapy. Dissertation Abstracts International, 25(2), 1395.

2482.   Harper, R.A. (1960), Marriage counseling as rational process-oriented psychotherapy. Journal of Individual Psychology, 16, 197-207.

2483.   Harper, R.A., and Hudson, J.W. (1952), The use of recordings in marriage counseling. Marriage and Family Living, 14, 133-140.

2484.   Harrell, L.F. (1983), The residue of alcoholism: A case study of the succeeding generation of an alcoholic marriage. Family Therapy, 10, 239-251.

2485.   Harrell, L.F. (1981), Family dependency as a transgenerational process: An ecological analysis of families in crisis. Dissertation Abstracts International, 41, 2762-B.

2486.   Harrington, J.A. (1982), Review of L.R. Wolberg and M.L. Aronson's Group and family therapy: 1981. British Journal of Psychiatry, 141, 435.

2487.   Harris, J. (1980), Psychiatric referrals by a juvenile court. British Journal of Guidance and Counseling, 8, 99-103.

2488.   Harris, J. (1984), Review of A. Treacher and J. Carpenter's Using family therapy. British Journal of Psychiatry, 145, 453.

2489.   Harris, J., and Mills, G.L. (1980), Current practice in a child and family psychiatric service: Analysis of 200 consecutive new referrals. Public Health, 94, 316-23.

2490.   Harris, O., and Janzen, C., Eds. (1980), Family treatment in social work practice. Itasca, IL: Peacock.

2491.   Harris, P. (1983), Support groups: The family connection. Free Association, 10, 1-4.

2492.   Harrison, M. (1981), Home-Start: A voluntary home-visiting scheme for young families. Child Abuse and Neglect, 5, 441-447.

2493.   Harrow, M., Astrachan, B.M., Detre, D., Schwartz, A.H., and Becker, R.E. (1967), An investigation into the nature of the patient-family therapy group. American Journal of Orthopsychiatry, 37, 888-899.

2494.   Hart, J.W. (1964), The use of the "gossip group" in a juvenile home setting. Federal Probation, 24, 57-59.

2495.   Hartman, L.M. (1983), Effects of sex and marital therapy on sexual interaction and marital happiness. Journal of Sex and Marital Therapy, 9, 137-151.

2496.   Hartman, L.M. (1980), The interface between sexual dysfunction and marital conflict. American Journal of Psychiatry, 137, 576-579.

2497.   Hartman, M. (1983), Review of D.H. Olson and R. Markoff's Inventory of marriage and family literature, Vol. 8. Journal of Sex and Marital Therapy, 9, 93.

2498.   Hartmann, H., Krane, R., and Becker, B. (1981), Toilet training and treatment of enuresis by instruments: Discussion and presentation of a new instrument. Zeitschrift Fur Kinder- Und Jugendpsychiatrie, 9, 152-159.

2499.   Hartmann, K., and Bush, M. (1975), Action-oriented family therapy. American Journal of Nursing, 75, 1184-1187.

2500.   Hartmann, S.S., and Hynes, J. (1975), Marriage education for mentally retarded adults. Social Casework, 56, 280-284.

2501.   Harvey, L.H. (1965), Communication, interaction and group experience in marriage therapy. Australian Journal of Social Issues, 2, 2-9.

2502.   Harvey, L.V. (1977), A comment on "argument for the use of paraprofessional counselors in premarital and marital counseling." Family Coordinator, 26(1), 69-70.

2503.   Harvey, M.A. (1980), On becoming a family therapist: The first three years. International Journal of Family Therapy, 2, 263-274.

2504.   Harvey, M.A. (1982), The influence and utilization of an interpreter for deaf persons in family therapy. American Annals of the Deaf, 127, 821-27.

2505.   Harvey, M.A. (1985), Toward a dialogue between the paradigms of family therapy and deafness. American Annals of the Deaf, 130, 305-310.

2506.   Harvey, M.A. (1984), Deafness in the family: Will the therapist listen - rejoinder. Family Process, 23(2), 216-222.

2507.   Harvey, M.A. (1984), Family therapy with deaf persons. Family Process, 23(2), 205-213.

2508.   Haskovcova, L. (1973), Group therapy of schizophrenic adolescents. Ceskoslovenska Psychiatrica, 69(6), 377.

2509.   Hassall, E., and Madar, D. (1980), Crisis group therapy with the separated and divorced. Family Relations, 29, 591-597.

2510.   Hastings, P.R., and Runkle, R.L. (1963), An experimental group of married couples with severe problems. International Journal of Group Psychotherapy, 13, 84-92.

2511.   Hatcher, C. (1978), Intra-personal and inter-personal models: Blending gestalt and family therapies. Journal of Marital and Family Therapy, 4, 63-68.

2512.   Hatfield, A.B. (1979), Family as partner in the treatment of mental illness. Hospital and Community Psychiatry, 30, 338-340.

2513.   Hatfield, A.B. (1979), Help seeking behavior in families of schizophrenics. American Journal of Community Psychology, 7, 563-569.

2514.   Hatfield, A.B. (1982), Meeting the needs of families of the psychiatrically disabled. Psychosocial Rehabilitation Journal, 6, 27-40.

2515.   Hatfield, F.E.S. (1982), Review of C. Wood's Health and the family. Journal of Family Therapy, 4, 399.

2516.   Hatterer, M.S. (1974), The problems of women married to homosexual men. American Journal of Psychiatry, 131, 275-278.

2517.   Hau, E.C. (1964), Family neurosis and family therapy. Discussion of new psychoanalytic results of W. Grotjahn. Archives of Psychosomatic Medicine, 10, 145-152.

2518.   Hau, E.C. (1964), Family neuroses and family therapy. Discussion of new psychoanalytic results obtained by M. Grotjahn. II. Aspects of treatment technique in psychoanalytic family therapy. Zietschrift fur Psycikosomatik Medizische, 10, 221-227.

2519.   Haug, M. (1971), Fokaltherapie der familie: Eine anwendung der psychoanalyse in der erziehungs berat ungsarbeit. (Focal therapy of the family: An application of psychoanalysis to child guidance.) Psyche, 25, 595-602.

2520.   Hausman, C.P. (1979), Short term counseling groups for people with elderly parents. Gerontology, 19, 102-107.

2521.   Hausman, M. (1974), Parents' groups: How group members perceive curative factors. Smith College, 44, 179-198.

2522.   Hausmann, B. (1974), Multi-family group treatment: Emphasizing the role of group members as therapeutic agents. American Journal of Orthopsychiatry, 44, 222-227.

2523.   Hautzinger, M., Linden, M., and Hoffman, N. (1982), Distressed couples with and without a depressed partner: An analysis of their verbal interaction. Journal of Behavior Therapy and Experimental Psychiatry, 13, 307-314.

2524.   Hawes, C.E. (1982), Couples growing together: A leader's guide for couple enrichment study groups. Second edition. Wooster, OH: Social Interest.

2525.   Hawkins, J., and Killorin, E. (1979), Family of origin: An experimental workshop. American Journal of Family Therapy, 7, 1-17.

2526.   Hawkins, J.L. (1976), Counselor involvement in marriage and family counseling. Journal of Marriage and Family Counseling, 2(1), 37-47.

2527.   Hawkins, S.P., Peterson, R.F., Schweid, E., and Byon, S.W. (1966), Behavior therapy in the home: Amelioration of problem parent-child relations with the parent in a therapeutic role. Journal of Experimental Child Psychology, 4, 99-107.

2528. Hawley, R.W. (1980), The marriage encounter experience and its effects on self-perception, mate-perception, and marital adjustment. Dissertation Abstracts International, 40, 5791-A.

2529. Hayez, J.Y. (1980), The guidance of parents in cases of marital tension (author's transl.). Neuropsychiatrie de L'Enfance et de L'Adolescence, 28, 411-6.

2530. Haynes, J.M. (1982), A conceptual model of the process of family mediation: Implications for training. American Journal of Family Therapy, 10, 5-16.

2531. Haynes, S.N., Jensen, B.J., Wise, E., and Sherman, D. (1981), The marital intake interview: A multimethod criterion validity assessment. Journal of Consulting and Clinical Psychology, 49(3), 379-387.

2532. Headings, V.E. (1980), Counseling in a hospital-based newborn screening service. Patient Counseling and Health Education, 2(2), 80-83.

2533. Heap, K.K. (1982), Work with parents of abused and neglected children. Child Abuse and Neglect, 6, 335-341.

2534. Heap, K.K. (1983), Working with parents in child abuse and neglect. Tidsskrift fur den Norske Laegeforening, 20, 537-40.

2535. Heath, A.W. (1983), Diagnosis and assessment in family therapy: VII. The live supervision form: Structure and theory for assessment in live supervision. Family Therapy Collections, 11, 143-154.

2536. Heath, A.W. (1982), Team family therapy training: Conceptual and pragmatic considerations. Family Process, 21, 187-94.

2537. Heath, D.H. (1978), Marital sexual enjoyment and frustration of professional men. Archives of Sexual Behavior, 7, 463-476.

2538. Heath, D.H. (1978), Personality correlates of the marital sexual compatibility of professional men. Journal of Sex and Marital Therapy, 4, 67-82.

2539. Heavilon, J.G. (1980), A critical evaluation of treatment modalities for hyperkinesis in children. Dissertation Abstracts International, 41, 1915-B.

2540. Heckel, R.V. (1975), A comparison of process data from family therapy and group therapy. Journal of Community Psychology, 3, 254-257.

2541. Hedblom, J.E. (1981), Anorexia nervosa: A multidisciplinary treatment program with the family. Social Work in Health Care, 7, 67-86.

2542. Heekerens, H.P. (1983), Institutional aspects of family therapy work in ambulatory care of children and adolescents. Praxis der Kinderpsychologie und Kinderpsychiatrie, 32, 98-105.

2543. Heersema, P.H., and Fry, W.F., Jr. (1963), Conjoint family therapy: A new dimension in psychotherapy. Topics and Problems in Psychotherapy, 4, 147-153.

2544.   Hefez, A. (1973), Neurosis and marriage: A phenomenological analysis of disturbed married couples. Human Heredity, 23, 59-68.

2545.   Hefez, A. (1973), Neurosis and marriage: A phenomenological analysis of disturbed married couples. Israel Annals of Psychiatry and Related Disciplines, 11, 81-90.

2546.   Hefner, C.W., and Prochaska, J.O. (1984), Concurrent vs. conjoint marital therapy. Social Work, 29(3), 287-294.

2547.   Heigl-Evers, A. (1967), The role of offense in marital conflicts and the resulting counseling problems. Praxis der Kinderpsychologie und Kinderpsychiatrie, 16, 33-41.

2548.   Heigl-Evers, A., and Heigl, F. (1975), The implicit marriage contract and its significance as a therapeutic concept. Praxis der Psychotherapie, 20(1), 25.

2549.   Heineman, R.K. (1973), The evolution of an abortion counseling service in an adoption agency. Child Welfare, 52(4), 253-260.

2550.   Heiner, H.G. (1970), An application of t-group method to the teaching of family relationships. Dissertation Abstracts International, 31, 3268-A.

2551.   Heinicke, C.M. (1976), Aiding 'at risk' children through psychoanalytic social work with parents. American Journal of Orthopsychiatry, 46, 89-103.

2552.   Heins, T. (1978), Marital interaction in depression. Australian and New Zealand Journal of Psychiatry, 12, 269-275.

2553.   Heins, T.J. (1978), Posted summaries in marital therapy. Australian and New Zealand Journal of Psychiatry, 12, 287.

2554.   Heisler, V. (1974), Dynamic group psychotherapy with parents of cerebral palsied children. Rehabilitation Literature, 35(11), 329-330.

2555.   Held, B.S., and Heller, L. (1982), Symptom prescription as metaphor: A systemic approach to the psychosomatic-alcoholic family. Family Therapy, 9, 133-145.

2556.   Held, J.P. (1978), The care and feeding of small group leaders of sex discussion groups. Journal of Sex and Marital Therapy, 4, 292.

2557.   Helfer, R.E., and Kempe, C.H. (Eds.) (1976), Child abuse and neglect: The family and the community. Cambridge, MA: Ballinger Publishers.

2558.   Helphand, M., and Porter, C.M. (1981), The family group within the nursing home: Maintaining family ties of long-term care residents. Journal of Gerontological Social Work, 4, 51-62.

2559.   Hemming, J. (1973), The new relationships in sex and marriage. Community Health, 4, 249-253.

2560.   Henderson, N.B. (1964), Married group therapy: A setting for reducing resistances. Psychological Reports, 16, 347-352.

2561.   Hendricks, G. (1979), The family centering book: Awareness activities the whole family can do together. Englewood Cliffs, NJ: Prentice-Hall.

2562.   Hendricks, J.J. (1983), The structural-strategic model of family therapy: Justification of a personal choice. Tijdschrift Voor Psychotherapie, 9, 130-139.

2563.   Hendricks, W.J. (1971), Use of multifamily counseling groups in treatment of male narcotic addicts. International Journal of Group Psychotherapy, 21, 84-90.

2564.   Hendrickson, W.E. (1978), An exploratory study of divorce as a potential differentiating factor among family therapists. Dissertation Abstracts International, 39, 2755-A.

2565.   Hendrickx, J. (1980), A structured program of contracts in family therapy. Tidjdschrift voor Psychotherapie, 6(1), 12-27.

2566.   Hendrickx, J., and Brand, D. (1983), Family orientation in the residential treatment of a child: The process of change in the child and the family. Tijdschrift Voor Psychotherapie, 9, 191-200.

2567.   Hendrickx, J., and Brand, D. (1983), Family orientation in the residential treatment of a child: A structured family therapy. Tijdschrift Voor Psychotherapie, 9, 246-251.

2568.   Henggeler, S.W., and Cohen, R. (1984). The role of cognitive development in the family ecological systems approach to childhood psychopathology. In B. Gholson and T.L. Rosenthal (Eds.), Applications of cognitive-developmental theory. Orlando, FL: Academic Press.

2569.   Henker, F.O. (1962), Married couples-group in therapy of psychoneuroses. Southern Medical Journal, 55, 401-405.

2570.   Henle, I. (1971), The group in marriage counseling. Wege zum Menschen, February, 43-53.

2571.   Henning, D. (1984), A study of the effects of post-wedding counseling with participants of pre-marital counseling groups. Dissertation Abstracts International, 45, 2416-A.

2572.   Henry, G. (1981), Psychic pain and psychic damage. In S. Box, B. Copley, J. Magagna, and E. Moustaki (Eds.), Psychotherapy with families: An analytic approach. London: Routledge and Kegan Paul Ltd.

2573.   Henry, P.W. (1983), The family therapy profession: University and institute perspectives. Dissertation Abstracts International, 44, 1961-B.

2574.   Henry, P.W., and Storm, C.L. (1984), The training metamorphosis: Teaching systemic thinking in family therapy programs. Journal of Strategic and Systemic Therapies, 3, 41-49.

2575.   Hentze, J. (1971), Family therapy. Praxis der Familienberatung, 1, 109-112.

2576.   Heppner, M.J. (1978), Counseling the battered wife: Myths, facts, and decisions. Personnel and Guidance Journal, 56(9), 522-525.

2577.   Herbert, W.L. (1960), The art of marriage counseling. New York:
        Emerson Books, Inc.

2578.   Hermalin, J., Mellendez, L., Kamarck, T., Klevans, F., Ballen, E., and
        Gordon, M. (1979), Enhancing primary prevention: Marriage of self-help
        groups and familial health care delivery systems. Journal of Clinical
        Child Psychology, 8, 125-129.

2579.   Herman, A.E. (1978), Review of C.J. Sager's Marriage contracts and
        couple therapy. Bulletin of the Menninger Clinic, 42, 175.

2580.   Hermannova, Z. (1965), Family centered therapy in Czechoslovakia.
        British Journal of Psychiatric Social Work, 8, 11-14.

2581.   Herndon, C.N., and Nash, E.M. (1962), Premarriage and marriage
        counseling. Journal of the American Medical Association, 180, 395-401.

2582.   Herold, P.L. (1980), The effects of psychosocial intervention with
        children who have asthma on children's locus of control and self-esteem
        scores, and measures of physical status. Dissertation Abstracts
        International, 40, 5075-B.

2583.   Hertzler, A.A., and Chun, H. (1979), The relationship of family
        structure and interaction to nutrition. Journal of American Diet
        Association, 74, 23-27.

2584.   Herzoff, N.E. (1979), A therapeutic group for cancer patients and their
        families. Cancer Nursing, 2(6), 469-474.

2585.   Hess, T. (1982), Individual psychotherapy for children and adolescents or
        family therapy: Combinable or mutually exclusive? Praxis Der
        Kinderpsychologie Und Kinderpsychiatrie, 31, 253-260.

2586.   Hessebiber, S., and Williamson, J. (1984), Resource theory and power in
        families: Life cycle considerations. Family Process, 23(2), 261-278.

2587.   Hesselnberg, M. (1982), Family therapy and its history. Soins
        Psychiatrie, 27, 41-4.

2588.   Hey, R.N., and Mudd, E.H. (1959), Recurring problems in marrige
        counseling. Marriage and Family Living, 21, 127-129.

2589.   Heynen, F.E. (1983), An examination of the relationship between sex
        roles of married couples and marital adjustment, marital
        communication, and quality of the marital relationship: Theoretical and
        practical implications for marital therapy. Dissertation Abstracts
        International, 43, 3269-A.

2590.   Hickman, M.E. (1970), Facilitation techniques in counseling married
        couples toward more effective communication. Dissertation Abstracts
        International, 31(5), 2107-A.

2591.   Hickok, J.E., and Komechak, M.G. (1974), Behavior modification in
        marital conflict: A case report. Family Process, 13, 111.

2592.   Hicks, P.S. (1981), Brief family therapy with military families. Military
        Medicine, 146, 573-6.

2593. Hiddema, F. (1974), Fighting couples. Nederlands Tijdschrift voor Geneeskunde, 118, 1079-1080.

2594. Hiesberger, J.M. (Ed.) (1979), Healing family hurts. Ramsey, NJ: Paulist Press.

2595. Higham, E. (1976), Case mangement of the gender incongruity syndrome in childhood and adolescence. Journal of Homosexuality, 2, 49-57.

2596. Hight, E.S. (1977), A contractual, working separation: A step between resumption and/or divorce. Journal of Divorce, 1(1), 21-30.

2597. Hightower, N.A., Rodriguez, S., and Adams, J. (1983), Ethnically mixed co-therapy with families. Family Therapy, 10, 105-110.

2598. Hightower, N.A., and Dimalanta, A.S. (1980), "Ma Bell": The other mother in family therapy. Family Therapy, 7, 147-151.

2599. Hill, P. (1976), Conjoint family therapy. Midwife Health Visit Community Nurse, 12, 355.

2600. Hill, P. (1983), Review of S. Skinner's Developments in family therapy - Walrond. Journal of Child Psychology and Psychiatry, 24, 328.

2601. Hill, P. (1984), Review of A. Bentovim, G. Correllbarnets and A. Cooklin's Family therapy: Complementary framework of theory and practice, Vol. I and II. British Journal of Psychiatry, 144, 219.

2602. Hill, S.G. (1983), The effects of a program of structured group counseling on the self-concept and leadership skills of disadvantaged gifted elementary school students. Dissertation Abstracts International, 43, 3510-A.

2603. Hillel, J.M., and Bordeleau, J.M. (1967), Treatment of a group of couples: Methodological approach. Laval Medicale, 38, 47-57.

2604. Hillman, B.W., and Perry, T. (1975), The parent-teacher education center: Evaluation of a program for improving family relations. Journal of Family Counseling, 3, 11-16.

2605. Hillman, C.H. (1954), An advice column's challenge for family-life education. Marriage and Family Living, 16, 51-54.

2606. Hills, D.S. (1982), Psychotherapy with high-achieving adolescent girls. Psychotherapy: Theory, Research and Practice, 19(1), 77.

2607. Hindman, M. (1976), Children of alcoholic parents. Alcohol Health and Research World, Exp. Iss., 2-6.

2608. Hindman, M. (1976), Family therapy in alcoholism. Alcohol Health and Research World, 1, 2-9.

2609. Hines, G.A. (1976), Efficacy of communication skills training with married partners where no marital counseling has been sought. Dissertation Abstracts International, 36, 5045-A.

2610. Hines, P.M. (1985), Review of C. E. Obudho's Black marriage and family therapy. Contemporary Psychology, 30(2), 146.

2611. Hines, P.M., and Hare-Mustin, R.T. (1980), Ethical concerns in family therapy. Advances in Family Psychiatry, 2, 65.

2612. Hinkle, D.E., Arnold, C.F., Croake, J.W., and Keller, J.F. (1980), Adlerian parent education: Changes in parents' attitudes and behaviors, and children's self-esteem. American Journal of Family Therapy, 8, 32-43.

2613. Hinman, L.M. (1983), Focus on the school-aged child in family intervention. Journal of School Health, 53, 499-502.

2614. Hirsch, R. (1961), Group therapy with parents of adolescent drug addicts. Psychiatric Quarterly, 35, 702-710.

2615. Hirsch, R., and Imhof, J.E. (1975), Family therapy approach to the treatment of drug abuse and addiction. Journal of Psychedelic Drugs, 7, 181-185.

2616. Hirschhorn, L., and Gilmore, T. (1980), The application of family therapy concepts to influencing organizational behavior. Administrative Science Quarterly, 25, 18-37.

2617. Hirschman, C., and Matras, J. (1971), A new look at the marriage market and nuptiality rates: 1915-1958. Demography, 8, 549-569.

2618. Hirschman, C., and Matras, J. (1974), A new look at the marriage market and nuptiality rates. Delaware Medical Journal, 46, 248-250.

2619. Hirschowitz, R.G. (1974-75), Family coping patterns in times of change. Social Psychology, 21, 37-43.

2620. Hitchens, E.Q. (1972), Denial: An identified theme in marital relationships of sex offenders. Perspectives in Psychiatric Care, 10(4), 152-159.

2621. Ho, M.K., and Settles, A. (1984), The use of popular music in family therapy. Social Work, 29(1), 65-66.

2622. Hoch, E.M. (1972), Hypno-behavioral approach for the non-consummated marriage. Journal of the American Society of Psychologists in Dental and Medical Schools, 19, 129-136.

2623. Hoch, Z. (1977), Sex therapy and marital counseling for the disabled. Archives of Physical Medicine and Rehabilitation, 58, 413-415.

2624. Hoch, Z. (1976), Sexual counseling and therapy. Journal of Family Counseling, 4(1), 7-13.

2625. Hoch, Z., Safir, M.P., Peres, Y., and Shepher, J. (1981), An evaluation of sexual performance: Comparison between sexually dysfunctional and functional couples. Journal of Sex and Marital Therapy, 7, 195-206.

2626. Hodes, M. (1985), Family therapy and the problem of cultural relativism: A reply to Dr. Law. Journal of Family Therapy, 7, 261-272.

2627. Hodges, J.M., Buch, L.C., Patrissi, G.A., and Liston, W. (1979), A model for family diagnostic procedures. Military Medicine, 144, 796-798.

2628.   Hodgson, J.W., and Lewis, R.A. (1979), Pilgrims' progress II. A trend analysis of family theory and methodology. Family Process, 18, 163–173.

2629.   Hoebel, F.C. (1976), Brief family–interactional therapy in the management of cardiac–related high–risk behaviors. Journal of Family Practice, 3, 613–618.

2630.   Hoek, A., and Wollstein, S. (1966), Conjoint psychotherapy of married couples: A clinical report. International Journal of Social Psychiatry, 12, 209–216.

2631.   Hof, L., and Dwyer, C.E. (1982), Overcoming ambivalence through the use of values analysis. American Journal of Family Therapy, 10, 17–26.

2632.   Hof, L., and Miller, W. (1980), Marriage enrichment: Philosophy, process, and program. Bowie, MD: Bradv.

2633.   Hoffman, L. (1983), Diagnosis and assessment in family therapy: II. A co–evolutionary framework for systemic family therapy. Family Therapy Collections, 11, 35–61.

2634.   Hoffman, L. (1981), Foundations of family therapy: A conceptual framework for system change. New York: Basic Books.

2635.   Hoffman, L. (1979), Review of L. Headley's Return to the source: Adults and their parents in family therapy. Family Process, 18, 360.

2636.   Hofling, C.K., and Lewis, J.M., Eds. (1980), The family: Evaluation and treatment. New York: Brunner/Mazel.

2637.   Hofstein, S. (1970), Modalities in the treatment of family discord. Journal of Jewish Community Service, 47, 20–29.

2638.   Hogan, P.D., and Royce, J.R. (1976), Four–way sessions: The co–therapy of couples in individual and conjoint treatment. Groups, 7, 7–11.

2639.   Hogg, W.F., and Northman, J.E. (1979), The resonating parental bind and delinquency. Family Therapy, 6(1), 21–26.

2640.   Hohenshil, T.H. (1979), Counseling handicapped persons and their families. Personnel and Guidance Journal, 58(4), 213.

2641.   Holdsworth, V. (1980), Marital therapy: A risky business. Introduction. Nursing Mirror, 151, 18–20.

2642.   Holis, F. (1968), Continuance and discontinuance in marital counseling and some observations on joint interviews. Social Casework, 99, 167–174.

2643.   Holland, C.J. (1976), Directive parental counseling: The parent's manual. Behavior Therapy, 7(1), 123–127.

2644.   Holland, M.J. (1984), Characteristics of family therapy terminators and continuers. Dissertation Abstracts International, 45, 2246–A.

2645.   Hollander, C.E. (1983), Comparative family systems of Moreno and Bowen. Journal of Group Psychotherapy, Psychodrama and Sociometry, 36, 1–12.

2646.   Hollander, S.L. (1981), Spontaneity, sociometry, and the warming up process in family therapy. Journal of Group Psychotherapy Psychodrama and Sociometry, 36, 44-53.

2647.   Hollander, W.M., and Hegreness, M.S. (1955), Group therapy with parents whose children are treated in a guidance center. Praxis der Kinderpsychologie und Kinderpsychiatrie, 4, 99-101.

2648.   Hollender, M.H., and Mercer, A.J. (1979), The wish to be held and hold in couples. Journal of Clinical Psychiatry, 40, 121-123.

2649.   Hollis, F. (1950), Evaluating marriage counseling. Marriage and Family Living, 12, 37-38.

2650.   Hollis, F. (1968), A profile of early interviews in marital counseling. Social Casework, 39, 35-43.

2651.   Holly, D.T. (1983), The relationship of couples' collaborative and adversarial behaviors to outcomes in marital therapy. Dissertation Abstracts International, 43, 2339-B.

2652.   Holmes, J. (1980), The sibling and psychotherapy: A review with clinical examples. British Journal of Medical Psychology, 53(4), 297-306.

2653.   Holmes, J. (1984), Review of C.E. Schaefer, J.M. Breimeister, and M.E. Fitton's Family therapy techniques for problem behaviors of children and teenagers. British Journal of Psychiatry, 45, 455.

2654.   Holoubek, A.B., and Holoubek, J.E. (1973), Pre-marriage counseling. Journal of Arkansas Medical Association, 70, 168-175.

2655.   Holt, S.J., and Robinson, T.M. (1979), The school nurse's 'family assessment tool.' American Journal of Nursing, 79, 950-953.

2656.   Holte, A., and Wormnes, B. (1980), Training family therapists: Salvador Minuchin. Tidsskrift For Norsk Psykologforening, 17, 27-35.

2657.   Holub, N., and Bernstein, H. (1975), Teaching the patient and the family. Family conferences as an adjunct to total coronary care...Mercy Hospital, Rockville Centre, Long Island, NY. Part 2. Heart Lung, 4, 767-769.

2658.   Holzman, C.G. (1973), Patterns of verbal interaction in couples seeking marital therapy. Dissertation Abstracts International, 34, 2934-B.

2659.   Homer, L.E. (1973), Community-based resource for runaway girls. Social Casework, 54, 473-479.

2660.   Hommond, J.M. (1980), A parent's suicide: Counseling the children. The School Counselor, 7, 385-388.

2661.   Hooper, D. (1981), Professional intervention in the parenting process. Proceedings of the Annual Symposium of the Eugenics Society, 167-175.

2662.   Hooper, D., Sheldon, A., and Kovmans, A.J.R. (1968), A study of group psychotherapy with married couples. 1: The group method. International Journal of Social Psychiatry, 15, 57-68.

2663.   Hooper, D., and Sheldon, A. (1970), A study of group psychotherapy with married couples. II: Evaluating the changes. International Journal of Social Psychiatry, 16, 299-305.

2664.   Hoover, M.J. (1979), Intensive care for relatives. Hospitals, 53, 219-220, 222.

2665.   Horejsi, C.R. (1974), Small group sex education for engaged couples. Journal of Family Counseling, 2, 23-27.

2666.   Horewitz, J. (1979), Transactional analysis and family therapy. New York: Aronson.

2667.   Horn, D. (1982), Family of origin technique. Canadian Journal of Psychiatry, 27, 616.

2668.   Horn, G. (1979), Open-house form of parental counseling. Praxis der Kinderpsychologie und Kinderpsychiatrie, 28, 100-110.

2669.   Horn, J.C. (1979), Family therapy for chimps. Psychology Today, 12, 36.

2670.   Hornby,G.H., and Singh, N.N. (1982), Reflective group counselling for parents of mentally retarded children. British Journal of Mental Subnoramlity, 28, 71-76.

2671.   Horne, A.M., and Graff, R.W. (1973), Married student concerns: Who counsels the married population? Journal of Counseling Psychology, 20, 384-385.

2672.   Horne, A.M., and Ohlsen, M.M. (1982), Family counseling and therapy. Itasca, IL: Peacock Publishers.

2673.   Horne, A.M., and Van Dyke, B. (1983), Treatment and maintenance of social learning family therapy. Behavior Therapy, 14, 606-613.

2674.   Horowitz, L. (1975), Treatment of family with a dying member. Family Process, 14, 95.

2675.   Horwitz, O., and Weber, J. (1973), Correlation between marital status and mortality. I. All Denmark. Ugeskrift for Laeger, 135, 1089-1095.

2676.   Horwitz, O., and Weber, J. (1973), Marital status and mortality. II. The capital, provincial towns, and rural districts. Ugeskrift for Laeger, 135, 1096-1104.

2677.   Hoskins, C.N. (1979), Level of activation, body temperature, and interpersonal conflict in family relationships. Nursing Research, 28, 154-160.

2678.   Hoster, K. (1979), Contemporary marriage: Structure, dynamics, and therapy. Family Coordinator, 28, 135.

2679.   House, A.E., and Stambaugh, E.E. (1979), Transfer of therapeutic effects from institution to home: Faith, hope, and behavior modification. Family Process, 18, 87-93.

2680.   Houseknecht, S.K., Vaughan, S., and Macke, A.S. (1984), Marital disruption among professional women: The timing of career and family events. Social Problems, 31(3), 273-284.

2681.   Houts, D.C. (1982), Marriage counseling with clergy couples. Pastoral Psychology, 30(3), 141.

2682.   Howard, Y., and Howard, E. (1979), Life and times of the Israel Association for Family Therapy. American Journal of Family Therapy, 1, 106-107.

2683.   Howe, B.J. (1975), The practice of psychotherapy as do-it-yourself treatment for a beginning therapist. Family Therapy, 2, 123128.

2684.   Howe, B.J. (1974), Family therapy and the treatment of drug abuse problems. Family Therapy, 1, 89-98.

2685.   Howell, D., and Parsloe, P. (1966), Working with a family in a child guidance setting. British Journal of Psychiatric Social Work, 8, 10-20.

2686.   Howell, E.L. (1982), Evaluation of a communications skills program with stepfather-adolescent-mother triads. Dissertation Abstracts International, 43, 1837-B.

2687.   Howells, J.G. (1980), Family diagnosis. Psychological Bulletin, 10(7), 6-14.

2688.   Howells, J.G. (1980), Review of M. Andolfi's Family therapy: An interactional approach. British Journal of Psychiatry, 136, 102.

2689.   Howells, J.G. (1980), An overview of family psychiatry. Psychiatric Annals, 10, 40-44.

2690.   Howells, J.G. (1980), Family diagnosis. Psychiatric Annals, 10, 248-252.

2691.   Howells, J.G. (1975), Vector therapy in family psychiatry. Child Psychiatry Quarterly, 8, 13-22.

2692.   Howells, J.G. (1975), Principles of family psychiatry. New York, NY: Brunner/Mazel.

2693.   Howells, J.G. (1972), Interpersonal transactions in the day of a seven year old boy. Acta Paedopsychiatrica, 38, 262-270.

2694.   Howells, J.G. (1970), Fallacies in child care: III. That children are brought up by parents. Acta Paedopsychiatrica, 37, 90-100.

2695.   Howells, J.G. (1969), Vector therapy in family therapy. Social Psychiatry, 4, 169-172.

2696.   Howells, J.G. (1965), Child psychiatry as an aspect of family psychiatry. Acta Paedopsychiatrica, 32, 35-44.

2697.   Howells, J.G. (1963), Extra-interview therapy in family psychiatry. Public Health, 77, 368-372.

2698.   Howells, J.G. (1969), A bridge between family psychiatry and psychiatry of the family. International Journal of Psychiatry, 89, 549-552.

2699.   Howells, J.G. (1968), Vector therapy as an aspect of family psychiatry.
        Psychotherapy and Psychosomatics, 16, 300-302.

2700.   Howells, J.G. (1979), Advances in family psychiatry. Advances in
        Family Psychiatry, 1, 542.

2701.   Howells, J.G. (Ed.) (1980), Advances in family psychiatry, Vol. 1.
        Madison, CT: International Universities Press.

2702.   Howells, J.G. (Ed.) (1980), Advances in family psychiatry, Vol. 2.
        Madison, CT: International Universities Press.

2703.   Howells, J.G., and Brown, A.W. (1985), Family diagnosis. Madison, CT:
        International Universities Press.

2704.   Howells, J.G., and Guirguis, W. (1985), The family and schizophrenia.
        Madison, CT: International Universities Press.

2705.   Hozman, T.L. (1974), A behavioral modification approach to marital
        counseling: The effect of two types of social modeling on the verbal
        interaction of a marital dyad. Dissertation Abstracts International, 34,
        5630-A.

2706.   Hozman, T.L., and Froiland, D.J. (1976), Families in divorce: A
        proposed model for counseling children. Family Coordinator, 25, 271-
        277.

2707.   Huber, C.H. (1979), Parents of the handicapped child: Facilitating
        acceptance through group counseling. Personnel and Guidance Journal,
        57, 267-268.

2708.   Huber, C.H. (1983), Divorce mediation: An opportunity for Adlerian
        counselors. Individual Psychology: Journal of Adlerian Theory,
        Research, and Practice, 39, 125-132.

2709.   Huber, C.H., and Milstein, B. (1985), Cognitive restructuring and a
        collaborative set in couples work. American Journal of Family Therapy,
        13, 17-27.

2710.   Huberty, C.E., and Huberty, D.J. (1976), Treating the parents of
        adolescent drug abusers. Contemporary Drug Problems, 5, 573-592.

2711.   Hudgens, G.J. (1979), Family-oriented treatment of chronic pain.
        Journal of Marital and Family Therapy, 5, 67-78.

2712.   Hudson, B.L. (1974), The families of agoraphobics treated by behavior
        therapy. British Journal of Social Work, 4(1), 51-59.

2713.   Hudson, J.A. (1979), Development and evaluation of problem-solving
        treatment package for marital therapy. Dissertation Abstracts
        International, 39, 5070-B.

2714.   Hudson, J.W., and Hudson, D.J. (1969), The marriage counselor, the
        child, and marital conflict. In: B.N. Ard, Jr., and C.C. Ard (Eds.),
        Handbook of marriage counseling. Palo Alto, CA: Science and Behavior
        Books.

2715.   Hudson, P. (1980), Different strokes for different folks: A comparative examination of behavioral, structural and paradoxical method in family therapy. Journal of Family Therapy, 2, 181-198.

2716.   Hudson, R.L. (1974), Married love in the middle years. Journal of Religion and Health, 13, 263-274.

2717.   Hughes, P. (1984), Review of A.S. Gurman's Questions and answers in the practice of family therapy, Vol. 2. British Journal of Psychiatry, 144, 224.

2718.   Humiston, K.E., Bondwin, J.W., and Num, W.E. (1967), Family therapy: Some contributions to treatment and training. Hospital and Community Psychiatry, 18, 40-43.

2719.   Humphrey, F.G. (1975), Changing roles for women: Implications for marriage counselors. Journal of Marriage and Family Counseling, 1, 219-227.

2720.   Humphrey, F.G. (1982), Extramarital affairs: Clinical approaches in marital therapy. Psychiatric Clinics of North America, 5, 581-593.

2721.   Humphrey, M., and Ounsted, C. (1964), Adoptive families referred for psychiatric advice: II. The parents. British Journal of Psychiatry, 110, 549-555.

2722.   Hunter, D.E.K. (1985), On the boundary: Family therapy in a long-term inpatient setting. Family Process, 24, 339-348.

2723.   Hunter, W.F. (1976), A selection of recent literature on human sexuality with special reference to marriage counseling practice. Journal of Psychology and Theology, 4(3), 233-252.

2724.   Huppert, P. (1976), The marriage counseling services in Australia. Medical Journal of Australia, 2, 142-144.

2725.   Hurley, R.P. (1982), The therapeutic advantage to the family therapist of intervening in the family-clinician system. Family Process, 21, 435-441.

2726.   Hurvitz, N. (1974), The family therapist as intermediary. Family Coordinator, 23, 145-158.

2727.   Hurvitz, N. (1975), The Miller family: Illustrating the symbolic interactionist approach to family therapy. Counseling Psychology, 5, 57-104.

2728.   Hurvitz, N. (1979), The sociologist as a marital and family therapist. American Behavioral Science, 22, 557-576.

2729.   Hurvitz, N. (1961), Group counseling with expectant mothers. Mental Hygiene in New York, 45, 439-449.

2730.   Hurvitz, N. (1967), Marital problems following psychotherapy with one spouse. Journal of Consulting Psychology, 31, 38-47.

2731.   Hurvitz, N. (1965), The marital roles inventory as a counseling instrument. Journal of Marriage and the Family, 27, 29-31.

2732.   Hutchinson, K.R., Nichols, W.C., and Hutchinson, I.W. (1980), Therapy for divorcing clergy: Implications from research. Journal of Divorce, 4(1), 83-94.

2733.   Hyer, L.A. (1983), Case history: Paradoxical letters in family therapy. Clinical Gerontologist, 2, 58-61.

2734.   Illingworth, R.S. (1967), Counseling the parents of the mentally handicapped child. Clinical Pediatrics, 6, 340-348.

2735.   Im, W.G., Wilner, R.S., and Breit, M. (1983), Jealousy: Interventions in couples therapy. Family Process, 22, 211-219.

2736.   Impey, L. (1981), Art media: A means to therapeutic communication with families. Perspectives in Psychiatric Care, 19, 70-77.

2737.   In, P.A., and McDermott, J.F., Jr. (1976), The treatment of child abuse: Play therapy with a 4-year-old. Journal of the American Academy of Child Psychiatry, 15(3), 430-440.

2738.   Inda, L.E. (1973), Family therapy and adolescence. Archivis Di Psicologia, Neurologia, e Psychiatria, 14, 117-121.

2739.   Ingoldsby, B.B. (1980), Review of P.J. Guerin's Family therapy: Theory and practice. Family Relations, 29, 134.

2740.   Ingram, G.L. (1974), Families in crisis. In R.E. Hardy and J.G. Cull (Eds.), Therapeutic needs of the family: Problems, descriptions and therapeutic approaches. Springfield, IL: Charles C. Thomas.

2741.   Insall, N. (1981), Use of an ending to work with a family's difficulty about differentiation. In S. Box, B. Copley, J. Magagna, and E. Moustaki (Eds.), Psychotherapy with families: An analytic approach. London: Routledge and Kegan Paul Ltd.

2742.   Ionedes, N.S. (1982), Therapy program for contemporary marital crises. Individual Psychology: Journal of Adlerian Theory, Research, & Practice, 38, 332-337.

2743.   Irish, G. (1967), Behavioral changes of participants in family group consultation Dissertation Abstracts International, 28, 467-468.

2744.   Irwin, C. (1985), Review of L.R. Wolberg and M.L. Aronson (Eds.), Group and family therapy. Australian and New Zealand Journal of Psychiatry, 19(1), 106.

2745.   Isaacs, C. (1983), Training family therapists: Identification and teaching of important therapist skills. Dissertation Abstracts International, 43, 3052-B.

2746.   Isaacs, C.D., Embry, L.H., and Baer, D.M. (1982), Training family therapists: An experimental analysis. Journal of Applied Behavior Analysis, 15, 505-520.

2747.   Isaacs, M.B. (1982), Helping Mom fail: A case of a stalemated divorcing process. Family Process, 21, 225-234.

2748. Isaacs, M.B. (1982), Therapy with remarriage families: IX. Facilitating family restructuring and relinkage. Family Therapy Collections, 2, 121-143.

2749. Ishizuka, Y. (1982), Divorce: Can and should it be prevented? Family Therapy, 9, 69-90.

2750. Ishizuka, Y. (1979), Causes of anxiety and depression in marriage. Psychiatric Annals, 9(6), 302-309.

2751. Ishizuka, Y. (1979), Conjoint therapy for marital problems. Psychiatric Annals, 9(6), 310-317.

2752. Isohanni, M. (1977), Experience of relatives' meetings in a therapeutic community. Psychiatria Fennica, 17, 171-180.

2753. Ito, K.L. (1985), Ho'oponopono, "To make right": Hawaiian conflict resolution and metaphor in the construction of a family therapy. Culture, Medicine and Psychiatry, 9(2), 201.

2754. Jackson, D.D. (1961), Family therapy in the family of the schizophrenic. In: M.I. Stein (Ed.), Contemporary psychotherapies. New York, NY: Free Press.

2755. Jackson, D.D. (Ed.) (1968), Communication, family and marriage. Palo Alto, CA: Science and Behavior.

2756. Jackson, D.D., Riskin, J., and Satir, V. (1961), A method of analysis of a family interview. Archives of General Psychiatry, 5, 321-339.

2757. Jackson, D.D., and Weakland, J.H. (1961), Conjoint family therapy: Some considerations on theory, technique, and results. Psychiatry, 24, 30-45.

2758. Jackson, D.D., and Yalom, I. (1964), Family homeostasis and patient change. Current Psychiatric Therapies, 4, 155-165.

2759. Jackson, J. (1962), A family group therapy technique for stalemate in individual treatment. International Journal of Group Psychotherapy, 12(2), 164-170.

2760. Jackson, J., and Grotjahn, M. (1959), The efficacy of group therapy in a case of marriage neurosis. International Journal of Group Psychotherapy, 9, 420-428.

2761. Jackson, J., and Grotjahn, M. (1958), The re-enactment of the marriage neurosis in group psychotherapy. Journal of Nervous and Mental Disease, 127, 503-510.

2762. Jackson, R.L. (1979), Maternal and infant nutrition and health in later life. Nutrition Review, 37, 33-37.

2763. Jacob, T., Favorini, A., Meisel, S.S., and Anderson, C.M. (1978), The alcoholic's spouse, children and family interactions: Substantive findings and methodological issues. Journal for Studies on Alcohol, 39, 1231-1251.

2764.   Jacob, T., Kornbut, S., Anderson, C., and Hartl, M. (1978), Role
        expectation and role performance in distressed and normal couples.
        Journal of Abnormal Psychology, 87, 286-290.

2765.   Jacob, T., and Grounds, L. (1978), Family interaction and
        communication deviance in pathological and normal families.
        Confusions and conclusions: A response to Doane. Family Process, 17,
        377-387.

2766.   Jacobs, L.I. (1975), Marital sex therapy. Current Psychiatric Therapies,
        15, 205-212.

2767.   Jacobson, C., and Mann, J. (1962), Families in treatment. Group
        Psychotherapy, Psychodrama and Sociometry, 15, 46-51.

2768.   Jacobson, G.F., and Portuges, H.S. (1978), Relations of marital
        separation and divorce to suicide: A report. Suicide and Life
        Threatening Behavior, 8, 217-224.

2769.   Jacobson, N.S. (1978), An experimental investigation of a behavioral
        approach to the treatment of marital discord. Dissertation Abstracts
        International, 38, 6158-6159-B.

2770.   Jacobson, N.S. (1978), Review of research on effectiveness of marital-
        therapy. In T.J. Paolini and B.S. McCardy (Eds.), Marriage and marital
        therapy: Psychoanalytic, behavioral, and systems theory perspectives.
        New York, NY: Brunner/Mazel.

2771.   Jacobson, N.S. (1978), Specific and nonspecific factors in the
        effectiveness of a behavioral approach to the treatment of marital
        discord. Journal of Consulting and Clinical Psychology, 46, 442-452.

2772.   Jacobson, N.S. (1977), Problem solving and contingency contracting in
        the treatment of marital discord. Journal of Consulting and Clinical
        Psychology, 45, 92-100.

2773.   Jacobson, N.S. (1978), Contingency contracting with couples:
        Redundancy and caution. Behavior Therapy, 9, 679.

2774.   Jacobson, N.S. (1978), A stimulus control model of change in behavioral
        couples' therapy: Implications for contingency contracting. Journal of
        Marital and Family Therapy, 4, 29-36.

2775.   Jacobson, N.S. (1977), Training couples to solve their marital
        problems: A behavioral approach to relationship discord: I. Problem-
        solving skills. International Journal of Family Counseling, 1, 22-31.

2776.   Jacobson, N.S. (1983), Beyond empiricism: The politics of marital
        therapy. American Journal of Family Therapy, 11, 11-24.

2777.   Jacobson, N.S. (1980), Behavioral marital therapy: Current trends in
        research, assessment and practice. American Journal of Family
        Therapy, 8(2), 3-5.

2778.   Jacobson, N.S. (1984), A component analysis of behavioral marital
        therapy: The relative effectiveness of behavior exchange and
        communication/problem-solving training. Journal of Consulting and
        Clinical Psychology, 52, 295-305.

2779.   Jacobson, N.S. (1985), Family therapy outcome research: Potential pitfalls and prospects. Journal of Marital and Family Therapy, 11(2), 149-158.

2780.   Jacobson, N.S., Follette, V.M., Follette, W.C., Holtzworthmunroe, A., Kait, J.L., and Schmaling, K.B. (1985), A component analysis of behavioral marital therapy: One year follow-up. Behaviour Research and Therapy, 23, 549-556.

2781.   Jacobson, N.S., Follette, W.C., and McDonald, D.W. (1982), Reactivity to positive and negative behavior in distressed and nondistressed married couples. Journal of Consulting and Clinical Psychology, 50, 706-14.

2782.   Jacobson, N.S., Waldron, H., and Moore, D. (1980), Toward a behavioral profile of marital distress. Journal of Consulting and Clinical Psychology, 48, 696-703.

2783.   Jacobson, N.S., and Anderson, E.A. (1980), The effects of behavior rehearsal and feedback on the acquisition of problem-solving skills in distressed and nondistressed couples. Behavior Research and Therapy, 18, 25-36.

2784.   Jacobson, N.S., and Follette, W.C. (1985), Clinical significance of improvement resulting from two behavioral marital therapy components. Behavior Therapy, 16(3), 249.

2785.   Jacobson, N.S., and Martin, B. (1976), Behavioral marriage therapy: Current status. Psychological Bulletin, 83, 540-556.

2786.   Jacobson, N.S., and Moore, D. (1981), Spouses as observers of the events in their relationship. Journal of Consulting and Clinical Psychology, 49, 269-77.

2787.   Jacobson, N.S., and Weiss, R.L. (1978), Behavioral marriage therapy: III. Contents of Gurman et al. May be hazardous to our health. Family Process, 17, 149-163.

2788.   Jaffe, D.T. (1978), The role of family therapy in treating physical illness. Hospital and Community Psychiatry, 29, 169-174.

2789.   Jaffe, M. (1976), Repatterning an ineffective mother-daughter attachment. Perspectives in Psychiatric Care, 14, 34-39.

2790.   Jaffe, P.G., Thompson, J.K., and Paquin, M.J. (1978), Immediate family crisis intervention as preventative mental health: The family consultant service. Professional Psychology, 9, 551.

2791.   Jakes, A., and Kratochvil, S. (1977), Short-term techniques of reducing tensions in married life. Ceskoslovenska Psychologia, 21(2), 121-125.

2792.   James, B. (1985), Review of C.B. Broderick's The therapeutic triangle: A sourcebook on marital therapy. Family Process, 34(1), 145.

2793.   James, K., and McIntyre, D. (1983), The reproduction of families: The social role of family therapy? Journal of Marital and Family Therapy, 9, 119-129.

2794. James, M. (1982), Review of F. Tustin's Autistic states in children. International Journal of Psychoanalysis, 63, 504-513.

2795. James, T.S. (1974), Why marry? African Journal of Medical Sciences, 48, 340-341.

2796. Janner, R., and Janner, J. (1966), Eheberatung als gruppenarbeit. (Marriage counseling as a group endeavor.) Psychotherapy and Psychosomatics, 14, 17-31.

2797. Jans-Dimond, R.J. (1983), The impact of a learning disability on children and their parents: A qualitative study of the individual perspectives. Dissertation Abstracts International, 43, 913-B.

2798. Jansma, T.J. (1972), Multiple vs. individual family therapy: Its effects on family concepts. Dissertation Abstracts International, 33, 128-1289-B.

2799. Janzen, C. (1978), Family treatment for alcoholism: A review. Social Work, 23, 135-141.

2800. Janzen, C. (1977), Families in the treatment of alcoholism. Journal of Studies on Alcohol, 38, 114-130.

2801. Jarvis, P., Esty, J., and Stutzman, L. (1969), Evaluation and treatment of families at the Fort Logan Mental Health Center. Community Mental Health Journal, 5, 14-19.

2802. Jeammet, P., Gorge, A., Zweiffel, F., and Flavigny, H. (1971), A study of familial interrelations in anorexia nervosa: Results of group psychotherapy of the parents. Revue de Neuropsychiatrie Infantile et D'Hygeine Mentale de L'Enfance, 1(11), 691.

2803. Jeammet, P., and Gorge, A. (1980), A form of family therapy: The patient's group. Results of 6-years' functioning of an open group of parents of anorexia nervosa adolescents. Psychiatrie de L'Enfant, 23, 587-636.

2804. Jefferson, C. (1978), Some notes on the use of family sculpture in therapy. Family Process, 17, 69-76.

2805. Jeineck, L.J. (1977), The special needs of the adolescent with chronic illness. American Journal of Maternal-Child Nursing, 2, 57-61.

2806. Jemail, J.A., and LoPiccolo, J. (1982), A sexual and a marital defensiveness scale for each sex. American Journal of Family Therapy, 10, 33-40.

2807. Jenkins, C. (1985), Orthodoxy in family practice as servant or tyrant. Journal of Family Therapy, 7(1), 19-31.

2808. Jenkins, H. (1981), Can I (let you let me) leave: Therapy with the adolescent and his family. Journal of Family Therapy, 3(2), 113-138.

2809. Jenkins, H. (1980), "Paradox: A pivotal point in therapy." Journal of Family Therapy, 2(4), 339-356.

2810. Jenkins, H. (1984), Which skills how: Options for family therapy training. Journal of Family Therapy, 6(1), 17-34.

2811. Jenkins, H. (1983), Review of R. Whiffen and J. Bynghall's Family therapy supervision: Recent developments in practice. Journal of Adolescence, 6, 106.

2812. Jenkins, J., Hildebrand, J., and Lask, B. (1982), Failure: An exploration and survival kit. Journal of Family Therapy, 4, 307.

2813. Jensen, G.D., and Wallace, J.G. (1967), Family mourning process. Family Process, 6, 56-66.

2814. Jensen, R. (1979), Review of H. Kwiatkowska's Family therapy and evaluation through art. Family Process, 4, 498.

2815. Jeppson, L., and Pruul, A. (1975), Reciprocity counseling in family therapy. Scandinavian Journal of Behavior Therapy, 4, 181-193.

2816. Jeri, F.R., and Sanchez, C. (1971), Psicosis en la ninez de comienzo tardio. (Late onset child psychosis.) Revue de Neuropsychiatrie Infantile et D'Hygeine Mentale de L'Enfance, 34, 91-109.

2817. Jersild, E.A. (1967), Group therapy for patient's spouses. American Journal of Nursing, 67, 544-549.

2818. Jessee, E., and L'Abate, L. (1981), Enrichment role-playing as a step in the training of family therapists. Journal of Marital and Family Therapy, 7, 507-514.

2819. Jessee, R.E., and Guerney, B.G. (1981), A comparison of Gestalt and relationship enhancement treatments with married couples. American Journal of Family Therapy, 9, 31-41.

2820. Jewson, R.H. (1980), The National Council on Family Relations: Decade of the seventies. Journal of Marriage and the Family, 40, 1017-1028.

2821. Jobin, H. (1979), Psychological problems of the child and his family. Canada's Mental Health, 27, 20-21.

2822. Joel, L.A. (1983), Review of I.W. Clements and D.M. Buchanan's Family therapy: A nursing perspective. American Journal of Nursing, 83, 102.

2823. Joffe, W.A. (1980), The effects of selected models of behavioral rehearsal upon the non-verbal communication of married couples. Dissertation Abstracts International, 40, 3937-B.

2824. Johnsen, A. (1983), Psychosis and family therapy. Tidsskrift for Norsk Psykologforening, 20, 315-323.

2825. Johnson, D. (Ed.) (1961), Marriage counseling: Theory and practice. Englewood Cliffs, NJ: Prentice-Hall.

2826. Johnson, D.M., and Sauage, M.J. (1967), The admission of mother and child: An approach to family therapy. Canadian Journal of Psychiatry, 12, 409-411.

2827. Johnson, E.M., and Stark, D.E. (1980), A group program for cancer patients and their family members in an acute care teaching hospital. Social Work and Health Care, 5, 335-349.

2828.   Johnson, E.S. (1969), Utilization of behavioral science concepts for a family in crisis. American Nursing Association Clinical Conference, 164.

2829.   Johnson, F.K. (1980), Notes on infant psychotherapy. Infant Mental Health Journal, 1(1), 19-33.

2830.   Johnson, F.L., Rudolf, L.A., and Hartmann, J.R. (1979), Helping the family cope with childhood cancer. Psychosomatics, 20, 241, 245-247, 251.

2831.   Johnson, G. (1968), Family treatment in psychiatric hospitals. Psychotherapy and Psychosomatics, 16, 333-338.

2832.   Johnson, J., Weeks, G.R., and L'Abate, L. (1979), Forced holding: A technique for treating parentified children. Family Therapy, 6, 123-132.

2833.   Johnson, J., and Watt, W. (1983), The survival to overachievement continuum: A new construct for clinical use. Family Therapy, 10, 77-90.

2834.   Johnson, J.L. (1976), A time-series analysis of the effects of therapy on family interaction. Dissertation Abstracts International, 36, 5796-B.

2835.   Johnson, K.P. (1968), Self-concept validation as the focus of marriage counseling. Family Coordinator, 17, 174-180.

2836.   Johnson, L.J. (1983), The effects of exploring family of origin on marital cohesion, adaptability, and family environment. Dissertation Abstracts International, 43, 2341-B.

2837.   Johnson, L.L. (1979), Kin selection in finite sibships (letter). Journal of Theoretical Biology, 77, 379-381.

2838.   Johnson, M.N., and Boren, Y. (1982), Sexual knowledge and spouse abuse: A cultural phenomenon. Issues in Mental Health Nursing, 4, 217-231.

2839.   Johnson, N.G. (1981), Child/family therapy: A question of whom and when. Family and Child Mental Health Journal, 7, 130-137.

2840.   Johnson, R.H. (1981), Preparation for family therapy: A videotaped procedure. Dissertation Abstracts International, 42, 1177-B.

2841.   Johnson, S.M., and Christenson, A. (1975), Multiple criteria follow-up of behavior modification with families. Journal of Abnormal Child Psychology, 3, 135-154.

2842.   Johnson, S.M., and Greenberg, L.S. (1985), Emotionally focused couples therapy: An outcome study. Journal of Marital and Family Therapy, 11, 313-318.

2843.   Johnson, T.F. (1977), Couple therapy as a method for treating male exhibitionism: Flashing. Journal of Marital and Family Therapy, 3, 33-38.

2844.   Johnson, T.F. (1975), Family therapy with families having delinquent offspring. Family Counseling, 3, 32-37.

2845.   Johnson, T.F. (1974), Hooking the involuntary family into treatment: Family therapy in a juvenile court setting. Family Therapy, 1, 79–82.

2846.   Johnson, T.F. (1977), The results of family therapy with juvenile offenders. Juvenile Justice, 28, 29.

2847.   Johnson, T.F. (1978), A contextual approach to treatment of juvenile offenders. Offender Rehabilitation, 3(2), 171–179.

2848.   Johnson, T.M. (1972), Effects of family therapy on patterns of verbal interchange in disturbed families. Dissertation Abstracts International, 32, 6650–6651-B.

2849.   Johnson, T.M., and Malony, H.N. (1977), Effects of short-term family therapy on patterns of verbal interchange in disturbed families. Family Therapy, 4, 207–215.

2850.   Jojic-Milenkovic, M. (1975), (Parallel interview in therapy with married couples.) Anali Zavoda za Mentalno Zdravije, 7, 57–61.

2851.   Jolly, J.D. (1977), Child care in North America. Child abuse: Can it be prevented? Part 5. Nursing Times, 73, 1994–1995.

2852.   Jones, E. (1983), Leaving whom – motherless families – problems of termination for the female family therapist. Journal of Family Therapy, 5, 11–22.

2853.   Jones, M.B. (1973), Nonassortative mating and small mean differences: A comment on the Reeds' family study. Social Biology, 20, 347–349.

2854.   Jones, M.C. (1968), An analysis of a family folder. Nursing Outlook, 16, 48–51.

2855.   Jones, R.M. (1978), An adolescent unit assessed: Attitudes to a treatment experience for adolescents and their families. Journal of Adolescence, 1, 371–384.

2856.   Jones, S.A. (1982), Review of M. Andolif and I. Zwerling's Dimensions of family therapy. Bulletin of the Menninger Clinic, 65, 294.

2857.   Jones, S.L. (1980), Family therapy: A comparison of approaches, Ed. 2. Bowie, MD: Brady.

2858.   Jones, S.L., and Dimond, M. (1982), Family theory and family therapy models: Comparative review with implications for nursing practice. Journal of Psychosocial Nursing and Mental Health Services, 20, 12–9.

2859.   Jones, W.L. (1969), Marriage: Growth or disaster? American Journal of Psychiatry, 125, 1115–1119.

2860.   Jones, W.L. (1967), The villain and the victim: Group therapy for married couples. American Journal of Psychiatry, 124, 351–354.

2861.   Jones, W.P. (1976), Some implications of the Sixteen Personality Factor Questionnaire for marital guidance. Family Coordinator, 25, 189–192.

2862.   Jongerius, P.J. (1979), All in the family. Group Analysis, 12, 13–16.

2863.   Jordan, J.R. (1985), Paradox and polarity: The tao of family therapy. Family Process, 24, 165-174.

2864.   Jordan, J.R. (1982), The use of history in family therapy: A brief rejoinder to Sluzki. Journal of Marital and Family Therapy, 8, 393-398.

2865.   Jordan, W. (1981), Family therapy: An outsider's view. Journal of Family Therapy, 3, 269-280.

2866.   Jorgensen, G.Q., Hammond, D.C., and Hardy, A. (1977), Saturation marathon couples' therapy in prison: A rationale. International Journal of Group Psychotherapy, 27, 97-103.

2867.   Jorne, P. (1979), Counseling sexually abused children: Further response. Personnel and Guidance Journal, 57(10), 502-506.

2868.   Jorstad, J., Ygelstad, E., and Mahabir, R.J. (1979), Schizophrenia 75: Psychotherapy, family studies, research. Canadian Journal of Psychiatry, 24(4), 370-371.

2869.   Joslyn, B.E. (1982), Shifting sex roles: The silence of the family therapy literature. Clinical Social Work Journal, 10, 39-51.

2870.   Josten, L. (1978), Out-of-hospital care for a pervasive family problem: Child abuse. American Journal of Maternal-Child Nursing, 3, 111-116.

2871.   Julian, A. (1979), Group treatment of juvenile delinquents: Review of the outcome literature. International Journal of Group Psychotherapy, 29, 3-38.

2872.   Julian, B., Ventola, L., and Christ, J. (1969), Multiple family therapy: The interaction of young hospitalized patients with their mothers. International Journal of Group Psychotherapy, 19, 501-509.

2873.   Julius, E.K. (1978), Family sculpting: A pilot program for a schizophrenic group. Journal of Marriage and Family Counseling, 4(3), 19-24.

2874.   Jung, M. (1983), Directions for building family development theory. Social Casework, 64, 363-370.

2875.   Jung, M. (1984), Structural family therapy: Its application to Chinese families. Family Process, 23(3), 635-674.

2876.   Juni, S. (1980), The stigma of mental illness as a cultural phenomenon: A study of schizophrenia in the Orthodox Jewish family. Family Therapy, 7(3), 223-236.

2877.   Junker, H. (1972), Experiences with group therapy in married couples of the upper lower class. Psyche, 26, 370-388.

2878.   Jurich, A.P., and Jurich, J.A. (1975), The lost adolescence syndrome. Family Coordinator, 24, 357-361.

2879.   Justice, B. (1978), Evaluating outcome of group therapy for abusing parents. Corrective and Social Psychiatry, 24(1), 45-52.

2880.   Justice, R., and Justice, B. (1976), The abusing family. New York: Human Science Press.

2881.   Kadis, A.L. (1956), Re-experiencing the family constellation in group psychotherapy. American Journal of Individual Psychology, 12, 63-68.

2882.   Kadis, A.L. (1964), A new approach to marital therapy. International Journal of Social Psychiatry, 10(4), 261-265.

2883.   Kadis, A.L. (1972), Current theories and basic concepts in family therapy. In: G.D. Goldman and D.S. Milman (Eds.), Innovations in psychotherapy. Springfield, IL: Charles C. Thomas.

2884.   Kadis, L.B., and McClendon, R.A. (1981), Redecision family therapy: Its use with intensive multiple family groups. American Journal of Family Therapy, 9, 75-83.

2885.   Kadis, L.B., and McClendon, R.A. (1983), Chocolate pudding and other approaches to intensive family therapy. Palo Alto, CA: Science and Behavior.

2886.   Kadushin, P. (1971), Toward a family diagnostic system. Family Coordinator, 20, 279-289.

2887.   Kadushin, P. (1969), The family story technique and intrafamily analysis. Journal of Project Technology, 33, 438-450.

2888.   Kadushin, P., Waxenberg, S.E., and Sager, C.J. (1971), Family story technique changes in interactions and effects during family therapy. Journal of Personality Assessment, 35, 62-71.

2889.   Kaffman, M. (1981), Paranoid disorders: The core of truth behind the delusional system. International Journal of Family Therapy, 3, 29-41.

2890.   Kaffman, M. (1965), Family diagnosis and therapy in child emotional pathology. Family Process, 4, 241-258.

2891.   Kaffman, M. (1985), Twenty years of family therapy in Israel: A personal journey. Family Process, 24(1), 113-128.

2892.   Kaffman, M. (1963), Short-term family therapy. Family Process, 2, 216-234.

2893.   Kaffman, M. (1969), Triadic-based family therapy: Six of one, half a dozen of another. International Journal of Psychiatry, 8, 553-556.

2894.   Kagan, E., and Zaks, M.S. (1972), Couple multi-couple therapy for marriages in crisis. Psychotherapy: Theory, Reserarch and Practice, 3, 332-336.

2895.   Kagan, H., and Zucker, A.H. (1970), Treatment of a "corrupted" family by rabbi and psychiatrist. Journal of Religion and Health, 9, 22-34.

2896.   Kagan, R.M. (1983), Engaging family competence to prevent repetitive and lengthy institutionalization of acting-out youth. Residential Group Care and Treatment, 15, 55-70.

2897.   Kahn, A.V. (1969), A therapeutic technique based on the interpersonal
        theory of psychiatry and the family dynamics. Psychotherapy,
        Psychodrama and Sociometry, 17, 226-240.

2898.   Kahn, C. (1984), Reviews of F. Bocus's Couples therapy, E.A. Carter and
        M. McGoldrick (Eds.). The family life cycle: A framework for family
        therapy, D.S. Freeman, Techniques of family therapy, and C.M. Hall,
        The Bowen family theory and its uses. The Psychoanalytic Review,
        71(4), 664-669.

2899.   Kahn, C. (1979), Review of P. Papp's, Family therapy: Full length case
        studies. Psychoanalytic Review, 66, 302.

2900.   Kahn, M.D. (1979), Organizational consultation and the teaching of
        family therapy: Contrasting case histories. Journal of Marital and
        Family Therapy, 5, 69-80.

2901.   Kahn, M.D., and Bank, S. (1981), In pursuit of sisterhood: Adult siblings
        as a resource for combined individual and family therapy. Family
        Process, 20, 85-95.

2902.   Kahn, M.D., and Bank, S. (1980), Therapy with siblings in reorganizing
        families: II. International Journal of Family Therapy, 2, 155-158.

2903.   Kahn, R., and Goodman, H. (1973), Successful adaptations of group
        therapy techniques in the treatment of socially and economically
        deprived mothers of school children. American Journal of
        Orthopsychiatry, 43(2), 262.

2904.   Kahn, S., and Kahn, M. (1982), Comment on readability of marital
        assessment measures used by behavioral marriage therapists.
        Psychological Reports, 45, 833-834.

2905.   Kalb, M. (1983), The conception of the alternative and the decision to
        divorce. American Journal of Psychotherapy, 37, 346-356.

2906.   Kales, J.D., and Kales, A. (1975), Managing the individual and family in
        crisis. American Family Physician, 12, 109-115.

2907.   Kaminski, Z. (1975), Case report: An asthmatic adolescent and his
        "repressed cry" for his mother. British Journal of Medical Psychology,
        48, 185-188.

2908.   Kane, B. (1970), Uncoupling marriages. Journal for Specialists in Group
        Work, 4(2), 87-93.

2909.   Kane, R.P. (1981), The family's role in primary prevention. Journal of
        Childhood and Contemporary Society, 14, 27-34.

2910.   Kanoff, H. (1978), Premarital counseling by the family physician.
        Medical Aspects of Human Sexuality, 12(9), 51-52.

2911.   Kanter, J., and Lin, A. (1980), Facilitating a therapeutic milieu in the
        families of schizophrenics. Psychiatry, 43, 106-119.

2912.   Kantor, D. (1983), The structural-analytic approach to the treatment of
        family developmental crisis. Family Therapy Collections, 8, 12-34.

2913.   Kantor, D. (1982), Review of D. Reiss' The family's construction of reality. Family Process, 21, 483-485.

2914.   Kantor, D., and Neal, J.H. (1985), Integrative shifts for the theory and practice of family systems therapy. Family Process, 24, 13-30.

2915.   Kantor, D., and Vickers, M.I. (1983), Divorce along the family life cycle. Family Therapy Collections, 8, 78-99.

2916.   Kantor, R.E., and Hoffman, L. (1966), Brechtian theater as a model for conjoint family therapy. Family Process, 5, 218-229.

2917.   Kaplan Denour, A., Fisher, G., Mass, M., and Czaczkes, J.W. (1974), Diagnosis and therapy of families of patients on chronic hemodialysis. Mental Health and Society, 1(304), 251-256.

2918.   Kaplan, A.H. (1969), Joint parent-adolescent interviews as a parameter in the psychoanalysis of the younger adolescent. Journal of Nervous and Mental Disease, 148, 550-558.

2919.   Kaplan, D., and Mearig, J.S. (1977), A community support system for a family coping with chronic illness. Rehabilitation Literature, 38, 79-82, 96.

2920.   Kaplan, J., Saayman, G.S., and Faber, P.A. (1981), An investigation of the use of nocturnal dream reports as diagnostic indices in the assessment of family problem solving. Journal of Family Therapy, 3, 227-242.

2921.   Kaplan, M.L., and Kaplan, N.R. (1978), Individual and family growth: A gestalt approach. Family Process, 17, 195-205.

2922.   Kaplan, M.L., and Kaplan, N.R. (1982), Organization of experience among family members in the immediate present: A Gestalt/systems integration. Journal of Marital and Family Therapy, 8, 5-14.

2923.   Kaplan, S.L. (1979), Behavior modification as a limit-setting task in the family psychotherapy of a disruptive boy. Journal of the American Academy of Child Psychiatry, 18, 492-504.

2924.   Kaplan, S.L. (1977), Structural family therapy for children of divorce: Case reports. Family Process, 16, 75-83.

2925.   Kaplan, S.L., and Escoll, P. (1973), Treatment of two silent adolescent girls. Journal of the American Academy of Child Psychiatry, 12, 59-72.

2926.   Kardener, S.H. (1970), Convergent internal security systems: A rationale for marital therapy. Family Process, 9(1), 83-91.

2927.   Karno, M., Brunon, J., Ishiki, D., and Wagniere, G. (1981), Therapeutic use of generative graphics: II. Application to family therapy. Journal of Mental Imagery, 1, 105-114.

2928.   Karofsky, P.S., Keith, D.V., Hoornstra, L.L., and Clune, C.S. (1983), A follow-up study of the impact of family therapy in the pediatric office. Clinical Pediatrics, 22, 351-355.

2929.   Karpel, M. (1976), Individuation: From fusion to dialogue. Family Process, 15, 65–82.

2930.   Karpel, M.A. (1977), Intrapsychic and interpersonal processes in the parentification of children. Dissertation Abstracts International, 38, 365B.

2931.   Karpel, M.A. (1980), Family secrets: I. Conceptual and ethical issues in the relational context. II. Ethical and practical considerations in therapeutic management. Family Process, 19, 295–306.

2932.   Karpel, M.A., and Strauss, E.S. (1983), Family evaluation. New York: Gardner Press.

2933.   Karpf, M. (1951), Marriage counseling and psychotherapy: A case. Marriage and Family Living, 13, 169–174.

2934.   Karpf, M.J. (1952), Premarital counseling and psychotherapy: Two cases. Marriage and Family Living, 14, 56–75.

2935.   Karson, M.A., and Karson, A. (1978), Counseling couples in their sixties. Social Work, 23, 243–244.

2936.   Kaslow, F. (1979), What personal photos reveal about marital sex conflicts. Journal of Sex and Marital Therapy, 5(2), 134–141.

2937.   Kaslow, F. (1980), Families, family therapy and the law. Journal of Marriage and Family Therapy, 6, 257–258.

2938.   Kaslow, F. (1985), Review of C.J. Falicov's Cultural perspectives in family therapy. Journal of Marital and Family Therapy, 11, 331.

2939.   Kaslow, F., and Hyatt, R. (1981), Divorce: A potential growth experience for the extended family. Journal of Divorce, 5, 115–126.

2940.   Kaslow, F.W. (1981), A dialectic approach to family therapy and practice: Selectivity and synthesis. Journal of Marital and Family Therapy, 7, 345–351.

2941.   Kaslow, F.W. (1980), History of family therapy in the United States: A kaleidoscopic overview. Marriage and Family Review, 3, 77–111.

2942.   Kaslow, F.W. (1978), Marital or family therapy for prisoners and their spouses or families. Federal Probation, 42, 53–60.

2943.   Kaslow, F.W. (1984), Divorce mediation and its emotional impact on the couple and their children. American Journal of Family Therapy, 12(3), 58–66.

2944.   Kaslow, F.W. (1981), Group therapy with couples in conflict: Its more better. Psychotherapy: Theory, Research and Practice, 18(4), 516.

2945.   Kaslow, F.W. (Ed.) (1982), The international book of family therapy. New York: Brunner/Mazel.

2946.   Kaslow, F.W., and Cooper, B. (1978), Family therapy with the learning disabled child and his/her family. Journal of Marital and Family Therapy, 4, 41–49.

180   Family Therapy

2947. Kaslow, F.W., and Friedman, J. (1977), Utilization of family photos and movies in family therapy. Journal of Marital and Family Therapy, 3, 19-25.

2948. Kaslow, F.W., and Friedman, J. (1980), Utilization of family photos and movies in family therapy. Advances in Family Psychiatry, 2, 257-266.

2949. Kaslow, F.W., and Ridenour, R.I. (Eds.) (1984), The military family: Dynamics and treatment. New York: Guilford Press.

2950. Kaslow, N.H., and Jackson, L.J. (1980), Review of N.S. Jacobson and G. Margolin's Marital therapy. Journal of Marital and Family Therapy, 6, 486.

2951. Katkin, S. (1979), Charting as a multipurpose treatment intervention for family therapy. Family Process, 17, 465-504.

2952. Katz, A.J., deKrasinski, M., Philip, E., and Wieser, C. (1975), Change in interactions as a measure of effectiveness in short-term family therapy. Family Therapy, 2, 31-56.

2953. Katz, B. (1981), Separation-individuation and marital therapy. Psychotherapy: Theory, Research, and Practice, 18, 195-203.

2954. Katz, J. (1982), Couples contracting workshops: A proactive counseling strategy. Personnel and Guidance Journal, 60, 567-571.

2955. Katz, J. (1979), Review of H. Stierlin's Psychoanalysis and family therapy. Psychoanalytic Review, 66, 301.

2956. Kaubish, V.K., and Nechaev, M.L. (1981), Couples psychotherapy of epileptic children in a psychiatric hospital. Zhurnal Neuropatologica Psikhiatrica, 28, 887-891.

2957. Kaufman, E. (1980), Myth and reality in the family patterns and treatment of substance abusers. American Journal of Drug and Alcohol Abuse, 7(3-4), 257-279.

2958. Kaufman, E. (1985), Family systems and family therapy of substance abuse: An overview of two decades of research and clinical experience. International Journal of the Addictions, 20, 879-916.

2959. Kaufman, E. (1985), Substance abuse and family therapy. New York: Grune and Stratton.

2960. Kaufman, E., and Kaufman, P. (1980), Family therapy of substance abusers. In: L. Brill and C. Winick (Eds.), Yearbook of substance use and abuse, Vol. 2. New York: Human Sciences Pres, pp. 113-143.

2961. Kaufman, E., and Kaufman, P. (1977), Multiple family therapy: A new direction in the treatment of drug abusers. American Journal of Drug and Alcohol Abuse, 4, 467-478.

2962. Kaufman, E., and Kaufman, P. (Eds.). (1979), Family therapy of drug and alcohol abuse. Pauline Kaufman, editor. National Council on Alcoholism. New York: Gardner Press.

2963.   Kaufman, E., and Pattison, E.M. (1981), Differential methods of family therapy in the treatment of alcoholism. Journal of Studies on Alcohol, 42, 951-71.

2964.   Kaufman, S.H. (1980), Review of E. Kaufman and P.N. Kaufman's Family therapy of drug and alcohol abuse. American Journal of Family Therapy, 8, 77-78.

2965.   Kaufmann, L. (1975), The therapy of schizophrenic families. Evolution Psychiatrique, 40, 363-378.

2966.   Kaufmann, L. (1969), Die handhabung der beziehung zwichen familie, patient und klinik. (The management of relations between the family, patient, and clinic.) Zeitschrift fur Psychotherapie und Medizinische Psychologie, 19, 221-229.

2967.   Kaufmann, L. (1969), Family research and therapy in schizophrenics. Nervenarzt, 40, 302-308.

2968.   Kaufmann, L. (1969), Family therapy. Bibliotheca Psychiatrica et Neurologica; Supplementa ad Psychiatria et Neurologia, 141, 103-118.

2969.   Kaufmann, L. (1969), Premieres experiences de la therapie de famille en clinique psychiatrique. (Initial experiences with family therapy in a psychiatric clinic.) Social Psychiatry, 4, 16-25.

2970.   Kaufmann, L., Masson, O., Masson, D., and Fivaz, E. (1978), Reflexions sur le decodage de la relation therapeutique en therapie de famille. Psychotherapy and Psychosomatics, 29, 221-227.

2971.   Kaufmann, P.N. (1967), Group therapy for pregnant, unwed adolescents in the prenatal clinic of a general hospital. International Journal of Group Psychotherapy, 17, 309-320.

2972.   Kay, D.W.K. (1978), Assessment of familial risks in functional psychoses and their application in genetic counseling. British Journal of Psychiatry, 133, 385-404.

2973.   Kaye, J. (1981), On the reification of systems in family therapy. Australian Journal of Family Therapy, 2(4), 199-203.

2974.   Kaye, J.W. (1984), Hypnotherapy and family therapy for the cancer patient: A case study. American Journal of Clinical Hypnosis, 27(1), 38-41.

2975.   Kaye, S., and Knapp, H.D. (1979), Child abuse: Prognostic factors in therapy effectiveness. Journal of Contemporary Psychotherapy, 10(2), 112.

2976.   Kazamias, N. (1979), Intervening briefly in the family system. International Journal of Group Psychotherapy, 25, 104-109.

2977.   Keane, V.R. (1969), The important others. Is the focus on the family? American Nursing Association Clinical Conference, 321.

2978.   Kearns, W.P. (1980), The development of a marriage enrichment program on conflict management for recently married couples. Dissertation Abstracts International, 41, 1087-A.

2979.   Keck, S.E. (1982), Behavioral diagnosis and assessment in marital therapy. Journal of Sex and Marital Therapy, 8, 119-134.

2980.   Keeney, B.P. (1981), Cybernetic patterns in family therapy: A Batesonian epistemology. Dissertation Abstracts International, 42, 2062-B.

2981.   Keeney, B.P. (1982), Not pragmatics, not aesthetics. Family Process, 21, 429-34.

2982.   Keeney, B.P. (1982), What is an epistemology of family therapy? Family Process, 21, 153-168.

2983.   Keeney, B.P. (1983), Diagnosis and assessment in family therapy: IX. Ecological assessment. Family Therapy Collections, 9, 155-169.

2984.   Keeney, B.P. (1979), Ecosystemic epistemology: An alternative paradigm for diagnosis. Family Process, 18, 117-129.

2985.   Keeney, B.P., and Cromwell, R.E. (1977), Toward systematic diagnosis. Family Therapy, 4, 225-236.

2986.   Keeney, B.P., and Ross, J.M. (1985), Mind in therapy: Constructing systemic family therapies. New York: Basic Books.

2987.   Keeney, B.P., and Sprenkle, D.H. (1982), Ecosystemic epistemology: Critical implications for the aesthetics and pragmatics of family therapy. Family Process, 21, 1-19.

2988.   Keith, D.V. (1980), The case of Helen D: A woman who learned to suffer...a biopsychosocial disorder. Family Process, 19, 269-275.

2989.   Keith, D.V. (1980), Family therapy and lithium deficiency. Journal of Marital and Family Therapy, 6, 49-54.

2990.   Keith, D.V. (1980), Review of M. Bowen's Family therapy in clinical practice. Psychosomatics, 21, 439.

2991.   Keith, D.V., and Whitaker, C.A. (1981), Play therapy: A paradigm for work with families. Journal of Marital and Family Therapy, 7, 243-254.

2992.   Keith, D.V., and Whitaker, C.A. (1978), Struggling with the impotence impasse: Absurdity and acting-in. Journal of Marital and Family Therapy, 4, 69-77.

2993.   Keith, P.M. (1981), Sex-role attitudes, family plans, and career orientations: Implications for counseling. Vocational Guidance Quarterly, 29(3), 244-252.

2994.   Keithlucas, H. (1978), Group child care as a family service. Adolescence, 13, 769.

2995.   Keller, J.E. (1978), Sexual behavior and guilt removing women: A cross-generational comparison. Journal of Sex and Marital Therapy, 4, 259.

2996.   Keller, J.F. (1983), Review of R.J. Freen, and J.L. Framo's Family therapy: Major contributions. Contemporary Psychology, 28, 227.

2997.   Keller, J.F., and Elliott, S.S. (1982), Reframing in marital therapy:
        From deficit to self-sacrifice as focus. Family Therapy, 9, 119-126.

2998.   Keller, J.F., and Elliott, S.S. (1980), Behavioral family therapy. Journal
        of Marital and Family Therapy, 6, 421-424.

2999.   Keller, J.F., and Elliott, S.S. (1980), Do personality changes occur in
        parents receiving behavioral family therapy? Journal of Marital and
        Family Therapy, 6(4), 421-424.

3000.   Keller, L.M. (1976), Marriage/family/child counselors' attitudes toward
        divorce as related to selected social characteristics. Dissertation
        Abstracts International, 37, 1806A.

3001.   Keller, M. (1985), Review of C.M. Anderson and S. Stewart's Mastering
        resistance: A practical guide to family therapy. Bulletin of the
        Menninger Clinic, 49(1), 78-80.

3002.   Keller, T. (1985), Review of The language of family therapy.
        Psychiatrische Praxis, 12(3), 89. Fol. 17, No. 30.

3003.   Kellerman, J. (1977), Childhood encopresis: A multimodal therapeutic
        approach. Psychiatric Quarterly, 14, 39-43.

3004.   Kellner, K.R., Best, E.K., Chesboro, S., Donnelly, W., and Green, M.
        (1981), Perinatal mortality counseling program for families who
        experience a stillbirth. Death Education, 5, 29-35.

3005.   Kelly, F.D., and Main, F.O. (1979), Sibling conflict in a single parent
        family: An empirical case study. American Journal of Family Therapy,
        7, 39-47.

3006.   Kemp, C.J. (1974), Family treatment within the milieu of a residential
        treatment center. Child Today, 3, 2-6.

3007.   Kemp, C.J. (1971), Family with the milieu of a residental treatment
        center. Child Welfare, 50, 229-235.

3008.   Kempe, C.H. (1982), Changing approaches to treatment of child abuse
        and neglect. Child Abuse and Neglect, 6, 491-493.

3009.   Kempler, H.L., and MacKenna, P. (1975), Drug abusing adolescents and
        their families: A structural view and treatment approach. American
        Journal of Orthopsychiatry, 45, 223.

3010.   Kempler, W. (1981), Experiential psychotherapy within families. New
        York: Brunner/Mazel.

3011.   Kempler, W. (1968), Experiential psychotherapy with families. Family
        Process, 7, 88-99.

3012.   Kempler, W. (1965), Experiential family therapy. International Journal
        of Group Psychotherapy, 15, 57-71.

3013.   Kempler, W. (1969), Family therapy of the future. International
        Psychiatry Clinics, 6, 135-158.

3014.   Kenkel, W.F. (1961), Sex of observer and spousal roles in decision making. Marriage and Family Living, 23, 185-186.

3015.   Kennedy, J.F. (1978), Transference problems encountered in psychoanalytically-oriented family therapy. International Journal of Group Psychotherapy, 28, 389-399.

3016.   Kennedy, K.M. (1979), Counseling the children of handicapped parents. Personnel and Guidance Journal, 58(4), 267.

3017.   Kennedy, M. (1969), Father-daughter incest: Treatment of the family. Lavel Medicine, 40, 946-950.

3018.   Kennedy, R., and Magagna, J. (1981), The aftermath of murder. In S. Box, B. Copley, J. Magagna and E. Moustaki (Eds.), Psychotherapy with families: An analytic approach. London: Routledge and Kegan Paul Ltd.

3019.   Kent, K., and Richie, J.L. (1976), Adoption as an issue in casework with adoptive parents. Journal of the American Academy of Child Psychiatry, 15, 510-522.

3020.   Kenward, K., and Rissover, J. (1980), A family systems approach to the treatment and prevention of alcoholism: A review. Family Therapy, 7(2), 97-106.

3021.   Kerner, J. (1979), The impact of grief: A retrospective study of family function following loss of a child with cystic fibrosis. Journal of Chronic Disease, 32, 221-225.

3022.   Kerr, M.E. (1983), Family evaluation and diagnosis. American Journal of Family Therapy, 11, 62-64.

3023.   Kersey, B.L., and Protinsky, H.O. (1985), Strategic treatment of families: An indirect method of indirect suggestion. Journal of Marital and Family Therapy, 323-326.

3024.   Kersey, F.L. (1983), Supervisor process and focus applied in the development and training of marriage and family therapists. Dissertation Abstracts International, 43, 2556-A.

3025.   Kerstetter, L.M. (1948), Variability of audience responses in the measurement of marriage partner roles. Sociatry, 2, 375-384.

3026.   Kerstetter, L.M. (1947), Role testing for marriage prediction. Sociatry, 1, 220-244.

3027.   Kesler, S. (1978), Building skills in divorce adjustment groups. Journal of Divorce, 2(2), 209-216.

3028.   Kessler, C.D. (1981), Follow-up of emotionally disturbed adolescents and their families who experienced long-term family therapy. Dissertation Abstracts International, 42, 1962-A.

3029.   Kessler, E.R., Mendelowitz, S., and Fischer, F.B. (1981), Family nurturing system. Family Therapy, 8(1), 1-8.

3030.   Kessler, S. (1976), Divorce adjustment groups. Personnel and Guidance Journal, 54, 251-255.

3031.   Ketai, R.M., and Brandwin, M.A. (1979), Childbirth-related psychosis and familial symbiotic conflict. American Journal of Psychiatry, 136, 190-193.

3032.   Kifer, R.E., Lewis, M.A., Green, D.R., and Phillips, E.L. (1974), Training predelinquent youths and their parents to negotiate conflict situations. Journal of Applied Behavioral Analysis, 7, 357-364.

3033.   Kiglore, J.E. (1975), Establishing and maintaining a private practice. Journal of Marriage and Family Counseling, 1, 145-148.

3034.   Kiglore, J.E. (1979), How to begin a psychotherapy group: Six approaches. Family Coordinator, 28, 142.

3035.   Kiglore, J.E. (1979), Marriage and family therapists use of media for public education. Journal of Marital and Family Therapy, 5, 87-92.

3036.   Kilgo, R.D. (1975), Counseling couples in groups: Rationale and methodology. Family Coordinator, 24, 337-342.

3037.   Kilmann, P.R. (1978), The impact of a marrige enrichment program on relationship factors. Journal of Sex and Marital Therapy, 4, 298-303.

3038.   Kilmann, P.R., Moreault, D., and Robinson, E.A. (1978), Effects of a marriage enrichment program: An outcome study. Journal of Sex and Marital Therapy, 4, 54-57.

3039.   Kilpatrick, A.C. (1968), Conjoint family therapy with geriatric patients. Journal of the Fort Logan Mental Health Center, 3, 29-35.

3040.   Kim, S.C. (1985), Family therapy for Asian Americans: A conceptual guide for use in psychotherapy. Psychotherapy, 22, 342-348.

3041.   Kimball, K.E., Healey, J.C., McIntyre, W.G., and Smith, D. (1982), Families in acoholic transaction: The family systems approach to alcoholism in the family and family rehabilitation. International Journal of Family Psychiatry, 3, 57-67.

3042.   Kimball, K.E., and Healey, J.C. (1982), An application of general systems theory to family theory and clinical practice. International Journal of Family Psychiatry, 3, 163-173.

3043.   Kimball, K.K., and McCabe, M.E. (1981), A decision-making group for couples. Personnel and Guidance Journal, 60(3), 153-156.

3044.   Kimber, J.A.M. (1961), An introduction to the marriage counselor and his work. Psychological Reports, 8, 71-75.

3045.   Kimbro, E.L., Taschman, H.A., Wylie, H.W., and MacLennan, B.W. (1967), A multiple family group approach to some problems of adolescence. International Journal of Group Psychotherapy, 17, 18-24.

3046.   King, B., Bissell, L., and Holding, E. (1978), The usefulness of the disease concept of alcoholism in working with wives of alcoholics. Social Work and Health Care, 3, 443-455.

3047.   King, C.H. (1967), Family therapy with the deprived family. Social Casework, 48, 203-208.

3048.   King, H.R. (1979), The identification of starters and nonstarters in family counseling. Dissertation Abstracts International, 40(9), 4487-B.

3049.   King, N.J. (1981), A multi-disciplinary approach to child abuse: The role of the nurse. Australian Nurses Journal, 11, 41-42.

3050.   Kingsley, S., and McEwan, J. (1978), Social classes for women of differing marital status. Journal of Biosocial Science, 10, 353-359.

3051.   Kingston, P. (1980), Review of T.J. Paolino and B.S. McCardy's Marriage and marital therapy: Psychoanalytic, behavioral and systems theory perspectives. British Journal of Social Work, 10, 390-391.

3052.   Kingston, P. (1982), Power and influence in the environment of family therapy. Journal of Family Therapy, 4, 211-228.

3053.   Kingston, P. (1984), 'But they aren't motivated....': Issues concerned with encouraging motivation for change in families. Journal of Family Therapy, 6(4), 381-404.

3054.   Kinney, J. (1978), Homebuilders: An in-home crisis intervention program. Children Today, 7, 15-17.

3055.   Kinney, J.M., Madsen, B., Fleming, T., and Haapala, D.A. (1977), Homebuilders: Keeping families together. Journal of Consulting and Clinical Psychology, 45, 667-673.

3056.   Kinsel, B.I., and Brubaker, T.H. (1983), Review of B. Silverstone, and H.K. Hyman's You and your aging parent. 2nd Edition. American Journal of Family Therapy, 11, 81-82.

3057.   Kinskern, D.P. (1985), Climbing out of the pit: Further guidelines for family therapy research. Journal of Marital and Family Therapy, 11(2), 159-162.

3058.   Kinsler, D.D. (1976), Life style: Marital stability versus the swinging singles existence. Journal of Psychiatric Nursing and Mental Health Services, 14, 20-21.

3059.   Kinsler, F. (1981), Second generation effects of the holocaust: The effectiveness of group therapy in the resolution of the transmission of parental trauma. Journal of Psychology and Judaism, 6(1), 53.

3060.   Kinston, W. (1982), Review of J.M. Gottman's Marital interaction: Experimental investigations. Journal of Family Therapy, 4, 321.

3061.   Kinston, W., and Bentovim, A. (1978), Brief focal family therapy when the child is the referred patient: II. Methodology and results. Journal of Child Psychology, Psychiatry and Allied Disciplines, 19, 119-143.

3062.   Kinston, W., and Loader, P. (1984), Eliciting whole-family interaction with a standardized clinical interview. Journal of Family Therapy, 6(4), 347-364.

3063. Kinzie, D., Sushama, P.C., and Lee, M. (1972), Cross-cultural family therapy: A Malaysian experience. Family Process, 11, 59-68.

3064. Kippes, D.E. (1981), Family therapy: An attempt to integrate models and modes into a structure of developing phases of therapy. Australian and New Zealand Journal of Psychiatry, 15(1), 11-17.

3065. Kirby, M.W., and Davis, K.E. (1972), Who volunteers for research on marital counseling? Journal of Marriage and the Family, 34(3), 469-473.

3066. Kirk, E.C. (1968), A mobility evaluation report for parents. Exceptional Child, 35, 57-62.

3067. Kirkendall, L.A. (1978), Review of C.J. Sager's Marriage contracts and couple therapy. Family Coordinator, 27, 294.

3068. Kirkendall, L.A. (1979), Review of J. Herr and J. Weakland's Counseling elders and their families: Practical techniques for applied gerontology. Journal of Marital and Family Therapy, 5, 113.

3069. Kirkendall, L.S. (1966), Using a student panel in teacher education on sex standards. Journal of Marriage and the Family, 28, 521-523.

3070. Kirkpatrick, M. (1982), Lesbian mother families. Psychiatric Annals, 12, 842-848.

3071. Kirschenbaum, M.J., and Blinder, M.G. (1972), Growth processes in married-couples group therapy. Family Therapy, 1, 85-104.

3072. Kirschner, C. (1979), Aging family in crisis: A problem in living. Social Casework, 60, 209-216.

3073. Kirschner, D.A., and Kirschner, S. (1985), Comprehensive family therapy: An integration of systemic and psychodynamic treatment models. New York: Brunner/Mazel.

3074. Kirshner, L.A. (1980), Review of S. Minuchin's Psychosomatic families. General Hospital Psychiatry, 2, 326-329.

3075. Kirshner, L.A. (1980), Review of F.M. Sander's Individual and family therapy: Toward an integration. General Hospital Psychiatry, 2, 326-329.

3076. Kishur, G.R. (1984), Review of E.J. Hunter's Families under the flag. American Journal of Family Therapy, 12(4), 73.

3077. Kisker, K.P. (1968), The egopath: Problem child of family investigation with schizophrenics. Psychotherapy and Psychosomatics, 16, 297-299.

3078. Kissel, S. (1974), Mothers and therapists evaluate long-term and short-term child therapy. Journal of Clinical Psychology, 30(3), 296-299.

3079. Kissen, M. (1983), Exploring object relations phenomenona in group settings. In L.R. Wolberg and M.L. Aronson (Eds.), Group and family therapy 1982. New York: Brunner/Mazel.

3080.   Kitson, G.C., and Langlie, J.K. (1984), Couples who file for divorce but change their minds. American Journal of Orthopsychiatry, 54(3), 469-489.

3081.   Kjaer, A. (1985), Abuse of women. The practicing physician. The entire family must be treated when abuse arises. Sygeplejersken, 85, 13-14.

3082.   Klapman, H.J., and Rice, D.L. (1965), An experience with combined milieu and family group therapy. International Journal of Group Psychotherapy, 15, 198-206.

3083.   Klapper, J.A., and Todd, D.A. (1968), Parent-couple group therapy on an adolescent inpatient service. American Journal of Orthopsychiatry, 38, 251-252.

3084.   Klawsnik, J. (1979), An evaluation of outreach family therapy performed by the learning intervention family team. Dissertation Abstracts International, 39, 6123-B.

3085.   Klees, P.S. (1980), Modifying defensive and supportive communication in families of delinquents. Dissertation Abstracts International, 40, 3940-B. (University Microfilms No. 8003365.)

3086.   Klein, A.F. (1963), Exploring family group counseling. Social Work, 8, 23-29.

3087.   Klein, D.F. (1980), Psychosocial treatment of schizophrenia, or psychosocial help for people with schizophrenia? Schizophrenia Bulletin, 6, 122-130.

3088.   Klein, H., Overbeck, A., and Brahler, E. (1983), Dimensions of the communication experience in family therapy interviews. Psychotherapie Psychosomatik Medizinische Psychologie, 33, 63-74.

3089.   Klein, H., and Erlich, H.S. (1978), Some psychoanalytic structural aspects of family function and growth. Adolescent Psychiatry, 6, 171-194.

3090.   Klein, H., and Erlich, H.S. (1975), Some dynamic and transactional aspects of family therapy with psychotic patients. Psychotherapy and Psychosomatics, 26, 148-155.

3091.   Klein, M. (1985), Canadian departments of pediatrics and family medicine: In need of family therapy. Canadian Medical Association Journal, 132, 629-633.

3092.   Klein, M.M., Plutchik, R., and Conte, H.R. (1973), Parental dominance - passivity and behavior problems of children. Journal of Consulting and Clinical Psychology, 40, 416-419.

3093.   Klein, N.C., Alexander, J.F., and Parsons, B.V. (1977), Impact of family systems intervention on recidivism and sibling delinquency: A model of primary prevention and program evaluation. Journal of Consulting and Clinical Psychology, 45, 469-474.

3094.   Klein, R.S., Altman, S.D., Dreisen, K., Friedman, R., and Powers, L. (1981), Restructuring dysfunctional parental attitudes toward children's

learning and behavior in school: Family-oriented psychoeducational
therapy: Part I. Journal of Learning Disabilities, 14, 15-19.

3095.   Klein, R.S., Altman, S.D., Dreisen, K., Friedman, R., and Powers, L.
(1981), Restructuring dysfunctional parental attitudes toward children's
learning and behavior in school: Family-oriented psychoeducational
therapy. II. Journal of Learning Disabilities, 14, 99-101.

3096.   Kleinberg, W.M. (1977), Counseling mothers in hospital post-partum
period: Comparison of techniques. American Journal of Public Health,
67(7), 672-673.

3097.   Kleinman, J., Rosenberg, E., and Whiteside, M. (1979), Common
developmental tasks in forming reconstituted families. Journal of
Marital and Family Therapy, 5, 79-86.

3098.   Klemer, R.H. (1966). Marriage counseling with the infertile couple.
Fertility and Sterility, 17, 104-109.

3099.   Klemer, R.H. (1965), Counseling in marital and sexual problems.
Baltimore, MD: Williams and Wilkins.

3100.   Klier, J., Fein, E., and Genero, C. (1984), Are written or verbal
contracts more effective in family therapy? Social Work, 29(3), 298-
300.

3101.   Klimenko, A. (1968), Multifamily therapy in the rehabilitation of drug
addicts. Perspectives in Psychiatric Care, 6, 220-223.

3102.   Klopper, E.J., Tittler, B.I., Friedman, S., and Hughes, S.J. (1978), A
multi-method investigation of two family constructs. Family Process,
17, 83-93.

3103.   Klosinski, G. (1979), Comments on the importance of domestic animals
for establishing equilibrium in family dynamics. Psychotherapy and
Psychosomatics, 29, 221-225.

3104.   Kluge, P. (1976), Therapy for married couples in the practice of the
established physician. Psychotherapie und Medizinische Psychologie,
26(4), 127-134.

3105.   Kluge, P. (1974), Group psychotherapy for married couples.
Psychotherapie und Medizinische Psychologie, 24, 132-137.

3106.   Klugman, J. (1977), Owning and disowning: The structural dimension.
Family Process, 16, 353-355.

3107.   Knapp, H.D. (1980), Review of L. Headley's Adults and their parents in
family therapy: A new direction in treatment. Journal of Contemporary
Psychotherapy, 11, 84.

3108.   Knapp, H.D. (1980), Review of T.J. Paolino and B.S. McCrady's Marriage
and marital therapy. Journal of Contemporary Psychotherapy, 11, 82.

3109.   Knapp, H.D., and Kaye S. (1980), Family patterns leading to learning
disability: A cognitive approach. Journal of Contemporary
Psychotherapy, 11(2), 167-177.

3110.   Knapp, J.J. (1975), Co-marital sex and marriage counseling: Sexually open marriage and related attitudes and practices of marriage counselors. Dissertation Abstracts International, 3(3), 1440-B.

3111.   Knapp, J.J. (1975), Some non-monogamous marriage styles and related attitudes and practices of marriage counselors. Family Coordinator, 24, 505-514.

3112.   Knauf, J.W. (1975), A study of growth toward self-actualization in a family life education program. Dissertation Abstracts International, 35, 5927-A.

3113.   Kniskern, D.P. (1980), Review of F.M. Sander's Individual and family therapy: Toward an integration. Contemporary Psychology, 25, 784.

3114.   Kniskern, D.P. (1979), Including children in marital and family therapy. American Journal of Family Therapy, 7, 76-79.

3115.   Kniskern, D.P., and Gurman, A.S. (1979), Research on training in marriage and family therapy. Journal of Marital and Family Therapy, 5, 83-94.

3116.   Knistern, D.P. (1978), Understanding and helping the individual in the family. International Journal of Family Counseling, 6, 92.

3117.   Knittle, B.J., and Tuana, S.J. (1980), Group therapy as primary treatment for adolescent victims of intrafamilial sexual abuse. Clinical Social Work Journal, 8(4), 236-242.

3118.   Knobloch, F. (1967), Die familien struktur als modell psychotherapeutischer methoden. (The family structure as a model psychotherapeutic method.) Praxis de Psychotherapie, 12, 257-264.

3119.   Knobloch, F. (1965), Family psychotherapy. Psychotherapy and Psychosomatics, 13, 155-163.

3120.   Knobloch, F., Knoblochova, J., and Sofrnova, M. (1964), La psicoterapia familiar. (Family psychotherapy.) Acta Psiquiatrica y Psychologica, 10, 17-30.

3121.   Knoblochova, J. (1967), Ehn-un familienpsychotherapie. (Marriage and family psychotherapy.) Psychotherapy and Psychosomatics, 15, 34-35.

3122.   Knoblochova, J. (1970), Family therapy in Czechoslovakia: An aspect of group-centered psychotherapy. International Psychiatry Clinics, 7, 55-80.

3123.   Knoblochova, J., and Knobloch, F. (1965), Family psychotherapy. World Health Organization - Public Health Papers, No. 28, 64-89.

3124.   Knox, D. (1976), Supervision in marriage counseling. Journal of Family Counseling, 4(2), 24-26.

3125.   Knox, D. (1973), Behavior contracts in marriage counseling. Journal of Family Counseling, 1, 22-28.

3126.   Knox, D. (1975), Affection vs. intercourse: Or, all he wants is my body. Journal of Family Counseling, 3, 65-66.

3127.   Knuckman, P. (1982), Modeling as an infant mental health intervention. Infant Mental Health Journal, 3, 184-186.

3128.   Knudson, R.M., Sommers, A.A., and Golding, S.L. (1980), Interpersonal perception and mode of resolution in marital conflict. Journal of Personality and Social Psychology, 38, 751-763.

3129.   Kobak, R.R., and Waters, D.B. (1984), Family therapy is a rite of passage: Play's the thing. Family Process, 23, 89-100.

3130.   Koch, A. (1973), Out-patient family therapy for a 14-year-old girl with anorexia nervosa. Ceskoslovenska Psychiatrie, 69, 387-392.

3131.   Koch, A. (1974), Out-patient family therapy for a 14-year-old girl with anorexia nervosa. Ugeskrift for Laeger, 136, 1031-1033.

3132.   Koch, J., and Koch, L. (1976), A consumer's guide to therapy for couples. Psychology Today, 9(10, 33-36.

3133.   Koch, U., and Schofer, G. (1978), (Relationships of aggressive and anxious affects to clinical conditions: An examination of married couples with the Gottschalk-Gleser method.) Zeitschrift fur Klinische Psychologie und Psychotherapie, 2, 110-125.

3134.   Kochne-Koplan, N.S. (1976), The use of self as a family therapist. Perspectives in Psychiatric Care, 14, 29-33.

3135.   Koff, G.L. (1983), Social values held by individually oriented therapists and family therapists regarding traditional family ideology. Dissertation Abstracts International, 43, 2343-B.

3136.   Kogan, K.L. (1978), Help seeking mothers and their children. Child Psychiatry and Human Development, 8(4), 204-208.

3137.   Koh, E.K. (1980), Family counseling in the east. Journal of the Royal College of General Practitioners, 10, 22-23.

3138.   Kohlmeyer, W.A., and Fernandes, X. (1963), Psychiatry in India: Family approach in the treatment of mental disorders. American Journal of Psychiatry, 119, 1033-1037.

3139.   Kohn, B. (1976), Simultaneous analysis of child and parent by the same analyst. Journal of the American Academy of Psychoanalysis, 4, 481-499.

3140.   Kohn, R. (1971), Treatment of married couples in a group. Group Process, 4, 96-105.

3141.   Kolevzon, M.S., and Green, R.G. (1983), Practice and training in family therapy: A known group study. Family Process, 22, 179-90.

3142.   Kolevzon, M.S., and Green, R.G. (1983), An experimentally based inductive approach to learning about family therapy. American Journal of Family Therapy, 11, 35-42.

3143.   Kolevzon, M.S., and Green, R.G. (1985), Family therapy models: Convergence and divergence. New York: Springer Publishing.

3144.   Kolko-Phillips, N., Davidson, M., and Auerbach, A.B. (1980), Discussion groups for mothers of high-risk infants and toddlers: An early intervention approach to treatment. Child Care Quarterly, 9(3), 206-208.

3145.   Kolter, T., and Chetwynd, J. (1980), Changes in family members during psychotherapy. Human Relations, 33, 101-110.

3146.   Komlos, P. (1976), (Family therapy with individual support.) Magyar Pszichologiai Szemle, 33(4), 346-363.

3147.   Kompass, F.R. (1983), Pastoral counseling with married couples when one of the partners wants the marriage to come to an end. Dissertation Abstracts International, 44, 1819-A.

3148.   Konanc, J.T., and Warren, N.J. (1984), Graduation: Transitional crisis for mildly developmentally disabled adolescents and their families. Family Relations: Journal of Applied Family and Child Studies, 31, 135-142.

3149.   Konopka, G. (1980), Family therapy by any other name. American Journal of Orthopsychiatry, 50, 567.

3150.   Koontz, J. (1983), Discovering the relevant metaphor: Diagnosis and treatment of a child with headache. Family Therapy, 10, 283-288.

3151.   Kopp, M.E. (1938), Marriage counseling in European countries. Journal of Heredity, 29, 153-160.

3152.   Korelitz, A., and Schulder, D. (1982), The lawyer-therapist consultation team. Journal of Marital and Family Therapy, 8, 113-119.

3153.   Korelitz, A.Z. (1982), Review of D.R. Freeeman's Marital crises and short-term counseling: A casebook. Family Process, 21, 501.

3154.   Koret, S. (1973), Family therapy as a therapeutic technique in residential treatment. Child Welfare, 52(4), 235-246.

3155.   Korn, G. (1984), Review of S. Zimberg's The clinical management of alcoholism. American Journal of Family Therapy, 12(4), 84.

3156.   Kornblit, A. (1982), About family therapy. Acta Psiquiatrica y Psychologia de America Latin, 28(2), 103.

3157.   Kornblit, A., and Demazieres, M.C. (1982), Seventh and eighth days sessions of the Society of Family Therapy. Acta Psiquiatrica y Psychologia de America Latin, 28(1), 11.

3158.   Kornfeld, M., Puntil, J., Duehn, W., Lane, B., Morrison, E., and Pepper, S. (1967), Community mental health project as a part of training in a traditional child guidance clinic. American Journal of Orthopsychiatry, 37, 364-365.

3159.   Kornfeld, M.S. (1980), Parental group therapy in the management of two fatal childhood diseases: A comparison. Health and Social Work, 5(4), 28-34.

3160.   Kornfeld, M.S. (1979), Parental group therapy in the management of
fatal childhood disease. Health and Social Work, 4(3), 99-118.

3161.   Korsch, B.M. (1980), Counseling patients and their families in a chronic
renal disease program. Patient Counseling and Health Education, 2(2),
87-91.

3162.   Kosinski, F.A. (1982), Standards, accreditation, and licensure in marital
and family therapy. Personnel and Guidance Journal, 60, 350-352.

3163.   Kosinski, F.A. (1983), Improving relationships in stepfamilies.
Elementary School Guidance and Counseling, 17, 200-207.

3164.   Koskas, E. (1978), (Review of P.J. Guerin's Family therapy: Theory and
practice.) L'Annee Psychologia, 78, 301.

3165.   Kossoris, P. (1970), Family therapy: An adjunct to hemodialysis and
transplantation. American Journal of Nursing, 70, 1730-1733.

3166.   Kosten, T.R., Jalali, B., Hogan, I., and Kleber, H.D. (1983), Family
denial as a prognostic factor in opiate addict treatment outcome.
Journal of Nervous and Mental Disease, 163, 611-616.

3167.   Kotis, J.P. (1965), A study of the verbal interaction in the initial session
of group counseling with marital pairs in which one spouse is alcoholic.
Dissertation Abstracts International, 2(3), 1814.

3168.   Kotkas, L.J. (1969), Informal use of the "interpersonal perception
method" in marital therapy. Canadian Journal of Psychiatry, 14, 11-14.

3169.   Kotlar, S.L. (1967), Role theory in marriage counseling. Sociology and
Social Research, 52(1), 50-62.

3170.   Kraemer, S. (1977), Tavistock family therapy conference: A review.
Bulletin of the British Psychological Society, 30, 408.

3171.   Kraemer, S. (1982), Leaving home, and the adolescent family
therapist. Journal of Adolescence, 5, 51-62.

3172.   Kraemer, S. (1982), A note on Spinoza's contribution to systematic
therapy. Family Process, 21, 353-357.

3173.   Kraemer, S. (1981), Why the question is missing: A reply to Kerreen
Reiger's paper. Journal of Family Therapy, 3, 309-312.

3174.   Kraft, S.P., and Demaio, T.J. (1982), An ecological intervention with
adolescents in low-income families. American Journal of
Orthopsychiatry, 52, 131-140.

3175.   Krakowski, A.J. (1981), Psychiatry in the general hospital: Liaison with
families. Psychiatric Journal of the University of Ottawa, 60, 175-179.

3176.   Kramer, C. (1974), Tips from a family therapist. Patient Care, 8, 241.

3177.   Kramer, C.H. (1980), Becoming a family therapist: Developing an
integrated approach to working with families. New York: Human
Sciences Press.

3178.   Kramer, D.A. (1982), The adopted child in family therapy. American Journal of Family Therapy, 110, 70-73.

3179.   Kramer, J.N. (1977), Family counseling as a key to successful alternative school programs for alienated youth. School Counselor, 24, 194-196.

3180.   Kramer, J.R., and Reitz, M. (1980), Using video playback to train family therapists. Family Process, 19, 145-50.

3181.   Kratochvil, S. (1979), Review of G.H. Zuk's Analysis of the family therapy: Intervention and therapeutic processes. Ceskoslovenska Psychologie, 23, 83.

3182.   Kratochvil, S. (1979), Analysis of the family therapy. Ceskoslovenska Psychologie, 23, 83.

3183.   Kratochvil, S. (1980), Sex therapy in an in-patient and out-patient setting. Journal of Sex and Marital Therapy, 6(2), 135-144.

3184.   Kratochvil, S. (1978), The course of therapeutic training for married couples in functional sexual disorders: Casuistics. Ceskoslovenska Psychiatrie, 74, 176-182.

3185.   Kratochvil, S. (1978), Therapeutic training for married couples with sexual dysfunctions: Principles and technique. Ceskoslovenska Psychiatrie, 74, 145-153.

3186.   Kratochvil, S. (1984), Review of D.B. Wile's Couples therapy: A non-traditional approach. Ceskoslovenska Psychologie, 27(5), 490.

3187.   Kratochvil, S. (1982), Review of M. Adolfi, and I. Zwerling's Dimensions of family therapy. Ceskoslovenska Psychologie, 26, 295.

3188.   Krebs, E. (1984), Family orientation in institutional rearing. The further conceptual development of the "Sommerberg House" therapeutic and pedagogic adolescent institution in Rosrath. Praxis de Kinderpsychologie und Kinderpsychiatrie, 33, 28-34.

3189.   Kreindler, S. (1976), Psychiatric treatment for the abusing parent and the abused child: Some problems and possible solutions. Canadian Journal of Psychiatry, 21, 275-280.

3190.   Kreische, R. (1983), Family therapy in inpatient clinics. Zeitschrift fur Psychosomatische Medizin und Psychoanalyse, 29, 37-48.

3191.   Kreitman, N., Collins, J., Nelsin, B., and Troop, J. (1971), Neurosis and marital interaction. IV. Manifest psychological interaction. British Journal of Psychiatry, 119, 243-252.

3192.   Kreitman, N., Collins, J., and Troop, J. (1970), Neurosis and marital interaction. I. Personality and symptoms. British Journal of Psychiatry, 117, 33-46.

3193.   Krell, R. (1982), Family therapy with children of concentration camp survivors. American Journal of Psychotherapy, 36, 513-522.

3194. Krell, R., and Miles, J.F. (1976), Marital therapy of couples in which the husband is a physician. American Journal of Psychotherapy, 30(2), 267-275.

3195. Krell, R., and Rabkin, L. (1979), The effects of sibling death on the surviving child: A family perspective. Family Process, 18, 471-477.

3196. Kressel, K. (1973), Resolving marital disagreements over money: A comparison of role reversal and self presentation Dissertation Abstracts International, 34, 3543A.

3197. Kressel, K., and Deutsch, M. (1977), Divorce therapy: An in-depth survey of therapists' views. Family Process, 16, 413-443.

3198. Kressel, K., and Slipp, S. (1975), Perceptions of marriage related to engagement in conjoint therapy. Journal of Marriage and Family Counseling, 1, 367-377.

3199. Krider, J.W., Jr. (1971), Desensitizing and resensitizing the schizogenic family system. Social Casework, 52, 370-376.

3200. Krieger, G.W., and Bascue, L.O. (1975), Terminal illness: Counseling with a family perspective. Family Coordinator, 24, 351-355.

3201. Krieger, M.J. (1980), Problems in the psychotherapy of children with histories of incest. American Journal of Psychotherapy, 34(1), 81-88.

3202. Krill, D.F. (1968), Family interviewing as an intake diagnostic method. Social Work, 13, 56-63.

3203. Krill, D.F. (1967), Loosening the oedipal bind through family therapy. Social Casework, 48, 563-569.

3204. Krishnamoorthy, S. (1979), Family formation and the life cycle. Demography, 16, 121-129.

3205. Krishtal, V.V. (1981), Conditions for the development and the variants in the manifestation of sexual disharmony in a married couple and its psychotherapeutic correction. Vrachebnoe Delo, 38, 85-8.

3206. Krivohlavy, J. (1980), Development of family therapy in California. Ceskoslovenska Psychologie, 24, 311-313.

3207. Krmpotic, E., Zellinger, B.B., and Gordon, C.L. (1970), Family counseling. Chicago Medical School Quarterly, 29, 134-152.

3208. Kroger, F., Petzold, E., and Ferner, H. (1984), Family therapy in clinical psychosomatics: Group work with the sculpture technique. Gruppenpsychotherapie und Gruppendynamik, 19(4), 361-379.

3209. Kronhausen, E.W., and Kronhausen, P.E. (1957), Family milieu therapy: The non-institutional treatment of severe emotional disturbances. Psychoanalysis, 5, 45-62.

3210. Kronick, D. (1978), Educational and counseling groups for parents. Academic Therapy, 13, 355-359.

3211.   Kronick, D. (1978), Parent education and counseling groups. Academic Therapy, 13(4), 485-490.

3212.   Krueger, D.W. (1979), Clinical considerations in the prescriptions of group, brief, long-term and couples therapy. Psychiatric Quarterly, 51(2), 92.

3213.   Krupinski, J., and Farmer, R. (1973), A study of aspects of marital life and roles in marriage guidance client and non-client marriages. Journal of Comparative Family Studies, 4, 295-308.

3214.   Kugel, L. (1974), Combining individual and conjoint sessions in marital therapy. Hospital and Community Psychiatry, 25, 795-798.

3215.   Kuhns, N.A. (1978), Relationship between Adlerian family counseling success and selected counselor variables. Dissertation Abstracts International, 39, 2066-2067A.

3216.   Kuipers, L., Berkowitz, R., Fries, R.E., and Leff, J. (1983), Family experiences with schizophrenia: Possibilities for modification. Nervenarzt, 54, 139-43.

3217.   Kuppersmith, J., Blair, R., and Slotnick, R. (1977), Training undergraduates as co-leaders of multi-family counseling groups. Teaching Psychology, 4, 3-6.

3218.   Kupst, M.J., Tylke, L., Thomas, L., Mudd, M.E., Richardson, C., and Schulman, J.L. (1982), Strategies of intervention with families of pediatric leukemia patients: A longitudinal perspective. Social Work in Health Care, 8, 31-47.

3219.   Kuriansky, J.B., and Sharpe, L. (1976), Guidelines for evaluating sex therapy. Journal of Sex and Marital Therapy, 2(4), 303-308.

3220.   Kurinansky, J.B., Sharpe, L., and O'Connor, D. (1982), The treatment of anorgasmia: Long-term effectiveness of a short-term behavioral group therapy. Journal of Sex and Marital Therapy, 8(1), 29.

3221.   Kurtz, D., and Marshall, E. (1984), Interviewing skills for family assistance workers. Knoxville, TN: University of Tennessee School of Social Work.

3222.   Kurtz, R.R., and Robbins, G.L. (1979), Family therapist as a change agent: Using principles and strategies of organization development in family therapy. American Journal of Family Therapy, 7, 31-40.

3223.   Kushner, S. (1965), The divorced, noncustodial parent and family treatment. Social Work, 10(3), 52-58.

3224.   Kuske, M. (1965), (New education methods applied at the "School for Mothers" in Bremen.) Schriftenreihe des Instituts fur Jugendkunde und Jugendbildung, 8, 37-47.

3225.   Kutter, P. (1984), Group and family: The therapy group as family. Gruppenpsychotherapie und Gruppendynamik, 20, 168-171.

3226.   Kwiatkowka, H.Y. (1967), Family art therapy. Family Process, 6, 37-55.

3227.   Kwiatkowka, H.Y. (1966), Arteterapia familial: Sua func ao na pesquisa
        e ne terapia. (The role of family art therapy in research and therapy.)
        Revue Psicologia Normal y Patological, 11, 90-103.

3228.   L'Abate, L. (1984), Beyond paradox: Issues of control. American
        Journal of Family Therapy, 12, 12-20.

3229.   L'Abate, L. (1985), The handbook of family psychology and therapy, Vol.
        1. Homewood, IL: Dorsey Press.

3230.   L'Abate, L. (1985), The handbook of family psychology and therapy, Vol.
        2. Homewood, IL: Dorsey Press.

3231.   L'Abate, L. (1985), Review of A. Lange and O. Van der Hart's Directive
        family therapy. Contemporary Psychology, 30(1), 23.

3232.   L'Abate, L. (1978), Review of P.A. Martin's A marital therapy manual.
        Journal of Marriage and the Family, 40, 642.

3233.   L'Abate, L. (1979), Review of T.J. Paolino and B.S. McCrady's Marriage
        and marital therapy: Psychoanalytic, behavioral and systems theory
        perspectives. Journal of Marital and Family Therapy, 5, 114.

3234.   L'Abate, L. (1977), Enrichment: Structured interventions with couples,
        families, and groups. Washington: University Press of America.

3235.   L'Abate, L. (1978), Psychopathology as transaction-historical note.
        International Journal of Family Counseling, 6, 60-65.

3236.   L'Abate, L. (1981), The role of family conferences in family therapy.
        Family Therapy, 8(1), 33-38.

3237.   L'Abate, L. (1974), Family enrichment programs. Journal of Family
        Counseling, 21, 32-38.

3238.   L'Abate, L. (1976), Understanding and helping the individual in the
        family. New York: Grune and Stratton.

3239.   L'Abate, L. (1975), Pathogenic role rigidity in fathers: Some
        observations. Journal of Marriage and Family Counseling, 1, 69-79.

3240.   L'Abate, L. (1984), Review of F.W. Kaslow's The international book of
        family therapy. Contemporary Psychology, 29(5), 408.

3241.   L'Abate, L., Berger, M., Wright, L., and O'Shea, M. (1979), Training
        family psychologists: The family studies program at Georgia State
        University. Professional Psychology, 10, 58-65.

3242.   L'Abate, L., Frey, J., and Wagner, V. (1982), Toward a classification of
        family therapy theories: Further elaborations and implication of the E-
        R-A-AW-C model. Family Therapy, 9, 251-262.

3243.   L'Abate, L., Weeks, G., and Weeks, K. (1979), Of scapegoats, strawmen
        and scarecrows. International Journal of Family Therapy, 1(1), 86-96.

3244.   L'Abate, L., and Allison, M.Q. (1977), Planned change intervention: The
        enrichment model with couples, families, and groups. Transatlantic
        Mental Health Research Newsletter, 19, 11-15.

3245. L'Abate, L., and Farr, L. (1981), Coping with defeating patterns in family therapy. Family Therapy, 8(2), 91-103.

3246. L'Abate, L., and Frey, J. (1981), The ERA model: The role of feelings in family therapy reconsidered. Journal of Marital and Family Therapy, 7, 143-150.

3247. L'Abate, L., and L'Abate, B.L. (1979), The paradoxes of intimacy. Family Therapy, 6, 175-184.

3248. L'Abate, L., and Thaxton, M.L. (1980), Popularity or influence: The use of citation index to identify leaders in family therapy. Family Process, 19, 337-340.

3249. L'Abate, L., and Weeks, G. (1978), A bibliography of paradoxical methods in psychotherapy of family systems. Family Process, 17, 95-98.

3250. L'Abate, L., and Weeks, G. (1976), Testing the limits of enrichment: When enrichment is not enough. Journal of Family Counseling, 4, 70-74.

3251. LaFollette, P. (1975), Family synergy: A variant family organization. Family Coordinator, 24, 561-562.

3252. LaPerriere, K. (1979), Family therapy training at the Ackerman Institute: Thoughts of form and substance. Journal of Marital and Family Therapy, 5, 53-58.

3253. LaPerriere, K. (1979), Toward the training of broad-range family therapists. Professional Psychology, 10, 880-883.

3254. LaPerriere, K. (1984), Review of M. McGoldrick, J.K. Pearce and J. Giordano's Ethnicity and family therapy. Contemporary Psychology, 29(6), 497-498.

3255. Laajus, S. (1981), Developmental phases of the family and developmental family therapy. Duodecim, 97, 142-52.

3256. Labarbera, J.D. (1980), Fathers who undermine children's treatment: A challenge for the clinician. Journal of Clinical Child Psychology, 9(3), 204-206.

3257. Labarge, E. (1981), Counseling patients with senile dementia of the Alzheimer type and their families. Personnel and Guidance Journal, 60(3), 139.

3258. Laborde, J.M. (1979), Symbolism and gift giving in family therapy. Journal of Psychiatric Nursing, 17(4), 32-35.

3259. Lachman, M., and Stuntz, E.C. (1975), Art therapy in the psychotherapy of a mother and her son. American Journal of Art Therapy, 14(4), 105-116.

3260. Ladame, F.G. (1978), (Mental disorders in adolescence and their therapeutic approach: Implications between theory and practice.) Annual Medical Psychology (Paris), 13, 46-67.

3261. Ladner, J.A. (1982), Adopting the cross-cultural child. Psychiatric Annals, 12, 849-854.

3262.   Lagos, J.M. (1981), Family therapy in the treatment of anorexia
nervosa: Theory and technique. International Journal of Psychiatry in
Medicine, 11, 291-302.

3263.   Lagrone, D.M. (1978), The military family syndrome. American Journal
of Psychiatry, 135, 1040-1043.

3264.   Laidlaw, R.W. (1967), The "constellation approach" to marriage
counseling. American Journal of Psychoanalysis, 27(2), 131-134.

3265.   Laidlaw, R.W. (1960), The psychotherapy of marital problems. Progress
in Psychotherapy, 5, 140-147.

3266.   Laird, R.A. (1982), The development of a rating scale for evaluating the
behaviors of family therapists. Dissertation Abstracts International, 42,
4725-A.

3267.   Lalive, J., and Manzano, J. (1982), Beyond post-partum psychosis: The
couple in question. Informentum Psychiatrique, 58, 633-645.

3268.   Laman, K.J. (1974), Selected behavioural characteristics of alcoholics
and their spouses. Canadian Journal of Public Health, 65, 221-223.

3269.   Laman, K.J. (1973), Selected behaviour characteristics of alcoholics and
their spouses. British Journal of Psychiatry, 123, 681-684.

3270.   Lambert, J.M. (1980), The life and death of a family therapy clinic.
Family Therapy, 7(2), 107-118.

3271.   Lamberton, M. (1977), Peer review in a family nurse clinician
program...University of Pennsylvania, School of Nursing, Philadelphia,
PA. Nursing Outlook, 25, 47-53.

3272.   Landau, J., and Griffiths, J. (1981), The South African family in
transition: Training and therapeutic implications. Journal of Marital
and Family Therapy, 7(3), 339-344.

3273.   Landau, J., and Griffiths, J.A. (1980), Family therapy in South Africa.
Journal of Marital and Family Therapy, 6(1), 83-84.

3274.   Landes, H.R. (1973), Treatment of anxiety in the families of children
undergoing tonsillectomy. Dissertation Abstracts International, 34,
2937-2938B.

3275.   Landes, J., and Winter, W. (1966), A new strategy for treating
disintegrating families. Family Process, 5, 1-20.

3276.   Landgarten, H. (1975), Group art therapy for mothers and daughters.
American Journal of Art Therapy, 14(2), 31.

3277.   Landgarten, H. (1981), Family art psychotherapy. International Journal
of Family Psychiatry, 2, 379-395.

3278.   Landgraf, J.R. (1973), The impact of therapeutic marital separation on
spouses in pastoral marriage counseling. Dissertation Abstracts
International, 33, 5021B.

3279.   Laner, M.R. (1978), Saving sinking ships: Implications from a theory of
        marital dissolution. Journal of Marriage and Family Counseling, 4, 51-
        57.

3280.   Laner, M.R. (1976), The medical model, mental illness, and metaphoric
        mystification among marriage and family counselors. Family
        Coordinator, 25(2), 175-181.

3281.   Lang, H., and Stierlin, S. (1979), Role of the father in the family
        therapy of a schizophrenic. In: C. Muller (Ed.), Psychotherapy of
        schiozphrenia. Amsterdam: Exerpta Medica.

3282.   Lang, J. (1974), Planned short-term treatment in a family agency.
        Social Casework, 55(6), 369.

3283.   Lang, M. (1980), Strategic family therapy: Three case histories.
        Australian Family Physician, 9(11), 780-785.

3284.   Lange, A., and Brinckmann, T. (1976), (Effects of a family relations
        course on attitude: Insight into personal problem-solving behavior of the
        participants.) Tijdschrif voor Psychologie, 4(3), 144-159.

3285.   Lange, A., and Van der Hart, O. (1983), Directive family therapy. New
        York: Brunner/Mazel.

3286.   Langer, M.F. (1959), Parent groups in total family therapy. Children, 6,
        69-71.

3287.   Langer, S.M. (1983), Marital therapy of chronic pain patients: A
        multiple-baseline study. Dissertation Abstracts International, 44, 1966-
        B.

3288.   Langmaier, J. (1975), Goals and possibilities of family therapy in the
        future socialist society. In M. Hausner, et al. (Eds.), Psychotherapie in
        Socialistschn Landern, Leipzig: Thieme, (133-137).

3289.   Langmeierova, D., and Langmeier, J. (1973), Theoretical basis for
        family therapy. Ceskoslovenska Psychiatrie, 69, 387-391.

3290.   Langsdorf, F. (1978), Understanding the role of extrafamilial social
        forces in family treatment: A critique of family therapy. Family
        Therapy, 5(1), 73-80.

3291.   Langsley, D.G. (1978), Three models of family therapy: Prevention,
        crisis treatment or rehabilitation. Journal of Clinical Psychiatry, 39,
        792-796.

3292.   Langsley, D.G., Fairbairn, R.H., and DeYoung, C.D. (1968),
        Adolescence and family crises. Canadian Journal of Psychiatry, 13, 125-
        133.

3293.   Langsley, D.G., Flomenhaft, K., and Machotka, P. (1969), Follow-up
        evaluation of family crisis therapy. American Journal of
        Orthopsychiatry, 39, 753-759.

3294.   Langsley, D.G., Pittman, F.S., Machotka, P., and Flomenhaft, K. (1968),
        Family crisis therapy: Results and implications. Family Process, 7, 145-
        158.

3295.   Langsley, D.G., Pittman, F.S., and Swank, G.E. (1969), Family crisis in schizophrenics and other mental patients. Journal of Nervous and Mental Disease, 149, 270-276.

3296.   Langsley, D.G., and Kaplan, D.M. (1968), The treatment of families in crisis. New York: Grune and Stratton.

3297.   Lansky, M. (1981), Family therapy and major psychopathology. New York: Grune and Stratton.

3298.   Lansky, M.R. (1980), Research in family therapy. Advances in Family Psychiatry, 2, 3-18.

3299.   Lansky, M.R. (1979), Research in family therapy. In: E.A. Serafetinedes (Ed.), Methods of biobehavioral research. New York, NY: Grune and Stratton.

3300.   Lansky, M.R. (1977), Establishing a family-oriented inpatient unit. Journal of Operational Psychiatry, 8, 66-74.

3301.   Lansky, M.R. (1982), Review of S. Box, B. Copley, J. Magagna, and E. Moustaki's Psychotherapy with families: An analytic approach. Family Process, 21, 492-493.

3302.   Lansky, M.R. (1984), Family therapy. In J. Yager (Ed.), Teaching psychiatry and behavioral science. New York: Grune and Stratton.

3303.   Lansky, M.R. (1984), Review of D. Bloch and R. Simon's The strength of family therapy: Selected papers of Nathan Ackerman. American Journal of Psychiatry, 141(6), 817.

3304.   Lansky, M.R., Bley, C.R., McVey, G.G., and Brotman, B. (1980), Multiple family groups as aftercare. Advances in Family Psychiatry, 2, 425-436.

3305.   Lansky, M.R., Bley, C.R., McVey, G.G., and Brotman, B. (1978), Multiple family groups as aftercare. International Journal of Group Psychotherapy, 28, 211-224.

3306.   Lansky, M.R., and Brotman, B. (1978), Family treatment training for psychiatric nurses: A report on social in-service workshops. Journal of Psychiatric Nursing, 16, 19-22.

3307.   Lansky, S.B. (1978), Childhood cancer: Parental discord and divorce. Pediatrics, 62, 184-188.

3308.   Lantz, J.E. (1978), Cotherapy approach in family therapy. Social Work, 23, 156-158.

3309.   Lantz, J.E. (1979), Extreme itching treated by a family systems approach. International Journal of Family Therapy, 1(3), 244-253.

3310.   Lantz, J.E. (1977), Family therapy: Using a transaction approach. Journal of Psychiatric Nursing, 15, 17-23.

3311.   Lantz, J.E. (1985), Extreme itching treated by a family systems approach. International Journal of Family Therapy, 7, 195-204.

3312. Lantz, J.E. (1982), Meaning in family therapy. International Forum for Logotherapy, 5, 44-46.

3313. Lantz, J.E., and Treece, N. (1982), Identity operations and family treatment. Journal Psychosocial Nursing and Mental Health Services, 20, 20-3.

3314. Lantz, J.E., and Werk, K. (1980), Family aspects of trichotillomania...a compulsion to pull one's hair...most frequently found with adolescent females. Journal of Psychiatric Nursing, 18, 32-37.

3315. Lapierre-Adamcy, E., and Burch, T.K. (1974), Trends and differentials in age at marriage in Korea. Studies in Family Planning, 5, 255-260.

3316. Lappin, J. (1983), On becoming a culturally conscious family therapist. Family Therapy Collections, 8, 122-136.

3317. Laqueur, H.P. (1968), Correlation between multiple family therapy, acute crises in a therapeutic community and drug levels. Diseases of the Nervous System, 29, Suppl., 188-192.

3318. Laqueur, H.P. (1968), General systems theory and multiple family therapy. In: J.H. Masserman (Ed.), Current psychiatric therapies. New York, NY: Grune and Stratton.

3319. Laqueur, H.P. (1973), Multiple family therapy: Questions and answers. Seminars in Psychiatry, 5(2), 195-205.

3320. Laqueur, H.P. (1970), Multiple family therapy and general systems theory. International Psychiatry Clinics, 7, 99-124.

3321. Laqueur, H.P., LaBurt, H.A., and Morong, E. (1964), Multiple family therapy. Current Psychiatric Therapies, 4, 150-154.

3322. Laqueur, H.P., LaBurt, H.A., and Morong, E. (1964), Multiple family therapy: Further developments. International Journal of Social Psychiatry, Special Edition, 2, 70-80.

3323. Laqueur, H.P., Wells, C.F., and Agresti, M. (1969), Multiple-family therapy in a state hospital. Hospital and Community Psychiatry, 20, 13-20.

3324. Laramore, D. (1979), Career counseling for families and other multi-age groups. Personnel and Guidance Journal, 57(10), 555-556.

3325. Larsen, F., and Mendelsohn, I. (1963), Group preparation of six problem patients for family care. Journal of the Fort Logan Mental Health Center, 1, 49-51.

3326. Larsen, G.R. (1974), An evaluation of the Minnesota Couple Communications Training Program's influence on marital communication and self and mate perceptions. Dissertation Abstracts International, 3(5-A), 2627-2628.

3327. Larsen, J.A. (1978), Dysfunction in the evangelical family: Treatment considerations. Family Coordinator, 27, 261-267.

3328.   Larson, C.C., and Gilbertson, D.L. (1977), Reducing family resistance to therapy through a child management approach. Social Casework, 58, 620-623.

3329.   Larson, C.C., and Talley, L.K. (1977), Family resistance to therapy: A model for services and therapists' roles. Child Welfare, 56, 121-126.

3330.   Larson, L.E., and Fraser, J.D. (1979), Family meal-time interaction: Understanding the family in its natural setting. Canadian Counselor, 13, 58-67.

3331.   Larson, N.W. (1981), An analysis of the effectiveness of a state-sponsored program designed to teach intervention skills in the treatment of family sexual abuse. Dissertation Abstracts International, 41, 4839-A.

3332.   Larson, R.S. (1972), Can parent classes affect family communication? School Counselor, 19, 261-270.

3333.   Lascari, A. (1978), The dying child and the family. Journal of Family Practice, 6, 1279-1286.

3334.   Lask, B. (1985) Review of R.F. Levant's Family therapy: A comprehensive overview. Journal of Family Therapy, 7(2), 184.

3335.   Lask, B. (1985), Review of S.R. Sauber's Family therapy: Basic concepts and terms. Journal of Family Therapy, 7(2), 184.

3336.   Lask, B. (1982), Family therapy in paediatric settings. In A. Bentovim, G.G. Barnes, and A. Cooklin (Eds.), Family therapy. 2. Complementary frameworks of theory and practice. London: Academic Press.

3337.   Lask, B. (1982), Physical illness and the family. In A. Bentovim, G.G. Barnes, and A. Cooklin (Eds.), Family therapy. 2. Complementary frameworks of theory and practice. London: Academic Press.

3338.   Lask, B., and Mathew, D. (1979), Childhood asthma: A controlled trial of family psychotherapy. Archives of Diseases of the Child, 54, 116-119.

3339.   Laskin, E.R. (1968), Breaking down the walls. Family Process, 7, 118-125.

3340.   Lassner, R., and Brassea, M. (1968), Family centered group therapy with chronic schizophrenic patients: A five-year follow-up study. Group Psychotherapy, 21, 247-258.

3341.   Lasswell, M., and Lobsenz, N.M. (1976), No fault marriage: The new technique of self-counseling and what it can help you do. Garden City, NY: Doubleday.

3342.   Lasswell, T.E., and Lasswell, M.E. (1976), I love you but I'm not in love with you. Journal of Marriage and Family Counseling, 2, 211-224.

3343.   Lastrucci, P. (1968), (Observations during psychotherapy of a family group in a psychiatric hospital.) Rivista Sperimentale di Freniatria e Medicina Legale delle Auenazioni Mentale, 92, 1731-1752.

3344.   Latham, J.D., and White, G.D. (1978), Coping with homosexual
expression within heterosexual marriages: Five case studies. Journal of
Sex and Marital Therapy, 4, 198-212.

3345.   Latham, N. (1979), The effect of marital adjustment of teaching basic
marital communication in a conjoint couples group using video
feedback. Dissertation Abstracts International, 40, 1425-B. (University
Microfilm No. 791973.)

3346.   Latham, T. (1982), The use of co-therapy as a training method. Journal
of Family Therapy, 4, 257-270.

3347.   Lathey, J.W. (1978), Assessing classroom environment and prioritizing
goals for severely retarded. Exceptional Children, 45, 190.

3348.   Lau, A. (1981), General systems theory and some clinical applications.
Journal of Family Therapy, 3, 313-326.

3349.   Lau, D. (1985), Cultural relativism, relative agreement. Journal of
Family Therapy, 7, 273-276.

3350.   Laughlin, J., and Weiss, H. (1981), An outpatient milieu therapy
approach to treatment of child abuse and neglect problems. Social
Casework, 62(2), 106-108.

3351.   Lav, A. (1984), Transcultural issues in family therapy. Journal of
Family Therapy, 6(2), 91-112.

3352.   Lavery, P.J. (1985), Differentiation of self and marital satisfaction: An
exploratory analysis based on the Bowen theory. Dissertation Abstracts
International, 45, 3321-B.

3353.   Lawson, B.A. (1977), Chronic illness in the school-aged child: Effects
on the total family. Journal of Maternal Child Nursing, 2, 49-56.

3354.   Lawton, M.P. (1979), Review of J.J. Herr and J.H. Weakland's
Counseling elders and their families: Practical techniques for applied
gerontology. Family Process, 18, 356-357.

3355.   Lazar, M.C., and Mason, S.M. (1981), Group counseling for victims of
sexual assault: Help unit program. Australian Journal of Sex, Marriage,
and Family, 3(2), 131-134.

3356.   Lazarus, L.W. (1976), Family therapy by a husband-wife team. Journal
of Marriage and Family Counseling, 2, 225-233.

3357.   Lazarus, P.J., Gavilo, H.M., and Moore, J.W. (1983), The treatment of
elective mutism in children within the school setting: Two case
studies. School Psychology Review, 12, 467-472.

3358.   Lazrus, A.A. (1981), Divorce counseling or marriage therapy? A
therapeutic option. Journal of Marital and Family Therapy, 7(1), 15-22.

3359.   LeBerre, F. (1984), Attempt at management of two brothers in a
distressing situation. Soins Psychiatrica, 44, 49-50.

3360.   LeBlang, T.R. (1979), The family stress consultation team: An Illinois
approach to protective services. Child Welfare, 58, 597-604.

3361. LeBow, M.D. (1973), The behavior modification process for parent-child therapy. Family Coordinator, 22, 313-319.

3362. LeFave, M.K. (1980), Correlates of engagement in family therapy. Journal of Marital and Family Therapy, 6, 75-81.

3363. LeMaire, J.G. (1973), Therapies for a couple. Perspectives in Psychiatric Care, 37, 29-39.

3364. LeMaire, J.G. (1972), Therapy for the couple. Paris: Payot.

3365. LeMaire, J.G. (1963), Essay on conjugal misunderstandings and the role of the marriage counselor. Hygiene Mentale (Paris), 52, 13-38.

3366. Lea, R.C. (1983), Acting up disorders in children: An evaluation of an intervention. Dissertation Abstracts International, 44, 611-B.

3367. Leadbeater, B., and Farber, B.A. (1983), The limits of reciprocity in behavioral marriage therapy. Family Process, 22, 229-37.

3368. Leader, A.L. (1975), The place of in-laws in marital relationships. Social Casework, 56, 486-491.

3369. Leader, A.L. (1964), The role of intervention in family-group treatment. Social Casework, 45, 327-332.

3370. Leader, A.L. (1980), Intergenerational separation anxiety in family therapy. Advances in Family Psychiatry, 2, 279-288.

3371. Leader, A.L. (1978), Intergenerational separation anxiety in family therapy. Social Casework, 59, 138-144.

3372. Leader, A.L. (1973), Family therapy for divorced fathers and others out of home. Social Casework, 54, 13-19.

3373. Leader, A.L. (1976), Denied dependency in family therapy. Social Casework, 57, 637-643.

3374. Leader, A.L. (1979), Notion of responsibility in family therapy. Social Casework, 60, 131-137.

3375. Leader, A.L. (1981), The centrality of the family in treating children. Family and Child Mental Health Journal, 7, 116-129.

3376. Leader, A.L. (1984), Therapeutic control in family therapy. Clinical Social Work Journal, 11(4), 351-361.

3377. Leahey, M., and Slive, A. (1983), Treating families with adolescents: An ecological approach. Canadian Journal of Community Mental Health, 10, 21-28.

3378. Leaman, D.R. (1983), Needs assessment: A technique to reverse marital burnout. Journal of Psychology and Christianity, 2, 47-51.

3379. Leavitt, S., Davis, M., Maloney, K.G., and Maloney, D.M. (1979), Parenting alone successfully: Development of a single parent training program. In: N. Stinnett, B. Chesser, and J. Defrain (Eds.), Building family strengths. Lincoln, NE: University of Nebraska Press.

3380. Lebedun, M. (1979), Measuring movement in group marital counseling. Social Casework, 51, 35-43.

3381. Lebovici, S. (1981), Family therapy. Psychiatrie de L'Enfant, 24, 541-83.

3382. Lebow, J. (1981), Issues in the assessment of outcome in family therapy. Family Process, 20(2), 167-188.

3383. Lebow, J.L. (1984), On the value of integrating approaches to family therapy. Journal of Marital and Family Therapy, 10(2), 127-138.

3384. Ledbetter, J.E. (1982), Systems theory in family and marital therapy. Psychiatric Forum, 11, 26-35.

3385. Lederer, M.L. (1967), Individual and group responses to control issues in family life education. Smith College, 38, 54-55.

3386. Lee, A.M., and Lee, E.B. (Eds.) (1961), Marriage and the family. New York, NY: Barnes and Nobel.

3387. Lefer, J. (1966), Counter-resistance in family therapy. Journal of Hillside Hospital, 15, 205-210.

3388. Leff, J. (1981), The role of maintenance therapy and relatives' expressed emotion in relapse of schizophrenia: A two-year follow-up. British Journal Psychiatry, 139, 102-104.

3389. Leff, J., Kuipers, L., Berkowitz, R., Eberlein, R., and Sturgeon, D. (1982), Social intervention in schizophrenic families. Lancet, 2, 1275.

3390. Leff, J., Kuipers, L., Berkowitz, R., Eberlein, R., and Sturgeon, D. (1982), A controlled trial of social intervention in the families of schizophrenic patients. British Journal of Psychiatry, 141, 121-134.

3391. Leff, J., Kuipers, L., Berkowitz, R., Fries, R.E., and Sturgeon, D. (1983), Social intervention in the families of schizophrenics: Addendum letter. British Journal of Psychiatry, 142, 311.

3392. Leff, J.P. (1980), Developments in family treatment of schizophrenia. Advances in Family Psychiatry, 2, 313-333.

3393. Legum, L. (1977), A comparison of two theoretical models of marital therapy in a group framework. Dissertation Abstracts International, 37(7), 3618-B.

3394. Lehnhardt, K. (1965), Practical experiences with open groups of parents in a child guidance center. Report based on a catamnestic interview with parents. Praxis der Kinderpsychologie und Kinderpsychiatrie, 14, 125-140.

3395. Lehnisch, E. (1983), Sleep disorders in young children: Psychological approach. Soins Gynecologie, Obstetrique, Puericulture, Pediatrie, Sfirec, 103, 43-45.

3396. Lehrman, N.S. (1963), The joint interview: An aid to psychotherapy and family stability. American Journal of Psychotherapy, 17, 83-94.

3397.   Lehtinen, M.W. (1978), Review of H. Grunebaum and J. Christ's
        Contemporary marriage: Structure, dynamics and therapy. Journal of
        Marriage and the Family, 40, 189.

3398.   Leiblum, S.R., and Rosen, R.C. (1979), The weekend workshop for
        dysfunctional couples: Assets and limitations. Journal of Sex and
        Marital Therapy, 5(1), 57-69.

3399.   Leichter, E. (1962), Group psychotherapy of married couples' groups:
        Some characteristic treatment dynamics. International Journal of Group
        Psychotherapy, 12, 154-163.

3400.   Leichter, E. (1973), Treatment of married couples groups. Family
        Coordinator, 22, 31-42.

3401.   Leichter, E. (1975), Treatment of married couples group. In: A.
        Gurman and D. Rice (Eds.), Couples in conflict. New York, NY: Jason
        Aronson.

3402.   Leichter, E. (1956), Family casework through the group method.
        Journal of the Jewish Community Service, 33, 376-387.

3403.   Leichter, E. (1979), Psychoanalysis and family therapy: Selected
        papers. International Journal of Group Psychotherapy, 29, 126-128.

3404.   Leichter, E., and Schulman, G. (1977), Multi-family group therapy: A
        multidimensional solution. Praxis der Kinderpsychologie und
        Kinderpsychiatrie, 26, 169-176.

3405.   Leichter, E., and Schulman, G.L. (1974), Multi-family group therapy.
        Family Process, 13, 95-110.

3406.   Leichter, E., and Schulman, G.L. (1972), Interplay of group and family
        treatment techniques in multifamily group therapy. International
        Journal of Group Psychotherapy, 22, 167-176.

3407.   Leichter, E., and Schulman, G.L. (1963), The family interview as an
        integrative device in group therapy with families. International Journal
        of Group Psychotherapy, 13, 335-345.

3408.   Leichter, E., and Schulman, G.L. (1968), Emerging phenomena in multi-
        family group treatment. International Journal of Group Psychotherapy,
        18, 59-69.

3409.   Leighton, D.J. (1969), Casework with the parents of autistic children.
        British Journal of Psychiatry, 10, 17-21.

3410.   Leighton, L.A., Stollak, G.E., and Ferguson, L.R. (1971), Patterns of
        communication in normal and clinic families. Journal of Consulting and
        Clinical Psychology, 36, 252-256.

3411.   Leik, R.K., and Northwood, L.K. (1964), Classification of family
        interaction problems for treatment purposes. Journal of Marital and
        Family Therapy, 26(3), 288-294.

3412.   Leik, R.K., and Northwood, L.K. (1964), Improving family guidance
        through the small-group experimental laboratory. Social Work, 9, 18-25.

3413.   Leler, H., Johnson, D.L., Cerrillo, F., and Buck, C. (1979), Building family strengths: Workshop model for enriching families. In: N. Stinnet, B. Chessler, and J. Defrain (Eds.), Building family strengths. Lincoln, NE: University of Nebraska Press.

3414.   Lemle, R. (1980), Review of I. Goldenberg and H. Goldenberg's Family therapy: An overview. Family Process, 19, 423-424.

3415.   Lenn, T.I., Lane, P.A., Merritt, E.T., and Silverstone, L. (1967), Parent group therapy for adolescent rehabilitation. V.O.C. Journal of Education, 7, 17-26.

3416.   Leon, A.M. (1969), Interferencias de los padres en el tratamiento de los ninos. (Parents' interference in their children's treatment.) Revista Argentina de Psicologia, 1, 101-106.

3417.   Leon, R.L. (1978), The generation gap: Adult and child psychiatry. Psychiatric Opinion, 15, 37-39.

3418.   Lerner, A. (1954), Attitudes of male alcoholic inmates toward marriage, family, and related problems. Mental Hygiene, 48, 468-482.

3419.   Lerner, B. (1978), Helping parents help their children. Acta Psiquiatrica y Psychologia, 24, 239.

3420.   Lerner, B.O. (1980), Third conference on family therapy. Acta, 26(3), 183-184.

3421.   Lerner, H.E. (1978), Adaptive and pathogenic aspects of sex role stereotypes: Implications for parenting and psychotherapy. American Journal of Psychiatry, 135(1), 49-52.

3422.   Lerner, H.E. (1979), Effects of the nursing mother-infant dyad on the family. American Journal of Orthopsychiatry, 49, 339-348.

3423.   Leroy, A. (1969), Family group therapy (A preliminary report.) Ugeskrift fur Laeger, 131, 851, 858.

3424.   Leslie, G.R. (1964), Conjoint therapy in marriage counseling. Journal of Marriage and the Family, 26, 65-71.

3425.   Leslie, G.R. (1964), The field of marriage counseling. In H.T. Christensen, Ed., Handbook of marriage and the family. Chicago, IL: Rand McNally.

3426.   Leslie, R.C., and Veldhuizen, J.F. (1974), Family counseling and the minister. Journal of Pastoral Care, 28, 3-12.

3427.   Lesoff, R. (1975), Foster's technique: A systematic approach to family therapy. Clinical Social Work Journal, 3, 32-45.

3428.   Lessin, S., and Jacob, T. (1979), Verbal-nonverbal congruence in normal and delinquent families. Journal of Clinical Psychology, 35, 391-395.

3429.   Lester, C.F., and Anderson, S. (1981), Counseling with families of gifted children: The school counselor's role. The School Counselor, 29, 147-151.

3430.   Lester, G.W. (1980), TA marital therapy. Transactional Analysis Journal, 10, 33-37.

3431.   Lester, G.W., Beckham, E., and Baucom, D.H. (1980), Implementation of behavioral marital therapy. Journal of Marital and Family Therapy, 6(2), 189-199.

3432.   Lester, M.E., and Doherty, W.J. (1983), Couples' long-term evaluations of their marriage encounter experience. Journal of Marital and Family Therapy, 9, 183-188.

3433.   Letulle, L.G. (1979), Family treatment in residential treatment for children. Social Work, 24, 49-51.

3434.   Levande, D.I. (1976), Family theory as a necessary component of family therapy. Social Casework, 57, 291-295.

3435.   Levant, R.F. (1978), Family therapy: A client-centered perspective. Journal of Marital and Family Counseling, 4, 35-42.

3436.   Levant, R.F. (1978), Client centered approaches to working with the family: An overview of new developments in therapeutic, educational and preventive methods. International Journal of Family Counseling, 1, 31-44.

3437.   Levant, R.F. (1980), Sociological and clinical models of the family: An attempt to identify paradigms. American Journal of Family Therapy, 8(4), 5-20.

3438.   Levant, R.F. (1980), A classification of the field of family therapy: A review of prior attempts and a new paradigmatic model. American Journal of Family Therapy, 8(1), 3-16.

3439.   Levant, R.F. (1983), Client-centered skills training programs for the family: A review of the literature. Counseling Psychologist, 12, 29-46.

3440.   Levant, R.F. (1983), Diagnostic perspectives on the family: Process, structural and historical contextual models. American Journal of Family Therapy, 11, 3-9.

3441.   Levant, R.F. (1983), Toward a counseling psychology of the family: Psychological-educational and skills-training programs for treatment, prevention, and development. Counseling Psychologist, 12, 5-27.

3442.   Levant, R.F. (1982), Client-centered family therapy. American Journal of Family Therapy, 10(2), 62.

3443.   Levant, R.F. (1984), Family therapy: A comprehensive overview. Englewood Cliffs, NJ: Prentice-Hall.

3444.   Levant, R.F., and Haffey, N.A. (1981), Toward an integration of child and family therapy. International Journal of Family Therapy, 9, 130-143.

3445.   Levay, A.N. (1983), Interminable sex therapy: Response. Journal of Marital and Family Therapy, 9, 15-18.

3446.   Levay, A.N., Kagle, A., and Weissburg, G.H. (1979), Issues of transference in sex therapy. Journal of Sex and Marital Therapy, 5(1), 15-21.

3447.   Levay, A.N., and Kagle, A. (1983), Interminable sex therapy: A report on 10 cases of therapeutic gridlock. Journal of Marital and Family Therapy, 9, 1-10.

3448.   Levay, A.N., and Weissberg, J. (1979), The role of dreams in sex therapy. Journal of Sex and Marital Therapy, 5(4), 334-339.

3449.   Levay, A.N., and Weissberg, J.H. (1981), The role of resistance in sex therapy. Journal of Sex and Marital Therapy, 7(2), 125.

3450.   Leveille, D.L. (1983), An evaluation of two modes of therapy for incestuous fathers. Dissertation Abstracts International, 44, 1388-A.

3451.   Levenburg, S.B. (1979), Studies in family-oriented crises intervention with hemodialysis patients. International Journal of Psychiatry in Medicine, 9, 83-92.

3452.   Levenson, J., and Berry, S.L. (1983), Family intervention in a case of multiple personality. Journal of Marital and Family Therapy, 9, 73-80.

3453.   Levenstein, S. (1981), Psychosomatic families and the general practitioner. South African Medical Journal, 16, 289-91.

3454.   Leventhal, T., and Weinberger, G. (1975), Evaluation of a large-scale brief therapy program for children. American Journal of Orthopsychiatry, 45, 119-133.

3455.   Leveton, A.F. (1964), Family therapy as the treatment of choice. Medical Bulletin of the United States Army in Europe, 21, 76-79.

3456.   Levi, L.D., Stierlin, H., and Savard, R.J. (1972), Fathers and sons: The interlocking crises of integrity and identity. Psychiatry, 35, 48-56.

3457.   Levick, M., and Herring, J. (1973), Family dynamics: As seen through art therapy. Art in Psychotherapy, 1, 45-54.

3458.   Levick, S.E., Jalali, B., and Strauss, J.S. (1981), With onions and tears: A multidimensional analysis of a counter-ritual. Family Process, 20, 77-83.

3459.   Levin, E.C. (1966), Therapeutic multiple family groups. International Journal of Group Psychotherapy, 16, 203-208.

3460.   Levine, B.L. (1985), Adolescent substance abuse: Toward an integration of family systems and individual adaptation theories. American Journal of Family Therapy, 13, 3-16.

3461.   Levine, L. (1956), Sex and marriage problems. In: S.R. Slavson (Ed.), The fields of group psychotherapy. New York, NY: International Universities Press.

3462.   Levine, L., and Brodsky, J. (1956), Taking stock of marriage: An illustration in group counseling. Marriage and Family Living, 18, 162-167.

3463. Levine, S.B. (1980), Conceptual suggestions for outcome research in sex therapy. Journal of Sex and Marital Therapy, 6(2), 102-108.

3464. Levine, S.B. (1978), The effectiveness of sex therapy for chronic secondary psychological impotence. Journal of Sex and Marital Therapy, 4, 235.

3465. Levine, S.B. (1982), A modern perspective on nymphomania. Journal of Sex and Marital Therapy, 8, 316-324.

3466. Levinson, E.D. (1969), Observations during the simultaneous psychiatric hospitalization of a three and one-half year old autistic girl, her psychotic mother, and eleven-day-old brother. Lavel Medicine, 40, 896-904.

3467. Levit, H.I. (1971), Marital crisis intervention: Hypnosis in impotence-frigidity cases. American Journal of Clinical Hypnosis, 14, 56-60.

3468. Levitt, M., and Rubenstein, B.O. (1957), The fate of advice: Examples of distortion in parental counseling. Mental Hygiene, 41, 213-216.

3469. Levitt, M.B. (1982), The impact of family intervention of attitudes of key relatives of psychiatric in-patients. Dissertation Abstracts International, 43, 1692-A.

3470. Levy, D.J. (1978), The relative efficacy of applied behavioral strategies in marital therapy. Dissertation Abstracts International, 39, 2507-2508-B.

3471. Levy, J., Rossman, B., Kravitz, H., Robertson, B., and Dow, T. (1973), Inpatients in love: Conjoint therapy of two adolescents. Canadian Psychiatric Association Journal, 18, 435-438.

3472. Levy, J., and Brown, R.D. (1980-81), The uncovering of projective identification in the treatment of the borderline adolescent. International Journal of Psychoanalytic Psychotherapy, 8, 137-149.

3473. Levy, J., and Weiss, A. (1966), Hearot teoretiyot al terapiat hamishpaha. (Theoretical notion about family therapy.) Megamot, 14, 312-321.

3474. Levy, R. (1979), Review of R.S. Ables and J.M. Brandsma's Therapy for couples. Social Work, 24, 439.

3475. Lewis, C.E., and Lewis, M.A. (1977), The content of care provided by family nurse practitioners. Journal of Community Health, 2, 259-267.

3476. Lewis, E. (1979), Mourning by the family after a stillbirth or neonatal death. Archives of Diseases of the Child, 54, 303-306.

3477. Lewis, H. (1980), Discussion: "International politics and family systems: Some observations on tactics." International Journal of Family Therapy, 2(4), 234-235.

3478. Lewis, J.C., and Glasser, N. (1965), Evolution of a treatment approach to families: Group family therapy. International Journal of Group Psychotherapy, 15, 506-515.

3479.   Lewis, J.M. (1979), The interface of family disturbance and individual patienthood. American Journal of Family Therapy, 7(3), 5-14.

3480.   Lewis, J.M. (1978), The adolescent and the healthy family. Adolescent Psychiatry, 6, 156-170.

3481.   Lewis, K.G. (1985), Review of C.M. Anderson and S. Stewart's Mastering resistance: A practical guide to family therapy. Journal of Marital and Family Therapy, 11(1), 102-103.

3482.   Lewis, S. (1983), Change in sex-role orientation as a function of brief marital therapy. Dissertation Abstracts International, 43, 2606-A.

3483.   Leyer, E., and Riedell, H. (1980), The relations between family, patient and clinic in inpatient psychiatric treatment and psychotherapy. Psychiatrische Praxis, 7(2), 65.

3484.   Liberman, R. (1970), Behavioral approaches to family and couple therapy. American Journal of Orthopsychiatry, 40, 106-118.

3485.   Liberman, R.P. (1972), Behavioral methods in group and family therapy. Seminars in Psychiatry, 4, 145-156.

3486.   Liberman, R.P. (1975), Behavioral methods in group and family therapy. In: M. Rosenbaum and M.M. Berger (Eds.), Group psychotherapy and group function. New York, NY: Basic Books.

3487.   Liberman, R.P. (1976), Marital therapy in groups: A comparative evaluation of behavioral and interactional formats. Copenhagen: Munksgaard.

3488.   Liberman, R.P., Levine, J., Wheeler, E., Sanders, N., and Wallace, C.J. (1976), Marital therapy in groups: A comparative evaluation of behavioral and interactional formats. Acta Psychiatrica Scandinavica, Suppl 266, 3-34.

3489.   Liberman, R.P., Wallace, C.J., Falloon, I.R., and Vaughn, C.E. (1981), Interpersonal problem-solving therapy for schizophrenics and their families. Comprehensive Psychiatry, 22, 627-630.

3490.   Liberman, R.P., Wheeler, E., and Sanders, N. (1976), Behavioral therapy for marital disharmony: An educational approach. Journal of Marriage and Family Counseling, 2, 383-395.

3491.   Liberthson, E. (1968), Helping families live with and for the mentally retarded child. Journal of Rehabilitation, 34, 24-26.

3492.   Libo, S.S., Palmer, C., and Archibald, D. (1971), Family group therapy for children with self-induced seizures. American Journal of Orthopsychiatry, 41, 506-509.

3493.   Libow, J.A., Raskin, P.A., and Caust, B.L. (1982), Feminist and family systems therapy: Are they irreconcilable? American Journal of Family Therapy, 10, 3-12.

3494.   Lichtenberg, J.D., and Pao, P.N. (1960), The prognostic and therapeutic significance of the husband wife relationship for hospitalized schizophrenic women. Psychiatry, 23, 209-213.

3495.   Liddle, H.A. (1980), On teaching a contextual or systemic therapy: Training content, goals, and methods. American Journal of Family Therapy, 8, 58-69.

3496.   Liddle, H.A. (1980), Review of M. Andolfi's Family therapy: An interactional approach. American Journal of Family Therapy, 8, 79-80.

3497.   Liddle, H.A. (1978), The emotional and political hazards of teaching and learning family therapy. Family Therapy, 5, 1-12.

3498.   Liddle, H.A. (1982), On the problems of eclecticism: A call for epistemologic clarification and human-scale theories. Family Process, 21, 243-50.

3499.   Liddle, H.A. (1983), Diagnosis and assessment in family therapy: I. A comparative analysis of six schools of thought. Family Therapy Collections, 11, 1-33.

3500.   Liddle, H.A. (1983), Review of T.C. Todd's The family therapy of drug abuse and addiction. Family Process, 22, 239-241.

3501.   Liddle, H.A. (1982), Family therapy training: Current issues, future trends. International Journal of Family Therapy, 4, 81-97.

3502.   Liddle, H.A. (1982), Review of S. Minuchin and C. Fishman's Family therapy techniques. American Journal of Family Therapy, 10, 82-87.

3503.   Liddle, H.A. (1984), Review of R. Whiffen and J. Bynghall's Family therapy supervision: Recent developments in practice. Journal of Marital and Family Therapy, 10(2), 197-199.

3504.   Liddle, H.A., Schwartz, R.C., Breunlin, D.C., and Constantine, J.A. (1984), Training family therapy supervisors: Issues of content, form and context. Journal of Marital and Family Therapy, 10(2), 139-150.

3505.   Liddle, H.A., Vance, S., and Pastushak, R.J. (1979), Family therapy training opportunities in psychology and counselor education. Professional Psychology, 10, 760-765.

3506.   Liddle, H.A., and Halpin, R.J. (1978), Family therapy training and supervision literature: A comparative review. Journal of Marriage and Family Counseling, 4, 77-98.

3507.   Liddle, H.A., and Saba, G.W. (1981), Systematic chic: Family therapy's new wave. Journal of Strategic and Systematic Therapies, 1(2), 36-40.

3508.   Liddle, H.A., and Saba, G.W. (1981), Systematic chic II: Can family therapy maintain its floy floy? Journal of Strategic and Systematic Therapies, 1(2), 40-42.

3509.   Liddle, H.A., and Saba, G.W. (1982), Teaching family therapy at the introductory level: A conceptual model emphasizing a pattern which connects training and therapy. Journal of Marital and Family Therapy, 8, 63-72.

3510.   Liddle, H.A., and Saba, G.W. (1983), Clinical use of the family life cycle: Some cautionary guidelines. Family Therapy Collections, 11, 161-176.

3511.   Liddle, H.A., and Schwartz, R.C. (1983), Live supervision/consultation:
         Conceptual and pragmatic guidelines for family therapy trainers.
         Family Process, 22, 477-490.

3512.   Lidz, T. (1972), Effect of family studies on the therapy of
         schizophrenia. Psyche, 26, 169-190.

3513.   Lieber, D.J. (1977), Parental focus of attention in a video-tape feedback
         task as a function of hypothesized risk for offspring schizophrenia.
         Family Process, 16, 467-475.

3514.   Lieberman, E.J. (1980), Review of M. Andolfi's Family therapy: An
         interactional approach. Journal of Marital and Family Therapy, 6, 353.

3515.   Lieberman, E.J. (1980), Review of C.P. Barnard and R.G. Corales's The
         theory and technique of family therapy. Journal of Marital and Family
         Therapy, 6, 353.

3516.   Lieberman, E.J. (1979), Review of H.Y. Kwiatkowska's Family therapy
         and evaluation through art. Journal of Marital and Family Therapy, 5,
         113.

3517.   Lieberman, E.J. (1966), Family therapy. Provo Papers, 77-91.

3518.   Lieberman, F. (1984), Reviews of C.M. Anderson and S. Stewart's
         Mastering resistance: A practical guide to family therapy and R.J.
         Marshall's Resistant interactions: Child, family and psychotherapist.
         Social Casework, 65, 189-190.

3519.   Lieberman, S. (1983), Marriage therapy. Recent Progress in Medicine,
         74, 227-48.

3520.   Lieberman, S. (1979), Transgenerational family therapy. Dover, NH:
         Longwood Publishing Group.

3521.   Lieberman, S. (1976), Letter: Family pathology and family treatment.
         British Medical Journal; Clinical Research Edition, 1, 1352.

3522.   Lieberman, S. (1982), Forging a marital bond. In A. Bentovim, G.G.
         Barnes, and A. Cooklin (Eds.), Family therapy. 2. Complementary
         frameworks of theory and practice. London: Academic Press.

3523.   Lieberman, S. (1982), Review of L. Headley's Adults and their parents in
         family therapy: A new direction in treatment. Journal of Family
         Therapy, 4, 328.

3524.   Lieberman, S. (1982), Going back to your own family. In A. Bentovim,
         G.G. Barnes, and A. Cooklin (Eds.), Family therapy. I. Complementary
         frameworks of theory and practice. London: Academic Press.

3525.   Lieberman, S., and Black, D. (1982), Loss, mourning and grief. In A.
         Bentovim, G.G. Barnes, and A. Cooklin (Eds.), Family therapy. 2.
         Complementary frameworks of theory and practice. London: Academic
         Press.

3526.   Lieberman, S., and Cooklin, A. (1982), Family therapy and general
         psychiatry. In A. Bentovim, G.G. Barnes, and A. Cooklin (Eds.), Family

therapy. 2. Complementary frameworks of theory and practice.
London: Academic Press.

3527.   Liebman, R., Honig, P., and Berger, H. (1976), An integrated treatment
program for psychogenic pain. Family Process, 15, 397-405.

3528.   Liebman, R., Minuchin, S., and Baker, L. (1974), The use of structural
family therapy in the treatment of intractable asthma. American
Journal of Psychiatry, 131(5), 535-540.

3529.   Liebman, R., Minuchin, S., and Baker, L. (1974), The role of the family
in the treatment of anorexia nervosa. Journal of the American Academy
of Child Psychiatry, 13, 264-274.

3530.   Liebman, R., Minuchin, S., and Baker, L. (1973), The role of the family
in the treatment of anorexia nervosa. Journal of American Academy of
Child Psychiatry, 12, 631-659.

3531.   Liebman, R., Minuchin, S., and Baker, L. (1974), The use of structural
family therapy in the treatment of intractable asthma. American
Journal of Pathology, 44, 611-619.

3532.   Liebman, R., Sargent, J., and Silver, M. (1983), A family systems
orientation to the treatment of anorexia nervosa. Journal of the
American Academy of Child Psychiatry, 22, 128-33.

3533.   Lief, H.I. (1982), The importance of marriage in mental health.
Psychiatric Annals, 12(7), 671.

3534.   Lief, H.I. (1982), Marital therapy in psychiatric practice. Psychiatric
Annals, 12(7), 670.

3535.   Lim-Meng, H., and Bottomley, V. (1983), A combined approach to the
treatment of effeminate behaviour in a boy: A case study. Journal of
Child Psychology and Psychiatry and Allied Disciplines, 24, 469-479.

3536.   Limerick, L. (1979), Counseling parents who have lost an infant.
Journal of the Royal College of Physicians of London, 13(4), 242-245.

3537.   Linden, M.E., Goodwin, H.M., and Resnik, H. (1968), Group
psychotherapy of couples in marriage counseling. International Journal
of Group Psychotherapy, 18, 313-324.

3538.   Lindenauer, G.G. (1971), Marriage education in a group therapy
setting. Journal of Emotional Education, 11, 165-177.

3539.   Lindenauer, G.G. (1969), Re-education in family living. Journal of
Emotional Education, 9, 25-27.

3540.   Lindenbaum, S., and Clark, D. (1983), Toward an integrative approach
to psychotherapy with children. American Journal of Orthopsychiatry,
53, 449-459.

3541.   Linder, S.B. (1974), The frequency of marriage once again.
Lakartidningen, 71, 152-153.

3542. Lindholm, B.W., and Touliatos, J. (1981), Parents and teachers perception of children in counseling and not in counseling. Journal of Psychology, 108(2), 283.

3543. Lindsay, J.S.B., and Pollard, D. (1974), Multiple family therapy. Australian and New Zealand Journal of Psychiatry, 8, 181-186.

3544. Lindt, H. (1948), Reactivation of mother child relationships in hospital group therapy. American Psychologist, 3, 346.

3545. Lingren, J.W. (1980), Procedures and materials for a marital growth group implementing the Adlerian lifestyle concept: Leader's manual; couple workbook. Dissertation Abstracts International, 40, 3784-A.

3546. Lipkin, G.B. (1980), The single parent. Journal of the New York State Nurses Association, 11, 10-16.

3547. Lipkin, G.B. (1978), The dysfunctional family. Journal of the New York State Nurses Association, 9, 32-43.

3548. Lippman-Hand, A. (1979), Genetic counseling: Parents' responses to uncertainty. Birth Defects, 15(50), 325-339.

3549. Lipsitt, D.R. (1981), The family in consultation-liaison psychiatry. General Hospital Psychiatry, 3, 231-236.

3550. Litman, T.J., and Veneers, M. (1979), Research on health care and the family: A methodological overview. Social Science Medicine, 13A, 379-385.

3551. Litovsky de Eiguer, D. (1980), An attempt to reconcile systems theory with group psychoanalytic theory within the context of their application in family therapy (author's transl.). Neuropsychiatrie de L'Enfance et de L'Adolescence, 28, 375-81.

3552. Littauer, C. (1980), Working with families of children in residential treatment. Child Welfare, 59, 225-34.

3553. Livesley, W.J. (1982), Review of L.R. Wolberg and M.L. Aronson's Group and family therapy 1980. Canadian Journal of Psychiatry, 27, 689.

3554. Livingood, A.B., and Cohen, S.R. (1980), Failures of individuation and communication disorders in children. Journal of Pediatric Psychology, 5, 179-187.

3555. Livsey, C.G. (1969), Family therapy: Role of the practicing physician. Modern Treatment, 6, 806-820.

3556. Lloyd, S.A., Cate, R.M., and Conger, J. (1983), Family violence and service providers: Implications for training. Social Casework, 64, 431-435.

3557. Lobato-Barrera, D.J. (1981), Multiple assessment of a workshop program for siblings of handicapped children. Dissertation Abstracts International, 41, 4674-B.

3558. Loeb, R.C. (1977), Group therapy for parents of mentally retarded children. Journal of Marriage and Family Counseling, 3(2), 77-84.

3559.   Lomax-Simpson, J.M. (1979), The large group as a vehicle for change, maturation and therapy for predominantly unsupported mothers and their children. Journal of Social Psychiatry, 25(4), 306-308.

3560.   Lonergan, E.C. (1983), Groups for medical patients: Coping mechanisms mobilized and revealed. In L.R. Wolberg and M.L. Aronson (Eds.), Group and family therapy 1982. New York: Brunner/Mazel.

3561.   Long, R.C. (1966), The path toward psychodrama family process. Group Psychotherapy, 19, 43-45.

3562.   Looney, J.G., Blotcky, M.J., Carson, D.I., and Gossett, J.T. (1980), A family-systems model for inpatient treatment of adolescents. Adolescent Psychiatry, 8, 499-511.

3563.   Lopes, L.M. (1980), A two-tiered ethnography of a couple in therapy: "I'm sorry I have to put it that way." But it is the only way he can. Dissertation Abstracts International, 40, 5921-A.

3564.   Loranger, P.D. (1973), An analysis of problem drinkers undergoing treatment through educational therapy, group therapy and family orientation. Dissertation Abstracts International, 3(9), 4350-B.

3565.   Lordi, W.M., and Silverberg, J. (1964), Infantile autism: A family approach. International Journal of Group Psychotherapy, 14, 360-365.

3566.   Losso, R.H. (1977), Psychoanalytic psychodrama for couples. Archiv Psicologia, Neurologia y Psichiariat, 38, 319-330.

3567.   Lott, E.B. (1981), The effects of pre-therapy training with lower-class families entering family therapy: Attendance and short-term subjective outcome. Dissertation Abstracts International, 41, 3897-B.

3568.   Lovern, J.D., and Zohn, J. (1982), Utilization and indirect suggestion in multiple-family group therapy with alcoholics. Journal of Marital and Family Therapy, 8, 325-333.

3569.   Low, B.J. (1984), A therapeutic use of the diagrammatic family tree. Child Welfare, 63, 37-43.

3570.   Low, P., and Low, M. (1975), Treatment of married couples in a group run by a husband and wife. International Journal of Group Psychotherapy, 25, 54-66.

3571.   Lowe, J. (1979), The psychological characteristics of professional marital/family therapists. Dissertation Abstracts International, 40, 2823-B.

3572.   Lowental, U. (1976), Multiple recurrent family model in the therapeutic community. International Journal of Social Psychology, 22, 19-24.

3573.   Lowman, J. (1980), Review of N.S. Jacobson and G. Margolin's Marital therapy: Strategies based on social learning and behavior exchange principles. Contemporary Psychology, 25, 995-996.

3574.   Lowry, T.S. (1975), Ethical considerations in sex therapy. Journal of Marriage and Family Counseling, 1(3), 229-236.

3575.   Luban-Plozza, B. (1979), Psychosomatic practice and the concept of family confrontation as therapeutic method. Psychotherapy and Psychosomatics, 31(1-4), 301-306.

3576.   Luban-Plozza, B. (1982), Family confrontation in clinical practice. Partnerberatung, 19, 79-90.

3577.   Luber, R.F. (1978), Teaching models in marital therapy: A review and research issue. Behavior Modification, 2, 77-91.

3578.   Luber, R.F. (1980), Review of T.J. Paolino and B.S. McCardy's Marriage and marital therapy. Behavior Modification, 5, 141.

3579.   Luber, R.F., and Wells, R.A. (1977), Structured, short-term multiple family therapy: An educational approach. International Journal of Group Psychotherapy, 27, 43-59.

3580.   Luckey, E.B. (1960), Implications for marriage counseling of self perceptions and spouse perceptions. Journal of Counseling Psychology, 7, 3-9.

3581.   Luders, W. (1983), Psychoanalysis versus family therapy. Psyche (Stuttg), 37, 462-69.

3582.   Luders, W. (1971), Church and family counseling. Praxis der Familienberatung Quarterly Supplement to Wege zum Menschen, 3, 373-377.

3583.   Luiz, G. (1978), Family therapy. South American Nursing Journal, 45, 12-13.

3584.   Lum, K. (1973), Towards multi-centered marital therapy. Psychotherapy: Theory, Research and Practice, 10, 208-211.

3585.   Lundin, T. (1982), Intervention in family therapy. Psykisk Halsa, 23, 189-193.

3586.   Lurie, A. (1984), Review of W.R. McFarlane's Family therapy in schizophrenia. Social Work, 29(3), 307.

3587.   Lurie, A., and Ron, H. (1971), Multiple family group counseling of discharged schizophrenic young adults and their parents. Social Psychiatry, 6, 88-92.

3588.   Lusterman, D.D. (1985), Review of J. Haley's Ordeal therapy: Unusual ways to change behavior. Journal of Marital and Family Therapy, 11(2), 211-12.

3589.   Lusterman, D.D. (1984), The family therapist's role in school consultation. American Journal of Family Therapy, 12(3), 67-68.

3590.   Lustig, F.W. (1978), Problem solving with families of retarded children. Australian Family Physician, 7, 824-826.

3591.   Lutahoire, S.K. (1975), The relevance of the human life cycle for marriage and family education and counseling among the Bantu in the west lake region of Tanzania, East Africa. Dissertation Abstracts International, 35, 6077-6078-B.

3592. Luther, G., and Loev, I. (1981), Resistance in marital therapy. Journal of Marital and Family Therapy, 10, 475-480.

3593. Luthman, S. (1972), The growth model in marital therapy. Family Therapy, 1, 63-83.

3594. Luthman, S. (1974), Techniques of process therapy. Family Therapy, 1, 141-162.

3595. Luthman, S.G. (1974), Watergate and the control framework. Family Therapy, 1(3), 211-218.

3596. Lutz, J. (1982), The psychotic child at home, in the educational therapy unit, and in the clinic: Therapeutic aspects. Acta Paedopsychiatricia, 48(2-3), 99.

3597. Lutz, S.E., and Medway, J.P. (1984), Contextual family therapy with the victims of incest. Journal of Adolescence, 7(4), 319-329.

3598. Lyles, M.R., and Carter, J.H. (1982), Myths and strengths of the black family: A historical and sociological contribution to family therapy. Journal of the National Medical Association, 74, 1119-1123.

3599. Lynch, C. (1982), A structured interview for working with couples at the point of separation. Family Therapy, 9, 21-34.

3600. Lynch, G., and Waxenberg, B. (1971), Marital therapy with the aging: A case study. Psychotherapy: Theory, Research and Practice, 8, 59-63.

3601. Lynch, M.A. (1978), Child abuse and the family: One way to see that they need help. Nursing Times, 74, 38-39.

3602. Lyons, M. (1978), Hospital provides special care for dying patients and their families. Hospitals, 52, 123-124, 126.

3603. Lyons, M.C. (1979), Marriage of convenience: An alternative to open marriage or creative divorce. Family Therapy, 6(3), 161.269

3604. Mabley, A. (1966), Group application interviews in a family agency. Social Casework, 47, 158-164.

3605. MacDonald, J.M. (1974), The emotional cripple: A family problem. Nursing Times, 70, 236-237.

3606. MacFarlane, K., and Korbin, J. (1983), Confronting the incest secret long after the fact: A family study of multiple victimization with strategies for intervention. Child Abuse and Neglect, 7, 225-237.

3607. MacGregor, R. (1970), Group and family therapy: Moving into the present and letting go of the past. International Journal of Group Psychotherapy, 20, 495-515.

3608. MacGregor, R. (1962), Multiple impact psychotherapy with families. Family Process, 1, 15-29.

3609. MacGregor, R., McDanald, C., and Goolishian, H.A. (1964), Multiple impact therapy with families. Hightstown, NJ: McGraw-Hill Book Co.

3610.   MacLean, G. (1976), An approach to the treatment of an adolescent with ulcerative colitis, conjoint therapy of the parents. Canadian Psychiatric Association Journal, 21, 287-293.

3611.   MacLean, G., Macintosh, B.A., Taylor, E., and Gerber, M. (1982), A clinical approach to brief dynamic psychotherapies in child psychiatry. Canadian Journal of Psychiatry, 27, 113-118.

3612.   Mace, D. (1948), Marriage counseling. London: Churchill.

3613.   Mace, D., and Marc, V. (1976), The selection, training and certification of facilitators for marriage enrichment programs. Family Coordinator, 25, 117-125.

3614.   Mace, D.R. (1973), Some experiments with marriage counseling procedures. Family Coordinator, 22(1), 23-30.

3615.   Mace, D.R. (1976), Marital intimacy and the deadly love-anger cycle. Journal of Marriage and Family Counseling, 2(2), 131-137.

3616.   Machotka, P., Pittman, F.S., and Flomenhaft, K. (1967), Incest as a family affair. Family Process, 6, 98-116.

3617.   Mackinnon, L., and Marlett, N. (1984), Social action perspective: The disabled and their families in context. Family Therapy Collections, 11, 111-126.

3618.   Mackle, R.E. (1967), Family problems in medical and nursing families. British Journal of Medical Psychology, 40, 333-340.

3619.   Mackler, J.L. (1982), Teaching an old dog new tricks in family therapy. Family Therapy, 9, 305-310.

3620.   Mackler, L., and Strauss, C. (1983), Berne, Eric, Lennard - 1910-1970 - Bibliography. In L.R. Wolberg and M.L. Aronson (Eds.), Group and family therapy 1982. New York: Brunner/Mazel.

3621.   Macon, L.B. (1975), A comparative study of two approaches to the treatment of marital dysfunction. Dissertation Abstracts International, 36, 4026-A.

3622.   Madanes, C. (1980), Marital therapy when a symptom is presented by a spouse. International Journal of Family Therapy, 2, 120-136.

3623.   Madanes, C. (1981), Strategic family therapy. San Francisco, CA: Jossey-Bass.

3624.   Madanes, C. (1981) Integrating ideas in family therapy. Family Therapy Network Newsletter, 5(3), 1-5.

3625.   Madanes, C. (1980), Protection, paradox, and pretending. Family Process, 19, 73-85.

3626.   Madanes, C. (1980), The prevention of rehospitalization of adolescents and young adults with severe problem behaviors. Family Process, 19, 179-191.

3627.   Madanes, C., and Haley, J. (1977), Dimensions of family therapy. Journal of Nervous and Mental Disease, 165, 88-98.

3628.   Maddison, D.C. (1961), The integrated therapy of family members: A case report. International Journal of Group Psychotherapy, 11, 33-48.

3629.   Madsen, M.K. (1979), Parenting classes for mentally retarded. Mental Retardation, 17, 195.

3630.   Magargee, A.B. (1977), The father in family therapy: An analysis of his verbal communication. Dissertation Abstracts International, 37, 5835-5836-B.

3631.   Magni, G. (1982), Managing psychologic crises in children and their families. Canadian Medical Association Journal, 127, 111-112.

3632.   Magnus, E.C. (1975), Measurement of counselor bias (sex-role stereotyping) in assessment of marital couples with traditional and nontraditional interaction patterns. Dissertation Abstracts International, 36, 2635A.

3633.   Magran, B.A. (1982), An integrative approach to marital therapy: Transactional analysis. Psychiatric Clinics of North America, 5, 529-542.

3634.   Mahon, E., and Egan, J. (1973), The use of family interviews in child psychotherapy. International Journal of Child Psychotherapy, 2, 365-377.

3635.   Mahoney, E.R. (1978), Large differences in attitude change toward premarital coitus. Archives of Sexual Behavior, 7, 493-501.

3636.   Main, F.O. (1978), Assessment of Adlerian family counseling styles as an aid in teacher training. Dissertation Abstracts International, 38(8), 4586-A.

3637.   Maizlish, I.L. (1957), Group psychotherapy of husband-wife couples in a child guidance clinic. Group Psychotherapy, Psychodrama and Sociometry, 10, 169-180.

3638.   Malageli-Tegliatti, M. (1974), Family psychotherapy and the work of denial. Rivista di Psichiatria, 9, 161-172.

3639.   Malazzoli, M.S., and Prata, G. (1982), Snares in family therapy. Journal of Marital and Family Therapy, 8(4), 443.

3640.   Maldonado, I., and Chagoya, L. (1979), Family therapy in Mexico - 1978. International Journal of Family Therapy, 1(1), 100.

3641.   Mallery, B., and Navas, M. (1982), Engagement of preadolescent boys in group therapy: Videotape as a tool. International Journal of Group Psychotherapy, 32, 453-468.

3642.   Mallouk, T. (1982), The interpersonal context of object relations: Implications for family therapy. Journal of Marital and Family Therapy, 8, 429-441.

3643.   Malon, D.W., and Spencer, D.M. (1985), Continuity and discontinuity in family therapy training. Journal of Social Work Education, 21(1), 66.

3644.   Malone, C.A. (1979), Child psychiatry and family therapy: Overview. Journal of the American Academy of Child Psychiatry, 18, 4-21.

3645.   Malone, C.A. (1974), Observations on the role of family therapy in child psychiatry training. Journal of the American Academy of Child Psychiatry, 13(3), 437-458.

3646.   Malone, V.S. (1982), Mutuality of relationship control and couple conflict. Dissertation Abstracts International, 43, 1047-A.

3647.   Maloney, M.J. (1981), The use of children's drawings in multiple family group therapy. Group, 5, 32-36.

3648.   Malouf, J.L., and Alexander, J.F. (1976), Family therapy research in applied community settings. Community Mental Health, 12, 61-71.

3649.   Malouf, R.E., and Alexander, F.J. (1974), Family crisis intervention: A model and technique of training. In: R.E. Hardy and J.G. Cull (Eds.), Therapeutic needs of the family: Problems, descriptions and therapeutic approaches. Springfield, IL: Charles C. Thomas.

3650.   Malpass, J.R. (1975), Family orientation program. American Correctional Therapy Journal, 29, 17-21.

3651.   Manair, E. (1976), The family role in the aetiology of schizophrenia in Iran. Acta Medica Iran, 19, 285-296.

3652.   Manalis-Swennen, R.G., and Querinjean, R. (1973), Comparative evaluation identification coordinates, admission channels, symptomatology, and modalities of organizing a university marriage counseling center and a traditional center. Acta Psychiatrica Belgica, 73, 785-802.

3653.   Manaster, A. (1967), The family group therapy program at Park View Home for the Aged. Journal of the American Geriatric Society, 15, 302-306.

3654.   Mancini, F., Sassaroli, S., Semerari, A., and Telfner, U. (1979), (Contribution to a falsifiable model of couples therapy.) Archiv of Psicologia, Neurologia y Psichiatrica, 40(2), 191-208.

3655.   Mandelbaum, A. (1976), Diagnosis in family treatment. Bulletin of the Menninger Clinic, 40, 497-504.

3656.   Mandelbaum, A. (1976), The inhibited child: A family therapy approach. In: E.J. Anthony and D.C. Gilpin (Eds.), Three clinical faces of childhood. Jamaica, NY: Spectrum.

3657.   Mandelbaum, A. (1977), Family treatment of borderline patient. In: P. Hartocollis (Ed.), Borderline personality disorders: The concept, the syndrome, the patient. New York, NY: International Universities Press.

3658.   Mandelbaum, A. (1977), A family centered approach to residential treatment. Bulletin of the Menninger Clinic, 41, 27-39.

3659.   Mandelbaum, A. (1971), Family process in the diagnosis and treatment of children and adolescents. Bulletin of the Menninger Clinic, 35, 153-166.

3660.   Mandelbaum, A. (1975), Review of S. Minuchin's Families and family therapy. Bulletin of the Menninger Clinic, 19, 199-203.

3661.   Mandelbaum, A. (1983), Review of J.L. Framo's Explorations in marital and family therapy: Selected papers of Framo, James L. Contemporary Psychology, 28, 216-217.

3662.   Mangold, B. (1982), Psychosomatic and family therapy: Theory and clinical practice. Praxis der Kinderpsychologie und Kinderpsychiatrie, 31, 207-213.

3663.   Mangold, B., and Obendorf, W. (1981), (The significance of the dynamics of family relationships in regard to management of retarded children.) Praxis der Kinderpsychologie und Kinderpsychiatrie, 30(1), 12-18.

3664.   Manjoney, D.M., and McKegney, F.P. (1979), Individual and family coping with polycystic kidney disease: The harvest of denial. International Journal of Psychiatry and Medicine, 9, 19-31.

3665.   Mann, A.M., and Lundell, F.W. (1977), Further experience in conjoint psychotherapy of marital pairs. Canadian Medical Association Journal, 116, 772-774.

3666.   Mann, J. (1978), Sharing orgasm. Journal of Sex and Marital Therapy, 4, 706.

3667.   Mann, J., and Starr, S. (1972), The self-report questionnaire as a change agent in family therapy. Family Process, 11, 95-105.

3668.   Mann, S.J. (1982), The integration of psychodrama and family therapy in the treatment of schizophrenia. Family Therapy, 9, 215-225.

3669.   Mannino, F.V. (1984), Areas of resistance in the beginning phase of family therapy. International Journal of Family Therapy, 6(1), 3-12.

3670.   Mannino, F.V., and Greenspan, S.I. (1976), Projection and misperception in couples treatment. Journal of Marriage and Family Counseling, 2(2), 139-143.

3671.   Mannino, F.V., and Shore, M.F. (1984), An ecological perspective on family intervention. In W.A. O'Connor and B. Lubin (Eds.), Ecological approaches to clinical and community psychology. New York: John Wiley and Sons.

3672.   Manosevitz, M., and Stedman, J.M. (1981), Some thoughts on training the novice family therapist in the art of family assessment. Family Therapy, 8, 67-76.

3673.   Mansheim, P. (1982), Parenting children with developmental disabilities. Journal of Psychosocial Nursing and Mental Health Services, 20, 24-26.

3674.   Manuel, M. (1979), Doing it the family way...a counseling "course" for stroke patients and their relatives. Nursing Mirror, 148, 28-29.

3675.   Manuel, P.E. (1971), Psychotherapy of married couples. Revista de Neuro-Psiquiatria (Stockholm), 34, 28-36.

3676.   Manus, G.I. (1966), Marriage counseling: A technique in search of a theory. Journal of Marriage and Family Counseling, 28(4), 449-453.

3677.   Marable, E.L. (1984), Review of V. Satir's Conjoint family therapy. Patient Education and Counseling, 6(3), 144.

3678.   Marahao, T. (1984), Family therapy and anthropology. Culture, Medicine and Psychiatry, 8(3), 255-280.

3679.   Marcelli, D., and Braconnier, A. (1980), The place of the "parental crisis" in the non-formalized treatment of the adolescent patient and his parents (author's transl.). Neuropsychiatrie de L'Enfance et de L'Adolescence, 28, 477-481.

3680.   Marcus, I.M. (1956), Psychoanalytic group therapy with fathers of emotionally disturbed preschool children. International Journal of Group Psychotherapy, 6, 61-79.

3681.   Marcus, I.M. (1951), Analytic group psychotherapy: Its pertinence to family disorders. Bulletin of Tulane University, 11.

3682.   Marcuse, B. (1974), The mini-marathon as part of ongoing group therapy in a couples' group. Canada's Mental Health, 22, 10-11.

3683.   Margalit, M. (1982), Learning disabled children and their families: Strategies of extension and adaptation of family therapy. Journal of Learning Disabilities, 15, 594-595.

3684.   Margolin, F.M. (1973), An approach to resolution of visitation disputes post-divorce: Short-term counseling. Dissertation Abstracts International, 34(4-B), 1754.

3685.   Margolin, G. (1978), A multi-level approach to the assessment of communication positiveness in distressed marital couples. International Journal of Family Counseling, 6(1), 81-89.

3686.   Margolin, G. (1979), Conjoint marital therapy to enhance anger management and reduce spouse abuse. American Journal of Family Therapy, 7(2), 13-23.

3687.   Margolin, G. (1983), Behavioral marital therapy: Is there a place for passion, play, and other non-negotiable dimensions? Behavior Therapist, 14, 65-68.

3688.   Margolin, G. (1982), Ethical and legal consideration in marital and family therapy. American Psychologist, 37, 788-801.

3689.   Margolin, G. (1980), Contingency contracting in behavioral marriage therapy. American Journal of Family Therapy, 8(3), 71-74.

3690.   Margolin, G. (1981), A behavioral-systems approach to the treatment of marital jealousy. Clinical Psychology Review, 34, 469-487.

3691. Margolin, G. (1984), Review of R.T. Seagreves' Marital therapy: A combined psychodynamic behavioral approach. Contemporary Psychology, 29(1), 6-7.

3692. Margolin, G., Talovic, S., Fernandez, V., and Onorato, R. (1983), Sex role considerations and behavioral marital therapy: Equal does not mean identical. Journal of Marital and Family Therapy, 9, 131-145.

3693. Margolin, G., and Wampold, B.E. (1981), Sequential analysis of conflict and accord in distressed and nondistressed marital partners. Journal of Consulting and Clinical Psychology, 49, 554-567.

3694. Margolin, G., and Weinstein, C.D. (1983), The role of affect in behavioral marital therapy. In L.R. Wolberg and M.L. Aronson (Eds.), Group and family therapy 1982. New York: Brunner/Mazel.

3695. Margolin, G., and Weiss, R.L. (1978), Comparative evaluation of therapeutic components associated with behavioral marital treatments. Journal of Consulting and Clinical Psychology, 46, 1476-1486.

3696. Marital therapy (editorial) (1979), Lancet, 1, 652-653.

3697. Mark, A.J., and Ludwig, A.M. (1969), Resurrection of the family of the chronic schizophrenic. American Journal of Psychotherapy, 23, 37-52.

3698. Markman, H.J., Jamieson, K.J., and FLoyd, F.J. (1983), The assessment and modification of premarital relationships: Preliminary findings on the etiology and prevention of marital and family distress. In J.P. Vincent (Ed.), Advances in family intervention, assessment and theory, Vol. 3. Greenwich: JAI Press.

3699. Markowitz, I. (1966), Family therapy in a child guidance clinic. Psychiatric Quarterly, 40, 308.

3700. Markowitz, I., Taylor, G., and Bokert, E. (1968), Dream discussion as a means of reopening blocked familial communication. Psychotherapy and Psychosomatics, 16, 348-356.

3701. Markowski, E.M. (1983), Live marital and family therapy supervision: A model for community mental health centers. Clinical Supervision, 1, 37-46.

3702. Markowski, E.M., and Cain, H.I. (1983), Marital and family therapy training and supervision: A regional model for rural mental health. Clinical Supervisor, 1, 65-75.

3703. Markowski, E.M., and Cain, H.I. (1984), Marital and family therapy certification and licensing examinations: One model. Journal of Marital and Family Therapy, 10(3), 289-296.

3704. Marriage and divorce. (1979), Statistical Bulletin of Metropolitan Life Insurance Company, 59, 7-15.

3705. Marriage guidance counseling in general practice (1980), Drug Therapy Bulletin, 18, 32.

3706. Marriage matters (editorial) (1979), British Medical Journal, 1, 1164.

3707.   Marsh, D.C., and Humphrey, N.D. (1953), Value congeries and marital counseling. Marriage and Family Living, 15, 28-32.

3708.   Marsh, J.C. (1976), The effects of modeling and instructions on changing communication in families. Dissertation Abstracts International, 36, 5268B.

3709.   Marticelli, A., and Speck, R.V. (1973), Social change, the family and you: How to tighten your own network. Journal of New York State School Nurse-Teacher Association, 4, 5-8.

3710.   Martin, B. (1977), Brief family intervention: Effectiveness and the importance of including the father. Journal of Counseling Psychology, 45, 1002-1010.

3711.   Martin, B. (1979), Of triangles and families: Review of M. Bowen's Family therapy in clinical practice. Contemporary Psychology, 24, 326.

3712.   Martin, F.E. (1977), Some implications from the theory and practice of family therapy for individual therapy. British Journal of Medical Psychology, 50, 53-64.

3713.   Martin, J.D. (1979), Violence and the family. British Journal of Psychiatry, 134, 120.

3714.   Martin, J.F. (1979), Family health and family planning in medical education. Tropical Doctor, 9, 85-88, 92.

3715.   Martin, P.A. (1979), Review of M. Bowen's Family therapy in clinical practice. American Journal of Family Therapy, 7, 99-100.

3716.   Martin, P.A. (1979), Training of psychiatric residents in marital therapy. Journal of Marital and Family Therapy, 5, 43-52.

3717.   Martin, P.A. (1979), Review of T.J. Paolini and B.S. McCrady's Marriage and marital therapy: Psychoanalytic, behavioral and systems theory perspectives. American Journal of Psychiatry, 136, 745.

3718.   Martin, P.A. (1976), A marital therapy manual. New York: Brunner/Mazel.

3719.   Martin, P.A. (1981), Defining normal values in marriage. International Journal of Family Psychiatry, 3, 105-114.

3720.   Martin, P.A. (1983), Review of F.G. Humphrey's Marital therapy. Journal of Marital and Family Therapy, 9, 217.

3721.   Martin, P.A. (1978), The normal value system technique in marital therapy. Current Psychiatric Therapies 18, 99-106.

3722.   Martin, P.A., and Bird, H.W. (1953), An approach to the psychotherapy of marriage partners. Psychiatry, 16, 123-127.

3723.   Martindale, B., and Bottomley, V. (1980), The management of families with Huntington's chorea: A case study to illustrate some recommendations. Journal of Child Psychology and Psychiatry, 21, 343-351.

3724.   Mas, C.H., Alexander, J.F., and Barton, C. (1985), Modes of expression in family therapy: A process study of roles and gender. Journal of Marital and Family Therapy, 11, 411-416.

3725.   Masimann, H., and Utrillo, M. (1975), Some thoughts concerning a family therapy experiment. Acta Psychiatrica Belgica, 75, 280-293.

3726.   Mason, M.J. (1981), Relationship enrichment: Evaluating the effects of a couples wilderness program. Dissertation Abstracts International, 42, 161-B.

3727.   Mason, M.J. (1984), Review of J.C. Hansen, J.D. Woody and R.H. Woody's Sexual issues in family therapy, Vol. 5. The family therapy collections. Contemporary Psychology, 29(8), 636.

3728.   Mason, M.J. (1983), Review of G.D. Erickson and T.P. Hogan's Family therapy: An introduction to theory and technique. 2nd Edition. Contemporary Psychology, 28, 58.

3729.   Mason, P.R. (1983), The pastor as initiator: Developing an alternative model for ministry to the recently married. Dissertation Abstracts International, 44, 1819-A.

3730.   Masserman, J.H. (1976), Comprehensive psychosomatic family therapy. Current Psychiatric Therapies, 16, 235-247.

3731.   Massey, R. (1983), Passivity, paradox, and change in family systems. Transactional Analysis Journal, 13, 33-41.

3732.   Massie, H.N., and Beels, C.C. (1972), The outcome of the family treatment of schizophrenia. Schizophrenia Bulletin, 6, 24-36.

3733.   Masson, D.O. (1980), Indications for family therapy. Revue Medicale de la Suisse Romande, 100, 577-582.

3734.   Masson, H.C., and O'Byrne, P. (1984), Applying family therapy: A practical guide for social workers. Elmsford, NY: Pergamon.

3735.   Masson, O. (1982), Child abuse and family therapy. Child Abuse and Neglect, 6, 47-56.

3736.   Masson, O. (1980), Family therapy in child and adolescent psychiatry. Revue Medical ede al Suisse Romande, 100, 583-589.

3737.   Masson, O. (1980), Systems psychotherapy in the family: Its place in child psychiatry (author's transl.). Neuropsychiatrie de L'Enfance et de L'Adolescence, 28, 367-73.

3738.   Masson, O. (1976), Possibilities of preventive and therapeutic treatment of children of schizophrenic mothers. Revue Neuropsychiatrie Infantile et D'Hygiene Mentale de L'Enfance, 24, 5-16.

3739.   Masson, O., and Pancheri, E. (1979), Family therapy in the treatment of adolescents. Acta Paedopsychiatrica, 44(3-4), 149-163.

3740.   Masten, A.S. (1979), Family therapy as a treatment for children: Critical review of outcome research. Family Process, 18, 323-336.

3741.   Master, R.S. (1978), Family therapy in child and adolescent psychiatry: A review of 35 families. Child Psychiatry Quarterly, 11, 70-82.

3742.   Matanovich, J.P. (1970), The effect of short-term group counseling upon positive perceptions of mate in marital counseling. Dissertation Abstracts International, 31, 2688A.

3743.   Mathieu, M. (1969), Reflections on the couple: On two formative seminars for marriage counseling. Hygiene Mentale, 53(2), 51-60.

3744.   Matousek, O. (1978), Techniques and means of family psychotherapy. Psychologica Patopsychologia Dielal, 13, 537-547.

3745.   Mattejat, F. (1983), Symptom fixation and resistance: Focal family therapy for psychosomatic symptoms in the context of enmeshed family systems. Zeitschrift Fur Kinder - Und Jugendpsychiatrie, 11, 203-233.

3746.   Mattejat, F., and Remschmidt, H. (1981), Effect of training on the assessment of families: Preliminary studies in the development of a family assessment training program. Zeitschrift Fur Kinder- Und Jugendpsychiatrie, 9, 317-333.

3747.   Mattejat, F., and Wiesse, J. (1983), The investigation of aspects of family pathology with interaction chronography: An exploratory study. Zeitschrift fur Klinische Psychologie, 31, 94-112.

3748.   Matter, B.R. (1980), Family therapy for continuing professional education. International Journal of Family Therapy, 2, 39-46.

3749.   Matteson, R. (1974), Adolescent self-esteem, family, communication, and marital satisfaction. Journal of Psychology, 86, 35-47.

3750.   Matthews, K.L. (1981), An interdisciplinary training model for family therapy. Family Therapy, 8, 179-185.

3751.   Matthews, K.L., and Cunningham, J.M. (1983), Combination of multiple-family therapy with parallel groups. American Journal of Psychotherapy, 37, 113-120.

3752.   Mattison, A.M. (1982), Review of S.J. Licata, and R.P. Petersen's Historical perspectives on homosexuality. American Journal of Family Therapy, 10, 83.

3753.   Mattson, A. (1976), Review of M. Sugar's The adolescent in group and family therapy. Journal of Nervous and Mental Disease, 163, 362.

3754.   Mattsson, A., and Agle, D.P. (1972), Group therapy with parents of hemophiliacs: Therapeutic process and observations of parental adaptation to chronic illness in children. Journal of the American Academy of Child Psychiatry, 11(3), 558-571.

3755.   Mattsson, B., and Dubinsky, L. (1977), Family therapy methods in the paranoia syndrome. Lakartidningen, 74, 1617-1618.

3756.   Matwiejczyk, H. (1978), Models and psychological problems of substitute family for orphaned children. Przeglad Psychologiczny, 21, 75-93.

3757.   Maugile, D. (1967), The concept of the couples as a unit during group
        psychotherapy of married couples. Laval Medicale, 38, 113-118.

3758.   Maurin, J. (1974). Conflict with the marital dyad. Journal of
        Psychiatric Nursing, 12, 27-31.

3759.   Mauroner, N.L. (1977), The family in psychosomatic medicine.
        Psychosomatics, 18, 8-10.

3760.   May, G.D. (1978), Review of C. Pomeroy's Fight it out, work it out, love
        it out: The story of a family in therapy. Contemporary Psycholology,
        23, 358.

3761.   May, G.D. (1978), Review of B.S. Ables' Therapy for couples: A
        clinician's guide for effective treatment. Contemporary Psychology,
        23, 358.

3762.   May, H.J. (1981), Integration of sexual counseling and family therapy
        with surgical treatment of breast cancer. Family Relations, 30(2), 291-
        295.

3763.   Mayadas, N.S., and Duehn, W.B. (1977), Stimulus modeling videotape for
        marital counseling: Method and application. Journal of Marriage and
        Family Counseling, 3(1), 35-42.

3764.   Mayer, L. (1970), Report on group therapy for mothers of children with
        intractable asthma. Medical Journal of Australia, 1, 887-889.

3765.   Mayo, J.A. (1979), Marital therapy with manic depressive patients
        treated with lithium. Comprehensive Psychiatry, 20(5), 419-426.

3766.   Maziade, M. (1980), Theoretical bases of family therapy (author's
        transl.). Neuropsychiatrie de L'Enfance et de L'Adolescence, 28, 253-8.

3767.   Mazur, V. (1973), Family therapy: An approach to the culturally
        different. International Journal of Social Psychiatry, 19, 110-113.

3768.   Mazza, N. (1981), The use of poetry in treating the troubled
        adolescent. Adolescence, 16, 403-408.

3769.   Mazza, N., and Prescott, B.U. (1981), Poetry: An ancillary technique in
        couples group therapy. American Journal of Family Therapy, 9, 53-57.

3770.   McAdoo, H. (1977), A review of the literature related to family therapy
        in the black community. Journal of Contemporary Psychotherapy, 9, 15-
        19.

3771.   McAdoo, H. (1977), Family therapy in the black community. American
        Journal of Orthopsychiatry, 47, 75-79.

3772.   McAndrews, M.M. (1982), Outreach family therapy in human service
        networks: Rationale and case study. Dissertation Abstracts
        International, 42, 3431-B.

3773.   McAuley, R. (1982), Behaviour therapy...Mrs. N was having difficulty
        managing her four-year-old-son. Nursing Times, 78, 2-5.

3774. McAuley, T., Longabaugh, R., and Gross, H. (1978), Comparative effectiveness of self and family forms of the Michigan Alcoholism Screening Test. Journal for Studies on Alcohol, 39, 1622-1627.

3775. McCarrick, A.K. (1979), Analysis of interaction sequences as a method of evaluating marital group psychotherapy. Dissertation Abstracts International, 39, 5751A.

3776. McCarrick, A.K., Manderscheid, R.W., Silbergeld, S., and McIntyre, J.J. (1982), Control patterns in dyadic systems: Marital group psychotherapy as change agent. American Journal of Family Therapy, 10, 3-14.

3777. McCarrick, A.K., Manderscheid, R.W., and Silbergeld, S. (1981), Gender differences in competition and dominance during the married-couples group therapy. Social Psychology Quarterly, 19, 164-77.

3778. McCarthy, J. (1978), Comparisons of the probability of the dissolution of first and second marriages. Demography, 15, 345-359.

3779. McCarthy, J., and Menken, J. (1979), Marriage, remarriage, marital disruption and age at first birth. Family Planning Perspectives, 11, 21-23, 27-30.

3780. McCarthy, J.J. (1977), Resolution of adolescent paradox through family treatment. In: T.J. Buckley, J.J. McCarthy, E. Norman, and M.A. Quaranta (Eds.), New directions in family therapy. Oceanside: Dabor Science Publications.

3781. McCartney, C.F. (1980), Counseling the husband and wife after the woman has been raped. Medical Aspects and Human Sexuality, 14(5), 121-122.

3782. McCary, J.L. (1978), Review of R.F. Stahmann and W.J. Hiebert's Klemer's counseling in marital and sexual problems: A clinician's handbook. Contemporary Psychology, 23, 669.

3783. McClellan, T.A., and Stieper, D.R. (1971), A structured approach to group marriage counseling. Mental Hygiene, 55, 77-84.

3784. McClendon, R. (1976), Multiple family group therapy with adolescents in a state hospital. Clinical Social Work, 4, 14-24.

3785. McClendon, R., and Kadis, L.B. (1983), Family therapy after Berne, Eric. In L.R. Wolberg and M.L. Aronson (Eds.), Group and family therapy 1982. New York: Brunner/Mazel.

3786. McColgan, E.B., Pugh, R.L., and Pruitt, D.B. (1985), Encopresis: A structural strategic approach to family treatment. American Journal of Family Therapy, 13, 46-54.

3787. McCollum, E.E. (1979), A family-oriented admission procedure on an inpatient psychiatric unit. Social Work in Health Care, 4, 423-430.

3788. McConaghy, N. (1978), Heterosexual experience, marital status, and orientation of homosexual males. Archives of Sexual Behavior, 7, 575-581.

3789.   McConnell, L.G. (1976), An examination of the counselors skill when counseling client with sexual problems. Family Coordinator, 25(2), 183–188.

3790.   McConville, B.J. (1973), Techniques of family therapy of adolescents. Australian and New Zealand Journal of Psychiatry, 7, 249–255.

3791.   McConville, B.J. (1979), Fragile families, troubled children: Aftermath of infant trauma. Canadian Journal of Psychiatry, 24, 269–270.

3792.   McConville, B.J. (1974), Proceedings: Techniques of family therapy of adolescents. Archives of General Psychiatry, 30, 381–389.

3793.   McCrady, B.S., Moreau, J., and Paolino, T.J. (1982), Joint hospitalization and couples therapy for alcoholism: A four-year follow-up. Journal of Studies on Alcohol, 43, 1244–1250.

3794.   McCrady, B.S., Paolino, T.J., Longabaugh, R., and Rossi, J. (1979), Effects of joint hospital admission and couples treatment for hospitalized alcoholics: A pilot study. Addictive Behavior, 4, 155–165.

3795.   McCrady, B.S., Paolino, T.J., and Langabaugh, R. (1978), Correspondence between reports of problem drinkers and spouses on drinking behavior and impairment. Journal of Studies on Alcohol, 39, 1252–1257.

3796.   McCubbin, H.I., and Boss, P.G. (1980), Family stress and coping: Targets for theory, research, counseling, and education. Family Relations, 29(4), 429–430.

3797.   McDaniel, S.H. (1981), Treating school problems in family therapy. Elementary School Guidance and Counseling, 15, 214–222.

3798.   McDaniel, S.H., Weber, T., and McKeever, J. (1983), Multiple theoretical approaches to supervision: Choices in family therapy training. Family Process, 22, 491–500.

3799.   McDermott, J.F. (1979), Family therapy in child psychiatry: Introduction. Journal of the American Academy of Child Psychiatry, 18, 1–3.

3800.   McDermott, J.F. (1979), Review of W.R. Beavers's Psychotherapy and growth: A family systems perspective. Journal of the American Academy of Child Psychiatry, 18, 186.

3801.   McDermott, J.F. (1979) Review of J.G. Howells's Principles of family psychiatry. Journal of the American Academy of Child Psychiatry, 18, 186.

3802.   McDermott, J.F. (1979), Review of A. Napier and C. Whitaker's Family crucible. Journal of the American Academy of Child Psychiatry, 18, 186.

3803.   McDermott, J.F. (1979), Review of C.R. Skinner's Systems of family and marital therapy. Journal of the American Academy of Child Psychiatry, 18, 186.

3804.   McDermott, J.F. (1979), Review of H. Stierlin's Psychoanalysis and
        family therapy. Journal of the American Academy of Child Psychiatry,
        18, 186.

3805.   McDermott, J.F., Jr. (1981), Indications for family therapy: Question or
        non-question? Journal of the American Academy of Child Psychiatry,
        20, 401-19.

3806.   McDermott, J.F., Jr., Char, W.F., Robillard, A.B., Hsu, J., Tseng, W.S.,
        and Ashton, G.C. (1983), Cultural variations in family attitudes and
        their implications for therapy. Journal of the American Academy of
        Child Psychiatry, 22, 454-458.

3807.   McDermott, J.F., Jr., and Char, W.F. (1974), The undeclared war
        between child and family therapy. Journal of the American Academy of
        Child Psychiatry, 13(3), 422-436.

3808.   McDonald, E.C. (1966), Out-patient therapy of neurotic families.
        Psychiatric Research Reports of the American Psychiatric Association,
        20, 206-211.

3809.   McDonald, G.W. (1975), Coalition formation in marital therapy triads.
        Family Therapy, 2, 141-148.

3810.   McDonald, P.L. (1983), The effects of participation in the family
        support program on the adaptive and maladaptive behaviors of
        developmentally disabled individuals. Dissertation Abstracts
        International, 44, 1055-A.

3811.   McDonough, J.J. (1976), Approaches to Adlerian family education
        research. Journal of Individual Psychology, 32, 224-231.

3812.   McDonough, J.J. (1978), Sibling ordinal position and family education.
        International Journal of Family Counseling, 6(2), 62-69.

3813.   McElroy, E., and Minard, J. (1979), Symposium on child psychiatric
        nursing. Sudden infant death syndrome: A framework for preventive
        mental health. Nursing Clinics of North America, 14, 391-403.

3814.   McFadden, V.M., and Doub, G. (1983), The therapist's new role:
        Training families for healthy survival. Family Therapy Collections, 11,
        134-160.

3815.   McGee, T.F. (1983), Long-term group psychotherapy with post-hospital
        patients. In L.R. Wolberg and M.L. Aronson (Eds.), Group and family
        therapy 1982. New York: Brunner/Mazel.

3816.   McGee, T.F., and Kostrubala, T. (1964), The neurotic equilibrium in
        married couples applying for group psychotherapy. Journal of Marriage
        and the Family, 26, 77-88.

3817.   McGill, C.W., Falloon, I.R., Boyd, J.L., Wood, and Siverio, C. (1983),
        Family educational intervention in the treatment of schizophrenia.
        Hospital and Community Psychiatry, 34, 934-938.

3818.   McGill, D. (1983), Cultural concepts for family therapy. Family
        Therapy Collections, 11, 108-121.

3819.   McGinnis, T.C. (1962), Joint interview counseling and psychotherapy
with married couples. Dissertation Abstracts International, 23(5), 1784.

3820.   McGoldrick, M. (1983), Review of E.O. Fisher and M.S. Fisher's
Therapists, lawyers and divorcing spouses. American Journal of Family
Therapy, 11, 80.

3821.   McGoldrick, M. (1982), Normal families: An ethnic perspective. In F.
Walsh (Ed.), Normal family processes. New York: Guilford Press.

3822.   McGoldrick, M. and Carter, E.A. (1982), The family life cycle. In F.
Walsh (Ed.), Normal family processes. New York: Guilford Press.

3823.   McGoldrick, M., Pearce, J.K., and Giordano, J. (Eds.). (1982), Ethnicity
and family therapy. New York: Guilford Press.

3824.   McGoldrick, M., and Pearse, J.K. (1981), Family therapy with Irish-
Americans. Family Process, 20(2), 223-244.

3825.   McGoldrick, M., and Preto, N.G. (1984), Ethnic intermarriage:
Implications for therapy. Family Process, 23, 347-364.

3826.   McGoldrick-Orfanidis, M., and Mueller, P.S. (1975), Family therapy in
the treatment of schizophrenia: A model of therapy based on
relabelling of schizophrenia as a family system disturbance. American
Journal of Orthopsychiatry, 45, 264.

3827.   McGoldrick-Orfanidis, M.M. (1979), Problems with family genograms.
American Journal of Family Therapy, 7(3), 74-75.

3828.   McGovern, K., Kirkpatrick, C., and LoPiccolo, J. (1976), A behavioral
group treatment program for sexually dysfunctional couples. Journal of
Marriage and Family Counseling, 2, 397-404.

3829.   McGuire, J.C., and Gottlieb, B.H. (1979), Social support groups among
new parents. Journal of Clinical Child Psychology, 8, 111-116.

3830.   McHolland, J.D. (1982), Chris: The "crazy" kid as a family hero.
International Journal of Family Therapy, 4, 115.

3831.   McInnis, K.M. (1982), Bibliotherapy: Adjunct to traditional counseling
with children of stepfamilies. Child Welfare, 61, 153-60.

3832.   McIntier, T.M. (1979), Hillhaven Hospice: A free-standing, family-
centered program. Hospital Progress, 60, 68-72.

3833.   McIntosh, D.M. (1975), A comparison of the effects of highly structured,
partially structured, and unstructured human relations training for
married couples on the dependent variables of communication, marital
adjustment, and personal adjustment. Dissertation Abstracts
International, 36, 1236A.

3834.   McKanny, L.R. (1976), Multiple family therapy on an alcohol treatment
unit. Family Therapy, 3, 197-209.

3835.   McKenzie, D.J. (1977), Family court counseling - one year after.
Mental Health in Australia, 1, 196-198.

3836.   McKeon, M.S. (1982), An analysis of healthy-family interactional research and its relationship to selected family-enrichment models. Dissertation Abstracts International, 42, 4726-A.

3837.   McKinley, C.K., Ritchie, A.M., Griffin, D., and Bondurant, W. (1970), The upward mobile negro family in therapy. Diseases of the Nervous System, 31, 710-715.

3838.   McLemore, C.W. (1973), Applications of balance theory to family relations. Counseling Psychologist, 20, 181-184.

3839.   McMahon, R.J., and Forehand, R. (1978), Nonprescription behavior therapy: Effectiveness of a brochure in teaching mothers to correct their children's inappropriate mealtime behavior. Behavior Therapy, 9(5), 814-821.

3840.   McManus, R. (1983), Facilitating family communication and family problem solving abilities through the family reunion game. Dissertation Abstracts International, 44, 612-B.

3841.   McMillan, E.L. (1969), Problem build-up: A description of couples in marriage counseling. Family Coordinator, 18(3), 260-267.

3842.   McMillan, J. (1978), Training for family living (proceedings). South African Medical Journal, 53, 836-838.

3843.   McNail, J.S. (1979), Group therapy with elusive parents. Social Casework, 60, 36-42.

3844.   McNall, S.A. (1977), Review of Guerin's Family therapy: Theory and practice. International Journal of the Sociology of the Family, 7, 265.

3845.   McNamee, S. (1983), Therapeutic change in family systems: A communication approach to the study of convoluted interactive patterns. Dissertation Abstracts International, 44, 1626-A.

3846.   McNeil, J.S., and Zondervan, R.C. (1971), The family in cultural isolation. Military Medicine, 136, 451-454.

3847.   McPherson, S.B., and Samuels, C.R. (1971), Teaching behavioral methods to parents. Social Casework, 52, 148-153.

3848.   McPherson, S.J. (1981), Family counseling for youthful offenders in the juvenile court setting: A therapy outcome study. Dissertation Abstracts International, 42, 382-B.

3849.   McPherson, S.R., Brackelmanns, W.E., and Newman, L.E. (1974), Stages in family therapy of adolescents. Family Process, 13, 77-94.

3850.   McRae, B.C. (1976), A comparison of a behavioral and a lecture discussion approach to premarital counseling. Dissertation Abstracts Internation, 36, 6391B.

3851.   McRae, M. (1977), An approach to the single parent dilemma...Jean Piaget's theory. American Journal of Maternal Child Nursing, 2, 164-167.

3852. McRee, S.L.V. (1978), A phenomenological study of the experience of a married couples' therapy group led by co-therapists. Dissertation Abstracts International, 39, 990B.

3853. McWhirter, D.P., and Mattison, A.M. (1978), The treatment of sexual dysfunction in gay male couples. Journal of Sex Marital Therapy, 4, 213-218.

3854. McWhirter, D.P., and Mattison, A.M. (1982), Psychotherapy for gay male couples. Journal of Homosexuality, 7(2-3), 79-91.

3855. McWhirter, J.J., and Kincaid, M. (1974), Family group consultation: Adjust to a parent program. Journal of Family Counseling, 2, 45-48.

3856. Meack, D.S., and LeUnes, A. (1977), Personality similarity-dissimilarity and underlying psychopathology in couples seeking marital counseling. Journal of Marital and Family Therapy, 3, 63-66.

3857. Mead, B.T. (1971), Marriage counseling: What to do before the police arrive. Journal of American Osteopathic Association, 70, 1357-1362.

3858. Mead, D.E. (1981), Reciprocity counseling: Practice and research. Journal of Marital and Family Therapy, 7, 189-200.

3859. Mead, E., and Crane, D.R. (1978), An empirical approach to supervision and training of relationship therapists. Journal of Marriage and Family Counseling, 4, 6775.

3860. Meade, E.S. (1982), A study of the orientations and attitudes of marriage counselors who handle marital separation cases. Dissertation Abstracts International, 42, 4302-A.

3861. Meadows, M.E., and Hetrick, H.H. (1982), Roles for counselor education departments in marriage and family counseling: Current status and projections. Counselor Education and Supervision, 22, 47-54.

3862. Meadows, M.E., and Taplin, J.F. (1970), Premarital counseling with college students: A promising triad. Journal of Counseling Psychology, 17(6), 516-518.

3863. Meck, D.S., and LeUnes, A. (1977), Marital instability in a semirural setting: Personality considerations. Journal of Community Psychology, 5, 278-281.

3864. Medalie, J.H. (1979), The family life cycle and its implications for family practice. Journal of Family Practice, 9, 47-56.

3865. Meedin, J., and Wattenberg, S.H. (1982), Students and short-term family therapy: An assessment. Social Casework, 63(4), 195.

3866. Meeks, D.E., and Kelly, C. (1970), Family therapy with the families of recovering alcoholics. Quarterly Journal of Studies on Alcohol, 31, 399-413.

3867. Meggs, G.A. (1974), A social worker's approach to marriage counseling problems: An explanation to lay people. Mental Health in Australia, 1(2), 58-60.

3868.   Mehlman, S.K. (1982), Behavioral marital therapy and the comparison of
         delayed treatment/immediate treatment and co-therapists/individual
         therapists in the treatment of distressed couples. Dissertation Abstracts
         International, 42, 4200-B.

3869.   Mehlman, S.K., Baucom, D.H., and Anderson, D. (1983), Effectiveness of
         co-therapists versus single therapists and immediate versus delayed
         treatment in behavioral marital therapy. Journal of Consulting and
         Clinical Psychology, 51, 258-266.

3870.   Meisel, S.S. (1977), The treatment of sexual problems in marital and
         family therapy. Clinical Social Work Journal, 5, 200-209.

3871.   Meiselman, K.C. (1980), Personality characteristics of incest history
         psychotherapy patients: A research note. Archives of Sexual Behavior,
         9(3), 195.

3872.   Meister, S.B. (1977), Charting a family's developmental status: For
         intervention and for the record. American Journal of Maternal Child
         Nursing, 2, 43-48.

3873.   Meitinger, H., and Heil, M. (1979), Family therapy and behavior
         modification. Zeitschrift fuet Kinder- und Jugendpsychiatrie, 7(4), 353.

3874.   Mejia, J.A. (1981), Contributions of therapist's relationship and
         structuring skills to marital therapy outcome variance in a Hispanic
         clinical couple population. Dissertation Abstracts International, 42, 779-
         B.

3875.   Meller, J., and Stone, G.Z. (1973), Marital problems in general
         practice. African Journal of Medical Sciences, 47, 1812-1814.

3876.   Melson, G.F. (1982), Review of J.T. Dempsey's The family and public
         policy: The issue of the 1980s. American Journal of Family Therapy, 10,
         78.

3877.   Melson, G.F. (1982), Review of G.Y. Steiner's The futility of family
         policy. American Journal of Family Therapy, 10, 78-79.

3878.   Mendell, D. (1975), Combined family and group therapy for problems of
         adolescents: A synergistic approach. In: M. Sugar (Ed.), The adolescent
         in group and family therapy. New York, NY: Brunner/Mazel.

3879.   Mendels, C.E., and Shemberg, K.M.(1976), Psychotherapy and
         consultation in the treatment of a schizophrenic child. Psychotherapy:
         Theory, Research and Practice, 13(4), 390-394.

3880.   Mendelsohn, M. (1979), Psychotherapy and growth: A family systems
         perspective. Social Casework, 60, 57.

3881.   Mendonca, J.D., Lumley, P., and Hunt, A. (1982), Brief marital therapy
         outcome: Personality correlates. Canadian Journal of Psychiatry, 27,
         291-295.

3882.   Meneghini, L.C., and Pinto de Abrev, J.R. (1973), Family crisis: A case
         study. Al Estudios Psicodinamic, 3, 34-41.

3883. Menzies, M.A. (1965), The angry parent in family-oriented therapy. Canadian Journal of Psychiatry, 10, 405-410.

3884. Mercer, R.T. (1977), Crisis: A baby is born with a defect. Nursing '77, 7, 45-47.

3885. Merei, V. (1976), Therapy of stuttering in the preschooler via group training of the mother: Indirect educational effect. In E. Loebell, (Ed.), XVIth International Congress of Logopedics and Phoniatrics, Basel, Karger, 325-329.

3886. Mereneas, D.A. (1968), Family therapy: An evolving role for the psychiatric nurse. Perspectives in Psychiatric Care, 6, 256-259.

3887. Merl, H. (1981), The effect of psychoanalysis on marriage and family therapy. Wiener Medizinische Wochenschrift, 131, 575-8.

3888. Merl, H. (1978), Psychoanalytic marital and family therapy. Gruppenpsychotherapie und Gruppendynamik, 13, 297-341.

3889. Merl, H. (1980), Psychotherapy adapted to family requirements. Gruppenpsychotherapie und Gruppendynamik, 16(1), 4.

3890. Merner, M.H. (1982), Partner similarity on the Myers-Briggs type indicator among functional and dysfunctional married couples. Dissertation Abstracts International, 42, 4772-A.

3891. Merrington, D., and Corden, J. (1981), Families' impressions of family therapy. Journal of Family Therapy, 3, 243-261.

3892. Messer, A.A. (1964), Family treatment of a school phobic child. Archives of General Psychiatry, 11, 548-555.

3893. Messina, J.J. (1975), A comparative study of parent consultation and conjoint family counseling. Dissertation Abstracts International, 35, 4188B.

3894. Messinger, L. (1976), Remarriage between divorced people with children from previous marriages: A proposal for preparation for remarriage. Journal of Marriage and Family Counseling, 2, 193-200.

3895. Messinger, L., Walker, K.N., and Freeman, S.J.J. (1978), Preparation for remarriage following divorce: The use of group techniques. American Journal of Orthopsychiatry, 48, 263-272.

3896. Messner, E., and Schmidt, D.D. (1974), Videotape in the training of medical students in psychiatric aspects of family medicine. International Journal of Psychiatric Medicine, 5, 269-273.

3897. Mester, R., Hazan, Y., Sella, A., and Klein, H. (1983), Therapeutic approaches to families of young Israeli soldiers. Family Process, 22, 61-68.

3898. Metcalf, S., and Williams, W. (1977), A case of male childhood transsexualism and its management. Australian and New Zealand Journal of Psychiatry, 11, 53-59.

3899.   Metcoff, J. (1980), Introducing videotape to the family in the role of a specialized member of the treatment system. Journal of Marital and Family Therapy, 7, 153-158.

3900.   Metcoff, J., and Whitaker, C.A. (1982), Family microevents: Communication patterns for problem solving. In F. Walsh (Ed.), Normal family processes. New York: Guilford Press.

3901.   Meth, R.L. (1985), Review of D. Bagarozi, A. Jurich, and R. Jackson's Marital and family therapy: New perspectives in theory, research and practice. Journal of Marital and Family Therapy, 11(1), 105.

3902.   Meyer, A. (1978), This stranger our son: Help for a child with behavior problems. Nursing Times, 74, 1975-1977.

3903.   Meyer, G.J. (1984), Innovations in family life styles. American Journal of Family Therapy, 12(3), 71-79.

3904.   Meyer, G.J., and Scherb, R. (1984), Keys to success: Unlocking the middle phases of family therapy. American Journal of Family Therapy, 12(2), 74-78.

3905.   Meyer, M. (1969), Family ties and the institutional child. Children, 16, 226.

3906.   Meyer, R. (1978), The critical situation of stillbirth: Demonstrated on a case of brief marital psychotherapy. Gynaexol Rundech, 18, 143-152.

3907.   Meyers, D.V. (1978), Toward an objective evaluation procedure of the Kinetic Family Drawings (KFD). Journal of Personality Assessment, 42, 358-365.

3908.   Meyers, S.V. (1984), Elective mutism in children: A family systems approach. American Journal of Family Therapy, 12(4), 39-45.

3909.   Meyerstein, I. (1979), The family behavioral snapshot: A tool for teaching family assessment. American Journal of Family Therapy, 7, 48-56.

3910.   Meyerstein, I. (1981), Unlearning myths about family therapy. International Journal of Family Psychiatry, 2, 203-219.

3911.   Meyerstein, I. (1977), Family therapy training for paraprofessionals in a community mental health center. Family Process, 16, 477-493.

3912.   Meyerstein, I., and Todd, J.C. (1980), On the witness stand: The family therapist and expert testimony. American Journal of Family Therapy, 8, 43-51.

3913.   Mezydlo, L., Wauck, L.A., and Foley, J.M. (1973), The clergy as marriage counselors: A service revisited. Journal of Religion and Health, 12, 278-288.

3914.   Miaoulis, C.N. (1976), A study of the innovative use of time and planned short-term treatment in conjoint marital counseling. Dissertation Abstracts International, 3(4), 1993-A.

3915.   Michaels, K.W., and Green, R.H. (1979), A child welfare agency
         project: Therapy for families of status. Child Welfare, 58(3), 216-220.

3916.   Michel, A. (1976), Ideologies, pressure groups, and family politics in
         France. Perspectives in Psychiatric Care, 55, 6-12.

3917.   Middleberg, C.V., and Gross, S.J. (1979), Family's affective rules and
         their relationships to the family's adjustment. American Journal of
         Family Therapy, 7(2), 37.

3918.   Midelfort, C.F. (1962), Symposium: Family treatment of
         schizophrenia. Use of members of the family in the treatment of
         schizophrenia. Family Process, 1(1), 114-118.

3919.   Midelfort, C.F. (1957), The family in psychotherapy. New York:
         McGraw-Hill.

3920.   Midelfort, C.F. (1982), Use of family in the treatment of schizophrenic
         and psychopathic patients. Journal of Marital and Family Therapy, 8, 1-
         11.

3921.   Milano, M.R. (1984), Review of M. McGoldrick, J.K. Pearce and J.
         Giordano's Ethnicity and family therapy. Family Process, 23(2), 288.

3922.   Milano, M.R. (1984), Review of J.M. Dillard's Marital counseling toward
         ethnic and cultural relevance in human encounters. Family Process,
         23(2), 288-289.

3923.   Miler, S. (Ed.) (1975), Marriages and families: Enrichment through
         communication. Small Group Behavior, 6, 1-120.

3924.   Miles, J.E. (1980), Motivation in conjoint therapy. Journal of Sex and
         Marital Therapy, 6(3), 205-213.

3925.   Milholland, T.A. (1980), The effects of marriage encounter on self-
         disclosure, trust, and marital satisfaction. Dissertation Abstracts
         International, 40, 3953-B.

3926.   Millard, J., and McLagan, J.R. (1972), Multifamily group work: A
         hopeful approach to the institutionalized delinquent and his family.
         Comprehensive Group Therapy, 3, 117-127.

3927.   Miller, C. (1980), Religious issues in family systems therapy. The
         Family, 8, 67-70.

3928.   Miller, D.K. (1975), Sexual counseling with spinal cord injured clients.
         Journal of Sex and Marital Therapy, 1(4), 312-318.

3929.   Miller, D.R. (1984), A family is a family is a family. Family Process,
         23(3), 389-394.

3930.   Miller, D.R., and Westman, J.C. (1964), Family teamwork and
         psychotherapy. American Journal of Orthopsychiatry, 34, 348-349.

3931.   Miller, D.R., and Westman, J.C. (1966), Family teamwork and
         psychotherapy. Family Process, 5, 49-59.

3932.   Miller, E. (1973), Treatment of a communal family. Social Casework,
        54, 331-341.

3933.   Miller, E. (1976), Psychotherapy of a child in a custody dispute. Journal
        of the American Academy of Child Psychiatry, 15(3), 441-452.

3934.   Miller, J. (1974), Cognitive dissonance in modifying families'
        perceptions. American Journal of Nursing, 74, 1468-1470.

3935.   Miller, J. (1981), Cultural and class values in family process. Journal of
        Marital and Family Therapy, 7, 467-473.

3936.   Miller, J. (1967), Concurrent treatment of marital couples by one or two
        analysts. American Journal of Psychoanalysis, 27(2), 135-139.

3937.   Miller, J.C. (1971), Systems theory and family psychotherapy. Nursing
        Clinics of North America, 6, 395-406.

3938.   Miller, J.R. (1980), Problems of single-parent families. Journal of the
        New York State Nurses Association, 11, 5-8.

3939.   Miller, M. (1972), Cooperation of some wives in their husband's
        suicides. Psychological Reports, 44, 39-42.

3940.   Miller, N. (1983), Group psychotherapy in a school setting for adolescent
        children of alcoholics. Group, 7, 34-40.

3941.   Miller, N.B., and Cantwell, D.B. (1976), Siblings as therapists: A
        behavioral approach. American Journal of Psychiatry, 133, 447-450.

3942.   Miller, S., and Winstead-Fry, P. (1982), Family systems theory and
        nursing practice. Englewood Cliffs, NJ: Reston.

3943.   Miller, S.O. (1985), Review of C.E. Obudho's Black marriage and family
        therapy. Social Casework, 66(5), 315-316.

3944.   Miller, T.W. (1976), The working mother: Issues and implications for
        family counselors. Journal of Family Counseling, 4, 61-65.

3945.   Miller, T.W. (1977), Impact of television programming for children on
        family life: Issues for family therapy. International Journal of Family
        Counseling, 5, 40-47.

3946.   Miller, T.W. (1984), Video feedback in marital therapy for schizophrenic
        patients. Hospital and Community Psychiatry, 35(10), 1078.

3947.   Miller, V., and Mansfield, E. (1981), Family therapy for the multiple
        incest family. Journal of Psychiatric Nursing, 19, 29-32.

3948.   Miller, V.H. (1974), An evaluation of the effect of sexual enrichment
        group experience on the sexual satisfaction and sexual pleasure of
        married couples. Dissertation Abstracts International, 34, 6218B.

3949.   Milloy, M. (1971). A look at the family and family interviewing. Child
        Welfare, 50, 40-46.

3950.   Mills, K.H., and Kilmann, P.R. (1982), Group treatment of sexual
        dysfunctions: A methodological review of the outcome literature.
        Journal of Sex and Marital Therapy, 8, 259-296.

3951.   Millstone, J. (1984), An analysis of the policy rationale for the Texas
        family code provision allowing courts to compel families of delinquent
        youth to participate in therapy. American Journal of Criminal Law, 12,
        169-188.

3952.   Milman, D.H. (1952), Group therapy with parents: An approach to the
        rehabilitation of physically disabled children. Journal of Pediatrics, 41,
        113-116.

3953.   Milosavljevic, P. (1972), Some aspects of work with psychiatric patients'
        families. Anali Zavoda Za Mentalno Zdravije, 4, 19-25.

3954.   Milosavljevic, P. (1977), Methodological approach to family therapy.
        Socijalna Psihijatrija, 5, 349-361.

3955.   Milosavljevic, P. (1977), The principles of family therapy. Psihijatrija
        Danas, 9(1), 99-107.

3956.   Milosavljevic, P. (1976), Emotional attitudes of parents of schizophrenic
        patients during family psychotherapy. Socijalna Psihijatrija, 4, 309-313.

3957.   Milosavljevic, P. (1975), Difficulties in group work with the parents of
        schizophrenic patients. Anali Zavoda Za Mentalno Zdravije, 7, 151-156.

3958.   Milosavljevic, P. (1975), Family psychotherapy within social
        psychiatry. Anali Zavoda Za Mentalno Zdravije, 7, 77-83.

3959.   Milosavljevic, P. (1982), The large group of psychotic patients' parents.
        Psihijatrija Danas, 14, 99-106.

3960.   Mintz, M.L. (1980), Validating a concept in family therapy: The
        interaction of subsystems. Dissertation Abstracts International, 41, 1119-
        B. (University Microfilms No. 8021154.)

3961.   Minuchin, P. (1985), Families and individual development: Provocations
        from the field of family therapy. Child Development, 56(2), 289.

3962.   Minuchin, S. (1984), Family Kaledioscope. Cambridge, MA: Harvard
        University Press.

3963.   Minuchin, S. (1979), Psychosomatic family in child psychiatry. Journal
        of the American Academy of Child Psychiatry, 18, 76-90.

3964.   Minuchin, S. (1974), Families and family therapy. Cambridge, MA:
        Harvard University Pres.

3965.   Minuchin, S. (1964), Family structure, family language and the puzzled
        therapist. American Journal of Orthopsychiatry, 34, 347-348.

3966.   Minuchin, S. (1965), Conflict-resolution family therapy. Psychiatry, 28,
        278-286.

3967.   Minuchin, S., Baker, L., Rosman, B.L., Liebman, R., Milman, L., and
        Todd, T.C. (1975), A conceptual model of psychosomatic illness in

children: Family organization and family therapy. <u>Archives of General Psychiatry</u>, <u>32</u>(8), 1031-1038.

3968.   Minuchin, S., Rosman, B.L., and Baker, L. (Eds.) (1978), <u>Psychosomatic families: Anorexia nervosa in context</u>. Cambridge, MA: Harvard University Press.

3969.   Minuchin, S., and Fishman, H.C. (1981), <u>Family therapy techniques</u>. Cambridge, MA: Harvard University Press.

3970.   Minuchin, S., and Montalov, B. (1967), Techniques for working with disorganized, low socioeconomic families. <u>American Journal of Orthopsychiatry</u>, <u>37</u>, 880-887.

3971.   Mirkin, M.P., Raskin, P.A., and Antognini, F.C. (1984), Parenting, protecting, preserving: Mission of the adolescent female runaway. <u>Family Process</u>, <u>23</u>, 63-74.

3972.   Misra, L.S., Saxena, N.K., and Pathak, M.P. (1982), Psycho-clinical symptoms and factors associated with natal history of mentally retarded children. <u>Child Psychiatry Quarterly</u>, <u>15</u>, 119-123.

3973.   Mitchell, C. (1982), Treatment of families in conflict: Recurrent themes in literature and clinical practice. <u>Journal of Contemporary Psychotherapy</u>, <u>13</u>, 29-60.

3974.   Mitchell, C. (1978), Review of H. Grunebaum and J. Christ's <u>Contemporary marriage: Structure, dynamics and therapy</u>. <u>Journal of Sex and Marital Therapy</u>, <u>4</u>, 226.

3975.   Mitchell, C.B. (1960), The use of family sessions in diagnosis and treatment of disturbances in children. <u>Social Casework</u>, <u>41</u>, 283-290.

3976.   Mitchell, C.B. (1979), The effects of short-term intensive training on family communication skills. <u>Dissertation Abstracts International</u>, <u>40</u>, 458B.

3977.   Mitchell, C.D. (1983), An exploratory analysis of specific therapist skills and corresponding changes in family behaviors during marital and family therapy sessions. <u>Dissertation Abstracts International</u>, <u>44</u>, 44-45A.

3978.   Mitchell, C.E. (1980), Tenacity in marriage and the positive effects of individual responsibility. <u>Family Therapy</u>, <u>7</u>(2), 119-124.

3979.   Mitchell, R.A. (1972), A marital therapy game identification, "You hold her I'm off." <u>Transactional Analysis Journal</u>, <u>2</u>, 161-162.

3980.   Mitsuyoshi, Y. (1973), Cotherapy for the family of schizophrenics and the nurses' role. <u>Kyoshitsu</u>, <u>25</u>, 18-25.

3981.   Mittelmann, B. (1949), Simultaneous treatment of both parents and their child. <u>Samiksa</u>, <u>3</u>, 212-221.

3982.   Miyoshi, N., and Liebman, R. (1969), Training psychiatric residents in family therapy. <u>Family Process</u>, <u>8</u>(1), 97-105.

3983.   Mjager, V.K. (1975), Psychotherapy and sociotherapy of neurotic patients from the viewpoint of family psychotherapy. In M. Hausner, et al., (Ed.), Psychotherapie in Sozialistischen Landern, Leipzig: Thieme, 139-141.

3984.   Mkhize, D.E. (1983), Growth marriage counseling as a means of liberation within the South African black parish situation. Dissertation Abstracts International, 44, 782-A.

3985.   Mladek, G. (1981), The influence of advice to the improvement of conflict-solving behavior of parents to children (author's transl.). Arztliche Jugendkdkunde, 72, 292-321.

3986.   Mlott, S., and Lira, F.T. (1977), Dogmatism, locus of control, and life goals in stable and instable marriages. Journal of Clinical Psychology, 33, 142-146.

3987.   Mlott, S.R., and Lira, F.T. (1975), A group therapy approach with hemodialysis patients and their families. Journal of the American Association of Nephrological Nurses and Technology, 2(3), 105-108.

3988.   Mlott, S.R., and Lira, F.T. (1975), Conceptual approaches to marital discordance: An overview for the physician. Journal of South Carolina Medical Association, 71, 287-291.

3989.   Mogey, J. (1961), Marriage counseling and family life education in England. Marriage and Family Living, 23, 146-154.

3990.   Mohamed, S.N., Weisl, G.M., and Waring, E.M. (1978), The relationship of chronic pain to depression: Marital adjustment and family dynamics. Pain, 5, 285-292.

3991.   Mohammed, Z. (1983), The effects of two methods of training and sequencing on structuring and relationship skills of family therapists. Dissertation Abstracts International, 43, 3512-A.

3992.   Molnar, G., and Cameron, P. (1975), Incest syndromes: Observations in a general hospital psychiatric unit. Canadian Psychiatric Association Journal, 20(5), 373-377.

3993.   Moloney, M.J. (1982), The use of children's drawings in multiple family group therapy. Group, 5(4), 32.

3994.   Money, J. (1981), Paraphilia and abuse-martyrdom: Exhibitionism as a paradigm for reciprocal couple counseling combined with antiandrogen. Journal of Sex and Marital Therapy, 7, 115-23.

3995.   Montalvo, B., and Gutierrez, M. (1978), The family and child placement practices. Family Process, 17, 287-337.

3996.   Montalvo, B., and Gutierrez, M. (1983), A perspective for the use of the cultural dimension in family therapy. Family Therapy Collections, 11, 15-32.

3997.   Montalvo, B., and Haley, J. (1973), In defense of child therapy. Family Process, 12(3), 227-244.

3998.   Montalvo, F.F. (1982), The third dimension in social casework: Mary E. Richmond's contribution to family treatment. Clinical Social Work Journal, 10, 103-112.

3999.   Montanari, J. (1969), A community-based residential program for disturbed children. Hospital and Community Psychiatry, 20, 103-108.

4000.   Montesarchio, G., Pontalti, C., and Ruggeri, G. (1978), (The couple: The reorganization of intrapsychic personal structures in mates.) Archivos Psicologia Neurologia y Psichiatria, 39(4), 453-472.

4001.   Moody, J.L. (1981), A strategy for salvaging young marriages. Dissertation Abstracts International, 42, 1012-A.

4002.   Moore, J.A., and Coulman, M.U. (1981), Anorexia nervosa: The patient, her family, and key family therapy interventions. Journal of Psychiatric Nursing, 19, 9-14.

4003.   Moore, J.B. (1982), Project Thrive: A supportive treatment approach to the parents of children with non-organic failure to thrive. Child Welfare, 61, 389-399.

4004.   Moore, R. (1974), Further thoughts on family therapy: Reply to Zaphiropoulos, Spiegel and Harrell. Contemporary Psychoanalysis, 10, 493-502.

4005.   Moos, R.H., Bromet, E., Tsu, V., and Moos, B. (1979), Family characteristics and the outcome of treatment for alcoholism. Journal of Studies on Alcoholism, 40, 78-88.

4006.   Moos, R.H., and Fuhr, R. (1982), The clinical use of social-ecological concepts: The case of an adolescent girl. American Journal of Orthopsychiatry, 52, 111-122.

4007.   Moran, J.J. (1982), Review of R.J. Green and J.L. Framo's Family therapy: Major contributions. Child Study Journal, 12, 299.

4008.   Morawetz, A., and Walker, G. (1984), Brief therapy with single-parent families. New York: Brunner/Mazel.

4009.   Mordock, J.B. (1974), Sibling sexual fantasies in family therapy: A case report. Journal of Family Counseling, 2, 60-65.

4010.   Morea, H.P. (1974), A family in trouble: A case study of a family in conjoint family therapy. Perspectives in Psychiatric Care, 12, 165-170.

4011.   Moreau, A., and Moreau, J. (1981), The doctor, his patient, and the family. Feuillets Psychiatriques de Liege, 14, 231-248.

4012.   Moreland, J., Schwebel, A.I., Fine, M.A., and Vess, J.D. (1982), Post-divorce family therapy: Suggestions for professionals. Professional Psychology, 13, 639-646.

4013.   Morello, P.A., and Factor, D.C. (1981), Therapy as prevention: An educational model for treating families. Canada's Mental Health, 29, 10-11.

4014.   Moreno, J.L. (1948), Psychodrama of a premarital couple. Sociatry, 2, 103-120.

4015.   Moreno, J.L. (1948), Psychodrama of a marriage. Sociatry, 2, 121-169.

4016.   Moreno, J.L. (1940), Psychodramatic treatment of marriage problems. Sociatry, 3, 1-23.

4017.   Moreno, J.L. (1941), The prediction and planning of success in marriage. Marriage and Family Living, 3, 83-84.

4018.   Moreno, J.L. (1966), Psychodrama of a marriage: A motion picture. Group Psychotherapy, Psychodrama and Sociometry, 19, 49-93.

4019.   Moreno, J.L., Moreno, Z., and Moreno, J. (1963), The first psychodramatic family. Group Psychotherapy, Psychodrama and Sociometry, 16, 203-249.

4020.   Moreno, J.L., Moreno, Z.T., and Moreno, J. (1964), The first psychodramatic family. Boston, MA: Beacon House.

4021.   Moreno, J.L., Moreno, Z.T., and Moreno, J. (1964), New Moreno legends, from the first psychodramatic family. Group Psychotherapy, Psychodrama and Sociometry, 17, 1-35.

4022.   Moreno, R. (1985), The effects of strategic-family therapy and client-centered therapy on selected personality variables of juvenile delinquents. Dissertation Abstracts International, 46, 1195-A.

4023.   Morgan, A.G., and Avery, A.W. (1982), Relationship enhancement with premarital couples: An assessment of effects on relationship quality. American Journal of Family Therapy, 10, 41-48.

4024.   Morgan, M.I. (1950), Course content of theory courses in marriage counseling. Marriage and Family Counseling, 12, 95-99.

4025.   Morgan, M.I., Johannis, T.B., Jr., and Fowler, S.E. (1952), Family counseling: Toward an analysis and definition. Marriage and Family Living, 15, 119-121.

4026.   Morgan, M.R. (1979), Counseling parents who have a handicapped child. Journal of the Royal College of Physicians of London, 13(4), 245-247.

4027.   Morgan, O.J. (1982), Runaways: Jurisdiction, dynamics, and treatment. Journal of Marital and Family Therapy, 8, 121-127.

4028.   Morgan, O.J. (1983), A contextual perspective: Process and action in psychotherapy. American Journal of Family Therapy, 11, 65-66.

4029.   Morgan, S.A., and Coles, J. (1978), Three assessment tools for family therapy. Journal of Psychiatric Nursing, 16, 39-42.

4030.   Morgillo, M.E. (1980), A comparison of the T-JTA and the MMPI profiles of married couples seeking counseling. Dissertation Abstracts International, 41, 1517-B.

4031.   Morley, W.E., and Brown, V.B. (1969), The crisis intervention group: A natural mating or a marriage of convenience. Psychotherapy: Theory, Research and Practice, 6, 30-36.

4032.   Morrice, J.K. (1981), Couple therapy in a therapeutic community setting. Journal of Family Therapy, 3(4), 353.

4033.   Morris, G.O., and Lyman, C.W. (1965), Schizophrenic offspring and parental styles of communication: A predictive study using excerpts of family therapy recordings. Psychiatry, 28, 19-44.

4034.   Morris, H.K. (1982), Reflections on one year in family therapy...from a client's perspective. The Family, 9(2), 109.

4035.   Morris, J.D., and Prescott, M.R. (1976), Adjustment to divorce through transactional analysis. Journal of Family Counseling, 4, 66-69.

4036.   Morris, J.D., and Prescott, M.R. (1975), Transition groups: An approach to dealing with post-partnership anguish. Family Coordinator, 24, 325-330.

4037.   Morris, M. (1978), Family play therapy: An extended treatment model. Ontario Psychologist, 10(4), 25-29.

4038.   Morrison, G.C. (1969), Therapeutic intervention in a child psychiatry emergency service. Journal of American Academy of Child Psychiatry, 8, 542-558.

4039.   Morrison, G.C., and Collier, J.C. (1969), Family treatment approaches to suicidal children and adolescents. Journal of the American Academy of Child Psychiatry, 8, 140-153.

4040.   Morrison, J.K. (1981), The use of imagery techniques in family therapy. American Journal of Family Therapy, 9, 52-56.

4041.   Morrison, J.K., Friedman, W., Lill, N., and Kaboyashi, N. (1979), Changing a mental health team's attitudes towards family therapy: A pilot study. American Journal of Family Therapy, 1, 57-60.

4042.   Morrison, J.K., Layton, B., and Newman, J. (1982), Values, ethics, legalities and the family therapist: V. Ethical conflict in clinical decision making: A challenge for family therapists. Family Therapy Collections, 1, 75-86.

4043.   Morrison, J.K., and Nevid, J.S. (1976), Demythologizing the attitudes of family caretakers about mental illness. Journal of Family Counseling, 4(1), 43-49.

4044.   Morrison, T.L., and Thomas, M.D. (1976), Judgments of educators and child-care personnel about appropriate treatment for mentally retarded or normal, overactive or withdrawn boys. Journal of Clinical Psychology, 32, 449-452.

4045.   Morrow, G.R., Hoagland, A.C., and Morse, I.P. (1982), Sources of support perceived by parents of children with cancer: Implications for counseling. Patient Counseling and Health Education, 4(1), 36.

4046.   Morrow, T. (1974), Flexibility in therapeutic work with parents and children. Bulletin of the Menninger Clinic, 38, 129-143.

4047.   Morse, J. (1979), A program for family management of the multiple handicapped child: TEMPO as a clinical model. Rehabilitation Literature, 40, 134-145.

4048. Moses, R. (1971), Some comments on family therapy in Israel. Israeli Annals of Psychiatry, 9, 132-137.

4049. Mosher, D.L. (1977), The Gestalt awareness expression cycle as a model for sex therapy. Journal of Sex and Marital Therapy, 3(4), 229-242.

4050. Mosher, D.L. (1979), Awareness in Gestalt sex therapy. Journal of Sex and Marital Therapy, 5(1), 41-56.

4051. Mosher, D.L. (1979), The Gestalt experiment in sex therapy. Journal of Sex and Marital Therapy, 5(2), 117-133.

4052. Mosher, D.L. (1979), Negative attitudes toward masturbation in sex therapy. Journal of Sex and Marital Therapy, 5(4), 315.

4053. Mosher, L.R. (1969), Schizophrenic communication and family therapy. Family Process, 8(1), 43-63.

4054. Mosher, L.R. (1976), Family therapy for schizophrenia: Recent trends. In: L.J. West and D.E. Flinn (Eds.), Treatment of schizophrenia. New York, NY: Grune and Stratton.

4055. Mosher, L.R., and Keith, S.J. (1980), Psychosocial treatment: Individual, group, family, and community support approaches. Schizophrenia Bulletin, 6, 10-41.

4056. Mosimann, H., and Utrilla, M. (1975), (Some thoughts concerning a family therapy experiment.) Acta Psychiatrica Belgica, 75(3), 280-293.

4057. Moss, S.Z. (1968), Integration of the family into the child placement process. Children, 15, 219-224.

4058. Moss, S.Z., and Moss, M.S. (1984), Threat to place a child. American Journal of Orthopsychiatry, 54, 168-173.

4059. Most, E. (1960), Casework results among married couples in conflict: A device to measure attitudinal change. Dissertation Abstracts International, 21, 2026.

4060. Mostwin, D. (1974), Multidimensional model of working with the family. Social Casework, 55, 209-215.

4061. Mostwin, D. (1980), Social dimension of family treatment. New York: National Association of Social Workers.

4062. Mottola, W.C. (1967), Family therapy: A review. Psychotherapy: Theory, Research and Practice, 4, 116-124.

4063. Moulton, P.G. (1982), A study of the viability of the concept of boundaries within family systems. Dissertation Abstracts International, 42, 3433-B.

4064. Moultrup, D. (1981), Towards an integrated model of family therapy. Clinical Social Work Journal, 9, 111-125.

4065. Mowatt, D.T., Vanduesen, J.M., and Wilson, D. (1984), Family therapy and the drug using offender: The organization of disability and treatment in a criminal justice context. Federal Probation, 48(2), 28-34.

4066.   Mowrer, O.H. (1975), New hope and help for the disintegrating American family. Journal of Family Counseling, 3, 17-23.

4067.   Moynihan, S.K. (1974), Home visits for family treatment. Social Casework, 55, 612-617.

4068.   Moynihan, S.K. (1978), Utilizing the school setting to facilitate family treatment. Social Casework, 59, 287-294.

4069.   Mozdzierz, G.J., and Friedman, K. (1978), The superiority-inferiority spouses syndrome: Diagnostic and therapeutic considerations. Journal of Individual Psychology, 34(2), 232-243.

4070.   Mozdzierz, G.J., and Lottman, T.J. (1973), Games married couples play: Adlerian view. Journal of Individual Psychology, 29, 182-194.

4071.   Mrazova, A., and Jochmanova, A. (1975), Course of psychotherapy group on marital consultations. Ceskoslovenska Psychologie, 19, 380-381.

4072.   Muacevic, V., and Hudolin, V. (1967), (The psychotherapy of neurotics with actual family conflicts.) Psychotherapy and Psychosomatics, 15, 48-49.

4073.   Muacevic, V., and Trbovic, M. (1973), (The therapeutic community and the isolated family of the patient.) Socijalna Psihijatrija, 1(1), 75-81.

4074.   Mudd, E.H. (1975), Marriage counseling and the related professions. Transactions and Studies of the College of Physicians at Philadelphia, 42(4), 433-440.

4075.   Mudd, E.H. (1980), The couples as a unit: Sexual, social, and behavioral considerations to reproductive barriers. Journal of Marital and Family Therapy, 6(1), 23-28.

4076.   Mudd, E.H. (1951), The practice of marriage counseling. New York: Association Press.

4077.   Mudd, E.H. (1945), A case study in marriage counseling. Marriage and Family Living, 7, 52-55.

4078.   Mudd, E.H. (Ed.) (1958). Marriage counseling: A casebook. New York: Association Press.

4079.   Mudd, E.H., Freeman, C.H., and Rose, E.K. (1941), Premarital counseling in the Philadelphia marriage counsel. Mental Hygiene, 25, 98-119.

4080.   Mudd, E.H., Preston, M.G., Froscher, H.B., and Peltz, W.L. (1950), Survey of a research project in marriage counseling. Marriage and Family Living, 12, 59-61.

4081.   Mueller, J.F. (1972), Casework with the family of the alcoholic. Social Work, 17, 79-84.

4082.   Mueller, P.S., and Orfanidis, M.M. (1976), A method of co-therapy for schizophrenic families. Family Process, 15, 179-191.

4083. Muir, R. (1975), The family and the problem of internalization. British Journal of Medical Psychology, 48, 267-272.

4084. Mulder, D.L. (1985), An integrative model of marital therapy based on the psychoanalytic, behavioral and systems approach. Dissertation Abstracts International, 46, 2051-B.

4085. Mumma, E.W. (1985), Looking beyond the one-way mirror: The scope of family therapy training is wider than it may appear. Public Welfare, 43, 20-29.

4086. Munford, P.R., and Chan, S.Q. (1980), Family therapy for the treatment of a conversion reaction: A case study. Psychotherapy: Theory, Research, and Practice, 17, 214-219.

4087. Munjack, D.J., and Oziel, L.J. (1978), Resistance in the behavioral treatment of sexual dysfunctions. Journal of Sex and Marital Therapy, 4, 122-138.

4088. Munson, C.E. (1980), Social work with families: Theory and practice. New York, NY: Free Press.

4089. Munson, C.E. (1980), Supervising the family therapist. Social Casework, 61, 131-137.

4090. Murphy, A., Pueschel, S.M., and Schneider, J. (1973), Group work with parents of children with Down's syndrome. Social Casework, 54, 114-119.

4091. Murphy, J.M. (1979), Use of non-verbal and body movement techniques in working with families with infants. Journal of Marital and Family Therapy, 5, 61-66.

4092. Murphy, M.J. (1983), The implications of intentionality for the theory of family therapy. Dissertation Abstracts International, 44, 1695-A.

4093. Murphy, N.M. (1980), Review of J.S. Horewitz's Family therapy and transactional analysis. American Journal of Psychiatry, 137, 759.

4094. Murphy, T.D. (1983), The meaning of counseling for families in a school setting. Dissertation Abstracts International, 44, 1695-A.

4095. Murra, J., and Novis, F.W. (1959), Family problems in rehabilitation counseling. Personnel and Guidance Journal, 38, 40-41.

4096. Murray, M.E (1979), Family character analysis. American Journal of Psychoanalysis, 9, 41-53.

4097. Murray, M.E. (1975), A model for family therapy integrating system and subsystem dynamics. Family Therapy, 2, 187-197

4098. Murrell, S.A. (1970), Intra-family variables and psychotherapy outcome research. Psychotherapy: Theory, Research and Practice, 7(1), 19-21

4099. Murrell, S.A., and Stachowiak, J.G. (1965), The family group: Development, structure, and therapy. Journal of Marriage and the Family, 27, 13-18.

4100. Murstein, B.I. (1974), Sex drive, person perception, and marital choice. Archives of Sexual Behavior, 3, 331-348.

4101. Musetto, A.P. (1981), The role of the mental health professional in contested custody: Evaluator of competence or facilitator of change. Journal of Divorce, 4, 69-79.

4102. Musliner, P. (1980), Strategic therapy with families and children. Journal of the American Academy of Child Psychiatry, 19, 101-17.

4103. Mutsaers, W. (1982), Myths in marriage and the family: A literature review. Tijdschrift Voor Psychotherapie, 8, 164-176.

4104. Myads, N.S., and Duehn, W.D. (1977), Measuring effects in behavioral sexual counseling with newly married couples. Journal of Sex Education and Therapy, 3(1), 33-37.

4105. Myers, C.R. (1946), Psychology in marriage and family counseling. Bulletin of Canadian Psychology, 6, 47-48.

4106. Myers, K.M., and Croake, J.W. (1984), Adlerian and analytic theory: A case presentation. American Journal of Family Therapy, 12(1), 48-58.

4107. Myers, M.F. (1982), Counseling the parents of young homosexual male patients. Journal of Homosexuality, 7(2-3), 131.

4108. Myers, M.F. (1984), Treating troubled marriages. American Family Physician, 27, 221-226.

4109. Myers, P.A., and Warkany, S.F. (1977), Working with parents of children with profound developmental retardation: A group approach. Clinical Pediatrics, 16, 367-370.

4110. Myers, R.F. (1959), The impact of psychotherapy on the spouse. Smith College Studies on Social Work, 29, 143-167.

4111. Myerswalls, J.A. (1983), Review of N.J. Anastasiow's The adolescent parent. American Journal of Family Therapy, 11, 83.

4112. NSPCC Battered Children Research Team. (1976), At risk: An account of the work of the Battered Child. Research Department NSPCC. London, England: Routledge and Kegan Paul.

4113. Nace, E.P. (1982), Therapeutic approaches to the alcoholic marriage. Psychiatric Clinics of North America, 5, 543-64.

4114. Nace, E.P., Dephoure, M., Goldberg, M., and Cammarota, C.C. (1982), Treatment priorities in a family-oriented alcoholism program. Journal of Marital and Family Therapy, 8, 143-150.

4115. Nadeau, K.G. (1972), An examination of some effects of the marital enrichment group. Dissertation Abstracts International, 33, 5453B.

4116. Nadelson, C., Bassuk, E.L., Hopps, C.R., and Boutelle, W.E. (1977), Conjoint marital psychotherapy: Treatment techniques. Diseases of the Nervous System, 38, 898-903.

4117.   Nadelson, C.C. (1977), Review of I.D. Glick's and D.R. Kessler's Marital and family therapy. American Journal of Psychiatry, 134, 829.

4118.   Nadelson, C.C. (1978), Marital-therapy from a psychoanalytic-perspective. In: T.J. Paolino and B.S. McCardy (Eds.), Marriage and marital therapy: Psychoanalytic, behavioral and systems theory perspectives. New York: Brunner/Mazel.

4119.   Nadelson, C.C., Bassuk, E.L., Hopps, C.R., and Boutelle, W.E. (1975), Evaluation procedures for conjoint marital psychotherapy. Social Casework, 56, 91-96.

4120.   Nadelson, C.C., Bassuk, E.L., Hopps, C.R., and Boutelle, W.E. (1977), The use of videotape in couples therapy. International Journal of Group Psychotherapy, 27, 241-254.

4121.   Nadelson, C.C., Palonsky, D.C., and Matthews, M.A. (1978), Marital stress and symptom formation in mid life. Psychiatric Opinion, 15(9), 29.

4122.   Nadelson, C.C., Polonsky, D.C., and Mathews, M.A. (1979), Marriage and midlife: The impact of social change. Journal of Clinical Psychiatry, 40, 292-298.

4123.   Nadler, J.H. (1983), Effecting change in stepfamilies: A psychodynamic behavioral group approach. American Journal of Psychotherapy, 37, 100-112.

4124.   Naess, P.O., and Spurkland, I. (1983), Family day treatment for children and adolescents. Acta Paedopsychiatrica, 19, 133-140.

4125.   Naess, P.O., and Spurkland, I. (1984), Family day care for children and adolescents. Tidsskrift fur Norske Laegeforening, 21, 436-439.

4126.   Nagaraja, J. (1974), Anorexia and cyclic vomiting in children: A psychogenic study. Child Psychiatry Quarterly, 7, 1-5.

4127.   Nagy, M. (1980), A multimethodical approach including family-therapeutic goals applied to institutional care. Praxis der Kinderpsychologie und Kinderpsychiatrie, 29, 152-158.

4128.   Nakhla, F., Lolkart, L., and Webster, J. (1969), Treatment of families as inpatients. Family Process, 8, 79-96.

4129.   Napier, A.Y. (1976), The consultation-demonstration interview. Family Process, 15, 419-426.

4130.   Napier, A.Y. (1982), Review of W. Kempler's Experiential psychotherapy within families. Family Process, 21, 494.

4131.   Napier, A.Y., and Whitaker, C.A. (1980), The family crucible. New York: Bantam.

4132.   Napolitani, D., Angelino, P., and Goria, I. (1973), The pathological family and the therapeutic community. Archivio di Psichologia, Neurologia, e Psichiatria, 34, 594-629.

4133.   Naraal, T., Meyer, A., and Brahler, E. (1983), Use of the Glessen Couple Test in family diagnosis. Praxis der Kinderpsychologie und Kinderpsychiatrie, 32, 278-285.

4134.   Narayanan, H.S. (1977), Experiences with group and family therapy in India. International Journal of Group Psychotherapy, 27, 517-521.

4135.   Nardini, M.D., and Ladame, F.G. (1980), Familal approach in adolescent psychiatry. Revue Medicale de la Suisse Remande, 100, 591-600.

4136.   Nash, E.M. (1962), Premarital and marital counseling: Study of practices of North Carolina physicians. Journal of the American Medical Association, 180, 395-401.

4137.   Nash, E.M., Jessner, L., and Abse, D.W. (Eds.) (1964), Marriage counseling in medical practice. Chapel Hill, NC: The University of North Carolina Press.

4138.   Naster, B.J. (1977), Reciprocity counseling: A behavioral approach to marital discords. Personnel and Guidance Journal, 55(9), 515-519.

4139.   Nathan, S.G. (1983), The uses of transference in the treatment of the individual patient in sex therapy. Journal of Sex and Marital Therapy, 9, 210-218.

4140.   National Institute on Drug Abuse, Division of Resource Development (1977), The use of family therapy in drug abuse treatment: A national survey. National Institute for Drug Abuse, Service and Research Report, No. 78, 62213P.

4141.   Nau, L. (1973), Why not family rehabilitation? Journal of Rehabilitation, 39, 14-17.

4142.   Navaitis, G.A. (1983), Experience in psychological consultation in matrimonial conflicts. Psikologicheskii Zhurnal, 4, 70-72.

4143.   Navak, T., Kovarik, J., and Capponi, V. (1983), Experiences with counseling services to foster families. Psychologia A Patopsychologia Dietata, 16, 271-276.

4144.   Negele, R.A. (1976), A study of the effectiveness of brief time-limited psychotherapy with children and their parents. Dissertation Abstracts International, 36, 3172B.

4145.   Neighbour, R. (1982), Family therapy by family doctors. Journal of the Royal College of General Practitioners, 32, 737-42.

4146.   Neilson, D.G. (1978), Communication in counseling marital problems: A survey. Patient Counseling and Health, 1, 13-17.

4147.   Neilson, D.G., and Knox, J.D. (1975), General practitioners and marriage guidance counseling. Journal of the Royal College of General Practitioners, 25, 462-464.

4148.   Nell, R. (1975), The use of dreams in couples' group therapy. Journal of Family Counseling, 3(2), 7-11.

4149.   Nelsen, J.C. (1983), Family treatment: An integrative approach. Englewood Cliffs, NJ: Prentice-Hall.

4150.   Nelson, B. (1970), Neurosis and marital interaction. II. Time sharing and social activity. British Journal of Psychiatry, 117, 47-58.

4151.   Nelson, G. (1973), Therapeutic communication with the alcoholic and his family. Canadian Journal of Psychiatric Nursing, 73, 2080-2086.

4152.   Nelson, J.C. (1985), Review of V. Satir's Conjoint family therapy. Third edition. Social Work, 30(1), 83-84.

4153.   Nelson, M.C. (1975), Psi in the family. Clinical Social Work Journal, 3, 279-285.

4154.   Nelson, R.C., and Friest, W.P. (1980), Marriage enrichment through choice awareness. Journal of Marital and Family Therapy, 6(4), 399-407.

4155.   Nelson, S.B. (1978), Some dynamics of medical marriages. Journal of the Royal College of General Practitioners, 28, 585-586.

4156.   Nelvey, J. (1984), Review of M.P. Nichols' Family therapy: Concepts and methods. American Journal of Psychotherapy, 38(4), 593.

4157.   Neraal, T. (1980), Autonomy—a multi-generational problem: A case of analytic family counseling. Praxis der Kinderpsychologie und Kinderpsychiatrie, 29, 286-292.

4158.   Neto, B.B. (1975), Group psychotherapy of married couples: Communications observed. In: L.R. Wolberg and M.L. Aronson (Eds.), Group therapy in 1975: An overview. New York: Stratton Intercontinental Medical Book Corporation.

4159.   Neto, B.B. (1974), Psychoanalytic therapy in a couples group. Archiv de Psicologia, Neurologia e Pichiatrica, 35(4), 597-607.

4160.   Netzer, C. (1980), Hubris in the family. International Journal of Family Therapy, 2, 22-38.

4161.   Neubeck, G. (1954), Factors affecting group psychotherapy with married couples. Marriage and Family Living, 16, 216-220.

4162.   Neubeck, G. (1950), Group therapeutic aspects of marriage education. Marriage and Family Living, 12, 142-143.

4163.   Neubeck, G. (1973), Toward a theory of marriage counseling: A humanistic approach. Family Coordinator, 22(1), 117-122.

4164.   Neuburger, M. (1983), Hypothesis for systematic work on two levels with families where the identified patient is designated as an addict. Etudes Psychotherapique, 14, 119-125.

4165.   Neumann, A. (1978), (Some aspects of couple therapy.) Analytische Psychologie, 9, 28-36.

4166.   Neumann, G.L. (1978), Beyond pregnancy and childbirth: The use of anticipatory guidance in preparing couples for postpartum stress. Dissertation Abstracts International, 38, 5582B.

4167. Nevejan, M. (1976), Family therapy and therapy for married couples. Nederlands Tijdschrift voor Generskunde, 120, 2314-2324.

4168. Neville, W.G. (1972), An analysis of personality types and their differential response to marital enrichment groups. Dissertation Abstracts International, 32, 6766A.

4169. Nevin, D. (1974), Multiple family therapy, the "overlooked" treatment approach: It's alive and ready for use. American Journal of Orthopsychiatry, 44, 223-227.

4170. New, D.C. (1980), A study of leisure activity patterns of couples in marital therapy. Dissertation Abstracts International, 41, 945-A.

4171. Newfield, N.A. (1985), Predicting divorce at marital therapy intake: A discriminant analysis model. Dissertation Abstracts International, 46, 1748-A.

4172. Newman, H.M. (1982), Talk about a past relationship partner: Metacommunicative implications. American Journal of Family Therapy, 10, 24-32.

4173. Newman, L.W. (1976), Treatment for the parents of feminine boys. American Journal of Psychiatry, 133, 683-687.

4174. Newman, M.B. (1969), Therapeutic intervention in a community child psychiatric clinic. Journal of the American Academy of Child Psychiatry, 8, 692-710.

4175. Ney, P.G. (1967), Combined therapies in a family group. Canadian Journal of Psychiatry, 12, 379-385.

4176. Ney, P.G. (1976), Combined approaches in the treatment of conflicted children and their families. Canada's Mental Health, 24, 2-6.

4177. Ney, P.G. (1976), Combined approaches in the treatment of latency children and their families. Canadian Psychiatric Association Journal, 21, 212-216.

4178. Ney, P.G., and Mills, W.A. (1976), A time-limited treatment program for children and their families. Hospital and Community Psychiatry, 27, 878-879.

4179. Nichols, J.F. (1980), The marital/family therapist as an expert witness: Some thoughts and suggestions. Journal of Marital and Family Therapy, 6, 293-299.

4180. Nichols, M.P. (1984), Family therapy: Concepts and methods. New York: Gardner Press.

4181. Nichols, W.C. (1980), Review of T.J. Paolino and B.S. McCrady's Marriage and marital therapy: Psychoanalytic, behavioral and systems theory perspectives. Family Relations, 29, 136.

4182. Nichols, W.C. (1979), Doctoral programs in marital and family therapy. Journal of Marital and Family Therapy, 5, 23-28.

4183.   Nichols, W.C. (1979), Education of marriage and family therapists: Some trends and implications. Journal of Marital and Family Therapy, 5, 19-28.

4184.   Nichols, W.C., Jr. (1973), The field of marriage counseling: A brief overview. Family Coordinator, 22(1), 3-13.

4185.   Nielsen, E., and Kaslow, F.W. (1980), Consultation in family therapy. American Journal of Family Therapy, 8, 35-42.

4186.   Nierenberg, M.A. (1972), Self-help first: A critical evaluation of "the family therapist's own family." International Journal of Psychiatry, 10, 34-41.

4187.   Nimorwicz, P., and Klein, R.H. (1982), Psychosocial aspects of hemophilia in families: II. Intervention strategies and procedures. Clinical Psychology Review, 35, 171-181.

4188.   Nobler, H. (1983), The effects of therapist variables in group psychotherapy. In L.R. Wolberg and M.L. Aronson (Eds.), Group and family therapy 1982. New York: Brunner/Mazel.

4189.   Nocetti, J.C. (1975), On couple and family therapy. Acta Psiquiatrica y Psicologia de America Latina, 21, 129-136.

4190.   Noone, R.J., and Reddig, R.L. (1976), Case studies in the family treatment of drug abuse. Family Process, 15, 325-332.

4191.   Nordlicht, S. (1979), Effects of stress on police officer and family. New York State Journal of Medicine, 79, 400-401.

4192.   Nordlie, E.B., and Reed, S.C. (1962), Follow-up adoption counseling for children of possible racial admixture. Child Welfare, 41, 297-304.

4193.   Noreen, C.S. (1975), Multiple family group treatment: A model of social work practice. Dissertation Abstracts International, 36, 4027A.

4194.   Norem, R.H., and Olson, D.H. (1983), Interaction patterns in premarital couples: Typological assessment over time. American Journal of Family Therapy, 11, 25-37.

4195.   Norfleet, M.A., Hammett, B.C., Lichte, S.L., Lukensmeyer, W.W., and Payne, B.A. (1983), Helping families cope with chronic pain: An integral part of an interdisciplinary and multimodal treatment program. In L.R. Wolberg and M.L. Aronson (Eds.), Group and family therapy 1982. New York: Brunner/Mazel.

4196.   Norman, E. (1977), Impact of changing sex roles and family therapy. In: T.J. Buckley, J.J. McCarty, E. Norman, and M.A. Quaranta (Eds.), New directions in family therapy. Oceanside Dabor Science Publications.

4197.   Norton, F.H. (1976), Counseling parents of the mentally retarded child. The School Counselor, 23(3), 200-205.

4198.   Norton, W.K. (1972), Empathic ability and adjustment in marriage. Dissertation Abstracts International, 32, 3571A.

4199.   Novak, D.W., and Busko, B.P. (1974), Teaching old dogs new tricks: Issues in the training of family therapists. Psychiatric Forum, 4, 14-20.

4200.   Novak, T., and Stepanik, J. (1975), The use of group psychagogics in children and parents to solve educational problems. Psychologia a Patopsychologia Dietata, 10, 351-357.

4201.   Nover, R.A., Williams, D.W., and Ward, D.B. (1981), Preventive intervention with infants in multi-risk-factor families. Childcare Today, 10, 27-31.

4202.   Nulman, E. (1983), Family therapy and advocacy: Directions for the future. Social Work, 28, 19-22.

4203.   Nunally, E.W., Miller, S., and Wackman, D.B. (1975), The Minnesota Couples Communication Program. Small Group Behavior, 6, 57-71.

4204.   Nurenberg, M.A. (1983), Review of M.R. Lansky's Family therapy and major psychopathology. Psychoanalysis Quarterly, 52, 301-304.

4205.   Nurse, J. (1972), Retarded infants and their parents: A group for fathers and mothers. British Journal of Social Work, 2, 159-174.

4206.   O'Brien, A., and Loudon, P. (1985), Redressing the balance: Involving children in therapy. Journal of Family Therapy, 7(2), 81.

4207.   O'Connor, F. (1972), Therapy for troubled marriages. Nebraska Medical Journal, 57, 93-96.

4208.   O'Connor, J.J. (1985), Family therapy with school-related problems. Family Process, 24(1), 131-132.

4209.   O'Connor, J.J. (1983), Why can't I get hives: Brief strategic therapy with an obsessional child. Family Process, 22, 201-209.

4210.   O'Connor, P.A. (1975), A model of power and coalition formation in conjoint marriage counseling. Family Coordinator, 24, 55-63.

4211.   O'Connor, W.J. (1977), Some observations on the use of T.A. in marriage counseling. Journal of Marriage and Family Counseling, 3, 27-34.

4212.   O'Dell, S.L. (1979), Media-assisted parent training: Alternative models. Behavior Therapy, 10, 103-110.

4213.   O'Farrel, T. (1979), Behavioral marital therapy for alcoholics and spouses: A comprehensive annotated bibliography. Catalog of Selected Documents in Psychology, 9, 8-9.

4214.   O'Farrel, T.J. (1983), Review of M.M. Ohlsen's Marriage counseling in groups. Journal of Marital and Family Therapy, 9, 109.

4215.   O'Farrell, T.J., Cutter, H.S.G., and Floyd, F.J. (1985), Evaluating behavioral marital therapy for male alcoholics: Effects on marital adjustment and communication from before to after treatment. Behavior Therapy, 16(2), 147.

4216.   O'Farrell, T.J., and Cutter, H.S.G. (1984), Behavioral marital therapy
        for male alcoholics: Clinical procedures from a treatment outcome
        study in progress. American Journal of Family Therapy, 12(3), 33-45.

4217.   O'Gara, E.A. (1959), A follow-up study of school referrals to a family
        agency. Smith College, 30, 36-62.

4218.   O'Hagan, K. (1984), Family crisis intervention in social services.
        Journal of Family Therapy, 6(2), 149-182.

4219.   O'Hare, C., and Ansel, A. (1975), Group training in family therapy: The
        student's perspective. Journal of Marriage and Family Counseling, 1,
        157-162.

4220.   O'Leary, K.D., Turkewitz, H., and Taffel, S.J. (1973), Parent and
        therapist evaluation of behavior therapy in a child psychological clinic.
        Journal of Consulting and Clinical Psychology, 41(2), 279-283.

4221.   O'Leary, K.D., and Arias, I. (1983), The influence of marital therapy on
        sexual satisfaction. Journal of Sex and Marital Therapy, 9, 171-181.

4222.   O'Leary, K.D., and Turkewitz, H. (1981), A comparative outcome study
        of behavioral marital therapy and communication therapy. Journal of
        Marital and Family Therapy, 7, 159-169.

4223.   O'Leary, K.D., and Turkewitz, H. (1978), Marital therapy from a
        behavioral perspective. In: T.J. Paolino and B.S. McCardy (Eds.),
        Marriage and marital therapy: Psychoanalytic, behavioral, and systems
        theory perspectives. New York: Brunner/Mazel.

4224.   O'Leary, K.D., and Turkewitz, H. (1978), Methodological errors in
        marital and child treatment research. Journal of Consulting and Clinical
        Psychology, 46(4), 747-758.

4225.   O'Neil, C.F. (1971), Family therapy in treatment of delinquency.
        American Journal of Orthopsychiatry, 41, 295.

4226.   O'Neil, C.F. (1969), Working with families of delinquent boys. Children,
        16, 198-202.

4227.   O'Neill, J. (1965), Siblings of the retarded. II. Individual counseling.
        Children, 12, 229-237.

4228.   O'Shea, M., and Jessee, E. (1982), Values, ethics, legalities and the
        family therapist: I. Ethical, value, and professional conflicts in systems
        therapy. Family Therapy Collections, 1, 1-21.

4229.   O'Sullivan, S., Berger, M., and Foster, M. (1984), The utility of
        structural family therapy nomenclature: Between clinician agreement in
        the conjoint family assessment interview. Journal of Marital and Family
        Therapy, 10(2), 179-184.

4230.   Oakey, R.C. (1961), Meeting the problems of intake in child guidance
        and marital counseling. Mental Hygiene, 45, 53-60.

4231.   Oancea, C. (1979), Family psychotherapy from the viewpoint of the
        child psychiatrist. Revue de Medicine Interne, 24, 161-172.

4232.   Oberfield, R., and Cilotta, C. (1983), A school-age boys/single mothers group. Journal of the American Academy of Child Psychiatry, 22, 375-381.

4233.   Oberfield, R.A. (1981), Family therapy with adolescents: Treatment of a teenage girl with globus hystericus and weight loss. Journal of the American Academy of Child Psychiatry, 20, 822-33.

4234.   Occhetti, A.E., and Occhetti, D.B. (1981), Group therapy with married couples. Social Casework, 62(2), 74-79.

4235.   Ockel, H.H. (1981), Potential interference in connection with intentional or unintentional transitions between individual and family therapy. Zeitschrift fur Psychosomatische Medizun und Psychoanalyse, 27, 307-317.

4236.   Ockel, H.H. (1970), Problems of parent counseling due to changes in our society. Praxis der Kinderpsychologie und Kinderpsychiatrie, 19(8), 282-287.

4237.   Odegard, M.M. (1983), The efficacy of a proactive marital enrichment program for dual-career couples. Dissertation Abstracts International, 44, 1736-A.

4238.   Offer, D., and Vanderstoep, E. (1974), Indications and contraindications for family therapy. Adolescent Psychiatry, 3, 249-262.

4239.   Offer, D., and Vanderstoep, E. (1975), Indications and contraindications for family therapy. In: M. Sugar (Ed.), The adolescent in group and family therapy. New York: Brunner/Mazel.

4240.   Ogden, G., and Zevin, A. (1976), When a family needs therapy: A practical assessment guide for parents, lay therapists, and professionals. New York: Harper and Row.

4241.   Ohlson, D.H., Russell, C.S., and Sprenkle, D.H. (1983). Circumplex model of marital and family systems: VI Theoretical update. Family Process, 22, 69-83.

4242.   Ohlson, E.L. (1974), The meaningfulness of play for children and parents: An effective counseling strategy. Journal of Family Counseling, 2(1), 53-54.

4243.   Ohlson, E.L., and Engin, A.W. (1975), IDENTICOM: A new marriage counseling strategy. Journal of Family Counseling, 3, 36-39.

4244.   Okun, B.F., and Rappaport, L.J. (1980), Working with families: An introduction to family therapy. Seituate, MA: Duxbury Press.

4245.   Olds, V. (1977), Use of co-therapists in family treatment. In: T.J. Buckley, J.J. McCarthy, E. Norman, and M.A. Quaranta (Eds.), New direction in family therapy. Oceanside: Dabor Science Publications.

4246.   Olie, D.A. (1982), The integration of family therapy in a psychiatric day hospital. Journal of Family Therapy, 4, 329-344.

4247.   Oliver, B.J. (1974), Family therapy: An institutional approach. Canadian Journal of Psychiatric Nursing, 15, 11-12.

4248.   Oliver, G.W. (1982), A cancer patient and her family: A case study. American Journal of Clinical Hypnosis, 24, 156-160.

4249.   Oliveri, M.E. (1981), Theory-based empirical classification of family problem-solving behavior. Family Process, 20, 409-418.

4250.   Oliveri, M.E., and Reiss, D. (1982), Family schemata of social relationships. Family Process, 21, 295-312.

4251.   Oliveri, M.E., and Reiss, D. (1982), Family styles of construing the social environment: A perspective on variation among non-clinical families. In F. Walsh (Ed.), Normal family processes. New York: Guilford Press.

4252.   Oliveri, M.E., and Reiss, D. (1984), Family concepts and their measurement: Things are seldom what they seem. Family Process, 23(1), 33-48.

4253.   Olsen, E.H. (1971), The marriage: A basic unit for psychotherapy. American Journal of Psychiatry, 127, 945-948.

4254.   Olsinski, P.K. (1980), A study of the effect of some Minnesota Multiphasic Personality characteristics on the adjustment of married, marriage-counseled, and divorced individuals. Dissertation Abstracts International, 41, 539-A.

4255.   Olson, D.H. (1979), Circumplex model of marital and family systems, cohesion and adaptability dimensions, family types, and clinical applications. Family Process, 18, 3-28.

4256.   Olson, D.H. (1970), Marital and family therapy: Integrative review and critique. Journal of Marriage and Family Counseling, 32, 501-538.

4257.   Olson, D.H., Russell, C.S. and Sprenkle, D.H. (1983), Circumplex model of marital and family systems: VI. Theoretical update. Family Process, 22, 69-83.

4258.   Olson, D.H., Russell, C.S., and Sprenkle, D.H. (1980), Marital and family therapy: A decade review. Journal of Marriage and the Family, 42(4), 973-993.

4259.   Olson, D.H., and Craddock, A.E. (1980), Circumplex model of marital and family systems: Application to Australian families. Australian Journal of Sex, Marriage and Family, 1(2), 53-69.

4260.   Olson, D.H., and Sprenkle, D.H. (1976), Emerging trends in treating relationships. Journal of Marriage and Family Counseling, 2(4), 317-329.

4261.   Olson, D.H., and Straus, M.A. (1972), A diagnostic tool for marital and family therapy: The SIMFAM technique. Family Coordinator, 21, 251-258.

4262.   Olson, U.F., and Pegg, P.F. (1979), Direct open supervision: A team approach. Family Process, 18, 463-469.

4263.   Oltmanns, T.F., Broderick, J.E., and Oleary, K.D. (1977), Marital adjustment and the efficacy of behavior therapy with children. Journal of Consulting and Clinical Psychology, 45(5), 724-729.

4264.   Openlander, P., and Searight, H.R. (1983), Family therapy perspectives in the college counseling center. Journal of College Student Personnel, 24, 423-427.

4265.   Opirhory, G., and Peters, G.A. (1982), Counseling intervention strategies for families with the less than perfect newborn. Personnel and Guidance Journal, 60, 451-455.

4266.   Opirhory, G.J. (1979), Counseling the parents of a critically ill newborn. Jogn Nursing, 8(3), 179-182.

4267.   Orchen, M.D. (1984), A treatment efficacy study comparing relaxation training, EMG biofeedback, and family therapy among heavy drinkers. Dissertation Abstracts International, 45, 2565-A.

4268.   Orcutt, B.A. (1977), Family treatment of poverty level families. Social Casework, 58, 92-100.

4269.   Orfanidis, M.M., and Mueller, P.S. (1976), Family therapy in the treatment of schizophrenia: A model of therapy based on a relabeling of schizophrenia as a family system disturbance. Family Process, 15(2), 179-191.

4270.   Orford, J. (1981), Review of I.D. Glick and D.R. Kessler's Marital and family therapy. 2nd Edition. British Journal of Clinical Psychology, 21, 231.

4271.   Orford, J. (1984), The prevention and management of alcohol problems in the family setting: A review of work carried out in English-speaking countries. Alcohol, 19, 109-122.

4272.   Orgun, I.N. (1973), Playroom setting for diagnostic family interviews. American Journal of Psychiatry, 130, 540-542.

4273.   Ormont, L.R. (1962), The use of group psychotherapy in the training of marriage counselors and family life educators. Marriage and Family Living, 24, 144-150.

4274.   Ormsby, R. (1950), Group psychiatric consultation in a family casework agency. Social Casework, 31, 361-365.

4275.   Orten, J.D. (1978), Organizing concepts in family therapy. International Journal of Family Counseling, 6(1), 9-16.

4276.   Osberg, J.W. (1962), Initial impressions of the use of short-term family group conferences. Family Process, 1(2), 236-244.

4277.   Osborn, E.B. (1983), Training paraprofessional family therapists in a Christian setting. Journal of Psychology and Christianity, 2, 56-61.

4278.   Osborne, D., Swensen, W.M., and Hardman, J.B. (1972), Counseling readiness and changes in perception of spouse during intensive group therapy. Psychological Reports, 31(1), 208-210.

4279.   Osborne, K. (1983), Women in families: Feminist therapy and family system. Journal of Family Therapy, 5, 1-10.

4280. Ostby, C.H. (1968), Conjoint group therapy with prisoners and their families. Family Process, 7, 184-201.

4281. Ostensen, K.W. (1981), The runaway crisis: Is family therapy the answer? American Journal of Family Therapy, 9, 3-12.

4282. Osterweil, J. (1962), Symposium: Family treatment of schizophrenia. Discussion. Family Process, 1(1), 141-145.

4283. Osterweis, M., Bush, P.J., and Zuckerman, A.E. (1979), Family context as a predictor of individual medicine use. Social Science Medicine, 12A, 287-291.

4284. Ostrov, S. (1978), Sex therapy with orthodox Jewish couples. Journal of Sex and Marital Therapy, 4, 266.

4285. Ottenberg, P. (1977), Violence in the family: Abused wives and children. Bulletin of The American Academy of Psychiatry and the Law, 5, 380-390.

4286. Otto, H.A. (1959), The use of inter-action centered schedules in group work with premarital couples. Group Psychotherapy, Psychodrama and Sociometry, 12, 223-229.

4287. Otto, H.A. (Ed.) (1976), Marriage and family enrichment: New perspectives and programs. Nashville, TN: Abingdon.

4288. Ounsted, C., Oppenheimer, R., and Lindsay, J. (1974), Aspects of bonding failure: The psychopathology and psychotherapeutic treatment of families of battered children. Developmental Medicine and Child Neurology, 16, 447-456.

4289. Overbeck, A. (1979), Reciprocity of intrapsychic disturbance and interpersonal processes in anorexia nervosa within the setting of family therapy. Zeitschrift fur Psychosomatiche Medizin und Psychoanalyse, 25, 216-239.

4290. Overbeck, A., Brahler, E., and Klein, H. (1982), The connection between verbal behavior and experience of communication in the family therapy interview. Praxis der Kinderpsychologie und Kinderpsychiatrie, 31, 125-143.

4291. Overbeck, A., Klein, H., Meyer, A., and Brahler, E. (1983), Communication experience in the in-family therapy initial interview. Psychotherapie Psychosomatik-Medizinische Psychologie, 33, 20-28.

4292. Overturf, J. (1976), Marital therapy: Toleration of differentness. Journal of Marriage and Family Counseling, 2(3), 235-241.

4293. Oxley, G.B. (1975), Short-term therapy with student couples. Social Casework, 54(4), 216-223.

4294. Padberg, J. (1975), Bargaining to improve communications in conjoint family therapy. Perspectives in Psychiatric Care, 13, 68-72.

4295. Padgett, V.R. (1983), Videotape replay in marital therapy. Psychotherapy: Theory, Research, and Practice, 20, 232-242.

4296.   Padreco, A.E. (1976), Interaction therapy: A behavioral approach to family psychotherapy. Dissertation Abstracts International, 37, 2520-2521B.

4297.   Paff-Bergen, L.A. (1985), Videotaped modeling of a strategic family therapy intervention: Impact of known and unknown models. Dissertation Abstracts International, 46, 2095-B.

4298.   Paget, H. (1982), The context of family therapy re-examined: Comment. Journal of Family Therapy, 4(2), 201.

4299.   Pakesch, E. (1972), Group therapy and family. Dynamische Psychiatrie, 5, 59-74.

4300.   Palacio, E.F. (1981), Possibilities for short-term parent-child therapy, with regard to questionable Oedipal development. Psychiatrie de L'Enfant, 24, 419-444.

4301.   Palazzoli, M.S. (1970), (Context and metacontext in family psychotherapy.) Archivo di Psicologia, Neurologia, e Psichiatria, 31, 203-211. (Italian)

4302.   Palazzoli, M.S., Boscolo, L., Cecchin, G.F., and Prata, G. (1974), The treatment of children through brief therapy of their parents. Family Process, 13(4), 429-442.

4303.   Palazzoli, M.S., Boscolo, L., Cecchin, G.F., and Prata, G. (1977), Family rituals: A powerful tool in family therapy. Family Process, 16, 445-453.

4304.   Palazzoli, M.S., Boscolo, L., Cecchin, G.F., and Prata, G. (1978), A ritualized prescription in family therapy: Odd days and even days. Journal of Marriage and Family Counseling, 4(3), 3-10.

4305.   Palisi, A.T., and Ruzicka, M.F. (1981), Panel analysis of approaches to family therapy. Small Group Behavior, 12(2), 159-166.

4306.   Palmer, S. (1983), Ethical and social issues in individual and family based theories: A framework for integration. Dissertation Abstracts International, 43, 3038-B.

4307.   Palmer-Erbs, V.K. (1978), Interventions with the adolescent drug user and the family. Issues in Comprehensive Pediatric Nursing, 3, 15-24.

4308.   Palombo, S.R. (1967), Recognition of parents of schizophrenics from excerpts of family therapy interviews. Psychiatry, 30, 405-412.

4309.   Panar, M.A., Jr. (1977), Toward an integrative approach in marriage counseling. International Journal of Family Counseling, 5(1), 41-43.

4310.   Panitz, D.R., McConchie, R.D., Sauber, S.R., and Fonseca, J.A. (1983), The role of machismo and the Hispanic family in the etiology and treatment of alcoholism in Hispanic American males. American Journal of Family Therapy, 11, 31-44.

4311.   Pannor, R., and Nerlove, E.A. (1977), Fostering understanding between adolescents and adoptive parents through group experiences. Child Welfare, 56, 537-545.

4312.   Paolino, T.J., and McCrady, B.S. (Eds.) (1978), Marriage and marital therapy: Psychoanalytic, behavioral and systems theory perspectives. New York: Brunner/Mazel.

4313.   Paolino, T.J., McCrady, B.S., and Diamond, S. (1978), Statistics on alcoholic marriages: An overview. International Journal of Addiction, 13, 1285-1293.

4314.   Papadopoulos, D.A., Buchinsky, V., and Powers, J. (1983), Senile dementia. Journal of Family Practice, 12, 201-218.

4315.   Papanek, H. (1965), Group psychotherapy with married couples. Current Psychiatric Therapy, 5, 157-163.

4316.   Papp, P. (1982), Staging reciprocal metaphors in a couples group. Family Process, 21, 453-467.

4317.   Papp, P.(Ed.) (1979), Family therapy: Full length case studies. New York: Gardner.

4318.   Papp, P., Silverstein, O., and Carter, E. (1973), Family sculpting in preventive work with "well families." Family Process, 12, 197-200.

4319.   Paquay-Weinstock, M. Appelboom-Fondu, J., and Dopchie, N. (1979), Influence of a chronic disease on the evolution of the family dynamics. Study of 25 families of hemophilic children. Acta Paedopsychiatrica, (Basel), 44, 219-228.

4320.   Paquin, M.J.R. (1977), The status of family and marital therapy outcomes: Methodological and substantive considerations. Canadian Psycholgical Review, 18, 221-232.

4321.   Paquin, M.J.R. (1981), Self-monitoring of marital communication in family therapy. Social Casework, 62, 267-272.

4322.   Parad, L.G. (1969), Planned short-term treatment: A study of 1656 family service and child guidance cases. Dissertation Abstracts International, 29, 3672A.

4323.   Pardeck, J.T. (1981), The current state and new direction of family therapy. Family Therapy, 8(1), 21-27.

4324.   Pardeck, J.T. (1982), Family policy: An ecological approach supporting family therapy treatment. Family Therapy, 9, 163-165.

4325.   Pardeck, J.T., Wolf, V., Killion, S., and Silverstein, G. (1983), Individual therapy vs. family therapy: Which is more effective? Family Therapy, 10, 173-181.

4326.   Parham, I.A., Priddy, J.M., Mcgovern, T.V., and Richman, C.M. (1982), Group psychotherapy with the elderly: Problems and prospects. Psychotherapy: Theory, Research and Practice, 19, 437-443.

4327.   Park, L.D. (1979), Summer family conference. Adventure in counseling families with handicapped children. Rehabilitation Literature, 40, 108-113.

4328.   Parker, G.W. (1981), Psychoanalysis and serendipity: Their place in family therapy. Journal of Child Psychotherapy, 7, 103-110.

4329.   Parker, S.B. (1977), The occurrence and sequence of positions and postural shifts during conjoint marital therapy. Dissertation Abstracts International, 38, 3900-B.

4330.   Parks, J.H. (1967), Group psychotherapy with married couples: New variations in technique. Pastoral Counseling, 3(1), 4-11.

4331.   Parloff, M.B. (1961), The family in psychotherapy. Archives of General Psychiatry, 4, 445-451.

4332.   Parry, J.K., and Young, A.K. (1978), The families as a system in hospital based social work. Health and Social Work, 3(2), 54-70.

4333.   Parsloe, P. (1967), Summing up of the study course: Thinking about the future of child guidance. British Journal of Psychiatric Social Work, 9, 90-96.

4334.   Parsons, B.V. (1972), Family crisis intervention: Therapy outcome study. Dissertation Abstracts International, 32, 6657-B.

4335.   Parsons, B.V., and Alexander, J.F. (1973), Short-term family intervention: A therapy outcome study. Journal of Consulting and Clinical Psychology, 41, 195-201.

4336.   Parsons, B.V., and Alexander, J.F. (1974), Short-term family intervention: A therapy outcome study. Journal of Asthma Research, 11, 127-138.

4337.   Partridge, W. (1960), Deadline for family care. Mental Hospital, 11, 21-24.

4338.   Pasmore, J. (1975), What is marital therapy? Psychotherapy and Psychosomatics, 25(1-6), 149-153.

4339.   Pasnau, R.O., Myer, M., Davis, L.J., Lloyd, R., and Kline, G. (1976), Coordinated group psychotherapy of children and parents. International Journal of Group Psychotherapy, 26(1), 89-103.

4340.   Paterson, E.S. (1978), Comparison of group marital treatments: Behavior modification, communication, and combined communication and behavior modification. Dissertation Abstracts International, 38, 5037-B.

4341.   Patrick, J.D., and Wander, R.S. (1974), Treatment of the adolescent crisis patient. Psychotherapy: Theory, Research and Practice, 11, 246-249.

4342.   Patterson, G.R. (1980), Social learning approach to family intervention: Coercive family process. 3. Eugene, OR: Castalia.

4343.   Patterson, G.R., and Reid, J.B. (1973), Intervention for families of aggressive boys: A replication study. Australian and New Zealand Journal of Psychiatry, 7, 146-154.

4344.   Patterson, G.R., Hops, H., and Weiss, R.L. (1975), Interpersonal skills
        training for couples in early stages of conflict. Journal of Marriage and
        the Family, 37, 295-304.

4345.   Patterson, J.M. (1984), Review of A.T. McCollum's The chronically ill
        child: A guide for parents and professionals. American Journal of
        Family Therapy, 12(1), 79-80.

4346.   Pattison, E.M. (1973), Group treatment methods suitable for family
        practice. Public Health Review, 2, 247-266.

4347.   Pattison, E.M. (1982), Management of religious issues in family
        therapy. International Journal of Family Therapy, 4, 140-163.

4348.   Pattison, E.M., DeFrancis, D., Wood, P., Frazier, H., and Crowder, J.
        (1975), A psychosocial kinship model for family therapy. American
        Journal of Psychiatry, 132, 1246-1251.

4349.   Patzer, H. (1969), Inclusion of the parents in the rehabilitation of the
        cerebral palsied child. Beitraege zur Orthopaedie und Traumatologie, 16,
        344-349.

4350.   Paul, K.L. (1982), Brief family therapy utilizing graph analysis.
        American Family Physician, 25, 183-187.

4351.   Paul, N.L. (1972), Changes?: A critical evaluation of "the family
        therapist's own family." International Journal of Psychiatry, 10, 42-44.

4352.   Paul, N.L. (1984), Review of J. Willi's Couples in collusion.
        Contemporary Psychology, 29(3), 256.

4353.   Paul, N.L., and Bloom, J.D. (1970), Multi-family therapy: Secrets and
        scapegoating in family crisis. International Journal of Group
        Psychotherapy, 20, 37-47.

4354.   Paul, N.L., and Grosser, G.H. (1965), Operational mourning and its role
        in conjoint family therapy. Community Mental Health, 1, 339-345.

4355.   Paul, N.L., and Paul, B.B. (1975), A marital puzzle: Transgenerational
        analysis in marriage counseling. New York: W.W. Norton.

4356.   Paul, N.L., and Paul, B.B. (1978), The use of EST as adjunctive therapy
        to family focused treatment. Journal of Marriage and Family
        Counseling, 4(1), 51-61.

4357.   Paul, N.L., and Paul, B.B. (1982), Death and changes in sexual
        behavior. In F. Walsh (Ed.), Normal family processes. New York:
        Guilford Press.

4358.   Paul, T.D., Brandt, I.K., Christian, J.C., Jackson, C.E., Nance, C.S., and
        Nance, W.E. (1978), Analysis of serus amino acid levels by the twin
        study method and comparison with family studies. Progress in Clinical
        and Biological Research, 24, 157-163.

4359.   Paulson, D. (1984), Review of A.S. Gurman's Questions and answers in
        the practice of family therapy. British Journal of Medical Psychology,
        57(1), 103.

4360.   Paulson, M.J. (1980), Review of J.A. Kroth's Child sexual abuse:
         Analysis of a family therapy approach. Contemporary Psychology, 25,
         728.

4361.   Paulson, M.J., Savino, A.B., Chaleff, A.B., Sanders, R.W., Frisch, F., and
         Dunn, R. (1974), Parents of the battered child: A multidisciplinary
         group therapy approach to life threatening behavior. Suicide and Life
         Threatening Behavior, 4(1), 18-31.

4362.   Paulson, M.J., Strouse, L., and Chaleff, A. (1980), Further observations
         on child abuse: An a posteriori examination of group therapy notes.
         Journal of Clinical Child Psychology, 9(3), 241-246.

4363.   Pavlin, S., and Rabkin, R. (1975), Family therapy: Some questions and
         answers. Journal of Family Counseling, 3, 16-26.

4364.   Paynan, H.M. (1979), Cancer in married couples. Southern Medical
         Journal, 72, 17-19.

4365.   Payne, J. (1978), Talking about children: An examination of accounts
         about reproduction and family life. Journal of Biosocial Science, 10,
         367-374.

4366.   Peabody, S.A. (1982), Alternative life styles to monogamous marriage:
         Variants of normal behavior in psychotherapy clients. Family Relations,
         31(3), 425.

4367.   Pearce, J., and Friedman, L. (Eds.) (1980), Family therapy: Combining
         psychodynamic and family systems approaches. New York: Grune and
         Stratton.

4368.   Pearlman, S. (1979), Convergence of therapist and client goals in the
         initial stage of marital counseling and its relationship to continuance in
         treatment. Dissertation Abstracts International, 39 4503-A.

4369.   Pearlman, T.W. (1974), Domestic relations: Advice for the physician.
         Rhode Island Medical Journal, 57, 108-109.

4370.   Pearne, D.H. (1977), Conjoint expressive drawing in couples
         psychotherapy. Dissertation Abstracts International, 38, 1897-B.

4371.   Pearson, D.H. (1978), A marriage enrichment program: Its effect on the
         intimacy of couples successfully terminated from remedial marriage
         therapy. Dissertation Abstracts International, 39, 2516-B.

4372.   Pearson, J.S. (1973), Family support and counseling in Huntington's
         disease. Psychiatric Forum, 4, 46-50.

4373.   Peck, B.B. (1974), Psychotherapy with fragmented (father-absent)
         families. Family Therapy, 1, 27-42.

4374.   Peck, B.B. (1971), Reading disorders: Have we overlooked something?
         Journal of School Psychology, 9, 182-190.

4375.   Peck, B.B. (1976), Therapy with disrupted families. Journal of
         Contemporary Psychotherapy, 7(1), 60-66.

4376.   Peck, B.B. (1975), Therapeutic handling of marital infidelity. Journal of Family Counseling, 3, 52-58.

4377.   Peck, B.B., and Schroeder, D. (1976), Psychotherapy with the father absent military family. Journal of Marriage and Family Counseling, 21(1), 23-30.

4378.   Peck, B.B., and Swarts, E. (1975), The premarital impasse. Family Therapy, 2, 1-10.

4379.   Peck, H.B. (1962), Group treatment approaches to the family. International Journal of Group Psychotherapy, 12, 131.

4380.   Pellman, R., and Platt, R. (1974), Three families in search of a director. American Journal of Orthopsychiatry, 44, 224-225.

4381.   Peltz, R.A. (1983), The war at home: Crisis of the contemporary couple and symptomatic child. Dissertation Abstracts International, 43, 3739-B.

4382.   Pendergrass, V.E. (1975), Marriage counseling with lesbian couples. Psychotherapy: Theory, Research and Practice, 12, 93-96.

4383.   Pent, C.M. (1968), Premarital and marriage counseling. American Annals of the Deaf, 113, 936-938.

4384.   Peplau, H.E. (1969), Professional closeness...as a special kind of involvement with a patient client, or family group. Nursing Forum, 8, 342.

4385.   Percy, W.H. (1982), Righting the wrongs: The impact of family therapy on everyday life. Dissertation Abstracts International, 42, 4246-B.

4386.   Perelman, J.S. (1960), Problems encountered in group psychotherapy of married couples. International Journal of Group Psychotherapy, 10, 136-142.

4387.   Perez, J.G. (1975), Child therapy conducted through family therapy. Revista Psicologie de al Universidad Monterrey, 4, 15-21.

4388.   Perez-Upegui, P. (1975), The method of personal interaction workshops applied to groups of married couples. Revista Colombia Psiquiatrica, 4(2), 209-221.

4389.   Perez-Upegui, P. (1975), Personal interaction laboratories for married couples. Acta Psiquiatrica y Psicologia de America Latina, 21, 28-34.

4390.   Perlberg, M. (1979), Family, heal thyself. Hospitals, 53, 82.

4391.   Perlman, L.M., and Bender, S.S. (1975), Operant reinforcement with structural family therapy in training anorexia nervosa. Journal of Family Counseling, 3, 38-46.

4392.   Perlmutter, L.H., Engel, T., and Sager, C.J. (1982), The incest taboo: Loosened sexual boundaries in remarried families. Journal of Sex and Marital Therapy, 8, 83-96.

4393.   Perlmutter, M.S., Loeb, D.G., Gumpert, G., Ohara, F., and Higbie, J.S. (1967), Family diagnosis and therapy using videotape playback. American Journal of Orthopsychiatry, 37(5), 900-905.

4394.   Perlmutter, M.S., and Hatfield, E. (1980), Intimacy, intentional metacommunication and second order change. American Journal of Family Therapy, 8, 17-23.

4395.   Perlmutter, R.A. (1983), Family involvement in psychiatric emergencies. Hospital and Community Psychiatry, 34, 255-257.

4396.   Perlmutter, R.A., and Babineau, R. (1983), The use of dreams in couples' therapy. Psychiatry, 46, 66-72.

4397.   Perosa, L.M., and Perosa, S.L. (1981), School counselor's use of structural family therapy with learning-disabled students. School Counselor, 29, 152-155.

4398.   Perr, M. (1979), Social and cultural influences on the doctor's family. American Journal of Psychoanalysis, 39, 71-80.

4399.   Perrault, C. (1979), Family support in the neonatal intensive care unit. Dimensions of Health Service, 56, 16-18.

4400.   Perrelman, J.S. (1960), Problems encountered in group psychotherapy of married couples. International Journal of Group Psychotherapy, 10, 136-142.

4401.   Perrez, M. (1980), Review of M. Andolfi's Family therapy: An interactional approach. Psychologie, 39, 172.

4402.   Perris, C., and Perris, H. (1978), Status within the family and early life experiences in patients with affective disordered and cycloid psychosis. Psychiatric Clinics (Basel), 11, 155-162.

4403.   Perry, C.P. (1979), Family-oriented obstetrics (editorial). Alabama Journal of Medical Science, 16, 69-70.

4404.   Perry, E. (1955), The treatment of aggressive juvenile delinquents in "family group therapy." International Journal of Group Psychotherapy, 5, 131-149.

4405.   Perry, R.M. (1977), The effects of counseling involvement on elementary school student behavior. Dissertation Abstracts International, 38, 2563-A.

4406.   Personett, J.D. (1978), Couples therapy: Treatment of choice with the drug addict. Journal of Psychiatric Nursing, 16(1), 18-21.

4407.   Peshkin, M.M., Kayer, L.C., and Abramson, H.A. (1976), Psychosomatic group therapy with parents of children with intractable asthma: II. The Temple family. Journal of Asthma Research, 13, 151-157.

4408.   Peshkin, M.M., and Abramson, H.A. (1976), Psychosomatic group therapy with parents of children with intractable asthma: VII. The Temple family. Journal of Asthma Research, 13(3), 151-157.

4409.   Peshkin, M.M., and Abramson, H.A. (1974), Psychosomatic group
        therapy with parents of children with intractable asthma: IV. The Saul
        family. Journal of Asthma Research, 11, 127-138.

4410.   Peshkin, M.M., and Abramson, H.A. (1974), Psychosomatic group
        therapy with parents of children with intractable asthma: V. The
        Temple family: I. Journal of Asthma Research, 12(1), 27-63.

4411.   Peshkin, M.M., and Abramson, H.A. (1974), Psychosomatic group
        therapy with parents of children with intractable asthma: VI. The
        Temple family: II. Journal of Asthma Research, 12(2), 95-122.

4412.   Peter, J.P., and Chinsky, R.R. (1974), Sociological aspects of cleft
        palate adults: I. Marriage. Canadian Journal of Public Health, 65, 221-
        223.

4413.   Peterman, K.O. (1983), You can improve family communication:
        Christian counseling aids. Grand Rapids, MI: Baker Books.

4414.   Petermann, F. (1982), Behavioral family therapy, counseling, and
        treatment. Therapeutische Gegenwande, 121, 416-421.

4415.   Petermann, F. (1981), Parents and educator training with regard to
        aggressive child's behavior. Praxis Der Kinderpsychologie Und
        Kinderpsychiatrie, 30, 217-222.

4416.   Peterson, B.P. (1980), Generality of treatment effects resulting from a
        behavioral parent-training program. Dissertation Abstracts
        International, 40, 3960-B.

4417.   Peterson, G.L., Frederiksen, L.W., and Rosenbaum, M.S. (1981),
        Developing behavioral competencies in distressed marital couples.
        American Journal of Family Therapy, 9, 13-23.

4418.   Peterson, J.A. (1973), Marital and family therapy involving the aged.
        Gerontologist, 13(1), 27-30.

4419.   Peterson, J.A. (1968), Marriage and family counseling: Perspective and
        prospect. New York: Association Press.

4420.   Peterson, R.W., and Brown, R. (1982), The child care worker as
        treatment coordinator and parent trainer. Child Care Quarterly, 8, 188-
        203.

4421.   Petri, H., and Hampel, C. (1983), Balint-group work with teacher-
        students. Gruppenpsychotherapie und Gruppendynamik, 18, 173-188.

4422.   Pettersen, F.A. (1983), Differentiation of the father's role in the
        infancy period. In J.P. Vincent (Ed.), Advances in family intervention,
        assessment and theory, Vol. 3. Greenwich: JAI Press.

4423.   Pettitt, G.A. (1979), Adjunctive trance and family therapy for terminal
        cancer. New Zealand Medical Journal, 89, 18-21.

4424.   Pety, J.R. (1983), The effects of marital expectation training on
        communication style and problem solving ability of couples.
        Dissertation Abstracts International, 44, 389-A.

4425.   Peuschel, S.M., and Yeatman, S. (1977), An educational and counseling program for phenylketonuric adolescent girls and their parents. Social Work in Health Care, 3, 29-36.

4426.   Pevsner, R. (1982), Group parent training versus individual family therapy: An outcome study. Journal of Behavior Therapy and Experimental Psychiatry, 13, 119-122.

4427.   Pevsner, R.K. (1981), Parent training and group therapy versus individual family therapy in the treatment of child behavior problems. Dissertation Abstracts International, 41, 3585-B.

4428.   Pew, M.L. (1972), Adlerian marriage counseling. Journal of Individual Psychology, 28, 192-202.

4429.   Pfeffer, C.R. (1982), Interventions for suicidal children and their parents. Suicide and Life-Threatening Behavior, 12, 240-248.

4430.   Pfeffer, D. (1976), Review of M. Sugar's The adolescent in group and family therapy. Clinical Social Work Journal, 4, 68.

4431.   Pfouts, J.H., Schopler, J.H., and Henley, H.C. (1982), Forgotten victims of family violence. Social Work, 27, 367-368.

4432.   Phelan, P.K. (1981), The process of incest: A cultural analysis. Dissertation Abstracts International, 42, 765-A.

4433.   Philage, M.L., Kuna, D.J., and Becerril, G. (1975), A new family approach to therapy for the learning disabled child. Journal of Learning Disablities, 8, 490-499.

4434.   Philage, M.L., and Kuna, D.L. (1975), The therapeutic contract and LD families. Academic Therapy, 10, 407-411.

4435.   Philippe, M.F. (1981), The application of family therapy in an acute situation of threat of suicide in an adolescent (author's transl). Neuropsychiatrie de L'Enfance et de L'Adolescence, 29, 373-377.

4436.   Phillips, C.E. (1980), Review of C.P. Barnard and R.G. Corrales's The theory and technique of family therapy. American Journal of Family Therapy, 8, 81.

4437.   Phillips, C.E. (1973), Some useful tests for marriage counseling. Family Coordinator, 22(1), 43-53.

4438.   Phillips, C.E. (1970), What marriage and family counseling is and how it works. Journal of Forensic Psychology, 2, 11-21.

4439.   Phillips, C.E. (1975), Marriage and family counseling in public schools. TPGA Journal, 4, 69-75.

4440.   Phillips, D. (1975), The family council: A segment of adolescent treatment. Journal of Behavior Therapy and Experimental Psychiatry, 6, 283-287.

4441.   Phillips, E.L., and Johnston, M.S.H. (1954), Theoretical and clinical aspects of short-term parent-child psychotherapy. Psychiatry, 17, 267-276.

4442. Phillips, E.M. (1977), Psychology and marriage counseling. Bulletin of the British Psychological Society, 30, 340-341.

4443. Phipps, S. (1981), Mourning response and intervention in stillbirth: An alternative genetic counseling approach. Social Biology, 28(1-2), 1.

4444. Pichler, E., Richter, R., and Jurgenssen, O.A. (1982), Concept for the total care of families of children with leukemia and tumors based on conversations with the parents. Onkologie, 5, 178-185.

4445. Piercy, F., Laird, R.A., and Mohammed, Z. (1982), A comprehensive training model for family therapists serving rural populations. Family Therapy, 9, 239-249.

4446. Piercy, F.P, and Hovestadt, A.J. (1980), Marriage and family therapy within counselor education. Counselor Education, Supplement, 20, 68-74.

4447. Piercy, F.P. (1984), Review of F. Kaslow's The international book of family therapy. Journal of Marital and Family Therapy, 10(2), 206-207.

4448. Piercy, F.P., Laird, R.A., and Mohammed, Z. (1983), A family therapist rating scale. Journal of Marital and Family Therapy, 9, 49-59.

4449. Piercy, F.P., and Sprenkle, D.H. (1984), The process of family therapy education. Journal of Marital and Family Therapy, 10, 399-408.

4450. Pierri, M., Santonstaso, P., and Viaro, M. (1975), Family psychotherapy: An experiment in supervison. Rivista di Psichiatrica, 10, 411-432.

4451. Pilalis, J. (1984), The formalization of family therapy training. Journal of Family Therapy, 6(1), 35-46.

4452. Pilisuk, M. (1978), Kinship, social networks, social support and health. Social Science Medicine, 12, 273-280.

4453. Pill, C.J. (1981), Family life education group for working with stepparents. Social Casework, 62, 159-166.

4454. Pillai, V., Collins, A., and Morgan, R. (1982), Family walk-in centre-Eton Socon: Evaluation of a project on preventive intervention based in the community. Child Abuse and Neglect, 6, 71-79.

4455. Pilowsky, I. (1979), Review of S. Minuchin's Families and family therapy. Australian and New Zealand Journal of Psychiatry, 13, 187.

4456. Pincus, L., and Dare, C. (1982), Family secrets. Acta Psiquiatrica y Psicologia de America Latina, 28, 175.

4457. Pines, M. (1984), Group analysis and family therapy: Discussion. International Journal of Group Psychotherapy, 34(2), 225-228.

4458. Pinney, E.L., Jr., and Slipp, S. (1982), Glossary of group and family therapy. New York: Brunner/Mazel.

4459. Pino, C.J. (1980), Research and clinical application of marital autopsy in divorce counseling. Journal of Divorce, 4, 31-48.

4460.   Pinsof, W.M. (1979), Family therapist behavior scale (FTBS):
        Development and evaluation of a coding system. Family Process, 18,
        451-462.

4461.   Pinsof, W.M. (1977), Family therapist verbal behavior: Development of
        a coding system. Dissertation Abstracts International, 38, 5587-B.

4462.   Pinsof, W.M. (1983), Integrative problem-centered therapy: Toward the
        synthesis of family and individual psychotherapies. Journal of Marital
        and Family Therapy, 9, 19-36.

4463.   Pinter, E. (1970), (Family psychotherapy.) Praxis, 59, 1066-1069.

4464.   Pipineli-Potamianov, A. (1973), Listening to the family interplay: A
        parent-child interview. International Journal of Group Psychotherapy,
        23, 338-345.

4465.   Piskin, H. (1983), Review of M.S. Bergmann and M.E. Jucovy's
        Generations of the holocaust. Family Process, 22, 246-248.

4466.   Pitman, E. (1985), Review of A. Treacher and J. Carpenter (Eds.), Using
        family therapy. British Journal of Social Work, 15(1), 95.

4467.   Pittman, F., DeYoung, C., Flomenhaft, K., Kaplan, D., and Langsley,
        D. (1966), Crisis family therapy. In J. Masserman (Ed.), Current
        psychiatric therapies, Vol. VI. New York: Grune and Stratton.

4468.   Pittman, F.S. (1966), Family therapy as an alternative to psychiatric
        hospitalization. Psychiatric Research Reports: American Psychiatric
        Association, 20, 188-195.

4469.   Pittman, F.S. (1979), Review of C.J. Sager's Marriage contracts and
        couple therapy. Family Process, 18, 358.

4470.   Pittman, F.S. (1979), Discussion: Family therapy approach to
        incapacitating migraine. International Journal of Family Therapy, 1(1),
        56-62.

4471.   Pittman, F.S. (1980), Review of M. Andolfi's Family therapy: An
        interactional approach. Family Process, 19, 313-314.

4472.   Pittman, F.S. (1984), Wet cocker spaniel therapy: An essay on
        technique in family therapy. Family Process, 23, 1-9.

4473.   Pittman, F.S. (1970), Critical incidents in the context of family
        therapy: Critical incident No. 7. International Psychiatry Clinics, 7,
        335-341.

4474.   Plank R. (1953), The family constellation of a group of schizophrenic
        patients. American Journal of Orthopsychiatry, 23, 817-825.

4475.   Plant, J.S. (1939), Present problems in marriage counseling. Mental
        Hygiene, 23, 353-362.

4476.   Platt, R. (1970), The myth and reality of the "matriarch": A case report
        in the family therapy. Psychoanalytic Review, 57(2), 203-223.

4477.   Pohlen, M., and Plankers, T. (1982), Family therapy: From
psychoanalysis to psychosocial action. Psyche: Zeitschrift fur
Psychoanalyse und Ihre Anwendungen, 36, 416-452.

4478.   Poichuk, N.B. (1980), I.V. therapy for children: Reducing parental and
patient fears. Dimensional Health Service, 57(8), 32.

4479.   Pokorney, D.H. (1968), Premarital counseling. American Annals of the
Deaf, 113, 939-941.

4480.   Pollak, O. (1964), Issues in family diagnosis and family therapy. Journal
of Marriage and Family Counseling, 26, 279-287.

4481.   Pollak, O., and Friedman, A.S. (1969), Family dynamics and female
sexual delinquency. Palo Alto, CA: Science and Behavior Books.

4482.   Polonsky, D.C., and Nadelson, C.C. (1982), Marital discord and the wish
for sex therapy. Psychiatric Annals, 12(7), 685.

4483.   Pontalti, C., Ancona, L., and Carafa, M. (1981), (Emotional significance
in couple transactions: Analysis with the Hostility Scale of
Gottschalk.) Archivi Psicologia, Neurologia e Psichiatria, 42, 228-245.

4484.   Pool M.L., and Frazier, J.R. (1973), Family therapy: A review of the
literature pertinent to children and adolescents. Psychotherapy:
Theory, Research and Practice, 10, 256-260.

4485.   Porter, J.L., and Dabul, B. (1977), The application of transactional
analysis to therapy with wives of adult aphasic patients. Journal of the
American Speech, Language, Hearing Association, 19, 244-248.

4486.   Porter, K., Zeigler, P., and Charles, E. (1976), A couples group for
medical students. Journal of Medical Education, 51, 418-419.

4487.   Porter, L.S., and Demeuth, B.R. (1979), The impact of marital
adjustment on pregnancy acceptance. Maternal and Child Nursing
Journal, 8, 103-113.

4488.   Portner, D.L. (1977), Hospitalization of the family in the treatment of
mental patients. Health and Social Work, 2, 110-122.

4489.   Portner, J. (1984), Review of S.B. Kamerman and C.D. Hayes' Families
that work: Children in a changing world. American Journal of Family
Therapy, 12(1), 82-83.

4490.   Possel, Z. (1975), Psychiatric problems in the light of Polish family code
legislation. Psychiatrica Polska, 9, 65-69.

4491.   Postner, R.S., Guttman, H.A., Sigal, J.J., Epstein, N.B., and Rakoff,
V.M. (1971), Process and outcome in conjoint family therapy. Family
Process, 10, 451-473.

4492.   Powell, G. (1979), Review of V. Satir's Conjoint family therapy.
Behavior Research Therapy, 17, 519.

4493.   Powell, G.S., and Gazda, G.M. (1979), "Cleaning out the trash": A case
study in Adlerian family counseling. Journal of Individual Psychology,
35(1), 45-57.

4494.   Powell, G.S., and Wampler, K.S. (1982), Marriage enrichment
         participants: Levels of marital satisfaction. Family Relations: Journal
         of Applied Family and Child Studies, 31, 389-393.

4495.   Powell, M., Taylor, J., and Smith, R. (1967), Parents and child in a child
         guidance clinic: Should they share the same therapist? International
         Journal of Group Psychotherapy, 17, 25-34.

4496.   Powell, M.B., and Monahan, J. (1969), Reaching the rejects through
         multifamily group therapy. International Journal of Group
         Psychotherapy, 19, 35-43.

4497.   Power, P.W. (1977), The adolescent's reaction to chronic illness of a
         parent: Some implications for family counseling. International Journal
         of Family Counseling, 5(1), 70-78.

4498.   Power, P.W. (1982), Family intervention in rehabilitation of patient
         with Huntington's disease. Archives of Physical Medicine and
         Rehabilitation, 63, 441-442.

4499.   Powers, J.R. (1982), Marriage encounter and the caring relationship
         inventory: An evaluation study. Dissertation Abstracts International,
         42, 4206-B.

4500.   Powers, R.L., and Hahn, J. (1979), Couple counseling: A "traditional"
         marriage in transition. Journal of Individual Psychology, 35, 26-44.

4501.   Poznanski, E., Maxey, A., and Maraden, G. (1974), Parental adaptations
         to maternal employment. Journal of the American Academy of Child
         Psychiatry, 13, 319-334.

4502.   Praszkier, R. (1980), (The community work with families of young (18-
         25) schizophrenic patients.) Przeglad Psychologiczny, 23(4), 729-745.

4503.   Prater, G.S. (1978), Family therapy with black families: Social workers'
         and clients perception. Dissertation Abstracts International, 38, 5056-
         5057-B.

4504.   Pratt, C., and Cove, L.A. (1971), The assembled foster family: A
         practical experiment. Paper Presented at the Annual Meetings of the
         American Orthopsychiatry Association, Washington, D.C.

4505.   Preneuf, C., and Collomb, H. (1971), Social change and family therapy
         in Senegal: Some practical problems. Revue de Neuropsychiatrie
         Infantile et D'Hygiene Mentale de L'Enfance, 66, 581-588.

4506.   Prescott-Hulnick, M. (1979), Counseling parents of handicapped
         children: Empathetic approach. Personnel and Guidance Journal, 58(4),
         263.

4507.   Press-Rigler, M. (1980), Parent aides: An intervention program in cases
         of child abuse and neglect. Journal of the Association of Child Care
         Hospitals, 8, 64-68.

4508.   Preuss, H.G. (1970), The "sick" marriage and its therapy. Therapeutisch
         Gegenwandte, 109, 680.

4509. Preuss, H.G. (1976), Die kranke ehe im brennpunkt analytischer psychotherapie. (The ailing marriage in the focus of analytic psychotherapy.) Praxis der Psychotherapie, 12, 275-280.

4510. Price, J.V. (1971), Adolescents/youth. American Journal of Orthopsychiatry, 41, 293-305.

4511. Price, M.G. (1978), The effects of mutual monitoring and immediate verbal feedback of spouse positive behaviors. Dissertation Abstracts International, 38, 6170-6171-B.

4512. Price, M.G., and Haynes, S.N. (1980), The effects of participant monitoring and feedback on marital interaction and satisfaction. Behavior Therapy, 11, 134-139.

4513. Price, S., Golden, J., and Golden, M. (1978), Training family planning personnel in sex counseling and sex education. Public Health Reports, 93(4), 328-334.

4514. Price, S., Heinrich, A.G., and Golden, J.S. (1980), Structured group treatment of couples experiencing sexual dysfunctions. Journal of Sex and Marital Therapy, 6(4), 247-257.

4515. Price-Bonham, S., and Murphy, D.C. (1980), Dual-career marriage: Implications for the clinician. Journal of Marital and Family Therapy, 6(2), 181-188.

4516. Primrose, D.A. (1975), Epiloia in twins: A problem in diagnosis and counseling. Journal of Mental Deficiency Research, 19(3-4), 195-203.

4517. Prochaska, J, and Fallon, B.C. (1979), Preparing a community for family life education. Child Welfare, 58, 665-672.

4518. Prochaska, J., and Coyle, J.R. (1979), Choosing parenthood: A needed family life education group. Social Casework, 60, 289-295.

4519. Prochaska, J., and Prochaska, J. (1978), 20th century trends in marriage and marital therapy. In T.J. Paolini and B.S. McCrady (Eds.), Marriage and marital therapy: Psychoanalytic, behavioral and systems theory perspectives. New York: Brunner/Mazel.

4520. Prochaska, J.O., and Heffner, C.W. (1985), Marital therapy: Reply. Journal of Marital and Family Therapy, 11(1), 96.

4521. Prodohl, D. (1979), Psychological aspects of partner and family therapy. In K. Guss (Ed.), Gestaltthorie und sozialarbeit (Gestalt theory and social work.) Darmstadt: Steinkopff, pp. 154-171.

4522. Prosen, S.S., and Farmer, J.H. (1982), Understanding stepfamilies: Issues and implications for counselors. Personnel and Guidance Journal, 60, 393-397.

4523. Prosky, P. (1984), Review of A. Bentovim, G. Correllbarnes and A. Cooklin's Family therapy: Complementary framework of theory and practice. Family Process, 23(1), 126.

4524. Prosky, P.S. (1974), Family therapy: An orientation. Clinical Social Work Journal, 2, 45-56.

4525.   Protinsky, B. (1984), Review of L. L'Abate and S. McHenry's Handbook of marital interventions. Family Process, 23(4), 579-580.

4526.   Protinsky, H., and Dillard, C. (1983), Enuresis: A family therapy model. Psychotherapy: Theory, Research, and Practice, 20, 81-89.

4527.   Protinsky, H., and Kersey, B. (1983), Psychogenic encopresis: A family therapy approach. Journal of Clinical Child Psychology, 12, 192-197.

4528.   Protinsky, H., and Quinn, W. (1981), Paradoxical marital therapy with symptom triangulation. Family Therapy, 8(2), 135-140.

4529.   Protinsky, H.O. (1977), Marriage and family therapy: Cognitive and behavioral approaches within a systems framework. Family Therapy, 4, 85-92.

4530.   Protinsky, H.O., Quinn, W., and Elliott, S.S. (1982), Paradoxical prescriptions in family therapy: From child to marital focus. Journal of Marital and Family Therapy, 8, 51-55.

4531.   Ptacek, P., and Tajcova, J. (1984), Experience with family therapy in general practice in a pediatric psychiatry outpatient department. Ceskoslovenska Psychiatrica, 27, 37-43.

4532.   Pthier, P.C., and Sherman, P. (1968), A clinical application of child psychiatric nursing concepts to expand the scope of community health nursing practice. American Nursing Association, Clinical Sessions, 125-130.

4533.   Pueschel, J., and Moglia, R. (1977), The effects of the penal environment on familial relationships. Family Coordinator, 26, 373-375.

4534.   Pueschel, S.M., and Murphy, A. (1977), Assessment of counseling practices at the birth of a child with Down's syndrome. American Journal of Mental Deficiency, 81(4), 325-330.

4535.   Quadrio, C. (1982), The Peter Pan and Wendy Syndrome: A marital dynamic. Australian and New Zealand Journal of Psychiatry, 16, 23-28.

4536.   Quaranta, M.A. (1977), Family group approach with families of children in placement. In: T.J. Buckley, J.J. McCarthy, E. Norman and M.A. Quaranta (Eds.), New directions in family therapy. Oceanside: Dabor Science Publications.

4537.   Quick, E., and Jacob, T. (1973), Marital disturbance in relation to role theory and relationship theory. Journal of Abnormal Psychology, 82, 309-316.

4538.   Quick, E., and Jacob, T. (1973), Marital disturbance in relation to role theory and relationship theory. Israel Annals of Psychiatry and Related Disciplines, 11, 81-90.

4539.   Quillen, M.A., and Denney, D.R. (1982), Group parent training versus individual family therapy: An outcome study. Journal of Behavior Therapy and Experimental Psychiatry, 13(2), 119.

4540. Quinn, W.H., and Davidson, B. (1984), Prevalence of family therapy models: A research note. Journal of Marital and Family Therapy, 10(4), 393-398.

4541. Quinn, W.H., and Keller, J.F. (1981), A family therapy model for preserving independence in older persons: Utilization of the family or procreation. American Journal of Family Therapy, 9(1), 79-84.

4542. Raasoch, J., and Laqueur, H.P. (1979), Learning multiple family therapy through simulated workshops. Family Process, 18, 95-102.

4543. Rabe, F. (1972), Induced abortion and marriage counseling in epilepsy. Medizinische Welt, 23, 330-331.

4544. Rabin, C. (1981), The single-case design in family therapy evaluation research. Family Process, 20, 351-366.

4545. Rabin, C., Rosenbaum, H., and Sens, M. (1982), Home-based marital therapy for multi-problem families. Journal of Marital and Family Therapy, 8, 451-461.

4546. Rabin, C.L. (1980), The effects of adding marital training to parent training on family interaction. Dissertation Abstracts International, 41, 404A.

4547. Rabiner, E.L., Molinski, H., and Gralnick, A. (1962), A conjoint family therapy in the inpatient setting. American Journal of Psychotherapy, 16, 618-631.

4548. Rabinowitz, M.D. (1984), Review of L. L'Abate's Family psychology: Theory, therapy and training. Journal of Marital and Family Therapy, 10(2), 215.

4549. Rachman, A.W. (1974), The role of "fathering" in group psychotherapy with adolescent delinquent males. Corrective and Social Psychiatry and Journal of Applied Behavior Therapy, 20(4), 11-22.

4550. Radlbeck, K.G. (1982), Expectations of seekers of marital and sexual counseling. Zeitschrift fur die Gesamte Hygiene und Ihre Grenzgebiete, 28, 580-584.

4551. Radochonski, M. (1982), Evolution of the concept of family therapy in the United States. Psychiatrica Polsak, 16, 187-194.

4552. Rahdert, R.F. (1982), Review of J.E. Simmons' Psychiatric evaluation of children. American Journal of Family Therapy, 10, 81.

4553. Rakoff, V., Sigal, J.J., and Epstein, N.B. (1967), Working through in conjoint family therapy. American Journal of Psychotherapy, 21, 782-790.

4554. Rakoff, V.M. (1984), The necessity for multiple models in family therapy. Journal of Family Therapy, 6, 199-210.

4555. Rakoff, V.M., Sigal, J.J., and Epstein, N.B. (1975), Predictions of therapeutic process and progress in conjoint family therapy. Archives of General Psychiatry, 32, 1013-1017.

4556.   Ramesar, S., and McCall, M. (1983), Coping with the negative therapeutic response in psychosocial problems in family medicine. Canadian Journal of Psychiatry, 28, 259-262.

4557.   Ranieri, R., and Pratt, T.C. (1978), Sibling therapy. Social Work, 23(5), 418.

4558.   Ransom, D.C. (1985), Review of W.J. Doherty and M.A. Baird's Family therapy and family medicine: Toward the primary care of families. Journal of Marital and Family Therapy, 11(1), 104-105.

4559.   Ransom, J.W., Schlesinger, S., and Derdeyn, A.P. (1979), A stepfamily in formation. American Journal of Orthopsychiatry, 49, 36-43.

4560.   Rao, V.N., Channabasavanna, S.M., and Parthasarathy R. (1982), Family situations of disturbed adolescents. Child Psychiatry Quarterly, 15, 113-118.

4561.   Rapoport, R. (1960), The family and psychiatric treatment: A conceptual approach. Psychiatry, 23, 53-62.

4562.   Rappaport, A.F., and Harrell, J. (1972), A behavioral-exchange model for marital counseling. Family Coordinator, 21, 203-212.

4563.   Rappeport, J.R. (1966), Sex in marriage counseling. Maryland State Medical Journal, 15, 35-40.

4564.   Rashkis, H.A. (1968), Depression as a manifestation of the family as an open system. Archives of General Psychiatry, 19, 57-63.

4565.   Rathbone-McCuan, E., and Pierce, R. (1978), Intergenerational treatment approach: An alternative model of working with abusive, neglectful and delinquent prone families. Family Therapy, 5(2), 121-141.

4566.   Rathbun, C., and Kolodny, R.L. (1967), A groupwork approach in cross-cultural adoptions. Children, 14, 117-121.

4567.   Ratliff, B.W., Moon, H.F., and Bonacci, G.A. (1978), Intercultural marriage: The Korean-American experience. Social Casework, 59(4), 221-226.

4568.   Ratna, L., and Davis, J. (1984), Family therapy with the elderly mentally ill: Some strategies and techniques. British Journal of Psychiatry, 145, 311-315.

4569.   Rau, H., and Wolf, C. (1980), Cooperation with parents in public youth welfare--demonstration of a specific family therapy. Praxis der Kinderpsychologie und Kinderpsychiatrie, 29, 8-13.

4570.   Raubolt, R.R. (1983), Brief, problem-focused group psychotherapy with adolescents. American Journal of Orthopsychiatry, 53, 157-165.

4571.   Raubolt, R.R. (1983), Treating children in residential group psychotherapy. Child Welfare, 11, 147-156.

4572.   Raundalen, M., and Dyregrov, A. (1983), Psychological intervention in families with a seriously ill child: Therapeutic means: II. Tidsskrift For Norsk Psykologforening, 20, 61-69.

4573. Rausch, R.A. (1981), A comparative study of structured and unstructured marriage enrichment programs. Dissertation Abstracts International, 42, 2078-B.

4574. Ravensborg, M.R. (1966), Separate workshops avoid the family pecking order. Hospital and Community Psychiatry, 17, 24-25.

4575. Ravich, R. (1969), Game-testing in conjoint marital psychotherapy. American Journal of Psychotherapy, 23, 217-229.

4576. Ravich, R.A. (1974), The origins of the concept of complementarity in Nathan Ackerman's family process theory. In L.R. Wolberg and M.L. Aronson (Eds.), Group therapy 1974: An overview. New York: Stratton Intercontinental Medical Book Corporation.

4577. Ravich, R.A. (1969), Triadic-based family therapy: Dyads, triads, and the sphere of between. International Journal of Psychiatry, 8, 557-561.

4578. Ray, J.S. (1974), The family training center: An experiment in normalization. Mental Retardation, 12, 12-13.

4579. Raymond, M., Slaby, A.E. and Lieb, J. (1977), The healing alliance: A new view of the family's role in the treatment of emotional problems. New York: Norton.

4580. Raymundo, M.A. (1981), A present trend in psychotherapy: Family therapy. Annales Medico-Psychologiques, 5, 661-668.

4581. Rayner, H. (1978), The Exter home-visiting project: The psychologist as one of several therapists. Child Care Quarterly, 4, 1-7.

4582. Rebner, I. (1972), Conjoint family therapy. Psychotherapy: Theory, Research and Practice, 9, 62-66.

4583. Rebner, I. (1974), Family therapy: The sum total of the individual. Canadian Journal of Psychiatric Nursing, 15, 1-2.

4584. Reckless, J. (1969), A confrontation technique used with married couples in a group therapy setting. International Journal of Group Psychotherapy, 19, 203-213.

4585. Reckless, J., and Byrd, P. (1980), A system of group therapy for the treatment of marital and sexual dysfunction. Journal of Sex and Marital Therapy, 6(3), 199-204.

4586. Reder, P. (1983), Disorganized families and the helping professions - who's in charge of what. Journal of Family Therapy, 5, 23-36.

4587. Reding, G.R., and Ennis, B. (1964), Treatment of the couple by a couple. British Journal of Medical Psychology, 37, 325-330.

4588. Rednour, R.C. (1982), A Delphi investigation of alternative futures for Texas marriage and family therapists. Dissertation Abstracts International, 43, 858B.

4589. Redwin, E. (1955), The behind-your-back technique in marriage counseling. Group Psychotherapy, 8, 40-46.

4590.   Reed, K.L. (1979), A practical guide to sexual counseling. Arizona Medicine, 36(11), 829-839.

4591.   Reed, S.C. (1974), A short history of genetic counseling. Social Biology, 21(4), 322-339.

4592.   Reese, D.J. (1982), Creatively managing conflict in marriage. Dissertation Abstracts International, 45, 832A.

4593.   Reese-Dukes, J.L., and Reese-Dukes, C. (1983), Pairs for pairs: A theoretical base for co-therapy as a non-sexist process in couple counseling. Personnel and Guidance Journal, 61, 99-101.

4594.   Reeves, A.C. (1971), Children with surrogate parents: Cases seen in analytic therapy with aetiological hypotheses. British Journal of Medical Psychology, 44(2), 155-172.

4595.   Regan, J.M., Connors, G.J., O'Farrell, T.J., and Jones, W.C. (1983), Services for the families of alcoholics: A survey of treatment agencies in Massachusetts. Journal of Studies on Alcohol, 44, 1072-1082.

4596.   Regas, S.J. (1984), A comparison of functional family therapy and peer group therapy in the treatment of hyperactive adolescents. Dissertation Abstracts International, 45, 2566-A.

4597.   Regas, S.J., and Sprenkle, D.H. (1984), Functional family therapy and the treatment of inhibited sexual desire. Journal of Marital and Family Therapy, 10, 63-72.

4598.   Reich, G. (1984), Influence in the therapist's family origin on the activity of therapists and counselors. Praxis der Kinderpsychologie und Kinderpsychiatrie, 33, 61-69.

4599.   Reich, G. (1982), Taboos and fears of the therapist dealing with his own family. Zeitschrift Fur Psychosomatische Medizin Und Psychoanalyse, 28, 393-406.

4600.   Reid, W.J. (1985), Family problem solving. New York: Columbia University Press.

4601.   Reiger, K. (1981), Family therapy's missing question: Why the plight of the modern family? Journal of Family Therapy, 3, 293-308.

4602.   Reilly, D.M. (1975), Family factors in the etiology and treatment of youthful drug abuse. Family Therapy, 2, 149-171.

4603.   Reilly, D.M. (1984), Family therapy with adolescent drug abusers and their families. Journal of Drug Issues, 14(2), 381-392.

4604.   Reilly, I., and Bayles, T. (1981), Family therapy training: Give the customers what they want. Journal of Family Therapy, 3(2), 167-176.

4605.   Reilly, P.R. (1975), Genetic counseling and the law. Houston Law Review, 12(3), 640-660.

4606.   Reimondi, R.A., Lockwood, B.W., and Brannigan, G.G. (1981), Family involvement in academic remediation. Academic Therapy, 16, 401-408.

4607.   Reinhardt, J.A. (1980), A tri-partite follow-up evaluation of residential treatment for emotionally disturbed children. Dissertation Abstracts International, 40, 4502-B.

4608.   Reiss, D. (1983), Sensory extendres versus meters and predictors: Clarifying strategies for the use of objective tests in family therapy. Family Process, 22, 165-171.

4609.   Reiss, D., Costell, R., Jones, C., and Berkman, H. (1980), The family meets the hospital: A laboratory forecast of the encounter. Archives of General Psychiatry, 37(4), 141-154.

4610.   Reiss, D., and Costell, R. (1977), The multiple family group as a small society: Family regulation of interaction with nonmembers. American Journal of Psychiatry, 134, 21-24.

4611.   Reiss, D., and Oliveri, M.E. (1983), Sensory experience and family proess: Perceptual styles tend to run in but not necessarily run families. Family Process, 22, 289-308.

4612.   Reiss, I.L. (1976), Family systems in America. Hinsdale, IL: Dryden.

4613.   Reiter, G.F. (1973), The effects of a systematic counseling program for mothers on family congruence, integration, positive and negative verbal responses, and a problem child's behavior. Dissertation Abstracts International, 34, 2793-2794A.

4614.   Reiter, G.F., and Kilmann, P.R. (1975), Mothers as family change agents. Journal of Counseling Psychology, 22, 61-65.

4615.   Reiter, L. (1983), Problems of diagnostic typology of married couples in therapy. Weiner Klinische Wochenschrift, 133, 478-480.

4616.   Reiter, L., and Steiner, E. (1982), (Conjoint marital therapy in a group and self help group.) Partnerberatung, 19, 133-144.

4617.   Reitl, M. (1984), Review of R.T. Seagraves' Marital therapy: A combined psychodynamic-behavioral approach. Social Work, 29(3), 308.

4618.   Rembar, J., Novick, J., and Kalter, N. (1982), Attrition among families of divorce: Patterns in an outpatient psychiatric population. Journal of the American Academy of Child Psychiatry, 21, 409-413.

4619.   Remschmidt, H. (1980), Review of W. Toman's Family therapy. Zeitschrift fur Knder-und Jugenpsychiatrie, 8, 342.

4620.   Remschmidt, H., and Mattejat, F. (1981), Construction of rating scales for family interviews: Factors affecting interrater reliability. Zeitschrift Fur Kinder- Und Jugendpsychiatrie, 9, 288-316.

4621.   Renner, R. (1976), Ambulatory therapy of a two-year old child, including parents and sister. Praxis der Kinderpsychologie und Kinderpsychiatrie, 25, 92-96.

4622.   Renzi-Guastalla, B., and Tremelloni, C.L. (1967), Psicoterapia coginunta individuale e familiare. (Combined individual and family psychotherapy.) Rivista di Psichiatria, 2(6), 574-582.

4623.   Reposa, R.E. (1979), Adolescent and family abandonment: Family systems approach to treatment. International Journal of Group Psychotherapy, 29, 359–368.

4624.   Resner, S.S. (1977), Utilization of the person-behavior matrix for the analysis of role-dimensions and role-perceptions of psychiatric mental health nurse family therapists. Dissertation Abstracts International, 37, 3872B.

4625.   Resnikoff, R.O. (1981), Teaching family therapy: Ten key questions for understanding the family as patient. Journal of Marital and Family Therapy, 7, 135–142.

4626.   Restak, R. (1975), Stimulus response: Genetic counseling for defective parents: The danger of knowing too much. Psychology Today, 9(4), 21.

4627.   Revenstorf, D., Schindler, L., and Hahlweg, K. (1983), Behavioral marital therapy applied in a conjoint and a conjoint-group modality: Short- and long-term effectiveness. Behavior Therapy, 14, 614–625.

4628.   Revesz, G., and Furedi, J. (1978), (The psychotherapy process when the group consists of several families.) Magyar Pszicholgie Szemle, 35(5), 459–465.

4629.   Review of A.M. Tansey's Where to get help for your family. (1978), Rehabilitation Literature, 39, 292.

4630.   Review of N.S. Jacobson and G. Margolin's Marital therapy. (1980), Acta Psiquiatrica y Psicologia de America Latina, 26, 85.

4631.   Review of T.J. Paolino and B.S. McCrady's Marriage and marital therapy: Psychoanalytic, behavioral and systems theory perspectives. (1980), Psychological Medicine, 10, 192.

4632.   Reynolds, B.D., Puck, M.H., and Robinson, A. (1974), Genetic counseling: An appraisal. Clinical Genetics, 5(3), 177–187.

4633.   Reynolds, M.K., and Corynes, J.T. (1970), A survey of the use of family therapy by caseworkers. Social Casework, 51, 76–81.

4634.   Rhodes, S.L. (1985), Reviews of W.R. McFarlane (Ed.), Family therapy in schizophrenia and W.J. Doherty and A.B. Macaran, Family therapy and family medicine: Toward the primary care of families. Social Casework, 66(2), 120–123.

4635.   Ribas, M. A. (1983), Parenting behavior as perceived by Chicano children during late childhood with implications for family therapy. Dissertation Abstracts International, 44, 323-B.

4636.   Rice, D.G. (1978), The male spouse in marital and family therapy. Counseling Psychologist, 7(4), 64–66.

4637.   Rice, D.G., and Rice, J.K. (1977), Non sexist "marital" therapy. Journal of Marriage and Family Counseling, 3(1), 3–10.

4638.   Rice, N., Satterwhite, B., and Pless, I.B. (1976–77), Family counselors in a pediatric specialty clinic setting. Social Work in Health Care, 2, 193–203.

4639.   Rich, P. (1980), Differentiation of self in the therapist's family of origin. Social Casework, 61, 394-399.

4640.   Richards, C.J., and Richards, C.S. (1979), Expectations and attitudes about marital counseling: A questionnaire survey of married individuals. Psychological Reports, 44(2), 582-583.

4641.   Richards, I.D., McIntosh, H.T., and Sweeney, S. (1979), A hundred vulnerable families. Public Health, 93, 16-24.

4642.   Richardson, R.W. (1984), Family ties that bind: A self-help guide to change through family of origin therapy. Seattle, WA: Self-Counsel Press.

4643.   Riche, M. (1979), Review of M. Bowen's, Family therapy in clinical practice. Social Service Review, 53, 140.

4644.   Richer, S. (1973), Mother-child psychotherapy in the one-parent family: A definition of objectives. Vie Medicale au Canada Francias, 2, 817-824.

4645.   Richman, J. (1979), Family therapy of attempted suicide. Family Process, 18, 131-142.

4646.   Richman, J. (1979), A couples therapy group on a geriatric service. Geriatric Psychiatry, 12(2), 203.

4647.   Richman, J. (1985), Family therapy for suicidal people. New York: Springer Publishing.

4648.   Richman, J. (1978). Symbiosis, empathy, suicidal behavior, and the family. Suicide and Life Threatening Behavior, 8, 139-149.

4649.   Richman, J., and Davidoff, I.F. (1971), Interaction testing and counseling as a form of crisis intervention during marital therapy. Proceedings of the Annual Convention of the American Psychological Association, 6, 439-440.

4650.   Richter, H.E. (1973), Two-week psychotherapy with couples. Psyche, 27, 889-901.

4651.   Richter, H.E. (1967), Die familie in der psychologischen medizin. (The family in psychological treatment.) Praxis der Psychotherapie, 12, 124-127.

4652.   Richter, H.E. (1970), Patient familie: Enstehung, struktur und therapie von konflikten in ehe und familie. (Family patient: The origin, structure and therapy of marital and family conflicts.) Hamburg, West Germany: Rowohlt Verlag.

4653.   Richter, H.E. (1977), Family therapy. In H.J. Haase (Ed.), Social psychiatrie. Stuttgart, West Germany: F.K. Schattauer Verlag.

4654.   Richter, H.E. (1968), Family therapy. Psychotherapy and Psychosomatics, 16, 303-318.

4655.   Rickarby, G., and Egan, P. (1981), Family therapy in the playroom. International Journal of Family Psychiatry, 2, 221-235.

4656.   Rickarby, G.A. (1981), A critique of some trends in family intervention. International Journal of Family Psychiatry, 2, 3-11.

4657.   Rickert, V.C., and Turner, J.E. (1978), Through the looking glass: Supervision in family therapy. Social Casework, 59(3), 131-137.

4658.   Ridenour, R.I. (1979), The family therapy literature: Often a difficult matter of choice. Review of H. Stierlin's Psychoanalysis and family therapy. Journal of Marital and Family Therapy, 5, 111-115.

4659.   Ridley, C.A. (1969), A study of work and marriage: The relationships of job satisfaction and job involvement to marital adjustment. Dissertation Abstracts International, 30, 5544A.

4660.   Ridley, C.A., Avery, A.W., Dent, J., and Harrell, J.E. (1981), The effects of relationship enhancement and problem solving programs on perceived heterosexual competence. Family Therapy, 8(2), 59-66.

4661.   Ridley, C.A., and Jorgensen, S.R. (1978), Relationship enhancement with premarital couples: An assessment of effects on relationship quality. American Journal of Family Therapy, 10, 41-48.

4662.   Rieger, W. (1973), A proposal for a trial of family therapy and conjugal visits in prison. American Journal of Orthopsychiatry, 43, 117-122.

4663.   Riess, B.F. (1976), Family therapy as seen by a group therapist. International Journal of Group Psychotherapy, 26, 301-311.

4664.   Rim, Y. (1979), Personality and means of influence in marriage. Human Relations, 32, 871-875.

4665.   Rim, Y. (1979), Reported means of influence in marriage, integrative complexity, and sex. European Journal of Social Psychology, 9, 101-104.

4666.   Rimmer, J. (1974), Psychiatric illness in husbands of alcoholics. Quarterly Journal of Studies on Alcohol, 35, 281-283.

4667.   Rinella, V. J., and Goldstein, M. R. (1980), Family therapy with substance abusers: Legal considerations regarding confidentiality. Journal of Marital and Family Therapy, 6, 319-326.

4668.   Ringstad, T., and Spurkland, I. (1981), Family therapy. Hospitalization of the entire family. Psychiatrica de L'Enfant, 24, 265-291.

4669.   Rinsley, D.B. (1973), Residential treatment: Should it be concomitant with family therapy? American Journal of Psychiatry, 130, 721.

4670.   Rippere, V. (1982), Review of S. Lieberman's Transgenerational family therapy. Behavior Research Therapy, 20, 531.

4671.   Riskin, J. (1982), Research on nonlabeled families: A longitudinal study. In F. Walsh (Ed.), Normal family processes. New York: Guilford Press.

4672.   Riskin, J., and McCorkle, M.E. (1979), Nontherapy family research and change in families: A brief clinical research communication. Family Process, 18, 161-162.

4673.   Riskind, J. (1977), Theoretical and practical differences between individual and family therapy. Dissertation Abstracts International, 38, 2882B.

4674.   Ritchie, A.M., and Serrano, A.C. (1974), Family therapy in the treatment of adolescents with divorced parents. In R.E. Hardy and J.G. Cull (Eds.), Therapeutic needs of the family: Problems, descriptions and therapeutic approaches. Springfield, IL: Charles C. Thomas.

4675.   Rittenhouse, J.D. (1970), Endurance of effect: Family unit treatment compared to identified patient treatment. Proceedings of the Annual Convention of the American Psychological Association, 5(pt.2), 535-536.

4676.   Ritterman, M. (1979), Outcome study for family therapy, Ritalin and placebo treatments of hyperactivity: An open systems approach. Dissertation Abstracts International, 39, 6138B. (University Microfilms No. 7910077.)

4677.   Ritterman, M. (1983), Using hypnosis in family therapy. San Francisco, CA: Jossey-Bass.

4678.   Ritterman, M.K. (1982), Hemophilia in context: Adjunctive hypnosis for families with a hemophiliac member. Family Process, 21, 469-476.

4679.   Ritterman, M.K. (1977), Paradigmatic classification of family therapy theories. Family Process, 16, 29-46.

4680.   Ro-Trock, G.K. (1977), A family therapy outcome study in an inpatient setting. American Journal of Orthopsychiatry, 47, 514-522.

4681.   Ro-Trock, G.K. (1976), Family therapy vs individual therapy in a public mental health facility. Dissertation Abstracts International, 36(11), 5523B.

4682.   Robbins, G., and Toomer, J.E. (1976), Innovative uses of the FIRO-B in couple counseling. Journal of Marriage and Family Counseling, 2(3), 277-282.

4683.   Roberts, F.J. (1971), Conjont marital therapy and the prisoner's dilemma. British Journal of Medical Psychology, 44, 67-74.

4684.   Roberts, J. (1983), Skill development in structural and strategic family therapy: Two models of live supervision. Dissertation Abstracts International, 43, 2610-A.

4685.   Roberts, J. (1985), Review of L.R. Wolbert and M.L. Aronson (Eds.), Group and family therapy 1983. The British Journal of Psychiatry, 146, 224.

4686.   Roberts, J. (1984), Families with infants and young children who have special needs. Family Therapy Collections, 11, 1-17.

4687.   Roberts, W. (1982), Preparations of the referral network - the professional and the family. In A. Bentovim, G.G. Barnes, and A. Cooklin (Eds.), Family therapy. I. Complementary frameworks of therapy and practice. London: Academic Press.

4688.   Roberts, W.L. (1968), Working with the family group in a child guidance clinic. British Journal of Psychiatric Social Work, 9, 175-179.

4689.   Robertson, N.C. (1974). The relationship between marital status and the risk of psychiatric referral. British Journal of Psychiatry, 124, 191-202.

4690.   Robin, A. L. (1981), A controlled evaluation of problem-solving communication training with parent-adolescent conflict. Behavior Therapy, 12, 593-609.

4691.   Robinson, A.L. (1983), Effects of a biofeedback monitored, guided imagery-based group counseling approach on post-divorce adjustment. Dissertation Abstracts International, 43, 3815A.

4692.   Robinson, L.D., and Weathers, O.D. (1973), Family therapy of deaf parents and hearing children: A new dimension in psychotherapeutic intervention. Acta Psychiatrica Scandinavica (Suppl.), 1-73.

4693.   Robinson, L.D., and Weathers, O.P. (1974), Family therapy of deaf parents and hearing children: A new dimension in psychotherapeutic intervention. American Annals of the Deaf, 119, 325-330.

4694.   Robinson, L.H. (1974), Group work with parents of retarded adolescents. American Journal of Psychotherapy, 28, 397-408.

4695.   Robinson, L.R. (1975), Basic concepts in family therapy: A differential comparison with individual treatment. American Journal of Psychiatry, 132, 1045-1048.

4696.   Robinson, M. (1968), Family-based therapy: Some thoughts on the family approach. British Journal of Psychiatric Social Work, 9, 188-192.

4697.   Robinson, M. (1982), Reconstituted families – some implications for the family therapist. In A. Bentovim, G.G. Barnes, and A. Cooklin (Eds.), Family therapy. 2. Complementary frameworks of theory and practice. London: Academic Press.

4698.   Robinson, M., Chandler, E., and Holden, H.M. (1967), Treatment of a "psychotic" family in a family psychiatric setting. Psychotherapy and Psychosomatics, 15, 56.

4699.   Robinson, M., and Parkinson, L. (1985), A family systems approach to concilliation in separation and divorce. Journal of Family Therapy, 7, 357-378.

4700.   Robinson, P.A. (1978), Parents of "beyond control" adolescents. Adolescence, 13, 109-119.

4701.   Robinson-Metz, M.E. (1983), A multidimensional study of marital and sexual dysfunctional couples: The role of conflict management style in symptom differentiation. Dissertation Abstracts International, 44, 925-B.

4702.   Roche, F.D. (1982), Approach of the family in general hospital psychiatry (author's transl.). Semain Des Hospitaux Therapeutic, Paris, 58, 877-880.

4703. Roche, F.D., and Schmit, G. (1983), Adolescence and family therapy. Semain Des Hospitaux Therapeutic, Paris, 59, 2309-2315.

4704. Rochford, G. (1981), Love, care, control and punishment. Journal of Family Therapy, 3, 281-291.

4705. Rock, N.L. (1974), Childhood psychosis and long term chemo and psychotherapy. Diseases of the Nervous System, 35(7), 303-308.

4706. Rodrian, J.L., and Weissenfluh, B. (1978), Counseling family of aphasic adult. In R.E. Hartbauer (Ed.), Counseling in communicative disorders. Chicago: Charles C. Thomas.

4707. Roffe, M.W., and Britt, B.C. (1981), A typology of marital interaction for sexually dysfunctional couples. Journal of Sex and Marital Therapy, 7, 207-222.

4708. Rogers, C.R. (1945), Counseling with the returned serviceman and his wife. Marriage and Family Living, 7, 82-84.

4709. Rogers, C.R. (1974), Wartime issues in family counseling. Marriage and Family Living, 6, 68-69.

4710. Rogers, J., Sheldon, A., Barwick, C., Letofsky, K., and Lancee, W. (1982), Help for families of suicide: Survivors support program. Canadian Journal of Psychiatry, 27, 444-449.

4711. Rohde, I.M. (1968), The nurse as family therapist. Nursing Outlook, 16, 49-52.

4712. Rohmer, L. (1969), Some issues in administering group therapy in the family focused setting. Journal of the Jewish Community Service, 45, 241-247.

4713. Rohrbaugh, M. (1984), Review of W.R. McFarlane's Family therapy in schizophrenia. Family Process, 23(2), 284-286.

4714. Rohrer, K., Adelman, B., Puckett, J., Toomey, B. Talbert, D., and Johnson, E.W. (1980), Rehabilitation in spinal cord injury: Use of a patient-family group. Archives of Physical Medicine Rehabilitation, 61, 225-229.

4715. Rolfe, D.J. (1976), Premarriage assessment of teenage couples. Journal of Family Counseling, 4(2), 32-39.

4716. Rollin, S.A., and Dowd, E.T. (1979), Conflict resolution: A model for effective marital and family relations. American Journal of Family Therapy, 7, 61-67.

4717. Roman, M. (1976), Symposium: Family therapy and group therapy-similarities and differences: Introduction. International Journal of Group Psychotherapy, 26, 281-287.

4718. Roman, M., Bauman, G., Borello, J., Meltzer, B., and Bregmanes, D. (1976), An effect of change in patient status on marital interaction. Family Process, 15(2), 251-258.

4719.   Romig, C.A. (1983), An empirical assessment of programs designed to enhance family emotional and educational resources. Dissertation Abstracts International, 43, 4058-A.

4720.   Rommers, M.S. (1979), Wives' evaluation of problems related to laryngectomy. Journal of Communication Disorder, 12, 411-430.

4721.   Ronald houses go up across nation. (1979), Modern Health Care, 9, 36-37.

4722.   Roness, A. (1980), Family therapy in Norway: Development and trends. International Journal of Family Therapy, 2, 200-204.

4723.   Roopman-Boyden, P.G. (1979), The problems arising from supporting the elderly at home. New Zealand Journal of Medicine, 89, 265-268.

4724.   Rose, J.A. (1949), Relation of therapy to reality of parental connection with children. American Journal of Orthopsychiatry, 19, 351-357.

4725.   Rose, R.J., Miller, J.Z., Grim, C.E., and Christian, J.C. (1979), Aggregation of blood pressure in families of identical twins. American Journal of Epidemiology, 109, 503-511.

4526.   Rosen, A., and Berry, K. (1978), Attribution of responsibility for marital sexual dysfunction and traditionalism. Journal of Social Service Research, 1(3), 287-297.

4727.   Rosen, E. (1979), Review of T.J. Paolino, Jr., and B.S. McCardy (Eds.), Marriage and marital therapy: Psychoanalytic, behavioral and systems theory perspectives. Clinical and Social Work Journal, 7, 221.

4728.   Rosen, R.C., and Schnapp, B.J. (1974), The use of a specific behavioral technique (thought-stopping) in the context of conjoint couples therapy: A case report. Behavior Therapy, 5, 261-264.

4729.   Rosenbaum, A., and O'Leary, K.D. (1981), Marital violence: Characteristics of abusive couples. Journal of Consulting and Clinical Psychology, 49(1), 63-71.

4730.   Rosenbaum, I.S., and Serrano, A.C. (1979), Rationale and outline for a training program in family therapy. Journal of Marital and Family Therapy, 5(3), 77-82.

4731.   Rosenbaum, M. (1974), The family under attack in an era of family therapy (or, whatever happened to the family?). In L.R. Wolberg and M.L. Aronson (Eds.), Group therapy 1974: An overview. New York: Stratton Intercontinental Book Corporation.

4732.   Rosenbaum, R. (1984), Review of A. Bross' Family therapy - principles of strategic practice. Family Process, 23(2), 287.

4733.   Rosenberg, E.B. (1980), Therapy with siblings in reorganizing families. International Journal of Family Therapy, 2(3), 139-150.

4734.   Rosenberg, J. (1974), Counseling the parent of the chronic delinquent. In R.E. Hardy and J.G. Cull (Eds.), Therapeutic needs of the family: Problems, descriptions and therapeutic approaches. Springfield, IL: Charles C. Thomas.

4735.   Rosenberg, J.B. (1978), Two is better than one: Use of behavioral
        techniques within a structural family therapy model. Journal of
        Marriage and Family Counseling, 4, 31-39.

4736.   Rosenberg, J.B., and Lindbald, M.B. (1978), Behavior therapy in a family
        context: Treating elective mutism. Family Process, 17, 77-82.

4737.   Rosenberg, P.P., and Rosenberg, L.M. (1976), A group experience in sex
        education for the family. International Journal of Group Psychotherapy,
        26, 235-241.

4738.   Rosenblatt, A., and Wiggins, L.M. (1967), Characteristics of the parents
        served. Social Casework, 48, 639-647.

4739.   Rosenblatt, P.C., Tino, S.L., and Cunningham, M.R. (1979), Disrespect,
        tension and togetherness-apartness in marriage. Journal of Marital and
        Family Therapy, 5(1), 47.

4740.   Rosenblatt, P.C., Titus, S.L., Nevaldine, A., and Cunningham, M.R.
        (1979), Marital system differences and summer-long vacations:
        Togetherness, apartness and tension. American Journal of Family
        Therapy, 7(1), 77.

4741.   Rosenbluth, M., and Cameron, P. M. (1981), Assessment, commitment,
        and motivation in marital therapy. Canadian Journal of Psychiatry, 26,
        151-154.

4742.   Rosenfeld, A.H. (1982), Closing the revolving door through family
        therapy. Hospital and Community Psychiatry, 33, 893-894.

4743.   Rosenfeld, J.P. (1980), Social strain of probate. Journal of Marital and
        Family Therapy, 6, 327-334.

4744.   Rosenheim, E. (1979), Short-term preventive therapy with children of
        fatally-ill parents. The Israel Annals of Psychiatry and Related
        Disciplines, 17(1), 67-73.

4745.   Rosenstock, H.A., and Cambor, C.G. (1979), Family therapy approach to
        incapacitating migraine. International Journal of Family Therapy, 1(1),
        46.

4746.   Rosenstock, H.A., and Vencent, K.R. (1979), Parental involvement as a
        requisite for successful adolescent therapy. Journal of Clinical
        Psychiatry, 40(3), 132-135.

4747.   Rosenthal, D., and Hansen, J. (1980), Working with single-parent
        families. Family Therapy, 7(2), 73-82.

4748.   Rosenthal, M. (1975), Effects of parent training groups on behavior
        change in target children: Durability, generalization and patterns of
        family interaction. Dissertation Abstracts International, 36, 4706-B.

4749.   Rosenthal, P., and Novey, T. (1976), Measurement of stroking behavior
        in couples. Transactional Analysis Journal, 6(2), 205-208.

4750.   Rosenthal, P.A. (1980), Short-term family therapy and pathological
        grief resolution with children and adolescents. Family Process, 19, 151-
        159.

4751. Rosenthal, P.A., Mosteller, S., Wells, J.L., and Rolland, R.S. (1974), Family therapy with multiproblem, multi-children families in a court clinic setting. Journal of the American Academy of Child Psychiatry, 13, 126-142.

4752. Rosenwaike, I. (1972), Factors associated with religious and civil marriages. Demography, 9, 129-141.

4753. Rosman, B.L., Minuchin, S., and Liebman, R. (1975), Family lunch session: An introduction to family therapy in anorexia nervosa. American Journal of Orthopsychiatry, 45, 846-853.

4754. Rosman, B.L., and Fishman, C. (Eds.) (1985), Evolving models for family change: A volume in honor of Salvador Minuchin. New York: Guilford Press.

4755. Rosman, B.L., and Kaplan, S.L. (1977), A family approach to anorexia nervosa: Study, treatment, and outcome. In R.A. Virgersky (Ed.), Anorexia nervosa. New York: Raven Press.

4756. Rosman, B.L., and Minuchin, S. (1976), Input and outcome of family therapy in anorexia nervosa. In J.L. Claghorn (Ed.), Successful psychotherapy. New York: Brunner-Mazel. 128-139.

4757. Rosoff, J.I. (1976), Pregnancy counseling and abortion referral for patients in federally funded family planning programs. Family Planning Perspectives, 8(1), 43-46.

4758. Ross, B. (1976), Adolescent therapists. Canada's Mental Health, 24, 15-16.

4759. Ross, E. (1982), Child and family counseling with particular reference to families containing deaf members. Rehabilitation, 26, 117-120.

4760. Ross, E.R. (1982), Comparative effectiveness of relationship enhancement and therapist-preferred therapy on marital adjustment. Dissertation Abstracts International, 42, 4610-A.

4761. Ross, J.H. (1977), The development and evaluation of a group pre-marital counseling workshop. Dissertation Abstracts International, 38, 6544-A.

4762. Ross, J.W. (1979), Coping with childhood cancer: Group intervention as an aid to parents in crisis. Social Work in Health Care, 4, 381-391.

4763. Ross, J.W. (1978), Social work intervention with families of children with cancer-changing critical phases. Social Work in Health Care, 3(3), 257.

4764. Ross, P.T. (1977), A diagnostic technique for assessment of parent-child and family interaction patterns: The family puppet technique for therapy with families with young children. Family Therapy, 4, 219-242.

4765. Ross, P.T. (1977), The little girl, the family therapist, and the fairy tale, a true fable: Based on an intensive family therapy with a low socioeconomic level family where a little child was identified patient. Family Therapy, 4, 143-150.

4766. Ross, T. (1980), A comparison of the family reconstruction process versus the expectancy demand effect. Dissertation Abstracts International, 41, 699-B.

4767. Ross, W.D. (1948), Group psychotherapy with psychotic patients and their relatives. American Journal of Psychology, 105, 383-386.

4768. Rothe, K. (1966), On marriage counseling and sex education from the viewpoint of the gynecologist. Zeitschrift fur Arztliche Fortbildung, 60, 1224-1226.

4769. Rotter, P. (1974), Working with parents of young deaf children. In R.E. Hardy and J.G. Cull (Eds.), Educational and psychosocial aspects of deafness. Springfield, IL: Charles C. Thomas.

4770. Rougeul, F. (1980), Introduction to systemic family therapies. Bulletin de Psychologie, 33, 891-893.

4771. Rounds, K.A. (1984), Review of W.J. Doherty and M.A. Baird's Family therapy and family medicine. Patient Education and Counseling, 5(4), 206.

4772. Rounsaville, B.J., Weisman, M.M., Prusoff, B.A., and Hercegbaum, R. (1979), Process of psychotherapy among depressed women with marital disputes. American Journal of Orthopsychiatry, 49, 505-510.

4773. Roy, R. (1984), Chronic pain: A family perspective. International Journal of Family Therapy, 6(1), 31-43.

4774. Ruback, R.B. (1982), Values, ethics, legalities, and the family therapist: VII. Issues in family law: Implications for therapists. Family Therapy Collections, 1, 103-123.

4775. Ruben, A.G. (1978), The family picture. Journal of Marriage and Family Counseling, 4(3), 25-27.

4776. Ruben, H.L. (1976), The office management of family crises. Connecticut Medicine, 40, 739-741.

4777. Rubenstein, B.O. (1957), Some observations regarding the role of fathers in child psychotherapy. Bulletin of the Menninger Clinic, 21, 16-27.

4778. Rubenstein, G. (1979), Program in 'psycho-obstetrics'. Health and Social Work, 4, 145-158.

4779. Rubenstein, J.S. (1982), Learning objectives in family therapy training. Canadian Journal of Psychiatry, 27, 556-558.

4780. Rubenstein, M.A., Nemiroff, R.A., and Chipman, A. (1967), Simultaneous hospitalization of a mother and daughter. American Journal of Orthopsychiatry, 37, 350-351.

4781. Rubin, S.S. (1983), Developing ego-focused family psychotherapy. Psychotherapy in Private Practice, 17, 53-58.

4782. Rubin, Z., and Mitchell, C. (1976), Couples research as couples counseling: Some unintended effects of studying close relationships. American Psychologist, 31(1), 17-25.

4783.   Rubinstein, D. (1967), Family therapy. Progress in Neurology and Psychiatry, 22, 435-444.

4784.   Rubinstein, D. (1968), Family therapy. Progress in Neurology and Psychiatry, 23, 469-481.

4785.   Rubinstein, D. (1963), Family therapy. Progress in Neurology and Psychiatry, 18, 542-548.

4786.   Rubinstein, D. (1964), Teaching of psychotherapy. Family therapy. International Psychiatry Clinics, 1, 431-442.

4787.   Rubinstein, D. (1980), Family psychiatry in psychosomatics: Problems of adolescence. Psychotherapy and Psychosomatics, 33, 112-120.

4788.   Rubinstein, D. (1974), Techniques in family psychotherapy of schizophrenia. In R. Cancro, N. Fox and L.E. Shapiro (Eds.), Strategic intervention in schizophrenia: Current developments in treatment. New York: Behavioral Publications.

4789.   Rubinstein, D. (1972), Family therapy. In E.A. Spiegel (Ed.), Progress in neurology and psychiatry: An annual review. XXVII. New York: Grune and Stratton.

4790.   Rubinstein, D. (1970), Family therapy. Progress in Neurology and Psychiatry, 25, 372-384.

4791.   Rubinstein, D. (1970), Critical incidents in the context of family therapy: Critical incident No. 5. International Psychiatry Clinics, 7, 309-326.

4792.   Rubinstein, D. (1971), Family therapy. Progress in Neurology and Psychiatry, 26, 459-472.

4793.   Rubinstein, D. (1974), Family therapy. Nursing Times, 30, 236-237.

4794.   Rubinstein, D. (1975), Family therapy of schizophrenia - where to? - what next? Psychotherapy and Psychosomatics, 25, 154-162.

4795.   Rubinstein, D. (1969), Family therapy. Progress in Neurology and Psychiatry, 24, 424-435.

4796.   Rucker-Embden-Jonasch, I. (1979), Practice of family therapy. Psychotherapie, 29, 214.

4797.   Rudestam, K.E., and Frankel, M. (1983), Treating the multiproblem family: A casebook. Monterey, CA: Brooks-Cole.

4798.   Rudin, J. (1983), Aid to ruptured family systems. Soins Gynecologie Obstetruie Pueric e Pediatriks, 103, 51-54.

4799.   Rudnitzki, G. (1979), Tentative model in family therapy. Psychotherapie, Psychosomatik, Medizinische Psychologie, 29(4), 142-146.

4800.   Rudolph, E. (1982), Sol Garfield, have you not heard about family psychotherapy? American Psychologist, 37, 98-99.

4801. Rueger, D.B., and Liberman, R.P. (1984), Behavioral family therapy for delinquent and substance abusing adolescents. Journal of Drug Issues, 14(2), 403-418.

4802. Ruestow, P., Dunner, D.L., Bleeker, B., and Fieve, R.R. (1978), Marital adjustment in primary affective disorder. Comprehensive Psychiatry, 19, 565-571.

4803. Rueveni, U. (1978), Review of B.S. Ables' Therapy for couples: Clinician's guide for effective treatment. Family Process, 17(1), 111.

4804. Rueveni, U. (1979), The family therapist as a system interventionist. International Journal of Family Therapy, 1(1), 67.

4805. Rueveni, U. (1979), Networking families in crisis. New York: Human Sciences Press.

4806. Rueveni, U. (1977), Family network intervention: Mobilizing support for families in crisis. International Journal of Family Counseling, 5, 77-83.

4807. Rueveni, U. (1984), Rebuilding family relationship bridges. International Journal of Family Therapy, 6(1), 44-52.

4808. Rueveni, U. (1984), Review of L.B. Kadis and R. McClendon's Chocolate pudding and other approaches to intensive multiple family therapy. Family Process, 23(2), 293.

4809. Rueveni, U., and Wiener, M. (1976), Network intervention of disturbed families: The key role of network activists. Psychotherapy: Theory, Research and Practice, 13, 173-176.

4810. Ruffin, R.A. (1969), Family therapy: Theoretical and practical considerations for nursing. American Nursing Association Clinical Conference, 332-337.

4811. Ruger, U. (1976), Review of C.J. Sager and H.S. Kaplan's Manual of marriage therapy, family therapy and group therapy. Zeitschrift fur Psychosomatische Medizin und Psychoanalyse, 22, 391-392.

4812. Rugg, J. (1980), Communication patterns of disorganized lower socioeconomic families: Nursing assessment and intervention. Military Medicine, 145(11), 776-779.

4813. Rule, W.R. (1983), Family therapy and the pie metaphor. Journal of Marital and Family Therapy, 9, 101-103.

4814. Rupel, L.W. (1983), The relationship of location to the effectiveness of marriage enrichment retreats and workshops. Dissertation Abstracts International, 44, 1737-A.

4815. Rushton, A. (1978), Group work with single parents—a single and separated parents' group. Health and Social Service Journal, 88, 27-29.

4816. Russell, A. (1976), Contemporary concerns in family therapy. Journal of Marriage and Family Counseling, 2(3), 243-250.

4817. Russell, A. (1976), Limitations of family therapy. Clinical Social Work, 4, 83-92.

4818.   Russell, A., Russell, L., and Waring, E.M. (1980), Cognitive family therapy: A preliminary report. Canadian Journal of Psychiatry, 25(1), 64-67.

4819.   Russell, A., and Russell, L. (1978), Exorcising the ghosts in the marital system. Journal of Marriage and Family Counseling, 4, 71-78.

4820.   Russell, C.S. (1979), Circumplex model of marital and family systems: III. Empirical evaluation with families. Family Process, 18, 29-45.

4821.   Russell, C.S., Anderson, S.A., Atilano, R.B., Jurich, A.P., and Bergen, L.P. (1984), Intervention strategies - predicting family therapy outcome. Journal of Marital and Family Therapy, 10(3), 241-252.

4822.   Russell, C.S., Bagarozzi, D.A., Atilano, R.B., and Morris, J.E. (1984), A comparison of two approaches to marital enrichment and conjugal skills training - Minnesota couples communication program and structured behavioral exchange contracting. American Journal of Family Therapy, 12(3), 13-25.

4823.   Russell, C.S., III. (1979), Empirical evaluation with families. Family Process, 18, 29-45.

4824.   Russell, C.S., Olson, D.H., and Sprenkle, D.H. (1983), From family symptom to family system: Review of family therapy research. American Journal of Family Therapy, 11, 3-14.

4825.   Russell, R.A. (1981), Assertiveness training and its effects upon the marital relationship. Family Therapy, 8(1), 9-20.

4826.   Rustin, S.L. (1973), Dehumanization and its effect on the ghetto family. Journal of Family Counseling, 1, 11-16.

4827.   Rutherford, B.B., and Bower, K.B. (1975), Behavioral contracting in conjoint family therapy. Family Therapy, 2, 215-226.

4828.   Rutledge, A.L. (1975), Treatment of male homosexuality through marriage counseling: A case presentation. Journal of Marriage and Family Counseling, 1(1), 51-62.

4829.   Rutledge, A.L. (1966), Premarital counseling. Cambridge, MA: Schenkman.

4830.   Rutledge, A.L. (1962), Husband-wife conferences in the home as an aid to marriage counseling. Marriage and Family Living, 24, 151-154.

4831.   Ryals, K., and Foster, D.R. (1976), Open marriage: A question of ego development and marriage counseling? Family Coordinator, 25, 297-303.

4832.   Ryan, B.A. (1980), Review of M. Bowen's Family therapy in clinical practice. Canada's Mental Health, 28, 23.

4833.   Ryan, F.G. (1983), The relationship of two models of supervision to structural family therapy outcome. Dissertation Abstracts International, 43, 2356-B.

4834. Rychener, D.L. (1983), Openness to dissonant or conflictual information over the developmental stages of dyadic formation and implications for premarital counseling. Dissertation Abstracts International, 43, 4058A.

4835. Ryder, N.B. (1974), The family in developed countries. Scientific American, 231, 122-128.

4836. Ryder, R.G., Kafka, J.S., and Olson, D.H. (1971), Separating and joining influences in courtship and early marriage. American Journal of Orthopsychiatry, 41, 450-464.

4837. Rydman, E.J. (1969), Membership categories in the American Association of Marriage Counselors. In B.N. Ard, Jr., and C.C. Ard (Eds.), Handbook of marriage counseling. Palo-Alto, CA: Science Behavior Books.

4838. Ryglewicz, H. (1982), Working with the family of the psychiatrically disabled young adult. New Directions for Mental Health Services, 14, 91-97.

4839. Ryle, A., and Lipshitz, S. (1975), Recording change in marital therapy with the reconstruction grid. British Journal of Medical Psychology, 48, 39-48.

4840. Sabin, S. M. (1983), Family involvement in the in-patient hospitalization of children. Dissertation Abstracts International, 44, 1976-B.

4841. Sabom, W.S. (1983), Review of L.R. Wolberg and M.L. Aronson's Group and family therapy 1981. Journal of Psychology and Theology, 11, 71.

4842. Sachs, L.J. (1972), Psychotherapy of mother and son producing chain reactions in untreated family members. Psychiatry Quarterly, 46, 187-198.

4843. Safer, D.J. (1968), Establishing boundary lines for families of children with behavior problems. Psychiatric Quarterly, 42, 86-97.

4844. Safer, D.J. (1966), Family therapy for children with behavior disorders. Family Process, 5, 243-255.

4845. Saffer, J.B. (1979), The awesome burden upon the child who must keep a family secret. Child Psychiatry and Human Development, 10, 35-40.

4846. Safir, M.P., and Hoch, Z. (1980), Couple interactional classification of sexual dysfunction: A new theoretical conceptualization. Journal of Sex and Marital Therapy, 6(2), 129-134.

4847. Sagatun, I.J. (1982), Attributional effects of therapy with incestuous families. Journal of Marital and Family Therapy, 8, 99-104.

4848. Sager, C.J. (1966), The development of marriage therapy: An historical review. American Journal of Orthopsychiatry, 36(5), 458-467.

4849. Sager, C.J. (1967), The conjoint session in marriage therapy. American Journal of Psychoanalysis, 27(2), 139-146.

4850. Sager, C.J. (1967), Marital psychotherapy. Current Psychiatric Therapies, 7, 92-102.

4851.   Sager, C.J. (1967), Transference in conjoint treatment of married
        couples. Archives of General Psychiatry, 16(2), 185-193.

4852.   Sager, C.J. (1968), An overview of family therapy. International
        Journal of Group Psychotherapy, 18(3), 302-312.

4853.   Sager, C.J. (1976), Marriage contracts and couple therapy: Hidden
        forces in intimate relationships. New York: Brunner/Mazel.

4854.   Sager, C.J. (1976), The role of sex therapy in marital therapy.
        American Journal of Psychiatry, 133(5), 555-558.

4855.   Sager, C.J. (1983), Treating the remarried family. New York:
        Brunner/Mazel.

4856.   Sager, C.J., Brayboy, T.L., and Watenberg, B.R. (1970), Black ghetto
        family in therapy: A laboratory experience. New York: Grove Press.

4857.   Sager, C.J., Kaplan, H.S., Gundlach, R.H., Kremer, M., Lenz, R., and
        Royce, J.R. (1971), The marriage contract. Family Practice, 10, 311-
        326.

4858.   Sager, C.J., Masters, Y.J., Ronall, R.E., and Normand, W.C. (1968),
        Selection and engagement of patients in family therapy. American
        Journal of Orthopsychiatry, 38(4), 715-723.

4859.   Sager, C.J., Masters, Y.J., Ronall, R.E., and Normand, W.C. (1967), The
        selection and engagement process for brief family therapy in a general
        hospital psychiatric walk-in clinic. American Journal of
        Orthopsychiatry, 37(2), 389-390.

4860.   Sager, C.J., Walker, E., Brown, H.S., Crohn, H.M., and Rodstein, E.
        (1981), Improving functioning of the remarried family system. Journal
        of Marital and Family Therapy, 7(1), 3-13.

4861.   Sager, C.J., and Kaplan, H.S. (Eds.) (1972), Progress in group and family
        therapy. New York: Brunner/Mazel.

4862.   Sahin, S.T. (1978), A new nursing perspective on the family with a
        special-needs child. Nursing Forum, 17(4), 356-375.

4863.   Sakamoto, Y. (1977), Some experiences through family psychotherapy
        for psychotics in Japan. International Journal of Social Psychiatry, 22,
        265-271.

4864.   Sakamoto, Y. (1977), Some experiences through family psychotherapy
        for psychotics in Japan. International Journal of Social Psychiatry, 22,
        265-271.

4865.   Sakamoto, Y., and Miura, T. (1976), An attempt to understand Japanese
        personality from a family psychiatry point of view. Australian and New
        Zealand Journal of Psychiatry, 10, 115-117.

4866.   Sakurai, Y., and Takanori, K. (1968), Study on the care and training of
        severely retarded children. Journal of Mental Health, 16, 1-28.

4867.   Salas, E., Forti, L., Saimovici, E., and Sirota, A. (1969), Group therapy
        for children and mothers in emergency situations arising from dental

treatment of the children. Revista de Psiquiatrica y Psicologia Medica, 9(1), 16-38.

4868. Salgado, R.M. (1974), The role of the Puerto Rican spiritist in helping Puerto Ricans with problems of family relations. Dissertation Abstracts Interational, 35, 3199A.

4869. Salin, L. (1978), Review of H. Stierlin's Psychoanalytic family therapy. Family Process, 17(2), 232.

4870. Salin, L. (1984), Review of L.G. Baruth and C.H. Huber's An introduction to marital theory and therapy. Family Process, 23(4), 578-579.

4871. Salin, L. (1984), Review of M. Nichols' Family therapy: Concepts and methods. Family Process, 23(4), 577-578.

4872. Salinger, R. (1979), Toward a biblical framework for family therapy. Psychology and Theology, 7, 241-250.

4873. Sallanranta, A. (1971), (Family therapy). Sairaanh Vuosik, 8, 86-102. (Finland)

4874. Salts, C.J. (1980), Effects of postseparation/postdivorce counseling groups on adjustment and self-concept. Dissertation Abstracts International, 40, 4262-A. (University Microfilms No. 80011114.)

4875. Salvino, C. (1974), A view of the role of family therapy in child psychiatry. Acta Paedopsychiarica (Basel), 40, 168-172.

4876. Sampaio, D. (1984), Systematic family therapy: A new concept, a new practice. Acta Medica Portugal, 5, 67-70.

4877. Sampaio, D. (1983), Individuals and families (editorial). Acta Medica Portugal, 4, 145-46.

4878. Sampel, D.D., and Seymour, W.R. (1980), A comparative analysis of the effectiveness of conciliation counseling on certain personality variables. Journal of Marital and Family Therapy, 6(3), 269-275.

4879. Sampson, N. (1972), Family therapy for the child with a communicative disorder. Journal of Communicative Disorders, 5, 205-211.

4880. Samuel, N. (1985), Living with psychiatric patients: The relationship between family burden and mental health among family members. Dissertation Abstracts International, 45, 3002-A.

4881. Samuma, K. (1978), The Japanese family in relation to people's health. Social Science Medicine, 12, 469-478.

4882. Sander, F.M. (1973), Touring the literature of family therapy. Seminars in Psychiatry, 5(2), 141-148.

4883. Sanders, G.L. (1984), Relationships of the handicapped: Issues of sexuality and marriage. Family Therapy Collections, 11, 63-74.

4884. Sandgrund, G. (1962), Group counseling with adoptive families after legal adoption. Child Welfare, 41, 248-252.

4885.   Sandholm, G.L. (1982), A systems perspective to marriage counseling. Pastoral Psychology, 30, 118-128.

4886.   Sandler, N. (1977), Working with families of chronic asthmatics. Journal of Asthma Research, 15, 15-21.

4887.   Sandler, N. (1977), Working with families of chronic asthmatics. Journal of Asthma Research, 15, 15-21.

4888.   Sands, R.M. (1965), A preventive clinical and educational program for children from two to three and their mothers. American Journal of Orthopsychiatry, 35, 295-296.

4889.   Santa Maria, L.J. (1969), Some traditional Philippine values and family therapy techniques. ANPHI Papers, 4, 11-15.

4890.   Santa-Barbara, J. (1983), Reply: Comments on research in family therapy. Family Process, 22, 338-339.

4891.   Santa-Barbara, J., Woodward, C.A., Levin, S., Goodman, J.T., Streiner, D., and Epstein, N.B. (1979), The McMaster family therapy outcome study: An overview of methods and results. International Journal of Family Therapy, 1(4), 304.

4892.   Santa-Barbara, J., and Epstein, N.B. (1973), Conflict behavior in clinical families: Interaction patterns and stable outcomes. Proceedings of the Annual Convention of the American Psychological Association, 8, 319-320.

4893.   Santa-Barbara, J., and Epstein, N.B. (1974), Conflict behavior in clinical families: Preasymptotic interactions and stable outcomes. Behavioral Science, 19, 100-110.

4894.   Santa-Barbara, J., and Epstein, N.B. (1973), Conflict behavior in clinical families: Preasymptotic interactions and stable outcomers. Behaviour Research and Therapy, 11, 383-394.

4895.   Santisteban, D. (1978), The process of cultural adaptation implications for individual and family functioning. Dissertation Abstracts International, 39, 1968B.

4896.   Sarembe, B. (1972), (Population structure in marital and sexual counseling.) Zeitschrift fur Arztliche Fortbildung, 66, 888-891.

4897.   Sargent, A.J. (1983), Family therapy: A view for pediatricians. Journal of Pediatrics, 102, 977-81.

4898.   Sargent, J. (1983), The family and childhood psychosomatic disorders. General Hospital Psychiatry, 5, 41-48.

4899.   Sargent, J. (1983), The sick child: Family complications. Journal of Developmental and Behavioral Pediatrics, 4, 50-56.

4900.   Sarphatie, H.R., and Tonino, J.F. (1968), Family therapy. Maanblad voor de geestelyke Volksgezondheid, 23(5), 206-209.

4901.   Sasano, E.M., and Reed, M. (1977), The family in physical therapy.....Family focus, Division of Physical Therapy, Stanford University. Physical Therapy, 57, 153-159.

4902.   Saslow, G. (1985), Review of W.R. McFarlane's (Ed.). Family therapy in schizophrenia. Contemporary Psychology, 30(3), 241.

4903.   Satir, V. (1967), Family systems and approaches to family therapy. Journal of the Fort Logan Mental Health Center, 4, 81-93.

4904.   Satir, V., Stachowiak, J., and Taschman, H.A. (1976), Helping families to change. New York: Aronson.

4905.   Satir, V.M. (1967), Conjoint family therapy. Palo Alto, CA: Science and Behavior Books.

4906.   Satir, V.M. (1964), Conjoint marital therapy. American Journal of Orthopsychiatry, 34, 277.

4907.   Sauber, S.R. (1971), Multiple family group counseling. Personnel and Guidance Journal, 49, 459-465.

4908.   Sauber, S.R., L'Abate, L., and Weeks, G.R. (1984), Family therapy: Basic concepts and terms. Rockville, MD: Aspen Systems.

4909.   Saucier, J.F. (1970), Psychodynamics of interethnic marriage. Canadian Psychiatric Association Journal, 15, 129-134.

4910.   Sauer, R.J. (1980), Family therapy with the individual patient. Family Therapy, 7(2), 125-130.

4911.   Sauer, R.J. (1981), The live-in boyfriend: A family arrangement. Family Therapy, 8, 203-210.

4912.   Saunders, A.L. (1975), Multiple family therapy in a community mental health center. Professional Psychology, 6, 140-144.

4913.   Saunders, D.G. (1977), Marital violence: Dimensions of the problem and modes of intervention. Journal of Marriage and Family Counseling, 3, 43-52.

4914.   Saunders, D.R., Kaplan, S.J., and Rodd, W.G. (1980), Implications of the personality assessment system for marital counseling: A pilot study. Psychological Reports, 46, 151-160.

4915.   Saunders, G., and Schuckit, M. (1980), Review of E. Kaufman and P.N. Kaufman's Family therapy of drug and alcohol abuse. American Journal of Drug and Alcohol Abuse, 7, 251.

4916.   Saunders, S. (1984), Violent individuals and families: A handbook for practitioners. Springfield, IL: C.C. Thomas.

4917.   Saur, W.G. (1975), An activity for exploring marital expectations. Family Coordinator, 24, 366-367.

4918.   Savitsky, E., and Sharkey, H. (1972), Study of family interaction in the aged. Journal of Geriatric Psychiatry, 5, 3-24.

4919.   Sawin, M.M. (1979), Family cluster model of family enrichment. In N. Stinnett, B. Chesser and J. Defrain (Eds.), Building family strengths. Lincoln, NE: University of Nebraska Press.

4920.   Scanzoni, J. (1965), Resolution of occupational-conjugal role conflict in clergy marriages. Journal of Marriage and the Family, 27(3), 396-402.

4921.   Scarth, L. (1984), Review of A. Bentovim, G. Correllbarnes and A. Cooklin's Family therapy: Complementary frameworks of theory and practice, Vol. I and II. Journal of Child Psychology and Psychiatry, 25(4), 655.

4922.   Schachter, R.S. (1978), Kinetic psychotherapy in the treatment of families. Family Coordinator, 27(3), 283-288.

4923.   Schaefer, C.E., Briesmeister, J.M., and Fitton, M.E. (Eds.) (1984), Family therapy techniques for problem behaviors of children and teenagers. San Francisco, CA: Jossey-Bass.

4924.   Schaefer, J.W., Palkes, H.S., and Stewart, M.A. (1974), Group counseling for parents of hyperactive children. Child Psychiatry and Human Development, 5(2), 89-94.

4925.   Schaeffer, D.S. (1969), Effects of frequent hospitalization on behavior of psychotic patients in multiple family therapy program. Journal of Clinical Psychology, 25(1), 104-105.

4926.   Schaffer, L., Wynne, L.C., Day, J., Ryckoff, I.M., and Halperin, A. (1962), On the nature and sources of the psychiatrist's experience with the family of the schizophrenic. Psychiatry, 25, 32-45.

4927.   Schaffer, M. (1981), An evaluation of the Minnesota couple communication program upon communication of married couples. Dissertation Abstracts International, 41, 4643-B.

4928.   Scharer, K. (1979), Nursing intervention with abusive and neglectful families within the community. Maternal-Child Nursing Journal, 8, 85-94.

4929.   Scharer, K. (1979), Nursing therapy with abusive and neglectful families. Journal of Psychiatric Nursing, 17, 12-16.

4930.   Scharf, C. (1984), Review of H.I. McCubbin an C.R. Figley's Stress and the family, Vol. 1. Coping with normative transition. Family Process, 23(3), 457.

4931.   Scharff, D.E. (1978), Truth and consequences in sex and marital therapy: The revelation of secrets in the therapeutic setting. Journal of Sex and Marital Therapy, 4(1), 35-49.

4932.   Scharfstein, B., and Libbey, M. (1982), Family orientation: Initiating patients and their families to psychiatric hospitalization. Hospital and Community Psychiatry, 33, 560-3.

4933.   Schauble, P.G., and Hil, C.G. (1976), A laboratory approach to treatment in marriage counseling: Training in communication skills. Family Coordinator, 25, 277-285.

4934.   Schechter, M.D. (1973), Psychoanalysis of a latency boy with neurodermatitis. Psychoanalytic Studies of the Child, 27, 529-564.

4935.   Schedler, D.E. (1980), The impact of the Ohlsen triad model of group counseling in treatment: Training workshops for clergy and spouses. Dissertation Abstracts International, 41, 2459-A.

4936.   Scheflen, A.E. (1978), Susan smiled: On explanation in family therapy. Family Process, 17(1), 59-68.

4937.   Scheideman, J. (1971), Student nurses lead family groups. Hospital and Community Psychiatry, 22, 378-380.

4938.   Scheidlinger, S., and Freeman, H. (1956), Family services. In S.R. Slavson (Ed.), The fields of group psychotherapy. New York: International Universities Press.

4939.   Scheiner, L.C., and Musetto, A.P. (1979), Redefining the problem: Family therapy with a severely symptomatic adolescent. Family Therapy, 6(3), 195.

4940.   Scheinfeld, D.R. (1970), Parent's values, family networks, and family development: Working with disadvantaged families. American Journal of Orthopsychiatry, 40, 413-425.

4941.   Scherz, F.H. (1966), Family treatment concepts. Social Casework, 47, 234-240.

4942.   Schetky, D.H. (1982), Corporate family lifestyles: A child psychiatrist's perspective. Psychiatric Annals, 12, 862-874.

4943.   Schibalski, K., and Harlander, U. (1982), Scapegoat dynamic in group psychotherapy of children. Dynamic Psychiatry, 15, 251-267.

4944.   Schild, S. (1982), Beyond diagnosis: Issues in recurrent counseling of parents of the mentally retarded. Social Work in Health Care, 8(1), 81.

4945.   Schiling, S., and Gross, E.J. (1979), Stages of family therapy: A developmental model. Clinical Social Work Journal, 7(2), 105-114.

4946.   Schiller, M.K. (1976), Family credit counseling: An emerging community service revisited. Journal of Consumer Affairs, 16(1), 97-100.

4947.   Schiller, P. (1960), Marriage counseling in a legal aid setting. Marriage and Family Living, 22, 213-215.

4948.   Schimel, J.L. (1979), Adolescents and families: An overview. Adolescent Psychiatry, 7, 362-370.

4949.   Schindler, R. (1983), Counseling Hassidic couples: The cultural dimension. Journal of Psychology and Judaism, 8(1), 52-62.

4950.   Schindler, W. (1966), The role of the mother in group psychotherapy. International Journal of Group Psychotherapy, 16, 198-202.

4951.   Schindler, W. (1955), Transference and countertransference in family pattern group psychotherapy. Acta Psychotherapie Psychosomatics Orthopsychiatria, 3, 345-353.

4952.   Schindler, W. (1953), Counter-transference in "family-pattern group psychotherapy." International Journal of Group Psychotherapy, 3, 424-430.

4953.   Schindler, W. (1951), "Family pattern" group therapy of sex disorders. International Journal of Sexology, 4, 142-149.

4954.   Schindler, W. (1980), Die analytische gruppentherapie nach dem familienmodell: Ausgew beitr. Munchen; Basel: E. Reinhardt.

4955.   Schjoth, A. (1973), Letter: The medical school course on contraception and family problems. The ideological manipulation of sexual pedagogy. Tidsskrift for den Norske Laegeforening, 93, 1797-1798.

4956.   Schlachter, R.H. (1975), Home counseling of adolescents and parents. Social Work, 20(6), 427-428.

4957.   Schlanger, P.H. (1978), Role playing used to elicit language from hearing impaired children. Group Psychotherapy, Psychodrama and Sociometry, 31, 136-143.

4958.   Schless, A.P., and Mendels, J. (1978), The value of interviewing family and friends in assessing life stressors. Archives of General Psychiatry, 35, 565-567.

4959.   Schmid, H. (1978), Review of J. Haley's Directed family therapy. Psychologie, 37(2), 169.

4960.   Schmidt, D.D., Hill, R., and Moir, R.N. (1980), Adolescent depression and family physician's approach to working with the family clinical conference. Journal of Family Practice, 9, 961-8.

4961.   Schmidt, R. (1978), The determination of focus in brief psychoanalytically-oriented family therapy. Praxis der Kinderpsychologie und Kinderpsychiatrie, 27(3), 87-92.

4962.   Schmidt, R. (1975), Psychoanalytically oriented family therapy according to the duplication theorem. Praxis der Kinderpsychologie und Kinder Psychiatrie, 24(7), 254-258.

4963.   Schmidt, S.A. (1970), Staff helps family help itself. Modern Nursing Home, 24, 35.

4964.   Schmidt, S.A., and Liebowitz, B. (1969), Adolescents and their families. American Journal of Orthopsychiatry, 39, 327-328.

4965.   Schmitt, B.D., and Beelley, P (1976), The long-term management of the child and family in child abuse and neglect. Pediatric Annals, 5, 59-78.

4966.   Schneer, H.I., and Hewlett, I.W. (1958), A family approach to stuttering with group therapy techniques. International Journal of Group Psychotherapy, 8, 329-341.

4967.   Schneider, T., Schonitzer, D., and Friedrichs, S. (1981), Graphic family therapy: An effective alternative to structure and strategy. Journal of Marital and Family Therapy, 7(1), 33.

4968.   Schneiderman, G., Lowder, J. A., and Grant, R.Q. (1983), Tay-Sachs and related lipid storage diseases: Family treatment. Psychiatric Journal of the University of Ottawa, 8, 113-115.

4969.   Schneiderman, G., and Evans, H. (1975), An approach to families of acting-out adolescents: A case study. Adolescence, 10, 495-498.

4970.   Schneiderman, G., and Pakes, E.H. (1976), The teaching of family therapy skills on an inpatient child psychiatry ward. Family Therapy, 3(1), 29-33.

4971.   Schneiderman, I. (1975), Family thinking in prevention of alcoholism. Preventive Medicine, 4, 296-309.

4972.   Schnell, R. (1974), Helping parents cope with the dying child with a genetic disorder. Journal of Clinical Child Psychology, 3, 34-35.

4973.   Schnitman, D.F. (1983), Cultural issues in family therapy: A systemic model. Dissertation Abstracts International, 44, 326-B.

4974.   Schodt, C.M., and Hayes, S.L. (1979), Counseling families after a SIDS loss: A Public Health Nursing Program in Philadelphia....The Pennsylvania Sudden Infant Death Syndrome (SIDS) Center. Pennsylvania Nurse, 34, 4-6.

4975.   Scholz, O.B. (1982), Utility of a goal-oriented strategy in marital therapy. Partnerberatung, 19, 69-78.

4976.   Schonfelder, T. (1979), Family therapy aspects in child and adolescent psychiatry. Acta Paedopsychiatrica, 44(3-4), 169-179.

4977.   Schover, L.R., and Von-Eschenbach, A.C. (1984), Sexual and marital counseling with men treated for testicular cancer. Journal of Sex and Marital Therapy, 10, 29-40.

4978.   Schreiber, L.E. (1966), Evaluation of family group treatment in a family agency. Family Process, 5(1), 21-29.

4979.   Schuham, A.I. (1972), Activity, talking time, and spontaneous agreement in disturbed and normal family interaction. Journal of Abnormal Psychology, 79, 68-75.

4980.   Schulman, G.L. (1973), Treatment of intergenerational pathology. Social Casework, 54, 462-472.

4981.   Schulman, G.L. (1976), Teaching family therapy to social work students. Social Casework, 57, 448-457.

4982.   Schulman, G.L. (1980), Therapy with siblings in reorganizing families: I. International Journal of Family Therapy, 2(3), 151-154.

4983.   Schulman, G.L. (1980), Review of T.J. Paolino and B.S. McCrady's Marriage and marital therapy: Psychoanalytic, behavioral and systems theory perspectives. International Journal of Group Psychotherapy, 30, 365.

4984.   Schulman, G.L. (1981), Divorce, single parenthood, and stepfamilies: Structural implications of these transactions. International Journal of Family Therapy, 3, 87-112.

4985.   Schulman, G.L. (1984), Review of M. Andolphi's Family therapy: An interactional approach. Social Work With Groups, 7(1), 105-107.

4986.   Schulman, G.L., and Leichter, E. (1968), Prevention of family break-up. Social Casework, 49, 143-150.

4987.   Schulman, S., and Klein, M.M. (1984), Resolution of transference problems in structural therapy of single-parent families by a male therapist. American Journal of Family Therapy, 12(2), 38-44.

4988.   Schulz, P.J. (1968), A group approach to working with families of the blind. New Outlook, 62, 82-86.

4989.   Schulz, P.M., Schulz, S.C., Dibble, E., Targum, S.D., VanKammen, D.P., and Gershon, E.S. (1982), Patient and family attitudes about schizophrenia: Implications for genetic counseling. Schizophrenia Bulletin, 8(3), 504.

4990.   Schumm, W.R. (1984), Review of D.H. Olson an R. Markoff's Inventory of marriage and family literature, Vol. 9, 1982. American Journal of Family Therapy, 12(3), 81.

4991.   Schumm, W.R., Bugaighis, M.A., and Jurich, A.P. (1985), Using repeated measures designs in program evaluation of family therapy. Journal of Marital and Family Therapy, 11(1), 87-94.

4992.   Schumm, W.R., and Bolsen, N.F. (1985), The family coping strategies scale. American Journal of Family Therapy, 13, 67-71.

4993.   Schumm, W.R., and Denton, W. (1980), Premarital counseling: Approaches, objectives, and evaluation: A bibliography. Pastoral Psychology, 28(3), 181.

4994.   Schumm, W.R., and Denton, W. (1979), Trends in premarital counseling. Journal of Marital and Family Therapy, 5(4), 23-32.

4995.   Schwab, L.O. (1975), Rehabilitation of physically disabled women in a family oriented program. Rehabilitation Literature, 36, 34-43.

4996.   Schwarts, L.L. (1984), Adoption, custody and family therapy. American Journal of Family Therapy, 12, 51-58.

4997.   Schwartz, R.C. (1981), The relationship among communication style, self-esteem, and the couple communication program. Dissertation Abstracts International, 41, 3198-B.

4998.   Schwartz, R.C. (1983), Review of R.J. Becvar and D.S. Becvar's Systems theory and family therapy - a primer. American Journal of Family Therapy, 11, 83.

4999.   Schwartz, R.C. (1982), Bulimia and family therapy: A case study. International Journal of Eating Disorders, 2, 75-82.

5000.   Schwartz, R.I. (1983), Concentric family therapy: Innovation in family treatment and training. Family Relations: Journal of Applied Family and Child Studies, 32, 485-488.

5001.   Schwartzman, J. (1983), Family ethnography: A tool for clinicians. Family Therapy Collections, 11, 137-149.

5002.   Schwartzman, J. (1984), Family theory and scientific method. Family Process, 23(2), 223-236.

5003.   Schwartzman, J. (1974), The individual, incest, and exogamy. Psychiatry, 37, 171-180.

5004.   Schwartzman, J. (1972), The individual, incest, and exogamy. Nebraska Medical Journal, 57, 93-96.

5005.   Schwarz, F. (1980), Individual and family therapy of schizophrenic psychoses (author's transl.). Nervenarzt, 51, 644-653.

5006.   Schwarz, F. (1981), Related persons in the psychotherapy of schizophrenic patients. Zeitschrift Fur Klinische Psychologie Und Psychotherapie, 29, 247-254.

5007.   Schween, P.A., and Gralnick, A. (1966), Factors affecting family therapy in the hospital setting. Comprehensive Psychiatry, 7, 424-431.

5008.   Schwertl, W. (1985), Review of The language of family therapy: A vocabulary. Praxis der Kinderpsychologie und Kinderpsychiatrie, 34(3), 110.

5009.   Schwietzer, J., and Weber, G. (1985), Family therapy with families of divorce: A survey. Praxis der Kinderpsychologie und Kinderpsychiatrie, 34(3), 96-109.

5010.   Schwoeri, L., and Schwoeri, F. (1981), Family therapy of borderline patients: Diagnostic and treatment issues. International Journal of Family Psychiatry, 2, 237-250.

5011.   Scoresby, A.L. (1973), The family as a subsystem. Journal of Employment Counseling, 10, 127-135.

5012.   Scott, E.M., and Manaugh, T.S. (1976), Territorial struggles in the marriages of alcoholics. Journal of Marriage and Family Counseling, 2(4), 341-345.

5013.   Scott, S. (1984), Deafness in the family - will the therapist listen? Family Process, 23(2), 214-215.

5014.   Scott, S. (1984), Mobilization: A natural resource of the family. Family Therapy Collections, 11, 98-110.

5015.   Scovern, A.W., Bukstell, L.H., Kilmann, P.R., Laval, R.A., Busemeyer, J., and Smith, V. (1980), Effects of parent counseling on the family system. Journal of Counseling Psychology, 27(3), 268-275.

5016.   Scully, T. M. (1983), Strategic family therapy with conduct disordered children and adolescents: An outcome study. Dissertation Abstracts International, 43, 3042-B.

5017.   Seawright, T.R. (1961), A social casework approach to marriage counseling. South Africa: Johannesburg Witwaterstrand University Press.

5018.   Sederer, L.I., and Sederer, N. (1979), Family myth: Sex therapy gone awry. Family Process, 18(3), 315-322.

5019.   Sedgwick, R. (1979), The use of psychoanalysis and family memorabilia in the study of family interaction. Corrective of Social Psychiatry, 25(4), 317.

5020.   Sedgwick, R. (1980), Family mental health: Theory and practice. St. Louis: Mosby.

5021.   Seeger, P.A. (1976), A framework for family therapy. Journal of Psychiatric Nursing and Mental Health Services, 14, 23-28.

5022.   Seeman, L. (1978), Early improvement in family therapy and its relationship to engagement and outcome. Dissertation Abstracts International, 39, 398B.

5023.   Seeman, L., Tittler, B.I., and Friedman, S. (1985), Early interactional change and its relationship to family therapy outcome. Family Process, 24(1), 59-68.

5024.   Seeman, L., Weitz, L.J., and Abramowitz, S.I. (1976), Do family therapists' family ideologies affect their impressions of families? Journal of Community Psychology, 4(2), 149-151.

5025.   Seeman, M.V., and Edwards-Evans, B. (1979), Marital therapy with borderline patients: Is it beneficial? Journal of Clinical Psychiatry, 40(7), 308-312.

5026.   Segal, R. (1981), Integrating art form therapies and family therapy. Social Casework, 62, 218-226.

5027.   Seghers, A. (1984), Study of a case of manic-depressive psychosis treated in the acute phase with drugs and family therapy. Acta Psychiatrica Belgica, 84, 38-49.

5028.   Segond, P. (1983), Marks for history of family therapies. Etudes Psychotherapiques, 14, 99-108.

5029.   Segraves, R.T. (1978), Conjoint marital therapy: A cognitive behavioral model. Archives of General Psychiatry, 35, 450-455.

5030.   Seidel, U. (1982), Techniques of therapeutic handling with constellation of family and brothers and sisters. Partnerberatung, 19, 124-132.

5031.   Seiden, A.M. (1976), Overview: Research on psychology of women: II. Women in families, work, and psychotherapy. American Journal of Psychiatry, 133(10), 1111-1128.

5032.   Seifert, M.H. (1974), Treating alcoholism, a family disease. American Annual for the Deaf, 119, 325-330.

5033.   Seifert, M.H., Jr. (1973), Treating alcoholism, a family disease. American Family Physician, 8, 150-153.

5034.   Seitz, S., and Riedell, G. (1974), Parent child interactions as the therapy target. Journal of Communication Disorders, 7(4), 295-304.

5035.   Selby, J.W., Calhoun, L.G., and Parrott, G. (1978), Attitudes toward seeking pastoral help in the event of the death of a close friend or relative. American Journal of Community Psychology, 6, 399-403.

5036.   Selig, A. (1976), Crisis theory and family growth. Family Coordinator, 25, 291-297.

5037.   Selig, A.L. (1979), Review of S. Walrondkinner's Family therapy: The treatment of natural systems. Canada's Mental Health, 27(3), 20.

5038.   Selig, A.L. (1982), Treating nocturnal enuresis in one session of family therapy: A case study. Journal of Clinical Child Psychology, 11, 234-237.

5039.   Selinger, D., and Barcal, A. (1977), Brief family therapy may lead to deep personality change. American Journal of Psychotherapy, 31, 302-309.

5040.   Selling, L.S. (1941), The adjustment of marital problems. Journal of Michigan Medical Society, 40, 789-794.

5041.   Selnes, B. (1980), The teenager as the one who carries the symptoms of his family: A clinical example. Tidsskrift For Norsk Psykologforening, 17, 542-548.

5042.   Selvin, M. and Marini, M.M. (1979), Can Ph.D.-M.D. intermarriages work: Letters. New England Journal of Medicine, 301, 278.

5043.   Selvini-Palazzoli, M. (1967), From the disturbed child to its family group: A new method of exploration and family. Rivista Sperimentale di Freniatria, 91, 1551-1555.

5044.   Selvini-Palazzoli, M., Boscolo, L., Cecchin, G., and Prata, G. (1977), Ritualized prescription in the therapy of the family: Odd and even days. Archivis di Psicologia, Neurologia y Psiquiatria, 38, 293-302.

5045.   Selvini-Palazzoli, M., and Prata, G. (1982), Snares in family therapy. Journal of Marital and Family Therapy, 8, 443-450.

5046.   Semmens, J.P. (1973), Counseling couples with sexual problems. Journal of the South Carolina Medical Association, 69, 390-395.

5047.   Semmens, J.P., and Semmens, F.J. (1973), Counseling couples with sexual problems. Journal of Psychosomatic Research, 17, 309-315.

5048.   Sencer, W. (1974), Family psychiatric treatment. Journal of Psychiatric Nursing, 12, 27-31.

5049.   Serayhorn, J. (1978), Social exchange theory: Cognitive restructuring in marital therapy. Family Process, 17(4), 427.

5050.   Serlin, E. (1982), Diagnosing family boundaries. American Journal of Family Therapy, 10, 73-78.

5051.   Serlin, E. (1983), Review of P. Daniels and K. Weingarten's Sooner or later - the timing of parenthood in adult lives. Journal of Marital and Family Therapy, 9, 107.

5052.   Serrano, A.C., Zuelzer, M.B., Howe, D.D., and Reposa, R.E. (1979). Ecology of abusive and nonabusive families: Implications for intervention. Journal of the American Academy of Child Psychiatry, 18, 67-75.

5053.   Serrano, A.C., and Wilson, N.J. (1963), Family therapy in the treatment of the brain-damaged child. Diseases of the Nervous System, 24, 732-735.

5054.   Serrano, F.H. (1977), Family psychotherapy in ISSSTE medical institutions. Arichivis di Psicologia, Neurologia 7 Psiquiatria, 38, 173-177.

5055.   Sevee, D. (1979), The family in family medicine (letter). Journal of Family Practice, 9, 26-28, 30.

5056.   Seymour, W. R. (1982), Values, ethics, legalities, and the family therapist: III. Counselor/therapist values and therapeutic style. Family Therapy Collections, 1, 41-60.

5057.   Seywert, F. (1981), On the "conjoint family therapy" in hospitalized schizophrenics (author's transl.). Psychotherapie, Psychosomatiks und Medicinishe Psycholocia, 31, 67-9.

5058.   Seywert, F. (1984), Therapies for the families of hospitalized psychotics. Revue Medicale de la Suisse Romande, 104, 125-30.

5059.   Sgroi, S.M. (1982), Family treatment of child sexual abuse. Journal of Social Work and Human Sexuality, 1, 109-128.

5060.   Shands, H.C. (1979), Review of C.E. Sluzki and D.C. Ransom's Double bind: Foundation of the communicational approach to the family. Family Process, 17, 492-496.

5061.   Shane, T.W. (1972), Conjoint therapy: One approach for treating dysfunctional marriage relationships. Dissertation Abstracts International, 32, 7080-A.

5062.   Shapiro, A. (1982), Marital problems presenting to a marriage counselor. British Medical Journal: Clinical Research Edition, 7, 797-8.

5063.   Shapiro, D.M. (1981), A family data base for the family oriented medical record. Journal of Family Practice, 13, 881-887.

5064.   Shapiro, E.R. (1982-3), The holding environment and family therapy with acting out adolescents. International Journal of Psychoanalytic Psychotherapy, 9, 209-26.

5065.   Shapiro, E.R. (1982), On curiosity: Intrapsychic and interpersonal boundary formation in family life. International Journal of Family Psychiatry, 3, 69-89.

5066.   Shapiro, E.R. (1978), Research on family dynamics: Clinical implications for the family of the borderline adolescent. Adolescent Psychiatry, 6, 360-376.

5067.   Shapiro, E.R., Shapiro, R.L., Zinner, J., and Berkowitz, D.A. (1977), The borderline ego and the working alliance: Indications for family and individual treatment in adolescence. International Journal of Psychoanalysis, 58, 77-87.

5068.   Shapiro, E.R., and Kolb, J.E. (1979), Engaging the family of the hospitalized adolescent: The multiple family meeting. Adolescent Psychiatry, 7, 322-342.

5069.   Shapiro, L.N., and Wild, C.M. (1976), The product of the consensus Rorschach in families of male schizophrenics. Family Process, 15, 211-224.

5070.   Shapiro, M.I., and Shapiro, G. (1958), Egotherapy with parents of the psychotic child. American Journal of Orthopsychiatry, 28, 786-793.

5071.   Shapiro, R. (1979), The problematic position of family therapy in professional training. Professional Psychology, 10, 876-879.

5072.   Shapiro, R.B. (1975), Short term family therapy outcome study: Interpersonal perception and communication patterns. Dissertation Abstracts International, 36, 1459-B.

5073.   Shapiro, R.J. (1975), Problems in teaching family therapy. Professional Psychology, 6, 41-44.

5074.   Shapiro, R.J. (1975), Some implications of training psychiatric nurses in family therapy. Journal of Marital and Family Counseling, 1, 323-330.

5075.   Shapiro, R.J. (1974), Therapist attitudes and premature termination in family and individual therapy. Journal of Nervous and Mental Disease, 159, 101-107.

5076.   Shapiro, R.J. (1980), Review of F.M. Sander's Individual and family therapy: Toward an integration. Family Process, 19, 420-422.

5077.   Shapiro, R.J. (1977), A family therapy approach to alcoholism. Journal of Marital and Family Counseling, 3, 71-78.

5078.   Shapiro, R.J. (1978), Family therapy for the drug user: Conceptual and practical considerations. Drug Forum, 6(3), 200-202.

5079.   Shapiro, R.J., and Budman, S.H. (1973), Defection, termination, and continuation in family and individual therapy. Family Process, 12, 55-68.

5080.   Shapiro, R.J., and Harris, R.I. (1976), Family therapy in treatment of the deaf: A case report. Family Process, 15, 83-96.

5081.   Shapiro, R.L. (1978), The adolescent, the therapist and the family: The management of external resistances to psychoanalytic therapy of adolescents. Journal of Adolescence, 1(1), 3-10.

5082.   Shapiro, R.L. (1979), Adolescents in family therapy: In J.R. Novello (Ed.), Short course in adolescent psychiatry. New York: Brunner/Mazel.

5083.   Shapiro, R.L. (1979), The problematic position of family therapy in professional training. Professional Psychology, 10(6), 876.

5084.   Shapiro, R.L. (1967), The origin of adolescent disturbances in the family: Some considerations in theory and implications for therapy. In G.H. Zuk and I. Boszormenyi-Nagy, (Eds.), Family therapy and disturbed families. Palo Alto, CA: Science and Behavior Books.

5085.   Shapiro, V., Fraiberg, S., and Adelson, E. (1976), Infant parent psychotherapy on behalf of a child in a critical nutritional state. Psychoanalytic Study of the Child, 31, 461-491.

5086.   Sharp, L. (1978), Relabeling in conjoint family therapy. Journal of Psychiatric Nursing, 16(7), 29-33.

5087.   Sharpe, R. (1975), Counseling services for school age pregnancy girls. Journal of School Health, 45(5), 284-285.

5088.   Shaw, J.A. (1979), The military family: Who has been scapegoated? (letter). American Journal of Psychiatry, 136, 351-352.

5089.   Shaw, R., Blumenfeld, H., and Sent, R. (1968), A short-term treatment program in a child guidance clinic. Social Work, 13, 81-90.

5090.   Sheedy, B.C. (1978), The creative encounter: Meeting through play in conjoint family therapy. Dissertation Abstracts International, 38(8), 3907B.

5091.   Sheehy, P.T. (1981), Family enrichment for stepfamilies: An empirical study. Dissertation Abstracts International, 42, 2317-A.

5092.   Sheely, M.D., Pulliam, G., and Goolishian, H.A. (1975), Developmental phases of co-therapy relationship and their effect on family systems. American Journal of Orthopsychiatry, 45, 265.

5093.   Sheinbein, M. (1976), Normal crises: Stage therapy and family therapy. Journal of Family Counseling, 4(1), 78-83.

5094.   Sheinbein, M. (1974), Feedback in conjoint marital interaction testing. Family Therapy, 1(3), 263-272.

5095.   Sheley, K.A. (1984), Review of A.S. Gurman's Questions and answers in the practice of family therapy, Vol. 2. Contemporary Psychology, 29(3), 254.

5096.   Shellow, R.S., Brown, B.S., and Osberg, J.W. (1963), Family group therapy in retrospect: Four years and sixty families. Family Process, 2, 52-67.

5097. Shelton, D. (1983), Documenting family therapy: One mental health clinic's experience. Journal of the American Medical Records Association, 54, 27-30.

5098. Shelton, P.R. (1982), Separation and treatment of child-abusing families. Family Therapy, 9, 53-60.

5099. Shen, J.T. (1982), Adolescent sexual counseling. Postgraduate Medicine, 71(5), 91-93, 96-97, 100.

5100. Shereshefsky, P.M. (1963), Family unit treatment in child guidance. Social Work, 8(4), 63-70.

5101. Sherman, B. (1972), The adolescent in family therapy. Family Therapy, 1, 35-48.

5102. Sherman, M.H., Ackerman, N.W., Sherman, S.N., and Mitchell, C. (1965), Non-verbal cues and reenactment of conflict in family therapy. Family Process, 4, 133-162.

5103. Sherman, M.H., Blair, A., Panken, S., Platt, R., and Schomer, J. (1972), Some dimensions of style in family therapy. Psychotherapy: Theory, Research and Practice, 9, 67-75.

5104. Sherman, R. (1983), Counseling the urban economically disadvantaged family: The action counseling method. American Journal of Family Therapy, 11, 22-30.

5105. Sherman, R. (1983), The power dimension in the family: A synthesis of Adlerian perspectives. American Journal of Family Therapy, 11, 43-53.

5106. Sherman, S.N. (1964), The sociopsychological character of family-group treatment. Social Casework, 45, 195-201.

5107. Sherman, S.N. (1962), Family treatment approaches: III. Discussion. American Journal of Orthopsychiatry, 32, 148-151.

5108. Sherman, S.N. (1961), The concept of the family in casework therapy. In N. Ackerman, F. Beatman, and S. Sherman, (Eds.), Exploring the base for family therapy. New York: Family Service Association.

5109. Sherman, S.N. (1967), Intergenerational discontinuity and therapy of the family. Social Casework, 48, 216-221.

5110. Sherman, S.N. (1966), Family treatment: An approach to children's problems. Social Casework, 47, 368-372.

5111. Sherman, S.N. (1966), Aspects of family interviewing critical for staff training and education. Social Service Review, 40, 302-308.

5112. Sherman, S.S. (1980), Discussion: "International politics and family systems: Some observations on tactics." International Journal of Family Therapy, 2, 230-233.

5113. Shernoff, M.J. (1984), Family therapy for lesbian and gay clients. Social Work, 29(4), 343-396.

5114.   Sherwood, J.J., and Scherer, J.J. (1975), A model for couples: How two can group together. Small Group Behavior, 6, 11-29.

5115.   Shields, L. (1969), Family crisis intervention. Journal of Psychiatric Nursing and Mental Health Service, 7, 222-225.

5116.   Shimada, T. (1959), A scientific study of marriage counseling: Especially as a part of family welfare casework. Bulletin of Kansaigakuin University, 766-792.

5117.   Shionott, H., and Kadowaki, J. (1979), The questionnaire to parents of children with the Down's syndrome: How to inform the parents and psychological responses to counseling. American Journal of Medical Genetics, 4(3), 215-218.

5118.   Shipman, G. (1945), Probation and the family. Probation, 23, 106-114.

5119.   Shipman, G. (1977), In my opinion: The role of counseling in the reform of marriage and divorce procedures. Family Coordinator, 26, 395-402.

5120.   Shmukler, D., and Friedman, M. (1983), Clinical implications of the family systems model. Journal of Family Therapy, 12, 51-58.

5121.   Shmukler, D., and Friedman, M. (1983), Clinical implications of the family systems model. Transactional Analysis Journal, 13, 94-96.

5122.   Shochet, B.R., and Lisansky, E.T. (1969), New dimensions in family practice. Psychosomatics, 10(2), 88-93.

5123.   Sholevar, G.P. (1975), A family therapist looks at the problem of incest. Bulletin of the American Academy of Psychiatry and the Law, 3, 25-31.

5124.   Sholtis, H.S. (1964), The management of marital counseling cases. Social Casework, 45, 71-78.

5125.   Shonick, H. (1975), Premarital counseling: Three years experience of a unique service. Family Coordinator, 24(3), 321-324.

5126.   Shore, M.F. (1984), Review of S.W. Henggeler's Delinquency and adolescent psychopathology: A family-ecological systems approach. Contemporary Psychology, 29(2), 145-146.

5127.   Shostak, D.A. (1977), Family vs. individual oriented behavior therapy as treatment approaches to juvenile delinquency. Dissertation Abstracts International, 38(7), 3474-B.

5128.   Shoulberg, D.J. (1980), Family therapy with unmarried young adults. The Family, 7(1), 17.

5129.   Showalter, D., and Jones, C.W. (1980), Marital and family counseling in prisons. Social Work, 25(3), 224.

5130.   Shulem, B.D. (1979), Dropping out after the initial family therapy interview. Dissertation Abstracts International, 40, 1079-A.

5131.   Shulman, S., and Klein, M.M. (1983), Distance-sensitive and consensus-
        sensitive families: The effect on adolescent referral for
        psychotherapy. American Journal of Family Therapy, 11, 45-58.

5132.   Sichlau, J.H. (1985), Predicting the organization effectiveness of Illinois
        hospital-based chemical dependency units using principles of family
        therapy. Dissertation Abstracts International, 46, 1154-A.

5133.   Sick, H. (1980), Abused women, abused children. Dynamische
        Psychiatrie, 13, 275-286.

5134.   Sideleau, B.F., and Light, N. (1981), Family treatment for the disturbed
        child? Perspectives in Psychatric Care, 19, 78-86.

5135.   Sider, R.C., and Clements, C. (1982), Family or individual therapy: The
        ethics of modality choice. American Journal of Psychiatry, 139, 1455-
        1459.

5136.   Siegel, J. (1981), Intrafamilial child sexual victimization: A role
        training model. Journal of Group Psychotherapy, Psychodrama and
        Socioimetry, 34, 37-43.

5137.   Siegel, R.J. (1982), The long-term marriage: Implications for therapy.
        Women and Therapy, 1, 3-11.

5138.   Sieh, M. (1978), The "what and why" of family therapy. Arizona Medical
        Journal, 35, 737-738.

5139.   Sieland, B. (1980), Case study: Behavior therapy of a mother-child
        interaction. Psychology in Education and Instruction, 27, 111.

5140.   Sieveking, N.A., Harrison, P.J., Ackerman, B.R., and Gorsuch, R.L.
        (1973), Moral judgments of psychotherapy clients and their parents.
        Journal of Clinical Psychology, 29(1), 103-105.

5141.   Sigal, J. (1971), A simple dynamic model for family diagnostic
        interviewing. Canadian Psychiatric Association Journal, 16, 87-91.

5142.   Sigal, J. (1969), Triadic-based family therapy. Power in family
        therapy: Why only triads? International Journal of Psychiatry, 8, 565-
        566.

5143.   Sigal, J., and Lewin, S. (1976), Teaching family therapy by simulation.
        Canada's Mental Health, 24, 6-9.

5144.   Sigal, J.J., Barrs, C.B., and Doubilet, A.L. (1976), Problems of
        measuring success of family therapy in a common clinical setting:
        Impasse and solutions. Family Process, 15, 225-233.

5145.   Sigal, J.J., Lasry, J.C., Guttman, H., Chayoga, L., and Pilon, R. (1977),
        Some stable characteristics of family therapists' intervention in real and
        simulated therapy sessions. Journal of Consulting and Clinical
        Psychology, 45, 23-26.

5146.   Sigal, J.J., Presser, G.B., Woodward, C.A., Santa-Barbara, J., Epstein,
        N.B., and Levin, S. (1980), Videotaped simulated families as a tool in
        family therapy outcome research. International Journal of Family
        Therapy, 2(4), 236-242.

5147. Sigal, J.J., Rakoff, V., and Epstein, N. (1967), Indicators of therapeutic outcome in conjoint family therapy. Family Process, 6, 215-226.

5148. Silbergeld, S. (1979), The group therapist leadership role: Assessment in adolescent coping courses. Small Group Behavior, 10, 176-199.

5149. Silbergeld, S., Thune, E.S., and Manderscheid, R.W. (1980), Marital role dynamics during brief group psychotherapy: Assessment of verbal interactions. Journal of Clinical Psychology, 36, 480-492.

5150. Silberstein, E.B., and Scott, C.J. (1978), An evaluation of undergraduate family care programs. Journal of Community Health, 3, 369-379.

5151. Silking, V.N. (1982), The protean shape and form of the black family. Psychiatric Annals, 12, 855-861.

5152. Silva, M.C. (1977), Spouses need nurses too. Canadian Nursing, 73, 38-41.

5153. Silva, M.C. (1979), Effects of orientation information on spouses' anxiety and attitudes toward hospitalization and surgery. Research in Nursing Health, 2, 127-136.

5154. Silverman, D.C. (1978), Sharing the crisis of rape: Counseling the mates and families of victims. American Journal of Orthopsychiatry, 48(1), 166-173.

5155. Silverman, H.L. (1974), Process and function in marital therapy: A psychological overview. Journal of Family Counseling, 2(1), 6-10.

5156. Silverman, H.L. (1973), Value issues in marriage counseling: Psychological and philosophical implications. Family Coordinator, 22(1), 103-110.

5157. Silverman, J. (1975), The woman's liberation movement: Its impact on marriage. Hospital and Community Psychiatry, 26, 39-40.

5158. Silverman, M.S., and Urbaniak, L. (1983), Marriage encounter: Characteristics of participants. Counseling and Values, 20, 42-51.

5159. Silverman, S.M. (1978), Review of P.J. Guerin's Family therapy: Theory and practice. Psychiatric Annals, 8(8), 94.

5160. Sim, J.H. (1978), A literature review on family therapy for psychiatric patients. Taehan Kanho, 17(4), 81-86.

5161. Simkinson, C.H. (1981), The new family therapy underground: A return to a context of collective meaning. Family Therapy Network Newsletter, 5(5), 21-22.

5162. Simon, F.B. (1980), Family therapy: Basis of social psychiatry. Psychiatrische Praxis, 7, 195-203.

5163. Simon, J., Wilkerson, J., and Keller, J.F. (1982), Marriage dilemma and an assessment device. Family Therapy, 9, 127-132.

5164. Simon, L. (1978), Marital counseling: A dynamic-holistic approach. American Journal of Psychoanalysis, 38(3), 243-254.

5165. Simon, M. (1981), Marital conflicts between love and sexuality. Therapeutische Gegenwantoe, 120, 681-9.

5166. Simon, R. (1984), Primary care physicians and family therapy. American Journal of Family Therapy, 12(3), 69-70.

5167. Simon, R. (1984), Review of W.J. Doherty and M.A. Baird's Family therapy and family medicine. Family Process, 23(1), 128-131.

5168. Simon, S.B. (1980), Values clarification in family groups. Journal for Specialists in Group Work, 5, 140-147.

5169. Simons, D.R. (1980), Accuracy of client self-reports of marital communications. Dissertation Abstracts International, 40, 3969-B.

5170. Simpson, G. (1960), People in families: Sociology, psychoanalysis and the American family. New York: Thomas Y. Crowell.

5171. Simpson, G. (1970), East-west conflict in a child of a "mixed" marriage. American Journal of Maternal Child Nursing, 131, 28.

5172. Singh, N. (1982), Notes and observations on the practice of multiple family therapy in an adolescent unit. Journal of Adolescence, 5, 319-32.

5173. Sipe, A.W.R. (1983), Review of A.S. Gurman's Questions and answers in the practice of family therapy. Psychiatric Annals, 13, 265.

5174. Siporin, M. (1980), Marriage and family therapy in social work. Social Casework: Journal of Contemporary Social Work, 61, 11-21.

5175. Siporin, M. (1984), Review of R.T. Seargreaves' Marital therapy and C.J. Sager's Treating the remarried family. Social Casework, 65, 58-59.

5176. Siporin, M. (1981), Teaching family and marriage therapy. Social Casework, 62(1), 20-29.

5177. Sites, H. J. (1983), Effects of maltreatment of children on development and learning achievement. Dissertation Abstracts International, 44, 1761-A.

5178. Sjovall, H. (1973), Marriage rate rise and fall: Swedish nuptiality 1861-1971. Lakartidningen, 70, 2465-2478.

5179. Sjovall, H. (1974), Marriage investigation: Motive, results and evaluation. Lakartidningen, 71, 153-154.

5180. Skarsten, S.S. (1978), An examination of the potential effectiveness of social work intervention into marital sexual dysfunctions. Dissertation Abstracts Intenational, 39, 1844-A.

5181. Skhiri, T., and Fournet, G. (1982), Case history of an intervention on family and larger social environment of an electively mute child and the impact on its development. Perspectives Psychiatriques, 20, 86-89.

5182. Skidmore, R.A., and Garrelt, H.V.S. (1955), The joint interview in marriage counseling. Marriage and Family Living, 17, 349-354.

5183.   Skidmore, R.A., and Skidmore, C.J. (1975), Marriage and family counseling in industry. Journal of Marriage and Family Counseling, 1, 135-144.

5184.   Skinner, C.J. (1980), A comparative analysis of behavioral training procedures for marital problem solving communication. Dissertation Abstracts International, 40, 3970-B.

5185.   Skynner, A., and Skynner, P.M. (1980), An open-systems approach to teaching family therapy. Group Analysis, 13, 31-41.

5186.   Skynner, A.C. (1974), School phobia: A reappraisal. British Journal of Medical Psychology, 47, 1-16.

5187.   Skynner, A.C. (1976), Systems of family and marital psychotherapy. New York: Brunner/Mazel.

5188.   Skynner, A.C. (1969), A group-analytic approach to conjoint family therapy. Journal of Child Psychology and Psychiatry, 10(2), 81-106.

5189.   Skynner, A.C. (1969), Indications and contraindications for conjoint family therapy. International Journal of Social Psychiatry, 15, 245-249.

5190.   Skynner, A.C. (1975), Some approaches to marital therapy. Proceedings of the Royal Society of Medicine, 68, 405-408.

5191.   Skynner, A.C.R. (1980), Recent developments in marital therapy. Journal of Family Therapy, 2, 271.

5192.   Skynner, A.C.R. (1979), Review of M. Bowen's Family therapy in clinical practice. Hospital and Community Psychiatry, 30, 276.

5193.   Skynner, A.C.R. (1984), Group analysis and family therapy. International Journal of Group Psychotherapy, 34(2), 215-224.

5194.   Skynner, A.C.R., and Skynner, P.M. (1979), Open systems approach to teaching family therapy. Journal of Marital and Family Therapy, 5(5), 5-16.

5195.   Skynner, R. (1982), Frameworks for viewing the family as a system. In A. Bentovim, G.G. Barnes, and A. Cooklin (Eds.), Family therapy. I. Complementary frameworks for theory and practice. London: Academic Press.

5196.   Slager-Jome, A., Smaby, M.H., and Tamminen, A.W. (1978), Counseling sexually abused children. Personnel and Guidance Journal, 57(2), 103-105.

5197.   Slavson, S.R. (1963), Steps in sensitizing parents (couples) in groups toward schizophrenic children. International Journal of Group Psychotherapy, 13, 176-186.

5198.   Slavson, S.R. (1965), Coordinated family therapy. International Journal of Group Psychotherapy, 15, 177-186.

5199.   Sletto, R.F. (1950), What is significant for research in marriage counseling? Marriage and Family Living, 12, 130-132.

5200.   Slipp, S. (1980), Marital therapy for borderline personality disorders. American Journal of Family Therapy, 8, 67-70.

5201.   Slipp, S. (1973), Family therapy with disorganized poor families. Groups, 5, 3-13.

5202.   Slipp, S. (1970), An overview of family therapy. Journal of Psychoanalytic Groups, 3, 1-7.

5203.   Slipp, S. (1982), Interface between psychoanalysis and family therapy. American Journal of Psychoanalysis, 42, 221-228.

5204.   Slipp, S. (1974), Factors associated with engagement in family therapy. Family Process, 13, 413-428.

5205.   Slipp, S., and Kressel, K. (1978), Difficulties in family therapy evaluation l. A comparison of insight vs. problem solving approaches II. Design critique and recommendations. Family Process, 17, 409-422.

5206.   Slivkin, S.E. (1977), Death and living: A family therapy approach. American Journal of Psychoanalysis, 37(4), 317-323.

5207.   Sloan, S.Z. (1984), Assessing the differential effectiveness of two enrichment formats in facilitating marital intimacy and adjustment. Dissertation Abstracts International, 45, 2569-A.

5208.   Sloman, L. (1981), Intrafamilial struggles for power: An ethological perspective. International Journal of Family Psychiatry, 2, 13-33.

5209.   Sluzki, C.E. (1983), Process, structure, and world views: Toward an integrated view of systematic models in family therapy. Family Process, 22, 469-476.

5210.   Sluzki, C.E. (1983), How to stake a territory in the field of family therapy in three easy lessons. Journal of Marital and Family Therapy, 11, 235-238.

5211.   Sluzki, C.E. (1978), Marital therapy from a systems-theory-perspective. In T.J. Paolini and B.S. McCrady (Eds.), Marriage and marital therapy: Psychoanalytic, behavioral and systems theory perspectives. New York: Brunner/Mazel.

5212.   Sluzki, C.E. (1968), Sintomas e interaccion familiar. (Symptoms and familial interactions.) Revista de Interamericana Psicologia, 2, 283-287.

5213.   Sluzki, C.E. (1979), Migration and family conflict. Family Process, 18, 379-390.

5214.   Sluzki, C.E. (1975), Coalitionary process in initiating family therapy. Family Process, 14, 67-78.

5215.   Small, A.C. (1980), The child's and parent's expectations of psychotherapy. Journal of Developmental and Behavioral Pediatrics, 1(2), 74-77.

5216.   Smilkstein, G. (1978), The family APGAR: A proposal for family function test and its use by physicians. Journal of Family Practice, 6, 1231-1239.

5217.   Smith, A.H. (1978), Encountering the family system in school related behavior problems. Psychology in the Schools, 15(3), 379-386.

5218.   Smith, B.J. (1982), Management of the patient with hyperemesis gravidarum in family therapy with hypnotherapy as an adjunct. Journal of New York State Nurses Association, 13, 17-26.

5219.   Smith, C.G. (1969), Alcoholics: Their treatment and their wives. British Journal of Psychiatry, 115, 1039-1042.

5220.   Smith, D.S., and Duane, M.J. (1980), Couples group treatment of chronic marital dysfunction. Journal of Psychiatric Nursing, 18, 30-6.

5221.   Smith, H.H. (1976), A clinic for sick marriages. Individual Psychology, 13(1), 6-11.

5222.   Smith, J.P. (1982), Social health concepts for family practice. Social Casework, 63, 363-369.

5223.   Smith, J.R. (1967), Suggested scales for prediction of client movement and the duration of marriage counseling. Sociology and Social Research, 52(1), 63-71.

5224.   Smith, J.R. (1970), Perception of self and other (mate) as motivation for marriage counseling: An interactional approach. Sociology and Social Research, 54, 466-476.

5225.   Smith, L.E. (1969), Intervention techniques and unhealthy family patterns. Perspectives in Psychiatry Care, 7, 112-119.

5226.   Smith, L.L., and McNamara, J.J. (1977), Social work services for radiation therapy patients and their families. Hospital and Community Psychiatry, 28(10), 752-754.

5227.   Smith, R.L., and Alexander, A.M. (Eds.) (1974), Counseling couples in groups: A manual for improving troubled relationships. Springfield, IL: Charles C. Thomas Publisher.

5228.   Smith, R.M. (1979), Marriage and family enrichment: A new professional area. Family Coordinator, 28, 87.

5229.   Smith, V.G., and Hepworth, D.W. (1967), Marriage counseling with one marital partner: Rationale and clinical implications. Social Casework, 48, 352-359.

5230.   Smith, V.G., and Nichols, W.C. (1979), Accreditation in marital and family therapy. Journal of Marital and Family Therapy, 5(14), 95-100.

5231.   Smith, V.L. (1980), Effects of group therapy on adolescents experiencing parental abuse due to divorce or marital separation. Dissertation Abstracts International, 41, 947A.

5232.   Smithells, T.A. (1983), Co-Pas: An Adlerian-based program for preparing physically handicapped preschool children for mainstreaming. Dissertation Abstracts International, 44, 391-A.

5233.   Smoyak, S.A. (1969), Threat: A recurring family dynamic. Perspectives of Psychiatric Care, 7, 267.

5234.   Smoyak, S.A. (1975), Family therapy. In F.L. Huey (Ed.), Psychiatric
        Nursing 1946-1974: A report on the state of the art. American Journal
        of Nursing, (pp. 36-49), New York.

5235.   Smoyak, S.A. (Ed.) (1975), The psychiatric nurse as a family therapist.
        New York: John Wiley and Sons.

5236.   Snodgrass, J.M. (1965), Counseling parents of the mentally retarded: An
        annotated bibliography. Mental Retardation Abstracts, 2, 265-270.

5237.   Snow, J.S. (1985), Individual and family therapy in the treatment of
        children: A study of therapists' opinions and practices. Dissertation
        Abstracts International, 45, 3347-B.

5238.   Snow, W. (1982), Review of L.R. Wolberg and M.L. Aronson's Group and
        family therapy 1980. Psychiatric Annals, 12, 892.

5239.   Snyder, A.I. (1978), Periodic marital separation and physical illness.
        American Journal of Orthopsychiatry, 48, 637-643.

5240.   Snyder, B.M. (1979), Marital difficulties. Primary Care: Clinics in
        Office Practice, 6, 365-390.

5241.   Snyder, D.K., and Regts, J.M. (1982), Factor scales for assessing marital
        disharmony and disaffection. Journal of Consulting and Clinical
        Psychology, 50, 736-43.

5242.   Sobel, A. (1982), Review of I.W. Clements and D.M. Buchanan's Family
        therapy - a nursing perspective. Family Process, 21, 499-500.

5243.   Sobesky, W.E. (1981), Coping with developmental transitions: Problems
        of a survivor family. Family and Child Mental Health Journal, 7, 100-115.

5244.   Sobol, B.S. (1982), Art therapy and strategic family therapy. American
        Journal of Art Therapy, 21, 43-56.

5245.   Soden, K.V. (1978), Therapy of children, adults and families. Praxis der
        Kinderpsychologie und Kinderpsychiatrie, 27(6), 197-201.

5246.   Soeken, D.R., Mandrescheid, R.W., Flatter, C.H., and Silbergeld, S.
        (1981), A controlled study of quantitative feedback in married-couples
        brief group psychotherapy. Psychotherapy: Theory, Research and
        Practice, 18(2), 204.

5247.   Sohni, H. (1984), Analytically-oriented family therapy in child and
        adolescent psychiatry—principles, indications, and goals. Praxis der
        Kinderpsychologie und Kinderpsychiatrie, 33, 9-18.

5248.   Soifer, R., Dio, E., Nachman, M., Morini, C., Alday, G., and Baza, B.
        (1964), (The family group as a method of diagnosis and therapeutic
        guidance in children.) Acta Psiquiatrica y Psicologia de America Latina,
        10(2), 97-103.

5249.   Sokoloff, B. (1979), Adoptive families: Needs for counseling. Clinical
        Pediatrics, 18, 184-190.

5250.   Solby, B. (1941), The psychodrama approach to marriage problems.
        American Sociological Review, 6, 523-530.

5251.   Solomon, A.P., and Greene, B.L. (1963), Marital disharmony:
        Concurrent therapy of husband and wife by the same psychiatrist.
        Disorders of the Nervous System, 24, 21-28.

5252.   Solomon, K., and Solomon, M. (1979), Jealousy and nontraditional
        marital units (letter). American Journal of Psychiatry, 136, 241-242.

5253.   Solomon, M.A. (1977), The staging of family therapy: An approach to
        developing the therapeutic alliance. Journal of Marriage and Family
        Counseling, 3, 59-66.

5254.   Solomon, M.A. (1974), Typologies of family homeostasis: Implications
        for diagnosis and treatment. Family Therapy, 1, 9-18.

5255.   Solomon, M.A. (1974), Resistance in family therapy: Some conceptual
        and technical considerations. Family Coordinator, 23, 159-163.

5256.   Solomon, M.A. (1973), A developmental, conceptual premise for family
        therapy. Family Process, 12, 179-188.

5257.   Solomon, M.A., and Hersch, L.B. (1979), Death in the family:
        Implications for family development. Journal of Marital and Family
        Therapy, 5, 43-49.

5258.   Solomon, M.F. (1985), Treatment of narcissistic and borderline disorders
        in marital therapy: Suggestions toward an enhanced therapeutic
        approach. Clinical Social Work Journal, 13(2), 141.

5259.   Solomon, M.L. (1969), Family therapy dropouts: Resistance to change.
        Canadian Psychiatric Association Journal, 14(1), 21-29.

5260.   Solomon, M.L. (1973), Considerations pratiques sur la therapie
        familiale. Canadian Psychiatric Association Journal, 18, 185-190.

5261.   Solomon, M.L. (1974), Transactional systems theory in family therapy:
        Its relevance to the definition of child psychiatry. Informentum
        Psychiatrique, 50, 1025-1031.

5262.   Solomon, M.L. (1975), Family psychiatry, transactional systems, and the
        frontiers of child psychiatry. Canadian Psychiatric Association Journal,
        20, 151-155.

5263.   Solomon, N. (1976), Homeostasis and family myth: An overview of the
        literature. Family Therapy, 3, 75-86.

5264.   Solow, R.A., and Cooper, B.M. (1975), Co-therapists as advocates in
        family therapy with crisis-provoking adolescents. In M. Sugar (Ed.), The
        adolescent in group and family therapy. New York: Brunner/Mazel.

5265.   Solow, R.A., and Cooper, B.M. (1974), Therapeutic mobilization of
        families around drug-induced adolescent crises. Adolescent Psychiatry,
        3, 237-248.

5266.   Somers, A.R. (1979), Marital status, health and use of health services.
        An old relationship revisited. Journal of American Medical Association,
        241, 1818-1822.

5267.   Sonne, J.C. (1972), Family therapy of sexually acting-out girls. In H.L. Resnik and M.E. Wolfgang (Eds.), Sexual behaviors: Social, clinical, and legal aspects. Boston, MA: Little, Brown.

5268.   Sonne, J.C. (1973), Insurance and family therapy. Family Process, 12, 399-414.

5269.   Sonne, J.C. (1974), On the question of compulsory marriage counseling as a part of divorce proceedings. Family Coordinator, 23, 303-306.

5270.   Sonne, J.C., Speck, R.V., and Jungreis, J.E. (1962), The absent-member maneuver as a resistance in family therapy of schizophrenia. Family Process, 1, 44-62.

5271.   Sonne, J.C., and Lincoln, G. (1965), Heterosexual co-therapy team experiences during family therapy. Family Process, 4, 177-196.

5272.   Sonne, J.C., and Lincoln, G. (1966), The importance of a heterosexual co-therapy relationship in the construction of a family image. Psychiatric Research Report of the American Psychiatric Association, 20, 196-205.

5273.   Sonnenshein-Schneider, M., and Baird, K.L. (1980), Group counseling children of divorce in the elementary school: Understanding process and technique. Personnel and Guidance Journal, 59(2), 88-92.

5274.   Sorenson, D.L. (1974), The relationship of perceptual incongruity and defensive style to marital discord. Dissertation Abstracts International, 35, 3037B.

5275.   Sorrells, J.M., and Ford, F.R. (1969), Toward an integrated theory of families and family therapy. Psychotherapy: Theory, Research and Practice, 6, 150-160.

5276.   Sorrels, J.P. (1978), Effectiveness and efficiency of family functioning: An experimental comparison of group dynamics and family dynamics. Dissertation Abstracts International, 40(1), 500-B.

5277.   Soucar, E. (1983), Comments on research in family therapy. Family Process, 22, 337-339.

5278.   Soumenkoff, G., Marneffe, C., Gerard, M., Limet, R., Beeckmans, M., and Hubinont, P.O. (1982), A coordinated attempt for prevention of child abuse at the antenatal care level. Child Abuse and Neglect, 6, 87-94.

5279.   Sourkes, B. (1977), Facilitating family coping with childhood cancer. Journal of Pediatric Psychology, 2, 65-67.

5280.   Sousa, S.B. (1983), A comparison of the effects of audio-video taping upon selected self-awareness factors with groups of family therapy trainees. Dissertation Abstracts International, 43, 3855-A.

5281.   Soyer, D. (1972), Helping the family to live with itself. Journal of Geriatric Psychiatry, 5, 52-76.

5282.   Spark, D. (1970), Critical incidents in the context of family therapy. Critical incident No. 3. International Psychiatry Clinics, 7, 291-298.

5283. Spark, D. (1970), Critical incidents in the context of family therapy. Critical incident No. 6. International Psychiatry Clinics, 7, 327-334.

5284. Spark, G.M. (1968), Parental involvement in family therapy. Journal of Marriage and the Family, 30, 111-118.

5285. Spark, G.M. (1977), Marriage is a family affair. Family Coordinator, 26, 167-174.

5286. Spark, G.M. (1974), Grandparents and intergenerational family therapy. Family Process, 13, 225-238.

5287. Sparks, B.L. (1981), Sexual counseling of the family. South Africa Medical Journal, 59(9), 291-293.

5288. Spears, R., and Lawlis, G.F. (1974), Marriage relationships shown by male alcoholics. Psychological Reports, 34, 944.

5289. Speck, R., and Speck, J. (1975), The urban commune; An alternative family style: Implications for family therapists. Family Therapy, 2, 181-186.

5290. Speck, R.V. (1967), Psychotherapy of the social network of a schizophrenic family. Family Process, 6, 208-214.

5291. Speck, R.V. (1964), Family therapy in the home. Journal of Marriage and the Family, 26, 72-76.

5292. Speck, R.V. (1964), Mental health problems involving the family, the pet, and the veterinarian. Journal of the American Veterinary Medicine Association, 145, 150-154.

5293. Speck, R.V., and Attneave, C.L. (1973), Family networks. New York: Pantheon.

5294. Speck, R.V., and Olans, J.L. (1967), The social networks of the family of a schizophrenic: Implications for social and preventive psychiatry. American Journal of Orthopsychiatry, 37, 206.

5295. Speck, R.V., and Speck, J.L. (1977), Treating the family in time of crisis. American Psychiatric Therapies, 17, 135-142.

5296. Spector, R.M., Guttman, H.A., Sigal, J.J., Rakoff, V.M., and Epstein, N.B. (1970), Time sampling in family therapy sessions. Psychotherapy: Theory, Research and Practice, 7, 37-40.

5297. Speed, B., Seligman, P., Kingston, P., and Cade, B. (1982), A team approach to therapy. Journal of Family Therapy, 4, 271-284.

5298. Speers, R.W. (1980), Review of H. Stierlin's Psychoanalysis and family therapy. Journal of the American Academy of Psychoanalysis, 28, 709-710.

5299. Speers, R.W. (1965), Group therapy in childhood psychosis. Chapel Hill, NC: University of North Carolina Press.

5300. Speers, R.W., and Lansing, C. (1964), Group psychotherapy with pre-school psychotic children and collateral group therapy of their parents. American Journal of Orthopsychiatry, 34, 659-666.

5301. Speigel, D.E., and Sperber, Z. (1967), Clinical experiment in short-term family therapy. American Journal of Orthopsychiatry, 37(2), 278-279.

5302. Spence, S.H. (1983), Review of A.S. Burman and D.P. Kniskern's Handbook of family therapy. Behavioural Psychotherapy, 11, 185.

5303. Spencer, W. (1974), Family psychiatric treatment. Mount Sinai Journal of Medicine, New York, 41, 520-523.

5304. Spengler, A. (1982), Couple therapy in the presence of severe physical disability —a case example. Rehabilitation, 43, 69-72.

5305. Sperling, E. (1969), Alters-und bezugsgruppen: Spezifische therapie-probleme; dargestellt am beimspiel der studenten-und familien behandlung. (Age and reference groups: Specific therapy problems exemplified by student and family treatment.) Zeitschrift fur Psychosomatische Medizin und Psychoanalyse, 15, 119-126.

5306. Sperling, E. (1975), Marriage and family treatment as super-ego therapy. Praxis der Psychotherapie, 20, 17-24.

5307. Sperling, E. (1973), Family therapy methods: Meanings, hopes and problems. Praxis der Psychotherapie, 18, 82-89.

5308. Sperling, E. (1979), Family therapy under the aspect of the three-generation problem. Psychotherapie, 29(6), 207-213.

5309. Sperling, E. (1978), Relevance of Gestalt therapy, primal therapy and family therapy for psychoanalysis. Zeitschrift fur Psychosomatische Medizin und Psychoanalyse, 24(2), 169-179.

5310. Sperling, E. (1970), The familial background of anorexia nervosa and the resulting therapeutic difficulties. Zeitschrift Fur Psychosomatische Meyazin und Psychoanalyse, 16, 130-141.

5311. Sperling, E. (1973), Technique of marriage and family therapy. Praxis der Kinderpsychologie und Kinderpsychiatrie, 22, 209-221.

5312. Sperling, E. (1973), Technique of marriage and family therapy. Zeitschrift fur Psychosomatische Medizin und Psychoanalyse, 19, 132-137.

5313. Sperry, L, (1984), Impasses in marital therapy: A time to consider nonpsychological factors. Individual Psychology, 40(2), 201-208.

5314. Spiegel, J.P. (1974), The family: The channel of primary care. Hospital and Community Psychiatry, 25, 785-788.

5315. Spielmacher, P.E. (1974), Patterns of power and interpersonal attraction in families receiving counseling. Dissertation Abstracts International, 35, 200-A.

5316. Spillane-Grieco, F. (1982), Increasing effectiveness in counseling runaways and their families. Juvenile and Family Court Journal, 33(3), 31.

5317. Spinelli, L.A., and Barton, K.S. (1980), Home management services for families with emotionally disturbed children. Child Welfare, 59, 43-52.

5318. Spitz, H.I. (1979), Group approaches to treating marital problems. Psychiatric Annals, 9(6), 50-72.

5319. Spitz, H.I. (1978), Structural-interactional group psychotherapy with couples. International Journal of Group Psychotherapy, 28, 401-414.

5320. Sporakowski, M.J. (1982), Values, ethics, legalities, and the family therapist: VII. The regulation of marital and family therapy. Family Therapy Collections, 1, 125-134.

5321. Sporakowski, M.J. (1985), Review of J.C. Hansen's (Ed.). The family therapy collections. Family Relations, 34(2), 299.

5322. Sporakowski, M.J., and Staniszewski, W.P. (1980), The regulation of marriage and family therapy: An update. Journal of Marital and Family Therapy, 6, 335-352.

5323. Sprenkle, D.H. (1982), Divorce mediation - a rational alternative to the adversary. American Journal of Family Therapy, 10, 80.

5324. Sprenkle, D.H., and Fisher, B.L. (1980), An empirical assessment of the goals of family therapy. Journal of Marital and Family Therapy, 6, 131-139.

5325. Sprenkle, D.H., and Fisher, B.L. (1978), Family therapy conceptualization and use of case materials. Family Therapy, 5(2), 177-183.

5326. Sprenkle, D.H., and Olson, D.H. (1978), Circumplex model of marital systems: An empirical study of clinical and non-clinical couples. Journal of Marriage and Family Counseling, 4, 59-74.

5327. Sprenkle, D.H., and Piercy, F.P. (1984), Research in family therapy - a graduate level course. Journal of Marital and Family Therapy, 10(3), 225-240.

5328. Sprenkle, D.H., and Storm, C.L. (1983), Divorce therapy outcome research: A substantive and methodological review. Journal of Marital and Family Therapy, 9, 239-258.

5329. Sprenkle, D.H., and Weis, D.L. (1978), Extramarital sexuality: Implications for marital therapists. Journal of Sex and Marital Therapy, 4(4), 279-291.

5330. Springer, A. (1980), Effects of physicians' early parental counseling on rearing of Down's syndrome children. American Journal of Mental Deficiency, 85(1), 1-5.

5331. Sprinks, S.H., and Birchler, G.R. (1982), Behavioral-systems marital therapy: Dealing with resistance. Family Process, 21, 169-85.

5332.   Spruiell, V. (1975), Adolescent narcissism and group psychotherapy. In M. Sugar (Ed.), The adolescent in group and family therapy. New York: Brunner/Mazel.

5333.   Sreenivasan, U. (1982), Review of K. Flomenhaft and A.E. Christ' The challenge of family therapy - a dialogue for child educators. Canadian Journal of Psychiatry, 27, 524.

5334.   Srinwasan, K., Reddy, P.H., and Raju, K.N. (1978), From one generation to the next: Changes in fertility, family size preferences, and family planning in an Indian state between 1951 and 1975. Studies of Family Planning, 9, 258-271.

5335.   Stachowiak, J.G. (1968), Psychological disturbances in children as related to disturbances in family interaction. Journal of Marriage and the Family, 30, 123-127.

5336.   Stackhouse, T.W. (1973), A communication analysis of the art of being stupid: A family systems and communication approach to the study of families with children having reading problems. Dissertation Abstracts International, 34, 3890-A.

5337.   Stafford, S., Olasov, B., Garrett, J.C., and Calhoun, J.F. (1983), Changing person perceptions in a marital simulation. Family Therapy, 10, 265-274.

5338.   Stagoll, B. (1981), Therapy with Greek families living in Australia. International Journal of Family Therapy, 3, 167-179.

5339.   Stagoll, B. (1983), Family therapy in Australia: Taking a squiz. American Journal of Family Therapy, 11, 16-21.

5340.   Stahmann, R.F., and Hiebert, W.J. (Eds.) (1977), Klemer's counseling in marital and sexual problems. A clinician's handbook. (2nd ed.) Baltimore, MD: Williams and Wilkins.

5341.   Stanley, S.F. (1978), Family education to enhance the moral atmosphere of the family and the moral development of adolescents. Journal of Counseling Psychology, 25(2), 110-118.

5342.   Stanton, M.D. (1978), Family therapy for the drug user: Conceptual and practical considerations. Drug Forum, 6(3), 203-205.

5343.   Stanton, M.D. (1978), Heroin addiction as a family phenomenon: A new conceptual model. American Journal of Drug and Alcohol Abuse, 5, 125-150.

5344.   Stanton, M.D. (1980), A critique of Kaufman's Myth and reality in the family patterns and treatment of substance abusers. American Journal of Drug and Alcohol Abuse, 7(3-4), 281-289.

5345.   Stanton, M.D. (1979), Family treatment approaches to drug abuse problems - review. Family Process, 18(3), 251-280.

5346.   Stanton, M.D. (1975), Psychology and family therapy. Professional Psychology, 6, 45-49.

5347.   Stanton, M.D. (1975), Family therapy training: Academic and internship opportunities for psychologists. Family Process, 14(3), 433-439.

5348.   Stanton, M.D. (1981), An integrated structural/strategic approach to family therapy. Journal of Marital and Family Therapy, 7, 427-439.

5349.   Stanton, M.D. (1983), Review of L. Hoffman's Foundations of family therapy - a conceptual model for systems change. Journal of Marital and Family Therapy, 9, 215.

5350.   Stanton, M.D. (1978), The family and drug misuse: A bibliography. American Journal of Drug and Alcohol Abuse, 5, 151-170.

5351.   Stanton, M.D., Steier, F., and Todd, T.C. (1982), Paying families for attending sessions: Counteracting the dropout problem. Journal of Marital and Family Therapy, 8, 371-373.

5352.   Stanton, M.D., Todd, T.C., and Steier, F. (1980), Outcome for structural family therapy with drug addicts. In: L.S. Harris (Ed.), Problems of drug dependence (pp. 415-421). Rockville, MD: National Institute of Drug Abuse, pp. 415-421.

5353.   Stanton, M.D., and Todd, T.C. (1980), A critique of the Wells and Dezen review of the results of nonbehavioral family therapy. Family Process, 19, 169-176.

5354.   Stanton, M.D., and Todd, T.C. (1981), Engaging "resistant" families in treatment. Family Process, 20, 261-93.

5355.   Stark, A.D., Meigs, J.W., Fitch, R.A., and DeLouise, E.R. (1978), Family operational co-factors in the epidemiology of childhood lead poisioning. Archives of Environmental Health, 33, 222-226.

5356.   Starr, A. (1959), Psychodrama with a family. Group Psychotherapy: Theory, Research and Practice, 12, 27-31.

5357.   Starr, P.H. (1956), The triangular treatment approach in child therapy: Complementary psychotherapy of mother and child. American Journal of Psychotherapy, 10, 40-53.

5358.   Startz, M.R., and Evans, C.W. (1981), Developmental phases of marriage and marital therapy. Social Casework, 62(6), 343.

5359.   Stauber, K.W. (1983), The use of family therapy theory in the development of a primary prevention program. Dissertation Abstracts International, 43, 3117-A.

5360.   Stauffer, M. (1951), Group psychotherapy in a family agency. International Journal of Group Psychotherapy, 1, 348-355.

5361.   Steadman, M. (1978), Ritual: A paradigm for family therapy. Dissertation Abstracts International, 38(8), 3911-B.

5362.   Stedman, J.M. (1977), Behavior therapy strategies as applied to family therapy. Family Therapy, 4, 217-224.

5363.   Stedman, J.M., Gaines, T., and Costello, R. (1983), Prediction of outcome in family-oriented therapy from family characteristics. Family Therapy, 10, 211-218.

5364.   Stedman, J.M., Gaines, T., and Morris, R. (1979), A study of conceptualization of family structure by experienced family therapists. Family Therapy, 6(3), 137.

5365.   Stedman, J.M., and Gaines, T. (1978), Trainee response to family therapy training. Family Therapy, 5, 81-90.

5366.   Steed, S.P. (1971), The influence of Adlerian counseling on familial adjustment. Dissertation Abstracts International, 31, 5782-A.

5367.   Steens, R. (1978), (A marital therapy.) Tidjskrift Voor Psychotherapie, 4(3), 141-150.

5368.   Steier, F. (1983), Family interaction and properties of self-organizing systems: A study of family therapy with addict families. Dissertation Abstracts International, 44, 863-A.

5369.   Steiger, T.B. (1973), Shadow child. American Journal of Nursing, 73, 2080-2086.

5370.   Stein, A., and Kleiman, J.A. (1984), A self-report family data form for family therapy. Journal of Family Therapy, 6(1), 63-68.

5371.   Stein, C. (1960), And now there are four: Minimal group psychotherapy in a family setting. Group Psychotherapy, 13, 14-21.

5372.   Stein, H.F. (1978), The Slovak-American swaddling ethos: Homeostat for family dynamics and cultural continuity. Family Process, 17, 31-45.

5373.   Stein, L.K. (1979), Counseling parents of hearing impaired children - psychotherapeutic model. In L.J. Bradford and W.G. Hardy, (Eds.), Hearing and hearing impairment. New York: Grune and Stratton.

5374.   Steinbauer, P.D. (1968), Reflections on criteria for selection and prognosis in family therapy. Canadian Psychiatric Association Journal, 13(4), 317-122.

5375.   Steinberg, D. (1978), The introduction of small group work to an adolescent unit. Journal of Adolescence, 4, 331.

5376.   Steinberg, J.L. (1980), Towards an interdisciplinary commitment: A divorce lawyer proposes attorney-therapist marriages or, at the least, an affair. Journal of Marital and Family Therapy, 6(3), 259-268.

5377.   Steinfeld, G.J. (1978), Decentering and family process: A marriage of cognitive therapies. Journal of Marriage and Family Counseling, 4(3), 61-69.

5378.   Steinfeld, G.J. (1975), Piaget's concept of decentering in relation to family process and therapy. In Proceedings fourth interdisciplinary seminar: Piagetian theory and its implications for the helping professions: February 15th, 1974: University of Southern California, Los Angeles: University of Southern California.

5379.   Steinglass, P. (1976), Experimenting with family treatment approaches to alcoholism, 1950-1975: A review. Family Process, 15(1), 97-123.

5380.   Steinglass, P. (1979), The Home Observation Assessment Method (HOAM): Real-time naturalistic observation of families in their homes. Family Process, 18, 337-354.

5381.   Steinglass, P. (1980), Assessing families in their own homes. American Journal of Psychiatry, 137, 1523-9.

5382.   Steinglass, P. (1984), Review of M.D. Stanton and T.C. Todd's The family therapy of drug abuse and addiction. Journal of Marital and Family Therapy, 10(4), 432-434.

5383.   Steinglass, P. (1984), Family systems theory and therapy: A clinical application of general systems theory. Psychiatric Annals, 14, 582-586.

5384.   Steinglass, P. (1982), Discussion groups for chronic hemodialysis patients and their families. General Hospital Psychiatry, 4, 7-14.

5385.   Steinglass, P. (1979), The alcoholic family in the interaction laboratory. Journal of Nervous Mental Disease, 167, 428-436.

5386.   Steinglass, P. (1979), An experimental treatment program for alcoholic couples. Journal of Study Alcohol, 40, 159-182.

5387.   Steinglass, P., Davis, D., and Berendson, D. (1977), Observations of conjointly hospitalized "alcoholic couples" during sobriety and intoxication: Implications for theory and therapy. Family Process, 1(1), 1-6.

5388.   Steinglass, P., Temple, S., Lisman, S. A, and Reiss, D. (1982), Coping with spinal cord injury: The family perspective. General Hospital Psychiatry, 4, 259-264.

5389.   Stemann, S. (1980), Review of H. Stierlin, I. Ruckerembden, N. Wetzel, and M. Wirsching's The first family interview. Gruppenpsycotherapie und Gruppendynamik, 16, 175-180.

5390.   Stempler, B.L. (1977), A group work approach to family group treatment. Social Casework, 58, 143-152.

5391.   Stenback, A. (1961), Marriage conflicts in marriage counseling. Nordisk Medicin, 6, 1053-1056.

5392.   Stepanik, J. (1978), The family therapy institute in Warsaw. Ceskoslovenska Psychiatrie, 74, 39-40.

5393.   Stephan-Jorgensen, C. J. (1983), Marriage, family, and child counseling: A study of the profession in California. Dissertation Abstracts International, 44, 1255-B.

5394.   Stephens, G.G. (1977), Update: The family practice movement today. Journal of Psychiatric Education, 1, 135.

5395.   Stern, D., and Kedem, A. (1983), Divorce and remarriage American style. American Journal of Family Therapy, 11, 60-61.

5396.   Stern, R.S., and Marks, J.M. (1973), Contract therapy in obsessive-
        compulsive neurosis and marital discord. British Journal of Psychiatry,
        123, 681-684.

5397.   Stern, S., Whitaker, C.A., Hagemann, N.J., Anderson, R.B, and Bargman,
        G.J. (1981), Anorexia Nervosa: The hospital's role in family
        treatment. Family Process, 20, 395-408.

5398.   Sternlicht, M., and Sullivan, I. (1974), Group counseling with parents of
        the mentally retarded: Leadership selection and functioning. Mental
        Retardation, 12(5), 11-13.

5399.   Stevens, D., and Johnson, A.R. (1969), Family group counseling.
        Hospital and Community Psychology, 20, 111.

5400.   Stewart, B. (1980), Counseling. Hidden conflicts: A case study of the
        Fisher family — 2. Occupational Health, 32(1), 22-29.

5401.   Stewart, B. (1980), Counseling. Hidden conflicts: A case study of the
        Fisher family - 3. Occupational Health, 32(2), 76-83.

5402.   Stewart, C.W. (1979), The minister as family counselor. Nashville, TN:
        Abingdon Press.

5403.   Stewart, D.W. (1972), Goal setting in marriage counseling. A
        protensive, timefinding method to facilitate coordination and
        cooperation of the marital pair. Dissertation Abstracts International,
        3(8), 4851B.

5404.   Stewart, R.H., Peters, T.C., Marsh, S., and Peters, M.J. (1975), Object
        relations approach to psychotherapy with marital couples, families, and
        children. Family Process, 14(2), 161-178.

5405.   Stewart, S., and Johansen, R. (1977), A family systems approach to
        home dialysis. Psychotherapy and Psychosomatics, 27, 86-92.

5406.   Stier, S., and Goldenberg, I. (1975), Training issues in family therapy.
        Journal of Marriage and Family Counseling, 1, 63-68.

5407.   Stierlin, H. (1975), Family therapy with adolescents and the process of
        intergenerational reconciliation. In M. Sugar (Ed.), The adolescent in
        group and family therapy. New York: Brunner/Mazel.

5408.   Stierlin, H. (1975), Von der psychoanalyses zur familientherapie:
        Theori, klinik. Stuttgart, West Germany: Keltt.

5409.   Stierlin, H. (1974), Shame and guilt in family relations. Theoretical and
        clinical aspects. Annual of New York Academy of Science, 223, 115-122.

5410.   Stierlin, H. (1974), Family theory: An introducton. In A. Burton (Ed.),
        Operational theories of personality. New York: Brunner/Mazel.

5411.   Stierlin, H. (1974), Shame and guilt in family relations. Archives of
        General Psychiatry, 30, 381-389.

5412.   Stierlin, H. (1973), A family perspective on adolescent runaways.
        Archives of General Psychiatry, 29, 56-62.

5413.   Stierlin, H. (1973), Group fantasies and family myths: Some theoretical and practical aspects. Family Process, 12, 111-125.

5414.   Stierlin, H. (1970), Family therapy with adolescents in light of the separation. Psyche, 24(10), 756-767.

5415.   Stierlin, H. (1979), Family therapy in German-speaking countries. Journal of Marital and Family Therapy, 5(4), 101-110.

5416.   Stierlin, H. (1979), Principles of family therapy. Psychotherapie, 29, 199-206.

5417.   Stierlin, H. (1980), Family therapy. Fortschrite der Medizin, 98, 1357-1358.

5418.   Stierlin, H. (1981), The patient's Nazi past and the dialogue between the generations. Family Process, 20, 379-390.

5419.   Stierlin, H. (1981), Family therapy--fashion or therapeutic breakthrough. Deutsch Medizinishe Wochenschrift, 106, 99-100.

5420.   Stierlin, H. (1983), Family therapy—a science or an art. Family Process, 22, 413-423.

5421.   Stierlin, H. (Ed.) (1977), Psychoanalysis family therapy. New York, NY: Aronson.

5422.   Stierlin, H., Wirsching, M., and Knauss, W. (1977), Family dynamics and psychosomatic disorders in adolescence. Psychotherapie und Psychosomatiks, 28, 243-251.

5423.   Stierlin, H., and Klugman, J. (1977), Family therapy as an empathetic process. Psyche, 31, 786-802.

5424.   Stierlin, H., and Rucker-Embden, I. (1980), The first interview with the family. New York: Brunner/Mazel.

5425.   Stinnett, N. (1979), Building family strengths: Blueprints for action. In N. Stinnett, B. Chesser and J. Defrain (Eds.), Building family strengths. Lincoln, NE: University of Nebraska Press.

5426.   Stix, E.M. (1979), The interaction TAT: An auxiliary method in the diagnosis of marital crises. Zeitschrift fur Klinische Psychologie und Psychotherapie, 27, 248-257.

5427.   Stockdale, J.S. (1981), Relationship of family counseling commitment to child self-concept and parent attitude. Dissertation Abstracts International, 41, 3496-A.

5428.   Stokes, W.R. (1951), A marriage counseling case: The married virgin. Marriage and Family Living, 13, 29-34.

5429.   Stokes, W.R. (1952), The concept of emotional maturity as related to marriage counseling. Marriage and Family Living, 14, 127-132.

5430.   Stolin, V.V. (1982), The psychological bases of family therapy. Voprosy Psikhologii, 4, 104-155.

5431. Stone, A. (1950), Marriage counseling today and tomorrow. Marriage and Family Living, 12, 39-40.

5432. Stone, A. (1949), Marriage education and marriage counseling in the United States. Marriage and Family Living, 11, 38-39.

5433. Stone, W.N. (1984), Review of L.R. Wolberg and M.L. Aronson's Group and family therapy: 1982. International Journal of Group Psychotherapy, 34(2), 299.

5434. Stork-Groeveld, I. (1973), Marital problems in the aged. Nederlands Tidschrift Voor Psychologie en Haar Grensegebieden, 117, 593-596.

5435. Storm, C.L., and Sprenkle, D.H. (1982), Individual treatment in divorce therapy: A critique of an assumption. Journal of Divorce, 6, 87-97.

5436. Stover, L., and Guerney, B.G., Jr. (1967), The efficacy of training procedures for mothers in family therapy. Psychotherapy: Theory, Research and Practice, 4(3), 110-115.

5437. Strachstein, H. (1977), Review of A.C.R. Skynner's Systems of family and marital psychotherapy. Group, 1(2), 143-144.

5438. Strain, P.S., Young, C.C., and Horowitz, J. (1981), Generalized behavior change during oppositional child training: An examination of child and family demographic variables. Behavior Modification, 5, 15-26.

5439. Straker, G., and Jacobson, R. (1979), A study of the relationship between family interaction and individual symptomology over time. Family Process, 18, 443-450.

5440. Stratford, J., Burck, C., and Kinston, W. (1982), The influence of context on the assessment of family interaction: A clinical study. Journal of Family Therapy, 4, 359-372.

5441. Straus, M.A. (1977), Societal morphogenesis and intrafamily violence in cross-cultural perspective. Annals of New York Academy of Science, 285, 717-730.

5442. Straus, M.A. (1974), Violence in the family. Nursing Digest, 2, 138-146.

5443. Strayhorn, J. (1978), Social-exchange theory: Cognitive restructuring in marital therapy. Family Process, 17, 437-448.

5444. Strean, H.S. (1962), A means of involving fathers in family treatment: Guidance groups for fathers. American Journal of Orthopsychiatry, 32(4), 719-727.

5445. Street, E. (1981), The family therapist and staff-group consultancy. Journal of Family Therapy, 3(2), 187-200.

5446. Street, E. (1984), Review of E.E. Filsinger's Marriage and family assessment: A sourcebook for family therapy. British Journal of Clinical Psychology, 23(3), 239.

5447. Street, E. (1983), Review of G.A. Walter, and S.E. Marks' Experiential learning and change: Theory, design and practice. Journal of Family Therapy, 5, 100.

5448.   Street, E. (1983), Review of D. Bloch and R. Simon's The strength of family therapy: Selected papers of Ackerman, Nathan W. Bulletin of the British Psychological Society, 36, 128.

5449.   Street, E., and Foot, H. (1984), Training family therapists in observational skills. Journal of Family Therapy, 6(4), 335-346.

5450.   Street, E., and Treacher, A. (1980), Microtraining and family therapy skills: Towards a possible synthesis. Journal of Family Therapy, 2, 243-258.

5451.   Street, E.C. (1982), Review of R.M. Lerrer and G.B. Spanier's Child influences on marital and family interaction: A life-span perspective. Journal of Family Therapy, 4, 322.

5452.   Strelnick, A. (1980), Multifamily group therapy for outpatients. American Journal of Family Therapy, 8, 72-74.

5453.   Strelnick, A.H. (1977), Multiple family group therapy: A review of the literature. Family Process, 16, 307-325.

5454.   Strich, S. (1980), Review of S. Lieberman's Transgenerational family therapy. Group Analysis, 13, 221-222.

5455.   Strickland, J.H. (1982), The effects of two marriage enrichment retreat models on marital satisfaction. Dissertation Abstracts International, 42, 4305-A.

5456.   Stricklin, G. (1985), Doctoral student-faculty relationships in marriage and family therapy programs as mediated by personal authority. Dissertation Abstracts International, 46, 1476-A.

5457.   Strochstein, H. (1978), Review of M. Sugar's The adolescent in group and family therapy. Group, 2(1), 62-64.

5458.   Strojnowski, J. (1980), Conflict solving in the family. Roczniki Filozoficzne: Psychologia, 39, 181-187.

5459.   Strojnowski, J. (1979), Psychotherapy in preventive health services with special regard to family and school problems. Psychiatrica Polska, 13, 383-389.

5460.   Stroup, A.L., and Galsser, P. (1959), The orientation and focus of marriage counseling. Marriage and Family Living, 21, 20-24.

5461.   Stroup, M. (1982), A preliminary study comparing two structured group treatments for stepfamilies: Couple/family treatment and family treatment. Dissertation Abstracts International, 43, 941-A.

5462.   Strozier, A.M. (1981), The effect of a selected marriage enrichment retreat upon relationship change, marital communication, and dyadic adjustment. Dissertation Abstracts International, 42, 1592-B.

5463.   Struck, G. (1971), Methods and tasks of marriage counseling: Setting of goals and future perspectives. Zurich: Institut fur Ehe und Familienkunde, 76-78.

5464.   Strus, D.F. (1975), The theory and practice of marital and family
        counseling: An overview of current conceptualizations. Dissertation
        Abstracts International, 36, 3649-A.

5465.   Stuart, R.B. (1969), Operant-interpersonal treatment for marital
        discord. Journal of Consulting and Clinical Psychology, 33, 675-682.

5466.   Stubblefield, K.S. (1977), A preventive program for bereaved families.
        Social Work Health Care, 2, 379-389.

5467.   Stultz, W.F. (1983), Review of M.W. Agopian's Parental child-stealing.
        American Journal of Family Therapy, 11, 85.

5468.   Sturges, J.S. (1977), Talking with children about mental illness in the
        family. Health and Social Work, 2, 87-109.

5469.   Sturm, I.E. (1971), An attempt to dramatize the double-bind hypothesis
        of the schizophrenogenic family. Journal of Psychology, 77, 55-66.

5470.   Stuttgen, T. (1978), (The prescribed separation of parents and patients
        in young schizophrenics.) Psychiatry Prax, 5, 127-132.

5471.   Suarez, J.M., Weston, N.L., and Hartstein, N.B. (1978), Mental health
        interventions in divorce proceedings. American Journal of
        Orthopsychiatry, 48, 273-283.

5472.   Suchotliff, L. (1978), Crisis induction and parental involvement: A
        prerequisite of successful treatment in an inpatient setting.
        Adolescence, 13, 697-702.

5473.   Sugar, M. (1979), Review of J.M. Lewis' How's your family. American
        Journal of Family Therapy, 7(3), 85.

5474.   Sugar, M. (1975), The structure and setting of adolescent therapy
        groups. In M. Sugar (Ed.), The adolescent in group and family therapy.
        New York: Brunner/Mazel.

5475.   Sugar, M. (1975), Defusing a high school critical mass. In M. Sugar
        (Ed.), The adolescent in group and family therapy. New York:
        Brunner/Mazel.

5476.   Sugar, M. (1975), Office network therapy with adolescents. In M. Sugar
        (Ed.), The adolescent in group and family therapy. New York:
        Brunner/Mazel.

5477.   Sugar, M. (1975), Group therapy for pubescent boys with absent
        fathers. In M. Sugar (Ed.), The adolescent in group and family therapy.
        New York: Brunner/Mazel.

5478.   Sugar, M. (Ed.) (1975), The adolescent in group and family therapy. New
        York: Brunner/Mazel.

5479.   Sugarman, S. (1984), Integrating family therapy training into psychiatry
        residency programs: Policy issues and alternatives. Family Process, 23,
        23-32.

5480.   Sugarman, S. (1981), Family therapy training in selected general
        psychiatry residency programs. Family Process, 20(2), 147-154.

5481.   Suh, M. (1979), Review of W.R. Beavers's Psychotherapy and growth: A family systems perspective. Psychiatric Journal of the University of Ottawa, 4, 274.

5482.   Sullaway, M., and Christensen, A. (1983), Couples and families as participant observers of their interaction. In J.P. Vincent (Ed.), Advances in family intervention, assessment and theory, Vol. 3. Greenwich: JAI Press.

5483.   Sullivan, B.P. (1982), An application of social learning theory to group marital therapy. Dissertation Abstracts International, 43, 888-B.

5484.   Summerlin, T.M.L., and Ward, G.R. (1978), Effect of parental participation in a parent group on a child's self-concept. Journal of Psychology, 100, 227.

5485.   Summers, F. (1978), Severe hypertension treated successfully by marital psychotherapy. American Journal of Psychiatry, 135, 989-990.

5486.   Summers, F. (1974), Successful treatment of hypertension: Compliance or marital therapy. American Journal of Psychiatry, 136, 464.

5487.   Summers, T.W. (1978), The examination of outcome evaluation procedures for a multiple family and adolescent group counseling. Dissertation Abstracts International, 38, 6180B.

5488.   Sunbury, J. (1980), Working with defensive projections in conjoint marriage counseling. Family Relations, 29(1), 107-110.

5489.   Sunbury, J.F. (1981), Marital therapy outcome: The influence of client, therapist, and treatment variables at follow-up. Dissertation Abstracts International, 42, 1195-B.

5490.   Sutcliff, P., Lovell, J., and Walters, S.M. (1985), New directions for family therapy: Rubbish removal as a task of choice. Journal of Family Therapy, 7(2), 175.

5491.   Sutherland, J.D. (1975), Review of C.J. Sager and H.S. Kaplan's (Eds.), Progress in group and family therapy. International Journal of Psychoanalysis, 56, 111-112.

5492.   Sutter, J.M. (1980), Role of the psychiatrist in marital problems. Anales de la Real Academia Nacional de Medicina (Madr.), 97, 544-50.

5493.   Swain, K. (1980), A comparison of state laws governing marriage and family therapy in the United States. Dissertation Abstracts International, 41, 822-A. (University Microfilms No. 8017122.)

5494.   Swain, K.L. (1975), Marriage and family counselor licensure: Special reference to Nevada. Journal of Marital and Family Counseling, 1, 149-155.

5495.   Swan, R.W. (1972), Differential counseling approaches to conflict reduction in the marital dyad. Dissertation Abstracts International, 32(11), 6629B.

5496.   Swap, S. (1984), Ecological approaches to working with families of disturbing children. In W.A. O'Connor and B. Lubin (Eds.), Ecological approaches to clinical and community psychology. New York: John Wiley and Sons.

5497. Sweeney, A. (1978), Genetic counseling in families with hearing impairment. Journal of Rehabilitation of the Deaf, 12(1), 1-13.

5498. Sweeney, B.T. (1970), Family-centered care in public health nursing. Nursing Forum, 9, 169.

5499. Swenson, C.M. (1980), A profile of marriage counselors at selected university counseling services in the midwest. Dissertation Abstracts International, 41, 1412-A.

5500. Swicegood, T.V. (1975), A marriage enrichment group for the newly married: A supplement to pre-marital pastoral counseling with description and analysis. Dissertation Abstracts International, 36, 4569A.

5501. Swift, W.J. (1981), Family availability for the working alliance: A neglected area in child psychiatry training. Journal of the American Academy of Child Psychiatry, 20, 810-21.

5502. Syerdahelyi, S. (1976), Experiences of family therapy in a psychiatric department. Magyar Psyichologiai Syemle, 33, 127-139.

5503. Sykes, B.W. (1978), The adaptation of the family training program to an office setting. Dissertation Abstracts International, 38, 3375B.

5504. Symonds, M. (1978), The psychodynamics of violence-prone marriages. American Journal of Psychoanalysis, 38, 213-222.

5505. Symonds, M. (1979), The wife as the professional. American Journal of Psychoanalysis, 39, 55-63.

5506. Symor, N.K. (1975), The dependency cycle: A social action theory developed through the use of family consciousness raising groups. Dissertation Abstracts International, 36 2531B.

5507. Sywvlak, A.E. (1978), The effect of filial therapy on parental acceptance and child adjustment. Dissertation Abstracts International, 38, 6180-6181B.

5508. Szalita, A.B. (1968), The combined use of family interviews and individual therapy in schizophrenia. American Journal of Psychotherapy, 22, 419-430.

5509. Szapocznik, J., Kurtines, W., Hervis, O., and Spencer, F. (1984), One person family therapy. In W.A. O'Connor and B. Lubin (Eds.), Ecological approaches to clinical and community psychology. New York: John Wiley and Sons.

5510. Szapocznik, J., Kurtines, W.M., Foote, F.H., Perez, V.A., and Hervis, O. (1983), Conjoint versus one-person family therapy: Some evidence for the effectiveness of conducting family therapy through one person. Journal of Consulting and Clinical Psychology, 51, 889-899.

5511. Szewczyk, Z. (1980), Training groups as a method of formation of parental attitude. Psychiatria Polska, 14, 283-6.

5512.   Szinetar, E. (1969), A csaladterapie nehany mozzanata. (Some factors of family therapy.) Magyar Pszichologie Szemle, 25, 416-424.

5513.   Szurek, S.A. (1952), Some lessons from efforts at psychotherapy with parents. American Journal of Psychiatry, 109, 296-302.

5514.   Szymanski, L.S., and Kiernana, W.E. (1983), Multiple family group therapy with developmentally disabled adolescents and young adults. International Journal of Group Psychotherapy, 33, 521-534.

5515.   Tabata, H. (1980), A study of the process of collaborative mothers counseling. Japanese Journal of Child and Adolescent Psychiatry, 21(4), 236-247.

5516.   Taft, J. (Ed.) (1948), Family casework and counseling: A functional approach. Philadelphia, PA: University of Pennsylvania Press.

5517.   Taggart, A.D., and Scheidlinger, S. (1953), Group therapy in a family service program. Social Casework, 24, 378-385.

5518.   Taggart, M. (1980), On saying goodbye to a deceased former parent. Journal of Marital and Family Therapy, 6(2), 117-122.

5519.   Taggart, M. (1982), Values, ethics, legalities, and the family therapist: II. Linear versus systematic values: Implications for family therapy. Family Therapy Collections, 1, 23-39.

5520.   Taggart, M. (1985), The feminist critique in epistemological perspective: Questions of context in family therapy. Journal of Marital and Family Therapy, 11(2), 113-126.

5521.   Taggart, M.E. (1979), Family crises in the "fourth trimester": The role of the nurse. Canada's Mental Health, 27, 9-11.

5522.   Taibbi, R. (1981), Use of the life-play fantasy with couples in conjoint marital therapy. Transactional Analysis Journal, 11(2), 138-141.

5523.   Taibbi, R. (1983), Handling extramarital affairs in clinical treatment. Social Casework, 64, 200-204.

5524.   Talmadge, J.M. (1975), Adler, Sullivan and family counseling. Family Therapy, 2, 173-180.

5525.   Talmadge, J.M. (1975), Psychiatric residents, medical students, and families: Teaching family dynamics to the uninitiated. Family Therapy, 2, 11-16.

5526.   Tamura, K. (1962), Joint interview in marriage counseling. Seishin Eisei (Kenkyu), 10, 42-52.

5527.   Tamura, K. (1964), The nature of marriage counseling and its trends. Kateisaiban-Geppo, 16(3), 1-41.

5528.   Tamura, K. (1965), Foundations of marriage counseling. Kaunseringu-No-Tembo Shinshin-Shobo, 163-177.

5529.   Tangari, A. (1974), Family involvement in the treatment of a psychiatric inpatient. Hospital and Community Psychiatry, 25, 792-794.

5530. Tangari, A., and Class, L. (1977), Advantages of multifamily therapy for families of psychiatric inpatients. Social Work in Health Care, 2, 399-406.

5531. Tapia, F. (1969), Family therapy simplified. Missouri Medicine, 66, 269-272.

5532. Tapp, J.T., Ryken, V., and Kaltwasser, C. (1974), Counseling the abusing parent by telephone. Crisis Intervention, 5(3), 27-37.

5533. Taragano, F. (1963), (The mental patient as emerging from the sickness of his internal family group.) Acta Psiquiatrica y Psicologia Argentina, 9(3), 232-235.

5534. Targow, J.G., and Zweber, R.V. (1969), Participants reactions to treatment in a married couples group. International Journal of Group Psychotherapy, 19, 221-225.

5535. Tarnow, J.D., and Tomlinson, N. (1978), Juvenile diabetes: Impact on the child and family. Psychosomatics, 19, 487-491.

5536. Tartter, A.R. (1977), The dynamics of abusive families and treatment considerations. Bulletin of the American Academy of Psychiatric Law, 8, 408-414.

5537. Tasem, M., and Augenbraun, B. (1965), Family group interviewing with the preschool child and both parents. Journal of the American Academy of Child Psychiatry, 4, 330-340.

5538. Taskinen, S. (1984), (Family guidance in child guidance centres.) Psykologia, 19, 35-37.

5539. Tatar, C.S. (1968), The marriage counselor—a neglected member of the psychotherapy team. Mental Hygiene, 52, 445-446.

5540. Tater, S.M. (1980), Psychodynamics of child abuse as seen through the conjoint psychotherapy of a mother and her abused child. Family Therapy, 7(3), 197.

5541. Taubman, L.C. (1981), The effects of the technique of the dialogue as taught in a marriage encounter weekend, upon self-disclosure, communication, satisfaction, and awareness. Dissertation Abstracts International, 42, 433-B.

5542. Tauss, V. (1976), Working wife-house husband: Implications for counseling. Journal of Family Counseling, 4, 52-55.

5543. Tavantzis, T.N. (1982), Family counseling, family drawings, and the initial interview. Journal for Specialists in Group Work, 7, 125-131.

5544. Tavormina, J.B. (1975), Relative effectiveness of behavioral and reflective group counseling with mentally retarded children. Journal of Consulting and Clinical Psychology, 43(1), 22-31.

5545. Tavormina, J.B. (1974), Basic models of parent counseling: A critical review. Psychological Bulletin, 81(11), 827-835.

5546.   Taylor, B. (1979), St. Thomas Hospital operates lodge for patients'
        families. Hospital Progress, 60, 24.

5547.   Taylor, D.C. (1982), Counseling the parents of handicapped children.
        British Medical Journal, 284, 1027-1028.

5548.   Taylor, F.A. (1977), Inpatient family therapy....Playfield House,
        Stratheden Hospital, Scotland. Nursing Mirror, 144, 62-64.

5549.   Taylor, H.E. (1977), Conducting and evaluating a family enrichment
        program for improving the quality of communication. Dissertation
        Abstracts International, 38, 2363A.

5550.   Taylor, H.J. (1977), The development of family counseling procedures in
        schools. Educational Psychology in Process, 4, 1-8.

5551.   Taylor, J.L. (1956), Psychiatric consultation in family counseling.
        Marriage and Family Living, 18, 259-266.

5552.   Taylor, J.L., and Sagin, S. (1975), A group counseling program for
        adopting parents. American Journal of Orthopsychiatry, 45(2), 266-267.

5553.   Taylor, R.B. (1979), Family behavior modification. American Family
        Physician, 19, 176-181.

5554.   Taylor, R.L. (1984), Marital therapy in the treatment of incest. Social
        Casework, 65(4), 195-202.

5555.   Tcheng-Loroche, F., and Prince, R.H. (1979), Middle income, divorced
        female heads of families: Their lifestyles, health and stress levels.
        Canadian Journal of Psychiatry, 24, 35-42.

5556.   Tearnan, B., and Lutzker, J.R. (1980), A contracting package in the
        treatment of marital problems: A case study. American Journal of
        Family Therapy, 8, 24-31.

5557.   Tec, L. (1972), Family therapy and drug abuse. International
        Pharmacopsychiatry, 7, 53-56.

5558.   Teicher, J.D., Sinay, R.D., and Stumphauser, J.S. (1976), Training
        community-based paraprofessionals as behavior therapists with families
        of alcohol-abusing adolescents. American Journal of Psychiatry, 133,
        847-850.

5559.   Teichman, Y. (1981), Family therapy with adolescents. Journal of
        Adolescence, 4, 87-92.

5560.   Teichman, Y., Spiegel, Y., and Teichman, M. (1978), Crisis intervention
        with families of servicemen missing in action. American Journal of
        Community Psychology, 6, 315-325.

5561.   Teisman, M.W., and Rodgers, B. (1982), A comparison of a traditional
        and marital approach to rehabilitation counseling. Journal of Marital
        and Family Therapy, 8(2), 91-92.

5562.   Teismann, M.W. (1979), Jealousy: Systematic problem-solving therapy
        with couples. Family Process, 18, 151-160.

5563.   Teismann, M.W. (1980), Convening strategies in family therapy. Family Process, 19(4), 393-400.

5564.   Tenenbaum, S. (1968), A psychologist looks at marriage. New York: A.S. Barnes.

5565.   Tennov, D., Jacobson, J.W., and Vittucci, M. (1980), Token economics and unpredictable reward in family settings: A descriptive report. Psychotherapy: Theory, Research, & Practice, 17, 220-226.

5566.   Terkelsen, K.G. (1983), Schizophrenia and the family: II. Adverse effects of family therapy. Family Process, 22, 191-200.

5567.   Terkelsen, K.G. (1982), Review of C.P. Barnard's Families, alcoholism and therapy. Family Process, 21, 490-491.

5568.   Terkelsen, K.G. (1984), Schizophrenia and the family. 2. Adverse effects of family therapy - response. Family Process, 23(3), 425-428.

5569.   Terkelsen, K.G. (1984), Review of W.R. McFarlane's Family therapy in schizophrenia. Journal of Marital and Family Therapy, 10(2), 211-212.

5570.   Terpstra, M.W. (1973), A language behavior therapy program for couples seeking a better sexual adjustment. Dissertation Abstracts International, 34(1), 428-B.

5571.   Terry, L.L. (1985), Toward the building of an ecosystemic model of organizational analysis and change processes: An application of family therapy theory to organizational psychology. Dissertation Abstracts International, 46, 2107-B.

5572.   Teruel, G. (1966), (New methods of diagnosis and treatment of marriage conflicts.) Psyche, 20, 600-621.

5573.   Textor, M. (1982), Family therapy in West Germany. International Journal of Family Therapy, 4, 60.

5574.   Textor, M.R. (1983), An assessment of prominence in the family therapy field. Journal of Marital and Family Therapy, 9, 317-320.

5575.   Textor, M.R. (1984), Review of C. Schneider's Family therapy from the viewpoint of psychotherapeutic schools. Psychologie in Erziehung und Unterricht, 31(3), 238.

5576.   Teyber, E. (1981), Structural family relations: A review. Family Therapy, 8(1), 39-48.

5577.   Teyber, E. (1983), Structural family relations: Primary dyadic alliances and adolescent adjustment. Journal of Marital and Family Therapy, 9, 89-100.

5578.   Thale, T., and Milloy, M. (1975), Training psychiatric residents in a family agency. Social Casework, 56(5), 292.

5579.   Thames, M.E. (1970), The effectiveness of group therapy in changing family role patterns toward disabled members. Dissertation Abstracts International, 31(4), 1911-A.

5580. Tharp, R.G. (1965), Marriage roles, child development and family treatment. American Journal of Orthopsychiatry, 35(3), 531-538.

5581. Thaxton, L., and L'Abate, L. (1982), The "second wave" and the second generation: Characteristics of new leaders in family therapy. Family Process, 21, 359-362.

5582. Theopold, G. (1973), A case of methodical social work. Praxis der Kinderpsychologie und Kinderpsychiatrie, 22, 295-303.

5583. Theopold, G., and Berendsen, D. (1974), A case analysis in methodical social work. Praxis der Kinderpsychologie und Kinderpsychiatrie, 23, 19-30.

5584. Thibault, D.R., and Rabiller, P. (1981), Schizophrenia and family therapy. Soins Psychiatrica, 26, 23-6.

5585. Thoen, G.A., and Russell, M.G. (1979), Child-free option: Workshop model for making one of life's major decisions: In N. Stinnett, B. Chesser, and J. Defrain (Eds.), Building family strengths. Lincoln, NE: Universtiy of Nebraska Press.

5586. Thomas, A. (1956), Simultaneous psychotherapy with marital partners. American Journal of Psychotherapy, 10, 716-727.

5587. Thomas, E.J., and Santa, C.A. (1982), Unilateral family therapy for alcohol abuse: A working conception. American Journal of Family Therapy, 10, 49-58.

5588. Thomas, J.L., and Simons, C.J.R. (1983), Normative history-graded processes: The changing social context of the family life cycle. American Journal of Family Therapy, 11, 71-73.

5589. Thompson, K.B. (1978), The effectiveness of couples communication training on interpersonal orientation, couple communication, perceptual congruence, and verbal communication style: A field study. Dissertation Abstracts International, 39, 3009-3010B.

5590. Thompson, R.A. (1980), Effects of videotape playback on casual attribution in distressed couples. Dissertation Abstracts International, 41, 1530-B.

5591. Thompson, R.W., and Wiley, E. (1970), Reaching families of hospitalized mental patients. A group approach. Community Mental Health, 6, 22-30.

5592. Thompson, S.V. (1980), Review of H.Y. Kwiatkowska's Family therapy and evaluation through art. American Journal of Psychotherapy, 34, 451.

5593. Thomstad, H. (1968), (Family psychiatry. Some practical and theoretical aspects.) Tidjschrift Voor Norske Laegeforening, 24, 2242-2245.

5594. Thorne, M.Q., Jr. (1967), Marital and LSD therapy with a transvestite and his wife. Journal of Sex Research, 3, 169-177.

5595. Thornton, A. (1978), Marital dissolution, remarriage and childbearing. Demography, 15, 361-380.

5596. Thornton, J.F., Plummer, E., Seeman, M.V., and Littman, S.K. (1981), Schizophrenia: Group support for relatives. Canadian Journal of Psychiatry, 26, 341-344.

5597. Thrower, S.M., Burce, W.E., and Walton, R.F. (1982), The family circle method for integrating family systems concepts in family medicine. Journal of Family Practice, 15, 451-457.

5598. Thweatt, R.W. (1980), Divorce: Crisis intervention guided by attachment theory. American Journal of Psychotherapy, 34(2), 240-245.

5599. Tiller, J.W. (1978), Brief family therapy for childhood tic syndrome. Family Process, 17, 217-223.

5600. Tinkelhor, D. (1978), Psychological, cultural and family factors in incest and family sexual abuse. Journal of Marriage and Family Counseling, 4, 41-49.

5601. Titchener, J.L. (1966), The problem of interpretation in marital therapy. Comprehensive Psychiatry, 7, 321-336.

5602. Titchener, J.L., and Golden, M. (1963), Prediction of therapeutic themes from observation of family interaction evoked by the 'revealed differences' technique. Journal of Nervous and Mental Disease, 136, 464-474.

5603. Tittler, B.I., Friedman, S., Blotcky, A.D., and Stedrak, J. (1982), The influence of family variables on an ecologically-based treatment program for emotionally disturbed children. American Journal of Orthopsychiatry, 52, 123-130.

5604. Tittler, B.I., Friedman, S., and Klopper, E.J. (1977), A system for tailoring change measures to the individual family. Family Process, 16, 119-121.

5605. Tiver, C. (1973), Family group therapy includes social dinner with treatment team. Hospital and Community Psychiatry, 24, 79.

5606. Todd, J., and Satz, P. (1980), The effects of long-term verbal memory deficits: A case study of an adolescent and his family. Journal of Marital and Family Therapy, 6, 431-438.

5607. Todd, T.C. (1977), Family therapy comes of age: Review of P.J. Guerin Jr.'s Family therapy: Theory and practice. New York: Gardner Press. Contemporary Psychology, 22, 441.

5608. Toeman, Z. (1945), Psychodramatic research of pre-marital couples. Sociometry, 8, 89.

5609. Toews, J. (1980), Adolescent developmental issues in marital therapy. Adolescent Psychiatry, 8, 244-252.

5610. Tomlinson, R., and Peters, P. (1981), Alternative to placing children: Intensive and extensive therapy with disengaged families. Child Welfare, 60, 95-103.

5611.   Tomm, K., and Sanders, G.L. (1983), Diagnosis and assessment in family therapy: V. Family assessment in a problem-oriented record. Family Therapy Collections, 8, 101-122.

5612.   Tomm, K., and Tomm, B. (1982), Review of S. Minuchin and H.C. Fishman's Family therapy techniques. Canadian Journal of Psychiatry, 27, 688.

5613.   Tomm, K.M., and Wright, L.M. (1979), Training in family therapy: Perceptual, conceptual and executive skills. Family Process, 18, 227-250.

5614.   Tomson, P.R. (1981), Why not be a family doctor? Journal of the Royal College of General Practioners, 31, 501.

5615.   Tonge, W.L. (1975), Marital therapy: How to choose the wrong treatment. Psychotherapy and Psychosomatics, 25(1-6), 163-167.

5616.   Tooley, K. (1970), The role of geographic mobility in some adjustment problems of children and families. Journal of the American Academy of Child Psychiatry, 9, 366-378.

5617.   Topel, S.I. (1967), Of crisis, family, and therapist: A preliminary guide to a therapeutic process in a disadvantaged Los Angeles community. American Journal of Orthopsychiatry, 37, 280.

5618.   Topham, M. (1967), Conjoint family therapy. Australian Journal of Social Work, 20(2), 2-7.

5619.   Toro, P.A. (1983), The strategies and effectiveness of three helping groups during marital disruption. Dissertation Abstracts International, 44, 1609-B.

5620.   Torpy, D.M., and Measey, L.G. (1974), Marital interaction in agoraphobia. Journal of Clinical Psychology, 30, 351-354.

5621.   Torpy, D.M., and Measey, L.G. (1973), Marital interaction in agoraphobia. Journal of Arkansas Medical Association, 70, 176-178.

5622.   Torrada, De Silva, M., and Aubert, C. (1980), The family approach to a case of a battered child. Helvetica Paediatrica Acta, 35, 225-32.

5623.   Tousley, M.M. (1982), The use of family therapy in terminal illness and death. Journal of Psychosocial Nursing and Mental Health Services, 20, 17-22.

5624.   Tovey, R. (1979), Marital group therapy. Clinical Social Work Journal, 7(2), 147-152.

5625.   Townsend, J.E. (1981), The effects of ego deficits on parenting an MBD child, examined in parental group therapy. Dissertation Abstracts International, 42, 2300-A.

5626.   Trabichet, J. (1981), Marriage counseling. Krankenpflege (Bern), 2, 22.

5627.   Tracey, J. (1970), Parent guidance groups: Is this therapy? Journal of Psychiatric Nursing, 8, 11-12.

5628.   Traditional large family of American Catholics is no longer the norm (news). (1978), Family Planning Perspectives, 10, 240-241.

5629.   Trafimow, E., and Pattak, S.I. (1982), Group treatment of primitively fixated children. International Journal of Group Psychotherapy, 32, 445-452.

5630.   Trainer, J.B. (1979), Premarital counseling and examination. Journal of Marital and Family Therapy, 5(2), 61-78.

5631.   Trainer, J.B. (Ed.) (1965), Physiological foundations for marriage counseling. St. Louis, MO: C.V. Mosby.

5632.   Trama, J.A. (1985), A comparison of the impact of an alcohol education program with Al-Anon on knowledge and attitudes about alcoholism and perceptions of the family environment. Dissertation Abstracts International, 45, 2668-A.

5633.   Trankina, F.J. (1975), Aggressive and withdrawn children as related to family perception and outcome of different treatment methods. Dissertation Abstracts International, 36, 924B.

5634.   Travis, R.P., and Travis, P.Y. (1975), The pairing enrichment program: Actualizing the marrige. Family Coordinator, 24, 161-165.

5635.   Travisono, A.P., and O'Neil, C.F. (1966), Intramitive family therapy. Corrective Psychiatry and Journal of Social Therapy, 12, 229-237.

5636.   Treacher, A. (1983), Review of C.H. Kramer's Becoming a family therapist: Developing an integrated approach to working with families. Journal of Family Therapy, 5, 98.

5637.   Treacher, A. (1982), Structural family therapy in context: Working with child focused therapy. Journal of Family Therapy, 4(1), 15.

5638.   Treacher, A., and Carpenter, J. (1982), Oh no not the Smiths again - an exploration of how to identify and overcome stuckness in family therapy. 1. Stuckness involving the contextual and technical aspects of therapy. Journal of Family Therapy, 4, 285-306.

5639.   Trends in living arrangement. (1978), Statistical Bulletin of Metropolitan Life Insurance Company, 59, 7-11.

5640.   Trenholme, A.K. (1975), Measuring family changes in therapy. Dissertation Abstracts International, 35, 4667-4668B.

5641.   Troemel-Ploetz, S. (1977), "She is just not an open person": A linguistic analysis of a restructuring intervention in family therapy. Family Process, 16, 339-352.

5642.   Trompetter, P.S. (1971), The elements and effects of a short program of marital fight training. Dissertation Abstracts International, 32(1), 573B.

5643.   Trotzer, J.P. (1981), The centrality of values in families and family therapy. International Journal of Family Therapy, 3, 42-55.

5644.   Trotzer, J.P. (1982), Engaging families in therapy: A pilot study. International Journal of Family Therapy, 4(1), 4.

5645.   Truitt, J. (1979), The family education association of west central
        Indiana: A grassroots prevention program for marital health.
        Contemporary Education, 50, 72-76.

5646.   Tseng, W.S. (1979), Triaxial family classification: Proposal. Journal of
        the American Academy of Child Psychiatry, 18, 22-43.

5647.   Tsoi-Hoshmand, L. (1975), The limits of quid pro quo in couple therapy.
        Family Coordinator, 24, 51-54.

5648.   Tsoi-Hoshmand, L. (1976), Marital therapy: An integrative behavioral-
        learning model. Journal of Marriage and Family Counseling, 2(2), 179-
        191.

5649.   Tsuang, M.T. (1978), Genetic counseling for psychiatric patients and
        their families. American Journal of Psychiatry, 135, 1465-1475.

5650.   Tubesing, N.L. (1977), Effects of a marriage counseling training
        program on Lutheran clergy couples. Dissertation Abstracts
        International, 38, 2191A.

5651.   Tucker, B.Z., Hart, G., and Liddle, H.A. (1976), Supervision in family
        therapy: A developmental perspective. Journal of Marriage and Family
        Counseling, 2, 269-276.

5652.   Tucker, B.Z., and Liddle, H.A. (1978), Intra- and interpersonal process in
        the group supervision of family therapists. Family Therapy, 5, 13-27.

5653.   Tucker, S.J. (1982), Evaluation of family therapy training. Dissertation
        Abstracts International, 42, 3926-A.

5654.   Tucker, S.J., and Pinsof, W.M. (1984), The empirical evaluation of
        family therapy training. Family Process, 23(3), 437-456.

5655.   Tullman, G. (1979), The measurement of communication skills in
        sexually dysfunctional couples. Dissertation Abstracts International, 40,
        2390-B. (University Microfilms No. 7923684.)

5656.   Tullman, G.M., Gilner, F.H., Kolodny, R.C., Dornbush, R.L., and
        Tuluman, G.D. (1981), The pre- and post-therapy measurement of
        communication skills of couples undergoing sex therapy at the Masters
        and Johnson Institute. Archives of Sexual Behavior, 1(2), 95-109.

5657.   Tunnadine, P. (1979), Marriage matters (letter). British Medical
        Journal, 1, 1485-1486.

5658.   Turkewitz, H. (1977), A comparative outcome study of behavioral
        marital therapy and communication therapy. Dissertation Abstracts
        International, 38, 2891B.

5659.   Turkewitz, H. (1980), Review of N.S. Jacobson and G. Margolin's Marital
        therapy: Strategies based on social learning and behavior exchange
        principles. Behavior Assessment, 2, 305-306.

5660.   Turkewitz, H., and O'Leary, K.D. (1981), A comparative outcome study
        of behavioral marital therapy and communication therapy. Journal of
        Marital and Family Therapy, 7(2), 159.

5661.   Turner, A.L. (1980), Therapy with families of a mentally retarded
        child. Journal of Marriage and Family Therapy, 6(2), 167-170.

5662.   Turner, F.B. (1954), Common characteristics among persons seeking
        professional marriage counseling. Marriage and Family Living, 16, 143-
        144.

5663.   Turner, M.B., and Gross, S.J (1976), An approach to family therapy: An
        affective rule-altering model. Journal of Family Counseling, 4, 50-56.

5664.   Turner, N.W. (1982), Conflict utilization in marital-dyadic therapy.
        Psychiatric Clinics of North America, 5, 503-518.

5665.   Tuson, G. (1985), Philosophy and family therapy: A study in
        interconnectedness. Journal of Family Therapy, 7, 277-296.

5666.   Twersky, R.K., and Williamson, P. (1983), Family conferences: An
        approach to teaching family systems care in a family practice
        residency. Social Work in Health Care, 9, 1-13.

5667.   Twitchell-Allen, D. (1954), Psychodrama in the family. Group
        Psychotherapy, 7, 167-177.

5668.   Tyler, A. (1980), Marriage, sex and counseling in Huntington's chorea.
        Sexuality and Disability, 3(3), 159-162.

5669.   Tyler, E.A., Truumaa, A., and Henshaw, P. (1962), Family group intake
        by a child guidance team. Archives of General Psychiatry, 6(3), 214-218.

5670.   Tyndall, N. (1972), The work of marriage guidance counselors.
        Postgraduate Medical Journal, 48, 563-568.

5671.   Tyndall, N. (1974), Marriage counselling. Work of marriage guidance
        councils. Part 1. Midwife and Health Visitor, 10, 298-300.

5672.   Tyndall, N.J. (1972), Marriage in difficulty: The work of marriage
        counseling. Commununity Health, 4, 28-33.

5673.   U.S. women marrying later, having babies later, spacing them further
        apart than in earlier years. (news). (1978), Family Planning
        Perspectives, 10, 302.

5674.   Udry, J.R., and Morris, N.M. (1978), Relative contribution of male and
        female age to the frequency of marital intercourse. Social Biology, 25,
        128-134.

5675.   Ulrici, D.K. (1983), The effects of behavioral and family interventions
        on juvenile recidivism. Family Therapy, 10, 25-36.

5676.   Umansky, J.A., and Umansky, S.J. (1976), Parents as behavior therapy
        technicians in treating reading deficits. Australian Psychologist, 11(3),
        305-312.

5677.   Umbarger, C. (1978), Redefining the problem: Individual symptoms and
        family system. International Journal of Family Counseling, 6, 19-24.

5678.   Umbarger, C. (1972), The paraprofessional and family therapy. Family
        Process, 11, 147-162.

5679.   Umbarger, C., and Hare, R. (1973), A structural approach to patient and therapist disengagement from a schizophrenic family. American Journal of Psychotherapy, 27, 274-284.

5680.   Umezu, K. (1970), The study of autistic children with behavior therapy. IV: Guidance meeting for mothers. Bulletin of the Seishin Igaku Institute, Institute of Psychiatry, 17, 71-84.

5681.   Underwood, D.M. (1980), The use of the Lasswell profile in marital therapy: A study of redefining dissimilarity in relationship treatment. Dissertation Abstracts International, 40, 3974-B. (University Microfilms No. 8003766.)

5682.   Urban, D. (1981), The short-term effects of a marital enrichment program on couple communication. Dissertation Abstracts International, 42, 93-A.

5683.   Urban, T.S., and Kelz, J.W. (1973), Wives' needs as related to perceptions of their husbands' post-mental hospital behavior. Community Health (Bristol), 4, 249-253.

5684.   Urbaniak, L. M. (1982), Marriage encounter: Description of participants and comparison to the caring relationship inventory norm groups. Dissertation Abstracts International, 42, 5030-A.

5685.   Urdal, B. (1968), The procedure in family group treatment. Nordisk Psychiatrie Tidsskrift, 22, 10-20.

5686.   Urdal, B. (1971), The differential indication for individual versus family therapy in adolescent psychiatry. Tidsskrift for den Norske Laegeforening, 91, 358-361. (Norweigen)

5687.   Usher, M.L., Jay, J., and Glass, D.R. (1982), Family therapy as a treatment modality for alcoholism. Journal of Studies on Alcoholism, 43, 927-938.

5688.   Uzoka, A.F. (1979), The myth of the nuclear family: Historical background and clinical implications. American Psychologist, 34, 1095-1106.

5689.   Vaglum, P. (1975), Family psychotherapy: A frame of reference for choosing methods for treatment in a psychiatric hospital. Psychotherapy and Psychosomatics, 25, 279-282.

5690.   Vaglum, P. (1973), The patient-centered family working group: A medium for collaboration with the "unmotivated" family members. A model and an example. Scandianavian Journal of Social Medicine, 1, 69-75.

5691.   Vaglum, P. (1973), The patient centered family working group: A medium for collaboration with the "unmotivated" family members. A model and an example. Rehabilitation Literature, 34, 358-363.

5692.   Valentine, D. (1980), The developmental approach to the study of the family: Implications for practice. Child Welfare, 59, 347-55.

5693. Valle, S.K., and Marinelli, R.P. (1975), Training in human relations skills as a preferred mode of treatment for married couples. Journal of Marriage and Family Counseling, 1, 359–365.

5694. Van Blaaderen-Stok, C.L. (1970), An approach to family therapy along analytic lines. International Journal of Group Psychotherapy, 20, 241–244.

5695. Van Deusen, J.M., Scott, S.M., and Stanton, M.D. (1980), Engaging "resistant" families in treatment. I. Getting the drug addict to recruit his family members. International Journal of the Addictions, 15, 1069–1089.

5696. Van Dyck, B.J. (1980), A multivariate analysis of a social learning approach to family intervention. Dissertation Abstracts International, 41, 2351–B. (University Microfilms No. 8029179.)

5697. Van Dyke, J., and Van Dyke, G. (1979), A medical student marriage. Journal of Florida Medical Association, 66, 537–538.

5698. Van Emde, B.C. (1962), Intensive group therapy with married couples. Revue Francaise de Psychoanalysis, 26, 446–465.

5699. Van Emde, B.C. (1953), The necessity of group therapy in marriage guidance clinics. International Journal of Sexology, 7, 79–80.

5700. Van Gee, S.J. (1979), Alcoholism and the family: A psychodrama approach. Journal of Psychiatric Nursing, 17, 9–12.

5701. Van Hagen, J. (1983), One residential center's model for working with families. Child Welfare, 62, 233–41.

5702. Van Krevelen, D.A. (1975), On the use of the family drawing test. Acta Paedopsychiatrica, 41, 104–109.

5703. Van Meerbeeck, P. (1979), (Image of body and family body.) Acta Psychiatrica Belgica, 79(6), 614–622.

5704. Van Ree, F. (1974), Couples group therapy in relation to continued education of nurses with diploma B. 2. Application as educational internship. Tijdschriff voor Ziekenverpleging, 2(37), 1062–1067.

5705. Van Suetendael, P.T. (1965), An exploration of the development of an instrument for assessing the ability of married couples to understand and interpret the intentions and feelings of others in episodes of interaction. Dissertation Abstracts International, 26, 2329.

5706. Van Veen, C.J.F. (1966), Concepts that are used in group dynamics: A discussion of the use of small group concepts for family therapy. Tijdschrift voor Maatschappelijk Were, 20(5), 93–100.

5707. Van Zoost, B. (1973), Premarital communication skills education with university students. Family Coordinator, 22, 187–191.

5708. Van den Blink, A.J. (1972), The helping response: A study and critique of family therapy with suggested implications for theological anthropology. Dissertation Abstracts International, 33(3), 1224–A.

5709.   Van den Blink, A.J. (1974), Family therapy and pastoral care. Journal of Pastoral Care, 28, 183-198.

5710.   Van den Heuvel, M., and Schaap, C. (1979), (Instruments to judge the effectiveness of therapy: II. With emphasis on marital therapy.) Tijdschirft voor Psychotherapie, 5(1), 55-66.

5711.   Van der Kleij, G. (1980), Review of D. Sandner's Walter Schindler: Die analytische gruppentherapie nach dem familienmodell. Group Analysis, 13, 222.

5712.   Vande Kemp, H. (1983), An annotated bibliography of selected references on family therapy. Journal of Psychology and Christianity, 2, 4-20.

5713.   Vande Kemp, H. (1983), Guide to family therapy journals and newsletters. Journal of Psychology and Christianity, 2, 62-63.

5714.   Vande Kemp, H. (1981), Teaching psychology of the family: An experimental approach and a working bibliography. Teaching of Psychology, 8, 152-156.

5715.   Vander-Vennen, M. (1983), The encounter with the family of origin. Journal of Psychology and Christianity, 2, 31-35.

5716.   Vangelder, D.W. (1974), Counseling families with behavioral disorders in children. Primary Care, 1(2), 243-252.

5717.   Vanitrommel, M.J. (1984), A consultation method addressing the therapist-family system. Family Process, 23, 469-480.

5718.   Vansteenwegen, A. (1978), Review of A. Vansteenwegen's, Residential family therapy. Family Process, 17(2), 244-246.

5719.   Vargo, J.W. (1979), The disabled wife and mother: Suggested goals for family counseling. Canadian Counselor, 13(2), 108-111.

5720.   Varilo, E. (1977), Family therapy for juvenile problems. Duodecim, 93, 872-882.

5721.   Vass, M., Jacobs, E., and Slavek, N. (1984), Live-in family counseling: An integrated approach. Personnel and Guidance Journal, 62, 429-431.

5722.   Vassil, T.V. (1978), Residential family camping. Altering family patterns. Social Casework, 59, 605-613.

5723.   Vassiliou, G.A. (1983), Analogic communication as a means of joining the family system in therapy. International Journal of Family Psychiatry, 4, 173-179.

5724.   Vaughan, M. (1979), Review of F. Johnson and S. Johnson's Families and family therapy. British Journal of Social and Clinical Psychology, 18, 446.

5725.   Vedeler, G. H. (1983), Family therapy as a method in child and adolescent psychiatry. Tidsskrift For Norsk Psykologforening, 20, 243-252.

5726.   Veltkamp, L.J., and Newman, K. (1976), Parent groups: How
        effective? Journal of Family Counseling, 4(2), 46-51.

5727.   Venables, E. (1977), Marriage counseling by members of the society.
        Bulletin of the British Psychological Society, 30, 44-46.

5728.   Venn, J. (1984), Family etiology and remission in a case of psychogenic
        fugue. Family Process, 23(3), 429-436.

5729.   Verdun, M.D. (1976), The judged effects on the family of teaching
        children Adlerian principles of democratic family counseling by a
        counseling or didactic method. Dissertation Abstracts International, 37,
        3432-A.

5730.   Verheij, F. (1980), The child and family therapy. Acta
        Paedopsychiatrica, 46, 161-174.

5731.   Verhulst, J. (1975), Marital change: An intensive, short-term
        approach. International Mental Health Research Newsletter, 17, 7-10.

5732.   Vernon, M. (1979), Counseling the parents of birth-defective children.
        Postgraduate Medicine, 65(3), 197-201.

5733.   Viaro, M. (1980), Case report: Smuggling family therapy through.
        Family Process, 19, 35-44.

5734.   Viaro, M., and Leonardi, P. (1983), Getting and giving information:
        Analysis of a family-interview strategy. Family Process, 22, 27-42.

5735.   Villeneuve, C. (1980), The child in family therapy. Current Psychiatric
        Therapy, 20, 29-34.

5736.   Villeneuve, C. (1979), The specific participation of the child in family
        therapy. Journal of the American Academy of Child Psychiatry, 18, 44-
        53.

5737.   Vincent, C. (Ed.) (1957), Readings in marriage counseling. New York:
        Cromwell.

5738.   Vincent, C.E. (1977), Barriers to the development of marital health as a
        health field. Journal of Marriage and Family Counseling, 3, 3-11.

5739.   Vincent, J.P. (1983), Review of E.E. Filsinger and R.A. Lewis' Assessing
        marriage: New behavioral approaches. Journal of Marital and Family
        Therapy, 9, 108.

5740.   Vincent, J.P. (Ed.) (1983), Advances in family intervention, assessment
        and theory, Vol. 3. Greenwich: JAI Press.

5741.   Vincent, J.P., Weiss, R.L., and Birchler, G.R. (1975), A behavioral
        analysis of problem solving in distressed and nondistressed married and
        stranger dyads. Behavior Therapy, 6, 475-487.

5742.   Vines, D. (1979), Division on maternal and child health nursing
        practice. Bonding, grief, and working through in relationship to the
        congenitally anomalous child and his family. American Nursing
        Association Publication of Division on Practice; Clinical and Scientific
        Sessions, 185-192.

5743.   Vines, N.R. (1979), Adult unfolding and marital conflict. Journal of
          Marriage and Family Therapy, 5(2), 5.

5744.   Visher, E.B. (1976), Conjoint collaborative marital therapy: A new
          approach. Current Concepts in Psychiatry, 2(4), 6-12.

5745.   Visher, E.B. (1978), Major areas of difficulty for stepparent couples.
          International Journal of Family Counseling, 6, 70-80.

5746.   Visher, E.B., and Visher, J.S. (1979), Stepfamilies: A guide to working
          with stepparents and stepchildren. New York: Brunner/Mazel.

5747.   Visher, E.B., and Visher, J.S. (1982), Therapy with remarriage families:
          VIII. Stepfamilies in the 1980's. Family Therapy Collections, 2, 105-119.

5748.   Visher, E.B., and Visher, J.S. (1982), Children in stepfamilies.
          Psychiatric Annals, 12, 832-841.

5749.   Visher, J.S., and Visher, E.B. (1982), Stepfamilies and stepparenting. In
          F. Walsh (Ed.), Normal family processes. New York: Guilford Press.

5750.   Vlatkovic, P.M., Vidovic, V., and Rudan, V. (1982), Indications for family
          psychotherapy. Psihijatrija Danas, 14, 343-348.

5751.   Voeller, M.N. (1982), Review of J.C. Hansen and D. Rosenthal's
          Strategies and techniques in family therapy. International Journal of
          Group Psychotherapy, 32, 561.

5752.   Vollmerhausen, J.W. (1980), A psychoanalyst glances at family
          therapists. Journal of the American Academy of Psychoanalysis, 8, 161-
          163.

5753.   Von Soden, K. (1978), (Therapy of children, adults and families.) Praxis
          der Kinderpsychologie und Kinderpsychiatrie, 27(6), 197-201.

5754.   Von Villiez, T. (1979), Therapy of enuresis from the family system
          perspective. Praxis der Kinderpsychologie und Kinderpsychiatrie, 28,
          43-46.

5755.   Von Villiez, T. (1982), "Heal"--"but whom?" The symptom-bearing child,
          his family, and the child psychiatrist. Acta Paedopsychiatrica, 48, 307-
          314.

5756.   Vore, D.A., and Wright, L. (1974), Psychological management of the
          family and the dying child. In R.E. Hardy and J.G. Cull (Eds.),
          Therapeutic needs of the family: Problems, descriptions and therapeutic
          approaches. Springfield, IL. Charles C. Thomas.

5757.   Voth, H.M. (1978), The family and the future of America. Alabama
          Journal of Medical Science, 15, 310-315.

5758.   Voth, H.M. (1979), Review of P. Papp's Family therapy: Full length case
          studies. Journal of Nervous and Mental Disease, 167, 715.

5759.   Voth, H.M. (1977), The family and the future of America. Journal of
          the Medical Association of the State of Alabama, 48, 17-21, 49.

5760.   Vroubkovaborzova, E. (1966), Attempt of a complex group therapy of children from alcoholic families. Protialkoholicky Obzor, 1(6), 206-209.

5761.   Vukov, M. (1979), Psychodynamics and therapy of functional sexual disorders in both marital partners. Psihijatrija Danas, 11(3-4), 351-356.

5762.   Vukov, M. (1980), Countertransference in marital therapy. Psihijatrija Danas, 12, 41-45.

5763.   Wachtel, E. (1979), Learning family therapy: Dilemmas of an individual therapist. Journal of Contemporary Psychotherapy, 10, 98-104.

5764.   Wachtel, E.F. (1982), The family psyche over three generations: The genogram revisited. Journal of Marital and Family Therapy, 8, 335-343.

5765.   Waddell, M. (1981), The family and its dynamics. In S. Box, B. Copley, J. Magagna, and E. Moustaki (Eds.), Psychotherapy with families: An analytic approach. London: Routledge and Kegan Paul Ltd.

5766.   Wade, B.K. (1980), The relationship between the disciplinary styles of black parents and preference for mode of family therapy. Dissertation Abstracts International, 40, 5835-B.

5767.   Wadeson, H. (1976), The fluid family in multi-family art therapy. American Journal of Art Therapy, 15, 115-118.

5768.   Wadeson, H. (1973), Art techniques used in conjoint marital therapy. American Journal of Art Therapy, 13, 147-164.

5769.   Wadeson, H. (1972), Conjoint marital art therapy techniques. Psychiatry, 35, 89-98.

5770.   Wagner, V., Weeks, G., and L'Abate, L. (1980), Enrichment and written messages with couples. American Journal of Family Therapy, 8(3), 36-44.

5771.   Wahler, R.G., and Afton, A.D. (1980), Attentional processes in insular and noninsular mothers: Some differences in their summary reports about child problem behaviors. Child Behavior Therapy, 2, 25-41.

5772.   Wahler, R.G., and Fox, J.J. (1980), Solitary toy play and time out: A family treatment package for children with aggressive and oppositional behavior. Journal of Applied Behavior Analysis, 13, 23-39.

5773.   Wahler, R.G., and Fox, J.J. (1982), Response structure in deviant child-parent relationships: Implications for family therapy. Nebraska Symposium on Motivation, 29, 1-46.

5774.   Wahlroos, S. (1976), Some limitations of family therapy. Journal of Family Counseling, 4, 8-11.

5775.   Wald, F.S. (1969), Development of an interdisciplinary team to care for dying patients and their families. American Nursing Association Clinical Conference, 47, 36-41.

5776.   Waldegrave, C. (1984), The butchers, an eclectic approach to family therapy. Journal of Family Therapy, 6, 247-263.

5777.   Waldegrave, C.T. (1981), Evaluating change in families: A follow-up study of the completed work with families in the first year of operation of a family therapy agency. Australian Journal of Family Therapy, 2(2), 76-82.

5778.   Waldo, M., and Guerney, B.G. (1983), Marital relationship enhancement therapy in the treatment of alcoholism. Journal of Marital and Family Therapy, 91, 321-323.

5779.   Walen, S.R. (1980), Cognitive factors in sexual behavior. Journal of Sex and Marital Therapy, 6(2), 87-101.

5780.   Waletzky, L.R. (1979), Husbands' problems with breast-feeding. American Journal of Orthopsychiatry, 49, 349-352.

5781.   Walk, D. (1983), Review of P. Barker's Basic family therapy. Journal of Child Psychology and Psychiatry, 24, 502.

5782.   Walker, B.A., Somerfeld, E., and Robinson, R. (1978), One-night stands: A challenge for family therapists. Family Therapy, 5, 259-265.

5783.   Walker, B.A., and Mehr, M. (1983), Adolescent suicide—a family crisis: A model for effective intervention by family therapists. Adolescence, 18, 285-292.

5784.   Walker, G. (1984), Review of M.I. Ritterman's Using hypnosis in family therapy. Family Process, 23, 581-583.

5785.   Walker, J.L., and White, N.J. (1975), The varieties of therapeutic experience: Conjoint therapy in a homosexual marriage. Canada's Mental Health, 23(2), 3-5.

5786.   Walker, K.N., and Messinger, L. (1979), Remarriage after divorce: Dissolution and reconstruction of family boundaries. Family Process, 18, 185-192.

5787.   Walker, L., Brown, H., Crohn, H., Rudstein, E., Zeisel, E., and Sager, C.J. (1979), Annotated bibliography of the remarried, the living together, and their children. Family Process, 18, 192-212.

5788.   Walker, L.R. (1978), The development, implementation, and evaluation of two educational models of family intervention. Dissertation Abstracts International, 39, 2160-A.

5789.   Walker, P.W. (1977), Premarital counseling for the developmentally disabled. Social Casework, 58(9), 475-479.

5790.   Walker, S.G. (1980), Factors associated with change in divorced and separated persons attending a didactic seminar. Dissertation Abstracts International, 40, 3975-B.

5791.   Wallace, D.H., and Barbach, L.G. (1974), Preorgasmic group treatment. Journal of Sex and Marital Therapy, 1, 146-154.

5792.   Wallace, M.E. (1982), A common base for psychotherapy and family therapy. Psychotherapy: Theory, Research and Practice, 19(3), 297-306.

5793.   Wallerstein, J.S. (1982), Review of F.M. Sanders' Individual and family therapy: Toward an integration. Psychoanalytic Quarterly, 51, 662-676.

5794.   Wallerstein, J.S., and Kelly, J.B. (1977), Divorce counseling: A community service for families in the midst of divorce. American Journal of Orthopsychiatry, 47, 4-22.

5795.   Walri, M. (1965), Nurse participation in family therapy. Perspectives in Psychiatric Care, 3, 8-13.

5796.   Walrond-Skinner, S. (1978), Indications and contraindications for the use of family therapy. Journal of Child Psychology and Psychiatry, 19(1), 57-62.

5797.   Walrond-Skinner, S. (1984), Whither family therapy? Twenty years on. Journal of Family Therapy, 6(1), 1-16.

5798.   Walrond-Skinner, S. (Ed.) (1979), Family and marital psychotherapy. Boston, MA: Routledge and Kegan Paul.

5799.   Walsh, B.M. (1972), Trends in age at marriage in postwar Ireland. Demography, 9, 187-202.

5800.   Walsh, F. (1983), Normal family ideologies: Myths and realities. Family Therapy Collections, 8, 1-14.

5801.   Walsh, F. (1983), The timing of symptoms and critical events in the family life cycle. Family Therapy Collections, 8, 120-133.

5802.   Walsh, F.W. (1978), Concurrent grandparent death and birth of schizophrenic offspring: An intriguing finding. Family Process, 17, 457-463.

5803.   Walsh, J.A. (1979), Decision-making processes in marital therapy: A clinician's dilemma. Dissertation Abstracts International, 40(7), 3427-B.

5804.   Walsh, T.C. (1981), Families in crisis: Relating vulnerability and family functioning to treatment. Family Therapy, 8(2), 105-112.

5805.   Walsh, W.M. (1980), A primer in family therapy. Springfield, IL: Charles C. Thomas.

5806.   Walter, J. (1962), A review of family research in 1959, 1960, and 1961. Marriage and Family Living, 24(2), 158-178.

5807.   Walters, L.H. (1983), The role of the family specialist and research in law. Family Relations: Journal of Applied Family and Child Studies, 32, 521-526.

5808.   Walters, S.M. (1983), Nursing care study: Parasuicide, crisis intervention and family therapy. Nursing Times, 79, 17-20.

5809.   Walz, T.H. (1975), The family, the family agency, and postindustrial society. Social Casework, 56, 13-20.

5810.   Wampler, K.D., and Sprenkle, D.H. (1980), The Minnesota Couple Communication Program: A follow-up study. Journal of Marriage and the Family, 42(3), 577-584.

5811. Wampler, K.S. (1980), Review of M. Andolfi's Family therapy: An
       interactional approach. Family Relations, 29, 263.

5812. Wampler, K.S. (1982), Bringing the review of literature into the age of
       qualification: Meta-analysis as a strategy for integrating research
       findings in family therapy. Journal of Marriage and the Family, 44(4),
       1009-1023.

5813. Wampler, K.S. (1982), The effectiveness of the Minnesota Couple
       Communication Program: A review of research. Journal of Marital and
       Family Therapy, 8, 345-355.

5814. Wampler, K.S. (1982), Counseling implications of the housework role.
       Counseling and Values, 26, 125-132.

5815. Wampler, K.S., and Powell, G.S. (1982), The Barrett-Lennard
       Relationship Inventory as a measure of marital satisfaction. Family
       Relatins, 3(1), 139-145.

5816. Warburton, J.R. (1982), Sex of client and sex of therapist variables in a
       family therapy study. Dissertation Abstracts International, 43, 1272-B.

5817. Ward, N. (1983), Review of A.S. Gurman's Questions and answers in the
       practice of family therapy. Canadian Journal of Psychiatry, 28, 325.

5818. Waring, E.M. (1980), Family therapy and psychosomatic illness.
       International Journal of Family Therapy, 2, 243-252.

5819. Waring, E.M. (1981), Cognitive family therapy in the treatment of
       schizophrenia. Psychiatric Journal of the University of Ottawa, 64, 229-
       233.

5820. Waring, E.M. (1981), Facilitating marital intimacy through self-
       disclosure. American Journal of Family Therapy, 9, 33-42.

5821. Waring, E.M. (1981), Towards a theory of family psychopathology. The
       Psychiatric Forum, 10(2), 1.

5822. Waring, E.M. (1978), Family therapy and schizophrenia. Canadian
       Psychiatric Association Journal, 23, 51-58.

5823. Waring, E.M. (1982), Marital intimacy and medical practice.
       International Journal of Psychiatric Medicine, 64, 59-66.

5824. Waring, E.M. (1982), Marriage and non-psychotic emotional illness.
       International Journal of Social Psychiatry, 28(2), 111.

5825. Waring, E.M. (1980), Marital intimacy, psychosomatic symptoms, and
       cognitive therapy. Psychosomatics, 21(7), 595-601.

5826. Waring, E.M., and Russell, L. (1980), Cognitive family therapy. Journal
       of Sex and Marital Therapy, 6(4), 258-273.

5827. Warkentin, J. (1960), Psychotherapy with couples and families. Medical
       Association of Georgia Journal, 49, 569-570.

5828.   Warmbrod, M.T. (1982), Alternative generation in marital problem solving. Family Relations: Journal of Applied Family and Child Studies, 31, 503–511.

5829.   Warner, J. (1980), Family therapy: A search for foundations. I. Systems and definitions. Journal of Family Therapy, 2, 259.

5830.   Warner, J. (1981), Family therapy: A search for foundations. II. Communications, boundaries and control. Journal of Family Therapy, 3(2), 201.

5831.   Warner, J. (1978), Anorexia nervosa and family therapy. British Medical Journal, 1, 303–304.

5832.   Warner, J. (1970), Conjoint family therapy. Royal Society of Health Journal, 90, 262–263.

5833.   Warner, M.D. (1982), Comparison of a religious marriage enrichment program with an established communication training enrichment program. Dissertation Abstracts International, 42, 3774-A.

5834.   Warner, W.J. (1982), Review of F. Bockus' Couple therapy. International Journal of Social Psychiatry, 28, 119.

5835.   Wasylenki, D.A. (1982), Problems in psychotherapy with women who leave their families. American Journal of Psychotherapy, 36(3), 408.

5836.   Waters, C.W., and Puller, M. (1968), Effect of the sudden departure and replacement of one member of a co-therapy team on a married couples group. Psychiatric Quarterly Supplement, 42(1), 65–74.

5837.   Waters, D.B. (1976), Family therapy as a defense. Journal of the American Academy of Child Psychiatry, 15, 464–474.

5838.   Watkins, J.M. (1981), Development, application, and evaluation of the marriage encounter relationship inventory. Dissertation Abstracts International, 42, 1467-A.

5839.   Watson, A.S. (1963), The conjoint psychotherapy of marriage partners. American Journal of Orthopsychiatry, 33, 912–922.

5840.   Watters, W.W. (1982), Conjoint couple therapy. Canadian Journal of Psychiatry, 27, 91.

5841.   Watts, E.M. (1969), Family therapy: Its use in mental retardation. Mental Retardation, 7, 41–44.

5842.   Watzlawick, P. (1966), A structured family interview. Family Process, 5, 256–271.

5843.   Watzlawick, P. (1982), Hermetic pragmaesthetics or unkempt thoughts about an issue of Family Process. Family Process, 21, 401-3.

5844.   Watzlawick, P., and Coyne, J.C. (1980), Depression following stroke: Brief problem-focused family treatment. Family Process, 19, 13-18.

5845.   Wauck, L.A. (1966), The clergy as marriage counselors. Journal of Religion and Health, 5(3), 252–259.

5846. Waxenberg, B.R. (1973), Therapist's empathy, regard, and genuineness as factors in staying in or dropping out of short-term, time-limited family therapy. Dissertation Abstracts International, 34, 1288B.

5847. Waydenfeld, S.W. (1979), Marriage matters (letter). British Medical Journal, 1, 1627.

5848. Weakland, J. (1962), Family therapy as a research area. Family Process, 1, 63-68.

5849. Weakland, J., Fisch, R., Watzlawick, P., and Bodin, A.M. (1974), Brief therapy: Focused problem resolution. Family Process, 13, 141-168.

5850. Weakland, J.H. (1977), Family somatics—a neglected edge. Family Process, 16, 263-272.

5851. Weakland, J.H. (1977), Paradigmatic classification of family therapy theories: Comments. Family Process, 16, 46-48.

5852. Weathers, L., and Liberman, R.P. (1975), The family contracting exercise. Journal of Behavior Therapy and Experimental Psychiatry, 6, 208-214.

5853. Weathers, L.R., and Liberman, R.P. (1978), Modification of family behavior. In D. Marholin (Ed.), Child behavior therapy. New York, NY: Gradner Press.

5854. Webb, N.L., Pratt, T.C., Linn, M.W., and Carmichael, J.S. (1978), Focus on the family as a factor in differential treatment outcome. International Journal of Addiction, 13, 783-795.

5855. Webb, R.A., and Bruen, W.J. (1967), Multiple child-parent therapy in a family therapeutic community. International Journal of Social Psychiatry, 14, 50-55.

5856. Webb-Woodard, L., and Woodard, B. (1982), A case of the blind leading the "blind": Reframing a physical handicap as competence. Family Process, 21, 291-294.

5857. Weber, G. (1982), How can we help adolescents in crisis? From the viewpoint of family therapists. Praxis der Psychotherapie und Psychosomatik, 31, 197-207.

5858. Weber, G.K. (1979), Family therapy education in schools of social work: A national survey. Dissertation Abstracts International, 40, 1687-A.

5859. Webster, C.T. (1974), Group therapy for behavior problem in a rural junior high school. Child Welfare, 53(10), 653.

5860. Webster, J. (1966), Nursing families in a therapeutic community. International Journal of Nursing Studies, 3, 1-7.

5861. Wechter, S.L. (1983), Separation difficulties between parents and young adults. Social Casework, 64, 97-104.

5862. Weeks, G., and L'Abate, L. (1978), Bibliography of paradoxical methods in psychotherapy of family systems. Family Process, 17(1), 95-98.

5863.   Weeks, G.R., and L'Abate, L. (1982), Paradoxical psychotherapy – theory
and practice with individuals, couples and families. Acta Psiquiatrica y
Psicologia de America Latina, 28, 176.

5864.   Weeks, G.R., and Wright, L. (1979), Dialects of the family life cycle.
American Journal of Family Therapy, 7, 85–91.

5865.   Weeks, M.O. (1978), Review of R.F. Stahmann and W.J. Hiebert's
Klemer's counseling in marital and sexual problems: A clinician's
handbook. 2nd ed. Personnel and Guidance Journal, 57, 175–176.

5866.   Weeks, R.B. (1976), Counseling parents of sexually abused children.
Medical Aspects of Human Sexuality, 10(8), 43–80.

5867.   Weiler, S.J. (1983), Review of D. Araoz's Hypnosis and sex therapy.
Journal of Marital and Family Therapy, 9, 219.

5868.   Weingarten, K. (1979), Family awareness for nonclinicians:
Participation in a simulated family as a teaching technique. Family
Process, 18, 143–150.

5869.   Weingarten, M.A., and Feuchtwanger, D. (1978), Group meetings with
new mothers in a family practice report of a pilot project. Israeli
Annals of Psychiatry, 16, 232–242.

5870.   Weinstein, C.D. (1983), Therapist and client in-session behaviors and
their relationship to client between session behaviors and outcome in
marital and family therapy: A microlevel analysis. Dissertation
Abstracts International, 44, 1612-B.

5871.   Weinstein, C.G. (1975), Differential change in self-actualization and
self-concept, and its effects on marital interaction, as an outcome of a
selected growth group experience. Dissertation Abstracts International,
33, 4067-A.

5872.   Weinstein, E. (1980), Family therapy: Analysis of a necessity. Revista
Chilena De Psicologia, 3, 7–13.

5873.   Weir, K. (1979), Psychological factors in feeding disorders occurring in
mentally or multiple handicapped children. Child Care, 5, 285–294.

5874.   Weise, K. (1968), (On the problem of family member participation in the
therapy of psychiatric patients.) Zeitschrift fur Arztliche Fortbildung,
62, 651–656.

5875.   Weisfeld, D., and Laser, M.S. (1977), Divorced parents in family therapy
in a residential treatment setting. Family Process, 16, 229–236.

5876.   Weiss, H.M. (1983), Role theory in practice and training: A unified
paradigm for family therapy. Dissertation Abstracts International, 43,
3777-B.

5877.   Weiss, R.L. (1980), Review of N.S. Jacobson and G. Margolin's Marital
therapy: Strategies based on social learning and behavior exchange
principles. American Journal of Family Therapy, 8, 84.

5878.   Weiss, R.L. (1979), Resistance in behavior marriage therapy. American
Journal of Family Therapy, 7(2), 3–6.

5879.   Weiss, R.L. (1978), Marital satisfaction and depression as predictors of physical health status. Journal of Consulting Clinical Psychology, 46, 1379-1384.

5880.   Weiss, R.L. (1975), Contracts, cognition, and change: A behavioral approach to marriage therapy. Counseling Psychologist, 5, 15-26.

5881.   Weiss, S.L. (1974), Parental expectations of psychotherapy. Journal of Psychology, 86, 71-80.

5882.   Weissman, H.W. (1975), The mental health team as a differential decision-maker for child patients: A national survey. Psychological Reports, 37, 643-650.

5883.   Weissman, S., and Montgomery, G. (1977), A family management training program. Individual Psychology, 14, 40-44.

5884.   Weissman, S., and Montgomery, G. (1980), Techniques for group family enrichment. Personnel and Guidance Journal, 59(2), 113-116.

5885.   Wellisch, D.K. (1980), Review of M. Bowen's Family therapy in clinical practice. American Journal of Psychotherapy, 34, 143-144.

5886.   Wellisch, D.K. (1976), A family therapy outcome study in an inpatient setting. Dissertation Abstracts International, 36, 3634-3635B.

5887.   Wellisch, D.K., Mosher, M.B., and Van Scoy, C. (1978), Management of family emotion stress: Family group therapy in a private oncology practice. International Journal of Group Psychotherapy, 28, 225-231.

5888.   Wellisch, D.K., and Ro-Trock, G.K. (1980), A three-year follow-up of family therapy. International Journal of Group Psychotherapy, 2, 169-175.

5889.   Wells, C.F. (1973), The conjoint family diagnostic interview and the family index of tension. Family Process, 12, 126-144.

5890.   Wells, R.A. (1980), Engagement techniques in family therapy. International Journal of Family Therapy, 2(2), 75-94.

5891.   Wells, R.A. (1980), Tempests, teapots (and research design): Rejoinder to Stanton and Todd. Family Process, 19, 177-8.

5892.   Wells, R.A. (1982), Discussion: Engaging families in therapy: A pilot study. International Journal of Family Therapy, 4(1), 20.

5893.   Wells, R.A. (1985), Marital therapy: Letter. Social Work, 30, 95.

5894.   Wells, R.A., Dilkes, T.C., and Trivelli, N. (1972), The results of family therapy: A critical review of the literature. Family Process, 11, 189-208

5895.   Wells, R.A., and Dezen, A.E. (1978), Ideologies, idols and graven images?: Rejoinder to Gruman and Kniskern. Family Process, 17(3), 283-286.

5896.   Wells, R.A., and Dezen, A.E. (1978), The results of family therapy revisited: The nonbehavioral methods. Family Process, 17, 251-274.

5897. Wells, S.J. (1981), A model of therapy with abusive and neglectful families. Social Work, 26(2), 113-118.

5898. Weltner, J.S. (1982), One- to three-session therapy with children and families. Family Process, 21, 281-289.

5899. Weltner, J.S. (1982), A structural approach to the single-parent family. Family Process, 21, 203-210.

5900. Weltner, J.S., and Dym, B. (1980), Shall we dance? Specialization of couple and therapist-patient relationships. Psychiatry, 43, 259-262.

5901. Wendorf, D.J. (1981), A data-based reply to Hare-Mustin on family therapy perils. Professional Psychology, 12, 665-667.

5902. Wendorf, D.J. (1978), Family therapy: An innovative approach in the rehabilitation of adult probationers. Federal Probation, 42, 40-44.

5903. Wendorf, D.J. (1984), A model for training practicing professionals in family therapy. Journal of Marital and Family Therapy, 10, 31-41.

5904. Wendorf, D.J., Wendorf, R.J., and Bond, D. (1985), Growth behind the mirror: The family therapy consortium's group process. Journal of Marital and Family Therapy, 11, 245-256.

5905. Wendorf, R.J., and Wendorf, D.J. (1981), Problems with family therapy in a community mental health center. Hospital and Community Psychiatry, 32, 852-5.

5906. Wendt, R.N., and Zake, J. (1984), Family systems theory and school psychology: Implications for training and practice. Psychology in the Schools, 21, 204-210.

5907. Wenz, F.V. (1979), Family constellation factors, depression, and parent suicide potential. American Journal of Orthopsychiatry, 49, 164-167.

5908. Werry, J.S. (1979), Family therapy: Behavioral approaches. Journal of the American Acadamy of Child Psychiatry, 18, 91-102.

5909. Wertheim, E.S. (1973), Family unit therapy and the science and typology of family systems. Family Process, 12(4), 361-376.

5910. Wertheim, E.S. (1973), Family therapy and its social implications. Australian and New Zealand Journal of Psychiatry, 7, 146-154.

5911. Wertheim, E.S. (1975), Family unit therapy, the institution of the family, and positive mental health. International Journal of Social Psychiatry, 21, 235-246.

5912. Wertheim, E.S. (1975), Positive mental health, western society and the family. International Journal of Social Psychiatry, 21(4), 247-255.

5913. Wertheimer, D. (1978), Family therapy training in Israel. Journal of Marriage and Family Counseling, 4, 83-90.

5914. Wesiack, W. (1971), Psychotherapeutic and general medical aspects of family therapy. Hippokrates, 42, 479-487.

5915.   Wesley, R. (1977), Marriage counseling: A new profession. Journal of Non-White Concilliation and Personnel Guidance, 6, 3-10.

5916.   West, B. (1981), Family involvement in psychosocial rehabilitation. Dissertation Abstracts International, 41, 2786-B.

5917.   West, J.D., and Zarski, J.J. (1983), The counselor's use of the paradoxical procedure in family therapy. Personnel and Guidance Journal, 61, 34-37.

5918.   West, J.D., and Zarski, J.J. (1983), Paradoxical interventions used during systematic family therapy: Considerations for practitioners. Family Therapy, 10, 125-134.

5919.   Wester, C.D., Somjen, L., Sloman, L., Bradley, S., Mooney, S.A., and Mack, J.E. (1979), The child care workers in the family: Some case examples and implications for the design of family centered programs. Child Care, 8(1), 5-18.

5920.   Westley, W.A., and Epstein, N.B. (1960), Family structure and emotional health: A case study approach. Marriage and Family Living, 22, 25-27.

5921.   Westman, J.C. (1981), A child psychiatrist's view of divorce counseling. Conciliation Courts Review, 19, 61-65.

5922.   Westman, J.C., Carek, D.J., and McDermott, J.F. (1965), A comparison of married couples in the same separate therapy groups. International Journal of Group Psychotherapy, 15, 274-281.

5923.   Westoff, C.F. (1978), Marriage and fertility in the developed countries. Scientific American, 239, 51-57.

5924.   Whan, M. (1983), Tricks of the trade: Questionable theory and practice in family therapy. British Journal of Social Work, 13, 321-337.

5925.   Wheeler, P.A. (1979), Locus of control and expectancies of parents applying for service at a children's clinic. Dissertation Abstracts International, 39, 4061-B.

5926.   Whelan, E.M. (1972), The temporal relationship of marriage, conception, and birth in Massachusetts. Demography, 9, 399-414.

5927.   Whitaker, C.A. (1969), Triadic-based family therapy. Dyads and triads. International Journal of Psychiatry, 8, 566-567.

5928.   Whitaker, C.A. (1966), Family treatment of a psychopathic personality. Comprehensive Psychiatry, 7, 397-402.

5929.   Whitaker, C.A. (1982), Comments on Keeney and Sprenkle's paper. Family Process, 21, 405-6.

5930.   Whitaker, C.A. (1978), Use of videotape in family therapy with special relation to therapeutic impasse. In M. Berger (Ed.), Videotape techniques in psychiatric training and treatment. New York, NY: Brunner/Mazel.

5931.   Whitaker, C.A. (1975), Psychotherapy of the absurd, with a special emphasis on psychotherapy of aggression. Family Process, 14(1), 1-16.

5932.   Whitaker, C.A. (1975), The symptomatic adolescent: An AWOL family member. In M. Sugar (Ed.), The adolescent in group and family therapy. New York, NY: Brunner/Mazel.

5933.   Whitaker, C.A., and Burdy, J. (1969), Family psychotherapy of a psychopathic personality: Must every member change? Comprehensive Psychiatry, 10(5), 361-364.

5934.   Whitaker, C.A., and Miller, M.H. (1969), A reevaluation of "psychiatric help" when divorce impends. American Journal of Psychiatry, 126, 611-618.

5935.   Whitaker, C.A., and Napier, A.Y. (1973), Techniques of the family therapy process. Revista del Neurologica y Psiquiatrica, 14, 79-105.

5936.   White, H. (1979), Your family is good for you. New York, NY: Random House.

5937.   White, H.C. (1944), An adventure in group therapy in a family agency setting. Mental Hygiene, 28, 423-430.

5938.   White, J. (1982), The application of Laing's Interpersonal Perception Method (I.P.M.) to the counseling context. Family Therapy, 9, 167-173.

5939.   White, M. (1981), Family therapy in Australia. Journal of Marital and Family Therapy, 10, 527-535.

5940.   White, M. (1979), Structural and strategic approaches to psychosomatic families. Family Process, 18, 303-314.

5941.   White, M. (1979), Distant family treatment: A case of school phobia. Australian Paediatric Journal, 15, 187-189.

5942.   White, M. (1983), Anorexia nervosa: A transgenerational system perspective. Family Process, 22, 255-273.

5943.   White, S.G., and Hatcher, C. (1984), Couple complementarity and similarity: A review of the literature. American Journal of Family Therapy, 12(1), 15-25.

5944.   White, S.L. (1976), Providing family-centered consultation to a juvenile court in Massachusetts. Hospital and Community Psychiatry, 27, 692-693.

5945.   White, S.L. (1978), Family therapy according to the Cambridge model. Journal of Marriage and Family Counseling, 4, 91-100.

5946.   Whiteside, M.F. (1985), Review of M.P. Nichols's Family therapy: Concepts and methods. Journal of Marital and Family Therapy, 11(1), 99-100.

5947.   Whiting, R.A. (1981), Practice of family therapy at a college counseling center. Journal of College Student Personnel, 22, 558-559.

5948.   Whiting, R.A., Terry, L.L., and Strom-Henriksen, H. (1984), From home to college, from college to home: An interactional approach to treating the symptomatic disabled college student. Family Therapy Collections, 11, 30-43.

5949.   Whitlock, G.E. (1961), Reply to the use of dreams in premarital counseling. Marriage and Family Living, 23, 258-262.

5950.   Whitney, F. (1976), Review of J.E. Bell's Family therapy. Social Service Review, 50, 671.

5951.   Wiedorn, W.S., Jr. (1961), Group therapy for families. Mental Hospital, 12, 21-22.

5952.   Wieman, R.J. (1974), Conjugal relationship modification and reciprocal reinforcement: A comparison of treatments for marital discord. Dissertation Abstracts International, 35, 493-B.

5953.   Wieman, R.J., Shoulders, D.I., and Farr, J.H. (1974), Reciprocal reinforcement in marital therapy. Journal of Behavior Therapy and Experimental Psychiatry, 5, 291-296.

5954.   Wiendorf, D.J., and Frey, J. (1985), Family therapy with the intellectually gifted. American Journal of Family Therapy, 13(1), 31-38.

5955.   Wijesinghe, O.B., and Wood, R.R. (1976), A reperatory grid study of interpersonal perception within a married couples psychotherapy group. British Journal of Medical Psychology, 49, 287-293.

5956.   Wikler, M. (1982), Another look at the diagnosis and treatment of Orthodox Jewish family problems. Journal of Psychology and Judaism, 1, 42-54.

5957.   Wiklinson, M. (1973), An information related systems theory of counseling. Family Coordinator, 22(4), 443-448.

5958.   Wilcoxon, A., and Fenell, D. (1983), Engaging the non-attending spouse in marital therapy through the use of therapist-initiated written communication. Journal of Marital and Family Therapy, 9, 199-203.

5959.   Wilcoxon, S.A. (1984), Review of C.C. Umbarger's Structural family therapy. Journal of Marital and Family Therapy, 10(4), 434-435.

5960.   Wilder, C. (1982), Muddles and metaphors: A response to Keeney and Sprenkle. Family Process, 21, 397-400.

5961.   Wildman, M. (1967), Communication in family therapy. British Journal of Psychiatric Social Work, 9, 75-79.

5962.   Wile, D.B. (1979), Insight approach to marital therapy. Journal of Marital and Family Therapy, 5, 43-52.

5963.   Wilfong, E.J. (1982), Enrichment through communication: Testing a cognitive-behavioral approach to marital communication skills training. Dissertation Abstracts International, 43, 1273-B.

5964.   Wilke, R.B. (1974), The pastor and marriage group counseling. Nashville, TN: Abingdon.

5965.   Wilkinson, C.B. (1965), An approach to the family therapy process. Diseases of the Nervous System, 26, 705-714.

5966.   Wilkinson, C.B. (1966), The psychodynamics of family interaction in family therapy. Journal of the National Medical Association, 58, 430-435.

5967.   Wilkinson, L. (1970), Death is a family matter. Registered Nurse, 33, 50.

5968.   Wilkinson, L.H. (1983), Consensus model training for couples: An outcome study of an integrated conflict management program for marriage enrichment. Dissertation Abstracts International, 44, 993-A.

5969.   Wilkinson, T. (1981), What about the family? Nursing young people in a psychiatric setting. Nursing, 1, 1301-1302.

5970.   Will, D. (1983), Approaching the incestuous and sexually abusive family. Journal of Adolescence, 6, 229-246.

5971.   Will, D. (1983), Some techniques for working with resistant families of adolescents. Journal of Adolescence, 6, 13-26.

5972.   Will, D., and Baird, D. (1984), An integrated approach to dysfunction in interprofessional systems. Journal of Family Therapy, 6, 275-290.

5973.   Willan, S., and Hugman, Y. (1982), Family therapy within a school's psychological service. Association of Educational Psychologists Journal, 5, 48-54.

5974.   Wille, A. (1982), The Family Sculpting Test. Praxis der Kinderpsychologie und Kinderpsychiatrie, 31, 150-4.

5975.   Willi, J. (1985), Couples in collusion: The unconscious dimension in partner relationships. San Bernardino, CA: Borgo Press.

5976.   Willi, J. (1985), Dynamics of couples therapy. San Bernardino, CA: Borgo Press.

5977.   Willi, J. (1970), On the specific structure and dynamics of group therapy of the couple. Ehe, 4, 162-168.

5978.   Willi, J. (1984), The concept of collusion: A combined systemic-psychodynamic approach to marital therapy. Family Process, 23, 177-185.

5979.   Williams, A.R., Trick, O.L., and Troum, R.A. (1981), The paranoid wife syndrome: Diagnosis and treatment. Journal of Marital and Family Therapy, 7, 75-79.

5980.   Williams, B.M., Wright, D., and Rosenthal, D. (1983), A model for intervention with latency-aged children of divorce. Family Therapy, 10, 111-124.

5981.   Williams, C.C., and Rice, D.G. (1977), The intensive care unit: Social work intervention with the families of critically ill patients. Social Work in Health Care, 2, 391-398.

5982.   Williams, D.M. (1979), Families of young, hearing-impaired children: The impact of diagnosis. Journal of Otolaryngology, 7, 500-506.

5983.   Williams, F.J. (1960), A community program of premarital counseling. Pastoral Psychology, 10, 39-44.

5984.   Williams, F.S. (1967), Family therapy: A critical assessment. American Journal of Orthopsychiatry, 37, 912-919.

5985.   Williams, F.S. (1975), Family therapy: Its role in adolescent psychiatry. In M. Sugar (Ed.), The adolescent in group and family therapy. New York, NY: Brunner/Mazel.

5986.   Williams, J. (1969), Feedback techniques in marriage counseling. In B.N. Ard, Jr., and C.C. Ard (Eds.), Handbook of marriage counseling. Palo Alto, CA: Science and Behavior Books.

5987.   Williams, M.J. (1952), Counseling parents and teachers on preschool level. Marriage and Family Living, 14, 19-22.

5988.   Williams, W.V., Lee, J., and Polak, P.R. (1976), Crisis intervention: Effects of crisis intervention of family survivors of sudden death situations. Community Mental Health Journal, 12, 128-136.

5989.   Williamson, D.S. (1973), Training opportunities in marriage and family counseling. Family Coordinator, 22, 99-102.

5990.   Williamson, D.S. (1978), New life at the graveyard: A method of therapy for individuation from a dead former parent. Journal of Marriage and Family Counseling, 4, 93-101.

5991.   Williamson, D.S. (1982), Personal authority in family experience via termination of the intergenerational hierarchical boundary: III. Personal authority defined, and the power of play in the change process. Journal of Marital and Family Therapy, 8, 309-323.

5992.   Williamson, D.S. (1981), Personal authority via termination of the intergenerational hierarchical boundary: A "new" stage in the family life cycle. Journal of Marital and Family Therapy, 7, 441-452.

5993.   Williamson, D.S. (1980), Review of L. Headley's Adults and their parents in family therapy: A new direction in treatment. Journal of Marital and Family Therapy, 6, 96.

5994.   Williamson, D.S. (1983), Coming of age in the fourth decade. Family Therapy Collections, 8, 66-77.

5995.   Williamson, D.S., and Malone, P.E. (1983), Systems-oriented, small group, family-of-origin family therapy: A comparison with traditional group psychotherapy. Journal of Group Psychotherapy, Psychodrama and Sociometry, 35, 165-177.

5996.   Willis, D.J. (1974), The families of terminally ill children: Symptomatology and management. Journal of Clinical Child Psychology, 3, 32-33.

5997.   Willmuth, M. (1979), The verbal diagnostic and art therapy combined: An extended evaluation procedure with family groups. Art Psychotherapy, 6, 11-18.

5998. Willrich, K.L. (1968), Familien therapie: Ein vielschichtiger weg zum psychisch kranken. (Family therapy: A multidimensional approach to mental illnesses.) Praxis der Psychotherapie, 13, 13-21.

5999. Wills, R.M., and Snyder, D.K. (1982), Clinical use of the Marital Satisfaction Inventory: Two case studies. American Journal of Family Therapy, 10, 17-26.

6000. Wilms, J.H. (1966), Counseling on premarital relationships. Journal of the American College Health Association, 15, 67-70.

6001. Wilner, R.S., and Rau, J.H. (1976), Family systems drawings. Family Therapy, 3, 245-267.

6002. Wilson, D.A. (1980), The effects of a partially structured Christian marriage enrichment program upon marital communication, general marital adjustment, and purpose in life. Dissertation Abstracts International, 41, 1506-A.

6003. Wilson, J.H. (1983), Review of A.S. Gurman's Questions and answers in the practice of family therapy. Behavioural Psychotherapy, 11, 192.

6004. Wilson, N.R. (1982), Family therapy in Kenya. Journal of Family Therapy, 4(2), 165.

6005. Wilson, S.L. (1971), Group therapy for parents of handicapped children. Rehabilitation Literature, 32(11), 332.

6006. Wiltz, N.A. (1973), Behavioral therapy techniques in treatment of emotionally disturbed children and their families. Child Welfare, 52, 483-492.

6007. Wiltz, N.A. (1971), Behavioral therapy techniques in treatment of emotionally disturbed children and their families. Child Welfare, 50, 40-46.

6008. Windell, J.O., and Woollams, S.J. (1976), The effects of training on marriages. Transactional Analysis Journal, 6(2), 209-212.

6009. Winder, A.E. (1965), Group therapy with parents of chldren in a residential treatment center. Child Welfare, 44, 266-271.

6010. Winder, A.E. (1978), Family therapy: A necessary part of the cancer patients care: A multidisciplinary treatment concept. Family Therapy, 5(2), 151-161.

6011. Winder, A.E., Greif, A.C., and Kelso, E.P. (1976), Family therapy: The single parent family and the battered child. Family Therapy, 3, 97-107.

6012. Winder, A.E., and Lamontca, E.L. (1978), Therapist for the cancer patient's family: A new role for the nurse. Journal of Psychiatric Nursing, 16, 22-27.

6013. Winer, L.R. (1971), The qualified pronoun count as a measure of change in family psychotherapy. Family Process, 10, 243-247.

6014. Winkelmann, F. (1975), The dying patient an his family: A Balint group experiences. Dynamische Psychiatrique, 8, 318-327.

6015.   Winkelpleck, J.M., and Westfield, J.S. (1982), Counseling considerations with gay couples. Personnel and Guidance Journal, 60(5), 294-296.

6016.   Winkle, C., Piercy, F.P., and Hovestadt, A.J. (1981), A curriculum for graduate-level marriage and family therapy education. Journal of Marital and Family Therapy, 7, 201-210.

6017.   Winkle, C.W. (1980), A graduate-level curriculum for marriage and family therapy education. Dissertation Abstracts International, 41, 2461A. (University Microfilms No. 8027689.)

6018.   Winkler, H.A. (1980), Review of E. Kaufman and P. Kaufman's Family therapy of drug and alcohol abuse. American Journal of Psychiatry, 137, 1287.

6019.   Winkler, I., and Doherty, W.J. (1983), Communication styles and marital satisfaction in Israeli and American couples. Family Process, 22, 221-228.

6020.   Winokur, M. (1982), A family systems model for supervision of psychotherapy. Bulletin of the Menninger Clinic, 46(2), 125.

6021.   Winston, A. (1978), Review of I.D. Glick and D.R. Kessler's Marital and family therapy. Social Service Review, 52, 501.

6022.   Winston, A., and Liberman, H.J. (1978), Family life in a community residence. Psychiatric Quarterly, 50, 50-54.

6023.   Wirsching, M. (1982), Family therapy—current status and prospects (author's transl.). Nervenarzt, 53, 1-6.

6024.   Wirsching, M. (1982), Marital crisis-family crisis. Analytische Psychologie, 13, 46-59.

6025.   Wirsching, M. (1984), Family dynamics and family therapy of ulcerative colitis and Crohn's disease. Zeitschrift fur Psychosomatische Medizin und Psychoanalyse, 30(3), 238-246.

6026.   Wirsching, M., Stierlin, H., Weber, G., and Wirsching, B. (1981), Family therapy with physically ill patients. Psychiatria Fennica (Supplement), 77, 111-118.

6027.   Wirsching, M., and Stierlin, H. (1979), Family dynamics and family psychotherapy of psychosomatic disorders. Psychotherapy and Psychosomatics, 32, 128-133.

6028.   Wirsching, M., and Stierlin, H. (1983), Psychosomatic families: Dynamics and therapy. Psyche: Zeitschrift Fur Psychoanalyse Und Ihre Anwendungen, 37, 596-623.

6029.   Wishart, J.T. (1981), The development and use of an instrument for family counseling: A Delphi-sage analysis approach. Dissertation Abstracts International, 42, 1968-A.

6030.   Withersty, D.J. (1977), Family involvement on a psychiatric inpatient service. American Journal of Psychiatry, 134, 93-94.

6031. Withersty, D.J., Linton, J., and Quarrick, E. (1975), Treating the hospitalized adolescent: A family approach. Family Therapy, 2, 129-135.

6032. Witkin, M.H. (1977), Sex therapy as an aid to marital and family therapy. Journal of Sex and Marital Therapy, 3, 19-30.

6033. Witkin, S.L. (1978), Group training in communication skills for couples: Preliminary report. International Journal of Family Counseling, 6, 45-56.

6034. Witt, J.A. (1972), Administrator to wife: "Will you love me as much in Montana as you did in New York?" Modern Hospital, 119, 76.

6035. Witt, J.A. (1973), Administrator to wife: "Will you love me as much in Montana as you did in New York?" Mental Retardation, 11, 31-34.

6036. Witte, P.G. (1977), Group therapy with multiple sclerosis couples. Health and Social Work, 2(3), 188-195.

6037. Wittrup, R.G. (1974), Marriage enrichment: A preventative counseling program designed to attain marriage potential. Dissertation Abstracts International, 34, 6399-A.

6038. Wodarski, J.S. (1981), Comprehensive treatment of parents who abuse their children. Adolescence, 16, 959-72.

6039. Wodarski, J.S., and Ammons, Paul W. (1981), Comprehensive treatment of runaway children and their parents. Family Therapy, 8, 229-240.

6040. Wolberg, L.R., and Aronson, M.L. (Eds.) (1981), Group and family therapy 1981. New York: Brunner/Mazel.

6041. Wolberg, L.R., and Aronson, M.L. (Eds.) (1980), Group and family therapy 1980: An overview. New York, NY: Brunner/Mazel.

6042. Wolberg, L.R., and Aronson, M.L. (Eds.) (1982), Group and family therapy 1982. New York: Brunner/Mazel.

6043. Wolberg, L.R., and Aronson, M.L. (Eds.) (1983), Group and family therapy 1983. New York: Brunner/Mazel.

6044. Wold, C.N., Betancourt, A., and Mayo, S. (1981), Use of task displacement in a family therapy process. Family Therapy, 8, 165-169.

6045. Wold, C.N., and Fagundes, J.O. (1977), Resolution of co-therapist's conflicts mirrored in brief family therapy. Family Therapy, 4, 31-41.

6046. Wolf, J.K. (1983), A study of two models for the prediction of outcome in family treatment for chemical dependency. Dissertation Abstracts International, 43, 2721-B.

6047. Wolf, S.S. (1980), A behavioral analysis of reciprocity marital counseling procedures. Dissertation Abstracts International, 40, 4006-B.

6048. Wolf, S.S., and Etzel, B. C. (1982), Reciprocity marital counseling: A replication and Analysis. Behavior Research and Therapy, 20, 407-410.

6049. Wolf, W. (1983), Relation between behavior and experience variables in the communication of happy and unhappy couples. Zeitschrift fur Kleinische Psychologie, Psychopathologie und Psychotherapie, 31, 352-368.

6050. Wolfe, D.A., Sandler, J., and Kaufman, K. (1981), A competency-based parent training program for child abusers. Journal of Counseling and Clinical Psychology, 49(5), 633-640.

6051. Wolfe, L.A., and Collins-Wolfe, J. A. (1983), Action techniques for therapy with families with young children. Family Relations: Journal of Applied Family and Child Studies, 32, 81-87.

6052. Wolin, S.J. (1984), Family rituals. Family Process, 23(3), 401-420.

6053. Wolin, S.J., Bennett, L.A., Noonan, D.L., and Eitelbaum, M.A. (1979), Family rituals and the recurrence of alcoholism over generations. American Journal of Psychiatry, 136, 589-593.

6054. Wolkenstein, A.S. (1977), The fear of committing child abuse: A discussion of eight families. Child Welfare, 56, 249-257.

6055. Wollstein, S., and Hock, A. (1962), Joint psychotherapy of couples. Harefuah, 62, 288-291.

6056. Wolman, B.B., and Stricker, G. (Eds.) (1983), Handbook of family and marital therapy. New York: Plenum Publishing.

6057. Wolper, B., and Scheiner, Z. (1981), Family therapy approaches and drug dependent women. National Institute on Drug Abuse: Treatment Research Monograph Series, 343-407.

6058. Wong, N. (1964), Family services offered by an evacuation neuropsychiatric section. A survey of 50 consecutive cases. Medical Bulletin of the U.S. Army in Europe, 21, 222-225.

6059. Wood, B., and Talmon, M. (1983), Family boundaries in transition: A search for alternatives. Family Process, 22, 347-357.

6060. Woodburn, L.T., and Barnhill, L.N. (1977), Applying family systems therapy principles to couples counseling. Personnel and Guidance Journal, 55(9), 510-514.

6061. Woodhouse, D. (1977), Marital counseling and the general practitioner: Referral from general practice to specialized agencies. Proceedings of the Royal Society of Medicine, 70, 498-502.

6062. Woods, R.B. (1977), A study of family life issues, counseling resource utilization and education program needs in the General Conference Mennonite Church. Dissertation Abstracts International, 38, 3219-3220-A.

6063. Woodward, C.A., Epstein, N.B., Santa Barbara, J., and Levin, S. (1980), The role of goal attainment scaling in evaluating family therapy outcome. Advances in Family Psychiatry, 2, 227-244.

6064.   Woodward, C.A., Santa Barbara, J., Levin, S., and Epstein, N.B. (1978),
         Aspects of consumer satisfaction with brief family therapy. Family
         Process, 17, 399–407.

6065.   Woodward, C.A., Santa Barbara, J., Levin, S., and Epstein, N.B. (1978),
         The role of goal attainment scaling in evaluating family therapy
         outcomes. American Journal of Orthopsychiatry, 48, 464–476.

6066.   Woodward, C.A., Santa Barbara, J., Streiner, D.L., Goodman, J.T.,
         Levin, S., and Epstein, N.B. (1981), Client, treatment, and therapist
         variables related to outcome in brief, systems-oriented family therapy.
         Family Process, 20(2), 189–97.

6067.   Woodward, L.E. (1947), Strengthening family life by educating for
         family living. Journal of Social Casework, 28, 363–369.

6068.   Woody, J.D. (1983), Sexuality in divorce and remarriage. Family
         Therapy Collections, 8, 62–81.

6069.   Woody, R.H. (1978), Family counseling and child custody. International
         Journal of Family Counseling, 6, 81–88.

6070.   Woody, R.H., Hansen, J.C., and Schauble, P.G. (1981), Trends in training
         marriage and family therapists. Academic Psychology Bulletin, 15, 75–
         88.

6071.   Woody, R.H., Woody, J.D., L'Abate, L., and Schauble, P.G. (1973),
         Sexual, marital, and familial relations: Therapuetic intervention for
         professional helping. Springfield, IL: Charles C. Thomas.

6072.   Woolf, V.V. (1983), Family network systems in transgenerational
         psychotherapy: The theory, advantages and expanded applications of the
         genogram. Family Therapy, 10, 219–237.

6073.   Worthington, B.C. (1979), Family therapy: An analysis of process and
         outcome in communications family therapy. Dissertation Abstracts
         International, 39, 5600–B.

6074.   Wrate, R.M. (1978), Family therapy. British Journal of Psychiatry, 132,
         415.

6075.   Wright, B.M. (1980), A study of family burden: An examination of the
         relationship between client problems and distress in a significant other.
         Dissertation Abstracts International, 40, 3979–B.

6076.   Wright, K.D., and Scott, T.B. (1978), The relationship of wives'
         treatment to the drinking status of alcoholics. Journal of Studies of
         Alcohol, 39, 1577–1581.

6077.   Wright, L., and L'Abate, L. (1977), Four approaches to family
         facilitation: Some issues and implications. Family Coordinator, 26, 176–
         181.

6078.   Wunderlin, R.F. (1974), The effects of communications training on
         verbal communications and relationship ratings of parents and
         adolescents. Dissertation Abstracts International, 34, 6400–A.

6079.   Wyckoff, P.J. (1978), Communication skills training: A treatment of marital discord. Dissertation Abstracts International, 39, 1509B.

6080.   Wylder, J. (1982), Including the divorced father in family therapy. Social Work, 27, 479–482.

6081.   Wylie, H.C., and Bluck, M.R. (1966), An approach to rapid involvement of parents in child guidance therapy. Psychological Reports, 19, 309–310.

6082.   Wylie, M. (1971), Maybe your whole family needs a psychiatrist and you don't know it. Ladies Home Journal, 88, 110.

6083.   Wynne, L.C. (1961), The study of intrafamilial alignments and splits in exploratory family therapy. In N. Ackerman, F.L. Bateman, and S.H. Sherman (Eds.), Exploring the base for family therapy. New York: Family Service Association of America.

6084.   Wynne, L.C. (1974), Family and group treatment of schizophrenia: An interim view. In R. Cancro, N. Fox, and L.E. Shapiro (Eds.), Strategic intervention in schizophrenia: Current developments in treatment. New York: Behavioral Publications.

6085.   Wynne, L.C. (1983), Family research and family therapy: A reunion. Journal of Marital and Family Therapy, 9, 113–118.

6086.   Wynne, L.C. (1984), Review of D.A. Bloch and R. Simon's The strength of family therapy – selected papers of Nathan W. Ackerman. Family Process, 23(2), 279–281.

6087.   Wynne, L.D., Jones, J.E., and Alkhayyal, M. (1982), Healthy family communication patterns: Observations in families at risk for psychopathology. In F. Walsh (Ed.), Normal family processes. New York: Guilford Press.

6088.   Yackulie, C.F. (1980), Review of F.M. Sander's Individual and family therapy: Toward an integration. American Journal of Family Therapy, 8, 82.

6089.   Yamprey, N. (1962), Asistencia psicoterapica a la familia nino enfermo. (Psychotherapy for the family of the mentally ill child.) Acta Psiquiatrica y Psicologia de Argentina, 8, 199–206.

6090.   Yarrow, L.J. (1979), Helping parents help their children. Contemporary Psychology, 24, 399–400.

6091.   Yassky, A.D. (1979), Review of A.Y. Napier and C.A. Whitaker's The family crucible. Group Analysis, 12, 174–177.

6092.   Yater, S. M. (1980), Psychodynamics of child abuse as seen through the conjoint psychotherapy of a mother and her abused child. Family Therapy, 7(3), 197–205.

6093.   Yek, K.F. (1977), Pastoral pre-marital counseling in Taiwan: An evaluative and descriptive study. Dissertation Abstracts International, 38(3), 1466–A.

6094.   Yelsma, P. (1984), Marital communication, adjustment and perceptual differences between happy and counseling couples. American Journal of Family Therapy, 12(1), 26-36.

6095.   Yogev, S. (1983), Dual-career couples: Conflicts and treatment. American Journal of Family Therapy, 11, 38-44.

6096.   York, J.B., and Weinstein, S.A. (1980-81), The effect of a videotape about death on bereaved children in family therapy. Omega: Journal of Death and Dying, 11(4), 355-361.

6097.   Youell, K.J. (1979), Family constellation and marital adjustment. Dissertation Abstracts International, 40(7), 3431-B.

6098.   Young, J. (1983), Implications of male and female co-therapists for a pastoral theology of family therapy. Journal of Psychology and Christianity, 2, 52-55.

6099.   Young, N.K. (1980), Parent and family guidance: A comparison of perceived and actual roles and functions of the secondary school counselor. Dissertation Abstracts International, 40, 4096-A.

6100.   Young-Kerr, K. (1979), Full length case studies. Family Coordinator, 28, 291.

6101.   Yuen, L. M. (1980), Family reconstruction: A study of its effects on self-concept, irrational beliefs, and interpersonal perception in college students. Dissertation Abstracts International, 41, 706-B.

6102.   Yule, V. (1965), Group differences in problems presented by marriage counseling clients. Australian Journal of Social Issues, 2, 38-58.

6103.   Z'elim, M. (1964), (The role of the family in the daily work of the general practitioner.) Harefuah, 67, 47-52.

6104.   Zaccheo, D. (1981), Group training for parents using didactic instruction in behavior principles as a precursor to individualized family behavior therapy. Dissertation Abstracts International, 41, 3597-B.

6105.   Zakharov, A. I. (1981), Psychology of the diagnostics and optimization of relations in the family. Voprosy Psikhologii, 3, 58-68.

6106.   Zakus, G., and Solomon, M. (1973), The family situation of obese adolescent girls. Adolescence, 8, 33-42.

6107.   Zaleski, Z., and Galkowski, M. (1978), Eroticism and marital satisfaction. Behavior Research and Therapy, 16, 285-286.

6108.   Zander, L., and Kraemer, S. (1984), Review of W. Doherty and M. Baird's Family therapy and family medicine. British Journal of Medical Psychology, 57, 199-200.

6109.   Zarski, J.J., Sonstegard, M.A., and Bitter, J.R. (1977), Training parents as functional professionals in a community setting. Individual Psychology, 14, 36-45.

6110.   Zauner, J. (1976), (Conflicts of separation in adolescents and therapeutic cooperation with their parents.) Praxis der Kinderpsychologie und Kinderpsychiatrie, 25(8), 306-310.

6111.   Zawada, S. (1981), An outline of the history and current status of family therapy. In S. Box, B. Copley, J. Magagna, and E. Moustaki (Eds.), Psychotherapy with families: An analytic approach. London: Routledge and Kegan Paul Ltd.

6112.   Zelitch, S.R. (1980), Helping the family cope: Workshops for families of schizophrenics. Health and Social Work, 5, 47-52.

6113.   Zentner, E.B. (1970), The amorphous family nexus. Psychiatric Quarterly, 44, 91-113.

6114.   Zerin, E. (1983), Finishing unfinished business: Applications of the drama triangle to marital therapy. Transactional Analysis Journal, 13, 155-157.

6115.   Zerof, H.G. (1968), An evaluation of a short-term course in teaching clergymen skills in family crisis intervention conducted in conjunction with a community mental health center. Dissertation Abstracts International, 29, 1115-1116A.

6116.   Zichittella, D.J. (1980), Couples' groups as an influence on love relationships. Dissertation Abstracts International, 41, 1938-B.

6117.   Ziegellaub, F. (1947), Requests for psychiatric treatment in a family agency. Mental Hygiene, 31, 582-589.

6118.   Ziegler, D.L., and Mazin, S.D. (1975), Contractual marriage counseling: A new look at intimate relationships. Journal of Family Counseling, 3, 29-35.

6119.   Ziegler, J.S. (1973), A comparison of the effect of two forms of group psychotherapy on the treatment of marital discord. Dissertation Abstracts International, 34(1), 143-A.

6120.   Ziegler, P., Porter, K., Charles, E., and Roman, M. (1977), Social stresses of medical students: A couples group approach. Group, 1, 235-244.

6121.   Ziegler, R.G. (1980), Task-focused therapy with children and families. American Journal of Psychotherapy, 34, 107-118.

6122.   Ziegler, R.G. (1982), Epilepsy: Individual illness, human predicament, and family dilemma. Family Relations: Journal of Applied Family and Child Studies, 31, 435-444.

6123.   Ziegler-Driscoll, G. (1977), Family research study at Eagleville Hospital and Rehabilitation Center. Family Process, 16, 175-189.

6124.   Zielan, V. (1979), The first family group session. Analytische Psychologie, 10, 71.

6125.   Zielan, V. (1979), From psychoanalysis to family therapy. Analytische Psychologie, 10, 69.

6126. Zierer, E., Sternberg, D., Finn, R., and Farmer, M. (1966), Family creative analysis: Its role in treatment: II. Bulletin of Art Therapy, 5(3), 87-104.

6127. Ziffer, R.L. (Ed.) (1985), Adjunctive techniques in family therapy. New York: Grune and Stratton.

6128. Zilbach, J.J. (1985), Young children in family therapy. New York: Brunner/Mazel.

6129. Zilbach, J.J. (1974), The family in family therapy: Discussion. Journal of the American Academy of Child Psychiatry, 13(3), 459-467.

6130. Zilbergeld, B. (1980), Alternatives to couples counseling for sex problems: Group and individual therapy. Journal of Sex and Marital Therapy, 6, 3-18.

6131. Zimmer, D. (1983), Interaction patterns and communication skills in sexually distressed, maritally distressed, and normal couples: Two experimental studies. Journal of Sex and Marital Therapy, 9, 251-265.

6132. Zimmerman, G.E. (1978), Review of P.A. Martin's A marital therapy manual. Family Coordinator, 27, 294.

6133. Zimmerman, I.M. (1979), Psychotherapy and growth: Family systems perspective. International Journal of Group Psychotherapy, 29, 121.

6134. Zimrin, H. (1984), Child abuse: A dynamic process of encounter between needs and personality traits within the family. American Journal of Family Therapy, 12(1), 37-47.

6135. Zinner, J. (1978), Combined individual and family therapy of borderline adolescents: Rationale and management of the elderly phase. Adolescent Psychiatry, 6, 420-433.

6136. Ziskin, J., and Ziskin, M. (1975), Comarital sex agreements: An emerging issue in sexual counseling. Counseling Psychologist, 5(1), 81-83.

6137. Zuckerman, E., and Jacob, T. (1979), Task effects in family interaction. Family Process, 18, 47-53.

6138. Zuk, G.H. (1979), Value systems and psychopathology in family therapy. International Journal of Family Therapy, 1, 133-151.

6139. Zuk, G.H. (1979), Theories of family pathology: In what direction? International Journal of Family Therapy, 1(4), 356.

6140. Zuk, G.H. (1980), Family therapy for the "truncated" nuclear family. International Journal of Family Therapy, 2(3), 193-199.

6141. Zuk, G.H. (1981), Style of relating as pathogenic relating: A family case study. International Journal of Family Therapy, 3(1), 16-28.

6142. Zuk, G.H. (1981), Family therapy: A triadic based approach. New York: Human Sciences Press.

6143.   Zuk, G.H. (1978), A therapist's perspective on Jewish family values.
        Journal of Marriage and Family Counseling, 4, 102-110.

6144.   Zuk, G.H. (1978), Values and family therapy. Psychotherapy: Theory,
        Research and Practice, 15, 48-55.

6145.   Zuk, G.H. (1976), Family therapy: Clinical hodgepodge or clinical
        science? Journal of Marriage and Family Counseling, 2, 299-303.

6146.   Zuk, G.H. (1973), Letter: Family therapy. Canadian Psychiatric
        Association Journal, 18, 543-544.

6147.   Zuk, G.H. (1973), Sources of anguish that affect commitment in family
        therapy. Neurologie e Psqiatria, 14, 107-116.

6148.   Zuk, G.H. (1970), Critical incidents in the context of family therapy.
        Critical incident No. 2 International Psychiatry Clinics, 7, 237-289.

6149.   Zuk, G.H. (1971), Family therapy during 1964-70. Psychotherapy:
        Theory, Research and Practice, 8, 90-97.

6150.   Zuk, G.H. (1972), Engagement and termination: The crucial reference
        points in family therapy. American Journal of Orthopsychiatry, 42, 323-
        324.

6151.   Zuk, G.H. (1966), The go-between process in family therapy. Family
        Process, 5, 162-178.

6152.   Zuk, G.H. (1967), Family therapy. Archives of General Psychiatry, 16,
        71-79.

6153.   Zuk, G.H. (1968), When the family therapist takes sides: A case report.
        Psychotherapy: Theory, Research and Practice, 5, 24-28.

6154.   Zuk, G.H. (1968), Prompting change in family therapy. Archives of
        General Psychiatry, 19, 727-736.

6155.   Zuk, G.H. (1968), The side-taking function in family therapy. American
        Journal of Orthopsychiatry, 38, 553-559.

6156.   Zuk, G.H. (1968), Family therapy: Formulation of a technique and its
        theory. International Journal of Group Psychotherapy, 18, 42-58.

6157.   Zuk, G.H. (1964), A further study of laughter in family therapy. Family
        Process, 3, 77-89.

6158.   Zuk, G.H. (1965), Preliminary study of the go-between process in family
        therapy. Proceedings of the Annual Convention of the American
        Psychological Association, 291-292.

6159.   Zuk, G.H. (1969), Triadic-based family therapy. International Journal of
        Psychiatry, 8, 539-548.

6160.   Zuk, G.H. (1969), Triadic-based family therapy. Reply to discussants.
        International Journal of Psychiatry, 8, 568-569.

6161.   Zuk, G.H. (1974), Letter: Family therapy. Canadian Medical
        Association Journal, 111, 277.

6162.   Zuk, G.H., Boszormenyi-Nagy, I., and Heiman, E. (1963), Some dynamics of laughter during family therapy. Family Process, 2, 302-314.

6163.   Zuk, G.H., and Boszormenyi-Nagy, I. (Eds.) (1967), Family therapy and disturbed families. Palo Alto, CA: Science and Behavior Books.

6164.   Zweben, A., and Pearlman, S. (1983), Evaluating the effectiveness of conjoint treatment of alcohol-complicated marriages: Clinical and methodological issues. Journal of Marital and Family Therapy, 9, 61-72.

6165.   Zwerling, I. (1954), Initial counseling of parents with retarded children. Journal of Pediatrics, 44, 469-479.

6166.   Zwerling, I. (1981), Family therapy and the alienation syndrome. Journal of Marital and Family Therapy, 7, 331-338.

6167.   Zwetschke, E.T., and Grenfell, J.E. (1965), Family group consultation: A description and a rationale. Personnel and Guidance Journal, 43(10), 974-980.

Author Index

Subject Index

Abuse, Violence:

137, 149, 252, 285, 311, 344, 347, 352, 355, 389, 447, 489, 505, 506, 693, 717, 752, 871, 943, 991, 1000, 1174, 1176, 1187, 1196, 1457, 1791, 1792, 1793, 1794, 1920, 2133, 2136, 2533, 2534, 2557, 2576, 2838, 2870, 2879, 2880, 2975, 3008, 3049, 3081, 3117, 3189, 3355, 3556, 3601, 3686, 3713, 4112, 4285, 4361, 4362, 4431, 4483, 4565, 4729, 4913, 4916, 4928, 4929, 4965, 5052, 5098, 5133, 5231, 5278, 5441, 5442, 5504, 5532, 5536, 5622, 5897, 6011, 6038

Abortion:

804, 2227, 2549, 4542, 4756

Adlerian Approach:

290, 450, 482, 806, 815, 1031, 1293, 1294, 1295, 1351, 1427, 1493, 1494, 1495, 1554, 1556, 1557, 1698, 1709, 1841, 2042, 2046, 2482, 2612, 2708, 2742, 3215, 3545, 3636, 3811, 4069, 4070, 4106, 4428, 4493, 4500, 5105, 5221, 5232, 5313, 5366, 5524, 5729, 5883

Adolescents, Adolescence:

9, 30, 57, 132, 188, 294, 297, 299, 325, 336, 349, 351, 365, 395, 402, 465, 471, 504, 551, 552, 557, 595, 638, 691, 692, 711, 723, 741, 755, 767, 808, 834, 875, 876, 893, 906, 934, 974, 980, 994, 1026, 1038, 1047, 1064, 1067, 1071, 1072, 1080, 1083, 1102, 1103, 1119, 1151, 1209, 1232, 1249, 1268, 1269, 1358, 1364, 1406, 1435, 1498, 1516, 1519, 1521, 1532, 1546, 1562, 1563, 1585, 1600, 1617, 1619, 1646, 1681, 1705, 1713, 1728, 1776, 1830, 1847, 1920, 1935, 1942, 1951, 1991, 1992, 2094, 2102, 2122, 2148, 2223, 2245, 2254, 2318, 2319, 2367, 2508, 2542, 2585, 2595, 2606, 2614, 2653, 2686, 2710, 2738, 2803, 2805, 2808, 2855, 2878, 2896, 2907, 2918, 2925, 2971, 3009, 3028, 3032, 3045, 3083, 3117, 3148, 3171, 3174, 3179, 3188, 3260, 3292, 3314, 3377, 3415, 3460, 3471, 3472, 3480, 3562, 3564, 3597, 3610, 3626, 3659, 3679, 3736, 3739, 3741, 3749, 3753, 3768, 3780, 3784, 3790, 3792, 3848, 3849, 3878, 3940, 3971, 4006, 4039, 4111, 4124, 4125, 4135, 4233, 4238, 4239, 4281, 4307, 4311, 4341, 4425, 4430, 4435, 4440, 4484, 4497, 4510, 4549, 4560, 4569, 4570, 4596, 4602, 4603, 4623, 4674,

4690, 4694, 4700, 4703, 4715, 4746, 4750, 4758, 4787, 4801, 4923, 4939, 4948, 4956,
4960, 4964, 4969, 4976, 5016, 5041, 5064, 5066, 5067, 5068, 5081, 5082, 5084, 5087,
5099, 5101, 5126, 5131, 5148, 5172, 5231, 5247, 5264, 5265, 5267, 5316, 5332, 5341,
5375, 5407, 5412, 5414, 5422, 5457, 5472, 5474, 5475, 5476, 5477, 5478, 5487, 5514,
5558, 5559, 5577, 5606, 5609, 5675, 5686, 5720, 5725, 5783, 5857, 5859, 5932, 5944,
5969, 5971, 5985, 6031, 6038, 6078, 6106, 6110, 6135

Alcoholism:

11, 154, 222, 244, 303, 494, 515, 620, 759, 763, 824, 910, 938, 951, 952, 953,
954, 956, 979, 1052, 1063, 1085, 1097, 1276, 1286, 1339, 1381, 1383, 1395, 1460, 1480,
1490, 1549, 1578, 1581, 1609, 1695, 1696, 1697, 1701, 1795, 1838, 1905, 2023,
2062, 2074, 2101, 2174, 2484, 2555, 2607, 2608, 2763, 2799, 2800, 2962, 2963, 2964,
3020, 3041, 3046, 3155, 3167, 3268, 3269, 3418, 3568, 3774, 3793, 3794, 3795, 3834,
3866, 3940, 4005, 4081, 4113, 4114, 4151, 4213, 4215, 4216, 4267, 4271, 4310, 4313,
4595, 4666, 4915, 4971, 5012, 5032, 5033, 5077, 5219, 5288, 5379, 5385, 5386, 5387,
5558, 5567, 5587, 5632, 5687, 5700, 5760, 5778, 6018, 6053, 6076, 6164

Anxiety, Stress:

543, 600, 602, 639, 743, 1013, 1291, 1423, 1509, 1519, 1817, 1969, 2750, 2791,
3133, 3274, 3360, 3370, 3371, 3796, 4121, 4166, 4191, 4930, 4958, 4992, 5148, 5153,
5555, 5887, 5889, 6120

Art Therapy (includes Music Therapy):

182, 940, 1038, 1107, 1218, 1458, 1579, 1896, 2088, 2090, 2115, 2621, 2736,
2804, 2814, 2873, 3208, 3226, 3227, 3259, 3276, 3277, 3457, 3516, 3647, 3768, 3769,
3993, 4318, 4370, 5026, 5244, 5543, 5592, 5702, 5767, 5768, 5769, 5974, 5997, 6001,
6126

Assessment, Scaling, Instruments, Testing:

62, 79, 119, 212, 214, 278, 283, 300, 329, 392, 400, 433, 441, 528, 571, 597, 608,
671, 685, 701, 718, 729, 731, 738, 831, 856, 920, 940, 1068, 1144, 1189, 1224, 1240,
1243, 1283, 1284, 1305, 1405, 1417, 1437, 1459, 1467, 1498, 1537, 1579, 1622, 1686,
1713, 1819, 1860, 1889, 1891, 1892, 1933, 2023, 2043, 2050, 2078, 2092, 2129, 2161,
2244, 2277, 2531, 2535, 2633, 2655, 2731, 2777, 2806, 2833, 2861, 2904, 2920, 2972,
2979, 2983, 3133, 3266, 3378, 3499, 3632, 3636, 3672, 3698, 3746, 3774, 3890, 3907,
3909, 4029, 4030, 4059, 4133, 4194, 4240, 4252, 4254, 4261,
4356, 4437, 4448, 4460, 4461, 4483, 4499, 4608, 4620, 4682, 4741, 4749, 4764, 4812,
4839, 4914, 4991, 4992, 5069, 5094, 5148, 5149, 5163, 5223, 5241, 5380, 5381, 5426,
5440, 5446, 5611, 5640, 5656, 5681, 5684, 5702, 5705, 5710, 5739, 5740, 5815, 5838,
5889, 5974, 5999, 6029, 6063, 6065

Behavior Therapy, Behavioral Emphasis:

100, 102, 190, 235, 258, 266, 277, 286, 288, 291, 310, 370, 390, 392, 495, 555,
605, 626, 627, 636, 663, 735, 736, 790, 820, 897, 898, 914, 958, 997, 1000, 1046, 1084,
1100, 1101, 1159, 1165, 1166, 1274, 1310, 1314, 1459, 1473, 1488, 1521, 1536, 1538,
1568, 1641, 1670, 1674, 1722, 1727, 1739, 1765, 1786, 1805, 1827, 1837, 1878, 1910,
1929, 1930, 1942, 1965, 2042, 2084, 2085, 2094, 2113, 2197, 2231, 2273, 2276, 2288,
2291, 2338, 2339, 2342, 2357, 2359, 2378, 2391, 2393, 2395, 2412, 2527, 2591, 2622,

2643, 2679, 2705, 2712, 2715, 2743, 2769, 2770, 2771, 2772, 2773, 2774, 2775, 2777, 2778, 2780, 2782, 2783, 2784, 2785, 2787, 2815, 2823, 2841, 2904, 2923, 2979, 2998, 2999, 3032, 3051, 3220, 3233, 3361, 3367, 3431, 3470, 3484, 3485, 3486, 3487, 3488, 3490, 3573, 3577, 3578, 3687, 3689, 3690, 3691, 3692, 3693, 3694, 3695, 3717, 3773, 3828, 3839, 3847, 3850, 3868, 3869, 3873, 3909, 3941, 4075, 4084, 4087, 4104, 4123, 4138, 4181, 4213, 4215, 4216, 4220, 4222, 4223, 4263, 4296, 4312, 4340, 4414, 4416, 4492, 4511, 4512, 4529, 4562, 4617, 4627, 4631, 4690, 4727, 4728, 4735, 4736, 4801, 4822, 4827, 4893, 4894, 4983, 5029, 5127, 5139, 5184, 5217, 5331, 5362, 5438, 5465, 5544, 5553, 5558, 5565, 5570, 5648, 5658, 5659, 5660, 5675, 5676, 5680, 5739, 5741, 5852, 5853, 5877, 5878, 5880, 5908, 5952, 5953, 5963, 6006, 6007, 6047, 6048, 6104, 6118

Bibliotherapy:

396, 3831

BOOKS:

Family Therapy:

28, 40, 48, 49, 99, 104, 138, 159, 162, 165, 234, 235, 281, 312, 326, 331, 338, 372, 414, 445, 508, 509, 520, 674, 680, 751, 753, 760, 781, 852, 879, 996, 1016, 1037, 1069, 1129, 1131, 1147, 1169, 1191, 1196, 1205, 1271, 1325, 1326, 1412, 1504, 1512, 1557, 1600, 1731, 1732, 1738, 1781, 1784, 1821, 1886, 1902, 1919, 1944, 1949, 1979, 1989, 1990, 2001, 2002, 2127, 2144, 2167, 2169, 2170, 2171, 2194, 2204, 2211, 2261, 2268, 2290, 2303, 2315, 2356, 2362, 2410, 2411, 2413, 2434, 2450, 2452, 2465, 2490, 2557, 2561, 2594, 2634, 2636, 2666, 2672, 2692, 2701, 2702, 2703, 2704, 2755, 2857, 2880, 2885, 2932, 2945, 2949, 2959, 2962, 2986, 3010, 3073, 3143, 3177, 3221, 3229, 323 , 3234, 3238, 3285, 3296, 3297, 3386, 3443, 3520, 3609, 3623, 3823, 3919, 3942, 3962, 3964, 3968, 3969, 4008, 4020, 4063, 4088, 4131, 4149, 4180, 4240, 4244, 4287, 4317, 4343, 4367, 4413, 4419, 4458, 4481, 4579, 4600, 4612, 4642, 4647, 4677, 4754, 4797, 4805, 4855, 4856, 4861, 4904, 4905, 4908, 4916, 4923, 5020, 5170, 5187, 5235, 5293, 5299, 5204, 5421, 5424, 5478, 5516, 5740, 5746, 5798, 5805, 5936, 6040, 6041, 6042, 6043, 6056, 6071, 6127, 6128, 6142, 6163

Marital Therapy:

104, 219, 281, 549, 851, 1318, 1821, 1944, 2073, 2170, 2171, 2180, 2434, 2577, 2632, 2825, 3099, 3234, 3341, 3386, 3487, 3718, 4076, 4078, 4137, 4287, 4312, 4355, 4419, 4829, 4853, 4855, 5017, 5187, 5227, 5340, 5564, 5631, 5737, 5798, 5964, 5975, 6056, 6071

Couples Therapy:

8, 888, 2180, 2524, 3234, 3364, 4829, 4853, 5227, 5976

Book Reviews:

98, 124, 198, 210, 232, 272, 280, 318, 352, 356, 364, 387, 416, 417, 448, 449, 458, 464, 494, 532, 564, 569, 573, 634, 635, 645, 693, 695, 696, 697, 698, 699, 700, 702, 726, 746, 799, 876, 903, 905, 941, 942, 947, 969, 997, 998, 1029, 1057, 1110, 1111, 1124, 1127, 1133, 1137, 1158, 1167, 1180, 1229, 1230, 1237, 1247, 1293, 1299, 1314, 1329, 1330, 1354, 1366, 1375, 1381, 1420, 1423, 1440, 1442, 1443, 1452, 1458, 1510, 1570, 1572, 1575, 1580, 1587, 1595, 1684, 1714, 1715, 1727, 1734, 1779, 1791, 1792, 1793, 1794, 1803, 1808, 1875, 1876, 1883, 1898, 1899, 1904, 1906, 1928, 1931, 1952, 1953, 1962, 1964, 1965, 1966, 1974, 1975, 1993, 1995, 2006, 2008, 2009, 2016, 2037, 2038, 2090, 2100, 2132, 2137, 2172, 2177, 2182, 2188, 2189, 2197, 2201, 2217, 2222, 2224, 2273, 2274, 2305, 2314, 2321, 2331, 2367, 2378, 2382, 2398, 2486, 2488, 2497, 2515, 2579, 2600, 2601, 2610, 2635, 2653, 2688, 2717, 2739, 2744, 2792, 2811, 2814, 2822, 2856, 2898, 2899, 2913, 2938, 2950, 2955, 2964, 2990, 2996, 3001, 3002, 3051, 3056, 3060, 3067, 3068, 3074, 3075, 3076, 3107, 3108, 3113, 3153, 3155, 3164, 3181, 3186, 3187, 3231, 3232, 3233, 3240, 3254, 3301, 3303, 3334, 3335, 3354, 3397, 3414, 3474, 3481, 3496, 3500, 3502, 3503, 3514, 3515, 3516, 3518, 3523, 3553, 3573, 3578, 3586, 3588, 3660, 3661, 3677, 3691, 3711, 3715, 3717, 3720, 3727, 3728, 3752, 3753, 3760, 3761, 3782, 3800, 3801, 3802, 3803, 3804, 3820, 3844, 3876, 3877, 3901, 3921, 3922, 3943, 3974, 4007, 4093, 4111, 4117, 4130, 4152, 4156, 4181, 4204, 4214, 4270, 4345, 4352, 4359, 4360, 4401, 4430, 4436, 4447, 4455, 4465, 4466, 4469, 4471, 4489, 4492, 4523, 4525, 4548, 4552, 4558, 4617, 4619, 4629, 4630, 4631, 4634, 4643, 4658, 4670, 4685, 4713, 4727, 4732, 4771, 4803, 4808, 4811, 4832, 4841, 4869, 4870, 4871, 4902, 4915, 4921, 4930, 4959, 4983, 4985, 4990, 4998, 5008, 5037, 5051, 5060, 5076, 5095, 5126, 5159, 5167, 5173, 5175, 5192, 5238, 5242, 5298, 5302, 5321, 5333, 5344, 5349, 5382, 5389, 5433, 5437, 5446, 5447, 5448, 5451, 5454, 5457, 5467, 5473, 5481, 5491, 5567, 5569, 5575, 5592, 5612, 5636, 5659, 5711, 5718, 5724, 5739, 5751, 5758, 5781, 5784, 5793, 5811, 5817, 5834, 5865, 5867, 5877, 5885, 5946, 5950, 5959, 5993, 6003, 6018, 6021, 6086, 6088, 6091, 6108, 6132

Eating Disorders:

929, 988, 1184, 1203, 1361, 1433, 1634, 1642, 1975, 2480, 2541, 2802, 2803, 3130, 3131, 3262, 3529, 3530, 3532, 3968, 4002, 4126, 4289, 4391, 4753, 4755, 4756, 4999, 5310, 5397, 5831, 5942

Personality Disorders, Borderline Affective Disorders:

149, 322, 427, 429, 430, 594, 723, 778, 837, 929, 934, 988, 1159, 1184, 1353, 1358, 1361, 1433, 1561, 1630, 1634, 1642, 1707, 1975, 2284, 2285, 2286, 2459, 2480, 2541, 2802, 2803, 3130, 3131, 3262, 3314, 3472, 3529, 3530, 3532, 3657, 3968, 4002, 4289, 4391, 4402, 4753, 4755, 4756, 4802, 4999, 5010, 5025, 5066, 5067, 5200, 5258, 5310, 5397, 5663, 5831, 5942, 6135

Cancer:

486, 1104, 1172, 1454, 2022, 2076, 2135, 2146, 2150, 2176, 2584, 2827, 2830, 2974, 3218, 3762, 4045, 4248, 4364, 4423, 4444, 4762, 4763, 4977, 5226, 5279, 5887, 6010, 6012

Case Studies, History:

18, 19, 20, 21, 22, 74, 79, 266, 419, 449, 463, 498, 606, 664, 884, 896, 927, 1004,

Divorce, Seperation:

Dreams, Dream Analysis:

Drugs-Abuse, Substance Abuse:

Family Therapy, Counseling:

2, 4, 5, 7, 9, 10, 11, 12, 13, 14, 15, 17, 18, 19, 20, 21, 22, 23, 25, 26, 27, 28, 29, 30, 31, 32, 33, 34, 35, 36, 37, 38, 39, 40, 41, 42, 43, 44, 45, 46, 47, 48, 49, 50, 51, 52, 53, 54, 56, 57, 58, 59, 60, 61, 63, 65, 66, 69, 70, 74, 75, 77, 78, 81, 83, 84, 85, 86, 88, 89, 90, 91, 94, 95, 96, 97, 98, 99, 100, 101, 102, 103, 104, 107, 108, 109, 110, 112, 115, 116, 117, 118, 119, 120, 123, 124, 125, 126, 127, 128, 129, 130, 131, 132, 133, 134, 135, 136, 137, 138, 139, 140, 141, 142, 143, 144, 145, 146, 147, 148, 149, 150, 151, 152, 153, 154, 155, 156, 157, 158, 159, 160, 161, 162, 163, 164, 165, 166, 167, 169, 170, 173, 174, 175, 176, 177, 178, 179, 182, 185, 186, 187, 188, 189, 191, 192, 193, 194, 196, 198, 199, 200, 201, 202, 203, 204, 205, 206, 207, 210, 211, 214, 222, 223, 224, 225, 226, 227, 228, 233, 234, 235, 236, 237, 238, 239, 240, 242, 243, 244, 245, 247, 248, 249, 250, 251, 252, 254, 255, 256, 260, 261, 262, 263, 265, 266, 267, 268, 269, 270, 272, 273, 274, 275, 276, 277, 278, 279, 280, 281, 282, 284, 285, 289, 290, 292, 294, 295, 296, 297, 299, 300, 301, 303, 304, 306, 309, 311, 312, 314, 315, 316, 317, 318, 319, 320, 321, 322, 323, 324, 325, 326, 327, 328, 329, 330, 331, 332, 333, 336, 337, 338, 339, 340, 341, 342, 343, 344, 346, 347, 348, 349, 350, 351, 352, 353, 354, 355, 356, 357, 358, 359, 360, 361, 362, 363, 364, 365, 366, 367, 368, 369, 370, 371, 372, 375, 376, 377, 378, 381, 382, 383, 385, 386, 387, 388, 393, 394, 395, 397, 398, 400, 402, 403, 404, 405, 406, 407, 408, 409, 412, 413, 414, 415, 417, 418, 419, 421, 422, 423, 424, 425, 426, 427, 428, 430, 431, 432, 434, 437, 438, 439, 440, 443, 444, 445, 447, 448, 449, 450, 451, 452, 453, 454, 455, 457, 458, 459, 462, 463, 464, 465, 466, 467, 468, 469, 470, 471, 472, 473, 474, 476, 477, 478, 479, 481, 484, 486, 487, 488, 489, 490, 491, 492, 493, 494, 496, 497, 499, 500, 501, 502, 503, 504, 505, 506, 507, 508, 509, 510, 511, 512, 513, 515, 516, 517, 518, 519, 520, 521, 522, 523, 525, 526, 527, 529, 530, 531, 532, 533, 534, 536, 538, 539, 540, 541, 542, 544, 547, 550, 551, 552, 553, 554, 556, 557, 558, 559, 561, 562, 563, 564, 567, 568, 569, 570, 572, 573, 574, 576, 578, 579, 580, 581, 582, 583, 584, 587, 588, 593, 594, 595, 596, 597, 598, 599, 603, 604, 607, 609, 610, 612, 615, 621, 622, 623, 624, 627, 628, 629, 630, 631, 634, 635, 636, 637, 639, 640, 644, 645, 646, 647, 648, 649, 650, 651, 652, 653, 654, 655, 656, 657, 658, 660, 661, 662, 663, 664, 665, 667, 668, 669, 671, 674, 675, 676, 677, 678, 679, 680, 681, 682, 683, 684, 685, 686, 687, 688, 689, 690, 691, 692, 693, 694, 697, 698, 699, 700, 702, 705, 706, 707, 708, 709, 710, 711, 713, 714, 715, 716, 717, 718, 719, 720, 721, 722, 723, 724, 725, 726, 727, 728, 729, 730, 732, 737, 738, 739, 740, 741, 744, 745, 746, 747, 748, 749, 750, 751, 752, 753, 754, 755, 756, 758, 759, 760, 761, 762, 763, 764, 765, 766, 767, 768, 769, 770, 771, 772, 773, 774, 776, 777, 780, 781, 782, 783, 786, 787, 788, 789, 791, 793, 795, 796, 797, 798, 799, 800, 802, 803, 804, 805, 806, 807, 808, 809, 810, 811, 812, 813, 814, 815, 816, 817, 819, 820, 821, 822, 825, 826, 828, 829, 830, 831, 832, 833, 834, 835, 839, 840, 841, 842, 846, 848, 849, 850, 852, 853, 854, 855, 865, 866, 869, 870, 871, 872, 873, 874, 875, 876, 877, 878, 879, 880, 881, 882, 884, 887, 890, 891, 892, 893, 894, 895, 899, 901, 902, 903, 904, 905, 906, 907, 909, 910, 911, 913, 914, 915, 916, 917, 918, 919, 920, 921, 922, 923, 925, 926, 927, 928, 929, 932, 933, 934, 935, 936, 937, 940, 941, 942, 943, 945, 946, 947, 949, 950, 955, 957, 959, 963, 964, 966, 967, 968, 969, 970, 971, 972, 974, 975, 976, 977, 978, 980, 981, 982, 983, 984, 985, 986, 987, 988, 989, 990, 991, 992, 993, 994, 995, 996, 998, 999, 1000, 1001, 1002, 1003, 1004, 1005, 1006, 1007, 1008, 1009, 1010, 1011, 1012, 1013, 1014, 1016, 1017, 1018, 1019, 1021, 1022, 1024, 1025, 1026, 1027, 1028, 1029, 1030, 1031, 1032, 1033, 1034, 1035, 1036, 1037, 1038, 1039, 1040, 1041, 1047, 1048, 1049, 1051, 1052, 1053, 1054, 1055, 1058, 1060, 1061, 1062, 1063, 1064, 1065, 1066, 1067, 1068, 1069, 1070, 1071, 1072, 1073, 1074, 1075, 1076, 1077, 1078, 1079, 1080, 1081, 1083, 1084, 1089, 1092, 1094, 1095, 1096, 1098, 1099, 1100, 1101, 1102, 1103, 1106, 1107, 1108, 1109, 1110, 1111, 1112, 1113, 1114, 1115, 1116, 1117, 1118, 1119, 1120, 1121, 1122, 1123, 1124, 1125, 1126, 1127, 1129, 1130, 1131, 1133, 1134, 1135, 1136, 1137, 1138, 1140, 1141, 1142, 1147, 1148, 1149, 1151, 1152, 1154, 1155, 1156, 1157, 1158, 1161, 1162, 1163, 1165, 1166, 1167, 1168, 1169, 1171, 1172, 1173, 1174, 1175, 1176, 1177, 1178, 1179, 1181, 1182, 1184, 1186, 1189, 1190, 1191, 1192, 1193, 1194, 1195, 1196, 1197, 1198, 1199, 1200, 1201, 1202, 1203, 1204, 1205, 1206, 1207, 1208, 1209, 1210, 1212, 1213, 1214, 1215,

Group Therapy/Psychotherapy:

Handicapped:

Home-Setting Therapy, Diverse Therapy Settings:

Hypnosis:

Individual and/or versus Family Therapy:

4163, 4166, 4167, 4170, 4171, 4172, 4179, 4181, 4182, 4183, 4184, 4194, 4198, 4207, 4210, 4211, 4213, 4214, 4215, 4216, 4221, 4222, 4223, 4224, 4230, 4234, 4237, 4241, 4243, 4253, 4254, 4255, 4256, 4257, 4258, 4259, 4260, 4261, 4263, 4270, 4273, 4278, 4284, 4286, 4287, 4292, 4295, 4309, 4312, 4313, 4315, 4320, 4321, 4329, 4330, 4338, 4340, 4344, 4352, 4355, 4364, 4366, 4368, 4369, 4371, 4376, 4378, 4381, 4382, 4383, 4386, 4388, 4389, 4400, 4412, 4417, 4418, 4419, 4424, 4428, 4437, 4438, 4439, 4442, 4446, 4452, 4459, 4469, 4475, 4479, 4482, 4487, 4494, 4499, 4500, 4508, 4509, 4511, 4512, 4514, 4515, 4519, 4520, 4521, 4525, 4528, 4529, 4530, 4535, 4537, 4538, 4543, 4545, 4546, 4550, 4562, 4563, 4567, 4573, 4575, 4584, 4585, 4588, 4589, 4590, 4591, 4592, 4615, 4616, 4617, 4627, 4630, 4631, 4636, 4637, 4640, 4649, 4652, 4659, 4660, 4661, 4664, 4665, 4666, 4699, 4701, 4704, 4707, 4708, 4715, 4716, 4718, 4720, 4726, 4727, 4729, 4739, 4740, 4741, 4743, 4752, 4757, 4760, 4761, 4768, 4772, 4778, 4802, 4811, 4814, 4819, 4820, 4822, 4825, 4828, 4829, 4830, 4831, 4834, 4836, 4837, 4839, 4846, 4848, 4849, 4850, 4851, 4853, 4854, 4857, 4870, 4874, 4878, 4883, 4885, 4896, 4906, 4909, 4913, 4914, 4917, 4920, 4927, 4931, 4933, 4935, 4947, 4975, 4977, 4983, 4984, 4990, 4993, 4994, 5012, 5017, 5025, 5029, 5040, 5042, 5046, 5047, 5049, 5061, 5062, 5094, 5099, 5116, 5119, 5124, 5125, 5128, 5129, 5137, 5149, 5152, 5153, 5154, 5155, 5156, 5157, 5158, 5163, 5164, 5165, 5169, 5171, 5174, 5175, 5176, 5178, 5179, 5180, 5182, 5183, 5184, 5187, 5190, 5191, 5199, 5200, 5207, 5211, 5219, 5220, 5221, 5223, 5224, 5228, 5229, 5230, 5231, 5239, 5240, 5241, 5246, 5250, 5251, 5252, 5258, 5266, 5269, 5272, 5273, 5274, 5285, 5288, 5306, 5311, 5312, 5313, 5318, 5322, 5323, 5326, 5328, 5329, 5331, 5337, 5340, 5367, 5376, 5386, 5387, 5391, 5393, 5395, 5396, 5403, 5426, 5428, 5429, 5431, 5432, 5434, 5435, 5437, 5443, 5446, 5451, 5455, 5456, 5460 5462, 5463, 5464, 5465, 5471, 5483, 5485, 5486, 5488, 5489, 5492, 5493, 5494, 5495, 5499, 5500, 5504, 5505, 5522, 5526, 5527, 5528, 5534, 5539, 5541, 5554, 5556, 5561, 5564, 5570, 5572, 5580, 5586, 5594, 5595, 5598, 5601, 5608, 5609, 5615, 5619, 5620, 5621, 5624, 5626, 5630, 5631, 5634, 5642, 5648, 5650, 5656, 5657, 5658, 5659, 5660, 5662, 5664, 5668, 5670, 5671, 5672, 5673, 5674, 5681, 5682, 5683, 5684, 5693, 5697, 5698, 5699, 5705, 5707, 5710, 5727, 5737, 5738, 5739, 5741, 5743, 5744, 5745, 5761, 5762, 5768, 5769, 5770, 5771, 5778, 5779, 5780, 5782, 5785, 5786, 5787, 5789, 5790, 5791, 5794, 5799, 5803, 5810, 5813, 5814, 5815, 5820, 5823, 5824, 5825, 5828, 5833, 5835, 5836, 5838, 5839, 5845, 5847, 5863, 5865, 5870, 5871, 5893, 5915, 5921, 5922, 5923, 5926, 5934, 5949, 5952, 5953, 5955, 5958, 5962, 5963, 5964, 5968, 5978, 5979, 5983, 5986, 5989, 5999, 6000, 6008, 6016, 6017, 6019, 6021, 6024, 6032, 6037, 6047, 6048, 6049, 6056, 6061, 6068, 6070, 6071, 6076, 6079, 6080, 6093, 6094, 6097, 6102, 6107, 6114, 6118, 6119, 6120, 6130, 6131, 6132, 6136, 6164

Marriage Enrichment, Family Enrichment Programs:

55, 253, 304, 396, 617, 900, 912, 1082, 1180, 1211, 1256, 1455, 1487, 1657, 1751, 1755, 1778, 1917, 2080, 2093, 2146, 2155, 2261, 2320, 2360, 2523, 2527, 2631, 2818, 2977, 3036, 3037, 3070, 3233, 3236, 3243, 3249, 3397, 3412, 3431, 3544, 3612, 3725, 3777, 3778, 3835, 3922, 3924, 3947, 4114, 4154, 4167, 4236, 4286, 4371, 4494, 4499, 4573, 4661, 4760, 4814, 4822, 4919, 5091, 5158, 5207, 5228, 5455, 5462, 5500, 5541, 5549, 5634, 5682, 5684, 5770, 5833, 5884, 5963, 5968, 6002, 6037

Marriage Process:

16, 24, 31, 55, 62, 73, 75, 76, 79, 92, 105, 152, 171, 172, 183, 184, 207, 227, 241, 253, 306, 308, 334, 345, 373, 399, 401, 429, 436, 440, 442, 446, 447, 456, 482, 535, 565, 575, 600, 602, 618, 619, 620, 638, 641, 659, 666, 701, 712, 742, 743, 775, 778, 793, 814, 823, 844, 845, 892, 924, 938, 1056, 1087, 1146, 1150, 1187, 1188, 1261, 1279, 1281, 1286, 1296, 1387, 1454, 1455, 1466, 1593, 1748, 1755, 1865, 1906, 1918, 1934, 1959, 1960, 1961, 1962, 1968, 1994, 2036, 2073, 2092, 2154, 2218, 2235, 2271, 2272, 2306, 2333, 2337, 2428, 2449, 2495, 2496, 2528, 2529, 2559, 2589, 2617, 2618, 2620, 2755, 2795, 2859, 3058, 3196, 3205, 3213, 3315, 3341, 3345, 3352, 3365, 3368,

3397, 3494, 3522, 3533, 3541, 3599, 3603, 3615, 3693, 3704, 3719, 3749, 3758, 3788, 3833, 3925, 3974, 3978, 3986, 3990, 4015, 4017, 4100, 4121, 4122, 4138, 4150, 4155, 4170, 4198, 4215, 4254, 4263, 4292, 4313, 4365, 4369, 4376, 4482, 4487, 4494, 4500, 4508, 4509, 4512, 4515, 4519, 4530, 4535, 4537, 4538, 4592, 4640, 4659, 4660, 4664, 4665, 4689, 4718, 4739, 4740, 4752, 4760, 4802, 4825, 4831, 4836, 4883, 4909, 4917, 5040, 5062, 5133, 5137, 5157, 5165, 5171, 5178, 5179, 5207, 5239, 5240, 5241, 5251, 5266, 5274, 5285, 5288, 5337, 5358, 5391, 5451, 5455, 5505, 5542, 5639, 5731, 5738, 5743, 5778, 5799, 5814, 5815, 5838, 5879, 5923, 5979, 6034, 6035, 6095, 6107

Mental Retardation:

3, 169, 171, 172, 196, 421, 687, 974, 1186, 1320, 1352, 1520, 1835, 2254, 2289, 2311, 2500, 2670, 2734, 3148, 3347, 3491, 3558, 3590, 3629, 3663, 3972, 4044, 4109, 4197, 4205, 4227, 4578, 4694, 4866, 4944, 5236, 5398, 5544, 5661, 5841, 5873, 6165

Multiple Family Therapy, Multiple Family Group Therapy, Family and Group Therapy, Family Groups:

23, 50, 81, 88, 90, 91, 133, 144, 185, 187, 301, 303, 323, 328, 365, 407, 432, 444, 457, 468, 471, 473, 474, 491, 492, 497, 499, 522, 530, 536, 538, 539, 540, 541, 570, 604, 671, 758, 866, 880, 887, 893, 955, 982, 1001, 1084, 1107, 1122, 1163, 1168, 1190, 1198, 1263, 1322, 1323, 1337, 1367, 1379, 1437, 1439, 1532, 1553, 1555, 1577, 1585, 1599, 1602, 1743, 1745, 1761, 1832, 1834, 1840, 1857, 1907, 1911, 1940, 1988, 2047, 2192, 2241, 2298, 2443, 2493, 2522, 2558, 2560, 2563, 2569, 2570, 2584, 2597, 2743, 2759, 2798, 2862, 2871, 2881, 2884, 2894, 2961, 3018, 3045, 3082, 3086, 3101, 3122, 3140, 3208, 3217, 3225, 3304, 3305, 3317, 3318, 3319, 3320, 3321, 3322, 3323, 3340, 3343, 3369, 3402, 3404, 3405, 3406, 3407, 3408, 3423, 3459, 3478, 3487, 3488, 3492, 3543, 3568, 3570, 3579, 3587, 3607, 3608, 3609, 3647, 3653, 3751, 3784, 3834, 3855, 3878, 3926, 3993, 4099, 4169, 4175, 4193, 4276, 4280, 4299, 4346, 4353, 4379, 4404, 4496, 4536, 4542, 4610, 4628, 4688, 4712, 4714, 4737, 4767, 4808, 4884, 4907, 4912, 4925, 4937, 4951, 4952, 4953, 4954, 4960, 4966, 4978, 4988, 5068, 5096, 5106, 5168, 5172, 5188, 5198, 5248, 5371, 5390, 5399, 5452, 5453, 5487, 5514, 5530, 5579, 5605, 5669, 5685, 5690, 5691, 5767, 5884, 5887, 5904, 5951, 5995, 5997, 6054, 6124

Neurosis:

76, 434, 455, 757, 788, 1160, 1521, 1827, 1862, 2110, 2111, 2209, 2300, 2303, 2313, 2388, 2517, 2518, 2544, 2545, 2569, 2760, 2761, 3191, 3192, 3808, 3816, 3983, 4072, 4150, 4233, 4314, 4705, 5396, 5606

Nurses, Mental Health Nurses, MH Care Providers/Team:

121, 146, 203, 204, 326, 327, 344, 350, 366, 407, 440, 523, 580, 650, 708, 732, 764, 765, 783, 784, 785, 803, 816, 870, 884, 921, 935, 957, 992, 1037, 1065, 1072, 1147, 1235, 1253, 1290, 1304, 1336, 1358, 1419, 1430, 1456, 1480, 1509, 1527, 1598, 1622, 1720, 1731, 1808, 1890, 1911, 2003, 2108, 2134, 2140, 2332, 2389, 2536, 2584, 2677, 2805, 2817, 2822, 2828, 2838, 2851, 2854, 2858, 2870, 2977, 3049, 3084, 3152, 3165, 3258, 3271, 3306, 3313, 3314, 3353, 3475, 3570, 3601, 3605, 3618, 3674, 3709, 3758, 3773, 3813, 3884, 3886, 3899, 3942, 3947, 3980, 4029, 4041, 4101, 4132, 4262, 4384, 4478, 4532, 4581, 4586, 4624, 4711, 4810, 4812, 4862, 4928, 4929, 4937, 4963, 4970, 4974, 5021, 5048, 5074, 5115, 5152, 5153, 5235, 5242, 5297, 5445, 5498, 5521, 5605, 5623, 5627, 5669, 5700, 5704, 5742, 5775, 5795, 5808, 5860, 5882, 5967, 5969, 6012

Review of Literature, History of Family Therapy, Marital Therapy or Couple Therapy, Historical Emphasis, Collections:

98, 173, 215, 520, 834, 946, 1206, 1502, 1745, 1759, 1903, 1940, 1944, 2028, 2053, 2070, 2204, 2301, 2325, 2352, 2404, 2438, 2475, 2497, 2587, 2723, 2770, 2794, 2869, 2871, 2941, 3235, 3303, 3439, 3440, 3598, 3661, 3770, 3950, 3973, 4103, 4484, 4551, 4658, 4754, 4824, 4848, 4882, 4990, 5028, 5160, 5263, 5321, 5448, 5453, 5688, 5713, 5806, 5812, 5894, 5943, 6086, 6111, 6149

Bibliographies:

372, 547, 1325, 1326, 2144, 2167, 2169, 2324, 2343, 3249, 3620, 4213, 4458, 4993, 5236, 5350, 5446, 5712, 5714, 5787, 5862

Role-Playing:

167, 846, 1023, 1252, 1721, 2818, 4957, 5102

School Counseling, School-Related, School Teacher, Students-All Ages, Student Issues:

127, 143, 150, 169, 170, 239, 240, 262, 290, 431, 459, 462, 513, 523, 543, 562, 582, 631, 777, 810, 839, 849, 907, 914, 917, 918, 919, 961, 1003, 1142, 1202, 1213, 1363, 1463, 1469, 1528, 1532, 1543, 1547, 1548, 1585, 1603, 1641, 1693, 1704, 1725, 1815, 1824, 1920, 1991, 2013, 2014, 2025, 2045, 2047, 2095, 2153, 2246, 2434, 2602, 2604, 2606, 2655, 2671, 2903, 3069, 3094, 3095, 3179, 3347, 3357, 3429, 3542, 3589, 3652, 3709, 3797, 3862, 3865, 3892, 3940, 4068, 4094, 4197, 4200, 4208, 4217, 4264, 4293, 4374, 4397, 4405, 4415, 4421, 4439, 4486, 4706, 4981, 5087, 5186, 5217, 5232, 5273, 5305, 5333, 5456, 5459, 5475, 5476, 5499, 5550, 5575, 5697, 5707, 5906, 5941, 5947, 5948, 5954, 5973, 5987, 6099, 6101, 6120

Sex-Roles:

12, 13, 14, 15, 101, 122, 227, 386, 585, 1252, 1466, 1550, 1721, 1772, 1855, 1900, 1959, 1960, 2157, 2209, 2267, 2449, 2453, 2462, 2468, 2469, 2589, 2731, 2764, 2869, 2993, 3014, 3025, 3026, 3169, 3196, 3213, 3239, 3421, 3482, 3535, 3632, 3692, 3724, 3777, 4173, 4196, 4537, 4538, 4550, 4624, 5149, 5580, 5814, 5876

Sex Therapy:

16, 67, 80, 190, 221, 843, 860, 962, 1020, 1090, 1091, 1132, 1144, 1145, 1182, 1183, 1185, 1261, 1378, 1476, 1518, 1523, 1549, 1628, 1651, 1710, 1803, 1806, 1958, 1974, 2032, 2064, 2184, 2328, 2336, 2432, 2495, 2556, 2622, 2623, 2624, 2766, 3099, 3110, 3126, 3183, 3184, 3185, 3205, 3219, 3344, 3398, 3445, 3446, 3447, 3448, 3449, 3463, 3464, 3574, 3762, 3781, 3789, 3928, 3994, 4049, 4050, 4051, 4052, 4104, 4139, 4284, 4482, 4513, 4590, 4854, 4896, 4931, 4977, 5018, 5099, 5287, 5340, 5656, 5791, 5865, 5867, 6032, 6071, 6130, 6136

Sex: Homosexual, Bisexual, Transvestite:

514, 690, 1185, 1195, 1340, 1402, 1468, 1963, 2516, 2595, 3070, 3344, 3535, 3752, 3788, 3853, 3854, 3898, 4107, 4382, 4828, 5113, 5594, 5785, 6015

2096, 2107, 2141, 2153, 2160, 2192, 2203, 2216, 2266, 2322, 2375, 2458, 2503, 2530, 2536, 2550, 2574, 2656, 2683, 2718, 2745, 2746, 2810, 2818, 2900, 3024, 3115, 3141, 3142, 3158, 3177, 3180, 3217, 3241, 3252, 3253, 3272, 3306, 3331, 3346, 3441, 3495, 3497, 3501, 3504, 3505, 3506, 3509, 3511, 3556, 3577, 3613, 3636, 3643, 3645, 3649, 3672, 3702, 3743, 3746, 3748, 3750, 3798, 3859, 3861, 3896, 3909, 3911, 3982, 3991, 4024, 4044, 4071, 4085, 4182, 4183, 4199, 4219, 4273, 4277, 4445, 4449, 4451, 4513, 4542, 4625, 4730, 4779, 4786, 4955, 4970, 4981, 5000, 5071, 5073, 5074, 5083, 5111, 5136, 5143, 5150, 5176, 5185, 5194, 5280, 5327, 5347, 5365, 5392, 5406, 5449, 5450, 5456, 5479, 5480, 5501, 5503, 5525, 5575, 5578, 5613, 5636, 5650, 5653, 5654, 5666, 5704, 5714, 5763, 5858, 5868, 5876, 5903, 5906, 5913, 5989, 6016, 6017, 6033, 6070, 6115

Therapy Process, Outcome, Drop-Outs:

16, 61, 74, 93, 100, 101, 103, 119, 125, 152, 153, 202, 223, 230, 236, 246, 259, 268, 281, 309, 340, 353, 363, 369, 376, 396, 408, 420, 425, 426, 457, 460, 495, 518, 519, 522, 531, 533, 552, 553, 562, 579, 596, 625, 643, 665, 689, 709, 718, 749, 770, 792, 801, 822, 833, 840, 889, 892, 939, 948, 949, 950, 959, 976, 980, 986, 1023, 1029, 1040, 1053, 1099, 1134, 1145, 1153, 1157, 1164, 1191, 1209, 1217, 1223, 1244, 1311, 1345, 1406, 1428, 1431, 1445, 1471, 1472, 1509, 1515, 1536, 1542, 1577, 1594, 1659, 1677, 1679, 1691, 1698, 1724, 1728, 1760, 1769, 1771, 1774, 1836, 1877, 1878, 1890, 1897, 1908, 1984, 1986, 2041, 2043, 2056, 2065, 2068, 2080, 2091, 2098, 2118, 2134, 2156, 2279, 2320, 2345, 2347, 2363, 2372, 2427, 2437, 2499, 2547, 2588, 2642, 2644, 2646, 2651, 2757, 2759, 2780, 2784, 2809, 2812, 2842, 2852, 2871, 2888, 2940, 2997, 3048, 3052, 3053, 3061, 3090, 3128, 3134, 3166, 3198, 3228, 3244, 3245, 3293, 3362, 3376, 3382, 3567, 3639, 3732, 3809, 3848, 3874, 3881, 3891, 3924, 3950, 3977, 4005, 4098, 4210, 4216, 4222, 4320, 4329, 4334, 4335, 4336, 4368, 4384, 4426, 4473, 4491, 4539, 4553, 4554, 4555, 4577, 4618, 4680, 4741, 4742, 4755, 4756, 4814, 4821, 4833, 4849, 4858, 4859, 4891, 4892, 4893, 4894, 4991, 5016, 5022, 5023, 5045, 5072, 5075, 5079, 5103, 5130, 5142, 5144, 5146, 5147, 5204, 5214, 5223, 5246, 5253, 5259, 5296, 5307, 5313, 5315, 5351, 5352, 5353, 5363, 5370, 5374, 5403, 5423, 5427, 5463, 5487, 5488, 5489, 5509, 5510, 5633, 5638, 5658, 5660, 5675, 5689, 5719, 5766, 5846, 5854, 5870, 5874, 5886, 5894, 5896, 5900, 5924, 5930, 5932, 5958, 5966, 6044, 6046, 6063, 6065, 6066, 6073, 6147, 6150

Therapists View/Role, Practicing Therapist, Co-Therapists:

47, 60, 61, 118, 161, 204, 215, 275, 370, 393, 398, 412, 426, 472, 480, 481, 517, 526, 534, 537, 542, 545, 550, 564, 588, 589, 590, 591, 592, 639, 670, 679, 684, 687, 776, 781, 807, 811, 813, 864, 935, 967, 1016, 1037, 1069, 1092, 1131, 1153, 1160, 1161, 1182, 1193, 1194, 1242, 1248, 1264, 1306, 1319, 1327, 1328, 1331, 1392, 1393, 1397, 1447, 1459, 1489, 1529, 1589, 1636, 1639, 1647, 1694, 1712, 1804, 1814, 1829, 1839, 1844, 1847, 1848, 1867, 1887, 1897, 1903, 1949, 1950, 1974, 1997, 2012, 2030, 2032, 2067, 2080, 2116, 2121, 2142, 2189, 2190, 2198, 2221, 2244, 2277, 2293, 2294, 2310, 2316, 2330, 2355, 2396, 2400, 2431, 2455, 2474, 2524, 2526, 2530, 2556, 2564, 2573, 2714, 2719, 2725, 2726, 2728, 2852, 2904, 3000, 3035, 3044, 3078, 3110, 3111, 3135, 3139, 3152, 3171, 3176, 3177, 3197, 3215, 3221, 3222, 3256, 3266, 3280, 3308, 3316, 3329, 3356, 3365, 3376, 3497, 3518, 3570, 3571, 3589, 3761, 3782, 3789, 3814, 3820, 3852, 3860, 3868, 3869, 3874, 3912, 3936, 3941, 3944, 3965, 3977, 3991, 4042, 4082, 4089, 4145, 4179, 4186, 4188, 4220, 4228, 4231, 4240, 4245, 4345, 4351, 4368, 4380, 4420, 4446, 4448, 4460, 4461, 4495, 4515, 4522, 4581, 4587, 4588, 4593, 4598, 4599, 4624, 4639, 4663, 4687, 4697, 4711, 4758, 4760, 4765, 4768, 4774, 4796, 4803, 4804, 4837, 4868, 4916, 4926, 4937, 4942, 4967, 4987, 5001, 5013, 5024, 5042, 5056, 5075, 5081, 5092, 5097, 5103, 5123, 5148, 5166, 5209, 5210, 5230, 5235, 5237, 5251, 5264, 5271, 5272, 5289, 5329, 5330, 5340, 5364, 5393, 5402, 5445, 5489, 5492, 5499, 5539, 5574, 5581, 5615, 5617, 5636, 5646, 5652, 5670, 5671, 5672, 5679, 5717, 5727,

About the Compilers

BERNARD LUBIN is a Professor of Psychology at the University of Missouri, Kansas City. He is a Diplomate (American Board of Professional Psychology) and a fellow of the American Psychological Association and the American Group Psychotherapy Association. Professor Lubin has published seven books and over 100 articles.

ALICE W. LUBIN, a former coordinator for Certified Consultants International and member of the Midwest Group for Human Resources, is coauthor of several books and author of many articles and book reviews. She has done graduate work at George Washington University, American University, and the Washington School of Psychiatry.

MARION G. WHITEFORD is a graduate student at Ohio State.

RODNEY V. WHITLOCK is a graduate student at the University of Missouri at Kansas City.